"Where, after all, do universal human rights begin? In small places, close to home—so close and so small that they cannot be seen on any map of the world. Yet they *are* the world of the individual person: the neighborhood he lives in; the school or college he attends; the factory, farm or office where he works. Such are the places where every man, woman and child seeks equal justice, equal opportunity, equal dignity without discrimination. Unless these rights have meaning there, they have little meaning anywhere. Without concerted citizen action to uphold them close to home, we shall look in vain for progress in the larger world."

Eleanor Roosevelt
*In Your Hands: A Guide for Community Action for the
Tenth Anniversary of the Universal Declaration of Human Rights*
United Nations, March 27, 1958

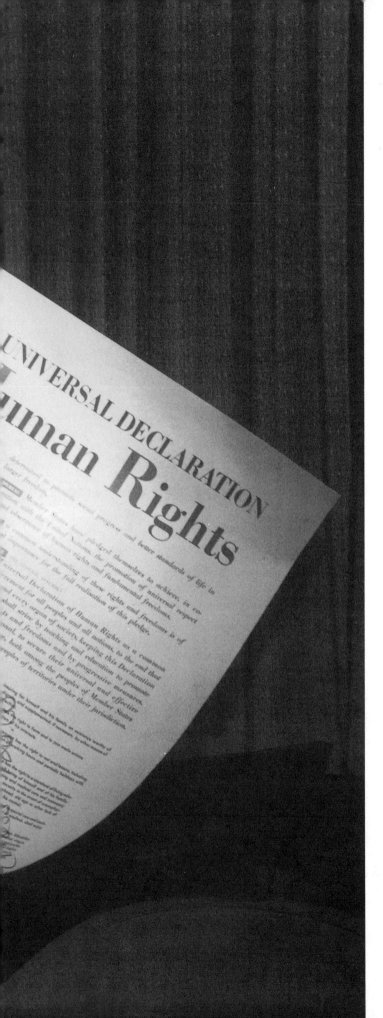

INTERNATIONAL ENCYCLOPEDIA OF

HUMAN RIGHTS

FREEDOMS, ABUSES, AND REMEDIES

ROBERT L. MADDEX

CQ PRESS

A DIVISION OF
CONGRESSIONAL QUARTERLY INC.

WASHINGTON, D.C.

CQ Press
A Division of Congressional Quarterly Inc.
1414 22nd Street, N.W.
Washington, D.C. 20037

(202) 822-1475; (800) 638-1710

www.cqpress.com

Printed and bound in the United States of America

04   03   02   01   00   5   4   3   2   1

Library of Congress Cataloging-in-Publication Data
Maddex, Robert L.
International encyclopedia of human rights : freedoms, abuses, and remedies / Robert L. Maddex.
p.   cm.
Includes bibliographical references and index.
ISBN 1-56802-490-8 (hardbound)
1. Human rights—Encyclopedias. 2. Civil rights—Encyclopedias.
I. Title.
JC571.M3243 2000
323'.03—dc21   00-042941

Produced by Archetype Press, Inc., Washington, D.C.

Project Director: Diane Maddex
Editor: Gretchen Smith Mui
Indexer: Deborah E. Patton
Designer: Robert L. Wiser

Cover: A rally in Great Britain to ban the testing of nuclear weapons. [Corbis-Bettmann]

Pages ii–iii: Eleanor Roosevelt reading the Universal Declaration of Human Rights in 1949. [United Nations]

Pages xviii–xix: Mary Robinson (right), the United Nations High Commissioner for Human Rights, comforts a woman in Grozny, the capital of Chechnya, in 2000. [Agence France-Presse].

Pages xx–xxi: Archbishop Desmond Tutu (right) with Nelson Mandela in South Africa in 1994. [Reuters/Corbis]

Pages xxii–xxiii: Women war workers in 1943 at a New Jersey shipyard. [UPI/Corbis-Bettmann]

Pages xxvi–xxvii: A youth imprisoned in a jail cell. [Corbis-Bettmann]

This book is dedicated to all those who have suffered and died to advance the cause of human rights.

CONTENTS

SUBJECTS

ENTRIES ARRANGED BY CATEGORY

Concepts

Documents

Human Rights Agencies

Nongovernmental Organizations

Biographies

INTERNATIONAL ENCYCLOPEDIA OF

HUMAN RIGHTS

FREEDOMS, ABUSES, AND REMEDIES

FOREWORD

The past fifty years have witnessed intense activity in the development of international norms and the setting of standards for human rights. Both the legislation and the literature on human rights have become increasingly complex. More than sixty international human rights treaties, covenants, and conventions have followed the Universal Declaration of Human Rights (1948), with more to come. Means of protecting human rights at regional and sub-regional levels are also expanding rapidly.

This encyclopedia serves a useful purpose by defining and explaining the evolving language of the field of international human rights. It will enable experts, students, and all those interested in human rights to become more familiar with key human rights documents, organizations, and personalities.

This publication comes at an appropriate time—during the United Nations Decade for Human Rights Education (1995–2004). The decade's purpose is to provide a framework for governments, international organizations, non-governmental organizations, and civil society generally to concentrate their efforts in the areas of human rights education, training, and public information. Educating everyone about human rights plays a vital role in the struggle to prevent human rights abuses and to embed a culture of respect for human rights in every part of the world.

Mary Robinson
United Nations High Commissioner for Human Rights

FOREWORD

Knowledge is the greatest ally in the continuous struggle to ensure that governments throughout the world recognize the human rights and the dignity of all people. To know what these rights are and how to pursue remedies when they are violated serves the interests of citizens of all countries.

The fight for freedom and democracy over my own country's discriminatory policy of apartheid was long and hard. In the end, however, right won out, and without widespread violence and bloodshed. God's divine justice is available to all who genuinely seek it, but the path to human justice is often strewn with obstacles. Reference works such as Robert Maddex's encyclopedia aid the pursuit of justice by opening the door to understanding our human rights and the ways in which we can claim and enforce these rights.

At the international and regional levels, the United Nations and regional human rights organizations in Africa, the Americas, and Europe are building systems for effective protection of human rights. At the national level, in constitutional democracies young and old, laws and court decisions define key terms in the burgeoning field of human rights. To be able to help ourselves and others promote and defend the human rights guaranteed in international documents such as the Universal Declaration of Human Rights (1948), in regional human rights documents, and in national and state constitutions and laws, we must be able to understand the history, theory, and language of human rights today.

I commend to you this *International Encyclopedia of Human Rights,* which contributes to codifying and illuminating the important and expanding field of human rights. God has given us the ability to reason, to create a better world on Earth for ourselves and our posterity, and to further human justice. May we rise to the challenge and the opportunity.

The Most Reverend Desmond Tutu
Archbishop Emeritus of Cape Town, South Africa

PREFACE

Since the end of World War II in 1945, striking progress has been made in protecting human rights. The number of nations with constitutional, democratic governments that guarantee some individual and minority rights has increased from a mere handful to a significant majority—well over one hundred—of the world's aproximately 190 countries. International agreements and national laws proclaim human rights for all people without distinction as to sex, race, color, language, national or social origin, religion, political or other opinion, property, birth, or other status—as called for in the Universal Declaration of Human Rights (1948). National, regional, and even several international tribunals for the adjudication of human rights violations are in place, and thousands of public and private institutions are advancing the cause of human rights concerns around the world. The number of government and quasi-government agencies devoted to human rights has proliferated along with nongovernmental organizations involved in defending human rights. The growth of Internet sites related to human rights activities confirms that public and private interest in the subject is continuing to grow worldwide, helping attract the attention of a new, electronic generation.

Although the tools have been created, the struggle to achieve a world in which all people are accorded the human rights to which they are entitled is just beginning. Human rights as a field of study remains in its infancy. An important step in the development of any new discipline is identifying, organizing, and illuminating the concepts, terms, documents, institutions, and people who have played a significant role. *The International Encyclopedia of Human Rights: Freedoms, Abuses, and Remedies* represents such a first step. Here the reader can find explanations of key concepts and terms in use at the national, regional, and international levels of human rights protection, focused not only on the rhetoric of human rights found in national and international documents but also on the discussion of such terms and concepts in decisions of national and international adjudicative bodies. Included here as well are summaries of significant documents themselves, information on key human rights agencies and advocacy groups, and profiles of people who have helped articulate and defend human rights over many centuries.

Concepts

More than one hundred fifty important concepts and terms—from abortion to youth—are described here, including such introductory ideas as rights, human rights, and international human rights instruments. Also included are a number of concepts and terms, such as the right to die and capital punishment, that are not fully developed or accepted as rights in all countries of the world. Many of these concepts and terms are derived from international and regional human rights agreements and decisions; others come from documents and decisions of specific nations as they address human rights concerns. Selection was based on the frequency of their use in significant human rights materials and their relative importance to the protection of human rights; more abstract or theoretical concepts or terms were avoided.

Entries discuss the current definition of the concept or term, its history, and what it means today in the context of human rights. Examples may be given to show how the word is used in national, regional, and international documents and in authoritative decisions. At the end of each entry are excerpts from documents—for example, national constitutions and international human rights instruments—as well as decisions of courts, commissions, and other adjudicatory bodies illustrating the use of the concept or term or illuminating its meaning. For both documents and decisions, two examples of each are generally given, the first representing a national document or decision, the second an international document or decision. Following these, where applicable, are suggested contacts, further reading, and cross-references to related entries in the encyclopedia.

Documents

One hundred documents significant to the historical development and the current state of human rights throughout the world have been selected for inclusion. These documents—predominantly international treaties, declarations, and statements of principles—represent a broad spectrum of human rights, including, for example, fundamental rights as well as the rights of children and juveniles, women, minorities, soldiers, prisoners, accused persons, and victims. Reference is made in the text to other human rights documents where they are relevant.

Also included are some national documents, such as England's Magna Carta (1215), the U.S. Declaration of Independence (1776), and France's Declaration of the Rights of Man and of the Citizen (1789)—ground-breaking statements that have greatly influenced the evolution of human rights beyond the borders of these nations. More recent examples, such as Czechoslovakia's Charter 77 (1977) and the Canadian Charter of Rights and Freedoms (1982), depart from the historical context of the countries in which they were developed. Drafted in a communist dictatorship, Charter 77 became an instrument for creating constitutional democracy; the Canadian charter similarly represents a break with the United Kingdom and other British Commonwealth nations, such as Australia and New Zealand, that have eschewed constitutional declarations or bills of rights guaranteeing individual freedoms and maintained the principle that their elected parliaments have absolute constitutional supremacy.

Each document is placed in its historical context, with background on its adoption. A detailed summary with excerpts from the document itself follows. One or more contacts are typically provided, usually the sponsoring agency or organization, together with reading entries where available and concluding with cross-references to entries of interest.

Agencies and Organizations

Among the thousands of public institutions and private organizations now involved in human rights activities are international agencies such as the United Nations; regional bodies such as the Council of Europe, Organization of American States, and Organization of African Unity; plus national offices and tribunals, as well as a growing number of nongovernmental organizations. Institutions included here have been selected for their importance and the varied interests they represent. Other organizations and institutions are mentioned in related entries. A great advantage is that most can now be located directly or indirectly through the Internet.

Biographies

The growth of human rights could be told almost entirely through the lives of great intellectuals, advocates, and activists in the field. The four dozen persons selected for profiles here illuminate the important efforts made in the long struggle—intellectual, political, legal, and cultural—toward the recognition and expansion of human rights today. Selections were based on the significance and the scope of each person's contribution to human rights, keeping in mind the role that the least powerful in society can play to achieve human rights—"the power of the powerless," as described by Václav Havel, the Czech author, human rights activist, and first president of the Czech Republic.

As all these entries show, the quest for human rights is rooted in the struggle for a balance of power between individuals and those people who control political power. The body politic, like the human body, works best when homeostasis—the state of physiological equilibrium produced by an organism's proper balance of functions and chemistry—is attained.

In preparing this encyclopedia, I was fortunate to have had the encouragement and assistance of several persons in particular. At CQ Press, first Shana Wagger and then Patricia Gallagher helped shape the concept of the book and saw it into publication under the guidance of Kathryn C. Suárez. Gretchen Smith Mui, editor for Archetype Press, gave the book her single-minded devotion for longer than we could ever have expected. To her I owe an immense debt for helping me clearly express the ideas presented on the following pages. My wife, Diane Maddex, president of Archetype Press, never stopped asking the right questions, prodding me to dig deeper and polishing my prose to the very end. Robert L. Wiser, Archetype Press's designer, took on the challenge of turning these many words into another handsome, readable volume for which Archetype Press is known. And in addition to the countless librarians, staff members of organizations, and others who helped answer specific questions, I want to single out Bruce Abramson, a human rights attorney in Geneva, for his valuable counsel. Like all human rights activities, this turned out to be a collaborative effort among dedicated people.

Key to the Symbols

⊠	Sources of information and assistance
☏	Telephone numbers
🖶	Facsimile numbers
✉	E-mail addresses
▯	Web sites

▤	Documents, including national constitutions and laws, international and regional declarations, agreements, standards, rules, and guidelines
▬▮	Court decisions and other legal judgments
▮	Further reading
☞	Related entries in the encyclopedia

INTRODUCTION

Human rights . . . belong inherently to each person, each individual, and are not conferred by or subject to any governmental authority. There is not one law for one continent, and one for another. And there should be only one single standard—a universal standard—for judging human rights violations.

—Kofi Annan, Secretary-General, United Nations

Several significant events in the evolution of human rights occurred in 1999. The member nations of the North Atlantic Treaty Organization (NATO) unanimously agreed to conduct a military campaign against the leader of Serbia, Slobodan Milosevic, for ordering genocidal ethnic cleansing in the Yugoslav province of Kosovo. And then the British House of Lords, by a majority vote, upheld a request by a Spanish judge that the former military ruler of Chile, General Augusto Pinochet, be extradited to Spain to be tried for allegations that he committed heinous crimes against his own citizens. In the same year Senegal became the first nation to ratify the Rome Statute (1998) establishing an International Criminal Court to prosecute, try, and punish perpetrators of the worst human rights abuses. (Ratification by sixty countries is necessary before the court becomes operational.)

The ultimate success or failure of these attempts to punish gross human rights abuses through military intervention, international and domestic legal action, and the establishment of an international criminal tribunal is not as important as the fact that such attempts are being made at all. The sovereign right of nations to conduct their internal affairs free of any judgment or reprisal by their peers—the other sovereign nations of the world—has for too long precluded the international community's attempts to punish national leaders. This principle of international law has meant that

political rulers were free to commit human rights abuses with impunity. The tide, however, is turning—slowly perhaps, but turning nonetheless.

Two interrelated victories for humankind during the past century were the spread of national democratic government and the international and national focus on human rights. Such progress has not come without great cost—two world wars and a genocidal Holocaust, among many other conflicts—and the road ahead is still long and steep. Atrocities in the former territory of Yugoslavia and in Rwanda, Iraq, Chechnya, and Sudan, together with the discriminatory and often violent treatment of women in countries such as Afghanistan and Pakistan, are constant reminders that the ideals of human rights have only a fragile foothold in the world.

Although we live in an era when more people then ever before enjoy freedom from oppression and protection of their rights, this achievement simply brings into sharper relief the plight of those not so fortunate. Every day, newspapers, news magazines, television news, and the Internet present human rights stories. Whether it is the abuse of children, repressive regimes, the lack of freedom and opportunity for women, war atrocities, police brutality, pollution of the environment, or campaigns for gay rights, minority rights, religious freedom, or nuclear disarmament, the public is continually made aware of the widespread lack of respect for the rights of others.

We have declarations of human rights in national constitutions and international agreements as well as mechanisms for expanding rights, but do we have the will and the courage to act in accordance with these noble sentiments? There can be no higher aspiration than confirming the oneness of all people by working to relieve oppression, overcome poverty, and create equal rights and opportunities. Although perhaps not as glamorous as walking on the moon or winning a world sports championship, releasing political prisoners, feeding starving children, and bringing to justice those responsible for the murder, torture, and rape of the innocent have to be far more rewarding. Protecting human rights for all will be the ultimate triumph of the human spirit.

Human Rights and Freedoms

A right is something a person ought to have or receive from another, a well-founded claim that may be asserted under law. A citizen in a democracy has the right to vote, for example, and if that right is denied the citizen may enforce it, and the official who wrongfully denied the right may be punished. Freedom is the basic right of all people to be left alone by their government as much as possible to pursue their own goals in life. "The only freedom which deserves the name," wrote John Stuart Mill in *On Liberty* (1859), "is that of pursuing our own good in our own way, so long as we do not attempt to deprive others of theirs, or impede their efforts to obtain it."

Human rights are rights to which every person is entitled simply by virtue of being a human living in a society of other humans. Among these are the right to life, liberty, and the security of the person. Strictly speaking, human rights arise out of the conflict between the goals of an individual in a political system and the goals of those who wield political power in that system. To reduce abuses of power and infringement of rights, a democracy or a constitutional monarchy places various limits on those who have political power. In an absolute monarchy or a dictatorship, however, all political power—including the power of life and death in many cases—is concentrated in the hands of a single person who is not accountable to anyone else for his or her actions. According to Thomas Paine, writing in *The Rights of Man* (1791) about the French Revolution of 1789, "The representatives of the people of France . . . [considered] that ignorance, neglect, or contempt of human rights are the sole cause of public misfortunes. . . ." A reaction to the excesses of the French monarchy, the French Revolution initiated a new wave of interest in human rights worldwide, but the Reign of Terror that followed demonstrated how the remedy could become as cruel and inhuman as any of the original violations.

Early civilizations gave little if any acknowledgment to human rights. Citizens of Athens and the other ancient Greek democracies probably had more protection for their rights than any people before their time or for centuries thereafter. In Athens every eligible citizen (excluding women and slaves) had the right to participate in the governing process of the city-state; in other parts of the world, an individual ruler or a small clique of aristocrats generally held absolute power. Athenian citizens had the right to a trial before being punished for breaking the law, to speak freely about the political questions of the day, and to criticize the government. These were the basic elements of Greek democracy—notions that would evolve into human rights—that the philosophers Plato and Aristotle were familiar with and that influenced their seminal works of political science such as *The Republic* and *The Politics*, respectively.

Cicero, the statesman and orator of ancient Rome, produced works that reflected the principles of the Roman Republic and the rights of its citizens. The concept of human rights, like that of democracy, then lay fairly dormant for centuries. Eventually, through the works of Christian scholars in Europe, such as St. Augustine in the fifth century and St. Thomas Aquinas in the thirteenth century, the concept of just governance was pursued. Magna Carta (1215), the Great Charter of liberties forced on King John of England, is an early example of attempts to remedy violations of rights. The right not to lose one's liberty except "by the lawful judgment of [one's] peers" or by the "law of the land" as set out in Magna Carta is a direct ancestor of the modern-day right to due process of law and to a trial by jury when accused of a crime.

Between the Middles Ages and the modern era, men such as the Dutch legal scholar Hugo Grotius, the English philosopher John Locke, and the French philosopher Jean-

Jacques Rousseau made significant contributions to the intellectual development of human rights concepts—Grotius in advancing the development of international and humanitarian law; Locke in asserting the fundamental rights of life, liberty, and property; and Rousseau in arguing for the sovereignty of citizens. In 1775, to redress their grievances against the British government for denial of their perceived rights, the American colonists went to war with Britain, fully aware that failure meant death for treason against the British Crown. The "unalienable Rights" of life and liberty enshrined in the colonists' Declaration of Independence (1776) are now universally acknowledged in national constitutions and international human rights documents to be fundamental human rights.

Today human rights often means different things to different people. The wealthy may focus on the right to property, while the poor may be more concerned with the right to work or an adequate standard of living. Members of minorities regard civil and cultural rights as vital to them, while a nation's majority group may emphasize the right to governance by majority rule. In addition to life, liberty, and personal security, fundamental human rights are now generally acknowledged to include a citizen's civil and political rights. Such rights include freedom of speech, thought, conscience, expression, opinion, religion, assembly, and association; equality; the right to vote and hold office; freedom of the press; privacy; the right to due process, a fair trial, and legal counsel; and guarantees against cruel or inhuman treatment and punishment. For those looking for a hierarchy of human rights in which some are considered more important than others, civil and political rights can be described as first-generation rights. Second-generation rights are positive rights that governments provide depending on their ability: economic and social entitlements such as welfare benefits. In a third generation of rights are such protections as collective and community rights.

Lists of human rights can be found in various national and international documents. At the national level, the most important rights are generally set out in constitutions, often as bills, charters, or declarations of rights. Rights are also identified in statutory law as well as in judicial opinions, which have, for example, helped create the common law of England. At the international level, the International Bill of Human Rights—a collective term encompassing the Universal Declaration of Human Rights (1948), International Covenant on Civil and Political Rights (1966), together with its two optional protocols, and International Covenant on Economic, Social and Cultural Rights (1966)—outlines most of the important human rights agreed to at least in theory by a consensus of the nations of the world: from equality and freedom from discrimination to freedom of thought to the right to take part in government to effective remedies for violations of fundamental rights. Other charters, conventions, covenants, guidelines, principles, and rules further identify international human rights norms or standards. Instruments developed by regional bodies of nations, such as the Council of Europe, Organization of American States, and Organization of African Unity, serve as regional statements of human rights; among them are the European Convention for the Protection of Human Rights and Fundamental Freedoms (1950), American Convention on Human Rights (1969), and African Charter on Human and Peoples' Rights (1981).

In Defense of Human Rights

Observance of human rights begins with such statements of rights in authoritative sources. Once asserted, human rights must be promoted and enforced if everyone is to benefit from the words on paper. People entitled to rights must know about those rights and how to exercise and enforce them. Knowledge is the first step in protecting rights and enjoying the benefits they provide.

Denials, abuses, and violations of human rights result from action or inaction by government officials in the face of established human rights. Such abuses may range from refusal to permit free expression of minority values or religious beliefs to arbitrary arrest and detention, torture, and summary execution. The abuses may infringe nationally declared or established rights or internationally recognized norms of human rights.

Although prevention of human rights violations through education is an important part of the enforcement process, a number of remedies exist for dealing with abuses. Victims can report violations to the proper local or national authorities, take legal action in domestic courts, or, after all domestic remedies have been exhausted, appeal to international human rights tribunals. Nongovernmental organizations are increasingly becoming involved in identifying and exposing human rights abuses as well as bringing pressure to bear on the governments responsible and on the world community at large to take action to stop the abuses and compensate the victims or their families.

The evolution of human rights protection is rooted in the actions of people as well as in documents and decisions, institutions and definitions. Throughout history individuals from Plato to Thomas Jefferson have developed ideas that laid the intellectual foundation of modern human rights. Defenders of human rights have given substance to these concepts and words and have acted, often in the face of great personal risk, to further the cause. Contemporary human rights leaders, such as Nelson Mandela and Archbishop Desmond Tutu of South Africa, Lech Walesa of Poland, and Václav Havel of the Czech Republic, have persevered in the face of great odds and at great personal risk to advance human rights in their respective countries. Aung San Suu Kyi of Burma (now Myanmar) and José Ramos-Horta of East Timor are just two of the many others who continue their struggle to bring democracy and respect for human rights to their homelands.

Toward Universal Sovereignty

The pursuit of human rights for all, both nationally and internationally, rests on a number of theoretical bases. Underlying one theory is the notion that there are laws of nature or natural laws that transcend human law and require that justice be done by rulers to those they rule. Another theory, as espoused by the eighteenth-century philosopher Jean-Jacques Rousseau among others, is based on a "social contract." In this view, individuals have rights from a presumed presocial state of existence that they delegate to others to create a social and political state for security and governance. Each person, according to this theory, retains as individual human rights those rights not delegated for that limited purpose. Yet another theory contends that human rights stem from religious and moral precepts that transcend laws created by people.

Because of the diversity of the human population and national traditions and laws, however, any theory of rights must address two basic problems: how to continue to expand human rights protection to every nation and person on Earth and how to create a consensus as to what human rights are, who is entitled to them, and why they must be vigorously enforced. The world has divided itself into so many national, ethnic, linguistic, religious, economic, and cultural camps that finding universally acceptable grounds for human rights appears to be almost insurmountable. Western cultural evolution has led to a standard of human rights, as expressed in the Universal Declaration of Human Rights, with which many Middle Eastern, Latin American, Asian, and African peoples do not readily identify—for example, that women and religious minorities should enjoy equal rights, that children should not be forced into labor, and that individual rights take precedence over group rights.

Another obstacle lies in a basic principle of international law: national sovereignty. For centuries the international community has legitimized the idea that every nation has the absolute right to govern its internal affairs without interference from other nations. This principle obviously provides little support for the people of one or more nations to intervene in order to expand awareness of human rights or punish violations in another nation. National sovereignty, therefore, may become a rationalization for failure to support human rights in another country.

When the principle of national sovereignty began developing five centuries ago, the world was far different than it is today. There were no true democracies, and absolute monarchs ruled most nations. The majority of countries are now governed by constitutional and democratic institutions, a fact that has led to increased observance of human rights. Popular sovereignty—the right of each citizen to participate equally in the governance of her or his country—is the basis of constitutional democracy, and a constitutional democracy has proven to be the best form of government to protect and expand citizens' human rights.

Whereas sovereignty originally conferred rights and privileges on a country's sovereign ruler or monarch, hereditary rulers have been replaced in modern democracies by temporary, elected officials who are accountable to the citizens. A democratic country's sovereignty is said to reside in the people, not in any one individual. If the people—the enfranchised citizenry of a constitutional democracy—have replaced the king, queen, emperor, or empress as the national sovereign, then, in theory, the citizens are each entitled to share in the same rights and privileges once accorded the monarch. And because sovereign nations have traditionally defended themselves against aggression as well as come to the aid of another threatened sovereign nation, the same right should be extended to any sovereign people with respect to the protection of human rights. Every constitutional democracy thus theoretically must have a right to intervene for its own protection, given that violations of human rights threaten all constitutional democracies and that sovereigns have an obligation to defend the rights of other sovereigns.

This theory has been employed, if only tacitly, on several occasions, including the Persian Gulf War in 1990–91 and the 1999 NATO intervention to stop Serbia's ethnic cleansing in Kosovo. Even the Charter of the United Nations (1945), it can be argued, sanctions the use of force to protect human rights. Although the charter bans aggression against the territorial integrity or political independence of any country "or in any other manner inconsistent with the Purposes of the United Nations," one of those purposes, set forth in the charter, is to "promote . . . universal respect for, and observance of, human rights and fundamental freedoms for all without distinction as to race, sex, language, or religion."

Cultural diversity throughout the world has led many nations and regions to reject numerous international norms of human rights as being reflective only of Western cultural ideals. Given a viable theory that legitimizes the right of democratic nations to intervene in countries whose rulers violate human rights norms, how can the problem of different standards of human rights among nations and cultures be overcome? The basic principle underlying all human rights documents, from the U.S. Declaration of Independence to the Universal Declaration of Human Rights, is the inherent equality of all human beings. This equality, on which popular sovereignty itself rests, underscores the universality of human rights as identified and defined in international human rights instruments, promulgated by international bodies such as the United Nations, approved by representatives of the world's nations, and ratified by a majority of the countries of the world. Observance of human rights strengthens individuals and nations by creating opportunities for all segments of the population, by freeing all people to be more creative and productive, and by making governments more responsive to the needs of all its citizens—not just a favored few. Where the norms came from, therefore, is immaterial.

Human Rights Systems

The systems that have developed for protecting human rights and remedying violations can be viewed vertically—on the national and international levels—as well as horizontally—by regions of the world.

Until recently rights and remedies, to the extent that any guarantees or enforcement existed, were the domain of national governments within their own political and territorial jurisdictions. Individual countries remain the primary protectors of the human rights of their citizens. One country may guarantee a bundle of constitutional rights under a relatively effective system of enforcing them. Another may promise similar rights but have an ineffective system of enforcement. And some countries simply ensure their citizens no rights at all.

The social and political interaction of national leaders and citizens, however, is complex. It would thus be unfair to judge a nation's level of human rights development simply by how many rights are guaranteed in a constitution or other national laws or how effective the government machinery is in enforcing them. Some countries rely on social, cultural, and religious institutions to reinforce human rights. In some cases these institutions may work just as well as political ones. But such institutions are also susceptible to abuse and discrimination, and the more local or provincial the society, the less likely it is that its human rights norms and enforcement procedures conform to international standards.

Before the creation of the United Nations in 1945, in the wake of World War II, significant progress in protecting human rights had been made. In the field of international humanitarian law—laws to relieve human suffering during armed conflict—the Geneva Convention of 1864, in which the International Red Cross was officially recognized, provided for the "Amelioration of the Wounded in Time of War." Hague conventions in 1899 and 1907 and a second Geneva Convention in 1906 continued the development of humanitarian law and the laws of warfare. In 1899 the Permanent Court of International Justice was established in The Hague to arbitrate disputes between nations. During the first half of the twentieth century both the International Labor Organization, through several conventions aimed at protecting workers around the world, and the League of Nations, by forming an alliance of nations for mutual benefit and expressly promoting some human rights efforts, increased protections on the international level.

The world community, however, would not see the need to address universal human rights as a whole until after two devastating world wars. Finally, in the wake of the Nazi Holocaust and the Japanese atrocities during World War II against people in occupied territory including China and Korea, the leaders of the victorious nations set about to create an international organization that would promote peace and understanding among all nations and extend human rights to everyone. The founding Charter of the United Nations in 1945 underscored the need for all nations to encourage respect for the human rights and fundamental freedoms of all persons. A major step in promoting human rights worldwide occurred three years later, when the UN General Assembly adopted the Universal Declaration of Human Rights in 1948 and then followed it in 1966 with the International Covenant on Civil and Political Rights and the International Covenant on Economic, Social and Cultural Rights. A second optional protocol to abolish capital punishment was added to the civil covenant in 1989. These later agreements helped move countries beyond the commendable rhetoric of the Universal Declaration to more binding treaties that required national ratification.

In 1993 the Office of the United Nations High Commissioner for Human Rights, headquartered in Geneva, was created to bring an executive focus and effective response to human rights problems around the world. Also set up under the UN charter is a Commission on Human Rights, which has a Subcommission on the Promotion and Protection of Human Rights and meets annually to review complaints of human rights abuses. Despite its ambitious human rights program, however, the amount of money the UN allocates for all its human rights activities is only about two percent of its annual budget.

Regional human rights systems have developed in Africa, the Americas, and Europe based on regional human rights documents and regional institutions; to a large extent, the more recently established African system is not nearly as effective as the European and inter-American systems, which have a longer history. As yet there is no similar Asian-Pacific system of human rights subscribed to by nations in that part of the world. In recent years, organizations representing Islamic countries have made an effort to promulgate cooperative human rights instruments; their positive effects, however, have yet to be realized.

The European system of human rights is sponsored by the Council of Europe and operates under the European Convention for the Protection of Human Rights and Fundamental Freedoms and a number of subsequent amending protocols; since 1999 the European Court of Human Rights has been the primary adjudicative body for human rights complaints against countries that are parties to the convention and protocols. In the Americas, the American Convention on Human Rights is implemented through the Inter-American Commission on Human Rights and the Inter-American Court of Human Rights. The African system operates under the African Charter on Human and Peoples' Rights and the African Commission on Human and Peoples' Rights.

Righting Wrongs

Remedies for human rights violations vary from nation to nation. Each of the separate branches of government can act to enforce rights established in constitutions and other national laws, including international treaty obligations. The legal profession, nongovernmental organizations, and the media can also play a role in seeing that justice is done. Nondemocratic countries have few if any independent institutions or reliable procedures for pressing human rights claims. The U.S. Department of State reports to Congress each year on the status of human rights in nations around the world, a project undertaken as well by organizations such as Amnesty International and Human Rights Watch.

Unlike individual nations, the international, UN-based human rights system and the regional systems share procedures necessitated by their lack of sovereignty, which precludes them from legislating or directly enforcing human rights principles. Therefore, they generally rely on three methods of addressing human rights problems: (1) promoting human rights through education, technical assistance, and promulgation of human rights instruments; (2) investigating and reporting on nations' compliance with their obligations under human rights agreements to which they are a party; and (3) adjudicating human rights complaints from other countries, groups, and individuals, as provided for in such agreements. The Commission on Human Rights also acts on complaints under limited authority granted by the Economic and Social Council (ECOSOC).

The regional human rights systems, like the international system, depend on the willingness of individual nations to make internal commitments to human rights and to enforce compliance with human rights norms. Regional systems must also contend with differences in traditions and customs and religious and cultural biases as well as dissimilar legal systems, any of which may be inimical to the promotion and protection of certain types of human rights. For example, because of religious or other traditional influences, the right to life may be interpreted in some countries to deny the right to abortion. The development of human rights law through regional systems is thus far from uniform.

The concept of cultural relativism raises difficulties in both regional and national human rights systems. Some nations contend that, because of their unique historic customs or traditions, they have the right to reject certain human rights or to maintain practices that violate international norms. Genital mutilation of females is one such practice that has been rationalized in some countries on the basis that cultural rights transcend individual human rights. Rights infringed by this practice, however, include the right of a girl or woman to be secure in her person; to be free from torture, discrimination, and violence; and to

withhold consent to dangerous and invasive medical practices. The procedure also ignores the need to respect each person's dignity and a child's right to have her best interests given paramount consideration.

Recognizing and enforcing human rights is a struggle to wrest power out of the hands of the few on behalf of the many. Any government, tradition, custom, or religion that promotes or condones the right of one person to exert absolute power over the life, death, or physical or mental well-being of another—simply because she is a woman or he is of a different racial or ethnic background, or because he is a child or she is impoverished or politically, culturally, or religiously different—becomes a weapon, one that must be rendered harmless.

In the Hands of All Citizens

The battle for human rights begins with each of us. The more that people are exposed to its language and concepts, the more difficult it will be for national governments or cultural institutions to deny or violate those rights. "The destiny of human rights is in the hands of all our citizens in all our communities," said Eleanor Roosevelt, the chair of the Commission on Human Rights, which drafted the Universal Declaration of Human Rights in 1948.

Starting at home and at school, young people should be taught that the rights of others must be respected, that they themselves possess dignity and worth, and that they should expect fair and equal treatment from those in authority. An equally important step is electing national and world leaders whose policies promote the expansion and enforcement of human rights. Supporting nongovernmental human rights organizations and individual human rights activists is another. Getting involved personally either through local or national political systems or in regional or international organizations dedicated to furthering human rights also advances the cause. Our own rights are enhanced when the rights of others are protected.

The power of the word defeats tyrants, because tyrants die and words are passed down from generation to generation. The words in this *International Encyclopedia of Human Rights*—the evolving language of human rights, human rights documents and institutions, and the lives of men and women who have defended human rights around the world—express the hope of the oppressed. Understanding all these aspects of human rights and the remedies that are available increases our potential as human beings and the awareness of our own humanity.

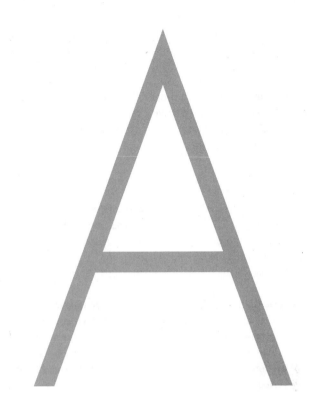

Rallies against U.S. participation in the Vietnam War mobilized Americans in the 1960s as few other issues had ever done. Exercising their constitutional right to freedom of assembly, young people marched, demonstrated, and held sit-ins to demand an end to the war. In 1967 thousands assembled outside the Pentagon, raising their hands in a call for peace.
[Library of Congress]

Aboriginal Peoples

See Indigenous Peoples

Abortion

The right to an abortion, along with family planning and contraception, is a reproductive right as well as a woman's right because it involves her body. As with the right to die and capital punishment, however, there is no international consensus on whether the right to have an abortion is a human right with the same status, for example, as freedom of conscience and freedom of religion. Proponents and opponents of abortion rights are also highly polarized, leaving little ground for compromise.

The act of procuring or inducing a premature delivery and thus the death of an offspring, called abortion, has been practiced since ancient times. Originally there was little if any moral condemnation of abortion (from the Latin *abortus,* meaning an untimely birth), but in many countries today abortions are illegal or restricted.

In the United States the demand for legal abortions grew out of the women's rights movement, which took the position that without the right to control their own reproduction, women could not fully realize other rights, particularly education and economic independence. In addition, a double standard existed: women of economic means could obtain an abortion, albeit illegally, while poor women, who could least afford to raise children properly, could not. Illegal abortions were often performed under less than adequate medical standards, thus greatly increasing the risk of harm to the woman.

The turning point in the United States came in 1973 with the U.S. Supreme Court's decision in the case of *Roe v. Wade.* Citing an implicit right of privacy in the U.S. Constitution, it struck down a one-hundred-year-old Texas state law prohibiting abortion except when the mother's life was endangered. From then on abortion became legal nationally. Subsequent Supreme Court decisions, however, have added some restrictions on the right to an abortion.

The Roman Catholic Church and a number of other religious organizations and sects oppose the right to an abortion on the grounds that it requires taking the life of an unborn child. Not all adherents of these religions hold the same views, however. And scientists, religious leaders, politicians, and lawyers are still debating the definition of life and when life begins for a human fetus.

Since the 1970s many but not all countries have liberalized their abortion laws. Great Britain did so in 1967, and in 1988 Canada's highest court voided that country's restrictive abortion law. In Ireland, where the influence of the Catholic Church is strong, abortions are banned, while in Italy the church's influence has not prevented the legalization of abortion. Other Western European countries permit legal abortion—for example, in 1998 Germany's constitutional court declared unconstitutional a Bavarian law that severely restricted access to abortions—although Finland has limited the grounds for abortion. Eastern European countries generally have liberalized their laws on abortion since the end of World War II. China, because of its overpopulation problem, actually encourages abortions, while India still has restrictive abortion laws, as do many countries in Africa. Latin America has some of the world's most restrictive abortion laws.

Constitution of Ireland (1937), Fundamental Rights, article 40, Personal Rights: "3. The State acknowledges the right to life of the unborn and, with due regard to the equal right to life of the mother, guarantees in its laws to respect, and, as far as practicable, by its laws defend and vindicate that right."

American Convention on Human Rights (1969), part I, State Obligations and Rights Protected, chapter II, Civil and Political Rights, article 4, Right to Life: "1. Every person has the right to have his life respected. This right shall be protected by law and, in general, from the moment of conception. No one shall be arbitrarily deprived of his life."

Supreme Court of Canada (1988): A law requiring women to obtain "a certificate from a therapeutic abortion committee" before having an abortion violated a woman's right to security under the Canadian Charter of Rights and Freedoms (1982), section 7.

European Court of Human Rights (1992): An Irish law made abortion illegal, but a restraint by the government on "providing information about lawful [abortion] services abroad . . . restrict[ed] freedom of expression across frontiers. . . . Since it was not against the criminal law for women to travel abroad to have an abortion, lawyers could reasonably have concluded that the provision of information [about the availability of abortion services abroad] did not involve a criminal offense."

American Civil Liberties Union (ACLU), Reproductive Freedom Project, 125 Broad Street, 18th Floor, New York, N.Y. 10004-2400. ☎ 212-549-2500. ✉ rfp@aclu.org. 🖥 www.aclu.org.

Catholics for Free Choice, 1436 U Street, N.W., Suite 301, Washington, D.C. 20009. ☎ 202-986-6093. 🖷 202-986-6093. ✉ cffc@catholicsforchoice.org. 🖥 www.catholicsforchoice.org.

National Abortion Rights Action League (NARAL), 1156 15th Street, N.W., Washington, D.C. 20005. ☎ 202-973-3000. 🖷 202-973-3096. ✉ naral@naral.org. 🖥 www.naral.org.

Planned Parenthood Federation of America, 810 Seventh Avenue, New York, N.Y. 10019. ☎ 212-541-7800. 🖷 212-245-1845. ✉ communications@ppfa.org. 🖥 www.plannedparenthood.org.

Fitzsimmons, Richard. *Pro-Choice/Pro-Life Issues in the 1990s.* Westport, Conn.: Greenwood, 1996.

Reynolds, Moira D. *Women Advocates of Reproductive Rights: Eleven Who Led the Struggle in the United States and Great Britain.* Jefferson, N.C.: McFarland, 1994.

Weddington, Sarah Ragle [legal counsel in *Roe v. Wade*]. *A Question of Choice.* New York: Penguin, 1993.

Civil Rights; Families; Life; Political Rights; Privacy; Women

Absolute Rights

See Fundamental Rights; Inviolable Rights

Accused

The notion that persons accused of crimes have certain rights is rooted in the ancient Greek democracies, where trials were decided by juries and penalties believed to be unjust, such as excessive fines, could be appealed. These rights were expanded by England's Magna Carta (1215), which provided that no official could place a person on trial solely on the basis of his own statement; credible witnesses to the truth of the accusation had to be found.

Under Anglo-American law, to accuse a person is to bring a charge or indictment alleging guilt of a crime or an offense before a court or a magistrate who has jurisdiction to inquire into the alleged crime. William Blackstone, the eighteenth-century commentator on the laws of England, wrote that "the finding of an indictment is only in the nature of an inquiry or accusation, which is afterwards to be tried and determined." English common law held that a person accused of a crime was presumed to be innocent until proven guilty by a jury of his or her peers (equals). To the framers of the U.S. Constitution, drafted in 1787, and the Bill of Rights, added to it in 1791, the presumption of innocence was a right so fundamental and so self-evident that it was not included in these documents. Today this right is guaranteed in all nations that observe the rule of law.

Most national constitutions refer to rights of the accused in differing degrees of detail. India's constitution (1950), for example, guarantees that "[n]o person accused of any offense shall be compelled to be a witness against himself," and Japan's constitution (1947) states that "in criminal cases the accused shall enjoy the right to a speedy and public trial by an impartial tribunal." The Draft Principles on Equality in the Administration of Justice, requested by the UN General

Assembly in 1973 and adopted by the Subcommission on the Promotion and Protection of Human Rights, sets forth ten rights to which every person should be entitled "in the examination of any criminal charge against him." These include the right of "access to tribunals," the right "to be heard ... by the competent [independent and impartial] tribunal previously established by law," the right "to be assisted and represented by counsel of his own choosing," the right to "a prompt and speedy" hearing as well as a public one, the right to presentation of a defense "in person or through counsel," the right to a decision "based only on the evidence placed before a court" and "rendered in public," and the opportunity "to appeal to a higher court."

Other international documents that extend rights to those accused of crimes include the Universal Declaration of Human Rights (1948), which recognizes the right, among others, of each person to "be presumed innocent until proven guilty according to law in a public trial at which he has had all the guarantees necessary for his defense." In addition, the International Covenant on Civil and Political Rights (1966) requires, for example, that "[a]nyone who is arrested shall be informed, at the time of arrest, of the reasons for his arrest and shall be promptly informed of any charges against him."

Constitution of Panama (1972), title III, Individual Rights and Social Rights and Duties, chapter 1, Fundamental Guarantees, article 22: "Persons accused of committing a crime have the right to be presumed innocent until proven guilty, at a public trial, under due process of law. Whoever is arrested shall have the right, from that moment, to legal counsel in all police and judiciary proceedings."

African Charter on Human and Peoples' Rights (1981), part I, Rights and Duties, chapter I, Human and Peoples' Rights, article 7: "1. Every individual shall have his cause heard. This comprises: a) the right to an appeal to competent national organs ... ; b) the right to be presumed innocent until proven guilty by a competent court or tribunal; c) the right to defense, including the right to be defended by counsel of his choice; and d) the right to be tried within a reasonable time by an impartial court or tribunal."

U.S. Supreme Court (1963): "The right of an indigent defendant in a criminal trial to have the assistance of counsel is a fundamental right essential to a fair trial, and ... [a] trial and conviction [in a state court] without the assistance of counsel violated the Fourteenth Amendment [to the U.S. Constitution, added in 1868]."

European Court of Human Rights (1984): The reliance on statements by anonymous informants for a conviction "involved limitations on the rights of the defense" of the accused that were irreconcilable with guarantees contained in the European Convention for the Protection of Human Rights and Fundamental Freedoms (1950), article 6, regarding the right to a fair trial.

Bassiouni, M. Cherif, with Alfred de Zayas. *The Protection of Human Rights in the Administration of Criminal Justice: A Compendium of United Nations Norms and Standards*. Geneva: Center for Human Rights, 1994.

Hertzberg, Sandra, and Carmela Zammuto. *The Protection of Human Rights in the Criminal Process under International Instruments and National Constitutions: A Study Project under the Direction of Cherif Bassiouni*. Toulouse, France: Erès, 1981.

Communication; Due Process of Law; Fair Trial; International Covenant on Civil and Political Rights; Judicial Independence; Magna Carta; Subcommission on the Promotion and Protection of Human Rights; Universal Delcaration of Human Rights; Youth

Adoption

Adoption is the process, formalized by social rules and laws, by which an orphan is made a member of another family. In most countries formal adoption is arranged through the courts and extends to adopted children the same legal rights as natural offspring; informal adoption generally does not confer legal rights.

In the process of adoption (from the Latin *adoptare*, meaning to choose for oneself), many interests have to be considered: those of the child, the adoptive parents and family, and the biological parents, if they are living, or other relatives. National governments also play a role in prescribing rules for the placement of children in institutions and foster homes. Because the social and legal implications of adoption have changed considerably, especially since World War II, the human rights implications of adoption have also been evolving.

The many interests at stake in adoption make it difficult to analyze the process in clear human rights terms. Privacy and freedom of information rights may conflict. In past years adoption agencies considered it best to fully disclose information about a child to the potential adoptive parents. By the 1950s, at least in the United States, the practice of selective disclosure became prevalent, the theory being that withholding negative information from the adoptive family put it on the same level as the biological family, which could not select a child based on information beforehand. By the 1990s, however, U.S. policy had reverted to full disclosure because of the importance of providing adoptive parents with information on the child's health and background. Another complicating factor is the right of adoptive children to information about their parents and background.

Interracial adoption, especially in the United States, continues to raise many contentious issues, as does the recent rise in intercountry adoptions, which require consideration of laws in the countries of both the adopters and the children being adopted. The Convention on the Rights of the Child (1989) sanctions such adoption "if the child cannot be placed in a foster or an adoptive family or cannot in any suitable manner be cared for in the child's country of origin." The convention urges all nations to "ensure that the best interests of the child shall be the paramount consideration" in all adoption procedures.

The European Convention on the Adoption of Children, which was approved by the Committee of Ministers of the Council of Europe in 1967 and became effective the following year, sets forth common principles and practices for adopting children in the countries that become parties to the agreement. In 1986 the UN General Assembly ratified a Declaration on Social and Legal Principles Relating to the Protection and Welfare of Children, with Special Reference to Foster Placement and Adoption Nationally and Internationally. Building on the UN document, the Convention on the Protection of Children and Co-operation in Respect of Intercountry Adoption was approved by the Hague Conference on Private International Law in 1993. The Hague convention requires that competent authorities in a child's state of origin find that intercountry adoption is in the child's best interests. Its aim is not to promote intercountry adoption but to ensure agreed-on procedures for protecting any children who are adopted.

U.S. Code, subsection 1996b, Adoption and Foster Care Rights: "(1) Prohibited conduct. A person or government that is involved in adoption or foster care placement may not—(A) deny to any individual the opportunity to become an adoptive or a foster care parent, on the basis of the race, color, or national origin of the individual, or of the child, involved; or (B) delay or deny the placement of a child for adoption or into foster care, on the basis of the race, color, or national origin of the adoptive or foster parent, or the child, involved."

African Charter on the Rights and Welfare of the Child (1990), article 24, Adoption: "States Parties which recognize the system of adoption shall ensure that the best interest of the child shall be the paramount consideration. . . ."

U.S. Supreme Court (1983): "If [an] unwed natural father fails to grasp the opportunity to develop a relationship with his child, the Constitution will not automatically compel a state to listen to his opinion of where the child's best interests lie."

European Commission of Human Rights (1992): The Irish government failed to respect the applicant's family life as required by the European Convention for the Protection of Human Rights and Fundamental Freedoms (1950), article 8, section 1, when it allowed an adoption of a child without the "the knowledge or consent of the natural father."

Joint Council on International Children's Services, 7 Cheverly Circle, Cheverly, Md. 20785-3040. (301-322-1906. 301-322-3425. mevans@jcics.org. www.jcics.org.

Bascom, Barbara B., and Carole A. McKelvey. *The Complete Guide to Foreign Adoption: What to Expect and How to Prepare Your New Child.* New York: Pocket Books, 1997.

International Adoption. Copenhagen: Danish State Information, 1997.

African Charter on the Rights and Welfare of the Child; Children; Convention on the Rights of the Child; Declaration on Social and Legal Principles Relating to the Protection and Welfare of Children, with Special Reference to Foster Placement and Adoption Nationally and Internationally; Families

Affirmative Action

See Race Discrimination

African Charter on Human and Peoples' Rights (Banjul Charter)

Colonialism has played a significant yet often deleterious role in the development of many nations of Africa. After World War I the League of Nations established a Permanent Mandates Commission to supervise the designated colonial powers' administration of their territories, but in none of its documents does the term *human rights* appear. The United Nations changed the mandate system to a trusteeship system, and because the UN charter (1945) encouraged self-government and independence, Africans sought to use the UN as a vehicle for emphasizing human rights.

The charter of the Organization of African Unity (OAU) (1963), an organization whose power rests in the hands of the political leaders of the African nations, contained some language promoting human rights. However, events in a number of African countries, such as Idi Amin's reign of terror in Uganda and similar abuses in the Central African Republic during the 1970s, impressed member countries with the urgency to do more to protect human rights in postcolonial and postindependence Africa.

As a result, the African Charter on Human and Peoples' Rights was drafted in Banjul, Gambia, and adopted by the heads of state and government of the OAU on June 28, 1981, in Nairobi, Kenya, entering into force on October 21, 1986. All of the fifty-three OAU member states except Eritrea, Ethiopia, and South Africa have ratified it to date. The document reflects Africa's history and traditions and takes a somewhat different approach from that of most other international instruments of its kind, enumerating individual rights but focusing to a greater extent on the collective rights of African peoples and the elimination of colonialism, neocolonialism, apartheid, Zionism, and "aggressive foreign military bases."

The other two regional systems of human rights, in Europe and in the Americas, provide for courts of human rights, but the Banjul Charter contains no reference to such a court to adjudicate violations and complaints against African governments. In 1997, however, an additional protocol to the charter was drafted to establish such a court with jurisdiction to consider cases submitted by the African Commission on Human and Peoples' Rights and states parties to the protocol that lodge a complaint or are the subject of such a complaint.

The charter's preamble acknowledges the inspiring influence of the OAU charter, which stipulates that "freedom, equality, justice and dignity are essential objectives for the achievement of legitimate aspirations of African peoples." The participating states, notes the preamble, have taken into consideration "the virtues of [the African states'] historical tradition and the values of African civilization which should inspire and characterize their reflection on the concept of human and peoples' rights." The document adds that it is the duty of government "to promote and protect human and peoples' rights and freedoms taking into account the importance traditionally attached to these rights and freedoms in Africa."

According to part I, Rights and Duties, chapter I, Human and Peoples' Rights, article 2, "Every individual shall be entitled to the enjoyment of the rights and freedoms recognized and guaranteed in the present Charter without distinction of any kind such as race, ethnic group, color, sex, language, religion, political or any other opinion, national and social origin, fortune, birth or other status."

Articles 3 through 17 set forth individual and citizen rights, such as equality before the law; equal protection of the law; respect for life and dignity; prohibitions against "[a]ll forms of exploitation and degradation of man, particularly slavery...."; liberty and security of the person; rights of the accused; freedom of conscience; the rights to receive information and express and disseminate opinions within the law; freedom of association; freedom of assembly; freedom of movement; equal access to participation in government and public service and to public property; the right to own property; the right "to work under equitable and satisfactory conditions"; and the right to education.

The state has a duty, as stipulated in article 18, to assist the family, "the natural unit and basis of society," and to ensure the protection of women, children, the aged, and the disabled. Articles 19 through 24 address peoples' rights,

declaring that all peoples are equal and have the "right to existence," to freely dispose of their wealth and natural resources, and to benefit from economic, social, and cultural development, which the state must ensure. The people are also guaranteed national and international peace and security and "a general satisfactory environment favorable to their development."

Chapter II, Duties, article 27, provides: "1. Every individual shall have duties towards his family and society, the State and other legally recognized communities and the international community. 2. The rights and freedoms of each individual shall be exercised with due regard to the rights of others, collective security, morality and common interest." Article 29 specifies the individual's duties, including preserving the "harmonious development of the family," serving the national community, working to the best of his or her abilities and competence and paying taxes, and "preserv[ing] and strengthen[ing] positive African cultural values in his relations with other members of the society...."

Part II, Measures of Safeguard, establishes the African Commission on Human and Peoples' Rights. According to chapter II, Mandate of the Commission, article 45, its purposes include promoting human and peoples' rights, ensuring the protection of those rights, interpreting the charter at the request of a state party or group affiliated with the OAU, and performing "any other tasks which may be entrusted to it by the Assembly of Heads of States and Government."

Organization of African Unity, P.O. Box 3243, Addis Ababa, Ethiopia. (251-1-51-7700. 🖨 251-1-51-2622. 🖳 y.afanou@telecom.net. 🖳 www.oau-oua.org.

African Commission on Human and Peoples' Rights; Apartheid; Collective Rights; Declaration on the Granting of Independence to Colonial Countries and Peoples; Development; Peoples' Rights; Self-Determination; Slavery

African Charter on the Rights and Welfare of the Child

Nearly a year after the UN General Assembly adopted the Convention on the Rights of the Child (1989), members of the Organization of African Unity (OAU) followed it with the African Charter on the Rights and Welfare of the Child on July 11, 1990, in Addis Ababa, Ethiopia. The OAU had already adopted the Declaration on the Rights and Welfare of the African Child in Monrovia, Liberia, in 1979. While the African charter contains much language that is similar to provisions in the UN convention, it mirrors the African

Charter on Human and Peoples' Rights in focusing on African cultural values and the child's role in that culture, demonstrated by the inclusion of article 31, which addresses responsibilities of the child.

The preamble to the charter notes that "the situation of most African children remains critical due to the unique factors of their socio-economic, cultural, traditional and developmental circumstances, natural disasters, armed conflicts, exploitation and hunger, and on account of the child's physical and mental immaturity he/she needs special safeguards and care. . . ." It further recognizes that "the child occupies a unique and privileged position in the African society and that for the full and harmonious development of his personality the child should grow up in a family environment in an atmosphere of happiness, love and understanding."

A child, as defined by article 2, is a person under the age of eighteen. Article 3 mandates nondiscrimination in the application of "the rights and freedoms recognized and guaranteed in this Charter"; and article 4 makes "the best interest of the child" the primary consideration and requires that children be given an opportunity to express their own views in "all judicial or administrative proceedings" affecting them. Articles 5 through 11 set forth basic rights of children, including the right to life; survival and development; a name and nationality; freedom of expression, association, thought, conscience, and religion; privacy; and education.

Articles 12 through 14, respectively, discuss leisure, recreation, and cultural activities; handicapped children; and health and medical services. Articles 15 through 30, respectively, address child labor, child abuse and torture, juvenile justice, the family, parental care and protection, parental responsibilities, harmful social and cultural practices, armed conflict, refugee children, adoption, separation from parents, apartheid and discrimination, sexual exploitation, drug abuse, the trafficking and abduction of children, and children of imprisoned mothers.

"Every child shall have responsibilities towards his family and society, the State and other legally recognized communities and the international community," requires article 31, Responsibilities of the Child. "The child, subject to his age and ability, and such limitations as may be contained in the present Charter, shall have the duty: (a) to work for the cohesion of the family, to respect his parents, superiors and elders at all times and to assist them in case of need; (b) to serve his national community by placing his physical and intellectual abilities at its service; (c) to preserve and strengthen social and national solidarity; (d) to preserve and strengthen African cultural values in his relations with other members of society. . . ; (e) to preserve and strengthen the independence and integrity of his country; (f) to contribute to the best of his abilities, at all times and at all levels, to the promotion and achievement of African unity."

Part II, chapter two, Establishment and Organization of the Committee on the Rights and Welfare of the Child, creates the African Committee of Experts on the Rights and Welfare of the Child, consisting of eleven members "of high moral standing, integrity, impartiality and competence in matters of the rights and welfare of the child." Candidates for membership on the committee are nominated by the states parties to the charter and are elected for five-year terms.

The purposes of the committee, set forth in chapter three, Mandate and Procedure of the Committee, include "promot[ing] and protect[ing] the rights enshrined in this Charter. . ."; monitoring its implementation; interpreting its provisions; and performing other tasks as assigned by the OAU or UN. Pursuant to article 43, each state party to the charter must submit reports on progress made in realizing the rights guaranteed in the charter, initially after two years and every three years thereafter. Article 44 authorizes the committee to "receive communications from any person, group or non-governmental organization recognized by the [OAU, member state, or the UN] relating to a matter covered by this Charter," while article 45 provides for investigations by the committee regarding such communications or complaints.

Chapter four, Miscellaneous Provisions, article 46, directs the committee to "draw inspiration from international law on human rights, particularly from the provisions of the African Charter on Human and Peoples' Rights, the Charter of the [OAU], the Universal Declaration of Human Rights, [and] the Convention on the Rights of the Child and other instruments adopted by the [UN] and by African countries in the field of human rights, and from African values and traditions."

Organization of African Unity, P.O. Box 3243, Addis Ababa, Ethiopia. (251-1-51-7700. 🖷 251-1-51-2622. 🖳 y.afanou@telecom.net. 🖳 www.oau-oua.org.

African Charter on Human and Peoples' Rights; Children; Convention on the Rights of the Child; Declaration on Social and Legal Principles Relating to the Protection and Welfare of Children, with Special Reference to Foster Placement and Adoption Nationally and Internationally; Declaration on the Rights of the Child

African Commission on Human and Peoples' Rights

The African Commission on Human and Peoples' Rights was established by the African Charter on Human and Peoples' Rights (Banjul Charter), adopted in 1981. Its purpose is "to promote human and peoples' rights and ensure their protection in Africa" while implementing the charter. In the decade after the commission began its work in 1986, it received seventy-two complaints. Of these the commission determined that fifty did not meet the criteria for admissibility set forth in its charter, five resulted in friendly settlements between the complainant and the government involved, and five were withdrawn. The commission took action on twelve cases, all of which resulted in determinations that the government involved had violated the charter.

Although the number of cases handled by the commission is far less than that handled by the European Commission of Human Rights or the Inter-American Commission on Human Rights during a similar period, it represents a beginning at focusing regional scrutiny and, through publication of its results, international attention on violations of human rights in Africa. The commission initially denied any role for nongovernmental organizations in their activities, but this position is eroding. In 1996, for example, one commission member described the working relationship between the commission and the organizations as "indispensable."

The commission consists of eleven members "chosen from amongst African personalities of the highest reputation, known for their high morality, integrity, impartiality and competence in matters of human and peoples' rights, particular consideration being given to persons having legal experience," as prescribed in the African Charter on Human and Peoples' Rights, part II, Measures of Safeguard, chapter I, article 30. Commission members are elected to six-year terms by the Assembly of Heads of States and Governments of the OAU from a list prepared by the states that are parties to the charter. Members serve in their individual capacities, not as representatives of their governments.

The commission's functions, like those of the Inter-American Commission on Human Rights, are both promotional and quasi-judicial. As set forth in chapter II, Mandate of the Commission, article 45, its promotional duties include collecting documents, conducting studies and research on African problems in the field of human rights, sponsoring seminars and conferences, publishing materials, disseminating information, and working with national and local institutions on human and peoples' rights issues. The commission also, as necessary, give its views and make recommendations to governments.

The commission's quasi-judicial functions, also delineated in article 45, include formulating "principles and rules aimed at solving legal problems relating to human and peoples' rights and fundamental freedoms upon which African Governments may base their legislations," interpreting the charter's provisions "at the request of a State Party, an institution of the OAU or an African organization recognized by the OAU," ensuring the protection of human and peoples' rights under conditions laid down by the charter, and carrying out any other work requested by the OAU.

Procedures for investigating violations of rights based on communications from member states and other complaints are established in chapter III, Procedure of the Commission. Article 47 authorizes the commission to receive communications from a state party to the charter alleging violations by another state party. The commission has three months to settle the matter between the states; if the attempt is unsuccessful, the matter may again be submitted to the commission. If an "amicable solution based on the respect of human and peoples' rights" is not reached, according to article 52, the commission is to prepare "within a reasonable period of time . . . a report stating the facts and its findings." The report is to be sent to the member states and communicated to the Assembly of Heads of State and Government.

The procedure for handling "communications other than those of States Parties to the present Charter" is spelled out in articles 55 and 56. As with communications from states parties to the African charter and in other international human rights systems, domestic remedies must first have been exhausted before the commission may act on the matter. An important aspect of these procedures is that the commission is authorized to handle "special cases which reveal the existence of serious or massive violations of human and peoples' rights." The matter is brought to the attention of the state concerned, and the commission reports its findings to the OAU's Assembly of Heads of State and Government.

Every two years, pursuant to article 62, the states parties to the charter submit a report on legislative or other measures that further the rights and freedoms recognized and guaranteed by the charter. In all its activities, according to chapter IV, Applicable Principles, the commission is to "draw inspiration from international law on human and peoples' rights, . . . the provisions of various African instruments on human and peoples' rights, the [UN] charter [1945] . . . , the Charter of the [OAU] [1963], the Universal Declaration of Human Rights [1948]," and other national and international human rights instruments.

African Commission on Human and Peoples' Rights, P.O. Box 673, Banjul, Gambia. (220-39-2962. ☎ 220-39-0764. 🖳umn.edu/humanrts/Africa/Commission.

Organization of African Unity, P.O. Box 3243, Addis Ababa, Ethiopia. (251-1-51-7700. ☎ 251-1-51-2622. 🖳 y.afanou@telecom.net. 🖳 www.oau-oua.org.

☞

African Charter on Human and Peoples' Rights; European Commission of Human Rights; Inter-American Commission on Human Rights; Regional Human Rights Systems

Aged

The elderly have long been accorded an honored place in human societies and cultures, and families have borne the responsibility for their care. But modern technological changes have brought about social changes, including the shifting of care for the aged from individuals to the government, especially in the more developed nations. Thus debate has intensified around the question of which rights of the aged (from the French *agé*, meaning having lived or existed a long time) must be assumed by the government.

As a result of longer life spans and lower birth rates, the number of elderly persons is increasing more rapidly in proportion to the total population and particularly the number of workers. The UN Committee on Economic, Social and Cultural Rights in 1995 projected that the number of persons over sixty years of age would reach 600 million by the year 2001 (triple the total for 1950) and would double again by the year 2025 to 1.2 billion. These increases, it stated, represent a "quiet revolution" that "is affecting the social and economic structures of societies both at the world level and at the country level, and will affect them even more in [the] future."

Almost all nations provide some form of social assistance to elderly citizens, usually in the form of social security and old-age benefits, including health care and assistance for persons who cannot afford necessities such as housing, food, and self-care. According to the Principles for Older Persons, adopted by the UN General Assembly in 1991, the aged should have, among other things, "access to adequate food, water, shelter, clothing and health care, . . . the opportunity to work or . . . access to other income-generating opportunities, . . . access to appropriate educational and training programs, . . . [and] be able to live in environments that are safe and adaptable to personal preferences and changing capacities. . . ."

Abuses of the elderly occur both in the family setting and in institutional facilities that are not properly monitored. Because of diminished physical and mental capacities and lack of adequate supervision, the aged often fall prey to the unscrupulous by fraud or outright thievery. In many ways the last stage of life can be like the first: requiring intensive care and supervision for safety, comfort, and well-being.

Argentina raised the issue of "old age rights" in the UN General Assembly in 1948, but it was not until 1970 that the secretary-general issued a preliminary report on the subject. The document warned that while the number of older persons was increasing, they were being neglected. Another UN report in 1973 singled out developed nations for age discrimination, economic insecurity, a reduced right to work, and inadequate provision for the elderly. Almost fifteen years later, in 1987, the Economic and Social Council (ECOSOC) authorized the establishment of the International Institute on Aging. Headquartered in Valletta, Malta, it provides training in gerontology, medical geriatrics, and social gerontology, as well as courses in income security for the elderly; it also issues a quarterly publication.

The Principles for Older Persons, a document based on the International Plan of Action on Aging, approved in 1982 by the World Assembly on Aging in Vienna, focuses on the issues of independence, participation, care, self-fulfillment, and dignity. The document begins by recognizing the "contributions that older persons make to their societies" and then sets forth specific recommendations that governments are encouraged to incorporate into their national programs. The General Assembly also designated 1999 as the International Year of the Elderly.

Canadian Charter of Rights and Freedoms (1982), Equality Rights: "15(1). Every individual is equal before and under the law . . . without discrimination and, in particular, without discrimination based on race, national origin, color, religion, sex, age. . . ."

American Convention on Human Rights (1969), Additional Protocol (1988), article 17: "Everyone has the right to protection in old age."

Canadian Federal Court of Appeals (1997): Regulations establishing compulsory retirement are not exceptions for purposes of human rights legislation, and compulsory retirement is not a bona fide occupational requirement.

Committee on Economic, Social and Cultural Rights (1995), General Comment no. 6, The Economic, Social and Cultural Rights of Older Persons: "3. Most of the States parties to the [International Covenant on Economic, Social and Cultural Rights (1966)], and the industrialized countries in particular, are faced with the task of adapting their social and economic policies to the aging of their populations, especially as regards social security. In the developing countries, the absence or deficiencies of social security coverage are being aggravated by the emigration of the younger members of the population and the consequent weakening of the traditional role of the family, the main support of older people."

International Federation on Aging, 425 Viger Avenue West, Suite 520, Montreal H2Z 1X2, Canada. ☎ 514-396-3358. 🖷 514-396-3378. 🖳 ifa@citenet.net. 🖳 www.ifa-fiv.org.

International Institute on Aging, 117 St. Paul Street, Valletta VLT 07, Malta. ☎ 356-24-30-44. 🖷 356-23-02-48. 🖳 inia@maltanet.net. 🖳 www.inia.org.

Formanek, Susanne, and Sepp Linhart, eds. *Aging: Asian Concepts and Experiences, Past and Present.* Vienna: Austrian Academy of Science, 1997.

Harris, Dan R., ed. *Aging Sourcebook: Basic Information on Issues Affecting Older Americans, Including Demographic Trends, Social Security, Medicare, Estate Planning, Legal Rights, Health and Safety,*

Elder Care Options, Retirement Lifestyle Options and End of Life Issues. Personal Concerns Series. Detroit: Omnigraphics, 1998.

Projects Assisting Older Workers in European Countries. Luxembourg: European Commission, Directorate-General for Employment, Industrial Relations, and Social Affairs, 1998.

Die, Right to; Discrimination; Domestic Violence; Families

AIDS

AIDS, an acronym for acquired immune deficiency syndrome, is a generally fatal disease that results in severe loss of cellular immunity. It is caused by an infection of a retrovirus known as HIV, which is transmitted in sexual fluids and blood and which can lie dormant for long periods of time. More than sixteen million people, including more than three million children, have died from the disease, and no cure or vaccine has yet been developed.

In 1987 a UN General Assembly resolution concluded that AIDS, which is concentrated in Africa, North and Latin America, south Asia, Western Europe, and the former Soviet Union, had reached pandemic proportions and threatened the health of the world's population. By the end of the 1990s, an estimated 34 million people worldwide were living with HIV/AIDS, an increase of a third over the figure reported by the United Nations in July 1996. Sub-Saharan Africa alone accounted for an estimated 23 million cases. The World Health Organization has taken a leading role in combating this virulent disease.

In addition to its physically debilitating effects, the AIDS epidemic raises a number of human rights issues for victims, medical personnel, government policy makers, and the general public. The fear of infection by the HIV virus has led to restrictions on people diagnosed with the virus or the disease. From what is known about transmission of HIV, these restrictions are not always justified. Also of concern are the stigmatization of people with the disease, which first manifested itself disproportionately among gay men; access to medical treatment; fears of contamination through donated blood; personal privacy; and discriminatory treatment. Discrimination may include refusal of authorities to grant health care, social security, or welfare benefits; loss of employment based on unwarranted fear of contamination; and denial of educational opportunities, housing, and the right to participate in sports, recreation, social activities, and trade unions.

"Since AIDS is a global problem that poses a serious threat to humanity," stated the London Declaration on AIDS Prevention, issued by delegates from 148 countries to the 1988 World Summit of Ministers of Health Programs for AIDS Prevention, "urgent action by all governments and people the world over is needed to implement [the World Health Organization's] global AIDS strategy.... We undertake to devise national programs to prevent and contain the spread of immunodeficiency virus (HIV) infection as a part of our countries' health systems."

U.K. AIDS (Control) Act 1987: "1.—(1) Reports shall be made in accordance with this section . . . [on] 1. The number of persons known . . . to be persons with AIDS at the end of the period to which the report relates . . . having been diagnosed as such . . . 2. The number of persons known . . . to have been diagnosed as persons with AIDS . . . in the reporting period and who have died. . . ."

Declaration of the Paris AIDS Summit (1994): The forty-two governments represented by the states parties to this document declare "our obligation as political leaders to make the fight against HIV/AIDS a priority,—our obligation to act with compassion for and in solidarity with those with HIV or at risk of becoming infected, both within our societies and internationally,—our determination to ensure that all persons living with HIV/AIDS are able to realize the full and equal enjoyment of their fundamental rights and freedoms without distinction and under all circumstances,—our determination to fight against poverty, stigmatization and discrimination. . . ."

French Special Court (1999): A special court composed of fifteen legislators and judges acquitted a former prime minister and minister but convicted a former health minister of delaying the introduction of an AIDS screening test, a delay that allowed some four thousand people to contract AIDS from blood transfusions and at least three hundred fifty to die.

European Court of Human Rights (1995): Under the European Convention for the Protection of Human Rights and Fundamental Freedoms (1950), article 6, an AIDS victim seeking damages was improperly barred from access to the courts by a 1991 French AIDS compensation law that was vague and did not contain sufficient safeguards.

UNAIDS, 20 avenue Appia, 1211 Geneva 27, Switzerland. (41-22-791-3666. 🖷 41-22-791-4187. 🖳 unaids@unaids.org. 🖳 www.unaids.org.

HIV/AIDS and Human Rights: International Guidelines. Geneva: United Nations, 1998.

Smith, Raymond A., ed. *Encyclopedia of AIDS: A Social, Political, Cultural, and Scientific Record of the AIDS Epidemic.* Chicago: Fitzroy Dearborn, 1998.

Discrimination; Health; World Health Organization

Alfonsín Foulkes, Raúl

Raúl Ricardo Alfonsín Foulkes (b. 1927) unflinchingly resisted the military junta that ruled Argentina from 1976 to 1982 and, when elected the country's president in 1983, helped bring to trial junta leaders who had abused human rights. For his efforts he received the Council of Europe's prize for human rights in 1986.

A native of Argentina's Buenos Aires province, Alfonsín Foulkes was graduated from military school and in 1945 joined the Radical Party, which was defeated when Juan Perón came to power the following year. After his graduation from law school in 1950, Alfonsín Foulkes returned to his hometown of Chascomús, where he practiced law, published a newspaper, and was elected to the city council. In 1953 the Perón government imprisoned him for his political activities.

After Perón's removal from office by a military coup in 1955, Alfonsín Foulkes became active in one of the two political parties formed from the Radical Party. He won a seat in the provincial legislature, was elected to the national congress in 1963 (his term was cut short by another military coup), and in 1972 founded a new reform movement. The Peronists returned to power in 1973 but were overthrown in 1976 by a military junta, which quickly became the most repressive government in Argentina's history.

Leading the criticism of the junta's violations of human rights, Alfonsín Foulkes helped form the Permanent Assembly for Human Rights, consisting of well-known jurists, politicians, and clergy. After Argentina's defeat in the Falklands-Malvinas War in 1982, the military regime crumbled, and in 1983 Alfonsín Foulkes was elected president of Argentina. Once in office he worked to rebuild Argentina's democratic institutions and brought members of the former juntas to trial for their acts. Defeated in a democratic election in 1989, he continued to play an active role in Argentina's political life.

Disappearance

Aliens

An alien (from the Latin *alienus,* meaning strange or hostile) is either a person of a foreign nation and allegiance or a nonnational (a stateless person, for example). The rights and obligations of aliens have been the subject of municipal and international law for thousands of years. In the fourth century B.C.E. the Greek philosopher Aristotle remarked in *The Politics:* "Resident aliens in many places do not possess even such rights [to sue or be sued] completely, for they are obliged to have a patron, so that they do but imperfectly participate in the community...."

Today a person's rights are generally predicated on his or her status in a particular political jurisdiction. Citizens of a state can expect certain rights, while aliens in the same jurisdiction are dependent on the state's willingness to extend rights to them. Theoretically the relationship between a citizen and the state is reciprocal, meaning that a citizen owes allegiance and certain duties to the state, and the state in return undertakes to protect the citizen and extend certain rights. However, no such reciprocity exists between one nation and a citizen of another nation; a country is thus under no obligation to extend to aliens any rights except those agreed to under international law and custom, although it may grant aliens certain rights in exchange for the extension of the same courtesy to its own citizens when in the alien country.

As long as aliens obey the laws of the host country, including laws regarding their alien status, they will generally receive certain basic rights as if they were citizens, although the rights to vote and hold office are usually reserved for citizens only. Often the treatment of aliens depends on such factors as religious and cultural differences, the number of aliens from a particular jurisdiction in the host country, and the host country's laws and economic conditions. Even foreigners who have acquired citizenship in the host country may find themselves discriminated against on the basis of race, ethnic origin, or religion. A number of other factors may determine whether a country will permit admission of aliens, and, once admitted, they may be expelled, deported, or extradited by the host country.

Because the treatment of aliens is not part of the relationship between citizens and their government, national constitutions generally do not expressly address the issue, except perhaps with regard to procedures for naturalization or becoming a citizen. The rights and duties of aliens are more likely to be covered in national laws and regulations. Relevant international human rights documents include the Convention Relating to the Status of Refugees (1951), Declaration on Territorial Asylum (1967), European Convention on the Legal Status of Migrant Workers (1977), and Declaration on the Human Rights of Individuals Who Are Not Nationals of the Country in Which They Live (1985).

Constitution of Colombia (1991), title III, Concerning Population and the Territory, chapter 3, Concerning Aliens, article 100: "Aliens in Colombia will enjoy the same civil rights as Colombians."

International Covenant on Civil and Political Rights (1966), article 13: "An alien lawfully in the territory of a State Party to the present Covenant may be expelled therefrom only in pursuance of a decision reached in accordance with law and shall, except where compelling reasons of national security otherwise require, be allowed to submit the reasons against his expulsion and to have his case reviewed by, and be represented for the purpose before, the competent authority or a person or persons especially designated by the competent authority."

U.S. District Court, Kansas (1980): "Excludable and excluded aliens who are not recognized under the law as having entered the United States do not enjoy the panoply of rights guaranteed to citizens and [legal aliens] by the [U.S.] Constitution [1789]."

Human Rights Committee (1994), General Comment 15: While the International Covenant on Civil and Political Rights (1966) "does not recognize the right of aliens to enter or reside in the territory of a State party" to it, the document does give aliens "all the protection regarding rights guaranteed therein, and its requirements should be observed by States parties in their legislation and in practice as appropriate."

Jacobson, David. *Rights across Borders*. Baltimore: John Hopkins University Press, 1996.

MacDonald, Ian A. *Immigration Law and Practice in the United Kingdom*. London: Butterworths, 1995.

Asylum; Convention Relating to the Status of Refugees; Declaration on Territorial Asylum; Declaration on the Human Rights of Individuals Who Are Not Nationals of the Country in Which They Live; Deportation; Diplomats and Consuls; Expulsion; Immigrants; Nationality; Refugees; Statelessness

Alma Ata, Declaration of

See Declaration of Alma Ata (Asian Press); Declaration of Alma Ata (Health)

American Convention on Human Rights

The American Convention on Human Rights, an inter-American human rights agreement sometimes referred to as the Pact of San José, Costa Rica, was opened for signature on November 22, 1969, and entered into force on July 18, 1978. Inspired by the American Declaration of the Rights and Duties of Man (1948), it was prepared under the auspices of the Organization of American States (OAS) after

the adoption by the UN General Assembly of the International Covenant on Civil and Political Rights in 1966.

The American Convention on Human Rights, like the European Convention for the Protection of Human Rights and Fundamental Freedoms (1950) and the African Charter on Human and Peoples' Rights (1981), is a regional approach to the promotion and enforcement of human rights. Such a system lies between the national approach, which relies on national institutions to enforce constitutional and other legal guarantees of rights, and the international system engendered by the documents and institutions of the United Nations, together with other international agreements and organizations, including nongovernmental ones. Two protocols were added: the first, relating to economic, social, and cultural rights, adopted in San Salvador, El Salvador, in 1988; and the second, relating to the abolition of the death penalty, adopted in Asunción, Paraguay, in 1990.

The preamble reaffirms the intention of the signatory states "to consolidate in this hemisphere, within the framework of democratic institutions, a system of personal liberty and social justice based on respect for the essential rights of man...." It also recognizes that the "essential rights of man are not derived from one's being a national of a certain state, but are based upon attributes of the human personality; and that they therefore justify international protection provided by the domestic laws of the American states."

Part I, State Obligations and Rights Protected, chapter I, General Obligations, article 1, Obligation to Respect Rights, declares: "1. The States Parties to this Convention undertake to respect the rights and freedoms recognized herein and to ensure to all persons subject to their jurisdiction the free and full exercise of those rights and freedoms, without discrimination for reasons of race, color, sex, language, religion, political or other opinion, national or social origin, economic status, birth, or any other social condition." Article 2, Domestic Legal Effects, states: "Where the exercise of any of the rights or freedoms referred to in Article 1 is not already ensured by legislative or other provisions, the States Parties undertake to adopt, in accordance with their constitutional process and the provisions of this Convention, such legislative or other measures as may be necessary to give effect to those rights or freedoms."

Chapter II, Civil and Political Rights, articles 3 through 25, address, among other issues, juridical personality (the right to be recognized everywhere as a person having rights and obligations), life, humane treatment, slavery, personal liberty, fair trial, privacy, conscience and religion, thought and expression, inaccurate or offensive statements by a regulated medium of communication, assembly, association, participation in government, equal protection before the law, and recourse to competent forums for protection against violations of fundamental rights.

States that are parties to the convention are required, according to chapter III, Economic, Social, and Cultural Rights, article 26, Progressive Development, to "adopt measures both internally and through international cooperation, especially those of an economic and technical nature, with a view to achieving progressively, by legislation or other appropriate means, the full realization of the rights implicit in the economic, social, educational, scientific, and cultural standards set forth in the Charter of the Organization of American States [1948] as amended by the Protocol of Buenos Aires."

As set forth in chapter IV, Suspension of Guarantees, Interpretation, and Application, article 27, Suspension of Guarantees, the convention's guarantees can be suspended and its provisions derogated from only in times of "war, public danger, or other emergency that threatens the independence or security of a State Party...." Article 28, Federal Clause, was added at the urging of the United States to allow a federal state such as itself to assume the obligations for only those subject areas over which it constitutionally exercises authority.

Chapter V, Personal Responsibilities, article 32, Relationship between Duties and Rights, declares: "1. Every person has responsibilities to his family, his community, and mankind. 2. The rights of each person are limited by the rights of others, by the security of all, and by the just demands of the general welfare, in a democratic society."

The Inter-American Commission on Human Rights and the Inter-American Court of Human Rights, according to part II, Means of Protection, chapter VI, Competent Organs, article 33, are the agencies designated for "the fulfillment of the commitments made by the States Parties to this Convention." Chapter VII, Inter-American Commission on Human Rights, articles 34 through 51, set forth the commission's organization, functions, competence, and procedures. The main function of the seven-member commission is "to promote respect for and defense of human rights." Among its duties is taking "action on petitions and other communications [from any] person or group of persons, or any nongovernmental entity ... containing denunciations or complaints of violations of this Convention by a State Party." The commission may transmit a report of its findings to the states concerned, "which shall not be at liberty to publish it." It may also refer the matter to the Inter-American Court of Human Rights or, after three months, publish the report. Chapter VIII, Inter-American Court of Human Rights, articles 52 through 73, discuss the organization, jurisdiction and functions, and procedures of the Inter-American Court of Human Rights.

Organization of American States, 17th Street and Constitution Avenue, N.W., Washington, D.C. 20006. ☏ 202-458-3000. 🖨 202-458-3967. 📧 pi@oas.org. 🖥 www.oas.org.

Buergenthal, Thomas. *International Human Rights Law in a Nutshell*. St. Paul, Minn.: West, 1995.

Davidson, J. Scott. *The Inter-American Human Rights System*. Hants, England: Dartmouth, 1997.

African Charter on Human and Peoples' Rights; American Declaration of the Rights and Duties of Man; European Convention for the Protection of Human Rights and Fundamental Freedoms; Inter-American Commission on Human Rights; Inter-American Court of Human Rights; Nongovernmental Organizations; Regional Human Rights Systems

American Declaration of the Rights and Duties of Man

The American Declaration of the Rights and Duties of Man is a resolution of the Organization of American States (OAS) adopted by the Ninth International Conference of American States on May 2, 1948, seven months before the Universal Declaration of Human Rights (1948). Although the drafters of the OAS declaration believed it to be without legal effect, respect for the document has grown. Today it is recognized as an authoritative statement of the accepted principles of the fundamental rights of the individual, and its authority is acknowledged in the OAS charter (1948).

Other human rights documents of importance to the inter-American regional system of human rights adopted by the conference on the same day that it adopted the declaration include the Inter-American Charter of Social Guarantees, Inter-American Convention on the Granting of Civil Rights to Women, and Inter-American Convention on the Granting of Political Rights to Women. More than twenty years later, in 1969, the American Convention on Human Rights was adopted.

The American Declaration of the Rights and Duties of Man begins by proclaiming that the "American peoples have acknowledged the dignity of the individual, and their national constitutions recognize that juridical and political institutions ... regulate life in human society." Further, they have as their principal aim "the protection of the essential rights of man and the creation of circumstances that will permit him to achieve spiritual and material progress and attain happiness...."

"All men are born free and equal, in dignity and in rights, and being endowed by nature with reason and conscience, they should conduct themselves as brothers one to another," states the preamble, adding that "fulfillment of duty by each individual is a prerequisite to the rights of all."

Chapter one, Rights, contains twenty-eight articles expressly acknowledging such rights as life, liberty, and security of the person; equality before the law, "without distinction as to race, sex, language, creed, or any other factor"; freedom "to profess a religious faith, and to manifest and practice it both in public and in private"; and "freedom of investigation, of opinion, and the expression of ideas, by any medium whatsoever." Other rights include protection of the law, protection of families, health care for mothers and children, freedom of movement, inviolability of the home and the "transmission of correspondence," preservation of health, education, the benefits of culture, work and fair remuneration, and other social benefits. Additional rights set forth in this chapter include recognition of the juridical personality (the right to be recognized everywhere as a person having rights and obligations) and civil rights, the right to a fair trial, the right of nationality, and the right to vote and participate in government, as well as the right of assembly, association, property, petition, protection from arbitrary arrest, due process of law, and asylum. Article XXVIII notes: "The rights of man are limited by the rights of others, by the security of all, and by the just demands of the general welfare and advancement of democracy."

Duties of individuals are set forth in chapter two, Duties, which consists of ten articles. "It is the duty of the individual so to conduct himself in relation to others," article XXIX provides, "that each and every one may fully form and develop his personality." In addition, each person has the duty, according to article XXX, "to aid, support, educate and protect his minor children. . ." and, states article XXXI, "to acquire at least an elementary education." Article XXXV addresses a person's duties with respect to social security and welfare. Other duties include the obligation to vote, to obey the law, to serve the community and the nation, to pay taxes, to work, and to refrain from political activities in a foreign country.

Organization of American States, 17th Street and Constitution Avenue, N.W., Washington, D.C. 20006. (202-458-3000. 202-458-3967. pi@oas.org. www.oas.org.

American Convention on Human Rights; Inter-American Charter of Social Guarantees; Inter-American Convention on the Granting of Civil Rights to Women; Inter-American Convention on the Granting of Political Rights to Women

Amnesty

The goal of amnesty is to make a new beginning, erase old animosities, or restore offenders or belligerents to a state of grace. The intentional overlooking or pardon for past offenses, *amnesty* is derived from the Greek *amnesis* and the Latin *amnestia*, both meaning oblivion. In national constitutions or laws, the power to grant amnesty—to forgive the illegal acts of a number of people, such as draft dodgers or

vanquished rebels—is one of the powers of the executive branch of government or the chief executive officer, although it sometimes involves the legislative branch as well. In international law, implied amnesty is the "burial in oblivion" of the particular causes of strife between belligerents encompassed in a treaty of peace.

Used for humanitarian reasons or political goodwill, amnesty today encompasses general grants of pardon and release of prisoners from detention. It is generally awarded to a group of people who meet certain criteria, whereas an executive pardon, offered by a government's chief executive, is typically extended to an individual. Government authorities may use humanitarian grounds as the basis for granting amnesty for ordinary criminal offenses—for example, to disabled persons, women, and children—as well as for relieving overcrowding in prisons, thus protecting the human rights of prisoners.

According to a special report for the Subcommission on the Promotion and Protection of Human Rights in 1985, amnesty for political offenses may be granted for a number of reasons. Political amnesty may be provided at regular intervals or, to alleviate internal political tensions, on special occasions such as national holidays or at the end of a state of emergency. To avoid punishment for crimes and human rights violations, leaders of authoritarian regimes, such as the recent military juntas in Argentina and Chile, may grant themselves amnesty just before a government's transition to a democracy, a process known as transitional justice; such amnesty, however, could be repealed by a new democratic regime. Political amnesty may also be granted to induce members of a guerrilla force to defect, thus weakening the faction's strength, and to encourage the return of exiles. A further use is under international peace treaties and in negotiations for the cessation of hostilities within a country.

Law on General Amnesty for the Consolidation of Peace, El Salvador (1993), article 1: "A broad, absolute and unconditional amnesty is granted in favor of all those who in one way or another participated in political crimes, crimes with political ramifications, or common crimes committed by no less than twenty people, before January 1st 1992, regardless of whether proceedings against them for the perpetration of these crime[s] have commenced or not, or whether they have received a sentence as a consequence."

American Convention on Human Rights (1969), chapter II, Civil and Political Rights, article 4: "6. Every person condemned to death shall have the right to apply for amnesty, pardon, or commutation of sentence, which may be granted in all cases."

Supreme Court of El Salvador (1993): Under constitutional principles, clemency is one manifestation of the sovereign power of the people; moreover, "individual grace develops in a parallel form with collective grace, the real predecessor of modern amnesty."

African Commission on Human and Peoples' Rights (1994): The claim of two journalists that their detention in Cote d'Ivoire was a violation of their rights must first be presented to the Cote d'Ivoire legal system, because the amnesty granted them "extirpated [voided] the legal effects of the detention."

Soyinka, Wole. *The Burden of Memory, the Muse of Forgiveness.* New York: Oxford University Press, 1998.

Justice; Prisoners; Punishment

Amnesty International

A worldwide volunteer movement, Amnesty International seeks to prevent governments from committing the gravest violations of fundamental human rights, such as deliberate and arbitrary executions, enforced disappearances, the taking of hostages, the use of children in armed conflict, and the infliction of severe suffering on people because of their identity or beliefs. This nongovernmental organization focuses mainly on freeing persons imprisoned because of their ethnic origin, sex, race, language, religion, national or social origin, or birth or economic status; ensuring fair and prompt trials for political prisoners; abolishing the death penalty and torture and cruel treatment of prisoners; and ending extrajudicial executions and involuntary disappearances.

The idea for Amnesty International came from a British barrister, Peter Benenson, who initiated an Appeal for Amnesty in 1961, an effort to aid people of all countries who had been imprisoned for their opinions. Originally a one-year campaign, it evoked a huge response and led to the establishment of a permanent, entirely voluntary organization pledged to securing worldwide observance of the Universal Declaration of Human Rights (1948). In 1977 the group was awarded the Nobel Peace Prize and in 1978 the United Nations Human Rights Prize.

A relatively large human rights organization, Amnesty International currently has more than one million members, subscribers, and donors in well over one hundred countries. It is headquartered in London but has offices in cities around the world, including New York City and Washington, D.C., and an urgent action office in Colorado. The organization's activities and budget are determined by an international council, which consists of voting representatives appointed by the national sections in fifty-five countries in proportion to their membership or groups.

In its 1998 annual report of human rights violations, Amnesty International concluded that extrajudicial executions occurred in fifty-five countries, people disappeared or continued to be classified as "disappeared" in thirty-one countries, torture and mistreatment by state authorities oc-

curred in 117 countries, and in forty-one countries prisoners were tortured, lacked adequate medical treatment, or were subjected to cruel, inhuman, or degrading medical conditions that led to their deaths. Also documented in many nations were prisoners of conscience, unfair trials of political prisoners, illegal detention, executions and sentences of death, and human rights abuses by armed opposition groups. Additional reports are issued by region and country.

Amnesty International, One Easton Street, London WC1X 8DJ, England. (44-207-413-5500. 🖷 44-207-956-1157. 🖳 amnestyis @amnesty.org. 🖳 www.amnesty.org.

Amnesty International USA, 322 Eighth Avenue, New York, N.Y. 10001. (212-807-8400. 🖷 212-627-1451. 🖳 admin-us@aiusa. org. 🖳 www.amnesty-usa.org.

Urgent Action Office, P.O. Box 1270, Nederland, Colo. 80466. (303-258-1170. 🖷 303-258-7881. 🖳 sharriso@aiusa.org. 🖳 www. amnesty-usa.org.

Capital Punishment; Detention; Disappearance; Fair Trial; Prisoners; Punishment; Summary Executions; Torture; Universal Declaration of Human Rights

Amparo

Amparo, from the Spanish word meaning protection, is a guarantee that citizens will be protected from government infringement of their civil rights. Similar to the Anglo-American concept of habeas corpus, which was developed to test the validity of a person's detention, *amparo* takes the form of a judicial proceeding. Developed in Mexico, it has spread throughout Latin America and is included in the constitutions of a number of Latin American countries.

The *amparo* provision of Mexico's 1917 constitution requires that a trial be held if requested by an injured party. In addition, any deficiency in a complaint filed by the injured party may also be corrected by the federal courts in an *amparo* trial. A finding in an *amparo* proceeding differs from a finding in other types of cases. The court's decision in an *amparo* trial does not necessarily bind the lower courts; thus, the only party that benefits from *amparo* is the petitioner.

Constitution of Nicaragua (1987), title IV, Rights, Duties, and Guarantees of the Nicaraguan People, chapter 1, article 45: "Persons whose constitutional rights have been violated or are in danger of violation shall have recourse to habeas corpus or protection *(mandamus),* according to the case and in accord with the law of *amparo.*"

**American Declaration of the Rights and Duties of Man (1948),
chapter one, Rights, article XVIII, Right to Fair Trial:** "Every person
may resort to the courts to ensure respect for his legal rights. There
should likewise be available to him a simple, brief procedure whereby the courts will protect him from acts of authority that to his prejudice violate any fundamental constitutional rights."

Supreme Court of Mexico (1925): An *amparo* proceeding was not
available to a Chinese national who was expelled from Mexico
because Mexico's constitution gave the president "the exclusive
power to expel from the national territory without a previous
judicial proceeding any alien whose stay is deemed inexpedient."

Human Rights Committee (1987): The complainant, an applicant
for civil service positions in Uruguay, had been rejected because of
a remedial law giving preference to former civil servants who had
been dismissed as ideologically incompatible during a period of
military rule. The committee held, however, that the complainant
was not a victim of discrimination under the International Covenant
on Civil and Political Rights (1966), even though he had exhausted
his local remedies, including having his action for *amparo* dismissed
by the supreme court of Uruguay.

Baker, Richard D. *Judicial Review in Mexico: A Study of the Amparo Suit.* Austin: University of Texas Press, 1971.

Habeas Corpus

Anthony, Susan B.

See Stanton, Elizabeth Cady

Apartheid

Apartheid (an Afrikaans word meaning separateness) was
South Africa's fifty-year policy of segregating inhabitants
of European descent from African blacks, people of mixed
race, and Indians. The word appeared as early as 1929 and
has since been used to refer to similar discriminatory
policies and forms of racial separation elsewhere.

The outbreak of World War II induced a wave of nationalism in South Africa and triggered a movement to pattern
society on the principle of racial purity, using Nazi Germany as a model. During the war, however, as a former
British colony, South Africa sent troops to fight for Britain.
The wartime economy drew a large influx of African blacks

into urban areas, distressing many white South Africans,
who in 1948 voted into power a political party with apartheid as its platform. Later renamed the National Party, it
remained in power for nearly a half century, until 1994.

Almost immediately the National Party pushed through
a number of laws to separate the races. The Population Registration Act of 1950 required the registration of all South
Africans by race or color; it was later amended to cover the
possibility of light-colored blacks' passing themselves off as
whites. The Group Areas Act of 1950 created separate areas
for the different races. The Prohibition of Mixed Marriages
Act of 1949 made marriages between whites and members
of other races illegal, and the Immorality Act of 1950 banned
sexual relations between whites and nonwhites. Other laws
implementing apartheid were enacted up until 1976.

In 1973 the UN General Assembly adopted the International Convention on the Suppression and Punishment of
the Crime of Apartheid, which entered into force in 1976.
That same year the General Assembly also undertook a program of action, noting that for thirty years the United Nations had made "patient efforts to persuade the racist minority regimes to abandon the bitter legacy of the past and
to work for a peaceful solution in accordance with the principles of human equality and international cooperation."

The struggle to eliminate apartheid was a long and difficult
one. Peaceful protests were repressed, some eighteen thousand demonstrators protesting South Africa's racist policy
were arrested, and the country's major antiapartheid organizations were outlawed. Influenced by the Black Power movement in the United States, Steve Biko, an African medical
student, became the leader of a student group in 1969 that
advocated nonviolent protests. Eventually Biko and others
were arraigned on charges of fomenting terrorism, and in
1977 Biko died of massive head injuries inflicted during police
interrogation. Another South African leader opposing the
apartheid regime was Archbishop Desmond Tutu, whose
international reputation and nonviolent approach to bringing about change made him a potent force in the campaign
against racial segregation and injustice. Even so, some of the
antiapartheid organizations turned to violence.

In 1986, partly in response to mounting international
disapproval, the all-white government began incrementally
dismantling apartheid. In 1990 South Africa's president,
Frederik de Klerk, lifted restrictions on the media, invited
antiapartheid activists to participate in writing a new multiracial constitution, and pledged an investigation of alleged human rights abuses by the government's security
forces. One significant event was the release from prison of
Nelson Mandela, the African National Congress party
leader, in 1990. On May 9, 1994, with apartheid now past,
the national legislature unanimously elected Mandela president of South Africa.

**Constitution of South Africa (1997), chapter 2, Bill of Rights,
section 25 [Property]:** "(8) No provision of this section may impede

the state from taking legislative and other measures to achieve land, water and related reform, in order to redress the results of past racial discrimination. . . ."

International Convention on the Suppression and Punishment of the Crimes of Apartheid (1973), article I: "1. The States Parties to the present Convention declare that *apartheid* is a crime against humanity and that inhuman acts resulting from the policies and practices of *apartheid* . . . are crimes violating the principles of international law, in particular the purposes and principles of the Charter of the United Nations [1945], and constituting a serious threat to international peace and security."

Supreme Court of Namibia (1992): "Throughout the preamble and substantive structures of the Namibian Constitution there is one golden and unbroken thread—an abiding 'revulsion' of racism and apartheid."

UN Security Council (1977): After much debate initiated by the massive use of violence against black citizens by the government of South Africa, including the shooting of antiapartheid demonstrators in Soweto in 1976, it was unanimously decided to impose a mandatory arms embargo on the country.

Butler, Anthony. *Democracy and Apartheid*. New York: St. Martin's, 1998.

Eades, Lindsay M. *The End of Apartheid in South Africa*. Westport, Conn.: Greenwood, 1999.

Declaration on Fundamental Principles Concerning the Contribution of the Mass Media to Strengthening Peace and International Understanding, to the Promotion of Human Rights and to Countering Racialism, Apartheid and Incitement to War; Declaration on the Elimination of All Forms of Racial Discrimination; International Convention on the Elimination of All Forms of Racial Discrimination; Mandela, Nelson; Race Discrimination; Tutu, Desmond

Appeals

The right to appeal a government decision, particularly a decision by a lower court, is a basic right in constitutional democracies. Both nationally and internationally, the human right to an impartial review of important decisions—those affecting a person's property, liberty, and life—is generally recognized. All modern nations have a judicial system and hierarchy through which appeals of lower court decisions may be made to higher courts. In some countries, however, the process is neither simple nor just.

Charles Dickens, writing to a friend in 1849, declared "[t]he indispensable necessity . . . for a public and solemn Court of Appeals in all criminal cases." The word *appeal* (from the French legal term *appel*, meaning to appeal to a higher court) carries with it the hope of having a decision reversed or at least modified in favor of the appellant. The term has been in use in English in this sense since at least the thirteenth century.

The right of appeal has a long history. The Athenian lawgiver Solon in 594 B.C.E. created a popular court of appeals where decisions of public officials might be challenged, and in the middle of the following century, when the court system was reformed, courts of first instance and appeals courts were established. Appeal rights developed in the common law of England, although one form, abolished by Parliament in 1816, provided for private prosecution of persons acquitted of crimes prosecuted by the government, thus constituting double jeopardy. In his commentaries on the laws of England, written in the eighteenth century, William Blackstone described the appeals process: "[T]he several courts had a gradual subordination to each other, the superior correcting and reforming the errors of the inferior. . . ."

Appeals may be of various types, and procedures for appealing decisions in criminal and civil cases differ. Some appeals are "of right," meaning that the law requires that the appeal be heard. Others, like certain appeals to the U.S. Supreme Court, are at the discretion of the higher court to accept for review. Some appeals are *de novo*, meaning that the appeals court uses the record of the trial court but reviews both the evidence and the law; in some cases, however, the reviewing court is limited to reviewing only how the law was interpreted or applied, not questions of fact. In Austria, Germany, and the United States, among many other countries, an important part of the process is the right of appeal, by which questions regarding the constitutionality of acts of the executive and legislative branches may be reviewed by the courts and declared invalid if found to be unconstitutional.

Some national constitutions, including those of Kenya, Nicaragua, and Peru, address the right of appeal, especially to the nation's supreme court. International documents that guarantee this right include the International Covenant on Civil and Political Rights (1966), American Convention on Human Rights (1969), and African Charter on Human and People's Rights (1981). Unfortunately, in many countries members of the judiciary are not truly independent or competent enough to adequately protect the average citizen's right of appeal. Like many other rights, the right of appeal depends heavily on the rule of law and an aggressive and independent legal system.

Constitution of Liberia (1986), article 69: "[T]he supreme court shall be the final arbiter of constitutional issues and shall exercise final appellate jurisdiction in all cases, both as to law and fact."

International Covenant on Civil and Political Rights (1966), part III, article 14: "5. Everyone convicted of a crime shall have the right to his conviction and sentence being reviewed by a higher tribunal according to law."

Federal Court of Appeals of Canada (1988): An appeal may not be reopened because opposing counsel misled appellants as to the powers of the Human Rights Tribunal. Such powers are purely a question of law about which opposing counsel has no duty to inform appellants.

African Commission on Human and Peoples' Rights (1995): Decrees of the Nigerian government nullifying the jurisdiction of the Nigerian courts to adjudicate the legality of the decrees constituted a breach of the African Charter on Human and Peoples' Rights (1981), article 7: "1. Every individual shall have the right to have his cause heard. This comprises: a) the right to an appeal to competent national organs against acts violating his fundamental rights as guaranteed by conventions, laws, regulations and customs in force."

Martineau, Robert J. *Appellate Justice in England and the United States: A Comparative Analysis.* Buffalo, N.Y.: W. S. Hein, 1990.

Due Process of Law; Fair Trial; Judicial Independence; Rule of Law

Aquinas, St. Thomas

See Thomas Aquinas, St.

Aquino, Corazon

Following the 1983 assassination of her husband, Benigno Aquino Jr., leader of the opposition to the Philippine dictator Ferdinand Marcos, Corazon Aquino (b. 1933), as she had vowed, dismantled the "dictatorial edifice" that Marcos had built and replaced it with "a genuine democracy" for the people.

Born on January 25, 1933, into a wealthy and politically powerful family, Maria Corazon (Cory) Cojuangco was educated in the United States, concentrating on French and mathematics. After returning to the Philippines, she studied law and married Aquino, who became a mayor, a governor, and a senator in the national legislature. His bid for the presidency of the Philippines in 1972 attracted great popular support and threatened to unseat Marcos, who declared martial law, arrested Benigno, and imprisoned him for seven years.

On his release from prison, Benigno was permitted to leave the Philippines and live in the United States, but when he tried to return to the Philippines in August 1983, Marcos had him assassinated as he disembarked from the plane. Although she had no political experience, Corazon Aquino, with the help of Cardinal Jaime Sin and the veteran politician Salvador H. Laurel, ran against Marcos for the presidency, with Laurel as her running mate. Although Marcos was declared the constitutionally elected winner, the discovery of extensive fraud led to widespread outrage and, ultimately, Marcos's exile.

Aquino was sworn in as president of the Philippines on February 25, 1986, and included human rights activists in her cabinet. A month after taking office, she dissolved the national legislature and established a "revolutionary" government under a "freedom" constitution to provide a transition from Marcos's dictatorial regime to genuine democracy. At the same time she also set in motion the process for creating a new democratic constitution, appointing forty-four of the fifty members of the commission created to draft the document.

Aquino took an active part in ensuring that the new constitution reflected reforms and checks and balances to limit the president's power as well as speeding up the drafting process. The new constitution was approved at the polls in February 1987. Aquino finished out her term of office, and on June 30, 1992, power was peacefully transferred to her elected successor, Fidel V. Ramos.

Although the Philippine people are still struggling to make democracy work, Corazon Aquino proves that courageous leadership can help topple dictatorships and restore human rights. The legacy of her vision now rests with the people of the Philippines and their will to stay the course she has charted for them.

Reid, Robert H., and Eileen Guerrero. *Corazon Aquino and the Brushfire Revolution.* Baton Rouge: Louisiana State University Press, 1995.

Constitutionalism; Democracy

Arab Charter on Human Rights

The Arab Charter on Human Rights was adopted on September 15, 1994, by the Council of the League of Arab States, which was founded in 1945 a few months before the United Nations. The League of Arab States consists of twenty-two Arab nations, including Egypt, Libya, Palestine, Saudi Arabia, Sudan, Syria, and Yemen. Most of the countries in the league are not democracies, and many have extremely poor records on human rights, for which they have been heavily criticized by non-Arab governments, international human rights bodies, and nongovernmental organizations such as the Lawyers Committee for Human Rights. The Arab Charter on Human Rights, like the earlier Cairo Declaration on Human Rights in Islam (1990), represents a response to world criticism that the Arab and Islamic worlds lack adequate human rights and personal protections especially in areas such as women's rights and religious tolerance. At the same time, the effort to present a positive position on many international human rights norms is a step in the right direction.

The preamble reaffirms "the Arab nation's belief in human dignity since God honored it by making the Arab World the cradle of religions and the birthplace of civilizations which confirmed its right to a life of dignity based on freedom, justice and peace...."

"All peoples have the right of self-determination and control over their natural wealth and resources," states part I, article 1(a), "and, accordingly, have the right to freely determine the form of their political structure and to freely pursue their economic, social and cultural development." Article 1(b) continues: "Racism, [Z]ionism, occupation and foreign domination pose a challenge to human dignity and constitute a fundamental obstacle to the realization of the basic rights of peoples. There is a need to condemn and endeavor to eliminate all such practices."

Part II, articles 5 through 8, respectively, guarantee that "[e]very individual has the right to liberty and security of person ..."; "[t]here shall be no crime or punishment except as provided by law ..."; "[t]he accused shall be presumed innocent until proven guilty at a lawful trial..."; and "[e]veryone has the right to liberty and security of person and no one shall be arrested, held in custody or detained without legal warrant and without being brought promptly before a judge."

Other rights enumerated in articles 9 through 18 include equality before the law and the right to a legal remedy, limitations on the death penalty, and the requirement that states parties to the charter "shall protect every person in their territory from being subjected to physical or mental torture or cruel and inhuman or degrading treatment." Imprisonment for debt is forbidden, prisoners are to be treated with humanity, double jeopardy is proscribed, privacy "shall be inviolable and any infringement thereof shall constitute an offense," and the "inherent right to recognition as a person before the law" is acknowledged. Article 19 declares that the people are the source of authority; articles 20, 21, and 22 guarantee freedom of movement within a country and between countries; and article 23 extends the right to seek political asylum.

Articles 25 through 33 guarantee a number of well-established human rights, including the right to private property; freedom of belief, thought, and opinion; freedom of religion and the right to peaceful assembly; the right to form trade unions; the right to work to secure "a standard of living that meets the basic requirements of life"; free choice of work; equality of opportunity in regard to work;

and access to public office. Article 34 targets illiteracy; article 35 confirms the right to live "in an intellectual and cultural environment in which Arab nationalism is a source of pride ..."; and articles 36 through 39 affirm the right to participate in cultural life, protect the culture and religions of minorities, extend care and protection to "the family, mothers, children and the aged," and extend to young persons "the most ample opportunities for physical and mental development."

Part III, article 40, creates a Committee of Experts on Human Rights to which the states parties to the charter submit reports.

League of Arab States, P.O. Box 11642, Cairo, Egypt. (20-2-750-511. 📠 20-2-740-331.

Arab Information Center, 1100 17th Street, N.W., Suite 901, Washington, D.C. 20036. (202-265-3210. 📠 202-331-1525.

Cairo Declaration on Human Rights in Islam; Cultural Rights; Lawyers Committee for Human Rights; Self-Determination; Regional Human Rights Systems

Aristotle

A student of Plato's, Aristotle (384–322 B.C.E.) has had the most profound impact on Western thought of any person. Political theory and ethics are just two of the fields his writings have influenced for more than two thousand years. His arguments that principles of justice depend on law and constitutional rule, which in turn rely on equity and equality before the law, have been the starting point for human rights theorists through the ages.

The son of the court physician to Philip I of Macedonia, Alexander the Great's grandfather, Aristotle was born in 384 B.C.E. in a small Greek township in northern Greece. He studied at Plato's academy in Athens for twenty years, until Plato's death in 347 B.C.E., and then traveled for twelve years, establishing academies in Assus and Mytilene and tutoring Philip's son Alexander in Macedonia.

Aristotle's scope of inquiry into the world about him was broader than his mentor's, including works on physics, botany, and art, which were largely unchallenged for two millennia after his death. Like Plato, however, he also wrote extensively about the relationship of the state to the lives of individuals. For him governments and constitutions were virtually identical concepts, constitutions being descriptions of how various types of governments worked rather than single documents containing supreme laws. His inquiries into politics and government included a compilation of 158 constitutions.

Aristotle argued that the state was a natural form of human organization, just like the family and the village, albeit a higher form. (He never questioned the relationship of master and slave or the superiority of the husband and father over the wife and mother, however.) He also contended that the purpose of the state was to promote the highest good for the citizens. This ultimate good, a composite of values such as honor, pleasure, reason, and other virtues, was called in Greek *eudaimonia.*

Because a government's treatment of its citizens affects their human rights, Aristotle's formulations of the nature and purpose of the state have had a great impact on human rights theory. Recognizing that people are the only animals with the power of speech and the need to form political associations, he also reasoned that "it is a characteristic of man that he alone has any sense of good and evil, of just and unjust, and the like. . . ." He concluded: "He who by nature and not by mere accident is without a state, is either a bad man or above humanity. . . ." Aristotle's works, especially *The Politics* and his two books on ethics, deal with democracy, constitutions, equity, justice, and equality before the law—concepts that play an important part in understanding human rights today.

Ackrill, J. L. *A New Aristotle Reader*. Princeton, N.J.: Princeton University Press, 1989.

Barnes, Jonathan, ed. *The Cambridge Companion to Aristotle*. New York: Cambridge University Press, 1995.

Constitutionalism; Democracy; Equality; Justice; Plato; Thomas Aquinas, St.

Artists

The creation of art is an attribute that sets humans apart from other animals. A small figure of a horse carved from the ivory tusks of a mammoth around 28,000 B.C.E. and the cave paintings in Lascaux, France, dating from 15,000 to 10,000 B.C.E. are among the earliest confirmations of the human proclivity to express symbolism and aesthetics. In fact, the history of our species can be told almost entirely in art forms such as architecture, painting, sculpture, and literature. That the ancient Greek philosopher Plato feared that artistic freedom would undermine the totalitarian basis of his new republic underscores the power of art.

Artistic freedom has been the subject of great debate throughout the ages. When they come in conflict with religious and moral beliefs, works of art may be denounced as blasphemy, obscenity, or pornography. Some government limits on the use of certain imagery may be legitimate—

for example, the official ban in post–Nazi Germany on the swastika, a traditional Indian artistic symbol. Movies and recordings, which are accepted means of artistic expression, have also been banned or destroyed by government authorities because they transgress societal standards.

To maintain their artistic integrity, artists need the freedom to control the use of their works and to profit from them, rights that are protected in most countries and internationally by copyright laws and agreements (with exceptions for legitimate research and scholarly pursuits). Faced with censorship of art and literary works, the right of free expression becomes equally important. James Joyce's now-classic *Ulysses* (1922) was initially banned in England and the United States. In 1994 the European Court of Human Rights held, by a vote of six to three, that the Austrian government's seizure and forfeiture of the film *Das Liebes-konzil*, deemed obscene by the Roman Catholic Church, did not violate article 10, Freedom of Expression, of the European Convention for the Protection of Human Rights and Fundamental Freedoms (1950).

Some national constitutions that address the rights of artists include those of Germany (1949) and Sweden (1975); Ireland's constitution (1937) actually makes provision for artists to be elected to the upper house of its national legislature. International human rights documents protecting artists' rights include the Berne Convention for the Protection of Literary and Artistic Works (1896, subsequently revised five times, most recently in 1971), Universal Copyright Convention (as revised in 1971), and International Convention for the Protection of Performers, Producers of Phonograms and Broadcasting Organizations (1961), adopted by ECOSOC. The latter, for example, extends protection for literary and artistic works to "actors, singers, musicians, dancers, and other persons who act, sing, deliver, declaim, play in or otherwise perform literary or artistic works" as well as "the person who, or the legal entity which, first fixes the sounds of a performance or other sounds" to a "phonogram," meaning "any aural fixation of sounds of a performance or other sounds." It also prohibits the broadcast or communication to the public of works of the performers and producers without their consent. States that are parties to the convention agree to provide legal protection for the rights of such artists.

Constitution of South Africa (1997), chapter 2, Bill of Rights, Freedom of Expression: "16. (1) Everyone has the right to freedom of expression, which includes . . . (c) freedom of artistic creativity. . . ."

Economic and Social Council Recommendation Concerning the Status of the Artist (1980): "[T]he artist plays an important role in the life and evolution of society and . . . should be given the opportunity to contribute to society's development and, as any other citizen, to exercise his responsibilities therein, while preserving his creative inspiration and freedom of expression. . . ."

U.S. Supreme Court (1909): An author who had "complied with the copyright statute and given up his common-law right of exclusive duplication prior to general publication ... obtained an exclusive right to multiply copies and publish the same for the term of years named in the statute. Congress did not sanction an existing right [in enacting the copyright statute]; it created a new one."

European Court of Human Rights (1988): "[T]hose who create, perform, distribute or exhibit works of art contribute to the exchange of ideas and opinions which is essential for a democratic society. Hence the obligation of the State not to encroach unduly on their freedom of expression."

International PEN, 9–10 Charterhouse Buildings, Goswell Road, London EC1M 7AT, England. (44-207-253-4308. 🖳 44-207-253-5711. 💻 intpen@gn.apc.org.

PEN American Center, 568 Broadway, New York, N.Y. 10012-3225. (212-334-1660. 🖳 212-334-2181. 💻 pen@pen.org. 🖥 www.pen.org.

PEN Canada, 24 Ryerson Avenue, Suite 401, Toronto, Ontario, M5T 2P3, Canada. (416-703-8448. 🖳 416-703-3870. 💻 pencan@web.net. 🖥 www.pencanada.ca.

Duboff, Leonard D., ed. *Art Law, Domestic and International.* South Hackensack, N.J.: F. B. Rothman, 1975.

Merryman, John H. *Law, Ethics and the Visual Arts.* The Hague: Kluwer Law International, 1998.

Expression; Plato; Universal Copyright Convention

Assembly

Citizens' freedom to gather to discuss politics, show support for government policies or changes to those policies, and present grievances to government authorities is a time-honored democratic procedure. Although electronic communications now make it possible for a group of citizens to assemble in cyberspace and petition their government by e-mail, the need for social interaction—to see one another and be seen as a group—will undoubtedly continue to be a critical element in the process of communication between citizens and their government. The human right to join together temporarily and peacefully in groups to promote common causes, therefore, remains essential.

A number of countries have adopted the term *assembly* (from Old French) as the name for their national legislatures, but the concept of a nongovernmental assembly of people who come together to protest or present grievances has been known for many centuries. In his work *The Politics,* written in the fourth century B.C.E., Aristotle described an assembly as a group of citizens meeting together to legislate, consult the constitution, and hear edicts of the magistrates. The thirteenth-century Icelandic tale *Njal's Saga* recounts that "Gunner rode to the Althing [the Icelandic parliament] accompanied by all the Sigfussons and by Njal and his sons; they went about together, and it was said that no other group there looked as formidable."

Today the right of assembly is guaranteed in most national constitutions and is proclaimed in many international human rights documents. Sometimes linked with the right of association, as in the Universal Declaration of Human Rights (1948), article 20, the right of assembly developed as part of Anglo-Saxon common law and the constitutional laws of England. Assembly for the purpose of peaceably petitioning the government to take or cease taking some action is implied in the English Bill of Rights (1689), a constitutional document of the United Kingdom. In the eighteenth century William Blackstone in his commentaries on the laws of England defined an assembly as the "concourse or meeting together of a considerable number of persons at the same place."

This right of the people to assemble peacefully and petition the government for the redress of grievances was included in a resolution of the First Continental Congress of Britain's colonies in America in 1774, two years before the Declaration of Independence was signed. It was subsequently included in the Bill of Rights (1791), appearing prominently in the First Amendment to the U.S. Constitution along with the right of free speech and freedom of religion and the press.

Freedom of assembly is basic to democratic government because it provides citizens an opportunity to demonstrate dissatisfaction with their government's actions and bring about change. Although this right carries the potential for unlawful mob action, governments are not justified in prohibiting peaceful assembly merely on this basis. Even if peaceable, however, the massing of large numbers of people may result in anxiety and inconvenience for other members of the public. The government thus has to weigh the type of response it will mount to any large demonstration. In some cases crowd control—additional police or even military personnel—is necessary. If counterdemonstrations occur at the same time, conflicts between assembled groups may break out. Overreaction by law enforcement officials to essentially peaceful assemblies sometimes leads to human rights abuses that special training, especially focusing on the constitutional and human rights of demonstrators, can alleviate.

Constitution of Germany (1949), I, Basic Rights, article 8, Freedom of Assembly: "(1) All Germans shall have the right to assemble peaceably and unarmed without prior notification or permission. (2) With regard to open-air meetings, this right may be restricted by or pursuant to a statute."

European Convention for the Protection of Human Rights and Fundamental Freedoms (1950), article 11: "1. Everyone has the right to freedom of peaceful assembly and to freedom of association with others, including the right to form and join trade unions for the protection of his interests."

U.S. Supreme Court (1937): A state law making it a crime to take part in a meeting sponsored by the Communist Party was repugnant to the guarantee of freedom of assembly set forth in the U.S. Constitution (1789).

European Commission of Human Rights (1979): The European Convention for the Protection of Human Rights and Fundamental Freedoms (1950), article 11(1), which guarantees the right of peaceful assembly, "leaves States parties an area of discretion in applying measures which restrict the exercise of a guaranteed right such as the right to peaceful assembly, [especially] when . . . the authority finds itself facing a foreseeable threat to public order and security and has to decide, often at very short notice, on which measures should be taken to protect against it."

Gora, Joel M., et al., eds. *The Right to Protest: The Basic ACLU Guide to Free Expression.* Carbondale: Southern Illinois University Press, 1991.

King, David C. *Freedom of Assembly.* Brookfield, Conn.: Millbrook, 1997.

Leahy, James E. *The First Amendment, 1791–1991: Two Hundred Years of Freedom.* Jefferson, N.C.: McFarland and Company, 1991.

Lumsden, Linda J. *Rampant Women: Suffragists and the Right of Assembly.* Knoxville: University of Tennessee Press, 1997.

Sherr, Avrom. *Freedom of Protest, Public Order, and the Law.* New York: Basil Blackwell, 1989.

Strum, Philippa. *When the Nazis Came to Skokie: Freedom for Speech We Hate.* Lawrence: University Press of Kansas, 1999.

Association; Bills of Rights; Law Enforcement; Petition

Assisted Suicide

See Die, Right to

Association

Forming associations is a basic social act. Even before recorded history people with like interests or goals probably formed bonds for concerted action, and since then associations (from the French word *association*, meaning society or union) have been made for social, professional, religious, and mystical purposes.

In medieval Europe, merchants formed associations called guilds for their mutual aid and protection and for the maintenance of standards. After the Renaissance in Europe, natural-law scholars developed a theory of association to account for the nature of prevalent human relationships such as the family and the state. Thomas Hobbes, the seventeenth-century English philosopher, concluded that the state and all other associations were alike in that they were based on either a republican or a monarchical constitution.

Today an association may be any type of organization, formal or informal, in which people join together for some mutual interest or purpose. The right of people to form associations with a minimum amount of restriction by the state is generally acknowledged in national and international law. Associations for political purposes in particular should be protected from unreasonable government interference, even though such associations are the ones that may threaten vested interests and incumbent governments.

The right of association is often linked with the right of assembly. However, the right of assembly as first guaranteed in the Bill of Rights (1791) of the U.S. Constitution secures the freedom to present grievances to the government, although this provision has been used to protect freedom of association as well. The right of association is also often linked with the right of workers to form a trade union.

In 1948 the general conference of the International Labor Organization (ILO) adopted the Convention Concerning Freedom of Association and Protection of the Right to Organize. This convention, which entered into force in 1950, provides in part I, Freedom of Association, article 2: "Workers and employers, without distinction whatsoever, shall have the right to establish and, subject only to the rules of the organization concerned, to join organizations of their own choosing without previous authorization." In the early 1950s the ILO established a Freedom of Association Committee and Freedom of Association Fact-Finding and Conciliation Commission to handle complaints of infringement of trade union rights.

Canadian Charter of Rights and Freedoms (1982), Fundamental Freedoms: "2. Everyone has the following fundamental freedoms: . . . (d) freedom of association."

International Covenant on Civil and Political Rights (1966), article 22: "1. Everyone shall have the right to freedom of association with others, including the right to form and join trade unions for the protection of his interests. 2. No restriction may be placed on the exercise of this right other than those which are prescribed by law and which are necessary in a democratic society in the interests of national security or public safety, public order . . . , the protection of public health or morals or the protection of the rights and freedoms of others. This article shall not prevent the imposition of lawful restrictions on members of the armed forces and of the police in their exercise of this right."

Federal Court of Canada (1995): An immigration law authorizing deportation of a resident alien on the grounds of membership in an organization that is "likely to engage in . . . acts of violence that would or might endanger the lives and safety of persons in Canada" infringes the constitutional guarantee of freedom of association.

European Court of Human Rights (1993): An Icelandic law requiring taxicab operators to be members of the Frami Automobile Association was a violation of the European Convention for the Protection of Human Rights and Fundamental Freedoms (1950), article 11, which guarantees "the right to freedom of peaceful assembly and to freedom of association with others. . . ."

Council of Europe. *Freedom of Association.* The Hague: Martinus Nijhoff, Kluwer Law International, 1994.

Freedom of Association: Digest of Decisions and Principles of the Freedom of Association Committee of the Governing Body of the International Labor Organization. 4th ed. Geneva: International Labor Office, 1996.

Assembly; Convention Concerning Freedom of Association and Protection of the Right to Organize; International Labor Organization; Workers

Asylum

Under international law, asylum is a right of a country, not an individual. However, many individuals who have been victims of persecution have sought and been granted asylum by countries with a policy of providing refuge to such persons. The Statue of Liberty in New York Harbor has represented the policy of the United States of welcoming refugees, including asylum seekers. For citizens of countries that deny them their rights to live in peace, seeking asylum is often the only way to enjoy such rights.

An ancient and widespread concept, asylum was practiced in the early cultures of the Middle East as well as by the Aztecs of Mexico. The right of asylum is related to the right of sanctuary, which originated during the Middle Ages in Europe, whereby a person on church property could be protected from arrest by secular authorities for alleged crimes. The Greek *asylos,* or *asylon,* means inviolate, while the Latin *asylum* means a place of refuge. The English term has been used in this latter sense since at least the fifteenth century.

Territorial asylum, as defined in 1950 by the International Law Institute in France, is the protection a state offers within its territory to a person who seeks refuge there. Diplomatic asylum, on the other hand, refers to the power of a foreign ambassador to grant refuge to a person on the embassy's property, which is extraterritorial and thus inviolable. The practice of establishing permanent diplomatic missions began during the Renaissance among the Italian states of Florence, Milan, Naples, and Venice.

The millions of refugees created by World War II and the concern of the United Nations about them led to the drafting in Geneva of the Convention Relating to the Status of Refugees (1951), which entered into force in 1954. In 1967 a protocol was added to provide for refugees resulting from events occurring after January 1, 1951.

Under international law today the right of asylum allows a person sought for political and related offenses in one country to request and be granted refuge by another country. Persons charged with nonpolitical crimes in one country are subject to extradition by the country in which refuge is sought, if there is an extradition agreement between the two. Deposed leaders as well as ordinary citizens who are being persecuted may seek asylum in another country.

The conditions for asylum are governed by both the laws of the country of refuge and international law. Under international law a person granted asylum must abide by the laws of the country granting asylum and may not commit any illegal acts while under its jurisdiction. However, under international law countries are not required to provide asylum, and those that do may impose such restrictions as limiting the number of people granted asylum and defining the nature of the offenses for which asylum will be granted.

During development of the International Covenant on Civil and Political Rights (1966), the nations involved strongly disagreed about the conditions under which the right of asylum would apply, so it was not incorporated into that human rights document. But the UN General Assembly did adopt the Declaration on Territorial Asylum in 1967. Some other international human rights documents—for example, the American Convention on Human Rights (1969) and the African Charter on Human and Peoples' Rights (1981)—also address the concept of asylum.

Constitution of Germany (1949), I. Basic Rights, article 16: "(2) No German citizen may be extradited to a foreign country. Persons persecuted on political grounds shall enjoy the right of asylum."

Universal Declaration of Human Rights (1948), article 14: "1. Everyone has the right to seek and to enjoy in other countries asylum from persecution. 2. This right may not be invoked in the case of prosecutions genuinely arising from non-political crimes or from acts contrary to the purposes and principles of the United Nations."

U.K. Court of Appeals (1991): Lebanese nationals who spent a night in an Austrian airport in transit to the United Kingdom could be denied asylum on the grounds that they were required to seek asylum in the "first safe country" they reached, which was Austria.

Human Rights Committee (1984): A Chilean citizen who had been refused asylum in the Netherlands had been "given ample opportunity in formal proceeding, including oral hearings, to present his case in the Netherlands" and therefore had "no claim under article 2 of the Optional Protocol" of the International Covenant on Civil and Political Rights (1966).

Plaut, W. Gunther. *Asylum: A Moral Dilemma.* Westport, Conn.: Praeger, 1995.

Representing Asylum Seekers. Boston: Massachusetts Continuing Legal Education, 1995.

African Charter on Human and Peoples' Rights; Aliens; American Convention on Human Rights; Convention Relating to the Status of Refugees; Declaration on Territorial Asylum; Declaration on the Human Rights of Individuals Who Are Not Nationals of the Country in Which They Live; Immigrants; Refugees

Augustine, St.

Influenced by Plato, the ancient Greek philosopher, and Cicero, the Roman orator and statesman of the first century B.C.E., St. Augustine (354–430) began to define the relationship among the church, the state, and the individual in the late fourth and early fifth century. Among his contributions to the development of human rights is his conclusion that peace and justice are dependent on just rulers who govern from a sense of duty rather than power.

Augustine was born in Tagaste, Souk-Ahras, in what is now Algeria, on November 13, 354. Educated in Latin grammar and literature, he studied rhetoric in Carthage. After reading the works of Marcus Tullius Cicero, he adopted Manichaeanism, the religion of Persia, and began his own school of rhetoric in 373. Losing faith in Manichaeanism, he traveled to Rome and Milan in 383 and adopted the Christian faith, later becoming a priest and then a bishop in Algeria.

A prolific writer, Augustine devoted much of his life to studying the Greek and Roman classics, especially Plato's works. During his lifetime the Visigoths sacked Rome, presaging the fall of the Roman Empire in the West. Augustine's writings, however, were preserved and became a part of the treasure of classical knowledge retained by the church during the Dark Ages.

Augustine's greatest contributions to the development of constitutional government and human rights stem from his influence on later scholars and thinkers such as St. Thomas Aquinas, the proponent of natural law. In his most famous work, *The City of God*, Augustine conceived of a city of man on Earth and a city of God as separate concepts. Because the divine justice of the spiritual world is lacking in the earthly sphere, he reasoned, governments on Earth must be instituted to maintain peace and dispense justice. If earthly justice is taken away, he believed, kingdoms become no more than excuses for "great robberies."

Augustine left a legacy of influential writings that prefigured the concepts of the separation of church and state and constitutional government based on the notion of the just state and the just citizen. Not until many centuries later, however, were such goals widely accepted in the world community.

Price, Richard. *Augustine.* Liguori, Mo.: Triumph, 1997.

Wills, Gary. *Saint Augustine.* New York: Viking, 1999.

Cicero, Marcus Tullius; Constitutionalism; Justice; Plato; Separation of Church and State; Thomas Aquinas, St.

Aung San Suu Kyi

The daughter of Aung San, considered the father of modern Burma (now called Myanmar), Aung San Suu Kyi (b. 1945) took a leading role in the democratic uprising against the country's military junta in 1988. Fearing her influence with the people, the military-dominated government placed her under house arrest in 1989 and refused to honor the national election results the next year when her National League for Democracy party overwhelmingly won. During six years of confinement to her home, Aung San Suu Kyi became a symbol of protest against tyranny and military oppression around the world.

Aung San Suu Kyi—her name, she says, means "a bright collection of strange victories"—was born on June 19, 1945, a month after British forces reentered Rangoon (now Yangon). Two years later her father, the country's revolutionary hero, was assassinated, six months before Burma became independent. Suu spent her high school years in New Delhi, where her mother was serving as ambassador to India, and while there was significantly influenced by the life and work of Mahatma Gandhi. Later, as a student at Oxford University in England, she became an admirer of the American civil rights leader Martin Luther King Jr. After graduation, Suu took an advisory position with the United Nations in New York City. In 1972 she married an Englishman, Michael Aris, and the couple made their home in England.

Burma had been in political and economic turmoil since the army overthrew the elected government on March 2, 1962. When Suu returned in the spring of 1988, the country was on the brink of social and economic disaster. Offering herself as a compromise candidate in August, she became the leader of the National League for Democracy. Despite her incarceration, her party overwhelmingly won the 1990 election—the first democratic contest in nearly three decades—although the military junta ignored the election results. Suu immediately began a hunger strike to underscore her plea for humane treatment for her supporters.

In 1990, while under house arrest, she was awarded both the Thorolf Rafto Prize for human rights and the European Parliament's Sakharov Award for Freedom of Thought, and the following year she won the Nobel Peace Prize. "Fear of losing power corrupts those who wield it and fear of the scourge of power corrupts those who are subjected to it," she observed in *Freedom from Fear*, a collection of her writings first published in 1991. She concluded by quoting Gandhi: "The greatest gift for an individual or a nation . . . [is] fearlessness, not merely bodily courage but absence of fear from the mind."

Following Suu's release in 1995, attempts by the National League for Democracy to organize active political opposition to the military rulers were quashed, many of her supporters were arrested, and she was again placed under house arrest. In March 1999 her husband died of cancer in England after being denied permission by Burmese authorities to pay a last visit to her. She continues to struggle for democracy and human rights in her native land.

Aung San Suu Kyi. *Freedom from Fear and Other Writings.* New York: Penguin, 1995.

Ling, Bettina. *Aung San Suu Kyi: Standing Up for Democracy in Burma.* New York: Feminist Press, City University of New York, 1998.

Gandhi, Mohandas K.; King, Martin Luther, Jr.; Sakharov, Andrei

Awards and Prizes

The most prestigious and remunerative award for human rights activities is the Nobel Peace Prize. Alfred Nobel (1833–96), the inventor of dynamite, created the Nobel Prize Fund under the terms of his will, which required the Norwegian parliament to appoint a committee to award a prize to an individual or organization that has significantly advanced the cause of peace (other prizes recognize contributions to the arts and sciences). The peace prize, which has been given annually since 1901, had a value of about $1 million in 1995. Recent recipients include José Ramos-Horta of East Timor, Nelson Mandela and Archbishop Desmond Tutu of South Africa, Rigoberta Menchú of Guatemala, and Aung San Suu Kyi of Myanmar (Burma).

Another prestigious award is the Right Livelihood Award, given to people or organizations for their contributions to solving such problems as war, poverty, environmental degradation, and social injustice. Sometimes referred to as the "alternative Nobel Prize," it is awarded by the Swedish parliament the day before the Nobel Prizes. Between two and five recipients share in the monetary award of $250,000, and one nonmonetary award is also presented. Past recipients of awards include Ken Saro-Wiwa, the Movement for the Survival of the Ogoni people in Nigeria for its fight against pollution, and Mary and Carrie Dann of the Western Shoshone Nation for defending the land rights of indigenous peoples.

Numerous other awards and prizes, such as the following, are given to individuals and organizations for their efforts in the field of human rights.

Baldwin Medal of Liberty Award (given in honor of Roger Baldwin, founder of the American Civil Liberties Union and the International League for Human Rights), American Civil Liberties Union (for U.S. achievements), 125 Broad Street, 18th Floor, New York, N.Y. 10004. (212-549-2500. 🖳 212-549-2646. 🖳 aclu@aclu.org. 🖳 www.aclu.org. Alternate years: Lawyers Committee for Human Rights (for non-U.S. achievements), 333 Seventh Avenue, 13th Floor, New York, N.Y. 10001-5004. (212-845-5200. 🖳 212-845-5299. 🖳 nyc@lchr.org. 🖳 www.lchr.org.

Carter-Menil Human Rights Award (established by former U.S. President Jimmy Carter and Dominique de Menil), The Carter Center, One Copenhill, 453 Freedom Parkway, Atlanta, Ga. 30307. (404-420-5100. 🖳 404-420-5145. 🖳 carterweb@emory.edu. 🖳 www.cartercenter.org.

European Human Rights Prize (given by the Council of Europe), P.O. Box 431 R6F, 67006 Strasbourg Cedex, France. (33-88-41-20-00. 🖳 33-88-41-27-81. 🖳 webmaster@coe.fr. 🖳 www.coe.fr.

Freedom Award (given by Freedom House), 120 Wall Street, New York, N.Y. 10005. (212-514-8040. 🖳 212-514-8050. 🖳 freehouse@igc.apc.org. 🖳 www.igc.apc.org.

Human Rights Award (given by the International League for Human Rights), 432 Park Avenue South, Room 1103, New York, N.Y. 10016. (212-684-1221. 🖳 212-684-1690. 🖳 ilhr@perfekt.net. 🖳 www.ilhr.org.

Human Rights Literary Award (given by the Nouveaux Droit de l'Homme), 14 cité Vaneau, 75007 Paris, France. (33-1-47-53-78-78. 🖳 33-1-45-56-07-06.

Minnesota Advocates International Human Rights Award (given by Minnesota Advocates for Human Rights), 310 Fourth Avenue South, Suite 1000, Minneapolis, Minn. 55401. (612-341-3302. 🖳 612-341-2971. 🖳 mnadvocates@igc.apc.org. 🖳 www.umn. edu/humanrts/mnadvocates.

Nobel Peace Prize (given by the Nobel Foundation), P.O. Box 5232, S-102 45 Stockholm, Sweden. (46-8-663-09-20. 🖳 46-8-660-38-47. 🖳 postmaster@nobel.no. 🖳 www.nobel.se.

PIOOM Award (given by Interdisciplinary Research Program on Root Causes of Human Rights Violations), PIOOM Foundation, c/o LISWO, Leiden University, Wassenaarseweg 52, 2333 AK Leiden, Netherlands. (31-71-527-38-61. 🖳 31-71-527-37-88. 🖳 schmid @rulfsw.leidenuniv.nl.

Reebok Human Rights Award (given by Reebok International), c/o Forefront, 333 Seventh Avenue, 13th Floor, New York, N.Y. 10001-5004. (212-845-5273. 🖳 212-253-4244. 🖳 forefront@fore-frontleaders.org. 🖳 www.forefrontleaders.org.

Right Livelihood Award, P.O. Box 15072, S-10465 Stockholm, Sweden. (46-8-702-03-40. 🖳 46-8-702-03-38. 🖳 info@right-livelihood.se. 🖳 www.rightlivelihood.se.

Robert F. Kennedy Human Rights Award (given by the Robert F. Kennedy Memorial Center for Human Rights), 1367 Connecticut Avenue, N.W., Suite 200, Washington, D.C. 20036. (202-463-7575. 🖳 202-463-6606. 🖳 hrcenter@rfkmemorial.org. 🖳 www. rfkmemorial.org.80/center_for_human_rights.

Roosevelt Four Freedoms Medals, Franklin and Eleanor Roosevelt Institute, 4079 Albany Post Road, Hyde Park, N.Y. 11238. (914-229-5321. 🖳 914-229-9046. 🖳 emurphy@idsi.net. 🖳 www. feri.org.

Sakharov Award for Freedom of Thought (given by the European Parliament), plateau du Kirchberg, BP 1601, L-2929 Luxembourg. (3-52-43-00-24-86. 🖳 3-52-43-00-22-74. 🖳 www.europarl. eu.int.

UNESCO Literacy and Peace Education Prizes, United Nations Educational, Scientific and Cultural Organization, 7 place de Fontenoy, 75700 Paris, France. (33-1-45-68-10-00 (literacy prizes); 33-1-45-68-38-14 (peace education prize). 🖳 33-1-40-65-98-71. 🖳 webmaster@unesco.org. 🖳 www.unesco.org.

United Nations Prizes in the Field of Human Rights (given by the United Nations High Commissioner for Human Rights), 8–14 avenue de la Paix, 1211 Geneva 10, Switzerland. (41-22-917-9000. 🖳 41-22-917-9016. 🖳 webadmin.hchr@unog.ch. 🖳 www.unhchr.ch.

☞

Aung San Suu Kyi; Carter, James Earl; Forefront; Freedom House; High Commissioner for Human Rights; International League for Human Rights; Lawyers Committee for Human Rights; Mandela, Nelson; Menchú, Rigoberta; Ramos-Horta, José; Tutu, Desmond; United Nations Educational, Scientific and Cultural Organization (UNESCO)

Congress OF THE United States,

begun and held at the City of New York, on

Wednesday, the fourth of March, one thousand seven hundred and eighty nine.

THE Conventions of a number of the States, having at the time of their adopting the Constitution, expressed a desire, in order to prevent misconstruction or abuse of its powers, that further declaratory and restrictive clauses should be added: And as extending the ground of public confidence in the Government, will best ensure the beneficent ends of its institution.

RESOLVED, by the Senate and House of Representatives of the United States of America in Congress assembled, two thirds of both Houses concurring, that the following Articles be proposed to the Legislatures of the several States, as amendments to the Constitution of the United States; all, or any of which Articles, when ratified by three fourths of the said Legislatures, to be valid to all intents and purposes, as part of the said Constitution, viz.

ARTICLES in addition to, and amendment of the Constitution of the United States of America, proposed by Congress, and ratified by the Legislatures of the several States, pursuant to the fifth Article of the original Constitution.

Article the first...... After the first enumeration required by the first Article of the Constitution, there shall be one Representative for every thirty thousand, until the number shall amount to one hundred, after which, the proportion shall be so regulated by Congress, that there shall be not less than one hundred Representatives, nor less than one Representative for every forty thousand persons, until the number of Representatives shall amount to two hundred, after which the proportion shall be so regulated by Congress, that there shall not be less than two hundred Representatives, nor more than one Representative for every fifty thousand persons.

Article the second.... No law, varying the compensation for the services of the Senators and Representatives, shall take effect, until an election of Representatives shall have intervened.

Article the third...... Congress shall make no law respecting an establishment of religion, or prohibiting the free exercise thereof; or abridging the freedom of speech, or of the press; or the right of the people peaceably to assemble, and to petition the Government for a redress of grievances.

Article the fourth... A well regulated Militia, being necessary to the security of a free State, the right of the people to keep and bear Arms, shall not be infringed.

Article the fifth...... No Soldier shall, in time of peace, be quartered in any house, without the consent of the owner, nor in time of war, but in a manner to be prescribed by law.

Article the sixth.... The right of the people to be secure in their persons, houses, papers, and effects, against unreasonable searches and seizures, shall not be violated, and no warrants shall issue, but upon probable cause, supported by oath or affirmation, and particularly describing the place to be searched, and the persons or things to be seized.

Article the seventh. No person shall be held to answer for a capital, or otherwise infamous crime, unless on a presentment or indictment of a grand jury, except in cases arising in the land or naval forces, or in the Militia, when in actual service in time of War or public danger; nor shall any person be subject for the same offence to be twice put in jeopardy of life or limb; nor shall be compelled in any criminal case, to be a witness against himself, nor be deprived of life, liberty, or property, without due process of law; nor shall private property be taken for public use, without just compensation.

Article the eighth.... In all criminal prosecutions, the accused shall enjoy the right to a speedy and public trial by an impartial jury of the State and district wherein the crime shall have been committed, which district shall have been previously ascertained by law, and to be informed of the nature and cause of the accusation; to be confronted with the witnesses against him; to have compulsory process for obtaining witnesses in his favor, and to have the assistance of counsel for his defence.

Article the ninth...... In suits at common law, where the value in controversy shall exceed twenty dollars, the right of trial by jury shall be preserved, and no fact, tried by a jury, shall be otherwise re-examined in any Court of the United States, than according to the rules of the common law.

Article the tenth...... Excessive bail shall not be required, nor excessive fines imposed, nor cruel and unusual punishments inflicted.

Article the eleventh. The enumeration in the Constitution, of certain rights, shall not be construed to deny or disparage others retained by the people.

Article the twelfth... The powers not delegated to the United States by the Constitution, nor prohibited by it to the States, are reserved to the States respectively, or to the people.

Frederick Augustus Muhlenberg, Speaker of the House of Representatives.

John Adams, Vice-President of the United States, and President of the Senate.

ATTEST,

John Beckley, Clerk of the House of Representatives.

Sam. A. Otis, Secretary of the Senate.

In 1789 the United States became the first country established under a written constitution. That same year the U.S. Congress adopted a resolution to amend the Constitution by adding a Bill of Rights guaranteeing to citizens certain rights, including freedom of religion, speech, and the press. Ratified in part in 1791, it became a model around the world for similar guarantees of rights. [Library of Congress]

Banishment

See Deportation; Expulsion; Forced Eviction

Banjul Charter

See African Charter on Human and Peoples' Rights

Basic Principles for the Treatment of Prisoners

The first comprehensive study of the treatment of prisoners dates from the eighteenth century: the Italian jurist Cesare Beccaria's *Treatise on Crimes and Punishment* (1764). Two centuries later, in the aftermath of World War II, the first international document addressing the issue appeared. The Geneva Convention Relative to the Treatment of Prisoners of War (1949) dealt with the imprisonment of "[p]ersons taking no active part in hostilities, including members of armed forces who have laid down their arms and those [disabled] by sickness, wounds, detention or any other cause ..." and "[m]embers of the armed forces of a Party to the conflict...."

The First United Nations Congress on the Prevention of Crime and the Treatment of Offenders in 1955 adopted the Standard Minimum Rules for the Treatment of Prisoners, and subsequent UN congresses have continued to address prisoners' human rights. On December 14, 1990, on the recommendation of the eighth such congress, the UN General Assembly affirmed the Basic Principles for the Treatment of Prisoners, a document that establishes guidelines for the humane treatment of prisoners throughout the world.

"All prisoners," declares paragraph 1, "shall be treated with the respect due their inherent dignity and value as human beings." Paragraph 2 stipulates: "There shall be no discrimination on the grounds of race, color, sex, language, religion, political or other opinion, national or social origin, property, birth or other status," although paragraph 3 notes that it is "desirable to respect the religious beliefs and cultural precepts of the group to which prisoners belong, whenever local conditions so require."

Paragraph 4 directs the state to discharge its duties with respect to the custody of prisoners and the protection of society against crime "in keeping with [its] other social objectives and its fundamental responsibilities for promoting the well-being and development of all members of society." While acknowledging that the principles are limited as "demonstrably necessitated by the fact of incarceration," paragraph 5 mandates that "all prisoners shall retain the human rights as set out in [the International Bill of Human Rights] as well as such other rights as are set out in other [UN] covenants."

"All prisoners shall have the right to take part in cultural activities and education aimed at the full development of the human personality," states paragraph 6, and paragraph 7 encourages the abolition of solitary confinement. Pursuant to paragraph 8, prisoners should be given the opportunity "to undertake meaningful remunerated employment which will facilitate their reintegration into the country's labor market and permit them to contribute to their own financial support and to that of their families."

Paragraphs 9, 10, and 11, respectively, provide that prisoners should have access to the country's health services, "favorable conditions shall be created for the reintegration of the ex-prisoners into society under the best possible conditions," and the document's principles "shall be applied impartially."

United Nations High Commissioner for Human Rights, 8–14 avenue de la Paix, 1211 Geneva 10, Switzerland. (41-22-917-9000. 🖳 41-22-917-9016. 🖳 webadmin.hchr@unog.ch. 🖳 www.unhchr.ch.

Beccaria, Cesare; Geneva Conventions; International Bill of Human Rights; Prisoners; Standard Minimum Rules for the Treatment of Prisoners

Basic Principles on the Role of Lawyers

Lawyers, judges, and the legal profession play a key role in ensuring equal justice for all under the law, especially in the Anglo-American legal system and the Western world. This relationship is crucial to development and enforcement of human rights. The right to counsel in a criminal prosecution, for example, is generally recognized as a fundamental human right without which a fair trial is not possible.

How lawyers can aid the pursuit of human rights, particularly at the international and regional levels, became a focus of the United Nations Congress on the Prevention of Crime and the Treatment of Offenders. The eighth such congress, which met in Havana, Cuba, in 1990, adopted the Basic Principles on the Role of Lawyers "to assist Member States in their task of promoting and ensuring the proper role of lawyers."

The document begins with a reference to the UN charter (1945), in which "the peoples of the world affirm, [among other things], their determination to establish conditions under which justice can be maintained" and goes on to acknowledge that "adequate protection of the human rights and fundamental freedoms to which all persons are entitled . . . requires that all persons have effective access to legal services provided by an independent legal profession. . . ." It adds that "professional associations of lawyers have a vital role to play in upholding professional standards and ethics, protecting their members from persecution and improper restrictions and infringements, providing legal services to all in need of them, and cooperating with gov-

ernmental and other institutions in furthering the ends of justice and the public interest. . . ." These principles have been formulated, therefore, to be "respected and taken into account by Governments" and to apply both to lawyers and to "persons who exercise the functions of lawyers without having the formal status of lawyers."

"All persons are entitled to call upon the assistance of a lawyer of their choice to protect and establish their rights and to defend them in all stages of criminal proceedings," states Access to Lawyers and Legal Services, paragraph 1. Paragraphs 2 and 3, respectively, direct governments to ensure "effective and equal access to lawyers . . . for all persons within their territory and subject to their jurisdiction, without distinction of any kind," as well as to provide "sufficient funding and other resources for legal services to the poor and, as necessary, to other disadvantaged persons." Paragraph 4 requires government and professional associations of lawyers to "promote programs to inform the public about their rights and duties under the law and the important role of lawyers in protecting their fundamental freedoms."

When arrested, detained, or charged with a criminal offense, all persons should be "immediately informed by the competent authority of their right to be assisted by a lawyer of their own choice," recommends Special Safeguards in Criminal Justice Matters, paragraph 5. Pursuant to paragraph 7, prompt access to a lawyer should occur "not later than forty-eight hours from the time of arrest or detention." Paragraph 8 states that legal services are to be provided "without payment if [those arrested or detained] lack sufficient means to pay for such services."

Qualifications and Training, paragraph 9, provides that "[g]overnments, professional associations of lawyers and educational institutions shall ensure that lawyers have appropriate education and training and be made aware of the ideals and ethical duties of the lawyer and of human rights and fundamental freedoms recognized by national and international law." Lawyers' responsibilities, enumerated in Duties and Responsibilities, paragraphs 12 and 13, include not only maintaining "the honor and dignity of their profession" but also advising clients on their legal rights and obligations, taking action to protect their interests, and assisting them before courts, tribunals, and administrative authorities. "Where the security of lawyers is threatened as a result of discharging their functions," notes Guarantees for the Functioning of Lawyers, paragraph 17, "they shall be adequately safeguarded by the authorities."

The remaining section headings address freedom of expression and association, professional organizations of lawyers, and disciplinary proceedings.

Lawyers Committee for Human Rights, 100 Maryland Avenue, N.E., Suite 500, Washington, D.C. 20002-5625. (202-547-5692. 🖳 202-543-5999. 🖳 wdc@lchr.org. 🖳 www.lchr.org.

United Nations High Commissioner for Human Rights, 8–14 avenue de la Paix, 1211 Geneva 10, Switzerland. ☎ 41-22-917-9000. 🖷 41-22-917-9016. 🖳 webadmin.hchr@unog.ch. 🖳 www.unhchr.ch.

☞

Accused; Counsel; Fair Trial; Judicial Independence; Justice; Lawyers Committee for Human Rights

Basic Principles on the Use of Force and Firearms by Law Enforcement Officials

How police and members of the military use force and firearms in performing their law enforcement duties, from apprehension to arrest and detention of suspected criminals, has important implications for the protection of human rights. In 1979 the UN General Assembly adopted the Code of Conduct for Law Enforcement Officials and Guidelines for Implementation to help ensure that persons who come in contact with domestic law enforcement officials will be treated in a humane manner that respects and protects their human rights. Eleven years later the Eighth United Nations Congress on the Prevention of Crime and the Treatment of Offenders, which met in Havana, Cuba, in 1990, produced the Basic Principles on the Use of Force and Firearms by Law Enforcement Officials.

The document reaffirms that "the work of law enforcement officials [defined according to the 1979 Code of Conduct for Law Enforcement Officials and including military authorities in those countries where they are used in the same capacity as domestic law enforcement officers] is a social service of great importance" and that the working conditions and status of these officials must be maintained and, where necessary, improved. Further, "with due regard to their personal safety," the document acknowledges that "consideration be given to the role of law enforcement officials in relation to the administration of justice, to the protection of the right to life, liberty and security of the person, to their responsibility to maintain public safety and social peace and to the importance of their qualifications, training and conduct. . . ." These principles were formulated, it adds, "to assist Member States in their task of ensuring and promoting the proper role of law enforcement officials, [and] should be taken into account and respected by Governments . . . and be brought to the attention of law enforcement officials as well as other persons, such as judges, prosecutors, lawyers, members of the executive branch and the legislature, and the public."

"Governments and law enforcement agencies shall adopt and implement rules and regulations on the use of force and firearms against persons by law enforcement officials," directs General Provisions, paragraph 1. "In developing such rules and regulations, [they] shall keep the ethical issues associated with the use of force and firearms constantly under review." According to paragraph 2, "Governments and law enforcement agencies should develop a range of means as broad as possible and equip law enforcement officials with various types of weapons and ammunition that would allow for a differentiated use of force and firearms. . . ." It further specifies that "[n]onlethal incapacitating weapons for use in appropriate situations" should also be developed, and law enforcement officials should be equipped with "shields, helmets, bullet-proof vests and bullet-proof means of transportation, in order to decrease the need to use weapons of any kind."

As far as possible, paragraph 4 recommends, "officials should apply non-violent means before resorting to the use of force and firearms." Paragraph 5 mandates: "Whenever the lawful use of force and firearms is unavoidable, law enforcement officials shall: (a) Exercise restraint in such use and act in proportion to the seriousness of the offense and the legitimate objective to be achieved; (b) Minimize damage and injury, and respect and preserve human life; (c) Ensure that assistance and medical aid are rendered to any injured or affected persons at the earliest possible moment; (d) Ensure that relatives or close friends of the injured or affected person are notified at the earliest possible moment."

Paragraphs 6, 7, and 8, respectively, require notification of superior officers in the case of death or injury caused by officials' use of force or firearms; mandate punishment for "arbitrary or abusive use of force or firearms"; and prohibit the excuse of "[e]xceptional circumstances such as internal political instability or any other public emergency . . . to justify any departure from these basic principles."

Law enforcement officials are prohibited from using firearms against persons "except in self-defense or defense of others[,] to prevent the perpetration of a particularly serious crime . . . and only when less extreme means are insufficient . . . ," notes Special Provisions, paragraph 9. This section also addresses warnings and identification by law enforcement officials, rules for the use of firearms, including authorization to carry them, the circumstances of their use, and the regulation and control of firearms and ammunition storage. Other sections of the Basic Principles address policing unlawful assemblies; policing persons in custody or detention; qualifications, training and counselling; and reporting and review procedures.

Reporting and Review Procedures, paragraph 25, recommends that "no criminal or disciplinary sanction [be] imposed on law enforcement officials who, in compliance with the Code of Conduct for Law Enforcement Officials and these basic principles, refuse to carry out an order to use force and firearms. . . ." Paragraph 26 states that "[o]bedience to superior orders shall be no defense [to improper use of force or firearms]. In any case, responsibility also rests on the superiors who gave the unlawful orders."

United Nations High Commissioner for Human Rights, 8–14 avenue de la Paix, 1211 Geneva 10, Switzerland. ☎ 41-22-917-9000. 📠 41-22-917-9016. 🖥 webadmin.hchr@unog.ch. 🖥 www.unhchr.ch.

☞

Code of Conduct for Law Enforcement Officials; Law Enforcement

Beccaria, Cesare

Cesare Bonesana, marchese di Beccaria (1738–94), an Italian jurist and economist, was the author of *Treatise on Crimes and Punishment* (1764), a monumental work that became the standard reference on criminal justice during his day. In it he argued against both the death penalty and the use of torture as a method for seeking truth and justice.

Born into a noble family in Milan on March 15, 1738, Beccaria studied at the University of Padua and was greatly influenced by the French Enlightenment movement, especially the French jurist known as Montesquieu (Charles-Louis de Secondat, baron de La Bréde et de Montesquieu). Beccaria's treatise, his most famous and influential work, was published under the title *Dei delitti e delle pene*. Then only twenty-six years old, he became an instant intellectual celebrity.

Basing his reasoning on the utilitarian proposition that the aim of government is the greatest good for the greatest number of people, Beccaria maintained that the severity of a punishment should be based on the extent to which the crime endangers society. A penalty should be no more severe, he argued, than required to deter a crime. Any excess punishment was tyrannical and self-defeating: "Every punishment which is not derived from absolute necessity is tyrannous, says the great Montesquieu, a proposition which may be generalized as follows: every act of authority between one man and another which is not derived from absolute necessity is tyrannous."

On torture, Beccaria held that "[n]o man may be called guilty before the judge has reached his verdict; nor may society withdraw its protection from him until it has been determined that he has broken the terms of the compact by which that protection is extended to him." And, he asked, "By what right, then, except that of force, does the judge have authority to inflict punishment on a citizen while there is doubt about whether he is guilty or innocent?"

Beccaria's proposals were promoted by Jeremy Bentham, the British utilitarian philosopher and reformer, and the treatise was a major influence on the reform of criminal law and criminal justice systems in Western Europe, particularly in Russia, Sweden, and the Hapsburg Empire, as well as in America. Beccaria's conclusions on criminal justice are as valid today as in the eighteenth century.

Beccaria, Cesare, Marchese di. *On Crimes and Punishments*. 1764. Reprint, Indianapolis: Hackett, 1986.

Caso, Adolph. *We, the People—: Formative Documents of America's Democracy*. Boston: Branden, 1995.

Basic Principles for the Treatment of Prisoners; Capital Punishment; Prisoners; Punishment; Torture

Beijing Rules

See Standard Minimum Rules for the Administration of Juvenile Justice

Bills of Rights

Constitutional government, whether a constitutional democracy or a constitutional monarchy, is government with circumscribed or limited powers. Constitutions contain rules for how a government operates as well as limitations on its powers, and many, including the U.S. Constitution (1789), also contain a specific list or bill of citizens' rights that the government is forbidden to encroach on—such as freedom of speech, thought, conscience, expression, religion, the press, assembly, and association; the right to life, liberty, and personal security; equality in all aspects of life; the right to vote and hold office; protection from unreasonable searches and seizures; the right to due process, a fair trial, and legal counsel; and guarantees against cruel and unusual punishment. Some constitutions acknowledge social rights, including health care, social security, and disability benefits, as well as minority rights. An alteration of the Latin *bulla* (in medieval times a seal, especially one appended to a charter), *bill*, meaning a sealed written document, has been in use in English since at least the fourteenth century.

Magna Carta, the Great Charter of English liberties forced on King John at Runnymede in 1215, is an early bill of rights. It is a component of the unwritten constitution of England and the United Kingdom, as is the Bill of Rights of 1688. The later bill of rights, however, was not a list of individual rights guaranteed by the government to its citizens but a statement of rights guaranteed by the English monarch to Parliament. The first modern bill of rights is the U.S. Bill of Rights—the first ten amendments to the U.S. Constitution, ratified in 1791.

Declarations or charters of rights and freedoms are similar to bills of rights. The Declaration of the Rights of Man and of the Citizen, promulgated in France in 1789, has been incorporated by reference into the country's current constitution (1958). The Canadian Charter of Rights and Freedoms (1982) has been acknowledged by the courts to be of constitutional stature; a bill of rights enacted by the Canadian parliament in 1960, however, was not intended to be of constitutional stature, because it did not bind the legislative branch of government and therefore did not prevent the parliament or provincial governments from acting in a manner inconsistent with its provisions.

A true bill of rights is one that protects citizens against government action and can be changed only by constitutional amendment. Not every bill of rights has such a guarantee. New Zealand's constitution is unwritten, and its parliament is technically supreme in relation to the other branches of government; New Zealand's bill of rights thus can be changed by the parliament without the consent of the citizens.

The Universal Declaration of Human Rights (1948) and two 1966 covenants—the International Covenant on Civil and Political Rights, including its two optional protocols, and the International Covenant on Economic, Social and Cultural Rights—have become known as the International Bill of Human Rights. Because only sovereign authorities can promulgate documents of constitutional stature, the International Bill of Human Rights, which relies on international law and the voluntary compliance of the nations that are parties to the covenants, is not a true bill of rights in the same sense as the U.S. Bill of Rights, France's Declaration of the Rights of Man and of the Citizen, and the Canadian Charter of Rights and Freedoms.

New Zealand Bill of Rights Act (1990), part I, General Provisions, 3, Application: "This Bill of Rights applies only to acts done— (a) By the legislative, executive, or judicial branches of the government of New Zealand; or (b) By any person or body in the performance of any public function, power, or duty conferred or imposed on that person by or pursuant to law."

Universal Declaration of Human Rights (1948), preamble: "The [UN] General Assembly proclaims this Universal Declaration of Human Rights as a common standard of achievement for all peoples and all nations, to the end that every individual and every organ of society, keeping this Declaration in mind, shall strive by teaching and education to promote respect for these rights and freedoms and by progressive measures, national and international, to secure their universal and effective recognition and observance, both among the peoples of Member States [of the United Nations] themselves and among the peoples of territories under their jurisdiction."

U.S. Supreme Court (1873): The U.S. Constitution's Thirteenth, Fourteenth, and Fifteenth Amendments, adopted in 1865, 1868, and 1870, respectively, were aimed at securing the freedom of the slaves; therefore, all the provisions of the U.S. Bill of Rights (1791) were not automatically incorporated into the Fourteenth Amend-

ment. By this the Court meant that it would enforce only some of the provisions of the Bill of Rights against action by the states. However, since 1873 the Court has gradually incorporated many of the other rights in the Bill of Rights into the Fourteenth Amendment so that they now apply to the states as well as to the national government.

Human Rights Committee (1992): A complaint filed by a Canadian citizen who claimed that his human rights had been violated by Canada and whose claim had been dismissed by an arbitration board as not being encompassed under the Canadian Charter of Rights and Freedoms (1982) was held to be inadmissible for failure to pursue all the remedies available in Canada.

Hickok, Eugene W., Jr., ed. *The Bill of Rights: Original Meaning and Current Understanding.* Charlottesville: University Press of Virginia, 1991.

Plescia, Joseph. *The Bill of Rights and Roman Law.* Bethesda, Md.: Austin and Winfield, 1995.

Canadian Charter of Rights and Freedoms; Declaration of the Rights of Man and of the Citizen; International Bill of Human Rights; International Covenant on Civil and Political Rights; International Covenant on Economic, Social, and Cultural Rights; Magna Carta; Universal Declaration of Human Rights

Body of Principles for the Protection of All Persons under Any Form of Detention or Imprisonment

In 1975 the UN General Assembly adopted the Declaration on the Protection of All Persons from Being Subjected to Torture and Other Cruel, Inhuman or Degrading Treatment or Punishment, which it followed in 1984 with the Convention against Torture and Other Cruel, Inhuman or Degrading Treatment or Punishment. Both documents address punishment of persons detained by government authorities for suspected acts or imprisoned for the commission of crimes. On December 9, 1988, the General Assembly approved the Body of Principles for the Protection of All Persons under Any Form of Detention or Imprisonment, which was drafted by the UN Subcommission on the Promotion and Protection of Human Rights, assisted by working groups under the Third (Social, Humanitarian and Cultural) Committee and the Sixth (Legal) Committee. The more recent document addresses a broader range of human rights concerns than those covered in the 1975 declaration and the 1984 convention on torture.

The Body of Principles begins by stating that its provisions "apply for the protection of all persons under any form of detention or imprisonment." The term *arrest* is defined as "the act of apprehending a person for the alleged commission of an offense or by the action of an authority"; *detained person* as "any person deprived of personal liberty except as a result of conviction for an offense"; and *imprisoned person* as "any person deprived of personal liberty as a result of conviction for an offence."

"All persons under any form of detention or imprisonment shall be treated in a humane manner and with respect for the inherent dignity of the human person," declares principle 1. According to principle 2, "Arrest, detention or imprisonment shall only be carried out strictly in accordance with the provisions of the law and by competent officials or persons authorized for that purpose." Principle 3 mandates: "There shall be no restriction upon or derogation from any of the human rights of persons under any form of detention or imprisonment recognized or existing in any State pursuant to law, conventions, regulations or custom on the pretext that this Body of Principles does not recognize such rights or that it recognizes them to a lesser extent." Furthermore, under principle 4, "Any form of detention or imprisonment and all measures affecting the human rights of a person under any form of detention or imprisonment shall be ordered by, or be subject to the effective control of, a judicial or other authority."

Principle 5(1) and (2) prohibits discrimination in the application of the principles on the basis of "race, color, sex, language, religion or religious belief, political or other opinion, national, ethnic or social origin, property, birth or other status" and requires the protection of "the rights and special status of women, especially pregnant women and nursing mothers, children, juveniles, aged, sick or handicapped persons." Principles 6 through 8, respectively, prohibit torture or cruel, inhuman treatment or punishment, with any interpretation extending the widest possible protection against abuses; direct how states, officials, and other persons should deal with complaints and violations; and require that detainees be accorded "treatment appropriate to their unconvicted status."

As set forth in principles 9 and 10, the powers of authorities who arrest or detain persons or who investigate them are limited to those granted to them by law and require that a person arrested be informed "at the time of his arrest of the reason for his arrest and ... be promptly informed of the charges against him." Principle 11(1) and (3) extends the right of detainees to defend themselves with the assistance of legal counsel and empowers judicial authorities "to review as appropriate the continuance of detention." According to principles 12, 13, and 14, records must be kept and rights must be explained, through the use of an interpreter if necessary.

Principles 15 through 33 expand on the right to legal counsel, address the rights of correspondence and visita-

tion with family members, and prohibit compelled confessions. Principle 34 outlines procedures in the case of the death or disappearance of a person detained or imprisoned; principle 35(1) extends the right to damages for "acts or omissions by a public official contrary to the rights contained in these principles"; and principle 38 requires a "trial within a reasonable time or ... release pending trial." A concluding General Clause provides: "Nothing in this Body of Principles shall be construed as restricting or derogating from any right defined in the International Covenant on Civil and Political Rights [1966]."

United Nations High Commissioner for Human Rights, 8–14 avenue de la Paix, 1211 Geneva 10, Switzerland. (41-22-917-9000. 📠 41-22-917-9016. 💻 webadmin.hchr@unog.ch. 🖥 www.unhchr.ch.

Accused; Convention against Torture and Other Cruel, Inhuman or Degrading Treatment or Punishment; Counsel; Declaration on the Protection of All Persons from Being Subjected to Torture and Other Cruel, Inhuman or Degrading Treatment or Punishment; Detention; Fair Trial; International Covenant on Civil and Political Rights; Prisoners; Punishment; Subcommission on the Promotion and Protection of Human Rights; Torture

Bonner, Yelena

See Sakharov, Andrei

Bunche, Ralph

The grandson of a slave, Ralph Bunche (1904–71) worked for both world peace and improved race relations in the United States. The recipient of the 1950 Nobel Peace Prize for his efforts to negotiate an armistice between the Arabs and the Israelis, he became an undersecretary of the United Nations in 1957 and undersecretary-general in 1969.

Born in Detroit on August 7, 1904, Bunche and his younger sister were raised by their maternal grandmother after the death of their parents when Ralph was thirteen years old. He attended the University of California on a scholarship, graduating in 1927, and in 1934 earned a graduate degree in government and international relations from Harvard University. Afterward he joined the faculty of Howard University, where he established the school's political science department.

While at Howard, with the help of a fellowship, Bunche began his study of Africa and colonial territories. He later focused on African colonial policy and assisted the Swedish sociologist Gunnar Myrdal in producing *An American Di-*

lemma (1944), his significant work on race relations in the United States. During World War II Bunche was employed by the Office of Strategic Services as an analyst of African and Far Eastern affairs and later by the State Department, where in 1944 and 1945 he became instrumental in establishing the UN.

Bunche's career with the UN began in 1947 as head of the new trusteeship division. His special skills landed him troubleshooting assignments, and in 1948, after the assassination of the chief mediator in the first Arab-Israeli war, he assumed the mediator's position. Bunche continued to rise in the UN hierarchy until his death in 1971 from complications of diabetes.

A leader in international human rights activities, Bunche also found time to play a major role in the civil rights struggle of African Americans in the United States. A member of the board of directors of the National Association for the Advancement of Colored People, he participated in civil rights marches in Selma and Montgomery, Alabama, led by Martin Luther King Jr. in 1965. For his promotion of human rights both nationally and internationally, Bunche received many honors and awards, including the Medal of Freedom, presented to him by President John F. Kennedy in 1963.

Herny, Charles P. *Ralph Bunche: Model Negro or American Other?* New York: New York University Press, 1999.

Keppel, Ben. *The Work of Democracy: Ralph Bunche, Kenneth B. Clark, Lorraine Hansberry, and the Cultural Politics of Race.* Cambridge, Mass.: Harvard University Press, 1995.

Civil Rights; King, Martin Luther, Jr.; Race Discrimination; United Nations

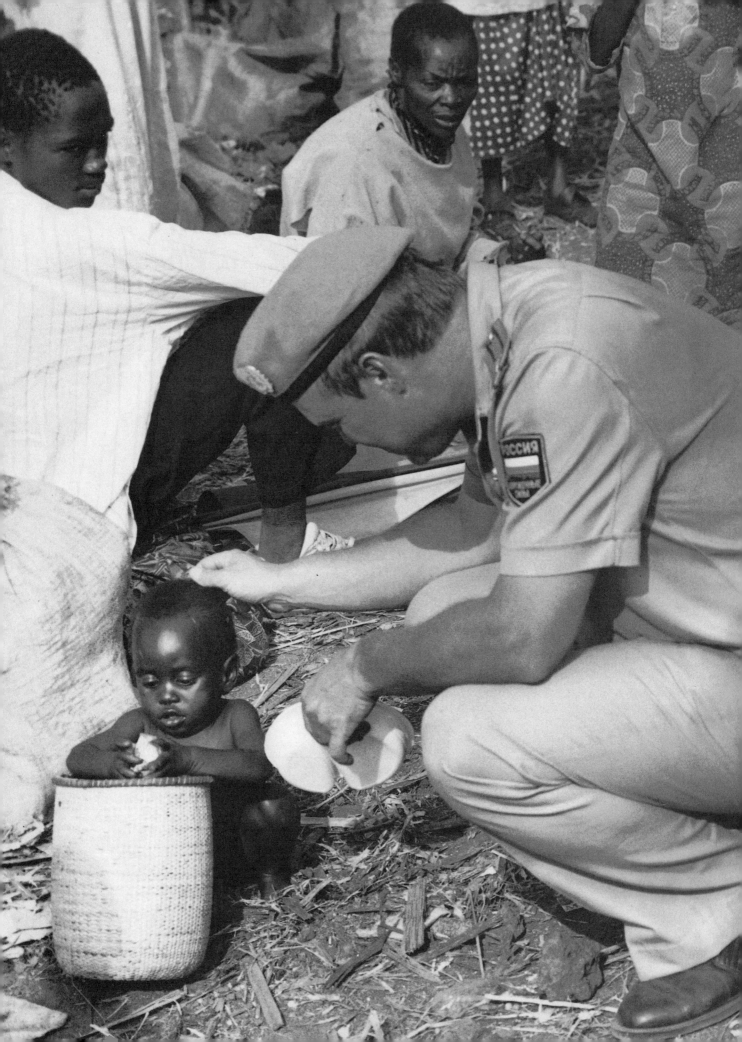

The human rights of children are among the most vulnerable to violations. The plight of children as the result of war, ethnic cleansing, forced eviction, and government-imposed starvation policies has become a major focus for human rights activists. Rwanda's internal conflict in the mid-1990s left many children uprooted, like these in a UN refugee camp in Ruhengeri.
[J. Isaac, United Nations]

Cairo Declaration on Human Rights in Islam

The word *Islam* means submission to God, and by implication it requires submission to those who rule in an Islamic state. Some tenets of the Islamic religion—for example, the unequal treatment of women, harsh and inhumane punishment for crimes, and an emphasis on subservience to leaders rather than on democratic accountability—have been seen as obstacles to the adoption of international human rights norms in Islamic countries, many of which have yet to embrace all the principles embodied in the Universal Declaration of Human Rights (1948) and other documents. Even the Arab Charter on Human Rights (1994), issued by the League of Arab States, has some glaring omissions with respect to slavery and religious tolerance.

Meeting in Cairo, Egypt, on August 5, 1990, the Organization of the Islamic Conference, whose fifty-six member countries include Afghanistan, Egypt, Indonesia, Pakistan, Palestine, Saudi Arabia, and Uganda, adopted the Cairo Declaration on Human Rights in Islam. Disseminated by the UN General Assembly and the World Conference on Human Rights, held in Vienna in 1993, the declaration sets forth the basic concepts of human rights and fundamental freedoms consonant with the Islamic religion. There is little evidence so far that it has had much positive influence in Islamic countries.

The document begins by reaffirming "the civilizing and historical role of the Islamic Ummah, which God made the best nation that has given mankind a universal and well-balanced civilization in which harmony is established between this life and the hereafter and knowledge is combined with faith. . . ." The document is based on the belief that "fundamental rights and universal freedoms in Islam are an integral part of the Islamic religion and that no one as a matter of principle has the right to suspend them in whole or in part or violate or ignore them in as much as they are binding divine commandments. . . ."

Article 1 proclaims: "(a) All human beings form one family whose members are united by submission to God and descent from Adam. . . ." Article 2(a) affirms that "[l]ife is a God-given gift and the right to life is guaranteed to every human being. It is the duty of individuals, societies and States to protect this right from any violation, and it is prohibited to take away life except for a *Shari'ah* [Islamic law] prescribed reason."

Rights and duties in the event of an armed conflict and with respect to a person's good name and honor, marriage, women, children, and legal capacity are addressed in articles 3 through 8, respectively. Articles 9 and 10 relate to education and religion; article 11 condemns slavery and colonialism; article 12 approves the right of asylum; article 13 guarantees the right to work; and article 14 prohibits usury.

Articles 15 through 21, respectively, cover the right to own property, the right to the fruits of one's own creations, the right to a clean environment, the right to security, equality before the law, rights of the accused, and the prohibition against taking hostages. The right "to express [one's] opinions in such manner as would not be contrary to the principles of the *Shari'ah*" is sanctioned in article 22, and article 23 grants the right "to assume public office in accordance with the provisions of *Shari'ah*." Pursuant to article 24, "All the rights and freedoms stipulated in this Declaration are subject to the Islamic *Shari'ah*," which, according to article 25, is "the only source of reference for the explanation or clarification of any of the articles of this Declaration."

Organization of the Islamic Conference, P.O. Box 178, Jeddah 21411, Saudi Arabia. (966-2-636-1400. 966-2-636-6871. idb.archive@mail.oicisnet.org. www.oicis.net.

United Nations High Commissioner for Human Rights, 8–14 avenue de la Paix, 1211 Geneva 10, Switzerland. (41-22-917-9000. 41-22-917-9016. webadmin.hchr@unog.ch. www.unhchr.ch.

Arab Charter on Human Rights; Regional Human Rights Systems; Vienna Declaration and Plan of Action

Canadian Charter of Rights and Freedoms

The United Kingdom and its former colony Australia do not have constitutional documents guaranteeing individual rights, such as the U.S. Bill of Rights (1791). However, another former colony, Canada, enacted such a document in 1982. Called the Canadian Charter of Rights and Freedoms, it has been held by the Canadian courts to be a part of Canada's constitution, and therefore laws passed by the parliament can now be invalidated by the courts if they are inconsistent with the charter.

Although Canada enacted a bill of rights in 1960, the jurisdiction of the provinces was not affected because the act lacked constitutional stature. The nation's Human Rights Act (1977) prohibited discrimination on certain grounds, including on the basis of race, color, and national or ethnic origin; in employment; and in the provision of goods, services, and accommodations. In 1983, a year after the Canadian Charter of Rights and Freedoms was adopted, the Human Rights Act was amended to prohibit harassment and discrimination by unions and employer organizations on similar grounds.

"Whereas Canada is founded upon principles that recognize the supremacy of God and the rule of law," begins the charter, which then guarantees in section 1, Guarantee of Rights and Freedoms, "the rights and freedoms set out

in it subject only to such reasonable limits prescribed by law as can be demonstrably justified in a free and democratic society."

Basic rights are set forth in Fundamental Freedoms, section 2, including freedom of conscience and religion; freedom of thought, belief, opinion, and expression, including freedom of the press and other media communication; freedom of peaceful assembly; and freedom of association.

The right "to vote in an election of members of the House of Commons or of a legislative assembly and to be qualified for membership therein" is guaranteed in Democratic Rights, section 3. Mobility rights include the right to enter, remain in, and leave Canada.

Legal Rights, sections 7 through 14, provide that everyone has the right to life, liberty, and personal security and the right not to be deprived of these except in accordance with the principles of fundamental justice. All citizens have enumerated rights relating to criminal charges and proceedings, as well as the right not to be subjected to cruel and unusual punishment. Certain rights are also extended to witnesses in legal proceedings.

According to Equality Rights, section 15: "(1) Every individual is equal before and under the law and has the right to the equal protection and equal benefit of the law without discrimination and, in particular, without discrimination based on race, national or ethnic origin, color, religion, sex, age or mental or physical disability."

Official Languages of Canada, sections 16 through 22, allow the use of two official languages: English and French. Citizens have the right to be taught in either English or French, pursuant to Minority Language Educational Rights, section 23.

Enforcement of the charter's provisions by the courts is authorized under Enforcement, section 24. General, section 25, provides, among other things, that the charter "shall not be construed so as to abrogate or derogate from any aboriginal treaty or other rights or freedoms [of] . . . aboriginal peoples of Canada. . . ." Application of Charter, sections 32 and 33, stipulates that the charter applies to "the Parliament and Government of Canada, . . . [including] the Yukon Territory and the Northwest Territories," as well as to the "legislatures and government of each province in respect to all matters within the authorities of the legislature[s] . . . ."

Department of Justice, Human Rights Law Division, 284 Wellington Street, K1A OH8, Ottawa, Ontario, Canada. (613-957-4938. 613-952-4137. dchartra@justice.gc.ca. www.canadajustice.gc.ca.

Gall, Gerald L. *The Canadian Legal System*. Toronto: Carswell Thomson, 1995.

Russell, Peter H., Rainer Knopff, and F. L. Morton. *Federalism and the Charter*. Ontario: Carlton University Press, 1989.

Bills of Rights; Constitutional Rights; Indigenous Peoples

Capital Punishment

Although the death penalty is denounced or prohibited in some international and regional human rights documents as well as in some national constitutions and laws, ninety countries, including the United States and China, still do not consider capital punishment a violation of human rights. Its use, however, is generally limited to certain types of crimes involving heinous offenses or the murder of law enforcement officers. The severity and finality of the death penalty, which make it impossible to correct a judicial error once a sentence of death has been carried out, have led to efforts to ensure that capital punishment is restricted to extreme crimes and that those accused of capital offenses receive a fair trial.

For at least as long as recorded history, the penalty for certain crimes has been capital punishment, a term derived from the Latin *caput* (head) that was used in England as early as the sixteenth century. Plato, the Greek philosopher of the fourth century B.C.E., devotes a section of his *Laws* to capital offenses—crimes that call for the death penalty—and includes among them robbery of temples, political subversion, and treason. The eighteenth-century French philosopher Jean-Jacques Rousseau argued that the death penalty was based on the consent of the people, because some citizens are asked to risk death in the defense of their country. Another French jurist and philosopher, Montesquieu, believed that the death penalty was too harsh a punishment for some crimes and could result in a reluctance by humane judges to impose it.

Cesare Beccaria, an eighteenth-century Italian jurist and criminologist, questioned the appropriateness of the death penalty in his *Treatise on Crimes and Punishment* (1764). The debate over the acceptability of capital punishment in an enlightened society has continued ever since, especially in the United States. In 1998, according to Amnesty International, eighty-six percent of all executions took place in China, the Democratic Republic of Congo, Iran, and the United States.

The arguments for and against capital punishment were summarized in a study requested by the UN General Assembly in 1959. The death penalty can be supported on the basis that it deters further crimes by the same offender, it punishes extreme antisocial behavior against which the state has the right to protect itself, it provides atonement for particularly heinous crimes, and it is an economical alternative to maintaining a criminal at government expense for a long period of time. Arguments against capital punishment include that it is a violation of the sanctity of life; the aim of penalties for crimes should be punishment and prevention (rather than atonement), which can be accomplished by means other than the death penalty; it is generally not an effective deterrent to crime; and it is a form of cruelty and inhumanity unworthy of a humane civilization. A tangential reasoning is that the death penalty often falls disproportionately on minorities or those charged with political crimes.

The International Covenant on Civil and Political Rights, adopted by the UN General Assembly in 1966, clearly supports abolition of capital punishment. Acknowledging the many countries that still allow it, however, article 6 sets out criteria for protecting the rights of persons sentenced to death for crimes. These include the right to due process and to seek a pardon or commutation of the sentence and a prohibition on capital punishment for pregnant women and anyone under eighteen years of age.

Reviewing the issue two decades later, the UN General Assembly in 1989 adopted the Second Optional Protocol to the 1966 covenant, Aiming at the Abolition of the Death Penalty. The introduction to the protocol enunciates the states parties' belief that "the abolition of the death penalty contributes to enhancement of human dignity and progressive development of human rights...." Article 1 mandates: "1. No one within the jurisdiction of a State Party to the present Protocol shall be executed. 2. Each State Party shall take all necessary measures to abolish the death penalty within its jurisdiction."

Constitution of Brazil (1988), title II, Fundamental Rights, chapter I, Individual and Collective Rights and Duties, article 5, 47: "[T]here shall be no punishment: a) of death, save in case of declared war...."

American Convention on Human Rights (1969), part I, State Obligations and Rights Protected, chapter II, Civil and Political Rights, article 4, Right to Life: "2. In countries that have not abolished the death penalty, it may be imposed only for the most serious crimes and pursuant to a final judgment rendered by a competent court and in accordance with a law establishing such punishment, enacted prior to the commission of the crime. The application of such punishment shall not be extended to crimes to which it does not presently apply."

Constitutional Court of South Africa (1995): Ten of eleven judges found that the death penalty constituted "cruel, inhuman or degrading treatment or punishment"; eight of the eleven found that it also violated the right to life; four found that it was a violation of the right to dignity; and one found that it infringed the right to equality.

African Commission on Human and Peoples' Rights (1994): Harassment of legal counsel by a Nigerian court, composed of one judge and four members of the military, forcing counsel's withdrawal and the subsequent imposition of the death penalty, violated the African Charter on Human and Peoples' Rights (1981), article 7, which mandates the right to appeal, the right to defense counsel, and the right to an impartial trial.

Amnesty International, Program to Abolish the Death Penalty, 600 Pennsylvania Avenue, S.E., Fifth Floor, Washington, D.C. 20003. (202-544-0200. 202-546-7142. dpprogram@aiusa.org. www.amnestyusa.org/abolish.

Derechos Human Rights, P.O. Box 2516, El Cerrito, Calif. 94530-5516. (510-483-4005. 603-372-9710. hr@derechos.org. www.derechos.org.

United Nations High Commissioner for Human Rights, 8–14 avenue de la Paix, 1211 Geneva 10, Switzerland. (41-22-917-9000. 41-22-917-9016. webadmin.hchr@unog.ch. www.unhchr.ch.

Gottfried, Ted. *Capital Punishment: The Death Penalty Debate*. Springfield, N.J.: Enslow, 1997.

Hood, Roger. *The Death Penalty: A Worldwide Perspective*. 2d ed. New York: Oxford University Press, 1996.

Wekesser, Carol, ed. *The Death Penalty: Opposing Viewpoints*. San Diego: Greenhaven, 1991.

Beccaria, Cesare; Fair Trial; International Covenant on Civil and Political Rights; International Covenant on Civil and Political Rights, Second Optional Protocol, Aiming at the Abolition of the Death Penalty; Plato; Principles on the Effective Prevention and Investigation of Extra-Legal, Arbitrary and Summary Executions; Rousseau, Jean-Jacques; Safeguards Guaranteeing Protection of the Rights of Those Facing the Death Penalty; Summary Executions

Carter, James Earl

Sometimes referred to as one of the greatest former presidents of the United States, James Earl (Jimmy) Carter (b. 1924) has made human rights an important part of his life, both in office and after his defeat in the 1980 U.S. presidential election. By his deeds, the former president has shown that the task of extending human rights requires personal commitment, not simply grand rhetoric.

Carter was born on October 1, 1924, in Plains, Georgia. On his graduation from the U.S. Naval Academy in 1946, he entered the navy and worked on the first nuclear-powered submarines. In 1953, on his father's death, he returned home to run the family business: peanut farming and warehousing. A strong supporter of racial equality, Carter entered politics in Georgia and was elected the state's governor in 1970. A leader in the national Democratic Party, he received its nomination for president and was elected to that office in 1976, becoming the first president since 1844 from a state in the Deep South.

Although his administration's foreign policy was not always a critical success, Carter's major achievements included facilitating the peace agreement between Israel and Egypt, known as the Camp David Accords, and taking a strong stand on human rights around the world. As Andrew Young, Carter's ambassador to the United Nations, observed: "Human rights is the greatest contribution of his [Carter's] presidency to the world. . . . [H]e made human rights the centerpiece of his administration." Believing that the United States had a significant role to play in promoting human rights around the world, Carter sought to limit or ban entirely U.S. foreign aid to nations guilty of human rights violations. "America didn't create human rights," he once commented. "Human rights created America."

After leaving office Carter established the Carter Center in Atlanta, Georgia, which promotes human rights in Third World nations, monitors elections in countries with new democratic governments, and assists in the eradication and prevention of diseases. Another major undertaking of the former president and his wife, Rosalynn, is Habitat for Humanity, the volunteer organization that provides low-income housing. In addition to these personal efforts, Carter has, as the official emissary of the United States, negotiated with the Nicaraguan Sandinista leader Daniel Ortega, North Korean dictator Kim Il Sung, and Haitian rebel leader Raoul Cedras, as well as acted as a mediator for the United States and the Somali warlord Mohamed Farrah.

The Carter Center, One Copenhill, 453 Freedom Parkway, Atlanta, Ga. 30307. (404-420-5100. 404-420-5145. carterweb@emory.edu. www.cartercenter.org.

Carter, Jimmy. *Keeping Faith*. New York: Bantam Books, 1982.

———. *Turning Point: A Candidate, a State, and a Nation Come of Age*. New York: Times Books, 1993.

Schraff, Anne E. *Jimmy Carter*. Springfield, N.J.: Enslow, 1998.

Center for Human Rights

In 1992 the UN General Assembly acknowledged the role of the Center for Human Rights in the "promotion, protection and implementation of human rights. . . ." Supervised by the Office of the High Commissioner for Human Rights, the center served as the UN division most directly concerned with human rights. On September 15, 1997, in connection with a general reform of the United Nations, however, it was merged into the High Commissioner's office in Geneva.

The center offered services on human rights issues and activities to many UN agencies, among them the General Assembly, Economic and Social Council (ECOSOC), Commission on Human Rights and its Subcommission on the Promotion and Protection of Human Rights, Human Rights Committee, and other bodies created under international human rights treaties. Other functions included coordination with specialized agencies, including the International Labor Organization, United Nations Educational, Scientific and Cultural Organization (UNESCO), and World Health Organization, as well as with regional intergovernmental human rights organizations, such as the Organization of American States, Organization of African Unity, and Council of Europe.

Among the center's other activities were providing advisory services and technical assistance on human rights to national governments; helping train government officials, judges, police, and military officers; creating legal studies programs and law libraries; drafting provisions required by international human rights documents; and disseminating information and publications on human rights.

United Nations High Commissioner for Human Rights, 8–14 avenue de la Paix, 1211 Geneva 10, Switzerland. ☎ 41-22-917-9000. 🖷 41-22-917-9016. 🖳 webadmin.hchr@unog.ch. 🖳 www.unhchr.ch.

High Commissioner for Human Rights

Charter of Paris for a New Europe

The Charter of Paris for a New Europe (1990) builds on the process begun by the Helsinki Final Act of 1975. While not legally binding, the charter reaffirms the commitment of the thirty-four member states, including France, Germany, the United Kingdom, Poland, Hungary, and the Czech Republic, as well as the United States and Canada, to certain democratic principles and human rights.

At the first world summit meeting, held in Helsinki, Finland, in 1975, the Conference on Security and Cooperation in Europe (CSCE), now called the Organization for Security and Cooperation in Europe (OSCE), adopted the Helsinki Final Act. Its creation of a framework for maintaining peace and security in Europe—the Helsinki process, as it came to be known—had an unexpected impact and culminated in the revolutionary events of 1989. The fall of the Berlin Wall and the rise of constitutional democracies in the former Soviet Union and its Eastern European communist satellite countries led to a new atmosphere in Europe regarding human rights.

A second summit meeting was held in Vienna in November 1990. There, on November 21, all the CSCE heads of state and government signed a new document, the Charter of Paris for a New Europe, confirming the end of confrontation and division in Europe and rededicating their countries to observe human rights and fundamental freedoms, which they called "an essential safeguard against an over-mighty State."

The charter has three major sections. The first, A New Era of Democracy, Peace and Unity, states in part: "Ours is a time for fulfilling the hopes and expectations our people have cherished for decades: steadfast commitment to democracy based on human rights and fundamental freedoms; prosperity through economic liberty and social justice; and equal security for all our countries." A subsection, Human Rights, Democracy and Rule of Law, proclaims in part: "Human rights and fundamental freedoms are the birthright of all human beings, are inalienable and are guaranteed by law. Their protection and promotion is the first responsibility of government." This subsection continues: "Democracy, with its representative and pluralist character, entails accountability to the electorate, the obligation of public authorities to comply with the law and justice administered impartially. No one will be above the law."

There follows a succinct recitation of certain basic human rights, including freedom of thought, conscience, religion or belief, expression, association and peaceful assembly, and movement; guarantees against arbitrary arrest or detention, torture, or other cruel, inhuman, or degrading treatment or punishment; and assurances of each person's right to know and act on his or her rights, to participate in free and fair elections, to receive a fair and public trial if charged with an offense, to own property, and to enjoy economic, social, and cultural rights. This section also declares "that the ethnic, cultural, linguistic and religious identity of national minorities will be protected and that persons belonging to national minorities have the right freely to express, preserve and develop that identity without any discrimination and in full equality before the law." The first section also addresses economic liberty and responsibility, friendly relations among participating states, security, unity, and the CSCE and the world.

The second major section is Guidelines for the Future. "We declare our respect for human rights and fundamental freedoms to be irrevocable," states the Human Dimension subsection. "We will fully implement and build upon the provisions relating to the human dimension of the CSCE." Other subsections cover security, economic cooperation, environment, culture, migrant workers, the Mediterranean, and nongovernmental organizations.

The last section, New Structures and Institutions of the

CSCE Process, begins: "Our common efforts to consolidate respect for human rights, democracy and the rule of law, to strengthen peace and to promote unity in Europe require a new quality of political dialogue and co-operation and thus development of the structures of the CSCE." A Supplementary Document was adopted along with the charter, containing procedures and organizational "modalities" relating to the charter's provisions.

Organization for Security and Cooperation in Europe (OSCE), Kärntner Ring 5–7, Fourth Floor, 1010 Vienna, Austria. ☎ 43-1-514-36-0. 🖨 43-1-514-36-96. 🖳 pm@osce.org. 🖳 www.osce.org.

European Convention for the Protection of Human Rights and Fundamental Freedoms; Helsinki Final Act; Organization for Security and Cooperation in Europe

Charter of the United Nations

The Covenant of the League of Nations (1919), the predecessor of the United Nations from 1920 to 1946, when it was officially dissolved, contained some human rights provisions. According to article 23, for example, its members were to "endeavor to secure fair and humane conditions of labor for men, women, and children" and "undertake to secure just treatment of the native inhabitants of territories under their control." As World War II was ending, representatives of the victorious nations met in San Francisco from April 25 to June 26, 1945, and adopted the Charter of the United Nations, which entered into force on October 24, 1945. Extending the human rights expressed in the earlier covenant, the charter specifically speaks of "promoting and encouraging respect for human rights and fundamental freedoms for all without distinction as to race, sex, language, or religion." The charter also envisaged in article 68 the establishment of the Commission on Human Rights, which was created by its Economic and Social Council (ECOSOC) in early 1946.

The UN charter established the United Nations as a body of member nations setting out their rights and obligations, set up the organization's offices and procedures, and codified major principles of international relations while recognizing the sovereignty of each nation-state and the basic human rights to which all persons are entitled. It also prohibited the use of force in international relations.

The charter begins: "We the Peoples of the United Nations, Determined to save succeeding generations from the scourge of war, which twice in our lifetime brought untold sorrow to mankind, and to reaffirm faith in fundamental human rights, in the dignity and worth of the human person, in the equal rights of men and women and of nations large and small, and to establish conditions under which justice and respect for the obligations arising from treaties and other sources of international law can be maintained, and to promote social progress and better standards of life in larger freedom, ... Have Resolved to Combine Our Efforts to Accomplish these Aims."

Chapter I, article 1, sets forth the purposes of the United Nations: "1. To maintain international peace and security ...; 2. To develop friendly relations among nations based on respect for the principle of equal rights and self-determination of peoples ...; 3. To achieve international cooperation in solving international problems of an economic, social, cultural, or humanitarian character, and in promoting and encouraging respect for human rights and for fundamental freedoms for all without distinction as to race, sex, language, or religion; and 4. To be a center for harmonizing the actions of nations in the attainment of these common ends."

The principles on which the organization and its members are to act, addressed by article 2, include the "principle of the sovereign equality of all its Members"; fulfillment "in good faith [of] the obligations assumed by them in accordance with the present Charter"; settlement of "international disputes by peaceful means ... [and refraining] in their international relations from the threat or use of force against the territorial integrity or political independence of any state...." Other principles to be observed, according to article 2, are giving "the United Nations every assistance in any action it takes in accordance with the present Charter ..." and refraining "from giving assistance to any state against which the United Nations is taking preventive or enforcement action." Article 2 also prohibits the UN from intervening "in matters which are essentially within the domestic jurisdiction of any state" or requiring "the Members to submit such matters to settlement under the present Charter...."

According to chapter II, articles 3 and 4, in addition to the countries that participated in the San Francisco conference, "Membership ... is open to all other peace-loving states which accept the obligations contained in the present Charter ..., [and] ... admission of any such state ... will be effected by a decision of the General Assembly upon the recommendation of the Security Council." Under article 5, a member "against which preventive or enforcement action has been taken by the Security Council may be suspended from the exercise of the rights and privileges of membership by the General Assembly upon the recommendation of the Security Council." Article 6 provides for expelling a member that "has persistently violated the Principles contained in the present Charter...."

Chapter III creates the principal agencies of the UN—the General Assembly, Security Council, ECOSOC, Trusteeship Council, International Court of Justice, and Secretariat—and authorizes the creation of subsidiary bodies. Article 8 states: "The United Nations shall place no restrictions on the eligibility of men and women to participate in any capacity and under conditions of equality in its principal and subsidiary organs." To date, however, no woman has served as UN secretary-general, its administrative head.

Chapter IV, articles 9 through 22, deal with the structure, functions, and procedures of the General Assembly, while chapter V, articles 23 through 32, address the structure, functions, and procedures of the Security Council. When the charter was adopted, the Security Council consisted of the Republic of China (later replaced by the People's Republic of China), France, the Union of Soviet Socialist Republics (succeeded by Russia), the United Kingdom of Great Britain and Northern Ireland, and the United States of America. Six additional nonpermanent members are to be elected by the General Assembly "for a term of two years" with "due regard . . . to the contribution of Members . . . to the maintenance of international peace and security. . . ." Chapter VI provides for the "pacific settlement" of disputes "by negotiation, enquiry, mediation, conciliation, arbitration, judicial settlement, resort to regional agencies or arrangements, or other peaceful means of [the parties'] own choice," giving the Security Council a significant role in investigating and hearing allegations of such controversies.

Chapter VII details the UN's courses of action with respect to "any threat to the peace, breach of the peace, or act of aggression," including the use of armed interventions. Its authority under this chapter was used in the 1990s to establish international tribunals to try alleged perpetrators of genocide in the former Yugoslavia (1993) and Rwanda (1994). Setting up such tribunals by Security Council resolutions allowed the UN to move quicker than it could have by trying to gain approval of an international convention.

"Nothing in the present Charter," states chapter VIII, article 52(1), "precludes the existence of regional arrangements or agencies for dealing with such matters relating to the maintenance of international peace and security. . . ." Article 54, however, requires that the "Security Council shall at all times be kept fully informed of activities undertaken or in contemplation under regional arrangements or by regional agencies for the maintenance of international peace and security."

Chapters IX and X, respectively, deal with international economic and social cooperation and the Economic and Social Council. Of particular significance for human rights is the language in chapter X, article 68: "The Economic and Social Council shall set up commissions in economic and social fields and for the promotion of human rights. . . ." Chapters XI, XII, and XIII, respectively, cover declarations regarding non-self-governing territories, the international trusteeship system (which replaced the mandate system of the League of Nations for guiding colonial territories to independence and self-government), and the Trusteeship Council, created to administer the trusteeship system.

The International Court of Justice, also known as the World Court, is established by chapter XIV, and the UN Secretariat, the organization's administrative operations, is created under chapter XV. The last chapters of the charter, XVI, XVII, XVIII, and XIX, respectively, are entitled Miscellaneous Provisions, Transitional Security Arrangements, Amendments, and Ratification and Signature. Amendments to the charter require a two-thirds vote of the members of the General Assembly and must be "ratified in accordance with [the member countries'] respective constitutional processes by two-thirds of the members of the United Nations, including all the permanent members of the Security Council."

There have been several amendments to the charter, including one to article 23, which entered into force in 1965 and increased from eleven to fifteen the number of members of the Security Council. An amendment to article 27, which became effective the same year, increased from seven to nine the number of affirmative votes necessary for a Security Council decision. Other amendments increased from eighteen to twenty-seven the number of members of ECOSOC, effective in 1965, and then to fifty-four, effective in 1973.

The goals of the charter, as set out in its preamble, remain "to practice tolerance and live together in peace with one another as good neighbors, and to unite our strength to maintain international peace and security, and to ensure . . . that armed force shall not be used, save in the common interest, and to employ international machinery for the promotion of the economic and social advancement of all peoples."

United Nations, New York, N.Y. 10017. (212-963-4475. 212-963-0071. inquiries@un.org. www.un.org.

Commission on Human Rights; Economic and Social Council (ECOSOC); International Criminal Court; International Court of Justice; United Nations

Charter 77 (Czechoslovakia)

In 1977 more than one thousand Czech intellectuals and artists signed a document called Charter 77 to protest the Czechoslovak government's disregard of the human rights provisions in the Helsinki Final Act (1975) and other human rights documents to which the country was a party. One of the signers was the renowned playwright and ardent human rights activist Václav Havel, who two years earlier at great personal risk had written an open letter to the leader of the repressive Czech regime, which he condemned for eroding values and fostering fear and apathy among the citizens. Following the "velvet revolution" in 1989, which toppled Czechoslovakia's communist regime, the Czech Republic came into being, and Havel was elected its first president in 1993.

The charter's first paragraph observes: "On 13 October 1976 [the Czechoslovak government] published the 'International

Covenant on Civil and Political Rights' [1966] and the 'International Covenant on Economic, Social and Cultural Rights' [1966] which had been signed in the name of our Republic in 1968, confirmed in Helsinki in 1975, and which acquired validity here on 23 March 1976. From that day our citizens have the right, and our State the duty, to be guided by them."

The fifth paragraph cites examples of violations of the right "to seek, receive and impart information and ideas of all kinds, regardless of frontiers ..." as guaranteed in the International Covenant on Civil and Political Rights, article 19, as well as violations of other provisions of that document relating to freedom of expression, thought, conscience, and religion. Charter 77 specifically condemns the Communist Party system in the eighth paragraph as "an instrument for restricting, and often completely suppressing, many civil rights ... whereby, in effect, all institutions and organizations of state are subordinated to the political directives from the apparatus of the ruling party and to the decisions of individuals influential in the power structure." Other human rights violations by the Czech government, as cited in the ninth, tenth, and eleventh paragraphs, include "arbitrary or unlawful interference with privacy, family, home or correspondence"; politically motivated prosecutions; and arbitrary denial of the right to leave the country.

In its penultimate paragraph the document authorizes three signatories, including Havel, to serve as spokesmen for the charter. The final paragraph asserts the belief that "Charter 77 will contribute to enabling all Czechoslovak citizens to live and work as free people." This document shows how a seemingly fruitless attempt by a relatively few people to hold a totalitarian regime responsible for human rights violations led to democracy and greatly expanded rights for millions of people.

Havel, Václav. *Disturbing the Peace: A Conversation with Karel Hvízdála.* New York: Knopf, 1990.

Havel, Václav; Helsinki Final Act; International Covenant on Civil and Political Rights; International Covenant on Economic, Social and Cultural Rights

Children

Under most nations' laws a child is considered a minor— a person who has not reached the age of majority—rather than an adult citizen, and thus is not accorded the full rights of citizenship. The idea that children, except perhaps those born to royal or ruling families, have rights is new, but human rights organizations are increasingly focusing on protecting children, especially in the Western world.

Underlying the Convention on the Rights of the Child (1989), a basic guide to the treatment of children adopted by the United Nations, is the philosophy that children have the same inherent value as adults as well as special needs, including the right to education and the right to play. "If we want to do a better job of teaching children how to be fair, we must set a better example by treating children fairly," says Marian Wright Edelman, chairman of the U.S.–based Children's Defense Fund.

In his *Politics*, written in the fourth century B.C.E., Aristotle quotes Homer's description of Greek households: "Each one [the male head of the family] gives laws to his children and his wives." Aristotle also refers to the republic envisioned by Plato, in which "citizens might have wives and children and property in common." For much of human history, children were simply considered the property of their parents and in many countries are still regarded this way. Today parents, whether natural or adoptive, are considered legally responsible for caring for and nurturing their children. Other family members or guardians may fill this role when the parents cannot, and in extreme cases foster parents or government and charitable institutions provide the necessary care for orphans, neglected or abandoned children, and children in abusive, unhealthy, or impoverished families.

Since the nineteenth century most Western countries have had laws regarding custody and guardianship of children, the rights and welfare of illegitimate children and orphans, and the property rights of minors. Enlightened societies now believe that children are entitled to food, housing, education, health care, an adequate standard of living, and child care while parents are working. It is estimated that some 250 million children themselves work around the world, half in Asia and a third in Africa, toiling at adult tasks from agriculture to manufacturing and mining. Children's rights also touch on a number of other issues, from illegitimacy, adoption, foster care, abuse, abduction, and family relations to drugs, work, military service, victimization by armed conflicts, torture, detention, disappearances, prostitution, and pornography. Other legal and social issues also come into play: the rights of women, mothers, fathers, families, grandparents, and guardians, along with cultural, religious, community, and government rights and responsibilities. Sexual abuse, exposure to violence in video games and the media, and Internet predators are just a few of the current concerns of children's rights activists. It is becoming clear that national attention alone is inadequate to address all these problems.

"[T]he well-being and interests of children and young adults are fundamental issues for any society," notes the Recommendation Concerning Sexual Exploitation, Pornography and Prostitution of, and Trafficking in, Children and Young Adults, adopted by the Committee of Ministers of the Council of Europe in 1991, "... [and] it is in the interests of member states of the Council of Europe to harmonize their national legislation ... in order to improve the co-ordination and effectiveness of action taken at [the] national and international level with a view to tackling this problem...."

Children's rights are addressed in some national constitutions—for example, those of Ireland (1937), India (1950), and Denmark (1953)—and in a number of international human rights documents. International conventions in 1919 and 1921 on the economic and sexual exploitation of children, respectively, were followed by the first international document embracing a wide range of children's rights: the Declaration of the Rights of the Child, adopted by the General Assembly of the League of Nations in 1924. This document preceded by nearly a quarter of a century the first general international document on human rights, the Universal Declaration of Human Rights (1948). In 1959 the UN General Assembly adopted its own Declaration of the Rights of the Child.

Other human rights documents specifically directed at children's rights include the Declaration on Social and Legal Principles Relating to the Protection and Welfare of Children, with Special Reference to Foster Placement and Adoption Nationally and Internationally (1986); Convention on the Rights of the Child (1989); and World Declaration on the Survival, Protection and Development of Children (1990). The African Charter on the Rights and Welfare of the Child (1990), in addition to recognizing that children require "particular care with regard to health, physical, mental, moral and social development," urges that "the virtues of their cultural heritage, historical background and the values of the African civilization . . . should inspire and characterize [the states parties'] reflection on the concept of the rights and welfare of the child." Under Responsibilities of the Child, the charter includes "placing his physical and intellectual abilities at [the] service" of the national community and preserving and strengthening "African cultural values in his relations with other members of the society. . . ." The European Convention on the Exercise of Children's Rights, opened for signature in 1996, focuses on procedural rights for children in judicial situations, such as the right to receive relevant information, to be consulted, to express personal views and to be informed of the consequences of acting in accordance with such views, and to be apprised of judicial decisions.

Provisions specifically relating to children can also be found in documents such as the Universal Declaration of Human Rights (1948), European Convention for the Protection of Human Rights and Fundamental Freedoms (1950), International Covenant on Economic, Social and Cultural Rights (1966), American Convention on Human Rights (1969) and its 1988 protocol, African Charter on Human and Peoples' Rights (1981), and Cairo Declaration on Human Rights in Islam (1990).

Constitution of India (1950, amended in 1977), part IV, Directive Principles of State Policy, article 39: "The State shall, in particular, direct its policy towards securing . . . (f) that children are given oppor-

tunities and facilities to develop in a healthy manner and in conditions of freedom and dignity and that childhood and youth are protected against exploitation and against moral and material abandonment."

Universal Declaration of Human Rights (1948), article 25(2): "Motherhood and childhood are entitled to special care and assistance. All children, whether born in or out of wedlock, shall enjoy the same social protection."

Supreme Court of Canada (1995): In dismissing an appeal by parents who wanted to withhold medical treatment for their child on religious grounds, the court held that the rights of a "child in need of protection" under the law outweighed any rights of the parents under the Canadian Charter of Rights and Freedoms (1982).

European Court of Human Rights (1999): The trial of two minors charged with killing a toddler in the United Kingdom was not a fair trial, because, by being tried as adults, the defendants could not participate in their own defense.

Children's Defense Fund, 25 E Street, N.W., Washington, D.C. 20001. (202-628-8787. 202-662-3510. cdfinfo@childrensdefense.org. childrensdefense.org.

Defense for Children International, P.O. Box 88, 1211 Geneva 20, Switzerland. (41-22-734-0558. 41-22-740-1145. dci-hq @pingnet.ch. www.childhub.ch/webpub/dcihome.

Free the Children, 1750 Steeles Avenue West, Suite 218, Concord, Ontario L4K 2L7, Canada. (404-760-9382. 404-760-9157. freechild@clo.com. www.freethechildren.org.

Human Rights Watch, Children's Rights Project, 350 Fifth Avenue, New York, N.Y. 10118-3299. (212-290-4700. 212-736-1300. www.hrw.org/about/projects/children.

International Save the Children Alliance, 275–81 King Street, London W6 9LZ, England. (44-208-748-2554. 44-208-237-8000. info@save-the-children-alliance.org. www.savethechildren.net.

United Nations Children's Fund (UNICEF), Three United Nations Plaza, New York, N.Y. 10017. (212-326-7000. 212-887-7465. addresses@unicef.org. www.unicef.org.

United Nations High Commissioner for Human Rights, 8–14 avenue de la Paix, 1211 Geneva 10, Switzerland. (41-22-917-9000. 41-22-917-9016. webadmin.hchr@unog.ch. www.unhchr.ch.

Franklin, Bob, ed. *The Handbook of Children's Rights: Comparative Policy and Practice.* Preface by Thomas Hammarberg. London: Routledge, 1995.

International Journal of Children's Rights. The Hague: Kluwer Law International, 1993–.

Malaspina, Ann. *Children's Rights.* San Diego: Lucent Books, 1998.

The Rights of the Child. Strasbourg, France: Council of Europe, 1996.

Adoption; African Charter on the Rights and Welfare of the Child; Convention on the Rights of the Child; Declaration on Social and Legal Principles Relating to the Protection and Welfare of Children, with Special Reference to Foster Placement and Adoption Nationally and Internationally; Declaration of the Rights of the Child; Declaration on the Protection of Women and Children in Emergency and Armed Conflict; Families; Maternity; United Nations Children's Fund (UNICEF); Women; World Declaration on the Survival, Protection and Development of Children; Youth

Cicero, Marcus Tullius

A Roman lawyer and statesman, Marcus Tullius Cicero (106–43 B.C.E.) contributed to the foundations of natural law and human rights in his work *The Laws.* His writings, along with those of the Greek philosopher Plato and the Roman historian Titus Livius Livy, were a wellspring for the Renaissance humanists who led Europe out of the Dark Ages on the path to the Enlightenment in the eighteenth century.

Born on January 3, 106 B.C.E., to a well-to-do Roman family, Cicero set his sights on being a politician. After military service, he served as an advocate, or lawyer, and in his first trial criticized the regime of the dictator Sulla. After marrying Terentia, the daughter of a wealthy family, he became a *quaestor* (a public official) and a member of the Roman senate. His career as a politician received a boost when he successfully prosecuted a leading official for gross mismanagement in Sicily in 70 B.C.E.

Cicero rose in the ranks of public officials from *aedile* to *praetor,* the latter position being of great judicial importance. He saw himself as a defender of the public good and helped thwart an attempt to seize power through an armed revolt. His call for a *concordia ordinum* (concord between the classes) resulted in his being praised as "the father of his country." Although an ambitious politician, he refused a invitation from Julius Caesar to join with him, Crassus, and Pompey—the first triumvirate—in a ruling alliance because he believed it to be unconstitutional.

As punishment for criticizing Caesar's harsh methods as Roman consul, Cicero was exiled from Rome. He sided with Pompey in the civil war against Caesar and after Pompey's death concentrated on writing. Following Caesar's assassination in 44 B.C.E., Cicero argued in the Roman senate for amnesty for the conspirators. In the power struggle that ensued, Cicero allied himself with Octavian, the adopted son of Julius Caesar, against Mark Anthony,

whom he feared as a threat as great to Roman freedom as Caesar had been. But when Octavian, later called Augustus and the first Roman emperor, seized power, he formed a ruling triumvirate with Lepidus and Mark Anthony. The three then set out to destroy their enemies, including Cicero.

Cicero died at the hands of an assassin sent by Mark Anthony in 43 B.C.E. Although unable to save the Roman Republic, his important written works, *The Republic* and *The Laws,* which extended Greek notions of government to include the Roman Republic, became valuable sources for future experiments in just and humane government. He also wrote a treatise on moral duties, and his *Hortensius,* a call to the study of philosophy, influenced St. Augustine, a significant figure in the development of modern government and human rights.

Cicero's legacy is that of a seeker of truth and justice in a world of power and corruption. His honesty and courage as a political leader are exemplary, and his writings, which transmitted and extended much of the best of the ideas of the ancient Greeks, have provided inspiration for the development of theories and practices of popular government and human rights.

Fuhrman, Manfred. *Cicero and the Roman Republic.* Oxford, England: Blackwell, 1992.

Powell, J.G.F., ed. *Cicero the Philosopher.* Oxford, England: Clarendon Press, Oxford University Press, 1995.

Augustine, St.; Plato

Citizenship

See Nationality

Civil Rights

Civil rights and civil liberties (from the Latin *civis,* citizen, and *civilis,* of or pertaining to the citizen) are the rights and freedoms that citizens possess in a civil society, from personal liberty and security to the right to move about the country and return from traveling abroad, use public facilities, and share equally in the rights and duties of citizenship. Civil rights are generally linked with political rights, such as the right to vote for government officials and be eligible to hold public office. Both civil rights and political rights are considered first-generation human rights because of their basic importance to democracy and the equal rights of all citizens; second-generation rights include economic, social, and cultural rights, and third-generation rights include collective rights.

Whereas economic, social, and cultural rights are considered positive rights, meaning that the government has to act to redistribute wealth, restrict class or social distinctions, or provide special accommodations for cultural minorities, civil rights are generally negative rights. The government fulfills its obligations by *not* doing something—for example, by not requiring a religious test for election or appointment to government office and not discriminating or allowing discrimination on the basis of such irrelevant classifications as sex, race, religion, or national origin. By guaranteeing fair and equal treatment, governments can protect the civil rights of their citizens in all interactions.

Like constitutional rights, civil rights can be traced from the ancient Greek democracies and the Roman Republic through England's Magna Carta (1215) to the American and French Revolutions in the late eighteenth century. Before then, the rights of individuals were largely unheard of. Although feudal lords and the clergy had some rights, the vast majority of vassals and serfs had only whatever rights were meted out to them by those higher up the pyramid of authority. Popular sovereignty—the supremacy of the people as opposed to that of a monarch, dictator, or junta—helps further equal rights for all citizens.

Civil rights are typically guaranteed in national constitutions, although implementation often falls short of the ideals expressed. In the United States, for example, advocates of full civil rights for blacks in the 1960s had to protest and openly defy discriminatory state segregation and election laws. Positive legislation, including the Civil Rights Act of 1964, was required to ensure that they receive the full civil rights to which they are entitled.

Civil rights are catalogued in the Universal Declaration of Human Rights (1948), but the most detailed international human rights document addressing civil rights is the International Covenant on Civil and Political Rights (1966). The Siracusa Principles on the Limitation and Derogation Provisions of the Covenant (1984), produced by a group of international law experts concerned that the civil and political rights in the 1966 covenant might be restricted or limited, establish guidelines for preventing arbitrary or unnecessary limitations on and derogations from these rights.

Constitution of Surinam (1987), chapter 5, Basic Rights, Individual Rights and Freedoms, article 13: "Loss of civil rights or the general forfeiture of all the goods of an offender may not be inflicted as a penalty or as a consequence of a penalty for any crime."

International Covenant on Civil and Political Rights (1966), part II, article 3: "The States Parties to the present Covenant undertake to ensure the equal right of men and women to the enjoyment of all civil and political rights set forth in the present Covenant."

High Court of Australia (1982): The Australian government had denied a lease of land to a group of aborigines on the grounds that its desegregation policy did not allow large areas of land for development by aborigines in segregated isolation. The court held that such discrimination was an infringement of a civil right under the Racial Discrimination Act of 1975, built on the International Convention on the Elimination of All Forms of Racial Discrimination (1965), which was signed and ratified by the Commonwealth.

European Court of Human Rights (1975): "The concept of 'civil rights and obligations' as found in the European Convention for the Protection of Human Rights and Fundamental Freedoms [(1950), article 6, paragraph 1] is not co-extensive with that of 'rights and freedoms as set forth in this Convention' [article 13], even if there may be some overlap. As to the 'right to liberty' [article 5], its 'civil' character is at any rate open to argument."

American Civil Liberties Union (ACLU), 125 Broad Street, 18th Floor, New York, N.Y. 10004-2400. (212-549-2500. 212-549-2648. rfp@aclu.org. www.aclu.org.

United Nations High Commissioner for Human Rights, 8–14 avenue de la Paix, 1211 Geneva 10, Switzerland. (41-22-917-9000. 41-22-917-9016. webadmin.hchr@unog.ch. www.unhchr.ch.

Civil and Political Rights: The Human Rights Committee. Geneva: Center for Human Rights, 1991.

Kramer, Daniel C. *Comparative Civil Rights and Liberties*. Washington, D.C.: University Press of America, 1982.

Accused; Constitutional Rights; Discrimination; Equality; International Covenant on Civil and Political Rights; King, Martin Luther, Jr.; Magna Carta; Political Rights; Race Discrimination

Code of Conduct for Law Enforcement Officials

Law enforcement is an important yet difficult part of maintaining order and compliance with the law. In fulfilling their duties, law enforcement officials are often called on to place their lives and health at risk. At the same time they are responsible for minimizing the force and violence necessary to accomplish their tasks.

To help ensure that those who enforce the law do so in a manner that respects the human rights of all citizens, the UN General Assembly adopted the Code of Conduct for Law Enforcement Officials on December 17, 1979. The code mandates that such officials, including members of the military when called on to perform law enforcement functions, carry out their duties with dignity and respect for human rights. Implementation guidelines for the code were endorsed by the Economic and Social Council (ECOSOC) in 1989, and in 1990 the Basic Principles on the Use of Force and Firearms by Law Enforcement Officials was adopted by the Eighth United Nations Congress on the Prevention of Crime and the Treatment of Offenders.

The General Assembly, notes the code's preamble, is "[m]indful that the nature of the functions of law enforcement in the defense of public order and the manner in which these functions are exercised have a direct impact on the quality of life of individuals as well as of society as a whole." It goes on to cite "the important task which law enforcement officials are performing diligently and with dignity, in compliance with the principles of human rights" and recognizes that "the establishment of a code of conduct for law enforcement officials is only one of several important measures for providing the citizenry served by law enforcement officials with protection of all their rights and interests." The code, says the General Assembly, is being transmitted to governments "with the recommendation that favorable consideration should be given to its use within the framework of national legislation or practice as a body of principles for observance by law enforcement officials."

Article 1 mandates that law enforcement officials "shall at all times fulfill the duty imposed upon them by law, by serving the community and by protecting all persons against illegal acts, consistent with the high degree of responsibility required by their profession." The following commentary provides that the "term 'law enforcement officials' includes all officers of the law, whether appointed or elected, who exercise police powers, especially the powers of arrest and detention," including military authorities in countries where they exercise police powers.

In the performance of their duty, law enforcement officials must "respect and protect human dignity and maintain and uphold the human rights of all persons," as directed in article 2. Pursuant to article 3, they may use force "only when strictly necessary and to the extent required for the performance of their duty." The commentary adds that "use of force by law enforcement officials should be exceptional. . . ." While officials "may be authorized to use force as is reasonably necessary under the circumstances . . . , no force going beyond that may be used."

Article 4 addresses the use of confidential matters in the possession of law enforcement officials; article 5 prohibits "any act of torture or other cruel, inhuman or degrading treatment or punishment"; and article 6 mandates that law enforcement officials "shall ensure the full protection of the health of persons in their custody and, in particu-lar, take immediate action to secure medical attention whenever required." Article 7 focuses on "acts of corruption" and directs that such acts be rigorously opposed and combated.

Article 8 states: "Law enforcement officials shall respect the law and the present Code" and must report suspected violations "to their superior authorities and, where necessary, to other appropriate authorities or organs vested with reviewing or remedial power." The commentary adds, among other things, that "[l]aw enforcement officials who comply with the provisions of this Code deserve the respect, the full support and the co-operation of the community and of the law enforcement agency in which they serve, as well as of the law enforcement profession."

United Nations High Commissioner for Human Rights, 8–14 avenue de la Paix, 1211 Geneva 10, Switzerland. (41-22-917-9000. 🖨 41-22-917-9016. 🖳 webadmin.hchr@unog.ch. 🖳 www.unhchr.ch.

Basic Principles on the Use of Force and Firearms by Law Enforcement Officials; Law Enforcement; Torture

Collective Rights

Collective rights are those rights to which a group or members of a group are entitled. They are often referred to as third-generation rights, after individual civil and political rights (first generation) and economic, social, and cultural rights (second generation). Because human rights are based on the principle of the equality of all human beings, it could be argued that collective rights are not human rights at all given that not everyone is equally entitled to them. Obviously, family rights are in some ways collective rights, as are the rights of groups such as women and minorities. Yet these rights are generally acknowledged to be related to civil and political rights, if not first-generation rights themselves. For example, the right to found a family and the duty of society and the state to protect the family as the natural and fundamental unit of society is set forth in the International Covenant on Civil and Political Rights (1966).

Collective rights are also characterized as peoples' rights and thus include the rights of self-determination and development, as well as the right to peace, utilization of natural resources, co-ownership of the common heritage of humankind, and a clean and healthy environment. Similarly, community rights—the collective rights of a group of people sharing common political aspirations—include the right of self-determination, the right to a common language and culture, and the right of development.

Because human beings are generally members of a number

of groups, it is difficult to distinguish individual rights from the rights of those who are members of specific groups. Whereas individual human rights are rights vis-à-vis the government, collective rights—at least in the narrow sense of self-determination and development—are really rights of groups of individuals vis-à-vis the traditional structure of the international community and international law. There are, of course, areas of conflict between collective or community rights and individual rights, and this will probably always be the case. For example, individual members of minority groups who wish to pursue a nontraditional education or occupation or who wish to marry outside the community may face coercive pressure from the community or be ostracized for trying to exercise their individual human rights.

Constitution of Colombia (1991), title I, Concerning Fundamental Principles, chapter 3, Concerning Collective Rights and the Environment, article 82: "It is the duty of the state to watch over the protection of the integrity of public space and for its assignment to common use, which has priority over the individual interest."

African Charter on Human and Peoples' Rights (1981), part I, Rights and Duties, chapter I, Human and Peoples' Rights, article 20.1: "All peoples shall have the right to existence. They shall have the unquestionable and inalienable right to self-determination."

Federal Court of Canada, Trial Division (1979): "An aboriginal title to . . . territory, carrying with it the right freely to move about and hunt and fish over it, vested at common law in the Inuit [aboriginal peoples once called Eskimos]. . . . The communal right of aborigines to occupy [such territory takes precedence over] the right of a private owner to peaceful enjoyment of his land."

European Commission of Human Rights (1974): "[N]either the existence nor the autonomy of a public body such as a commune, nor the official functions exercised within such a body, are protected by article 11, or any other provision of the [European Convention for the Protection of Human Rights and Fundamental Freedoms (1950)]. The Commission observes in this connection that communes are not associations formed and freely joined by individuals but bodies established and governed by public law."

Gewirth, Alan. *The Community of Rights*. Chicago: University of Chicago Press, 1996.

Development; Environment; Natural Resources; Peace; Peoples' Rights; Self-Determination

Commission on Human Rights

The Commission on Human Rights is authorized by a 1970 resolution of the Economic and Social Council (ECOSOC) to consider and act on complaints that "appear to reveal a consistent pattern of gross and reliably attested violations of human rights and fundamental freedoms." The commission submits proposals, recommendations, and reports on human rights concerns to the UN General Assembly through ECOSOC, aided by the commission's Subcommission on the Promotion and Protection of Human Rights.

Composed of fifty-three representatives from UN member states, who are elected by ECOSOC for three-year renewable terms using a formula to ensure an equitable geographical distribution, the commission meets annually for six weeks in Geneva. It is one of three UN commissions directly involved with human rights issues. The other two, which also report to ECOSOC, are the Commission on the Status of Women and the Commission on Crime Prevention and Criminal Justice.

Unlike the Human Rights Committee, a treaty-based agency established to monitor compliance with the International Covenant on Civil and Political Rights (1966) and to consider human rights complaints against countries party to the covenant and its protocols, the Commission on Human Rights grew out of the Charter of the United Nations (1945). Article 68 directed ECOSOC to "set up commissions in economic and social fields and for the promotion of human rights." The commission was created in 1946 and held its first meeting in 1947. At that time its sole function was to draft the Universal Declaration of Human Rights, which was adopted by the General Assembly in 1948.

For the next twenty years the commission focused on creating documents that defined and promoted human rights worldwide. This work culminated in the creation of the International Covenant on Civil and Political Rights and the International Covenant on Economic, Social and Cultural Rights, both adopted by the General Assembly in 1966. Together with the Universal Declaration of Human Rights and the two protocols to the first covenant, these documents have been called the International Bill of Human Rights.

The creation of the United Nations, its Commission on Human Rights, and the Universal Declaration of Human Rights erroneously raised hopes and expectations that some action would be taken about human rights violations brought to the UN's attention. Between 1947 and 1957 some sixty-five thousand complaints, called communications, from individuals and organizations asserted human rights violations, and the number has increased dramatically since then to about twenty thousand annually. In 1947, however, the commission had officially recognized its lack of authority to deal with such complaints. While confirming this inability, ECOSOC nevertheless requested, by Resolution 728F (1959), that the UN secretary-general confidentially compile complaints for members to consult before each session of the commission. The resolution also requested that each UN member country be informed anonymously of complaints against it; governments had the option of having any replies to the commission presented "in summary form or in full."

The commission's continuing lack of authority to act on complaints led ECOSOC in 1967 to approve, by Resolution 1235, the commission's request to examine allegations of gross human rights violations contained in the lists compiled under Resolution 728F. It was also authorized to make a "thorough study" of cases that revealed a consistent pattern of abuse. This 1235 procedure extended the same authority to the commission's Subcommission on the Promotion and Protection of Human Rights.

To make the commission's work more effective, in 1970 ECOSOC adopted Resolution 1503, which further defined the processes contained in the earlier resolution and extended the commission's authority to take action on individual complaints alleging consistent and gross violations. Procedures were refined to include a three-step review of the communications by a working group of the subcommission and then by the subcommission and the commission. Review of and comments on government replies to allegations were also allowed, although the matters considered were still to remain confidential.

Today the commission has two basic functions: it has primary responsibility for UN human rights policy in cooperation with the Office of the High Commissioner for Human Rights, and it serves as the enforcement arm of the UN human rights system, albeit with limited means to enforce compliance or ensure that justice is done within particular nations. The commission also seeks to devise more effective ways to implement international human rights policies, a difficult task because such procedures may threaten national sovereignty under international law. Better implementation, short of an international police force, is therefore highly problematic.

In furthering UN human rights policy, the commission initiates studies and fact-finding missions, drafts conventions and declarations for the approval of ECOSOC and the General Assembly, and discusses human rights violations in public and private meetings. For assistance the commission may call on working groups and special rapporteurs (experts), in addition to its subcommission. Working groups have been set up on topics including contemporary forms of slavery, indigenous populations, minorities, administration of justice, compensation, enforced disappearances, and arbitrary detention. Rapporteurs address similar subjects or broad themes, among them states of emergency, impunity, extreme poverty, torture, arbitrary executions, religious intolerance, and sale of children. In 1994, for example, one special rapporteur on religious intolerance visited China and another studying contemporary forms of racism visited the United States. Rapporteurs have also been appointed for specific countries such as Afghanistan, Cambodia, Cuba, Guatemala, Haiti, Iran, Iraq, Myanmar (Burma), Palestine, Rwanda, and Yugoslavia.

In the last decade the commission has increasingly focused on providing advisory services and technical assistance on human rights to UN member countries. As set forth in the Vienna Declaration and Program of Action, adopted by the World Conference on Human Rights in 1993, emphasis is now being placed on promoting economic, social, and cultural rights, especially the rights to development and an adequate standard of living. The commission is also paying closer attention to protecting the rights of vulnerable groups such as minorities and indigenous people, children, and women. According to a report of decisions adopted by the commission at its fifty-fifth session in 1999, questions addressed included human rights in Cyprus, systematic rape, sexual slavery, slavelike practices during armed conflict, affirmative action, and human rights in Central America during the reconstruction after Hurricane Mitch.

The commission's success in acting on communications that indicate a pattern of gross human rights violations is difficult to assess. Because proceedings relating to a complaint are closed, communications remain confidential. And because of the rigorous filtering process by the working groups, subcommission, and commission, only relatively few of the thousands of annual complaints are acted on. Its enforcement techniques are limited: it may refer a matter to ECOSOC, appoint a special rapporteur to conduct a study of the case, or recommend that ECOSOC or the General Assembly adopt a resolution calling for the nation involved to correct the abuse indicated. If a country refuses to follow such a resolution, the only recourse is public condemnation by the UN. It is nonetheless likely that the commission's procedures, together known as the Resolution 1503 Procedure, have in fact had positive impacts on some countries' human rights policies given, for example, that the commission now publicly identifies the countries involved in its deliberations.

United Nations High Commissioner for Human Rights, 8–14 avenue de la Paix, 1211 Geneva 10, Switzerland. (41-22-917-9000. 41-22-917-9016. webadmin.hchr@unog.ch. www.unhchr.ch.

Flood, Patrick James. *The Effectiveness of UN Human Rights Institutions*. Westport, Conn.: Praeger, 1998.

Charter of the United Nations; Economic and Social Council (ECOSOC); High Commissioner for Human Rights; Human Rights Committee; International Bill of Human Rights; International Covenant on Civil and Political Rights; Resolution 1503 Procedure; Subcommission on the Promotion and Protection of Human Rights; United Nations; Vienna Declaration and Program of Action; Working Groups

Committee on the Elimination of Discrimination against Women

In 1946 the Economic and Social Council (ECOSOC) created a forty-five-member Commission on the Status of Women. Concerned with establishing an international norm of equality for women, the UN General Assembly in 1952 adopted the Convention on the Political Rights of Women and then the Convention on the Nationality of Married Women in 1957. Five years later, in 1962, the UN adopted the Convention on Consent to Marriage, Minimum Age for Marriage and Registration of Marriages, which promoted national legislation granting equal rights for both spouses. Then in 1967 the Declaration on the Elimination of Discrimination against Women pointed out that women were still being denied "participation, on equal terms with men, in the political, social, economic and cultural life of their countries. . . ." Because such discrimination continued in many countries and cultures, the General Assembly in 1979 adopted the Convention on the Elimination of All Forms of Discrimination against Women, which established the Committee on the Elimination of Discrimination against Women to monitor its implementation.

Article 2 of the convention specifies that signatory nations agree to pursue equality in their national constitutions "or other appropriate legislation if not yet incorporated therein," to adopt laws prohibiting discrimination against women, to enforce protection of women's rights, to avoid discrimination, to take "measures to eliminate discrimination against women by any person, organization or enterprise," to modify or abolish existing discriminatory laws, and to repeal all penal provisions that constitute discrimination against women.

The committee now consists of twenty-three experts who serve in their personal capacity. Members are elected to four-year terms by secret ballot by the states parties to the convention from a list of persons nominated by them. Each state party is allowed to nominate one person from its own country. The committee is authorized to adopt rules of procedure and elect its officers for terms of two years. Meetings are generally held at the UN headquarters in New York City or in Vienna.

The committee's main function is outlined in the convention's article 18. Paragraph 1 requires that "States Parties undertake to submit to the [UN] Secretary-General, for consideration by the Committee, reports on the legislative, judicial, administrative or other measures which they have adopted to give effect to the provisions of the Convention and on the progress made in this respect. . . ." Reports are to be sent "(a) Within one year after the entry into force for the State concerned; (b) Thereafter at least every four years and further whenever the Committee so requests."

According to article 21, "The Committee shall, through the Economic and Social Council, report annually to the General Assembly . . . on its activities and may make suggestions and recommendations based on the examination of reports and information received from the States Parties." The UN secretary-general is then to transmit committee reports to the Commission on the Status of Women. Article 22 provides that "specialized agencies shall be entitled to be represented at the consideration of the implementation of such provisions of the present Convention as fall within the scope of its activities. The Committee may invite the specialized agencies to submit reports on the implementation of the Convention in areas falling within the scope of their activities."

As of January 2000 the committee has considered 101 initial periodic reports on activities to improve the protection of women in countries that are states parties to the convention as well as 130 subsequent reports. At its twenty-second session, at the beginning of 2000, it reviewed initial reports from India and Myanmar (formerly Burma) as well as other reports from Jordan, Democratic Republic of the Congo, Burkino Faso, Belarus, Luxembourg, and Germany.

Through this procedure of reviewing country reports and making recommendations, the committee acts to effect antidiscriminatory changes in national constitutions, laws, and administrative procedures. Besides evaluating the progress made by the states parties to the convention, the committee makes general recommendations on strategies to eliminate discrimination against women.

The committee's effectiveness should be increased as a result of a new procedure authorizing the committee to receive individual complaints and transmit its findings to the states involved under an optional protocol to the convention that was opened for signature on December 10, 1999. According to article 7 of the protocol, the committee will examine and consider in closed meetings all information provided in the complaint, and its views and recommendations will be communicated to the parties concerned. The state party against which the complaint is made will then have six months to consider the committee's findings, provide a response, and take remedial action. As with all international and regional human rights decisions, it is up to the offending country to act in good faith to carry out the committee's recommendations.

United Nations High Commissioner for Human Rights, 8–14 avenue de la Paix, 1211 Geneva 10, Switzerland. (41-22-917-9000. 📠 41-22-917-9016. 📧 webadmin.hchr@unog.ch. 🖥 www.unhchr.ch.

Convention on Consent to Marriage, Minimum Age for Marriage and Registration of Marriages; Convention on the Elimination of All Forms of Discrimination against Women; Convention on the

Political Rights of Women; Declaration on the Elimination of Discrimination against Women; Economic and Social Council (ECOSOC); Sex Discrimination; Women

Committee on the Elimination of Racial Discrimination

In 1963 the UN General Assembly adopted the Declaration on the Elimination of All Forms of Racial Discrimination, which it followed in 1965 with the International Convention on the Elimination of All Forms of Racial Discrimination, a document that entered into force in 1969. Part II of the convention establishes a Committee on the Elimination of Racial Discrimination, consisting of "eighteen experts of high moral standing and acknowledged impartiality elected by the States Parties [to the convention] from among their nationals. . . ." They are elected for four-year terms, one-half every two years, and generally meet at UN headquarters in New York City and in Geneva. Article 10 authorizes the committee to adopt its own rules of procedure and elect its officers for terms of two years and also specifies that a committee secretariat is to be provided by the UN secretary-general.

Under the terms of the convention, the committee has three basic functions. Pursuant to article 9, the states parties are "to submit to the Secretary-General of the United Nations for consideration by the Committee a report on the legislative, judicial, administrative or other measures which they have adopted and which give effect to the provisions of the Convention. . . ." The committee is to report annually to the General Assembly "and may make suggestions and general recommendations based on the examination of the reports and information received from [them]."

Article 11 specifies that the committee may also receive communications from one state party that another state party "is not giving effect to the provisions of [the] Convention. . . ." The committee transmits the communication, or complaint, to the state accused of the offense. If a settlement of the dispute cannot be worked out within six months, the committee chair appoints an ad hoc conciliation commission, which reports its findings and recommendations to the chair, who in turn sends them to the parties involved.

Although the committee is prohibited from receiving anonymous petitions, article 14 authorizes it to consider complaints "from individuals and groups ... within its jurisdiction claiming to be victims of a violation" by a state party. Such petitions are confidentially brought to the attention of the state party alleged to be in violation of the convention, which has three months in which to respond. As with most international human rights remedies, before the committee can take action all domestic remedies must first be exhausted unless unreasonable delay has occurred.

The committee may then forward its recommendations to the state and the complaining party and summarizes such matters in its annual report.

Under article 15, the committee was also given a role in dealing with inhabitants of non-self-governing territories and territories governed under a UN trusteeship. All such trusteeships have now ended.

As of October 1999, the committee had one pending active case, an individual complaint regarding Australia, and had found three such complaints inadmissible under the convention's terms. On the basis of article 9, which requires that states parties file reports, the committee tries to measure its impact in effecting change in national constitutions and statutory laws, introducing educational programs, and creating national agencies to help deal with the problems of race discrimination, among other efforts.

According to the committee, its work has been hampered by the failure of some countries to file their reports and the tardiness of such reports, both of which impede the process of monitoring actions to eliminate discrimination. Another problem has been the failure of some countries to meet their monetary commitments to support the committee's work and the UN's lack of funding support, a result of its own financial difficulties.

United Nations High Commissioner for Human Rights, 8–14 avenue de la Paix, 1211 Geneva 10, Switzerland. (41-22-917-9000. 🖨 41-22-917-9016. 🖳 webadmin.hchr@unog.ch. 🖳 www.unhchr.ch.

Declaration on the Elimination of All Forms of Racial Discrimination; International Convention on the Elimination of All Forms of Racial Discrimination; Race Discrimination

Communication

Communication (from the Latin *communicatio*) refers to the exchange of information and ideas in any form but particularly via telephone or the mail, which is susceptible to invasion of privacy. Communications technology and the means of intervention have advanced exponentially since the days of messengers on foot and horseback. Worldwide postal service, the telegraph and telephone, satellite and e-mail are all forms of communication in which the privacy of the information exchanged may be compromised by the government.

The Bill of Rights (1791) of the U.S. Constitution does not expressly guarantee freedom of communication. However, governmental invasion of privacy by tapping the telephone line of a person suspected of a crime (wiretapping), without approval by a court of law, has been prohibited under the Fourth Amendment, which guarantees the "right of the people to be secure in their persons, houses, papers, and effects, against unreasonable searches and seizures...."

Some more recent national constitutions, however, expressly provide for freedom of communication, including the constitutions of Turkey (1982) and Brazil (1988). A number of international human rights documents also contain declarations of the right or freedom of communication, although they may be couched in terms of the right to privacy, especially with regard to correspondence. Such documents include the European Convention for the Protection of Human Rights and Fundamental Freedoms (1950) and the American Convention on Human Rights (1969). (Some international and regional human rights systems use the term *communication* to refer to formal allegations or complaints of human rights abuses.)

Arrested persons also have a right to communicate with others to ensure their defense against criminal charges. A resolution by the Commission on Human Rights in 1961 called for a study on this subject in the context of arbitrary arrest, detention, and exile. The study addressed a person's right to notify others of his or her arrest, receive visits, and correspond; remedies and sanctions available for the denial of such rights; and detention under emergencies and the practice of holding a person *incommunicado* (without access to communication).

On November 22, 1978, the United Nations Educational, Scientific and Cultural Organization (UNESCO) adopted the Declaration on Fundamental Principles Concerning the Contribution of the Mass Media to Strengthening Peace and International Understanding, to the Promotion of Human Rights and to Countering Racialism, Apartheid and Incitement to War. Endorsed by the UN General Assembly in 1982, this document focuses on the role of radio, television, and the print media in promoting human rights and disseminating accurate information to mass audiences. The European Declaration on Mass Communication Media and Human Rights (1970) defines freedom of expression in the context of mass communications media as "freedom to seek, receive, impart, publish, and distribute information and ideas. There shall be a corresponding duty for the public authorities to make available information on matters of public interest within reasonable limits and a duty for mass communication media to give complete and general information on government affairs."

Constitution of Sweden, The Instrument of Government (1974), chapter 2, Fundamental Rights and Freedoms, article 1: "All citizens shall be guaranteed the following in their relations with the public administration: 1.... The freedom to communicate information and express ideas, opinions, and emotions...."

American Declaration of the Rights and Duties of Man, chapter one, Rights, article X: "Every person has the right to the inviolability and transmission of his correspondence."

Supreme Court of Canada (1991): A communication made to a religious adviser who is not an ordained priest "will not bar the possibility of the communication being found to be privileged, and thus inadmissible [as evidence]," according to the Canadian Charter of Rights and Freedoms (1982), which requires the court "to begin any analysis with a non-denominational approach."

Inter-American Commission on Human Rights (1995): Members of the Peruvian army who invaded the home of the former president of Peru threatened his safety and that of his wife and their children, held them *incommunicado* and under house arrest, and removed a number of private family documents solely on the basis of "a superior order of arrest against them." The commission found that the government had violated the rights of the former president and his family as guaranteed by the American Convention on Human Rights, article 11, which states in part: "2. No one may be the object of arbitrary or abusive interference with his private life, his family, his home, or his correspondence...."

Ploman, Edward W., ed. *International Law Governing Communications and Information: A Collection of Basic Documents*. Westport, Conn.: Greenwood, 1982.

Zelezny, John D. *Communications Law: Liberties, Restraints, and the Modern Media*. Belmont, Calif.: Wadsworth, 1997.

American Convention on Human Rights; Commission on Human Rights; Complaints; Declaration on Fundamental Principles Concerning the Contribution of the Mass Media to Strengthening Peace and International Understanding, to the Promotion of Human Rights and to Countering Racialism, Apartheid and Incitement to War; European Convention for the Protection of Human Rights and Fundamental Freedoms; Expression; Information; Privacy; Regional Human Rights Systems

Compensation

"An eye for an eye and a tooth for a tooth" is an ancient rule of compensation. As societies evolved, an injured or aggrieved party would make a claim or demand on the person who caused damage, his or her relatives, or persons who had authority to decide such matters. The modern legal definition of compensation (from the Latin *compensare*, meaning to weigh one thing against another or to counterbalance) is an act that a court orders to be done or money that a court or other tribunal directs be paid by a person whose acts or omissions have caused loss or injury to another. The object is to make the injured party whole or restore the victim to his or her condition or position before the injury or loss occurred. In some cases, of course, what is lost is irreplaceable or cannot be restored, as in the loss of life. Thus, compensation generally refers to money paid to the injured party or his or her heirs in accordance with traditional or statutory standards of justice.

Compensation may be required for the government's taking of private property, thus recognizing the right to ownership of private property. It may also be specified by law or legal determination for other violations of rights, such as illegal detention or other miscarriage of justice. Compensation or money damages may be required in cases of personal injury and suffering or death. In international law there is also a recognized right to compensation for the property losses of foreign nationals resulting from government action, including the nationalization of such property, although the question of fair, just, and prompt payment is not always respected in international claims settlement agreements.

Many national constitutions, including those of South Korea (1948) and Germany (1949), guarantee the right to compensation for the taking of private property for public use, and many national laws authorize compensation for other public as well as private wrongs. The Federal Tort Claims Act, for example, provides a legal mechanism for compensating people injured by negligent or wrongful acts of federal employees in the United States that are committed within the scope of their duty but that otherwise would be barred by the principle of sovereign immunity.

At the international and regional levels, human rights courts and tribunals generally have authority to make awards or recommendations for compensation as a part of their decisions. The European Convention for the Protection of Human Rights and Fundamental Freedoms (1950), article 50, expressly authorizes the European Court of Human Rights to "afford just satisfaction to the injured party," which, according to the court's decisions, includes monetary compensation. In addition, a special UN compensation commission was established in 1991 under Security Council Resolution 687 to handle claims for damage by Iraq during the Gulf War. The concept of exacting compensation from nations for wrongful acts is not new, however. Throughout history nations, on behalf of their governments or nationals, have exacted reparations or compensation from other nations for wartime and peacetime damages. After World War II, for example, a number of countries presented claims to Germany and received compensation for damages resulting from the war and the discriminatory actions of the Nazi regime.

Constitution of Japan (1947), chapter III, Rights and Duties of the People, article 29: "Private property may be taken for public use upon just compensation therefor."

American Convention on Human Rights (1969), article 10, Right to Compensation: "Every person has the right to be compensated in accordance with the law in the event he has been sentenced by a final judgment through a miscarriage of justice."

Human Rights Committee (1994): The complaint of a Uruguayan civil servant who had been dismissed from his post was found inadmissible "given that [he] was reintegrated into the civil service and . . . granted compensation for the prejudice he had suffered."

National Court of Estonia, Constitutional Review Chamber (1995): "Property rights are inviolable and enjoy equal protection. Forced alienation [or transfer] may take place only for public purposes in return for fair and prompt compensation."

Compensation for Expropriation: A Comparative Study. Proceedings of the 1990 Conference of the United Kingdom National Committee of Comparative Law. Oxford, England: Jason Reese in association with the United Kingdom National Committee of Comparative Law, 1990.

Pross, Christian. *Paying for the Past: The Struggle over Reparations for Surviving Victims of the Nazi Terror.* Baltimore: Johns Hopkins University Press, 1998.

European Convention for the Protection of Human Rights and Fundamental Freedoms; European Court of Human Rights; Property; War Crimes

Complaints

Complaints, like petitions, communications, and applications, are formal written documents alleging a violation of human rights. Such complaints may be filed with various international, regional, and national human rights agencies, commissions, courts, and tribunals established to investigate allegations of abuse, or with a special government official such as an ombudsman. *Complaint*, meaning a statement of injury or grievance laid before a court or judicial authority for the purposes of prosecution or redress, has been in use in English since at least the fifteenth century.

Regarding an act of the British Parliament pertaining to the performance of justices of the peace, William Blackstone, the eighteenth-century commentator on English law, noted: "[I]n all cases where an *information* or *complaint* in writing and upon oath is laid before any justice of the peace, that any person has committed, or is suspected to have committed, any . . . indictable offense whatsoever . . . such justice may issue his *warrant* to apprehend such person. . . ." In Anglo-American law, a complaint is one of a number of formal methods by which a court's power is invoked to investigate and adjudicate charges of wrongdoing.

When making a complaint about a human rights violation, a person, an organization, or even another government must communicate the complaint in the manner prescribed by the competent authority. The terminology for this action varies; sometimes the method of filing a complaint is by a *communication* of the allegations; in other cases, the requirements may call for a *petition* or an *application* to be submitted. In all instances, the assistance of a lawyer with experience in prosecuting human rights complaints is helpful.

In concreto complaints allege actual violations of human rights, as opposed to *in abstracto* complaints, which are abstract questions about human rights. Incompatible complaints are those not in accord with the requirements of a governing treaty or other authority that provides for complaint adjudication; therefore, they are generally found inadmissible or not capable of being acted on by the commission or tribunal with which they have been filed.

Information on where to file human rights complaints in a specific country can usually be obtained from government information listings, offices of elected officials, nongovernmental organizations active in prosecuting human rights violations, or lawyers. International and regional human rights organizations make available instructions and forms for filing complaints, as well as a list of the countries that are parties to international human rights agreements under which redress may be sought. The Inter-American Commission on Human Rights, for example, publishes a manual on how to present a petition in the Inter-American human rights system. It explains in simple language the functions of the commission and the rights protected by the American Convention on Human Rights (1969) and contains information on who may present a petition, conditions for presenting one, when a petition may be presented, and what a petition should include to be valid; forms for filing a complaint or petition are included.

Constitution of Namibia (1990), chapter 10, Ombudsman, article 91, Functions: "The functions of the Ombudsman . . . shall include the following: (a) the duty to investigate complaints concerning alleged or apparent instances of violations of fundamental rights and freedoms, abuse of power, unfair, harsh, insensitive or discourteous treatment of an inhabitant of Namibia by an official in the employ of any organ of Government. . . ."

European Convention for the Protection of Human Rights and Fundamental Freedoms (1950), section IV, article 48: "The following may bring a case before the [European Court of Human Rights] . . . (a) the Commission: . . . (d) a High Contracting Party against which the complaint has been lodged."

Constitutional Court of Germany (1957): "[S]ince there are no rules of international law to be found that afford any greater protection of private property than the Basic Law [Constitution of Germany (1949)] . . . , it need not be discussed whether a constitutional complaint can actually be founded on Art. 25 [which incorporates the general rules of public international law into German federal law] of the Basic Law."

European Court of Human Rights (1994): "The applicant lastly brought forward a series of grievances which may be summarized as a complaint that in [his] judgment the Dutch Industrial Appeals Tribunal did not, or not sufficiently, deal with various arguments advanced by him [in support of his appeal against the milk quota allotted him by the Dutch authorities]."

African Commission on Human and Peoples' Rights, P.O. Box 673, Banjul, Gambia. (220-39-2962. 🖷 220-39-0764. 🖳umn.edu/humanrts/Africa/Commission.

European Court of Human Rights, Council of Europe, F-67075 Strasbourg Cedex, France. (33-3-88-41-20-18. 🖷 33-3-88-41-27-30. 🖳 dhcourt@court1.coe.fr. 🖳 www.ei-ie.org.

Human Rights Committee, Communications Branch, 8–14 avenue de la Paix, 1211 Geneva 10, Switzerland. (41-22-917-1234. 🖷 41-22-917-0123. 🖳 webadmin.hchr@un.org.ch. 🖳 www.unhchr.ch/htm/menu2/6/hrd.

Inter-American Commission on Human Rights, 1889 F Street, N.W., Washington, D.C. 20006. (202-458-6002. 🖷 202-458-3992. 🖳 cidhoea@oas.org. 🖳 cidh.oas.org.

International (Criminal) Tribunal for Rwanda, P.O. Box 6016, Arusha, Tanzania. (255-57-4369 (via satellite link at 212-963-2850). 🖷 255-57-4000 (via satellite link at 212-963-2848). 🖳 codrington@un.org. 🖳 www.un.org/ictr.

International (Criminal) Tribunal for Yugoslavia, P.O. Box 13888, 2501 EW The Hague, Netherlands. (31-70-416-5000. 🖷 31-70-416-5345. 🖳 www.un.org/icty.

United Nations High Commissioner for Human Rights, 8–14 avenue de la Paix, 1211 Geneva 10, Switzerland. (41-22-917-9000. 🖷 41-22-917-9016. 🖳 webadmin.hchr@unog.ch. 🖳 www.unhchr.ch.

Coomans, Fons, ed. *The Right to Complain about Economic, Social and Cultural Rights.* Proceedings of the Expert Meeting on the Adoption of an Optional Protocol to the International Covenant on Economic, Social and Cultural Rights, January 25–28, 1995. Utrecht, Netherlands: Netherlands Institute of Human Rights, 1995.

Martin, Francisco F., et al. *International Human Rights Law and Practice: Cases, Treaties, and Materials.* The Hague: Kluwer Law International, 1997.

American Convention on Human Rights; Inter-American Commission on Human Rights; Nongovernmental Organizations; Ombudsmen; Remedies; Violations

Conscience

Conscience is the sense of morality or principle that guides an individual in making decisions—the personal morality that lies somewhere between simple thought and the more complex dogma of religion. An individual's right to act on his or her conscience alone is a relatively new concept. Throughout most of history a person's actions, in order to be acceptable, had to be based on the laws and social and cultural mores of the society in which he or she lived; to act in accordance simply with one's own beliefs was often a punishable offense.

Freedom of conscience (from the Latin *conscientia*, meaning knowledge within oneself) recognizes the right of every person to the unfettered development of his or her personality, as long as it does not infringe on the rights of others or the legitimate responsibilities of the state. Freedom of conscience means that a person must be allowed not only to have and exhibit a personal belief but also to disseminate such belief.

Those who refuse to participate directly in warfare on the grounds that killing another human being is against their personal principles are known as conscientious objectors. In 1993 the Commission on Human Rights adopted a resolution that drew attention "to the right of everyone to have conscientious objections to military service as a legitimate exercise of the right to freedom of thought, conscience, and religion as laid down in article 18 of the Universal Declaration of Human Rights [1948] as well as article 18 of the International Covenant on Civil and Political Rights [1966]."

Freedom of conscience raises other issues concerning human rights. Does freedom of conscience allow a person or family to require their children to hold the same convictions? Does conscientious objection to war permit a person to refuse to pay a percentage of his or her taxes earmarked for the country's military budget? May a person claiming freedom of conscience refuse to take an oath to tell the truth in court? And, in the case of medical treatment or procedures for a minor child, does the parents' refusal to accept a blood transfusion on the grounds of freedom of conscience legally protect the parents and the medical personnel if death or injury to the child results? Generally, such situations are addressed by specific laws and judicial opinions in each country. As with many other human rights, however, there are few absolutes and many points of conflict.

Constitution of Germany (1949), I, Basic Rights, article 4: "(1) Freedom of faith, of conscience, and freedom to profess a religion or a particular philosophy (Weltanschauung) shall be inviolable."

European Convention for the Protection of Human Rights and Fundamental Freedoms (1950), section 1, article 9: "1. Everyone has the right to freedom of thought, conscience and religion. . . ."

Constitutional Court of Germany (1960): "Conscience is to be understood as an experiential and spiritual phenomenon that absolutely compels a person, in demonstrating his concern for fellow human beings, to commit himself unreservedly to an ideal."

European Commission of Human Rights (1977): With regard to the European Convention for the Protection of Human Rights and Fundamental Freedoms (1950), article 4, paragraph 3(b), which states in part that "the term 'forced or compulsory labor' shall not include . . . any service of a military character or, in case of conscientious objectors in countries where they are recognized, service exacted instead of compulsory military service," the commission "expressly recognized that civilian service may be imposed on conscientious objectors as a substitute for military service. . . ."

Miller, Richard W. *Moral Differences: Truth, Justice, and Conscience in a World of Conflict.* Princeton, N.J.: Princeton University Press, 1992.

Shapiro, Ian, and Robert Adams, eds. *Integrity and Conscience.* New York: New York University Press, 1998.

Commission on Human Rights; Personality; Religion; Thought

Conscientious Objectors

See Conscience; Military Personnel

Constitutional Rights

A constitution (from the Latin *constitutum*, meaning agreement, and *constituo*, meaning to establish or arrange) may simply be a description of how a particular government actually works, or it may be a written or unwritten plan of how a particular government should work. In addition to setting out the government's operations, most modern constitutions also state the rights and freedoms guaranteed to the people. The word *constitutional,* meaning ruling according to a constitution or constitutional forms that limit arbitrary power, has been used in English since the beginning of the nineteenth century and even earlier in the sense of something in harmony with or authorized by the political constitution.

Constitutional rights are those rights guaranteed to citizens in their supreme laws—their constitutions—as opposed to statutory rights, which are subject to change by the government through its procedures for creating laws. Constitutional and statutory rights differ further from international and regional espoused or guaranteed rights, such as those in the Universal Declaration of Human Rights (1948) and the European Convention for the Protection of Human Rights and Fundamental Freedoms (1950). Theoretically, a state or a nation has the power to enforce constitutional rights, while internationally declared rights require the voluntary cooperation of each country for enforcement. Not all constitutional rights are human rights. There is no international consensus, for example, that the right of citizens to bear arms, which has been guaranteed under the U.S. Constitution since the adoption of the Bill of Rights in 1791, is a universal human right.

Many written national constitutions include a declaration or bill of rights, which generally encompass such rights as freedom of speech, the press, and religion; the right to vote and hold office; the right to due process of law and equality before the law; and the right of peaceable assembly and association. Some constitutions include social rights, such as the right to health care, social security, and disability benefits. Often the rights of persons accused of crimes are specified, such as the right to counsel and a fair trial. Some constitutions—for example, those of India (1950) and Malaysia (1957)—make provisions for the rights of certain minority groups.

Countries generally have procedures, either constitutional, statutory, or traditional, to help ensure that constitutional provisions are adhered to by the government. These procedures include judicial review or institutions such as constitutional courts, councils, or legislative committees. The constitutions of the United States and some Latin American countries, for instance, allow for judicial review—the power of the regular courts of law to review acts of the executive and legislative branches of government and void acts that are inconsistent with the constitution and the rights declared therein. Austria and Germany, on the other hand, each have a special constitutional court to ensure conformance with their constitutions. France has a constitutional council, and Sweden has a parliamentary constitutional committee that may review laws before they become effective to ensure conformance with their constitutions.

Because constitutional rights are specifically within the purview of sovereign states, they tend not to be mentioned in international human rights documents. However, a number of such documents, including the Convention on the Elimination of All Forms of Discrimination against Women (1979) and the Declaration of Basic Principles of Justice for Victims of Crime and Abuse of Power (1985), direct nations to take measures necessary to ensure that internationally recognized human rights are enshrined in their laws; presumably, such measures would include incorporating those rights into constitutional documents.

Some cases heard by international bodies, particularly the European Court of Human Rights, deal with the implications of specific national constitutions on human rights issues. The human rights and fundamental freedoms in the court's founding document, the European Convention for the Protection of Human Rights and Fundamental Freedoms, may appear to be inconsistent either with provisions of the national constitutions of the European countries under the court's jurisdiction or with the application of such provisions by government authorities in those countries. The court, therefore, may have to reconcile constitutional rights with human rights enshrined in the controlling 1950 convention. And, under the American Convention on Human Rights (1969), language concerning the right to life may conflict with a nation's constitutionally sanctioned use of the death penalty in certain criminal cases.

Constitution of Ireland (1937), Fundamental Rights, Private Property, article 43: "1.1. The state acknowledges that man, in virtue of his rational being, has the natural right, antecedent to positive law, to the private ownership of external goods. 1.2. The state accordingly guarantees to pass no law attempting to abolish the right of private ownership or the general right to transfer, bequeath, and inherit property."

Convention on the Elimination of All Forms of Discrimination against Women (1979), part I, article 2: "States Parties condemn discrimination against women in all its forms, agree to pursue by all appropriate means and without delay a policy of eliminating discrimination against women and, to this end, undertake: (a) To embody the principle of the equality of men and women in their national constitutions or other appropriate legislation if not yet incorporated therein and to ensure, through law and other appropriate means, the practical realization of this principle."

Declaration on the Right and Responsibility of Individuals, Groups and Organs of Society to Promote and Protect Universally Recognized Human Rights and Fundamental Freedoms (1998), article 2: "1. Each State has a prime responsibility and duty to protect, promote and implement all human rights and fundamental freedoms, *inter alia,* by adopting such steps necessary . . . [including] the legal guarantees required to ensure that all persons under its jurisdiction, individually and in association with others, are able to enjoy all those rights and freedoms in practice."

Queen's Bench, Manitoba, Canada (1985): The Canadian Charter of Rights and Freedoms (1982) is a constitutional document intended to govern rights between the government and citizens. It is not determinative of rights between private citizens and private organizations.

European Court of Human Rights (1996): Although it dismissed a case involving freedom of expression because domestic remedies had not been exhausted, the court nevertheless found that certain provisions of Greece's constitution (1975) are relevant, including article 14, [section] 1: "Every person may express and propagate his thoughts orally, in writing and through the press in compliance with the laws of the State."

Cohen, William, and David J. Danelski. *Constitutional Law, Civil Liberty and Individual Rights.* 4th ed. Westbury, N.Y.: Foundation, 1997.

Moore, Wayne D. *Constitutional Rights and Powers of the People.* Princeton, N.J.: Princeton University Press, 1996.

Bills of Rights; Constitutionalism; Judicial Review

Constitutionalism

The evolution of constitutionalism—the concept that government powers should be dispersed and limited by laws that rulers must obey—has had a significant, positive impact on human rights. Because these rights involve the relationship between citizens and their government, the laws and institutions of constitutional government that seek accountability of government officials, place checks and balances on the separate power centers of government, and ensure adherence to the rule of law are primary protectors of human rights. *Constitutionalism* (from the French *constitutionel,* meaning relating to a constitution, in harmony with a constitution, or ruling according to a constitution that limits arbitrary power) can mean either a constitutional system of government or adherence to constitutional principles.

The ancient Greek philosopher Aristotle concluded that constitutional governments—ones other than tyrannies—try to combine oligarchy (rule by the few) with democracy (rule by the many); he claimed that democracy is safer because there is strength in numbers and because people who are equal are more contented. Plato, Aristotle's older contemporary, however, was suspicious of democracy and believed that the best government is one that operates according to philosophical principles.

Ancient Greece spurred the evolution of constitutional democracy, which is centered around governments in which all citizens have an equal right to vote and hold office and in which agreed-upon principles limit the majority's

absolute power. The Roman Republic (509–27 B.C.E.); the Icelandic parliament (the Althing), which first met in 930; Magna Carta (1215) and the unwritten British constitution, which evolved from common law and tradition; the U.S. Constitution (1789); and the French constitutions first adopted in the late eighteenth century—all have helped advance constitutional democracy as practiced today in the majority of the world's countries.

The philosophical principles that now define constitutionalism and constitutional government include regular elections, accountability of governing officials, protection of individual and minority rights, checks and balances within the government, separation of government powers, and the rule of law. Constitutionalism creates checks on arbitrary and capricious decisions by persons holding political power and thus helps ensure that all citizens are treated equally before the law, that those in power are held accountable for their acts, and that questions regarding human rights are adjudicated by independent and impartial tribunals. So-called human rights constitutionalism is based on recognition of each person's equal dignity and entitlement to those rights inherent in being human.

Although the term *constitutionalism* is generally not found in national constitutions or international human rights documents, the government structure that is described in constitutions and the adherence by government officials to their country's constitution reflect the degree to which a government is based on the principles of constitutionalism.

Constitution of Portugal (1976), Fundamental Principles, article 3, Sovereignty and Legality: "1. Sovereignty, one and indivisible, rests with the people, who shall exercise it in accordance with the forms laid down in the constitution. 2. The state shall be subject to the constitution and based on democratic legality. 3. The validity of the laws or other acts of the state . . . shall depend on their being in accordance with the constitution."

Charter 77 (Czechoslovakia) (1977), paragraph 8: "The Constitution of the C.S.S.R [Czechoslovak Soviet Socialist Republic, then dominated by the Soviet Union] and the other laws and legal norms give no authority either for the content and form, nor for the making and application of . . . [the] decisions [by the Communist Party rulers of Czechoslovakia; such decisions] are often purely verbal, entirely unknown to citizens, and uncontrollable by them. . . ."

Constitutional Court of South Africa (1996): Acting as an independent arbiter under provisions of the 1993 interim constitution of South Africa, the court declared that not all of the provisions of the country's proposed new constitution complied with the Constitutional Principles set forth in the 1993 constitution and agreed on by the former government of South Africa, the liberation movements, and other minority groups.

European Court of Justice (1986): The fact that the European Community was based on the fundamental constitutional principle of the rule of law gives the court the power to overrule measures taken by the European Parliament.

Alexander, Larry, ed. *Constitutionalism: Philosophical Foundations.* New York: Cambridge University Press, 1998.

Thompson, Kenneth W., and Rett R. Ludwikowski. *Constitutionalism and Human Rights: America, Poland, and France. A Bicentennial Colloquium at the Miller Center.* Lanham, Md.: University Press of America, 1989.

Aristotle; Constitutional Rights; Democracy; Magna Carta; Majority Rule; Plato; Rule of Law

Consular Rights

See Diplomats and Consuls

Convention against Discrimination in Education

The Universal Declaration of Human Rights (1948) calls for education to "be directed to the full development of the human personality." On December 14, 1960, the Convention against Discrimination in Education was adopted by the General Conference of the United Nations Educational, Scientific and Cultural Organization (UNESCO). The convention was based on the recommendation of a special rapporteur of the Subcommission on the Promotion and Protection of Human Rights and was endorsed by the subcommission, Commission on Human Rights, and Economic and Social Council (ECOSOC). The document aims to eradicate discrimination and ensure equal treatment of all persons in the field of education. In 1962 UNESCO's General Conference adopted a protocol to the 1960 convention that created a Conciliation and Good Offices Commission to assist in implementing the provisions of the earlier document.

The convention opens by recalling that "the Universal Declaration of Human Rights asserts the principle of non-discrimination and proclaims every person has the right to education." It adds that UNESCO, "while respecting the diversity of national educational systems, has the duty not only to proscribe any form of discrimination in education but also to promote equality of opportunity and treatment for all in education."

Article 1 defines *discrimination* to include "any distinction, exclusion, limitation or preference which, being based on race, color, sex, language, religion, political or other opinion, national or social origin, economic condition or birth, has the purpose or effect of nullifying or impairing equality of treatment in education. . . ." Article 1 continues by giving specific examples of discrimination, such as: "(a) Of depriving any person or group of persons of access to education of any type or at any level; (b) Of limiting any person or groups of persons to education of an inferior standard; (c) [Of] establishing or maintaining separate educational systems or institutions for persons or groups of persons . . . or, (d) Of inflicting on any person or group of persons conditions which are incompatible with the dignity of man." The same article notes that "all types and levels of education" are included in its scope.

Under article 2 is a list of three "situations [that] shall not be deemed to constitute discrimination." They include separate sex institutions for education as long as they are otherwise equal; certain religious or linguistic schools; and private educational facilities that meet certain standards. Article 3 details measures to be taken by the parties to the convention in order "to eliminate and prevent discrimination," such as abolishing existing discriminatory laws and practices, enacting positive legislation, prohibiting discrimination in the matter of fees, scholarships, and public assistance to educational institutions, and providing to foreign nationals "the same access to education as that given to their own nationals."

Article 4 addresses the formulation, development, and application of national policy "to promote equality of opportunity and treatment in the matter of education. . . ." Article 5 provides that education "shall be directed to the full development of the human personality and to strengthening of respect for human rights . . ."; that the "liberty of parents" is to be respected; and that the "rights of members of national minorities to carry on their own educational activities," with certain limitations, are to be observed.

According to article 8, disputes arising under the convention that are not settled by negotiation are to be taken to the International Court of Justice, at the request of the parties. Reservations to the convention are prohibited by article 9; and article 10 mandates that the convention "shall not have the effect of diminishing the rights which individuals or groups may enjoy by virtue of agreements concluded between two or more States, where such rights are not contrary to the spirit of this Convention."

United Nations Educational, Scientific and Cultural Organization (UNESCO), 7 place de Fontenoy, 75352 Paris 07 SP, France. (31-1-45-68-10-00. 31-1-45-67-16-90. webmaster@unesco.org. www.unesco.org.

☞

Commission on Human Rights; Discrimination; Education; Sub-commission on the Promotion and Protection of Human Rights; Economic and Social Council (ECOSOC); United Nations Educational, Scientific and Cultural Organization (UNESCO)

Convention against Torture and Other Cruel, Inhuman or Degrading Treatment or Punishment

The Convention against Torture and Other Cruel, Inhuman or Degrading Treatment or Punishment was adopted by the UN General Assembly and opened for signature, ratification, and accession on December 10, 1984; it entered into force on June 26, 1987. This convention builds on the Declaration on the Protection of All Persons from Being Subjected to Torture and Other Cruel, Inhuman or Degrading Treatment or Punishment, which was adopted by the General Assembly in 1975. Other international documents relating to torture include the Inter-American Convention to Prevent and Punish Torture (1985) and the European Convention for the Prevention of Torture and Inhuman or Degrading Treatment or Punishment (1987).

The convention's introductory material underscores that everyone should be free from cruel, inhuman, and degrading treatment and punishment, as asserted in both the Universal Declaration of Human Rights (1948) and the International Covenant on Civil and Political Rights (1966). "[I]n accordance with the principles proclaimed in the Charter of the United Nations [1945]," it also observes, "recognition of the equal and inalienable rights of all members of the human family is the foundation of freedom, justice and peace in the world," noting that "those rights derive from the inherent dignity of the human person." The present convention is adopted, it adds, "to make more effective the struggle against torture and other cruel, inhuman or degrading treatment or punishment throughout the world."

Torture is defined in part I, article 1, as "any act by which severe pain or suffering, whether physical or mental, is intentionally inflicted on a person for such purposes as obtaining from him or a third person information or a confession, punishing him for an act he or a third person has committed or is suspected of having committed, or intimidating or coercing him or a third person, or for any reason based on discrimination of any kind, when such pain or suffering is inflicted at the instigation of or with the consent or acquiescence of a public official or other person acting in an official capacity. It does not include pain or suffering arising only from, inherent in or incidental to lawful sanctions."

According to article 2: "1. Each State Party shall take effective legislative, administrative, judicial or other measures to prevent acts of torture in any territory under its jurisdiction. 2. No exceptional circumstances whatsoever, whether a state of war or a threat of war, internal political instability or any other public emergency, may be invoked as a justification of torture. 3. An order from a superior officer or a public authority may not be invoked as a justification of torture."

Articles 3 and 4, respectively, prohibit expelling, returning, or extraditing "a person to another State where there are substantial grounds for believing that he would be in danger of being subjected to torture"; and require states to make torture and related offenses punishable as crimes. The convention also requires under article 5 that states parties establish their jurisdiction in a number of situations, including aboard ships and aircraft and in cases where their nationals are the offenders or victims.

Measures for taking alleged offenders into custody, notifying their state of nationality or residence, and prosecuting or extraditing them for prosecution in another state are outlined in article 6. Under articles 9 and 10, signatory states are required to cooperate with each other in connection with criminal proceedings and to "ensure that education and information regarding the prohibition against torture are fully included in the training of law enforcement personnel, civil or military, medical personnel, public officials and other persons who may be involved in the custody, interrogation or treatment of any individual subjected to any form of arrest, detention or imprisonment."

Article 13 mandates that "[e]ach State Party shall ensure that any individual who alleges he has been subjected to torture in any territory under its jurisdiction has the right to complain to, and to have his case promptly and impartially examined by, its competent authorities. Steps shall be taken to ensure that the complainant and witnesses are protected against all ill-treatment or intimidation as a consequence of his complaint or any evidence given."

Under Part II, the convention establishes a Committee against Torture, consisting "of ten experts of high moral standing and recognized competence in the field of human rights, who shall serve in their personal capacity." The members are elected for four-year terms by secret ballot by the signatory states. The committee, through the UN secretary-general, receives reports from the states as to "measures they have taken to give effect to their undertakings under this Convention" and may make comments on the reports and include any of its comments in the committee's annual report.

As specified in article 20, "If the Committee receives reliable information which appears to it to contain well-founded indications that torture is being systematically practiced in the territory of a State Party, the Committee shall invite that State Party to co-operate in the examination of the information and to this end to submit observations with regard to the information concerned." The committee may then make a "confidential inquiry" and transmit its findings to the party concerned "together with any comments or suggestions which seem appropriate in view of the situation." Allegations that a state party is in violation of the convention's provisions may also be brought to the committee's attention by another state party, according to article 21. The committee reviews referred matters "only after it has ascertained that all domestic remedies have been invoked and exhausted," except for apparent emergencies.

Committee against Torture, Office of United Nations High Commissioner for Human Rights, 8–14 avenue de la Paix, 1211 Geneva 10, Switzerland. 41-22-917-3456. 41-22-917-0213. webadmin.hchr@unog.ch. www.unhchr.ch.

Declaration on the Protection of All Persons from Being Subjected to Torture and Other Cruel, Inhuman or Degrading Treatment or Punishment; Detention; European Convention for the Prevention of Torture and Inhuman or Degrading Treatment or Punishment; Inter-American Convention to Prevent and Punish Torture; Law Enforcement; Punishment; *Refoulement;* Torture

Convention Concerning Freedom of Association and Protection of the Right to Organize

On July 9, 1948, the General Conference of the International Labor Organization (ILO) adopted Convention no. 87, Concerning Freedom of Association and Protection of the Right to Organize, which entered into force on July 4, 1950. Subsequently, the ILO adopted a number of conventions, nos. 98 (1949), 135 (1971), 151 (1978), and 154 (1981), all of which relate to the right of workers to organize.

The preamble notes in part that the principles embodied in this document, adopted unanimously, were intended to form the basis for international regulation, adding that "the General Assembly of the United Nations, at its second session, endorsed these principles and requested the [ILO] to continue every effort in order that it may be possible to adopt one or several international Conventions...."

Part I, Freedom of Association, article 2, declares: "Workers and employers, without distinction whatsoever, shall have the right to establish and, subject only to the rules of the organization concerned, to join organizations of their own choosing without previous authorization." According

to article 3: "1. [Such] organizations shall have the right to draw up their constitutions and rules, to elect their representatives in full freedom, to organize [themselves] and to formulate their programs. 2. The public authorities shall refrain from any interference which would restrict this right or impede the lawful exercise thereof."

Workers and employers and their organizations, as set forth in article 8, "shall respect the law of the land [and it] shall not ... impair, nor shall it be so applied as to impair, the guarantees provided for in this Convention." Article 10 defines *organization* to mean "any organization of workers or of employers for furthering and defending the interests of workers or of employers."

Part II, Protection of the Right to Organize, article 11, provides that each member of the ILO "undertakes to take all necessary and appropriate measures to ensure that workers and employers may exercise freely the right to organize."

Part III, Miscellaneous Provisions, article 13, states in part: "2. A declaration accepting the obligations of this Convention may be communicated to the Director-General of the International Labor Office: (a) By two or more Members of the Organization in respect of any territory which is under their joint authority; or (b) By any international authority responsible for the administration of any territory, in virtue of the Charter of the United Nations [1945] or otherwise, in respect of such territory."

International Labor Organization, 4 route des Morillons, 1211 Geneva 22, Switzerland. 41-22-799-6111. 41-22-798-8685. somavia@ilo.org. www.ilo.org.

Association; International Labor Organization; Workers

Convention Concerning the Protection of the World Cultural and Natural Heritage

To ensure the conservation of important world cultural treasures by both the countries in which they are located and the international community as a whole, the United Nations Educational, Scientific and Cultural Organization (UNESCO) in 1954 adopted the Convention on the Protection of Cultural Property in the Event of Armed Conflict. In 1966 the UN General Assembly adopted the International Covenant on Economic, Social and Cultural Rights, which recognizes the right of everyone to take part in cultural life and notes the conservation responsibilities of

countries party to the covenant. Then in 1970 UNESCO addressed the issue of stolen artifacts when it adopted the Convention on the Means of Prohibiting and Preventing the Illicit Import, Export and Transfer of Ownership of Cultural Property.

Formalizing worldwide heritage preservation and conservation efforts, the UNESCO General Conference, meeting in Paris on November 16, 1972, adopted the Convention Concerning the Protection of the World Cultural and Natural Heritage, which entered into force on December 17, 1975. The convention begins by noting that "the cultural heritage and the natural heritage are increasingly threatened with destruction not only by the traditional causes of decay, but also by changing social and economic conditions which aggravate the situation with even more formidable phenomena of damage or destruction" and recalling that UNESCO's constitution "provides that it will maintain, increase, and diffuse knowledge, by assuring the conservation and protection of the world's heritage...." The preamble adds that "in view of the magnitude and gravity of the new dangers threatening them, it is incumbent on the international community as a whole to participate in the protection of the cultural and natural heritage of outstanding universal value, by the granting of collective assistance which, although not taking the place of action by the State concerned, will serve as an effective complement thereto...."

Under part I, Definitions of the Cultural and the Natural Heritage, article 1, the convention includes the following in the category of cultural heritage: "Monuments: architectural works, works of monumental sculpture and painting, elements or structures of an archaeological nature, inscriptions, cave dwellings and combinations of features, which are of outstanding universal value from the point of view of history, art or science; Groups of buildings ... which, because of their architecture, their homogeneity or their place in the landscape, are of outstanding universal value from the point of view of history, art or science; [and] Sites: works of man or the combined works of nature and of man, and areas including archaeological sites which are of outstanding universal value from the historical, aesthetic, ethnological or anthropological points of view." Article 2 defines natural heritage areas, including physical, biological, geological, and physiographical formations, the habitats of threatened animal and plant species, and natural areas significant to science or conservation or for their natural beauty.

According to part II, National Protection and International Protection of the Cultural and Natural Heritage, article 4, "Each State Party to this Convention recognizes that the duty of ensuring the identification, protection, conservation, presentation and transmission to future generations of the cultural and natural heritage referred to in Articles 1 and 2 and situated on its territory, belongs primarily to that State. It will do all it can to this end, to the utmost of its own resources and, where appropriate, with any international assistance and cooperation, in particular,

financial, artistic, scientific and technical, which it may be able to obtain."

Article 5 recommends measures to be "taken for the protection, conservation and presentation of the cultural and natural heritage" in each nation. These measures include adoption of an appropriate general policy, establishment of services related to the convention's goals, development of scientific and technical studies, and support for training and scientific research. According to article 6, states must recognize their duty to the international community as a whole and must not "take any deliberate measures which might damage directly or indirectly [their] cultural and natural heritage."

An Intergovernmental Committee for the Protection of the Cultural and Natural Heritage of Outstanding Universal Value, called the World Heritage Committee, is established under UNESCO by part III, articles 8 through 15. One of the committee's key responsibilities is to maintain and accept new entries for a World Heritage List of cultural and natural properties "having outstanding universal value." Consent of the country concerned is required for inclusion of a site on the list. To date, 630 sites have been added to the list. The committee also produces a List of World Heritage in Danger, places threatened by "serious and specific dangers, such as ... accelerated deterioration, large-scale public or private projects or rapid urban or tourist development projects ... abandonment ... the outbreak or the threat of an armed conflict; [or] calamities and cataclysms...." Requests for protection, conservation, or rehabilitation of cultural and natural sites are also directed to the World Heritage Committee.

Part IV establishes a Fund for the Protection of the World Cultural and Natural Heritage, which accepts contributions to further its preservation and conservation responsibilities. The remaining sections of the convention deal with conditions and arrangements for international assistance, education programs, and reports.

International Council on Monuments and Sites, 49–51 rue de la Fédération, 75015 Paris, France. (33-1-45-67-67-70. 🖳 33-1-45-66-06-22. 🖳 secretariat@icomos.org. 🖳 www.icomos.org.

U.S. Committee, International Council on Monuments and Sites, 401 F Street, N.W., Room 331, Washington, D.C. 20001. (202-842-1862. 🖳 202-842-1861.

World Heritage Committee, UNESCO, 7 place de Fontenoy, 75352 Paris 07 SP France. (33-1-45-68-10-00. 🖳 33-1-45-67-16-90. 🖳 wh-info@unesco.org. 🖳 www.unesco.org/whin.

☞

Environment; International Covenant on Economic, Social and Cultural Rights; Natural Resources; United Nations Educational, Scientific and Cultural Organization (UNESCO)

Convention for the Suppression of the Traffic in Persons and of the Exploitation of the Prostitution of Others

Although the international slave trade ended early in the nineteenth century and the Slavery Convention entered into force in 1927, prostitution (known as white slavery) and the transportation of women and children for sexual exploitation remain as contemporary forms of slavery. These issues were addressed in separate international agreements in 1904, 1910, 1921, and 1933. In 1937 the League of Nations prepared a draft convention extending the scope of these four agreements, but the outbreak of World War II and the collapse of the League postponed international initiative on these issues until after the war.

In 1948, at the request of the Economic and Social Council (ECOSOC), the UN secretary-general prepared a draft of the Convention for the Suppression of the Traffic in Persons and of the Exploitation of the Prostitution of Others. The convention, which unified the four earlier international human rights documents on the subject, was adopted by the UN General Assembly on December 2, 1949, and entered into force on July 25, 1951.

"[P]rostitution and the accompanying evil of the traffic in persons for the purpose of prostitution," notes the convention's preamble, "are incompatible with the dignity and worth of the human person and endanger the welfare of the individual, the family and the community." It then takes note of the four international agreements and the 1937 League of Nations draft convention, adding that "developments since 1937 make feasible the conclusion of a convention consolidating [these] instruments and embodying the substance of the 1937 draft convention as well as desirable alterations therein."

"The Parties to the present Convention," according to article 1, "agree to punish any person who, to gratify the passions of another: 1. Procures, entices or leads away, for the purposes of prostitution, another person, even with the consent of that person; 2. Exploits the prostitution of another person even with the consent of that person." Under article 2, the parties "further agree to punish any person who: 1. Keeps or manages, or knowingly finances or takes part in the financing of a brothel; 2. Knowingly lets or rents a building or other place or any part thereof for the purpose of the prostitution of others."

Articles 3 and 4 urge that, to "the extent permitted by domestic law, attempts to commit any of the offenses referred to in articles 1 and 2, and acts preparatory to the commission thereof" and "intentional participation in [such] acts shall also be punishable." Pursuant to article 5, injured parties who are aliens should be treated the same as nationals in domestic proceedings against violators. And, according to article 6, parties to the convention agree "to take all necessary steps to repeal or abolish any existing law, regulation or administrative provisions [whereby] persons engaged in or suspected of engaging in prostitution are subject to either special registration or the possession of a special document or any other exceptional requirement for supervision or notification." Article 7 addresses the use of "previous convictions in foreign States" as a basis for establishing recidivism and disqualifying the offender from the exercise of civil rights. Article 8 makes the offenses in articles 2 and 3 extraditable offenses.

"Each Party to the present Convention," according to article 14, "shall establish or maintain a service charged with the coordination and centralization of the results of investigations of offenses referred to in the present Convention." Article 15 requires that parties, to "the extent permitted by the domestic law and to the extent to which the authorities responsible ... may judge desirable," make available to each other: "1. Particulars of any offense referred to in the present Convention or any attempt to commit such offense; 2. Particulars of any search for and any prosecution, arrest, conviction, refusal of admission or expulsion of persons guilty of any offenses referred to in the convention, the movements of such persons, and any other useful information with regard to them." The information so furnished "shall include descriptions of the offenders, their fingerprints, photographs, methods of operation, police records and records of conviction."

Article 20 mandates that the parties "shall ... take the necessary measures for the supervision of employment agencies in order to prevent ... , in particular women and children, from being exposed to the danger of prostitution." Each party is directed under article 21 to "communicate to the Secretary-General of the United Nations such laws and regulations as have already been promulgated in their States, and thereafter [on an annual basis.]"

Article 28, the last article, states that the "provisions of the present Convention shall supercede [the four previous] international instruments referred to in the Preamble. . . ." A Final Protocol provides that "[n]othing in the present Convention shall be deemed to prejudice any legislation which ensures ... stricter conditions than those provided by the present Convention."

United Nations High Commissioner for Human Rights, 8–14 avenue de la Paix, 1211 Geneva 10, Switzerland. (41-22-917-9000. 41-22-917-9016. webadmin.hchr@unog.ch. www.unhchr.ch.

Slavery; Slavery Convention; Women

Convention on Consent to Marriage, Minimum Age for Marriage and Registration of Marriages

The right to marry and the rights within a marriage are important to those aspiring to begin family life as a married couple. Because many women have traditionally been denied rights to consent to marriage or to have equal rights in marriage, these rights have special relevance for them. The rights of male spouses and the parents of those who marry have long been enforced by society, religions, and the state. But with the acknowledgment since World War II of the equality of women and men, the need to guarantee the rights of persons in marriage and the family created by a marriage has been raised to the level of international significance.

By a resolution dated November 7, 1962, the UN General Assembly opened the Convention on Consent to Marriage, Minimum Age for Marriage and Registration of Marriages for signature and ratification, and the document entered into force on December 9, 1964. The convention is supplemented by a Recommendation on Consent to Marriage, Minimum Age for Marriage and Registration of Marriages, which the General Assembly adopted on November 1, 1965, to recognize that "the family group should be strengthened because it is the basic unit of every society...."

The 1962 convention opens by noting that the contracting states, in conformity with the Charter of the United Nations (1945), desire "to promote universal respect for, and observance of, human rights and fundamental freedoms for all, without distinction as to race, sex, language or religion." It continues by recalling that "article 16 of the Universal Declaration of Human Rights [1948] states that: '(1) Men and women of full age, without any limitation due to race, nationality or religion, have the right to marry and to found a family. They are entitled to equal rights as to marriage, during marriage and at its dissolution. (2) Marriage shall be entered into only with the free and full consent of the intending spouses.'" The preamble continues by urging signatory states to "take all appropriate measures with a view to abolishing ... customs, ancient laws and practices [that are inconsistent with the UN Charter and the Universal Declaration of Human Rights by] ensuring [among other things] complete freedom in the choice of a spouse, eliminating completely child marriages and the betrothal of young girls before the age of puberty, establishing appropriate penalties where necessary and establishing a civil or other register in which all marriages will be recorded."

Article 1 states: "1. No marriage shall be legally entered into without the full and free consent of both parties, such consent to be expressed by them in person after due publicity and in the presence of the authority competent to sol-emnize the marriage and of witnesses, as prescribed by law. 2.... [I]t shall not be necessary for one of the parties to be present when the competent authority is satisfied that the circumstances are exceptional and that the party has, before a competent authority and in such manner as may be prescribed by law, expressed and not withdrawn consent."

According to article 2, the "States Parties ... shall take legislative action to specify a minimum age for marriage. No marriage shall be legally entered into by any person under this age, except where a competent authority has granted a dispensation as to age, for serious reasons, in the interest of the intending spouses." Article 3 mandates that "[a]ll marriages shall be registered in an appropriate official register by the competent authority." The remaining seven articles address procedural issues.

The supplemental 1965 UN recommendation invites the Commission on the Status of Women to examine reports received from member states and "to report thereon to the Economic and Social Council with such recommendations as it may deem fitting."

United Nations High Commissioner for Human Rights, 8–14 avenue de la Paix, 1211 Geneva 10, Switzerland. (41-22-917-9000. 🖳 41-22-917-9016. 🖳 webadmin.hchr@unog.ch. 🖳 www.unhchr.ch.

Families; Marriage; Women

Convention on Prohibitions or Restrictions on the Use of Certain Conventional Weapons ...

The Convention on Prohibitions or Restrictions on the Use of Certain Conventional Weapons Which May Be Deemed to Be Excessively Injurious or to Have Indiscriminate Effects and three annexed protocols were drafted by a UN conference on the subject in Geneva. The document was adopted on October 10, 1980, and opened for signature on April 10, 1981; it entered into force on December 2, 1983. The convention and its protocols represent an important addition to international humanitarian law, supplementing a number of Geneva Conventions relating to the treatment of prisoners of war, civilians in time of war, and the protection of victims of conflicts. The parties to the convention have agreed to reduce unnecessary suffering in an armed conflict caused by excessively dangerous weapons or ones that indiscriminately cause injuries, such as mines, booby-traps, incendiary devices, and fragmentary weapons.

The convention, it notes in the preamble, is based on international law principles that civilian populations should be protected during hostilities, that "the right of the parties to an armed conflict to choose methods or means of warfare is not unlimited," and that "the employment in armed conflicts of weapons, projectiles and material and methods of warfare of a nature to cause superfluous injury or unnecessary suffering" is prohibited. The document also points out that "it is prohibited to employ methods or means of warfare which are intended, or may be expected, to cause widespread, long-term and severe damage to the natural environment" and states that the contracting parties wish "to prohibit or restrict further the use of certain conventional weapons" and believe that "the positive results achieved in this area may facilitate the main talks on disarmament with a view to putting an end to the production, stockpiling and proliferation of such weapons."

Article 1 declares: "This Convention and its annexed Protocols shall apply in the situations referred to in Article 2 common to the Geneva Conventions of 12 August 1949 for the Protection of War Victims, including any situation described in paragraph 4 of Article 1 of Additional Protocol I to these Conventions." Article 2 expressly states that this convention does not abrogate any other obligations of states under "international humanitarian law applicable in armed conflict." According to article 6, the parties to the convention "undertake, in time of peace as in time of armed conflict, to disseminate this Convention and those of its annexed Protocols by which they are bound as widely as possible in their respective countries and, in particular, to include the study thereof" in their military instruction programs. . . ." Article 7 sets forth how states parties and others must relate to each other with respect to its terms, stating that "[w]hen one of the parties to a conflict is not bound by an annexed Protocol, the parties bound by this Convention and that annexed Protocol shall remain bound by them in their mutual relations."

Protocol on Non-Detectable Fragments (Protocol I), in its entirety, prohibits "any weapon the primary effect of which is to injure by fragments which in the human body escape detection by X-rays."

Protocol on Prohibitions or Restrictions on the Use of Mines, Booby-Traps and Other Devices (Protocol II), article 1, provides that it does not apply "to the use of antiship mines at sea or in inland waterways." The protocol continues by defining *mine, booby-trap, other devices, military objective, civilian objects,* and *recording,* the latter meaning "registration in the official records [of] all available information facilitating the location of minefields, mines and booby-traps." Article 3 addresses general restrictions on the use of mines, booby-traps, and other devices, prohibiting their use against civilian individuals or groups and limiting them to military objectives; article 4 details restrictions on the use of mines and other devices in populated areas; and article 5 sets forth restrictions on the use of remotely delivered mines, calling for advance warning if

any such devices may affect civilian populations. Articles 6, 7, 8, and 9, respectively, prohibit the use of certain booby-traps; require that the location of minefields, mines, and booby-traps be recorded and published; protect UN forces and missions from the effects of these weapons; and direct international cooperation in their removal. Guidelines on recording locations of weapons are provided in the Technical Annex to the protocol.

Protocol on Prohibitions or Restrictions on the Use of Incendiary Weapons (Protocol III), article 1, defines an *incendiary weapon* as "any weapon or munition which is primarily designed to set fire to objects or to cause burn injury to persons through the action of flame, heat, or a combination thereof, produced by chemical reaction of a substance delivered on the target." Article 2 addresses the protection of civilians and civilian objects, stating: "It is prohibited in all circumstances to make any military objective located within a concentration of civilians the object of attack by air-delivered incendiary weapons." In addition to banning the weapons' use on civilians, the provision also prohibits attacks on "forests or other kinds of plant cover . . . except when such natural elements are used to cover, conceal or camouflage combatants or other military objectives, or are themselves objectives. . . ."

United Nations High Commissioner for Human Rights, 8–14 avenue de la Paix, 1211 Geneva 10, Switzerland. (41-22-917-9000. 🖷 41-22-917-9016. 🖳 webadmin.hchr@unog.ch. 🖳 www.unhchr.ch.

☞

Declaration on the Prohibition of the Use of Nuclear and Thermo-Nuclear Weapons; Environment; Geneva Conventions; War; Weapons

Convention on the Elimination of All Forms of Discrimination against Women

Social justice and human rights in democratic societies are based on the inherent worth, dignity, and equality of all human beings. Historically, however, women have been systematically excluded from overt participation in the important decision-making processes of society. The tide of discrimination against women began to turn at 11:45 A.M. on September 19, 1893, when the governor-general of New Zealand formally assented to the first national law granting suffrage to women. Since then, the vote has been extended to women in all democratic countries and many national laws have been enacted granting women equality in economic and family matters.

In 1967 the UN General Assembly adopted the Declaration on the Elimination of Discrimination against Women, which called discrimination against women "fundamentally unjust and . . . an offense against human dignity." Then on December 18, 1979, it adopted the Convention on the Elimination of All Forms of Discrimination against Women. While the purpose of the convention, which entered into force on September 3, 1981, is to remove the centuries-old practice of treating women as inferior to men and to ensure that the states parties to the document take all necessary steps to remove government roadblocks to the elimination of "all forms of discrimination against women," many religions, traditions, and social customs still keep women from participating equally with men in important areas of daily life.

The introduction notes the states parties' concern "that despite [international human rights documents] extensive discrimination against women continues to exist, [and] . . . that discrimination against women violates the principles of equality of rights and respect for human dignity, is an obstacle to the participation of women, on equal terms with men, in the political, social, economic and cultural life of their countries, hampers the growth of the prosperity of society and the family and makes more difficult the full development of the potentialities of women in the service of their countries and of humanity, [and] that in situations of poverty women have the least access to food, health, education, training and opportunities for employment and other needs. . . ."

Part I, article 1, defines the term *discrimination against women* as "any distinction, exclusion or restriction made on the basis of sex which has the effect or purpose of impairing or nullifying the recognition, enjoyment or exercise by women, irrespective of their marital status, on a basis of equality of men and women, of human rights and fundamental freedoms in the political, economic, social, cultural, civil or any other field." Article 2 outlines a number of measures that governments can take to implement the convention's goals, including embodying "the principle of the equality of men and women in national constitutions or other appropriate legislation," adopting "appropriate legislative and other measures . . . prohibiting all discrimination against women," establishing "legal protection of the rights of women on an equal basis with men . . . ," refraining "from engaging in any act or practice of discrimination against women . . . ," and repealing "all national penal provisions which constitute discrimination against women."

According to article 3, the states parties to the convention "shall take in all fields . . . all appropriate measures, including legislation, to ensure the full development and advancement of women. . . ." Article 4 declares that "temporary special measures aimed at accelerating *de facto* equality between men and women shall not be considered discrimination as defined in the present Convention. . . ." Article 5 requires that measures be taken to "modify the social and cultural patterns of conduct of men and women, with a view to achieving the elimination of prejudices and cus-

tomary and all other practices which are based on the idea of the inferiority or the superiority of either of the sexes or on stereotyped roles for men and women." Article 6 requires that the signatory nations "suppress all forms of traffic in women and exploitation of prostitution of women."

Part II, article 7, addresses the elimination of discrimination against women "in the political and public life of the country," guaranteeing the right to vote and hold office and to participate in the formulation of government policy and in nongovernmental organizations. Articles 8 and 9, respectively, require states parties to ensure that women have the opportunity to represent their country at the international level as well as equal rights with men regarding their own nationality and the nationality of their children.

Part III mandates equal rights for women in the areas of education, employment, and health care, as well as other areas of economic and social life, providing means to these ends. Article 14 addresses the roles of women in rural areas. Part IV calls for equality before the law and in marriage.

Part V establishes a Committee on the Elimination of Discrimination against Women. Members are elected for four-year terms by secret ballot of the states parties from a list of persons nominated by the states. Each state party may nominate one person from among its own nationals. The committee considers reports filed by the states "on the legislative, judicial, administrative or other measures adopted to give effect to the provisions" of the convention. The committee in turn reports on its activities and makes annual comments and recommendations to the UN General Assembly, through the Economic and Social Council (ECOSOC). The committee's reports are also transmitted to the UN Commission on the Status of Women, created in 1946 by ECOSOC to promote and determine the progress toward women's rights worldwide.

When it becomes effective, an optional protocol opened for signature on December 10, 1999, will allow women or their representatives to bypass their governments and file human rights complaints under the convention directly with the committee. Article 7 of the protocol authorizes the committee to examine and consider information provided in complaints and communicate its views and recommendations to the concerned parties. The nation in which the abuse is alleged to have occurred will be allowed six months to consider the committee's findings, provide a response, and take remedial action.

Committee on the Elimination of Discrimination against Women, Division for Advancement of Women, Room DC2-1236, United Nations, New York, N.Y. 10017. (212-963-3162. 🖷 212-963-3463. 🖳 daw@un.org 🖳 www.un.org/dpcsd/daw/cedaw.

Committee on the Elimination of Discrimination against Women; Convention for the Suppression of the Traffic in Persons and of

Exploitation of the Prostitution of Others; Convention on Consent to Marriage, Minimum Age for Marriage and Resolution of Marriages; Declaration on the Elimination of Discrimination against Women; Marriage; Sex Discrimination; Women

Convention on the International Right of Correction

In a 1946 resolution, shortly after the United Nations was founded, the General Assembly proclaimed that "freedom of information is a fundamental right and is the touchstone of all freedoms to which the United Nations is consecrated." These sentiments were incorporated into a series of general principles adopted by the Conference on Freedom of Information held in Geneva in 1948. Although no declaration on freedom of information had yet been adopted by the General Assembly, on December 16, 1952, the Convention on the International Right of Correction was opened for signature. Intended to counteract—that is, correct—propaganda and false information disseminated especially by some communist countries, it entered into force on August 24, 1962.

The convention's preamble begins by noting that the contracting states desire "to implement the right of their peoples to be fully and reliably informed, . . . to improve understanding between their peoples through the free flow of information and opinion, . . . [and] thereby to protect mankind from the scourge of war, to prevent the recurrence of aggression from any source, and to combat all propaganda which is either designed or likely to provoke or encourage any threat to peace, breach of the peace, or act of aggression. . . ." The preamble concludes by pointing out "that the legislation of certain States does not provide for a right of correction of which foreign governments may avail themselves, and that it is therefore desirable to institute such right on the international level. . . ."

Article I defines the terms *news dispatch* as "news material transmitted in writing or by means of telecommunications, in the form customarily employed by information agencies . . ."; *information agency* as "a press, broadcasting, film, television or facsimile organization, public or private, regularly engaged in the collection and dissemination of news material . . ."; and *correspondent* as "a national of a Contracting State or an individual employed by an information agency of a Contracting State, who in either case is regularly engaged in the collection and the reporting of news material, and who when outside his State is identified as a correspondent by a valid passport or by a similar document internationally acceptable."

Article II, paragraph 1, recognizes "that the professional responsibility of correspondents and information agencies requires them to report facts without discrimination and in their proper context and thereby to promote respect for human rights and fundamental freedoms, to further inter-national understanding and co-operation and to contribute to the maintenance of international peace and security." It also notes that, "as a matter of professional ethics, all correspondents and information agencies should, in case of news dispatches transmitted or published by them and which have been demonstrated to be false or distorted, follow the customary practice of transmitting through the same channels, or of publishing corrections of such dispatches." It continues: "The Contracting States agree that in cases where a Contracting State contends that a news dispatch capable of injuring its relations with other States or its national prestige or dignity transmitted from one country to another by correspondents or information agencies of [any state] and published or disseminated abroad is false or distorted, it may submit its version of the facts (hereinafter called 'communiqué') to the Contracting States within whose territories such dispatch has been published or disseminated. A copy of the communiqué shall be forwarded at the same time to the correspondent or information agency concerned to enable that correspondent or information agency to correct the news dispatch in question." Paragraph 2 provides that a "communiqué may be issued only with respect to news dispatches and must be without comment or expression of opinion."

Article III, paragraph 1, sets a time limit of "five clear days" in which the contracting state receiving the communiqué shall: "(a) Release the communiqué to the correspondents and information agencies . . . ; and (b) Transmit the communiqué to the headquarters of the information agency whose correspondent was responsible for originating the dispatch in question, if such headquarters are within its territory." According to paragraph 2, "In the event that a Contracting State does not discharge its obligation under this article, with respect to the communiqué of another Contracting State, the later may accord, on the basis of reciprocity, similar treatment to a communiqué thereafter submitted to it by the defaulting State."

Article IV gives the UN secretary-general a role in enforcing the provisions, and article V designates the International Court of Justice as the forum for the settlement of disputes under the convention that cannot otherwise be settled by negotiations.

A draft Declaration on Freedom of Information prepared by the Economic and Social Council (ECOSOC) in 1960 has never been considered or approved by the General Assembly.

United Nations High Commissioner for Human Rights, 8–14 avenue de la Paix, 1211 Geneva 10, Switzerland. (41-22-917-9000. 🖶 41-22-917-9016. 🖳 webadmin.hchr@unog.ch. 🖳 www.unhchr.ch.

Information; International Court of Justice; The Press

Convention on the Political Rights of Women

Since the Convention on the Political Rights of Women became effective in 1954, the political rights of women around the world have improved, at least with respect to the extension of voting rights and the increasing number of women in positions of political power. However, in some areas of the world, such as Afghanistan, the role of women in political life and leadership and other important aspects of society has been significantly reduced. A major challenge in improving political rights for women is the perpetuation of the historic and traditional differentiation in the roles of men and women, so that in many countries even salutary changes in national laws and policy still do not translate into equality of political opportunity for women.

In 1948 the Organization of American States adopted the Inter-American Convention on the Granting of Civil Rights to Women and the Inter-American Convention on the Granting of Political Rights to Women. The same year, in the Universal Declaration of Human Rights, the UN General Assembly proclaimed, "Everyone is entitled to the rights and freedoms set forth in this Declaration, without distinction of any kind, such as race, color, sex. . . ." Around the same time the Commission on the Status of Women, established in 1946 by the Economic and Social Council (ECOSOC), produced the Convention on the Political Rights of Women, which was adopted by the General Assembly on December 20, 1952, opened for signature on March 31, 1953, and entered into force on July 7, 1954.

The Convention begins by noting that the contracting parties desire "to implement the principle of equality of rights for men and women contained in the Charter of the United Nations [1945]. It goes on to recognize that "everyone has the right to take part in the government of his country directly or indirectly through freely chosen representatives, and has the right to equal access to public service in his country." The goal, states the document, is to "equalize the status of men and women in the enjoyment and exercise of political rights, in accordance with the provisions of the Charter . . . and of the Universal Declaration of Human Rights."

"Women shall be entitled to vote in all elections on equal terms with men, without any discrimination," declares article 1. Article 2 provides that "[w]omen shall be eligible for election to all publicly elected bodies, established by national law, on equal terms with men, without any discrimination," while article 3 asserts that "[w]omen shall be entitled to hold public office and to exercise all public functions, established by national law, on equal terms with men, without any discrimination."

Article 7 describes procedures for lodging reservations to any of the articles and objections to such reservations;

and article 8 outlines procedures for denunciations of the convention and the effects thereof, including a provision that the convention "shall cease to be in force as from the date when the denunciation which reduces the number of parties to less than six becomes effective." A dispute that "may arise between any two or more Contracting States concerning the interpretation or application of this Convention, which is not settled by negotiation," according to article 9, "shall at the request of any one of the parties to the dispute be referred to the International Court of Justice for decision, unless they agree to another mode of settlement."

United Nations High Commissioner for Human Rights, 8–14 avenue de la Paix, 1211 Geneva 10, Switzerland. (41-22-917-9000. 41-22-917-9016. webadmin.hchr@unog.ch. www.unhchr.ch.

Convention on the Elimination of All Forms of Discrimination against Women; Declaration on the Elimination of Discrimination against Women; Economic and Social Council (ECOSOC); Inter-American Convention on the Granting of Civil Rights to Women; Inter-American Convention on the Granting of Political Rights to Women; International Court of Justice; Political Rights; Women

Convention on the Prevention and Punishment of the Crime of Genocide

The Nazi Holocaust in Europe before and during World War II, which exterminated some six million Jews, impelled the international community to take action against genocide. In 1946 the UN General Assembly affirmed that genocide is a crime under international law and that persons guilty of genocide are to be punished for their acts. To ensure recognition of this principle of international law, the General Assembly requested the Economic and Social Council (ECOSOC) to draft a convention on the crime of genocide. The final draft of the convention was adopted on December 9, 1948, and went into force on January 12, 1951.

In its preamble the convention observes that "genocide is a crime under international law, contrary to the spirit and aims of the United Nations and condemned by the civilized world" and notes that "at all periods of history genocide has inflicted great losses on humanity," adding that international cooperation is required "to liberate mankind from such an odious scourge."

According to article 1, the parties to the convention undertake to prevent and punish the crime of genocide "whether committed in time of peace or in time of war." Article 2 defines *genocide* as "acts committed with intent to destroy, in whole or in part, a national, ethnical, racial or religious group." Such acts include: "(a) Killing members of the group; (b) Causing serious bodily or mental harm to members of the group; (c) Deliberately inflicting on the group conditions of life calculated to bring about its physical destruction in whole or in part; (d) Imposing measures intended to prevent births within the group; (e) Forcibly transferring children of the group to another group."

Punishable acts, as set forth in article 3, include "(a) Genocide; (b) Conspiracy to commit genocide; (c) Direct and public incitement to commit genocide; (d) Attempt to commit genocide; (e) Complicity in genocide." Article 4 declares: "Persons committing genocide or any of the other acts enumerated in article 3 shall be punished, whether they are constitutionally responsible rulers, public officials or private individuals."

Articles 5, 6, and 7, respectively, require that the parties to the convention enact necessary legislation to provide effective penalties, that persons charged with genocide "be tried by a competent tribunal of the State in the territory of which the act was committed, or by such international penal tribunal as may have jurisdiction . . . ," and that acts of genocide "shall not be considered as political crimes for the purpose of extradition." Articles 8 and 9 authorize a party to the convention to call on the United Nations for assistance in "the prevention and suppression of acts of genocide" and require that disputes under the convention "be submitted to the International Court of Justice at the request of any of the parties to the dispute."

Following its effective date, the convention was to remain in effect for ten years, after which it stays in force for successive periods of five years for those nations that still adhere to it. If the number of states parties diminishes to fewer than sixteen, the convention ceases to remain in force.

The genocide convention provides guidance and definitions of types of crimes (although not legal authority) for international war crimes tribunals. It played a key role in the 1961 trial in Israel of the Nazi official Adolph Eichmann for his participation in atrocities against Jews and others and in the war crimes tribunals covering the former Yugoslavia (1993) and Rwanda (1994). While the statutes creating these two criminal tribunals reproduce some language from the genocide convention, each was set up by the UN Security Council through a resolution rather than by the more cumbersome process used to create most international conventions.

United Nations High Commissioner for Human Rights, 8–14 avenue de la Paix, 1211 Geneva 10, Switzerland. ☎ 41-22-917-9000. 🖨 41-22-917-9016. 🖳 webadmin.hchr@unog.ch. 🖳 www.unhchr.ch.

Crimes against Humanity; Genocide; International Court of Justice; International Criminal Court; Rome Statute of the International Criminal Court; War Crimes

Convention on the Rights of the Child

The first international human rights instrument addressing children's rights was the Geneva Declaration of the Rights of the Child (1924). The Universal Declaration of Human Rights (1948) has provisions relating to children, as do other international human rights documents, including the European Convention for the Protection of Human Rights and Fundamental Freedoms (1950) and the American Convention on Human Rights (1969). In 1959 the UN General Assembly adopted the Declaration of the Rights of the Child, stating in part that "the child, by reason of his physical and mental immaturity, needs special safeguards and care, including appropriate legal protection, before as well as after birth." Three decades later, on November 20, 1989, the General Assembly adopted and opened for signature the Convention on the Rights of the Child, which entered into force on September 2, 1990. This document, which was drafted by the Committee on the Rights of the Child, provides a basic guide for the protection, care, and empowerment of children.

The major points of the convention are that the first consideration should be what is best for children; that their views, to the extent they are capable of expressing them, should be taken into consideration; and that children should be guaranteed a right of survival and healthy development through such measures as immunization and a nutritious diet. Equal opportunity for boys and girls is also stressed. A ten-member Committee on the Rights of the Child is created to review the progress made by states parties in meeting the convention's objectives.

The preamble observes that "in accordance with the principles proclaimed in the Charter of the United Nations [1945], recognition of the inherent dignity and of the equal and inalienable rights of all members of the human family is the foundation of freedom, justice, and peace in the world." It goes on to state that the signatory nations believe "that the family, as the fundamental group of society and the natural environment for the growth and well-being of all its members and particularly children, should be afforded the necessary protection and assistance so that it can fully assume its responsibilities within the community, . . . [and recognize] that the child, for the full and harmonious development of his or her personality, should grow up in a family environment, in an atmosphere of happiness, love, and understanding." The preamble also indicates "that the child should be fully prepared to live an individual life in society, and brought up in the spirit of the ideals proclaimed in the Charter of the United Nations, and in particular in the spirit of peace, dignity, tolerance, freedom, equality and solidarity. . . ."

Part I, article 1, of the convention provides that "a child means every human being below the age of eighteen years unless, under the law applicable to the child, majority is attained earlier." Article 2 declares: "1. States Parties shall respect and ensure the rights set forth in the present Convention to each child . . . without discrimination of any kind. . . . 2. [They] shall take all appropriate measures to ensure that the child is protected against all forms of discrimination or punishment on the basis of the status, activities, expressed opinions, or beliefs of the child's parents, legal guardians, or family members."

According to article 3: "1. In all actions concerning children, whether undertaken by public or private social welfare institutions, courts of law, administrative authorities or legislative bodies, the best interests of the child shall be the primary consideration. 2. States Parties undertake to ensure the child such protection and care as is necessary for his or her well-being. . . . 3. [They] shall ensure that the institutions, services and facilities responsible for the care or protection of children shall conform with the standards established by competent authorities. . . ." Pursuant to article 4, states parties are to "undertake all appropriate legislative, administrative, and other measures for the implementation of the rights recognized in the present Convention. . . ." Article 5 mandates that they "shall respect the responsibilities, rights and duties of parents or [others] responsible for the child. . . ."

"[E]very child has the inherent right to life," provides article 6, which also requires states parties to "ensure to the maximum extent possible the survival and development of the child." Article 7 addresses the right of the child to a name, a nationality, and "the right to know and be cared for by his or her parents," while article 8 deals with "the right of the child to preserve his or her identity, including nationality, name and family relations. . . ." Articles 9 through 11, respectively, focus on situations where the child is separated from his or her parents; family reunification; and "the illicit transfer and non-return of children abroad." Children's right to have their views considered in matters affecting them and their right to freedom of expression and information are emphasized in articles 12 and 13. Freedom of thought, conscience, and religion; freedom of association and peaceable assembly; and the right of privacy for children are the subjects of articles 14, 15, and 16.

Articles 17 through 23 cover situations involving the mass media and the child's access to information, assistance by the states to parents, and "appropriate legislative, administrative, social and educational measures to protect the child," as well as situations where the child is "deprived of his or her family environment" or is physically or mentally disabled. According to articles 24 and 25, states parties "recognize the right of the child to the enjoyment of the highest attainable standards of health. . . ." Articles 26 through 30 address the child's "standard of living" and his or her "physical, mental, spiritual, moral and social development"; right to education; and entitlement to ethnic, religious or linguistic minority rights. The remaining articles in part I deal with other specific problems for children, including becoming victims of abuse and being brought into the criminal justice system.

Part II establishes the Committee on the Rights of the Child, which consists of "ten experts of high moral standing and recognized competence in the field" for "the purpose of examining the progress made by the States Parties in achieving the realization of the obligations undertaken" in the convention.

In September 1990, the same month that the convention became effective, the World Summit for Children, meeting in New York City, adopted the World Declaration on the Survival, Protection and Development of Children. Focusing on education and health, including nutrition, safe water, and sanitation, the conferees set goals to be reached by the year 2000. Among them were the reduction of infant mortality and increased access to primary education.

Defense for Children International, P.O. Box 88, 1211 Geneva 20, Switzerland. (41-22-734-0558. 🖷 41-22-740-1145. 🖳 dci-hq @pingnet.ch.

United Nations High Commissioner for Human Rights, 8–14 avenue de la Paix, 1211 Geneva 10, Switzerland. (41-22-917-9000. 🖷 41-22-917-9016. 🖳 webadmin.hchr@unog.ch. 🖳 www.unhchr.ch.

Children; Declaration of the Rights of the Child; Declaration on Social and Legal Principles Relating to the Protection and Welfare of Children, with Special Reference to Foster Placement and Adoption Nationally and Internationally; Declaration on the Protection of Women and Children in Emergency and Armed Conflict; Families; International Labor Organization; Standard Minimum Rules for the Administration of Juvenile Justice; Youth

Convention Relating to the Status of Refugees

The devastation caused by World War I and the resulting dislocation of many thousands of people focused the world's concern on the plight of international refugees. In 1919 the League of Nations established an Office of the High Commissioner for Refugees, and in response to new waves of refugees after World War II, the new United Nations created its own Office of the High Commissioner for Refugees.

The Convention Relating to the Status of Refugees was adopted on July 28, 1951, by the UN Conference of Plenipotentiaries on the Status of Refugees and Stateless Persons and entered into force on April 22, 1954. In 1966 the Economic and Social Council (ECOSOC) approved the Protocol Relating to the Status of Refugees, which was opened for ratification in 1967 and expanded the definition of refugees to include persons who had become refugees after January 1, 1951. Both the convention and the protocol required the signatory nations to cooperate with the UN on refugee matters.

The preamble to the 1951 convention acknowledges the UN's "profound concern for refugees" and its endeavors to ensure their fundamental freedoms. Recognizing "the social and humanitarian nature of the problems of refugees," the document encourages the contracting states to "do everything within their power to prevent this problem from becoming a cause of tension between States. . . ."

A refugee, as defined by chapter I, General Provisions, article 1, is a person who, "[o]wing to well-founded fear of being persecuted for reasons of race, religion, nationality, membership of a particular social group or political opinion, is outside the country of his nationality and is unable, or owing to such fear, is unwilling to avail himself of the protection of that country; or who, not having a nationality and being outside of the country of his former habitual residence . . . is unable or unwilling to return to it."

Article 1.c. stipulates that the convention ceases to apply to a refugee under certain conditions: "(1) He has voluntarily re-availed himself of the protection of the country of his nationality; or (2) Having lost his nationality, he has voluntarily reacquired it; or (3) He has acquired a new nationality, and enjoys the protection of the country of his new nationality; or (4) He has voluntarily re-established himself in the country which he left or outside which he remained owing to fear of persecution; or (5) He can no longer, because the circumstances in connection with which he has been recognized as a refugee have ceased to exist, continue to refuse to avail himself of the protection of the country of his nationality." A number of further details in the definition follow.

Articles 2, 3, 4, and 5, respectively, address general obligations of refugees, nondiscrimination by contracting states, freedom of religion for refugees, and rights granted apart from the convention. Article 10 deals with "continuity of residence" for refugees, and article 11 provides guidance for handling refugee seamen on board a ship of a contracting state.

According to chapter II, Juridical Status, article 12, a refugee's personal status "shall be governed by the law of the country of his domicile or, if he has no domicile, by the law of the country of his residence." Chapter II also focuses on movable and immovable property, artistic rights and industrial property, the right of association, and access to courts. Chapters III and IV cover gainful employment and welfare.

Chapter V, Administrative Measures, article 25, provides in part: "1. When the exercise of a right by a refugee would normally require the assistance of authorities of a foreign country to whom he cannot have recourse, the Contracting States in whose territory he is residing shall arrange that such assistance be afforded to him by their own authorities or by an international authority. 2. The authority or authorities . . . shall deliver or cause to be delivered under their supervision to refugees such documents or certifications as would normally be delivered to aliens by or through their national authorities." Chapter V also addresses, among other things, freedom of movement, identity papers, travel documents, expulsion, and prohibition of expulsion or return (*refoulement*). Chapter VI deals with executory and transitory provisions. Chapter VII, Final Clauses, article 43, states in part: "1. This Convention shall come into force on the ninetieth day following the day of the deposit of the sixth ratification or accession."

Although refugee problems around the world have not diminished since the adoption of the 1951 convention and the 1967 protocol—in 1991 there were an estimated seventeen million legal refugees and some twenty-four million internally displaced persons (potential refugees)—the plight of such refugees has been greatly mitigated by the cooperative efforts promoted by the document. The recent displacement of citizens in Kosovo and Rwanda, for example, confirms the need for international cooperation on refugee problems under the UN aegis.

Refugees International, 1705 N Street, N.W., Washington, D.C. 20036. 202-828-0110, 800-REFUGEE. 202-828-0819. ri@refintl.org. www.refintl.org.

United Nations High Commissioner for Refugees, C.P. 2500, 1211 Geneva 2, Switzerland. 41-22-729-8111. 41-22-731-9546. hqpioo@unhcr.ch. www.unhcr.ch.

Weis, Paul. *The Refugee Convention, 1951: The Travaux Preparatiores Analysed, with a Commentary*. New York: Cambridge University Press, 1995.

High Commissioner for Refugees; *Refoulement;* Refugees; Statelessness

Conventions

See International Human Rights Instruments; Treaties; *and specific documents*

Council of Europe

See Regional Human Rights Systems

Counsel

A vigorous and independent legal profession, like an independent and protected judiciary, is a bulwark against infringements of human rights. Even countries without written constitutions, such as New Zealand and the United Kingdom, have extremely good human rights records, in part because of their long histories of professional and aggressive legal representation. If true equality before the law is to be maintained, access to competent legal counsel —through some form of court-appointed counsel or legal aid—is equally important for those who cannot afford to retain an attorney on their own.

Counsel, counselor, advocate, pleader, lawyer, and *attorney* are various titles for persons who are qualified members of the legal profession and who may represent others in matters before a court of law. *Counsel* (from the Latin *consilium,* meaning policy and advice, and *consiliarius,* meaning adviser) has been in use in English since about the fourteenth century. In England a solicitor may advise clients about legal matters, but only barristers who have been "admitted to the bar" are eligible to appear on behalf of a client in court. The word *attorney* comes from ancient English and means a person who is placed in the turn (*turne*), or stead, of another. The ancient Romans understood the concept of legal representation. Like many other members of the senatorial class in Rome, Marcus Tullius Cicero, who died in 43 B.C.E., occasionally spoke on behalf of others in legal proceedings.

The importance of the right to legal counsel or representation in legal matters cannot be overemphasized, especially in cases that concern the deprivation of liberty or life. Not only is the law more complicated in the modern age, but the state also has a virtual monopoly on the ability to collect evidence and coerce witnesses in support of the prosecution of citizens. A criminal defendant's representation by an impartial and professionally trained attorney helps ensure that the prosecution make its case honestly, within the bounds of the law, and that any guilty verdict may be appealed.

There are many reasons for guaranteeing the right of defendants to legal representation. Suspects are often held in jail pending a trial and are therefore greatly hampered in mounting their own defense. In addition, persons who are accused of serious crimes are under psychological pressure that can prevent them from acting in their own best interests. Professional advocates also have a number of tools and talents at their disposal with which to defend their clients' interests.

The right to free legal assistance or legal aid is a related

issue. In a significant precedent in 1963, the U.S. Supreme Court held that "assistance of counsel is a fundamental right essential to a fair trial and that conviction without the assistance of counsel violated the Fourteenth Amendment [to the U.S. Constitution, added in 1868]." The Court thus held unconstitutional the conviction of a person who had no funds and had been denied a court-appointed attorney in a noncapital felony case.

Some national constitutions and laws—for example, the constitutions of the United States (1789) and India (1950) and—guarantee the right to counsel. A number of international human rights documents, such as the International Covenant on Civil and Political Rights (1966) and the European Convention for the Protection of Human Rights and Fundamental Freedoms (1950), also guarantee this human right.

Constitution of Japan (1947), chapter III, Rights and Duties of the People, article 34: "No person shall be arrested or detained without being at once informed of the charges against him or without the immediate privilege of counsel; nor shall he be detained without adequate cause; and upon demand of any person such cause must be immediately shown in open court in his presence and the presence of his counsel."

International Covenant on Civil and Political Rights (1966), part III, article 14: "3. In the determination of any criminal charge against him, everyone shall be entitled to the following minimum guarantees, in full equality; . . . (d) To be tried in his presence, and to defend himself in person, or through legal assistance of his own choosing; to be informed, if he does not have legal assistance, of this right; and to have legal assistance assigned to him, in any case where the interests of justice so require, and without payment by him in such case if he does not have sufficient means to pay for it. . . ."

Queen's Bench, Alberta, Canada (1990): "Although there is no absolute right to legal counsel, the court has an inherent power to appoint counsel where an applicant may be deprived of his liberty." The following criteria were identified as determinants of whether an individual is entitled to publicly funded legal counsel: the applicant's educational level, an ability to present his case, the relative simplicity of the issues, the seriousness of the charge and the potential penalty, especially whether the outcome of the hearing might be confinement or imprisonment, the simplicity of the evidence and the lack of procedural difficulties, and the defendant's ability to pay for legal services.

International (Criminal) Tribunal for the Former Yugoslavia (1996): "While the defense has full discretion over the strategy it decides to adopt in response to the Prosecution, the [tribunal] must nonetheless ensure that the rights of the accused are actually respected and, more specifically, the accused's right to counsel."

Puritz, Patricia, et al. *A Call for Justice: An Assessment of Access to Counsel and the Quality of Representation in Delinquency Proceedings.* Chicago: American Bar Association Juvenile Justice Center, Youth Law Center, 1995.

Regan, Francis, et al., eds. *The Transformation of Legal Aid: Comparative and Historical Studies.* New York: Oxford University Press, 1999.

Accused; Basic Principles on the Role of Lawyers; Cicero, Marcus Tullius; Due Process of Law; European Convention for the Protection of Human Rights and Fundamental Freedoms; Fair Trial; International Covenant on Civil and Political Rights; Lawyers Committee for Human Rights

Courts of Law

See Fair Trial; Judicial Independence; Judicial Review

Covenants

See Treaties; *and specific documents*

Crimes against Humanity

Under international law the concept of crimes against humanity has roots in the ethics propounded by the ancient Greek philosophers Plato and Aristotle. St. Thomas Aquinas continued to develop the idea in his work on natural law, arguing that the divine law of God prohibited injustice in the secular world. In the sixteenth century Franciscus de Victoria, a major contributor to the development of international law, concluded that even in war both sides were bound to do as little harm as necessary to the other. The mass killing of innocents was condemned in the same century, and a century later Samuel Pufendorf declared that under international law human beings owed each other the duties of humanity. The Hague peace conferences in 1899 and 1907 recognized expressly the "laws of humanity" and the notion of the public conscience.

The Rome Statute (1998), which established the International Criminal Court, defines *crimes against humanity* as "any of the following acts when committed as a part of widespread or systematic attack directed against any civilian population, with knowledge of the attack: (a) Murder; (b) Extermination; (c) Enslavement; (d) Deportation or forcible transfer of population; (e) Imprisonment or other severe deprivation of physical liberty in violation of fundamental

rules of international law; (f) Rape, sexual slavery, enforced prostitution, or any other form of sexual violence of comparable gravity; (g) Torture; (h) Persecution against any identifiable group . . ."; (i) Enforced disappearance of persons; (j) The crime of apartheid; (k) Other inhumane acts of a similar character intentionally causing great suffering, or serious injury to body or to mental or physical health."

International law holds certain acts such as piracy and slavery as crimes against the community of nations. However, the concept of national sovereignty—the international law principle that no state may interfere in the internal affairs of another—curtails what nations can do with respect to another nation's treatment of its own citizens. But a precedent was set when world opinion denounced as a crime against humanity the Turkish government's massacre of its Armenian minority in 1915. And in 1919 an Allied commission recommended punishment for those responsible for barbaric actions that violated the laws of humanity during World War I, although this recommendation and similar provisions in peace treaties at that time were never enforced.

The atrocities of World War II, however, raised the conscience of the world community with regard to crimes against humanity and gross violations of human rights that such crimes represent. As a result, international law precedent was again set by the prosecution of Nazi war criminals at the Nuremberg trials in Germany and similar war crimes trials in Tokyo, the indictments for which specified "[o]ther conventional war crimes and crimes against humanity." In 1999 the nineteen member states of the North Atlantic Treaty Organization (NATO) made their first concerted effort to stem mass violations of human rights by punishing militarily the Yugoslav Serbians for conducting a program of ethnic cleansing in the Yugoslav province of Kosovo. NATO actions included aerial bombing and occupation of the province of Kosovo by international peacekeeping forces

Crimes against humanity by a nondemocratic ruler can sometimes be atoned for through the process of transitional justice, in which through a negotiated agreement the ruler relinquishes power voluntarily so that democracy can be restored. How to deal with crimes against humanity resulting from the use of biological, chemical, and nuclear weapons of mass destruction remains an intractable problem, however.

Report of the Commission of Inquiry into the Crimes and Misappropriations Committed by Ex-President Habré [of Chad], His Accomplices and/or Accessories (1992): "To prevent Chad from falling again into the horrors and injustice of the past; To guarantee present and future generations that their basic rights and dignity will be respected; To enable Chad and Chadians to return to peace, stability, and national concord; And finally to bar the road to any sanguinary [bloody] and despotic regime in the future, the Commission of Inquiry recommends: . . . 6) prosecution without delay of the authors of this horrible genocide, who are guilty of crimes against humanity. . . ."

Rome Statute of the International Criminal Court (1998), article 5, Crimes within the Jurisdiction of the Court: "1. The jurisdiction of the Court shall be limited to the most serious crimes of concern to the international community as a whole. The Court has jurisdiction in accordance with this Statute with respect to the following crimes: . . . (b) Crimes against humanity. . . ."

Supreme Court of Canada (1994): In the case of crimes against humanity, incorporated by statute into Canadian criminal law in 1987, the defense that an act was done in obedience to orders by a superior or by an officer of the law is not available where the order was manifestly unlawful and the accused had a moral choice whether or not to obey the order.

Supreme Court of Israel (1962): "Not only do all crimes attributed to the appellant [Adolf Eichmann] bear an international character, but their harmful and murderous effects were so embracing and widespread as to shake the international community to its very foundations. The State of Israel therefore was entitled, pursuant to the principle of universal jurisdiction and in the capacity of a guardian of international law and an agent for its enforcement, to try the appellant."

Kritz, Neil J., ed. *Transitional Justice: How Emerging Democracies Reckon with Former Regimes*. Washington, D.C.: U.S. Institute for Peace, 1995.

Minow, Martha. *Between Vengeance and Forgiveness: Facing History after Genocide and Mass Violence*. Boston: Beacon, 1998.

Aristotle; Convention on the Prevention and Punishment of the Crime of Genocide; Disappearance; Genocide; International Criminal Court; North Atlantic Treaty Organization (NATO); Plato; Rome Statute of the International Criminal Court; Thomas Aquinas, St.; Torture; War Crimes

Cruel and Unusual Punishment

See Capital Punishment; Punishment; Torture

Cultural Rights

The population of most countries includes peoples of different cultures. The notion that a society should tolerate ethnic, racial, and religious diversity—pluralism—has been accepted as the policy of most nations, especially democratic ones, while ethnic or racial purity as a national goal has been discredited. "Every people has the right and duty to develop its culture," proclaims the Declaration of the Principles of International Cultural Cooperation, adopted by the General Conference of the United Nations Educational, Scientific and Cultural Organization (UNESCO) in 1966. "Cultural cooperation is a right and duty for all people and all nations," it adds.

Like economic and social rights, cultural rights have been called second-generation rights—as opposed to first-generation political and civil rights—because they are relative to the rights of others rather than absolute. Among them is the right of members of a minority culture to take part in the cultural life of their people, to maintain key elements of their culture (such as language and religion), and to pass along to their children information about their culture. Another cultural right is freedom from discrimination because of one's cultural background.

Cultural rights, however, may conflict with individual rights. In some societies the practice of female genital mutilation, for example, is a cultural tradition, but it is also a significant violation of a person's rights and as such is widely condemned regardless of its cultural status. Cultural and individual rights also conflict in the case of persons who wish to leave the culture into which they were born in order to become a member of a different culture or to renounce cultural ties. In addition, the cultural rights of one group may interfere with the cultural rights of another, and cultural conflicts may occur among countries and private interests—for example, when a government or a private entity illegally appropriates the cultural artifacts of a group or a nation.

A number of cultural rights issues arise frequently. One is the criteria used to identify a culture or membership in a culture and the authority to claim rights or benefits guaranteed by national law or policy. Another is cultural relativism—the influence of the cultural context in determining the extent to which human rights are to be protected; as with female genital mutilation, an argument is sometimes made that human rights are not the same for citizens everywhere in the world but may be limited by culture, religion, form of government, and tradition. The historical trend in human rights development, however, indicates movement away from limited rights toward full rights for all individuals, unless a person freely waives his or her human rights because of sincerely held cultural principles.

Some national constitutions and international human rights documents expressly provide for some form of cultural rights. Of particular significance is the International Covenant on Economic, Social and Cultural Rights (1966), which guarantees the right of everyone to take part in cultural life. The United Nations Educational, Scientific and Cultural Organization (UNESCO) has established a number of conventions regarding cultural matters, including the Convention for the Protection of Cultural Property in the Event of Armed Conflict (1954), Convention on the

Means of Prohibiting and Preventing the Illicit Import, Export and Transfer of Ownership of Cultural Property (1970), and Convention Concerning the Protection of the World Cultural and Natural Heritage (1972).

Constitution of Belgium (1831), heading III, Concerning Authorities, chapter I, Concerning the Houses of Parliament, section III, Concerning the Community Councils, article 59b: "2. The community council, each in its own sphere [Flemish and French], shall regulate by decree: 1. cultural matters. . . ."

Universal Declaration of Human Rights (1948), article 27: "1. Everyone has the right freely to participate in the cultural life of the community. . . ."

Constitutional Court of South Africa (1996): South Africa's constitution (1993) protects the right to establish schools on the basis of, among other things, a common culture; however, it does not require the government to establish such schools.

Human Rights Committee (1993): A member of the Wiradjuri Nation of New South Wales, Australia, alleged that his and his children's cultural rights were violated when a family court in Australia awarded custody of his children to his nonaboriginal ex-wife, thereby depriving the children of their cultural membership and heritage guaranteed by the International Covenant on Civil and Political Rights (1966), article 27. His claim was denied on the basis that he failed to exhaust domestic remedies.

United Nations High Commissioner for Human Rights, 8–14 avenue de la Paix, 1211 Geneva 10, Switzerland. (41-22-917-9000. 🖳 41-22-917-9016. 🖳 webadmin.hchr@unog.ch. 🖳 www.unhchr.ch.

Alston, Philip, ed. *Human Rights Law*. New York: New York University Press, 1996.

Lury, Celia. *Cultural Rights: Technology, Legality, and Personality*. London: Routledge, 1993.

Collective Rights; Convention Concerning the Protection of the World Cultural and Natural Heritage; International Covenant on Economic, Social and Cultural Rights; Language; Limburg Principles on the Implementation of the International Covenant on Economic, Social and Cultural Rights; Minorities; Pluralism; Religion; Tolerance; United Nations Educational, Scientific and Cultural Organization (UNESCO)

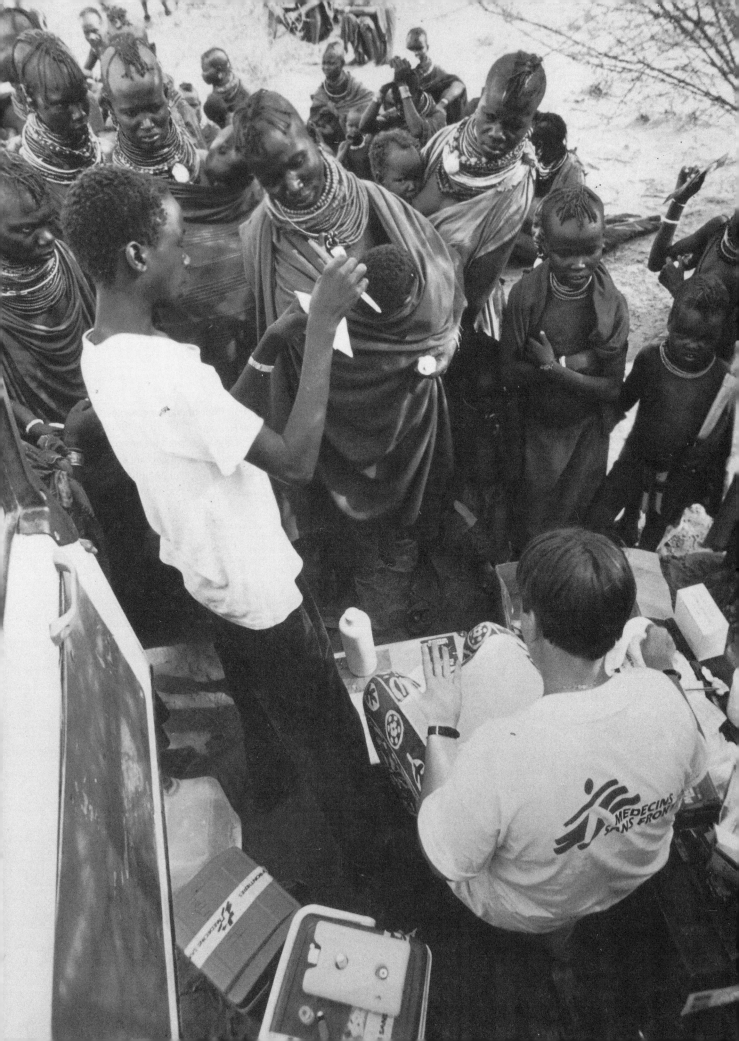

Providing medical attention and health care to victims of epidemics, war, and natural disasters is an important humanitarian activity. Doctors without Borders (Médecins sans Frontières), which recently received the Nobel Peace Prize for its work, sent one of its volunteer medical teams to conduct field checkups at a remote health post in the African country of Kenya. [Doctors without Borders]

Death Penalty

See Capital Punishment

Declaration of Alma Ata (Asian Press)

Because a vigorous, free, and independent press is necessary to the protection of democratic government as well as human rights, a seminar sponsored jointly by the United Nations and the United Nations Educational, Scientific and Cultural Organization (UNESCO) held in Alma Ata, Kazakhstan, between October 5 and 9, 1992, produced a Declaration of Alma Ata encouraging independent and pluralistic media in Asia. The declaration follows the Declaration of Windhoek (1991), which promotes an independent and pluralistic African press and was adopted in Windhoek, Namibia, also under the joint sponsorship of the UN and UNESCO.

"In Asia and the Pacific, including the newly independent Central Asian Republics of the former Soviet Union, which identify with the Asian region," begins the declaration, "we seek practical application of the principles enshrined in the Declaration of Windhoek, in conjunction with relevant national and international professional organizations and relevant United Nations agencies, in

the following specific project proposals and in the following fields."

Under section I, Legislation, the participants seek "expert advice and legal drafting assistance to replace redundant press laws inherited at independence with laws that create enforceable rights to freedom of expression, freedom of opinion, access to information and freedom of the press; to abolish monopolies and all forms of discrimination in broadcasting and allocation of frequencies, in printing, newspaper and magazine distribution, and in newsprint production and distribution; and to abolish barriers to launching new publications, and discriminatory taxation."

Section II addresses training, including "the rights of women in the media, and the rights of minority groups within societies." Section III deals with the free flow of information, section IV with the safety of journalists, section V with public service broadcasting, and section VI with professional associations. Section VII, the last item, covers special economic issues, "and in particular ... arrang[ing] a feasibility study into alternative methods of acquiring and distributing newsprint, alternative facilities for printing and distributing newspapers and magazines and alternative means of obtaining low-interest credit."

United Nations Educational, Scientific and Cultural Organization (UNESCO), 7 place de Fontenoy, 75352 Paris 07 SP, France. (33-145-68-10-00. 🖶 33-145-67-16-90. 🖳 webmaster@unesco.org. 🖳 www.unesco.org.

United Nations High Commissioner for Human Rights, 8–14 avenue de la Paix, 1211 Geneva 10, Switzerland. (41-22-917-9000. 📠 41-22-917-9016. 🖳 webadmin.hchr@unog.ch. 🖳 www.unhchr.ch.

Declaration on Fundamental Principles Concerning the Contribution of the Mass Media to Strengthening Peace and International Understanding, to the Promotion of Human Rights and to Countering Racialism, Apartheid and Incitement to War; Expression; Information; Opinion; The Press

Declaration of Alma Ata (Health)

The first Declaration of Alma Ata, Kazakhstan (then a part of the Soviet Union), was adopted by the International Conference on Primary Health Care in 1978 and endorsed by the UN General Assembly on November 29, 1979. The main goal of the declaration—to achieve health care for all by the year 2000—obviously was not reached worldwide or even in the United States, a developed country, where the extension of health care coverage to millions of uninsured citizens, including mothers and children, was still being debated by political candidates the election year of 2000.

The declaration, prepared under the joint sponsorship of the World Health Organization and the United Nations Children's Fund (UNICEF), opens by expressing "the need for urgent action by all governments, all health and development workers, and the world community to protect and promote the health of all the people of the world."

In paragraph I, the conference "strongly affirms that health, which is a state of complete physical, mental and social well-being, and not merely the absence of disease or infirmity, is a fundamental human right. . . ." Paragraph II notes that the "existing gross inequality in the health status of the people particularly between developed and developing countries as well as within countries is politically, socially and economically unacceptable and is, therefore, of common concern to all countries." Paragraphs III and IV address economic and social development as well as planning and implementation of health care.

According to paragraph V, "Primary health care is the key to attaining [health care for all by 2000] as part of development in the spirit of social justice." Primary care, explains paragraph VI, "is essential health care based on practical, scientifically sound and socially acceptable methods and technology made universally accessible to individuals and families in the community through their full participation and at a cost that the community and country can afford to maintain. . . ."

Paragraph IX provides that "[a]ll countries should coop-

erate in a spirit of partnership and service to ensure primary health care for all people since the attainment of health by people in any one country directly concerns and benefits every other country." The final item, paragraph X, suggests that an "acceptable level of health care for all the people of the world by the year 2000 can be obtained through a fuller and better use of the world's resources, a considerable part of which is now spent on armaments and military conflicts."

✉️

United Nations Children's Fund (UNICEF), Three United Nations Plaza, New York, N.Y. 10017. (212-326-7000. 📠 212-887-7465. 🖳 addresses@unicef.org. 🖳 www.unicef.org.

World Health Organization, avenue Appia 20, 1211 Geneva 27, Switzerland. (41-22-791-2111. 📠 41-22-791-3111. 🖳 info@who.int. 🖳 www.who.org.

Health; United Nations Children's Fund (UNICEF); World Health Organization

Declaration of Basic Principles of Justice for Victims of Crime and Abuse of Power

The Universal Declaration of Human Rights (1948) provides that "everyone has the right to an effective remedy . . . for acts violating fundamental human rights," while the more recent International Covenant on Civil and Political Rights (1966) refers to "victims rights." Based on the recommendation of a United Nations Congress on the Prevention of Crime and the Treatment of Offenders, the UN General Assembly on November 29, 1985, adopted the Declaration of Basic Principles of Justice for Victims of Crime and Abuse of Power. The declaration's purpose is to influence governments to recognize and alleviate the problems suffered by victims of crime and government abuse and by their families and witnesses who assist in the prosecution of criminal offenders. To date more than half of the U.S. states have added victims' rights amendments to their constitutions. Compared to these state provisions, national constitutions generally do not specify the rights of victims in such detail, but the constitutions of some countries— Zimbabwe (1980) and Slovenia (1991), for example—expressly sanction the right of persons harmed by government officials or institutions to be compensated or receive restitution.

In A, Victims of Crime, paragraph 1, the declaration states that the word *victims* "means persons who, individually or collectively, have suffered harm, including physical or mental injury, emotional suffering, economic loss or substantial impairment of their fundamental rights, through acts or omissions that are in violation of criminal laws operative within Member States [of the United Nations], including those laws proscribing criminal abuse of power." Paragraph 2 notes that a "person may be considered a victim, under this Declaration, regardless of whether the perpetrator is identified, apprehended, prosecuted or convicted and regardless of the familial relationship between the perpetrator and the victim. The term 'victim' also includes, where appropriate, the immediate family or dependents of the direct victim and persons who have suffered harm in intervening to assist victims in distress or to prevent victimization." Paragraph 3 prohibits discrimination against victims on the basis of a number of factors, including race, color, sex, age, family status, disability, property, and political opinion.

"Victims should be treated with compassion and respect for their dignity," observes paragraph 4 in the subsection Access to Justice and Fair Treatment. "They are entitled to access to the mechanisms of justice and to prompt redress, as provided for by national legislation, for the harm they have suffered." Paragraph 5 recommends that "[j]udicial and administrative mechanisms should be established and strengthened where necessary to enable victims to obtain redress through formal or informal procedures that are expeditious, fair, inexpensive and accessible. Victims should be informed of their rights in seeking redress through such mechanisms."

A number of ways to meet the needs of victims are listed in paragraph 6. Among them are "a) Informing victims of their role and the scope, timing and progress of the proceedings and of the disposition of their cases...; b) Allowing the views and concerns of victims to be presented and considered at appropriate stages of the proceedings...; c) Providing proper assistance to victims throughout the legal process; d) Taking measures to minimize inconvenience to victims, protect their privacy, when necessary, and ensure their safety, as well as that of their families and witnesses on their behalf, from intimidation and retaliation; e) Avoiding unnecessary delay in the disposition of cases and the execution of orders or decrees granting awards to victims." Paragraph 7 suggests "[i]nformal mechanisms for the resolution of disputes... where appropriate to facilitate conciliation and redress for victims."

Under the subsection Restitution, paragraphs 8 through 11, the procedures for returning property or paying compensation to victims are addressed. Restitution is to be considered "as an available sentencing option in criminal cases"; where the environment is affected, its restoration should be taken into account along with other forms of restitution; and where public officials are at fault, "the victims should receive restitution from the State...."

Paragraphs 12 and 13, in the subsection Compensation, state in part that when "compensation is not fully available from the offender or other sources, States should endeavor to provide financial compensation to: 1) Victims who have sustained significant bodily injury or impairment of physical or mental health as a result of serious crimes; b) The family, in particular dependents of persons who have died or become physically or mentally incapacitated as a result of such victimization."

Paragraphs 14 through 17 deal with assistance to victims, calling for "the necessary material, medical, psychological and social assistance through governmental, voluntary, community-based and indigenous means." Paragraph 16 advises that "[p]olice, justice, health, social service and other personnel concerned should receive training to sensitize them to the needs of victims, and guidelines to ensure proper and prompt aid."

In B, Victims of Abuse of Power, paragraph 18 defines *victims* as in paragraph 1 concerning victims of crime, except that instead of being based on violations of national laws, the status of a victim of an abuse of power is based on violations "of internationally recognized norms relating to human rights." According to paragraph 19, "States should consider incorporating into the national law norms proscribing abuses of power and providing remedies to victims of such abuses...." In paragraph 20, nations are urged to "consider negotiating multilateral international treaties relating to victims, as defined in paragraph 18." The last item, paragraph 21, calls on nations to "periodically review existing legislation and practices to ensure their responsiveness to changing circumstances" and to "enact and enforce, if necessary, legislation proscribing acts that constitute serious abuses of political or economic power ... and make readily available appropriate rights and remedies for victims of such acts."

United Nations High Commissioner for Human Rights, 8–14 avenue de la Paix, 1211 Geneva 10, Switzerland. (41-22-917-9000. 🖨 41-22-917-9016. 🖳 webadmin.hchr@unog.ch. 🖳 www.unhchr.ch.

Compensation; Declaration on the Protection of All Persons from Enforced Disappearance; Disappearance; Impunity; Victims

Declaration of Independence (United States)

The U.S. Declaration of Independence (1776) has been heralded around the world as one of the most important expressions of human rights and freedoms. Other nations since then, including Brazil, Israel, Venezuela, and Zimbabwe, have likewise declared their independence in similar documents, and its language has been used by other nations to express similar human rights principles. For example, South Korea's constitution (1948, revised 1988), chapter 2, Rights and Duties of Citizens, article 10, proclaims: "All citizens shall be assured of human worth and dignity and have the right *to pursue happiness* [emphasis added]."

The clash between American colonists and British troops in Massachusetts in the spring of 1775—the "shot heard 'round the world"—signaled the beginning of an important event in the history of human rights. Some of the thirteen colonies immediately began planning for a war of independence from Great Britain, and early in 1776 *Common Sense*, the incendiary pamphlet by the recently arrived British subject Thomas Paine, became an instant bestseller. The case Paine made for the colonies' separation from Britain fanned revolutionary fervor and led to the drafting of the Declaration of Independence.

The Second Continental Congress, composed of delegates from all thirteen colonies, convened in Philadelphia in May 1775. On June 7, 1776, Richard Henry Lee of Virginia, the largest colony, introduced a resolution that called for severing all ties with Britain. It passed, and a committee of five delegates, headed by Thomas Jefferson, also of Virginia, was assigned the task of drafting a declaration of independence.

Benjamin Franklin of Pennsylvania and John Adams of Massachusetts were also members of the drafting committee, but they and the others deferred to Jefferson, who had already proposed a constitution for Virginia and so had material to draw on. Jefferson additionally had available the Virginia Declaration of Rights, drafted by George Mason and adopted by a convention on June 12, 1776.

Adams made several changes in Jefferson's draft, and the congress removed some of his impassioned language against the slave trade. After discussion on July 3, the document was approved and signed on July 4, 1776, by the congress's president, John Hancock, and its secretary, Charles Thomson. Other members signed it on or after August 2.

When Jefferson arrived in Philadelphia in 1776, he brought his reputation as a man knowledgeable about literature and science and possessing a talent for writing. Clearly the seventeenth-century English philosopher John Locke's basic principles of human rights—the right to life, liberty, and property—were well known to Jefferson. The Virginia Declaration of Rights provided one model, and Jefferson's own draft constitution for Virginia, which had been rejected, included charges against George III similar to those in the less well known parts of the Declaration of Independence.

Much of the declaration's language relates specifically to the cause of separating from Britain but transcends that goal to achieve timelessness. "When in the Course of human Events," begins the document, "it becomes necessary for one People to dissolve the Political Bands which have connected them with another, and to assume among the Powers of the Earth, the separate and equal Station to which the Laws of Nature and of Nature's God entitle them...."

The most-quoted portion is the second paragraph, which begins: "We hold these Truths to be self-evident, that all Men are created equal, that they are endowed by their Creator with certain unalienable Rights, that among these are Life, Liberty, and the Pursuit of Happiness—That to secure these Rights, Governments are instituted among Men, deriving their just Powers from the Consent of the Governed, that whenever any Form of Government becomes destructive of these Ends, it is the Right of the People to alter or to abolish it, and to institute new Government, laying its Foundation on such Principles, and organizing its Powers in such Form, as to them shall seem most likely to effect their Safety and Happiness."

These few words have laid the basis for a noble quest: a world in which all persons are accorded the equal rights and dignity to which they are entitled as human beings.

The Declaration of Independence. Milestone Documents in the National Archives series. Rev. ed. Washington, D.C.: National Archives and Records Administration, 1992.

Eicholz, Hans L. *Thomas Jefferson and the Origins and Implications of the Declaration of Independence.* New York: Peter Lang, 1998.

Malone, Dumas. *The Story of the Declaration of Independence.* New York: Oxford University Press, 1954.

Human Rights; Jefferson, Thomas; Liberty; Life; Locke, John; Mason, George; Paine, Thomas; Political Rights

Declaration of the Rights of Man and of the Citizen (France)

Forged in 1789 during the French Revolution, the Declaration of the Rights of Man and of the Citizen predates by two years the incorporation of the Bill of Rights into the U.S. Constitution (1789), although it lacks the broad personal protections of that seminal document. Adopted by the French National Assembly, the revolutionary ruling body of France, on August 6, 1789, the declaration was intended to be a statement of principles on which the National Assembly would base its reform of the French government. A statement of rights, not duties, it asserted new claims for political, social, and constitutional rights and was designed to have universal appeal, hence the inclusion of the word *man* in the title.

The declaration's principles have been incorporated in

France's current constitution (1958), and the document has inspired similar expressions of rights in other national constitutions, particularly those of countries in which French influence has been significant. The constitution of Algeria (1976), for example, provides: "The fundamental liberties and the Rights of Man and the Citizen are guaranteed. They constitute the patrimony of all Algerians . . . who have the task of transmitting it from generation to generation in its integrity and inviolability."

"The representatives of the French people," begins the declaration, "formed into a National Assembly considering that ignorance, disregard or contempt of the rights of man are the sole causes of public misfortunes and corruption of governments, have resolved to set forth in solemn declaration the natural, inalienable and sacred rights of man. . . . Accordingly, the National Assembly recognizes and proclaims, in the presence and under the auspices of the Supreme Being, the following rights of man and of the citizen."

Article 1 declares: "Men are born free and remain free and equal in rights. Social distinctions may be based only upon considerations of general usefulness." Article 2 states that the purpose of every political association is to preserve humankind's inalienable rights, which are liberty, property, security, and resistance to oppression. "All sovereignty resides essentially in the nation," observes article 3.

Political rights are guaranteed in article 6, as is the equality of citizens before the law and for high office and public employment. Article 7 extends rights to those accused of crimes, and article 8 prohibits ex post facto laws. Article 9 states: "Since every man is presumed innocent until declared guilty, if arrest be deemed indispensable, all unnecessary severity for securing the suspect must be severely repressed by law." Article 10 provides that no person "is to be importuned because of his opinions, even religious ones, provided their manifestation does not disturb the public order established by law." Article 11 sets forth in part: "Free communication of ideas and opinions is one of the most precious rights of man."

Article 15 acknowledges the right to require an accounting of every public official; article 16 requires the guarantee of rights and the separation of powers for a constitution; and article 17 protects private property rights and calls for just compensation for any taking of private property for public use.

Thomas Paine, author of the revolutionary pamphlet *Common Sense* (1776), later wrote *Rights of Man* (1791) and served as a delegate to the French constitutional convention in 1792. In *Rights of Man,* he reproduced and commented on the French declaration, noting in one part: "A Declaration of Rights is, by reciprocity, a Declaration of Duties also. Whatever is my right as a man, is also the right of another; and it becomes my duty to guarantee, as well as to possess. . . . I will close the subject with the energetic apostrophe of M. de la Fayette—May this great monument raised to Liberty, serve as a lesson to the oppressor, and an example to the oppressed!"

Bills of Rights; Paine, Thomas

Declaration of the Rights of the Child

"Motherhood and childhood are entitled to special care and assistance," notes the Universal Declaration of Human Rights (1948). Affirming children's right to special protection, opportunities, and facilities for a healthy and normal development into adulthood, the Declaration of the Rights of the Child was adopted by the UN General Assembly on November 20, 1959. Thirty years later the General Assembly followed this document with the Convention on the Rights of the Child (1989), which entered into force in 1990.

Although the care and development of children have traditionally been the responsibility of their families, compulsory public education, national health care programs, government-supported facilities for orphans and homeless children, and programs for children with special needs had by 1959 made children's welfare a matter of national and international concern. The 1959 declaration attempts to formalize each nation's duties to children and their families based on the principles that "mankind owes the child the best it has to give" and that "the best interests of the child shall be the paramount consideration."

The preamble observes that "the child, by reason of his physical and mental immaturity, needs special safeguards and care, including appropriate legal protection, before as well as after birth." It notes that the declaration has been adopted "to the end that [each child] may have a happy childhood and enjoy for his own good and for the good of society the rights and freedoms herein set forth. . . ."

Principle 1 provides that the rights enumerated are to be enjoyed without "distinction or discrimination on account of race, color, sex, language, religion, political or other opinion, national or social origin, property, birth or other status, whether of himself or of his family." According to principle 2, "The child shall enjoy special protection, and shall be given opportunities and facilities, by law and by other means, to enable him to develop physically, mentally, morally, spiritually and socially in a healthy and normal manner and in conditions of freedom and dignity. In the enactment of laws for this purpose, the best interests of the child shall be the paramount consideration."

Principles 3 and 4, respectively, mandate that the child is "entitled from his birth to a name and a nationality" and "shall enjoy the benefits of social security," including prenatal and postnatal care, adequate nutrition, housing, recreation, and medical services. Principle 5 asserts that disabled children are entitled to "special treatment, education and care." Principle 6 advocates that a child, "wherever possible, grow up in the care and under the responsibility of his parents," but if necessary "public authorities shall have the duty to extend particular care to children without a family and to those without adequate means of support. Payment of State and other assistance towards the maintenance of children of large families is desirable."

Principle 7 addresses a child's right to "free and compulsory" education "to become a useful member of society" as well as a "full opportunity for play and recreation," while principle 8 provides that a child "shall in all circumstances be among the first to receive protection and relief." Under principle 9, children are to be protected from "neglect, cruelty and exploitation . . . [and] shall not be the subject of traffic [for prostitution, for example], in any form." This item also recommends that children "not be admitted to employment before an appropriate minimum age," adding that they "shall in no case be caused or permitted to engage in any occupation or employment which would prejudice [their] health or education, or interfere with [their] physical, mental or moral development."

The last item, principle 10, directs that children "shall be protected from practices which may foster racial, religious and any other form of discrimination. [They] shall be brought up in a spirit of understanding, tolerance, friendship among peoples, peace and universal brotherhood, and in full consciousness that [their] energies and talents should be devoted to the service of [others]."

United Nations Children's Fund (UNICEF), Three United Nations Plaza, New York, N.Y. 10017. (212-326-7000. ☎ 212-887-7465. ▯ addresses@unicef.org. ▯ www.unicef.org.

United Nations High Commissioner for Human Rights, 8–14 avenue de la Paix, 1211 Geneva 10, Switzerland. (41-22-917-9000. ☎ 41-22-917-9016. ▯ webadmin.hchr@unog.ch. ▯ www.unhchr.ch.

Adoption; African Charter on the Rights and Welfare of the Child; Children; Convention on the Rights of the Child; Declaration on Social and Legal Principles Relating to the Protection and Welfare of Children, with Special Reference to Foster Placement and Adoption Nationally and Internationally; Declaration on the Protection of Women and Children in Emergency and Armed Conflict; Families; United Nations Children's Fund (UNICEF); World Declaration on the Survival, Protection and Development of Children

Declaration on Environment and Development

See Rio Declaration on Environment and Development

Declaration on Fundamental Principles Concerning the Contribution of the Mass Media . . .

The Declaration on Fundamental Principles Concerning the Contribution of the Mass Media to Strengthening Peace and International Understanding, to the Promotion of Human Rights and to Countering Racialism, Apartheid and Incitement to War was adopted by the General Conference of the United Nations Educational, Scientific and Cultural Organization (UNESCO) on November 28, 1978. The UN General Assembly endorsed the declaration on December 10, 1978, in a resolution calling on the countries and organizations of the UN to promote its principles through every means at their disposal.

The declaration's aim is to make sure that the rights set forth in the International Covenant on Economic, Social and Cultural Rights (1966), such as equal rights for men and women, self-determination, and the rights to work, to the enjoyment of just and favorable conditions of work, to form trade unions, to social security, to an adequate standard of living and the highest attainable standard of physical and mental health, to education, and to participation in cultural life, are exercised in a nondiscriminatory manner. It also seeks to promote national recognition of "the benefits to be derived from the encouragement and development of international contacts and cooperation in the scientific and cultural fields," as contained in the covenant's part II, article 15, paragraph 4. While expressly recognizing freedom of opinion, expression, and information, however, the declaration underscores the importance of the mass media in ensuring wide distribution of accurate information and counteracting many types of propaganda against human rights.

The preamble begins by recalling that "by virtue of its Constitution the purpose of UNESCO is to 'contribute to peace and security by promoting collaboration among the nations through education, science and culture in order to further universal respect for justice, for the rule of law and for the human rights and fundamental freedoms' (Art. I, 1), and that to realize this purpose the organization will strive 'to promote the free flow of ideas by word and image' (Art. I, 2)." It goes on to recognize "the Universal Declaration of Human Rights [1948] . . . and particularly article 19 thereof, which provides that 'everyone has the right to freedom of opinion and expression; this right includes freedom to hold opinions without interference and to seek, receive and impart information and ideas through any media and regardless of frontiers'; and the International Covenant on Civil and Political Rights [1966] . . . , article 19 of which proclaims the same principles and article 20 of which condemns incitement to war, the advocacy of national, racial or religious hatred and any form of discrimination, hostility or violence. . . ."

Article I emphasizes the mass media's contribution to the declaration's goals, stating: "This contribution will be more effective to the extent that the information reflects the different aspects of the subject dealt with." According to article II: "1. The exercise of freedom of opinion, expression and information, recognized as an integral part of human rights and fundamental freedoms, is a vital factor in the strengthening of peace and international understanding." Paragraph 2 requires that public access to information "be guaranteed by the diversity of the sources and means of information available to it. . . ." Adds paragraph 4: "If the mass media are to be in a position to promote the principles of this Declaration in their activities, it is essential that journalists and other agents of the mass media, in their own country or abroad, be assured of protection guaranteeing them the best conditions for the exercise of their profession."

Under article III, the mass media can support the principles of the declaration "by disseminating information on the aims, aspirations, cultures and needs of all peoples, contribute to [the elimination of] ignorance and misunderstanding between peoples, to make nationals of a country sensitive to the needs and desires of others, to ensure the respect of the rights and dignity of all nations, all peoples and all individuals without [discrimination] . . . and to draw attention to the great evils which afflict humanity, such as poverty, malnutrition and diseases. . . ."

"The mass media," states article IV, "have an essential part to play in the education of young people in a spirit of peace, justice, freedom, mutual respect and understanding. . . ." Article V reiterates the need for information to reflect all points of view; article VI urges a correction in the "inequalities in the flow of information to and from developing countries"; and article VII focuses on "disseminating more widely all of the information concerning the universally accepted objectives and principles which are the bases of the resolutions" adopted by UN organs.

Articles VIII, IX, and X, respectively, address the training of journalists, the need "for the international community to contribute to the creation of the conditions for a free flow and wider and more balanced dissemination of information . . . ," and the need "to create and maintain throughout the world the conditions which make it possible . . . to achieve the objectives of this Declaration." Article XI calls on UN members "to guarantee the existence of favorable conditions for the operation of the mass media, in conformity with the provisions of the Universal Declaration of Human Rights and . . . the International Covenant on Civil and Political Rights."

United Nations Educational, Scientific and Cultural Organization (UNESCO), 7 place de Fontenoy, 75352 Paris 07 SP, France. (33-145-68-10-00. 🖷 33-145-67-16-90. 🖷 addresses@unesco.org. 🖷 www.unesco.org.

Apartheid; Convention on the Elimination of All Forms of Racial Discrimination; Convention on the International Right of Correction; Expression; Information; Opinion; The Press; Race Discrimination; Speech; War

Declaration on Human Settlements

See Vancouver Declaration on Human Settlements

Declaration on Principles of International Law Concerning Friendly Relations and Co-operation among States . . .

On October 24, 1970—the twenty-fifth anniversary of the United Nations—the UN General Assembly adopted the Declaration on Principles of International Law Concerning Friendly Relations and Co-operation among States in Accordance with the Charter of the United Nations. In attempting to promote the rule of law throughout the world and to strengthen world peace, the declaration converts concepts in the UN charter (1945) regarding how nations are to deal peacefully with one another into basic principles of international law, applicable to all nations. The fact that conflicts among nations have continued to occur does not diminish the importance of the declaration's lofty ideals.

The resolution approving the declaration begins by emphasizing "the paramount importance of the Charter of the United Nations for the maintenance of international peace and security and for the development of friendly relations and co-operation among States." In the Annex containing the declaration, the General Assembly notes that "the peoples of the United Nations are determined to practice tolerance and live together in peace with one another as good neighbors" and points out "the importance of maintaining and strengthening international peace founded upon freedom, equality, justice and respect for fundamental human rights. . . ."

The Annex goes on to itemize seven "progressive" principles proclaimed by the General Assembly that should be codified in international law, and then, in the following part, discusses each principle in more detail, providing rules for their interpretation and application.

The principles and excerpts from the commentary are as follows:

Principle (a) asserts that "States shall refrain in their international relations from the threat or use of force against the territorial integrity or political independence of any State, or in any other manner inconsistent with the purposes of the United Nations." The declaration observes that every nation "has the duty to refrain from any forcible action which deprives peoples ... of their right to self-determination and freedom and independence.... All States," it adds, "shall comply in good faith with their obligations under the generally recognized principles and rules of international law with respect to the maintenance of international peace and security, and shall endeavor to make the United Nations security system based on the Charter more effective."

According to principle (b), "States shall settle their international disputes by peaceful means. . . ." The commentary admonishes that nations "shall accordingly seek early and just settlement of their international disputes by negotiation, inquiry, mediation, conciliation, arbitration, judicial settlement, resort to regional agencies or arrangements or other peaceful means of their choice."

Principle (c) mandates that nations have the "duty not to intervene in matters within the domestic jurisdiction of any [other] State, in accordance with the Charter." The text adds that the "use of force to deprive peoples of their national identity constitutes a violation of their inalienable rights and of the principle of non-intervention."

Nations have the duty, under principle (d), "to co-operate with one another in accordance with the Charter." Comments recommend that nations "co-operate in the economic, social and cultural fields as well as in the field of science and technology and for the promotion of international cultural and educational progress. States should co-operate in the promotion of economic growth throughout the world, especially that of the developing countries."

Principle (e) underscores national obligations to observe "the principle of equal rights and self-determination of peoples." The document notes that every country "has the duty to promote through joint and separate action universal respect for and observance of human rights and fundamental freedoms in accordance with the Charter."

Each nation must adhere to the "principle of sovereign equality of States," notes principle (f). The observation is made that sovereignty includes the following elements: juridical equality, "rights inherent in full sovereignty," "the duty to respect the personality of other States," the inviolability of "territorial integrity and political independence," "the right [of a nation] freely to choose and develop its political, social, economic and cultural systems," and "the duty to comply fully and in good faith with its international obligations and to live in peace with other States."

According to principle (g), "States shall fulfill in good faith the obligations assumed by them in accordance with the Charter; so as to secure their more effective application within the international community [to] promote the realization of the purposes of the United Nations." The commentary requires, among other things: "Where obligations arising under international agreements are in conflict with the obligations of Members of the United Nations under the Charter of the United Nations, the obligations under the Charter shall prevail."

"In their interpretation and application," adds the declaration's second part, "the above principles are interrelated and each principle should be construed in the context of the other principles." The document concludes by stating that the "principles of the Charter which are embodied in this Declaration constitute basic principles of international law, and consequently [the General Assembly] appeals to all States to be guided by these principles in their international conduct and to develop their mutual relations on the basis of the strict observance of these principles."

United Nations, One United Nations Plaza, New York, N.Y. 10017. (212-963-4475. 🖷 212-963-0071. 🖳 inquiries@un.org. 🖳 www. un.org.

Charter of the United Nations; Equality; Fundamental Rights; International Law; Justice; Peace; Rule of Law; Self-Determination; Sovereignty; United Nations

Declaration on Social and Legal Principles Relating to the Protection and Welfare of Children . . .

Children are among the most vulnerable members of society, even more so when the protection and care traditionally given by their families is not available. Recognizing the importance of protecting the rights and well-being of children in foster or adoptive care, including sparing them from abuse or neglect by the government itself, the UN General Assembly adopted a declaration to this effect on December 3, 1986. The aim of the Declaration on Social and Legal Principles Relating to the Protection and Welfare of Children, with Special Reference to Foster Placement and Adoption Nationally and Internationally is to provide international guidance for the care and placement of children who, for various reasons, cannot be cared for by their parents or other relatives. The declaration came almost three decades after the General Assembly adopted the Declaration of the Rights of the Child (1959) and three years before its Convention on the Rights of the Child (1989).

The declaration begins by expressing concern over "the large number of children who are abandoned or become orphans owing to violence, internal disturbance, armed conflicts, natural disasters, economic crises or social problems" and observing that "in all foster placement and adoption procedures the best interests of the child should be the paramount consideration." It adds that "only where a particular institution is recognized and regulated by the domestic law of a State would the provisions of this Declaration relating to that institution be relevant and that such provisions would in no way affect the existing institutions in other legal systems," such as those available under Islamic law, for example. The prefatory statement concludes by noting that the universal principles enumerated in the document "do not impose on States such legal institutions as foster placement or adoption."

The first part, A, General Family and Child Welfare, article 1, urges that every nation "should give a high priority to family and child welfare." Articles 2 and 3, respectively, provide that child welfare "depends upon good family welfare" and that a child's first priority "is to be cared for by his or her own parents." "When care by the child's own parents is unavailable or inappropriate," adds article 4, "care by relatives of the child's parents, by another substitute—foster or adoptive—family or, if necessary, by an appropriate institution should be considered."

"In all matters relating to the placement of a child outside the care of the child's own parents," states article 5, "the best interests of the child, particularly his or her need for affection and right to security and continuing care, should be the paramount consideration." According to article 6, "Persons responsible for foster placement or adoption procedures should have professional or other appropriate training." Article 7 requires that governments "determine the adequacy of their national child welfare services and consider appropriate actions."

Under article 8, the child must "at all times have a name, a nationality and a legal representative. The child should not, as a result of foster placement, adoption or any alternative regime, be deprived of his or her name, nationality or legal representative unless the child thereby acquires a new name, nationality or legal representative." Adds article 9: "The need of a foster or an adopted child to know about his or her background should be recognized by persons responsible for the child's care unless this is contrary to the child's best interests."

In section B, which addresses foster placement, article 10 requires that such care "be regulated by law." Section C is devoted to adoption. According to article 13, "The primary aim of adoption is to provide the child who cannot be cared for by his or her own parents with a permanent family." Articles 14 through 16, respectively, address the "most appropriate environment for the child," "adequate counseling" for all parties, and the need for "prospective adoptive parents [to] be observed by child welfare agencies or services prior to the adoption." Article 16 also suggests legislation to "ensure that the child is recognized in law as

a member of the adoptive family and enjoys all the rights pertinent thereto."

Intercountry adoption as an option is discussed in article 17, and government policy and laws regarding "effective supervision for the protection of children involved in intercountry adoption" are covered in article 18. Article 19 directs that policies and laws prohibit "abduction and . . . any other act for illicit placement of children." Articles 20 and 21, the last two articles, urge safeguards and standards for intercountry adoption placements as well as special precautions where agents for prospective parents are involved.

United Nations High Commissioner for Human Rights, 8–14 avenue de la Paix, 1211 Geneva 10, Switzerland. (41-22-917-9000. 🖨 41-22-917-9016. 🖳 webadmin.hchr@unog.ch. 🖳 www.unhchr.ch.

Adoption; African Charter on the Rights and Welfare of the Child; Children; Convention on the Rights of the Child; Declaration of the Rights of the Child; Families; United Nations Children's Fund (UNICEF)

Declaration on Social Progress and Development

Social rights are generally called second-generation rights, because they are a nation's obligations to provide benefits to its citizens, rather than fundamental rights—freedom from discrimination and due process of law, for example—that protect individuals from government actions. Most social rights—such as freedom from hunger, national health care, and social security—are contingent on a nation's wealth and conditions from population size and level of technological development to its general social and political climate.

The Universal Declaration of Human Rights (1948) called the realization of social rights, along with economic and cultural rights, indispensable for every member of society and for the development of each individual's personality. Nearly two decades later, the International Covenant on Economic, Social and Cultural Rights (1966) specifically addressed social rights. To emphasize the need to improve social programs to better human life, the UN General Assembly on December 11, 1969, adopted the Declaration on Social Progress and Development, which observes that "international peace and security on the one hand, and social progress and economic development on the other, are closely interdependent and influence each other."

The lengthy declaration begins by recalling the pledge made by UN members in the Charter of the United Nations (1945) "to take joint and separate action in co-operation with the Organization to promote higher standards of living, full employment and conditions of economic and social progress and development." It goes on to refer to "the standards already set for social progress in the constitutions, conventions, recommendations and resolutions of the International Labor Organization, the Food and Agricultural Organization of the United Nations, the United Nations Educational, Scientific and Cultural Organization [UNESCO], the World Health Organization, the United Nations Children's Fund [UNICEF] and of other organizations. . . ."

The document emphasizes that "the primary responsibility for the development of the developing countries rests on those countries themselves" and acknowledges "the pressing need to narrow and eventually close the gap in the standards of living between economically more advanced and developing countries and, to that end, that Member States shall have the responsibility to pursue internal and external policies designed to promote social development throughout the world, and in particular to assist developing countries to accelerate their economic growth." Stating that it recognizes "the urgency of devoting to works of peace and social progress resources being expended on armaments and wasted on conflict and destruction," the declaration suggests that "the primary task of all States and international organizations is to eliminate from the life of society all evils and obstacles to social progress, particularly such evils as inequality, exploitation, war, colonialism and racism." The introduction ends by calling for "national and international action for [the declaration's] use as a common basis for social development policies."

"All peoples and all human beings, without distinction as to race, color, sex, language, religion, nationality, ethnic origin, family or social status, or political or other conviction," proclaims part I, Principles, article 1, "shall have the right to live in dignity and freedom and to enjoy the fruits of social progress and should, on their part, contribute to it." According to article 2: "Social progress and development shall be founded on respect for the dignity and value of the human person and shall ensure the promotion of human rights and social justice, which requires: (a) The immediate and final elimination of all forms of inequality, exploitation of peoples and individuals, colonialism and racism, including nazism and *apartheid,* and all other policies and ideologies opposed to the purposes and principles of the United Nations; (b) The recognition and effective implementation of civil and political rights as well as of economic, social and cultural rights without any discrimination."

Article 3 sets forth certain "primary conditions of social progress and development," including: "(a) National independence based on the right of people to self-determination; (b) The principle of non-interference in the internal affairs of States; . . . (d) Permanent sovereignty of each nation over its natural wealth and resources; (e) The right and responsibility of each State and, as far as they are concerned, each nation and people to determine freely its own objectives of social development, to set its own priorities and to decide in conformity with the principles of the Charter of the

United Nations the means and methods of their achievement without any external interference. . . ."

Article 4 calls for assistance and protection for the "family as a basic unit of society," noting that "[p]arents have the exclusive right to determine freely and responsibly the number and spacing of their children." Article 5 addresses "the full utilization of human resources" required for social progress and development, while article 6 predicates social development on everyone's right "to work and the free choice of employment." Articles 7, 8, and 9, respectively, focus on the need for "rapid expansion of national income and wealth and their equitable distribution among all members of society"; the government's "primary role and ultimate responsibility of ensuring the social progress and well-being of its people"; and international recognition "of the common interest of all nations in the exploration, conservation, use and exploitation, exclusively for peaceful purposes" of areas of the environment, such as "outer space and the sea-bed and ocean floor . . . , beyond the limits of national jurisdiction, in accordance with the . . . Charter of the United Nations."

Part II, Objectives, spells out how social progress and development are to be achieved. Article 10 lists a number of rights and goals, including the right to work and form trade unions, as well as promotion of full productive employment; the elimination of hunger, malnutrition, and poverty; health protection for the entire population, "if possible free of charge"; the eradication of illiteracy; the right to universal access to culture, free compulsory education, and adequate housing; and the sharing of scientific and technological advances.

Part III, Means and Methods, focuses on planning and the adoption of specific measures to attain the declaration's goals. Article 26 provides for compensation for damages, "be they social or economic in nature . . . caused as a result of aggression and of illegal occupation of territory by the aggressor." The last item, article 27, addresses disarmament and urges "the complete prohibition of tests of nuclear weapons, the prohibition of the development, production and stockpiling of chemical and bacteriological (biological) weapons and the prevention of the pollution of oceans and inland waters by nuclear wastes."

United Nations High Commissioner for Human Rights, 8–14 avenue de la Paix, 1211 Geneva 10, Switzerland. (41-22-917-9000. 🖶 41-22-917-9016. 🖳 webadmin.hchr@unog.ch. 🖳 www.unhchr.ch.

Development; Economic Rights; Environment; Health; International Covenant on Economic, Social and Cultural Rights; International Labor Organization; Peace; Social Rights; Sovereignty; United Nations Children's Fund (UNICEF); United Nations Educational, Scientific and Cultural Organization (UNESCO); Weapons; World Health Organization

Declaration on Territorial Asylum

Sovereign jurisdictions have long granted protection to persons fleeing persecution in other countries. The right of territorial asylum—refuge in another nation, as opposed to diplomatic asylum in an embassy in one's own country—is recognized in a number of international human rights documents, including the Universal Declaration of Human Rights (1948) and the American Convention on Human Rights (1969). The law of asylum was codified by the International Law Commission in 1959, and then in 1966 the UN General Assembly adopted a resolution stating a need for a declaration on the right of asylum. Drafted by a legal committee of the General Assembly, the Declaration on Territorial Asylum was adopted on December 14, 1967. The right of territorial asylum continues to be claimed by millions of refugees fleeing persecution, including many Kosovars who fled the ethnic cleansing carried out in 1999 by Serbian government forces.

The declaration begins by reiterating that the Universal Declaration of Human Rights (1948), article 14, mandates that "[e]veryone has the right to seek and to enjoy in other countries asylum from persecution." It further recognizes that "the grant of asylum by a State to persons entitled to invoke article 14 . . . is a peaceful and humanitarian act and that, as such, it cannot be regarded as unfriendly by any other State." The document then recommends that, "without prejudice to existing instruments dealing with asylum and the status of refugees and stateless persons, States should base themselves in their practices relating to territorial asylum on the following principles."

Article 1 declares: "1. Asylum granted by a State, in the exercise of its sovereignty, to persons entitled to invoke article 14 of the Universal Declaration of Human Rights, including persons struggling against colonialism, shall be respected by all other States. 2. The right to seek and to enjoy asylum may not be invoked by any person with respect to whom there are serious reasons for considering that he has committed a crime against peace, a war crime or a crime against humanity, as defined in the international instruments drawn up to make provision in respect of such crimes. 3. It shall rest with the State granting asylum to evaluate the grounds for the grant of asylum."

According to article 2, persons needing asylum are "of concern to the international community. Where a State finds difficulty in granting or continuing to grant asylum," it adds, "States individually or jointly or through the United Nations shall consider, in a spirit of international solidarity, appropriate measures to lighten the burden on that State." Article 3 bars countries from rejecting asylum seekers at their borders or expelling them once in their territory if such persons "may be subjected to persecution." Exceptions are permitted in the case of national security and the safety of the receiving country's population, "as in the case of a mass influx of

persons." Article 3 continues by recommending that conditional or provisional asylum be provided and that those seeking asylum be allowed to proceed to another country rather than being rejected or expelled.

Article 4, the final item, mandates: "States granting asylum shall not permit persons who have received asylum to engage in activities contrary to the purposes and principles of the United Nations."

United Nations High Commissioner for Human Rights, 8–14 avenue de la Paix, 1211 Geneva 10, Switzerland. (41-22-917-9000. ▤ 41-22-917-9016. ▣ webadmin.hchr@unog.ch. ▣ www.unhchr.ch.

United Nations High Commissioner for Refugees, C.P. 2500, 1211 Geneva 2, Switzerland. (41-22-729-8111. ▤ 41-22-731-9546. ▣ hqpioo@unhcr.ch. ▣ www.unhcr.ch.

Asylum; Convention Relating to the Status of Refugees; Deportation; Diplomats and Consuls; Expulsion; Forced Eviction; Immigrants; High Commissioner for Refugees; Nationality; *Refoulement;* Refugees; Statelessness; Territorial Jurisdiction

Declaration on the Control of Drug Trafficking and Drug Abuse

In 1946 the United Nations, a year after its creation, gained primary responsibility for the control of international drug trafficking under a protocol whereby countries that had concluded narcotics agreements before World War II transferred to it the authority previously granted to the League of Nations. Within the UN, the Economic and Social Council (ECOSOC) was given direct responsibility for drug trafficking.

By 1961 the Single Convention on Narcotic Drugs had been adopted to govern means of interdicting illicit drug traffic while protecting the legal trade in drugs required for medical and scientific use. Over the next two decades the increasing flow and use of illicit drugs, together with related national and international crime problems, resulted in the UN General Assembly's adoption of the Declaration on the Control of Drug Trafficking and Drug Abuse on December 14, 1984.

The declaration begins by noting the General Assembly's awareness that "the international community has expressed grave concern at the fact that trafficking in narcotics and drug abuse constitutes an obstacle to the physical and moral well-being of peoples and of youth in particular." It goes on to note "the urgency of preventing and punishing the illicit demand for, abuse of and illicit production of and traffic in drugs." The preamble adds that "the Quito Declaration against Traffic in Narcotic Drugs of 11 August 1984 and the New York Declaration against Drug Trafficking and the Illicit Use of Drugs of 1 October 1984 recognize the international nature of this problem and emphasize that it should be solved with the firm support of the entire international community."

"Drug trafficking and drug abuse," proclaims paragraph 1, "are extremely serious problems which, owing to their magnitude, scope and widespread pernicious effects, have become an international criminal activity demanding urgent attention and maximum priority." Paragraph 2 adds that the "illegal production of, illicit demand for, abuse of and illicit trafficking in drugs impede economic and social progress, constitute a grave threat to the security and development of many countries and peoples and should be combated by all moral, legal and institutional means, at the national, regional and international levels."

According to paragraph 3, "The eradication of trafficking in narcotic drugs is the collective responsibility of all States, especially those affected by problems relating to illicit production, trafficking or abuse." UN members are called on in paragraph 4 to "utilize the legal instruments against the illicit production of and demand for, abuse of and illicit traffic in drugs and adopt additional measures to counter new manifestations of this shameful and heinous crime." Paragraph 5, the last item, requests UN members to "undertake to intensify efforts and to coordinate strategies aimed at the control and eradication of the complex problem of drug trafficking and drug abuse through programs including economic, social and cultural alternatives."

Economic and Social Council (ECOSOC), One United Nations Plaza, Room s-2963, New York, N.Y. 10017. (212-963-4640. 212-963-5935. esa@un.org. www.ecosoc.org.

Drugs; Economic and Social Council (ECOSOC)

Declaration on the Elimination of All Forms of Intolerance and of Discrimination Based on Religion or Belief

Strongly held beliefs make it difficult for many people to tolerate the different beliefs and opinions of others. But the clash of ideas ultimately fuels the progress of humanity, and tolerance of the ideas and beliefs of others—rather than its opposite, intolerance—makes those clashes pos-

sible as well as nonviolent. Discrimination on the basis of religion or personal beliefs unjustly punishes a person for his or her thoughts and conscience.

The Universal Declaration of Human Rights (1948) and the International Covenant on Civil and Political Rights (1966) and Interntional Covenant on Economic, Social and Cultural Rights (1966), together with many other international human rights documents and national constitutions, mandate freedom from discrimination based on religious and other beliefs. The UN General Assembly underscored this right on November 25, 1981, when it adopted the Declaration on the Elimination of All Forms of Intolerance and of Discrimination Based on Religion or Belief.

The declaration begins by observing that infringements of the right to freedom of thought, conscience, religion, and belief "have brought, directly or indirectly, wars and great suffering to mankind, especially where they serve as a means of foreign interference in the internal affairs of other States and amount to kindling hatred between peoples and nations." It adds that "religion or belief, for anyone who professes either, is one of the fundamental elements in his conception of life and that freedom of religion or belief should be fully respected and guaranteed." The document then acknowledges that "it is essential to promote understanding, tolerance and respect in matters relating to freedom of religion and belief and to ensure that the use of religion or belief for ends inconsistent with the Charter of the United Nations [1945], other relevant instruments of the United Nations and the purposes and principles of the present Declaration is inadmissible.... [F]reedom of religion and belief," it continues, "should also contribute to the attainment of the goals of world peace, social justice and friendship among peoples and to the elimination of ideologies or practices of colonialism and racial discrimination." The preamble concludes by expressing the General Assembly's concern over "manifestations of intolerance and ... the existence of discrimination in matters of religion or belief still in evidence in some areas of the world."

Article 1 declares: "1. Everyone shall have the right to freedom of thought, conscience and religion. This right shall include freedom to have a religion or whatever belief of his choice, and freedom, either individually or in community with others and in public or private, to manifest his religion or belief in worship, observance, practice and teaching. 2. No one shall be subject to coercion which would impair his freedom to have a religion or belief of his choice. 3. Freedom to manifest one's religion or belief may be subject only to such limitations as are prescribed by law and are necessary to protect public safety, order, health or morals or the fundamental rights and freedoms of others."

Discrimination "by any State, institution, group of persons or person on the grounds of religion or other belief" is prohibited under article 2, which defines the expression *intolerance and discrimination based on religion or belief* as "any distinction, exclusion, restriction or preference based on religion or belief and having as its purpose or as its effect nullification or impairment of the recognition, enjoyment or exercise of human rights and fundamental freedoms on an equal basis." According to article 3, such discrimination "constitutes an affront to human dignity and a disavowal of the principles of the Charter of the United Nations. . . ." Article 4 directs the countries of the world to "take effective measures to prevent and eliminate discrimination on the grounds of religion or belief."

Article 5 addresses the rights of parents and children with respect to, among other things, religious education, tolerance, and universal brotherhood, while article 6 enumerates the panoply of rights entailed by freedom of thought, conscience, religion, and belief, among them: "(a) To worship or assemble in connection with a religion or belief, and to establish and maintain places for these purposes; (b) To establish and maintain appropriate charitable or humanitarian institutions; (c) To [have] materials related to the rites or customs of a religion or belief; (d) To write, issue and disseminate relevant publications . . . ; (e) To teach a religion or belief in places suitable for these purposes; . . . (h) To observe days of rest and to celebrate holidays and ceremonies in accordance with one's religion or belief. . . ."

Article 7 mandates that the "rights and freedoms set forth in the present Declaration shall be [codified] in national legislation. . . ." Article 8, the final item, declares: "Nothing in the present Declaration shall be construed as restricting or derogating from any right defined in the Universal Declaration of Human Rights and the International Covenants on Human Rights."

United Nations High Commissioner for Human Rights, 8–14 avenue de la Paix, 1211 Geneva 10, Switzerland. ☎ 41-22-917-9000. 🖷 41-22-917-9016. 🖳 webadmin.hchr@unog.ch. 🖳 www.unhchr.ch.

Conscience; Opinion; Religion; Separation of Church and State; Thought; Tolerance

Declaration on the Elimination of All Forms of Racial Discrimination

Discrimination on the basis of race has plagued humankind throughout history, bringing suffering both to those people who have been discriminated against and to those who, on the basis of perceived distinctions, have treated others as unequal or less than fully human. In 1950 the United Nations Educational, Scientific and Cultural Organization (UNESCO) concluded that "'race' is not so much a biological phenomenon as a social myth." On November 20, 1963, the UN General Assembly adopted the Declaration on the Elimination of All Forms of Racial Discrimination, which affirms the fundamental equality of all human beings and confirms that discrimination on the basis of race, color, or ethnic origin is an offense to human dignity and a contravention of the basic principles of the United Nations. The declaration was followed two years later with the International Convention on the Elimination of All Forms of Racial Discrimination (1965), which entered into force in 1969.

The declaration begins with a reminder that "the Charter of the United Nations [1945] is based on the principles of the dignity and equality of all human beings and seeks, among other basic objectives, to achieve international cooperation in promoting and encouraging respect for human rights and fundamental freedoms for all without distinction as to race, sex, language or religion." After pointing out that the UN has "condemned colonialism and all practices of segregation and discrimination associated therewith," the document observes that "any doctrine of racial differentiation or superiority is scientifically false, morally condemnable, socially unjust and dangerous, and that there is no justification for racial discrimination either in theory or in practice." The opening concludes by noting alarm at "the manifestations of racial discrimination still in evidence in some areas of the world" and stating that "racial discrimination harms not only those who are its objects but also those who practice it."

"Discrimination between human beings on the ground of race, color or ethnic origin," declares article 1, "is an offense to human dignity and shall be condemned as a denial of the principles of the Charter of the United Nations, as a violation of the human rights and fundamental freedoms proclaimed in the Universal Declaration of Human Rights [1948], as an obstacle to friendly and peaceful relations among nations and as a fact capable of disturbing peace and security among peoples."

According to article 2: "1. No State, institution, group or individual shall make any discrimination whatsoever in matters of human rights and fundamental freedoms in the treatment of persons, groups of persons or institutions on the ground of race, color or ethnic origin. 2. No State shall encourage, advocate or lend its support, through police action or otherwise, to any [such] discrimination. . . . 3. Special concrete measures shall be taken in appropriate circumstances in order to secure adequate development or protection of individuals belonging to certain racial groups with the object of ensuring the full enjoyment by such individuals of human rights and fundamental freedoms. These measures shall in no circumstances have as a consequence the maintenance of unequal or separate rights for different racial groups."

Article 3 directs particular attention to "civil rights, access to citizenship, education, religion, employment, occupation and housing" as well as "equal access to any place or facility intended for use by the general public. . . ." Article 4 addresses effective measures to be taken by all nations to eliminate race discrimination; article 5 calls for an end to "policies of racial segregation and especially policies of *apartheid* . . ."; and article 6 bars discrimination in voting and participation in government. Article 7 confirms the right of everyone "to equality before the law and to equal justice under the law," as well as "the right to an effective remedy and protection against any discrimination he may suffer . . . through independent national tribunals competent to deal with such matters."

Teaching, education, and information to counteract race discrimination and prejudice are mandated in article 8. Article 9 condemns propaganda based on ideas or theories of racial superiority and calls for punishing incitement to racial violence, while article 10 pledges the UN, specialized agencies, national governments, and nongovernmental organizations to "do all in their power to promote energetic action which . . . will make possible the abolition of all forms of racial discrimination." The last item, article 11, directs every nation to "promote respect for and observance of human rights and fundamental freedoms. . . ."

United Nations High Commissioner for Human Rights, 8–14 avenue de la Paix, 1211 Geneva 10, Switzerland. (41-22-917-9000. 🖶 41-22-917-9016. 🖳 webadmin.hchr@unog.ch. 🖳 www.unhchr.ch.

☞

Apartheid; Civil Rights; Committee on the Elimination of Racial Discrimination; Discrimination; International Convention on the Elimination of All Forms of Racial Discrimination; Race Discrimination

Declaration on the Elimination of Discrimination against Women

The first international human rights document to mention the equal rights of women and men was the Charter of the United Nations (1945), which was followed a year later by the creation of the Commission on the Status of Women by the Economic and Social Council (ECOSOC). Then in 1948 the Universal Declaration of Human Rights proclaimed that "[a]ll human beings are born free and equal in dignity and rights, [and e]veryone is entitled to all the rights and freedoms set forth in this Declaration, without distinction of any kind," including on the basis of sex. That same year three other human rights documents addressed the rights of women: the two inter-American declarations granting civil rights and

political rights to women and the International Labor Organization's Night Work (Women) Convention. These were soon supplemented with additional conventions regarding the political rights of women (1952), the nationality of married women (1957), and marriage (1962), in which wives were expressly made equal to husbands.

However, in the face of evidence that women were still being discriminated against in many of the basic arenas of life—politics, economic opportunities, and social and cultural activities—the UN General Assembly on November 7, 1967, took a further step to advance women's rights by adopting the Declaration on the Elimination of Discrimination against Women. The declaration begins by noting that despite adoption of other basic human rights documents "and despite the progress made in the matter of equality of rights, there continues to exist considerable discrimination against women." It goes on to observe that such discrimination "is incompatible with human dignity and with the welfare of the family and of society, prevents [women's] participation, on equal terms with men, in the political, social, economic and cultural life of their countries and is an obstacle to the full development of the potentialities of women in the service of their countries and of humanity."

"Discrimination against women, denying or limiting as it does their equality of rights with men," notes article 1, "is fundamentally unjust and constitutes an offense against human dignity." According to article 2, "All appropriate measures shall be taken to abolish existing laws, customs, regulations and practices which are discriminatory against women, and to establish adequate legal protection for equal rights of men and women, in particular: (a) The principle of equality of rights shall be embodied in the constitution or otherwise guaranteed by law; (b) The international instruments of the United Nations and the specialized agencies relating to the elimination of discrimination against women shall be ratified or acceded to and fully implemented as soon as practicable."

Article 3 calls for the education of public opinion and eradication of practices "based on the idea of the inferiority of women." Article 4 focuses on voting and political rights; article 5 affirms equal rights for women with respect to nationality; and article 6 sets forth a number of specific rights, including equal rights in property ownership, marriage, and parenting; it also prohibits child marriage and "the betrothal of young girls before puberty." Article 7 mandates that "[a]ll provisions of penal codes which constitute discrimination against women shall be repealed." Article 8 urges that all appropriate measures, including legislation, be taken "to combat all forms of traffic in women and exploitation of prostitution of women."

Equal educational opportunities are addressed in article 9, while article 10 focuses on economic and social equality but includes some special protections in the case of maternity and the nature of work to be performed by women. The last item, article 11, urges governments, nongovernmental organizations, and individuals "to do all in their power to promote the implementation of the principles contained in this Declaration."

In 1979 the UN went a step further by adopting the Convention on the Elimination of All Forms of Discrimination against Women, which created the Committee on the Elimination of Discrimination against Women to monitor implementation of its provisions.

United Nations High Commissioner for Human Rights, 8–14 avenue de la Paix, 1211 Geneva 10, Switzerland. ☏ 41-22-917-9000. 🖷 41-22-917-9016. 🖳 webadmin.hchr@unog.ch. 🖳 www.unhchr.ch.

☞

Committee on the Elimination of Discrimination against Women; Convention for the Suppression of the Traffic in Persons and of the Exploitation of the Prostitution of Others; Convention on Consent to Marriage, Minimum Age for Marriage and Registration of Marriages; Convention on the Elimination of All Forms of Discrimination against Women; Convention on the Political Rights of Women; Declaration on the Elimination of Violence against Women; Inter-American Convention on the Granting of Civil Rights to Women; Inter-American Convention on the Granting of Political Rights to Women; Maternity; Sex Discrimination; Women

Declaration on the Elimination of Violence against Women

The United Nations has undertaken a number of initiatives on behalf of women's rights in addition to recognizing the equality of women and men in the Universal Declaration of Human Rights (1948) as well as in the International Covenant on Civil and Political Rights (1966) and the International Covenant on Economic, Social and Cultural Rights (1966). In 1952 the UN General Assembly adopted the Convention on the Political Rights of Women, followed by the Convention on the Nationality of Married Women in 1957; in 1979 the Convention on the Elimination of All Forms of Discrimination against Women was added to its roster of documents on women.

Recognizing that women's basic human rights are denied by violence against them—a historical manifestation of the unequal physical, and often social, power of women and men—the General Assembly unanimously adopted the Declaration on the Elimination of Violence against Women on December 20, 1993. The declaration acknowledges that the domination and discrimination that often breed violence against women have prevented their full advancement. It singles out certain particularly vulnerable women, among them those who are minorities, indigent, refugees, institutionalized, prisoners, children, elderly, disabled, and besieged during armed conflicts.

The declaration begins by noting that the General Assembly recognizes "the urgent need for the universal application to women of the rights and principles with regard to equality, security, liberty, integrity and dignity of all human beings." It then notes its concern "that violence against women is an obstacle to the achievement of equality, development and peace, as recognized in the Nairobi Forward-looking Strategies for the Advancement of Women (1984), in which a set of measures to combat violence against women was recommended, and to the full implementation of the Convention on the Elimination of All Forms of Discrimination against Women, ... [and] ... that in light of the above there is a need for a clear and comprehensive definition of violence against women, a clear statement of the rights to be applied to ensure the elimination of violence against women in all its forms, a commitment by States in respect of their responsibilities, and a commitment by the international community at large to the elimination of violence against women...."

Article 1 defines *violence against women* as "any act of gender-based violence that results in, or is likely to result in, physical, sexual or psychological harm or suffering to women, including threats of such acts, coercion or arbitrary deprivation of liberty, whether occurring in public or in private life." According to article 2: "Violence against women shall be understood to encompass, but not be limited to, the following: a) Physical, sexual and psychological violence occurring in the family, including battering, sexual abuse of female children in the household, dowry-related violence, marital rape, female genital mutilation and other traditional practices harmful to women, non-spousal violence and violence related to exploitation; b) Physical, sexual and psychological violence occurring within the general community, including rape, sexual abuse, sexual harassment and intimidation at work, in educational institutions and elsewhere, trafficking in women and forced prostitution; c) Physical, sexual and psychological violence perpetrated or condoned by the State, wherever it occurs."

The rights of women are catalogued in article 3. They include "all human rights and fundamental freedoms in the political, economic, social, cultural, civil or any other field," such as the right to life, equality, liberty and security of the person, equal protection under the law, freedom from all forms of discrimination, the highest health standard attainable, just and favorable conditions of work, and freedom from torture or other cruel, inhuman, or degrading treatment or punishment.

In article 4 signatory nations are urged to "condemn violence against women and ... not invoke any custom, tradition or religious consideration to avoid their obligations with respect to its elimination." The article lists seventeen ways to pursue the declaration's goals, including "Exercising due diligence to prevent, investigate and, in accordance with national legislation, punish acts of violence against women ...; Developing ... preventive approaches and all those measures of a legal, political, administrative and cultural nature that promote the protection of women ...; Recognizing the important role of the women's movement and non-governmental organizations world wide in raising awareness and alleviating the problem of violence against women...."

The role of the UN is delineated in article 5. Some of the ways the document suggests it can help include fostering "international and regional cooperation ..."; promoting "the formulation of guidelines or manuals relating to violence against women ..."; considering "the issue of the elimination of violence against women, as appropriate, in fulfilling their mandates with respect to the implementation of human rights instruments ..."; and cooperating "with non-governmental organizations in addressing the issue of violence against women." The last article, article 6, declares that nothing in the declaration "shall affect any provision that is more conducive to the elimination of violence against women" in other domestic or international human rights laws.

United Nations High Commissioner for Human Rights, 8–14 avenue de la Paix, 1211 Geneva 10, Switzerland. (41-22-917-9000. 🖶 41-22-917-9016. 🖳 webadmin.hchr@unog.ch. 🖳 www.unhchr.ch.

☞

Convention for the Suppression of the Traffic in Persons and of the Exploitation of the Prostitution of Others; Convention on the Elimination of All Forms of Discrimination against Women; Convention on the Political Rights of Women; Convention on the Rights of the Child; Domestic Violence; International Covenant on Civil and Political Rights; International Covenant on Economic, Social and Cultural Rights; Sex Discrimination; Universal Declaration of Human Rights; Women

Declaration on the Eradication of Hunger and Malnutrition

See Universal Declaration on the Eradication of Hunger and Malnutrition

Declaration on the Granting of Independence to Colonial Countries and Peoples

"Equal rights and self-determination of peoples" were sanctioned in 1945 by the Charter of the United Nations, which fifteen years later decided to reaffirm its support of aspirations for independence and self-government held by many colonies and administered territories. On December 14, 1960, the UN General Assembly adopted the Declaration on the Granting of Independence to Colonial Countries and Peoples. Although colonialism has greatly diminished since 1960, ethnic, religious, and linguistic minorities throughout the world still desire territorial independence, from the rebels in the Russian province of Chechnya to Basque separatists in Spain and many French-speaking citizens of the Canadian province of Quebec. The conflict between the right of sovereign nations to unfettered governance within their territories and the right of all peoples to self-determination and independence still leads to tensions and warfare.

In the declaration, the General Assembly recognizes "the passionate yearning for freedom in all dependent peoples and the decisive role of such peoples in the attainment of their independence" and "the increasing conflicts resulting from the denial of or impediments in the way of the freedom of such peoples, which constitute a serious threat to world peace." It goes on to affirm that "peoples may, for their own ends, freely dispose of their natural wealth and resources without prejudice to any obligations arising out of international economic co-operation, based upon the principle of mutual benefit, and international law." The document underscores "the necessity of bringing to a speedy and unconditional end colonialism in all its forms and manifestations."

Paragraph 1 asserts that the "subjection of peoples to alien subjugation, domination and exploitation constitutes a denial of fundamental human rights...." "All peoples," adds paragraph 2, "have the right to self-determination; by virtue of that right they freely determine their political status and freely pursue their economic, social and cultural development."

According to paragraphs 3 and 4, the "[i]nadequacy of political, economic, social or educational preparedness should never serve as a pretext for delaying independence. All armed action or repressive measures of all kinds directed against dependent peoples shall cease in order to enable them to exercise peacefully and freely their right to complete independence...." But, according to paragraph 6, "Any attempt aimed at the partial or total disruption of the national unity and the territorial integrity of a country is incompatible with the purposes and principles of the Charter of the United Nations."

Paragraph 7, the declaration's final item, calls on all states, among other things, to observe the UN documents regarding this matter "on the basis of equality, non-interference in the internal affairs of all States, and respect for the sovereign rights of all peoples and their territorial integrity."

United Nations High Commissioner for Human Rights, 8–14 avenue de la Paix, 1211 Geneva 10, Switzerland. (41-22-917-9000. 🖶 41-22-917-9016. 🖳 webadmin.hchr@unog.ch. 🖳 www.unhchr.ch.

Charter of the United Nations; Cultural Rights; Declaration on the Right to Development; Declaration on the Rights of Persons Belonging to National or Ethnic, Religious and Linguistic Minorities; Development; International Covenant on Economic, Social and Cultural Rights; Self-Determination; Sovereignty

Declaration on the Human Genome and Human Rights

See Universal Declaration on the Human Genome and Human Rights

Declaration on the Human Rights of Individuals Who Are Not Nationals of the Country in Which They Live

The treatment of aliens, including immigrants, has historically been an internal matter to be determined, in accordance with the principle of national sovereignty, by each nation. Diplomats residing in a foreign country, on the other hand, have been entitled to special treatment under international law. The concept of reciprocity between nations—that the treatment of one country's nationals living in another country is predicated on similar treatment in turn—generally provides protection for most aliens in a foreign country.

To state some basic international rights of persons other than diplomats who reside in a foreign country, a draft declaration on the rights of aliens was prepared based on a report by a special rapporteur (expert) appointed by the Subcommission on the Promotion and Protection of Human Rights of the Commission of Human Rights. On December 13, 1985, the UN General Assembly then adopted the Declaration on the Human Rights of Individuals Who Are Not Nationals of the Country in Which They Live.

The declaration begins by reiterating that "the Universal Declaration of Human Rights [1948] proclaims ... that everyone has the right to recognition everywhere as a person before the law, that all are equal before the law and entitled without any discrimination to equal protection of the law, and that all are entitled to equal protection against any discrimination in violation of that Declaration and against any incitement to such discrimination." The document next recognizes that, "with improving communications and the development of peaceful and friendly relations among countries, individuals increasingly live in countries of which they are not nationals ... [and] ... that the protection of human rights and fundamental freedoms provided for in international instruments should be ensured for individuals who are not nationals of the country in which they live."

Article 1 declares that the term *alien* "shall apply, with due regard to qualifications made in subsequent articles, to any individual who is not a national of the State in which he or she is present." Article 2 disclaims any interpretation of the declaration that could be seen as "legitimizing the illegal entry into and the presence in a State of any alien, ... [or] as restricting the right of any State to promulgate laws and regulations concerning the entry of aliens and the terms and conditions of their stay or to establish diffferences between nationals and aliens."

According to article 3, "Every State shall make public its national legislation or regulations affecting aliens." Article 4 requires that aliens "observe the laws of the State in which they reside or are present and regard with respect the customs and traditions of the people of that State." Under article 5 is a list of the rights that aliens should enjoy in the host country, including the "right to life and security of person"; rights with respect to "privacy, family, home or correspondence"; the "right to be equal before the courts, tribunals and all other organs and authorities administering justice ..."; the "right to choose a spouse, to marry, to found a family"; "freedom of thought, opinion, conscience and religion"; the "right to retain their own language, culture and tradition"; and the "right to transfer abroad earnings, savings or other personal monetary assets, subject to domestic currency regulations." Other rights to be guaranteed, "[s]ubject to such restrictions as are prescribed by law," include the "right to leave the country," "freedom of expression," "peaceful assembly," and the "right to own property alone as well as in association with others, subject to domestic law."

Article 6 prohibits torture or "cruel, inhuman or degrading treatment or punishment, and in particular, no alien shall be subjected without his or her free consent to medical or scientific experimentation." Article 7 mandates that aliens not be expelled except "in pursuance of a decision reached in accordance with law and shall, except where compelling reasons of national security otherwise require, be allowed to submit the reasons why he or she should not be expelled...." Article 7 also requires that aliens facing expulsion be allowed to "have [their] case reviewed by, and be represented for the purpose before, the competent authority or a person or persons specially designated by the competent authority. Individual or collective expulsion of such aliens on grounds of race, color, religion, culture, descent or national origin is prohibited."

The rights to safe and healthy working conditions, fair wages, equal pay for equal work, trade union membership, and health protection, medical care, social security, social services, education, rest and leisure are extended in article 8. Article 9 provides that "[n]o alien shall be arbitrarily deprived of his or her lawfully acquired assets"; and article 10, the last item, declares: "Any alien shall be free at any time to communicate with the consulate or diplomatic mission of the State of which he or she is a national or, in the absence thereof, with the consulate or diplomatic mission of any other State entrusted with the protection of the interests of the State of which he or she is a national in the State where he or she resides."

United Nations High Commissioner for Human Rights, 8–14 avenue de la Paix, 1211 Geneva 10, Switzerland. (41-22-917-9000. 🖷 41-22-917-9016. 🖳 webadmin.hchr@unog.ch. 🖳 www.unhchr.ch.

☞

Aliens; Deportation; Diplomats and Consuls; Expulsion; Forced Eviction; Immigrants; Minorities; Nationality; Subcommission on the Promotion and Protection of Human Rights

Declaration on the Prohibition of the Use of Nuclear and Thermo-Nuclear Weapons

The two atomic bombs dropped by the United States on Hiroshima and Nagasaki, Japan, ending World War II in the Pacific in September 1945, left the world a lasting impression of the devastation that can be wrought by nuclear and thermonuclear weapons. With the increasing power and buildup of such weapons during the early days of the Cold War, led by the United States and the Soviet Union, the UN General Assembly took steps to formalize its opposition to these destructive weapons. The most important of the General Assembly's resolutions condemning the use of atomic devices was the November 24, 1961, Declaration on the Prohibition of the Use of Nuclear and Thermo-Nuclear Weapons. In it the UN calls the use of such weapons "a crime against mankind and civilization." The vote was not unanimous, however: there were fifty-five votes for the resolution, twenty votes against, and twenty-six abstentions.

The declaration requests that the UN secretary-general consult with member nations concerning a convention to prohibit nuclear weapons, and a number of treaties and agreements limiting or banning such weapons have subsequently been adopted, among them the Nuclear Test Ban Treaty (1963), Treaty on the Non-Proliferation of Nuclear Weapons (1968), Strategic Arms Limitation Treaty (SALT I, 1972, and II, 1979), South Pacific Nuclear-Free Zone Treaty (1985), Strategic Arms Reduction Treaty (START I, 1991, and II, 1993), and Comprehensive Nuclear-Test-Ban Treaty (1996).

The UN's 1961 declaration begins by pointing to the General Assembly's "responsibility under the Charter of the United Nations [1945] in the maintenance of international peace and security, as well as in the consideration of principles governing disarmament." It goes on to state that "the use of nuclear and thermo-nuclear weapons would bring about indiscriminate suffering and destruction to mankind and civilization to an even greater extent than the use of [weapons of mass destruction that in the past have been] declared ... to be contrary to the laws of humanity and a crime under international law," concluding that "the use of weapons of mass destruction, such as nuclear and thermo-nuclear weapons, is a direct negation of the high ideals and objectives which the United Nations has been established to achieve through the protection of succeeding generations from the scourge of war and through the preservation and promotion of their cultures."

In paragraph 1, the first of the document's two items, the General Assembly declares: "(a) The use of nuclear and thermo-nuclear weapons is contrary to the spirit, letter and aims of the United Nations and, as such, [is] a direct violation of the Charter of the United Nations; (b) The use of [such] weapons would exceed even the scope of war and cause indiscriminate suffering and destruction to mankind and civilization and, as such, is contrary to the rules of international law and to the laws of humanity; (c) The use of [such] weapons is a war directed not against an enemy or enemies alone but also against mankind in general, since the peoples of the world not involved in such a war will be subjected to all the evils generated by the use of such weapons; (d) Any State using [such] weapons is to be considered as violating the Charter of the United Nations, as acting contrary to the laws of humanity and as committing a crime against mankind and civilization."

The General Assembly in paragraph 2 requests that the UN secretary-general "consult the Governments of Member States to ascertain their views on the possibility of convening a special conference for signing a convention on the prohibition of the use of nuclear and thermo-nuclear weapons for war purposes and to report on the results of such consultation to the General Assembly. . . ."

International Atomic Energy Agency, P.O. Box 100, Wagramer Strasse 5, A-1400 Vienna, Austria. (43-1-20600. 🖷 43-1-20607. 🖳 official.mail@iaea.org. 🖳 www.iaea.org.

United Nations, One United Nations Plaza, New York, N.Y. 10017. (212-963-4475. 🖷 212-963-0071. 🖳 inquires@un.org. 🖳 www. un.org.

Convention on Prohibitions or Restrictions on the Use of Certain Conventional Weapons Which May Be Deemed to Be Excessively Injurious or to Have Indiscriminate Effects; Peace; War; Weapons

Declaration on the Promotion among Youth of the Ideals of Peace, Mutual Respect and Understanding between Peoples

On December 7, 1965, the UN General Assembly launched its campaign to address the issue of youth involvement in the struggle for human rights by adopting the Declaration on the Promotion among Youth of the Ideals of Peace, Mutual Respect and Understanding between Peoples. The declaration's aim was to promote the improvement in international relations, world peace, security, and human rights by educating young people. Following up on the declaration in 1979, the General Assembly designated 1985 as International Youth Year. A conference on youth held that year adopted guidelines for a further long-term global strategy for youth involvement. Promoting the guidelines has entailed assisting governments with the development of policies for young people and using the United Nations Youth Fund to support projects involving them.

The declaration begins by recalling, in part, that "the purpose of the United Nations Educational, Scientific and Cultural Organization [UNESCO] is to contribute to peace and security by promoting collaboration among nations through education, science and culture" and recognizing "the role and contributions of that organization towards the education of young people in the spirit of international understanding, co-operation and peace." The document goes on to observe that "young people wish to have an assured future" and that "peace, freedom and justice are among the chief guarantees that their desire for happiness will be fulfilled." It further notes that "the education of the young and exchanges of young people and of ideas in a spirit of peace, mutual respect and understanding between peoples can help to improve international relations and to strengthen peace and security."

Principle I declares: "Young people shall be brought up in the spirit of peace, justice, freedom, mutual respect and understanding in order to promote equal rights for all human beings and all nations, economic and social progress, disarmament and the maintenance of international peace and security." According to principle II, "All means of education, including as of major importance the guidance given by parents or family, instruction and information intended for the young should foster among them the ideals of peace, humanity, liberty and international solidarity and all other ideals which help to bring peoples closer together, and acquaint them with the role entrusted to the United Nations as a means of preserving and maintaining peace and promoting international understanding and co-operation." Principle III directs that young people "shall be brought up in the knowledge of the dignity and equality of all men, without distinction as to race, color, ethnic origins or beliefs,

and in respect for fundamental human rights and for the right of peoples to self-determination."

Principle IV recommends that "[e]xchanges, travel, tourism, meetings, the study of foreign languages, the twinning of [creation of mutual relationships between] towns and universities [in different countries and cultures] . . . should be encouraged and facilitated," while principle V suggests "[n]ational and international associations of young people . . . to promote the purposes of the United Nations. . . ." The last item, principle VI, underscores the role of the family in training young people "to acquire higher moral qualities, to be deeply attached to the noble ideals of peace, liberty, the dignity and equality of all men, and imbued with respect and love for humanity and its creative achievements." Young people are urged to "become conscious of their responsibilities in the world they will be called upon to manage and should be inspired with confidence in a future of happiness for mankind."

United Nations Educational, Scientific and Cultural Organization (UNESCO), 7 place de Fontenoy, 75352 Paris 07 SP, France. (33-145-68-10-00. ☎ 33-145-67-16-90. ✉ addresses@unesco.org. ⊞ www.unesco.org.

Voices of Youth (UNICEF): ⊞ www.unicef.org/voy.

Education; Equality; Peace; Self-Determination; United Nations; United Nations Educational, Scientific and Cultural Organization (UNESCO); Youth

Declaration on the Protection of All Persons from Being Subjected to Torture . . .

"No one," mandates the Universal Declaration of Human Rights (1948), "shall be subjected to torture or to cruel, inhuman or degrading treatment or punishment." Torture as an instrument of the state violates an individual's inherent dignity and right to be secure in his or her person. Even legally sanctioned punishment for crime, according to national and international standards of human rights, must be humane and not cruel or degrading or take the form of torture. Cruel and unusual punishment was constitutionally proscribed as early as the U.S. Bill of Rights (1791).

To underscore international repugnance over torture, the UN General Assembly on December 9, 1975, adopted the Declaration on the Protection of All Persons from Being Subjected to Torture and Other Cruel, Inhuman, or Degrading Treatment or Punishment. A convention on the same subject was subsequently adopted in 1984 by the General Assembly, which two years earlier had issued the Principles of Medical Ethics Relevant to the Role of Health Personnel, Particularly Physicians, in the Protection of Prisoners and Detainees against Torture and Other Cruel, Inhuman and Degrading Treatment or Punishment. A number of other international and regional human rights documents similarly ban torture.

The declaration contains no preamble and begins with article 1, which states: "1. For the purposes of this Declaration, torture means any act by which severe pain or suffering, whether physical or mental, is intentionally inflicted by or at the instigation of a public official on a person for such purposes as obtaining from him or a third person information or confession, punishing him for an act he has committed or is suspected of having committed, or intimidating him or other persons. It does not include pain or suffering arising only from, inherent in or incidental to, lawful sanctions to the extent consistent with the Standard Minimum Rules for the Treatment of Prisoners. 2. Torture constitutes an aggravated and deliberate form of cruel, inhuman or degrading treatment or punishment."

According to article 2, "Any act of torture or other cruel, inhuman or degrading treatment or punishment is an offense to human dignity and shall be condemned as a denial of the purposes of the Charter of the United Nations [1945] and as a violation of the human rights and fundamental freedoms proclaimed in the Universal Declaration of Human Rights." Article 3 mandates that no nation "may permit or tolerate torture or other cruel, inhuman or degrading treatment or punishment. Exceptional circumstances such as a state of war or a threat of war, internal political instability or any other public emergency may not be invoked as a justification of torture or other cruel, inhuman or degrading treatment."

Articles 4, 5, and 6, respectively, require nations to "take effective measures to prevent torture . . ."; ensure that law enforcement personnel are given training regarding "the prohibition against torture . . ."; and specify that countries "keep under systematic review interrogation methods and practices as well as arrangements for the custody and treatment of persons deprived of their liberty . . . , with a view to preventing any cases of torture. . . ." Article 7 requires states to make torture a criminal offense; article 8 mandates an impartial examination of complaints regarding torture; and article 9 urges an impartial investigation even without a specific complaint wherever "there is reasonable ground to believe that an act of torture . . . has been committed. . . ."

The last items, articles 10, 11, and 12, respectively, address punishment for committing acts of torture, redress and compensation for torture victims, and evidence, such as confessions, obtained as the result of torture.

United Nations High Commissioner for Human Rights, 8–14 avenue de la Paix, 1211 Geneva 10, Switzerland. (41-22-917-9000. 📠 41-22-917-9016. 🖳 webadmin.hchr@unog.ch. 🖳 www.unhchr.ch.

Basic Principles for the Treatment of Prisoners; Beccaria, Cesare; Body of Principles for the Protection of All Persons under Any Form of Detention or Imprisonment; Code of Conduct for Law Enforcement Officials; Convention against Torture and Other Cruel, Inhuman or Degrading Treatment or Punishment; Detention; Disappearance; European Convention for the Prevention of Torture and Inhuman or Degrading Treatment or Punishment; Geneva Conventions; Inter-American Convention to Prevent and Punish Torture; Principles of Medical Ethics Relevant to the Role of Health Personnel, Particularly Physicians, in the Protection of Prisoners and Detainees against Torture and Other Cruel, Inhuman and Degrading Treatment or Punishment; Prisoners; Punishment; Rules for the Protection of Juveniles Deprived of Their Liberty; Standard Minimum Rules for the Treatment of Prisoners; Torture

Declaration on the Protection of All Persons from Enforced Disappearance

Enforced or involuntary disappearance is a gross violation of human rights that came to the world's attention in the 1970s and 1980s. Particularly in military-ruled countries in South America's "Southern Cone"—primarily Argentina, Chile, and Uruguay—citizens have been abducted and often tortured and murdered with the government's authorization or approval. "Enforced disappearances occur," explains the UN General Assembly, "in the sense that persons are arrested, detained or abducted against their will or otherwise deprived of their liberty by officials of . . . Government, or by organized groups or private individuals acting on behalf of, or with the support, direct or indirect, consent or acquiescence of the Government, followed by a refusal to disclose the fate or whereabouts of the persons concerned or a refusal to acknowledge the deprivation of their liberty, which places such persons outside the protection of the law." In 1980 the Commission on Human Rights created a Working Group on Enforced or Involuntary Disappearances, which heard reports of more than fifty thousand disappearance cases from more than seventy countries. Declaring the practice "a crime against humanity," the General Assembly on December 18, 1992, adopted the Declaration on the Protection of All Persons from Enforced Disappearance.

In the introduction, the General Assembly expresses its deep concern that "in many countries, often in a persistent manner, enforced disappearances occur. . . ." The practice, it continues, "undermines the deepest values of any society committed to respect for the rule of law, human rights and fundamental freedoms, and . . . is of the nature of a crime against humanity." The declaration further urges governments to follow the Standard Minimum Rules for the

Treatment of Prisoners (1955), Code of Conduct for Law Enforcement Officials (1979), Declaration of Basic Principles of Justice for Victims of Crime and Abuse of Power (1985), Basic Principles on the Use of Force and Firearms by Law Enforcement Officials (1990), and similar human rights documents, as well as to make the present declaration "generally known and respected."

"Any act of enforced disappearance is an offense to human dignity," states article 1. "It is condemned as a denial of the purposes of the Charter of the United Nations and as a grave and flagrant violation of human rights and fundamental freedoms. . . ." It adds that any such act "places the persons subjected thereto outside the protection of the law and inflicts severe suffering on them and their families. It constitutes a violation of the rules of international law guaranteeing [among other things] the right to recognition as a person before the law, the right to liberty and security of the person and the right not to be subjected to torture and other cruel, inhuman or degrading treatment or punishment. It also violates or constitutes a grave threat to the right to life."

Article 2 mandates: "1. No state shall practice, permit or tolerate enforced disappearances. 2. States shall act at the national and regional levels and in cooperation with the United Nations to contribute by all means to the prevention and eradication of enforced disappearance." Article 3 directs that each state "shall take effective legislative, administrative, judicial or other measures to prevent and terminate acts of enforced disappearance in any territory under its jurisdiction." According to article 4: "1. All acts of enforced disappearance shall be offenses under criminal law punishable by appropriate penalties which shall take into account their extreme seriousness. 2. Mitigating circumstances may be established in national legislation for persons who, having participated in enforced disappearances, are instrumental in bringing the victims forward alive or in providing voluntarily information which would contribute to clarifying cases of enforced disappearance."

Article 5 adds civil penalties to criminal ones for involvement in enforced disappearances; article 6 prohibits reliance on a superior's order as protection against liability for such acts and directs that training of law enforcement personnel emphasize this requirement; article 7 bars use of emergency conditions as an excuse for such acts; and article 8 prohibits the return (*refouler*) of any person to a state where he or she "would be in danger of enforced disappearance." Articles 9 through 18 address the nature of judicial remedies and proper handling of victims and perpetrators.

"The victims of acts of enforced disappearance and their family," states article 19, "shall obtain redress and shall have the right to adequate compensation, including the means for as complete a rehabilitation as possible. In the event of the death of the victim as a result of an act of enforced disappearance, their dependents shall also be entitled to compensation." Article 20 addresses the abduction of children, which it terms "an extremely serious offense, which shall be punished as such." It also calls for the annulment "of any adoption which originated in enforced disappearance."

Article 21 provides that the "provisions of the present Declaration are without prejudice to the provisions enunciated in the Universal Declaration of Human Rights or in any other international instrument, and shall not be construed as restricting or derogating from any of those provisions."

Derechos Human Rights, P.O. Box 2516, El Cerrito, Calif. 94530-5516. (510-483-4005. 603-372-9710. hr@derechos.org. www.derechos.org.

United Nations High Commissioner for Human Rights, 8–14 avenue de la Paix, 1211 Geneva 10, Switzerland. (41-22-917-9000. 41-22-917-9016. webadmin.hchr@unog.ch. www.unhchr.ch.

Basic Principles on the Use of Force and Firearms by Law Enforcement Officials; Charter of the United Nations; Code of Conduct for Law Enforcement Officials; Commission on Human Rights; Compensation; Crimes against Humanity; Declaration of Basic Principles of Justice for Victims of Crime and Abuse of Power; Disappearance; Punishment; *Refoulement;* Standard Minimum Rules for the Treatment of Prisoners; Torture; Universal Declaration of Human Rights; Victims

Declaration on the Protection of Women and Children in Emergency and Armed Conflict

Concerned about reports of suffering by civilians, especially women and children, during war and emergencies, the UN General Assembly decided to encourage the nations of the world to emphasize protection of women and children during such conflicts, ensuring that they have food, shelter, and medical care and that their inalienable rights are guaranteed. On December 14, 1974, it adopted the Declaration on the Protection of Women and Children in Emergency and Armed Conflict, which follows a number of international humanitarian agreements such as the Geneva Conventions (1949) and underscores general principles of international humanitarian law aimed at securing civilian populations and noncombatants during war and other national emergencies.

The declaration begins by expressing the General Assembly's deep concern "over the sufferings of women and children belonging to the civilian population who in periods of emergency and armed conflict in the struggle for peace, self-determination, national liberation and independence are too often the victims of inhuman acts and consequently suffer serious harm." It goes on to deplore "the fact that grave attacks are still being made on fundamental freedoms and the dignity of the human person and that colonial and racist foreign domination Powers continue to violate international humanitarian law" and further notes the UN's "responsibility for the destiny of the rising generation and for the destiny of mothers, who play an important role in society, in the family and particularly in the upbringing of children." The preamble concludes by calling on all UN member nations to strictly observe the following declaration.

"Attacks and bombings on the civilian population, inflicting incalculable suffering, especially on women and children, who are the most vulnerable members of the population, shall be prohibited, and such acts shall be condemned," states paragraph 1. According to paragraph 2, "The use of chemical and bacteriological weapons in the course of military operations constitutes one of the most flagrant violations of the Geneva Protocol of 1925, the Geneva Conventions of 1949 and the principles of international humanitarian law and inflicts heavy losses on civilian populations, including defenseless women and children, and shall be severely condemned."

Paragraph 3 directs that all states "abide fully by their obligations [under international law] relative to respect for human rights in armed conflicts, which offer important guarantees for the protection of women and children." According to paragraph 4, "All efforts shall be made by States involved in armed conflicts . . . to spare women and children from the ravages of war. All the necessary steps shall be taken to ensure the prohibition of measures such as persecution, torture, punitive measures, degrading treatment and violence, particularly against that part of the civilian population that consists of women and children." Paragraph 5 states: "All forms of repression and cruel and inhuman treatment of women and children, including imprisonment, torture, shooting, mass arrests, collective punishment, destruction of dwellings and forcible eviction, committed by belligerents in the course of military operations or in occupied territories shall be considered criminal."

The last item, paragraph 6, proclaims: "Women and children belonging to the civilian population and finding themselves in circumstances of emergency and armed conflict in the struggle for peace, self-determination, national liberation and independence, or who live in occupied territories, shall not be deprived of shelter, food, medical aid or other inalienable rights, in accordance with the provisions of the Universal Declaration of Human Rights [1948], the International Covenant on Civil and Political Rights [1966], the International Covenant on Economic, Social and Cultural Rights [1966], the Declaration of the Rights of the Child [1959] or other instruments of international law."

United Nations High Commissioner for Human Rights, 8–14 avenue de la Paix, 1211 Geneva 10, Switzerland. (41-22-917-9000. 🖳 41-22-917-9016. 🖳 webadmin.hchr@unog.ch. 🖳 www.unhchr.ch.

Children; Convention on Prohibitions or Restrictions on the Use of Certain Conventional Weapons Which May Be Deemed to Be Excessively Injurious or to Have Indiscriminate Effects; Declaration of the Rights of the Child; Declaration on the Prohibition of the Use of Nuclear and Thermo-Nuclear Weapons; Geneva Conventions; International Covenant on Civil and Political Rights; International Covenant on Economic, Social and Cultural Rights; Universal Declaration of Human Rights; War; Weapons; Women

Declaration on the Right and Responsibility . . . to Promote and Protect Universally Recognized Human Rights . . .

According to the Charter of the United Nations (1945), the organization's mandate includes "promoting and encouraging respect for human rights and fundamental freedoms." Since its inception the UN and its agencies have promulgated various documents, including those that make up the International Bill of Human Rights, to carry out this responsibility. To reemphasize that the UN's mission requires the cooperation of individuals and organizations, not just national governments, the UN General Assembly on December 9, 1998, adopted the Declaration on the Right and Responsibility of Individuals, Groups and Organs of Society to Promote and Protect Universally Recognized Human Rights and Fundamental Freedoms.

This document largely acknowledges and encourages the work carried out by human rights advocates, defenders, activists, and the growing number of private, nongovernmental organizations that are not a part of any national government or international or regional treaty organization such as the UN or the regional human rights systems. The declaration notes that although "the prime responsibility and duty to promote and protect human rights and fundamental freedoms lie with the State," nongovernmental human rights defenders also share the responsibility "to promote respect for and foster knowledge of human rights and fundamental freedoms at the national and international levels."

The resolution adopting the declaration begins by noting that the General Assembly reaffirms "the importance of the observance of the purposes and principles of the Charter of the United Nations for the promotion and protection of all human rights and fundamental freedoms for all persons in all countries of the world." It further invites "[g]overnments, agencies and organizations of the United Nations system and intergovernmental and non-governmental organizations to intensify their efforts to disseminate the Declaration and to promote universal respect and understanding thereof. . . ."

The Annex to the resolution, which contains the declaration's text, stresses that "all members of the international community shall fulfill, jointly and separately, their solemn obligation to promote and encourage respect for human rights and fundamental freedoms...." It proceeds to acknowledge "the important role of international cooperation for, and the valuable work of individuals, groups and associations in contributing to, the effective elimination of all violations of human rights and fundamental freedoms of peoples and individuals, including [those] in relation to mass, flagrant or systematic violations such as those resulting from apartheid, all forms of racial discrimination, colonialism, foreign domination or occupation, aggression or threats to national sovereignty, national unity or territorial integrity and from the refusal to recognize the right of peoples to self-determination and the right of every people to exercise full sovereignty over its wealth and natural resources."

"Everyone has the right, individually and in association with others," declares article 1, "to promote and to strive for the protection and realization of human rights and fundamental freedoms at the national and international levels." Article 2 mandates that each nation "has a prime responsibility and duty to protect, promote and implement all human rights and fundamental freedoms" through legislative, administrative, and other steps. According to article 3, "Domestic law consistent with the Charter of the United Nations and other international obligations of the State in the field of human rights and fundamental freedoms ... should be implemented...." Articles 5 through 8 set forth specific rights associated with promoting and protecting human rights, including the rights of peaceful assembly and to "know, seek, obtain, receive and hold information about all human rights and fundamental freedoms," including to publish information. Each person's entitlement to remedies for human rights violations is set out in article 9, which sanctions the freedom to complain about government policies and to monitor compliance in forums such as public hearings and trials. Article 10 provides that "[n]o one shall participate, by act or by failure to act where required, in violating human rights and fundamental freedoms and no one shall be subjected to punishment or adverse action of any kind for refusing to do so." The list of specific rights is continued in articles 11 through 13, which guarantee the lawful exercise of a profession and the right to participate in peaceful human rights activities. Articles 14 and 15 address national responsibilities to promote citizens' understanding of their civil, political, economic, social, and cultural rights.

Article 16 declares: "Individuals, non-governmental organizations and relevant institutions have an important role to play in contributing to making the public more aware of questions relating to all human rights and fundamental freedoms through activities such as education, training and research in these areas to strengthen ... understanding, tolerance, peace and friendly relations among nations and among all racial and religious groups, bearing in mind the various backgrounds of the societies and communities in which they carry out their activities."

Limitations on the rights stated in the declaration, according to article 17, must be "in accordance with applicable international obligations and ... determined by law solely for the purpose of securing due recognition and respect for the rights and freedoms of others and of meeting the just requirements of morality, public order and the general welfare in a democratic society."

Article 18 specifies that individuals have "duties towards and within the community" and "a responsibility in safeguarding democracy, promoting human rights and fundamental freedoms and contributing to the promotion and advancement of democratic societies, institutions and processes." Articles 19 and 20 disavow any interpretation of the declaration implying the right to act contrary to the rights guaranteed, including national support for activities of organizations contrary to the UN charter.

United Nations High Commissioner for Human Rights, 8–14 avenue de la Paix, 1211 Geneva 10, Switzerland. ☏ 41-22-917-9000. 🖷 41-22-917-9016. 🖳 webadmin.hchr@unog.ch. 🖳 www.unhchr.ch.

☞

Charter of the United Nations; Defenders of Human Rights; International Bill of Human Rights; Nongovernmental Organizations; Race Discrimination; Regional Human Rights Systems; Remedies; Self-Determination

Declaration on the Right of Peoples to Peace

The preamble to the Charter of the United Nations (1945) underscores the organization's determination "to save succeeding generations from the scourge of war" by urging nations to practice tolerance and live together "in peace with one another as good neighbors." To further its mission to maintain world peace, four years later the UN General Assembly adopted the Declaration on the Essentials of Peace (1949). In 1978 the UN reaffirmed the right of individuals and nations to peace with its Declaration on the Preparation of Societies for Life in Peace. Then in 1982 the General Assembly announced that 1986 would be the International Year of Peace, and on November 12, 1984, it adopted the Declaration on the Right of Peoples to Peace. The aim of this relatively short declaration is to emphasize that without peace the implementation of all other human rights is in constant jeopardy.

The declaration begins by reiterating that "the principal aim of the United Nations is the maintenance of international peace and security" and expressing "the will and the aspirations of all peoples to eradicate war from the life of mankind and, above all, to avert a world-wide nuclear catastrophe." It goes on to observe that "life without war serves as the primary international prerequisite for the material well-being, development and progress of countries, and for the full implementation of the rights and fundamental human freedoms proclaimed by the United Nations." The preamble concludes by stressing the General Assembly's awareness that "in the nuclear age the establishment of a lasting peace on Earth represents the primary condition for the preservation of human civilization and the survival of mankind" and that "the maintenance of a peaceful life for peoples is the sacred duty of each State."

In the declaration's four main sections, the General Assembly:

"1. Solemnly proclaims that the peoples of our planet have a sacred right to peace;

"2. Solemnly declares that the preservation of the right of peoples to peace and the promotion of its implementation constitute a fundamental obligation of each State;

"3. Emphasizes that ensuring the exercise of the right of peoples to peace demands that the policies of States be directed towards the elimination of the threat of war, particularly nuclear war, the renunciation of the use of force in international relations and the settlement of international disputes by peaceful means on the basis of the Charter of the United Nations;

"4. Appeals to all States and international organizations to do their utmost to assist in implementing the rights of peoples to peace through the adoption of appropriate measures at both the national and the international level."

✉

United Nations High Commissioner for Human Rights, 8–14 avenue de la Paix, 1211 Geneva 10, Switzerland. ☎ 41-22-917-9000. 🖨 41-22-917-9016. 🖳 webadmin.hchr@unog.ch. 🖳 www.unhchr.ch.

Charter of the United Nations; Declaration on Principles of International Law Concerning Friendly Relations and Co-operation among States in Accordance with the Charter of the United Nations; Declaration on the Prohibition of the Use of Nuclear and Thermo-Nuclear Weapons; Declaration on the Promotion among Youth of the Ideals of Peace, Mutual Respect and Understanding between Peoples; Peace; Tolerance; War

Declaration on the Right to Development

The right of all peoples to "dispose of their natural wealth and resources" is set forth in both the International Covenant on Civil and Political Rights (1966) and the International Covenant on Economic, Social and Cultural Rights (1966), which are part of what is called the International Bill of Human Rights. A right of "economic, social and cultural development" is also created in the African Charter on Human and Peoples' Rights (1981). Related to the right of self-determination in the wake of colonialism, the right to development has become linked as well with environmental rights, particularly with sustainable development policies aimed at avoiding harmful consequences from manufacturing, mining, chemical production, deforestation, and other development activities.

Proclaiming the right to development to be inalienable and the basis for the enjoyment of economic, social, cultural, and political benefits by individuals and groups, the UN General Assembly on December 4, 1986, adopted the Declaration on the Right to Development. The document opens by noting that "development . . . aims at the constant improvement of the well-being of the entire population." It proceeds to recall "the right of peoples to self-determination, by virtue of which they have the right freely to determine their political status and to pursue their economic, social and cultural development" and to consider that "the elimination of the massive and flagrant violations of the human rights of the peoples and individuals affected by situations such as those resulting from colonialism, neocolonialism, *apartheid*, all forms of racism and racial discrimination, foreign domination and occupation, aggression and threats against national sovereignty, national unity and territorial integrity and threats of war would contribute to the establishment of circumstances propitious to the development of a great part of mankind." The document then states that "international peace and security are essential elements for the realization of the right to development." It also observes the "close relationship between disarmament and development" and points out that "progress in the field of disarmament would considerably promote progress in the field of development. . . ." The declaration concludes by recognizing that "the human person is the central subject of the development process" and thus should be its main participant and beneficiary.

Article 1 declares: "1. The right to development is an inalienable human right by virtue of which every human person and all peoples are entitled to participate in, contribute to, and enjoy economic, social, cultural and political development, in which all human rights and fundamental freedoms can be fully realized. 2. The right to development also implies the full realization of the right of peoples to self-determination, which includes, subject to the relevant provisions of both International Covenants on Human Rights, the exercise of their inalienable right to full sovereignty over all their natural wealth and resources."

Focusing on the "human person" at the center of development, article 2 states that people "have a responsibility for development, individually and collectively," and that nations "have the right and duty to formulate appropriate national development policies. . . ." According to article 3, governments "have the primary responsibility for the creation of national and international conditions favorable to the realization of the right to development." That realization, it adds, "requires full respect for the principles of international law concerning friendly relations and co-operation among States...." Article 3 further mandates that states also "have the duty to co-operate with each other in ensuring development and eliminating obstacles to development ... as well as to encourage the observance and realization of human rights."

Article 5 requires nations to "take resolute steps to eliminate the massive and flagrant violations of the human rights of peoples and human beings affected by ... apartheid ... racism and racial discrimination, colonialism, foreign domination and occupation, [and] aggression ... ," among other abuses. Article 6 suggests that nations give "equal attention and urgent consideration ... to the implementation, promotion and protection of civil, political, economic, social and cultural rights." Article 7 urges all nations to promote international peace and security; and article 8 suggests, among other things, that states "should undertake, at the national level, all necessary measures ... [to] ensure ... equality of opportunity for all in their access to basic resources, education, health services, food, housing, employment and the fair distribution of income."

Article 9 declares that "[a]ll the aspects of the right to development set forth in the present Declaration are indivisible and interdependent and each of them should be considered in the context of the whole." It adds that "[n]othing in the present Declaration shall be construed as being contrary to the purposes and principles of the United Nations...." Article 10, the last item, provides: "Steps should be taken to ensure the full exercise and progressive enhancement of the right to development, including the formulation, adoption and implementation of policy, legislative and other measures at the national and international levels."

United Nations High Commissioner for Human Rights, 8–14 avenue de la Paix, 1211 Geneva 10, Switzerland. (41-22-917-9000. 🖷 41-22-917-9016. 🖳 webadmin.hchr@unog.ch. 🖳 www.unhchr.ch.

Apartheid; Collective Rights; Declaration on Social Progress and Development; Development; Economic Rights; Environment; Natural Resources; Rio Declaration on Environment and Development; Self-Determination

Declaration on the Rights of Disabled Persons

In 1971 the UN General Assembly adopted the Declaration on the Rights of Mentally Retarded Persons, which confirms that the mentally retarded have the same rights as other people, including access to proper medical care, economic security, rehabilitation, and training, along with the right to live with one's own family or foster parents. The mentally retarded are part of a much larger group of approximately half a billion disabled persons worldwide.

Extending these guarantees to all people suffering from disabilities, the UN General Assembly on December 9, 1975, adopted the Declaration on the Rights of Disabled Persons. This document addresses civil and political rights, as well as equal treatment and services to develop the full capabilities of the disabled. The declaration, together with the Guidelines for Action on Human Resources Development in the Field of Disability (Tallinn Guidelines) (1989), Standard Rules on the Equalization of Opportunities for Persons with Disabilities (1993), and Long-term Strategy (1994) for implementing the World Program of Action (1982), is a primary source of international rights for the disabled.

The document's introduction begins by noting that "the Declaration on Social Progress and Development [1969] has proclaimed the necessity of protecting the rights and assuring the welfare and rehabilitation of the physically and mentally disadvantaged." It goes on to underscore "the necessity of preventing physical and mental disabilities and of assisting disabled persons to develop their abilities in the most varied fields of activities and of promoting their integration as far as possible in normal life." Calling for "national and international action to ensure that [the declaration] will be used as a common basis and frame of reference for the protection of these rights," the declaration next outlines thirteen points and goals.

Paragraph 1 defines *disabled person* as "any person unable to ensure by himself or herself, wholly or partly, the necessities of a normal individual and/or social life, as a result of a deficiency, either congenital or not, in his or her physical or mental capabilities." Paragraph 2 guarantees the rights of the disabled without exception, distinction, "or discrimination on the basis of race, color, sex, language, religion, political or other opinions, national or social origin, state of wealth, birth or any other situation applying ... to the disabled person ... or to his or her family."

Paragraphs 3, 4, and 5, respectively, provide that disabled persons "have the inherent right to respect for their human dignity"; "have the same civil and political rights as other human beings"; and "are entitled to the measures designed to enable them to become as self-reliant as possible." Paragraphs 6 through 8, respectively, address the rights of the disabled to "medical, psychological and functional treatment," "economic and social security and to a decent level of living," and consideration of "their special needs ... at all stages of economic and social planning." Paragraph 9 guarantees them the right to "live with their families or with foster parents and to participate in all social, creative or recreational activities." According to paragraph 10, disabled persons are to "be protected against all exploitation, all regulations and all treatment of a discriminatory, abusive or degrading nature."

Under paragraph 11, they are to be allowed access to "qualified legal aid" and special consideration in judicial proceedings. Paragraph 12 observes that organizations of disabled persons "may be usefully consulted in all matters regarding [their] rights." The final item, paragraph 13, requires that "[d]isabled persons, their families and communities shall be fully informed, by all appropriate means, of the rights contained in this Declaration."

United Nations High Commissioner for Human Rights, 8–14 avenue de la Paix, 1211 Geneva 10, Switzerland. (41-22-917-9000. 🖳 41-22-917-9016. 🖳 webadmin.hchr@unog.ch. 🖳 www.unhchr.ch.

☞

Declaration on Social Progress and Development; Disabled Persons; Guidelines for Action on Human Resources Development in the Field of Disability (Tallinn Guidelines); Health; Rehabilitation

Declaration on the Rights of Persons Belonging to National or Ethnic, Religious and Linguistic Minorities

On November 18, 1992, the UN General assembly adopted the Declaration on the Rights of Persons Belonging to National or Ethnic, Religious and Linguistic Minorities, whose aim is to proclaim support for minorities as set forth in the International Covenant on Civil and Political Rights (1966). Article 27 of the covenant provides that "[i]n those States in which ethnic, religious or linguistic minorities exist, persons belonging to such minorities shall not be denied the right, in community with other members of their group, to enjoy their own culture, to profess and practice their own religion, or to use their own language." The 1992 declaration was the product of a Commission on Human Rights working group established in 1978 and was based on a draft declaration submitted by Yugoslavia. A final draft was prepared in 1981 and became the basis for the text adopted a decade later.

The declaration begins by noting that "the constant promotion and realization of the rights of persons belonging to national or ethnic, religious and linguistic minorities, as an integral part of the development of society as a whole and within a democratic framework based on the rule of law, would contribute to the strengthening of friendship and cooperation among peoples and States." It goes on to recognize "the need to ensure even more effective implementation of international human rights instruments with regard to the rights of persons belonging to national or ethnic, religious and linguistic minorities."

Article 1 mandates: "1. States shall protect the existence and the national or ethnic, cultural, religious and linguis-

tic identity of minorities within their respective territories and shall encourage conditions for the promotion of that identity. 2. States shall adopt appropriate legislative and other measures to achieve those ends." According to article 2, minorities are to have certain rights, including "to enjoy their own culture, to profess and practice their own religion, and to use their own language, in private and in public, freely and without interference or any form of discrimination." They are also to be free "to participate effectively in cultural, religious, social, economic and public life . . . [as well as] in decisions on the national and, where appropriate, regional level concerning the minority to which they belong or the regions in which they live, in a manner not incompatible with national legislation." Other rights proclaimed include "to establish and maintain their own associations" and "to establish and maintain, without discrimination, free and peaceful contacts with other members of their group and with persons belonging to other minorities. . . ."

The ability of minorities to exercise their rights "individually as well as in community with other members of their group, without any discrimination" as well as not to exercise such rights are set forth in article 3. Article 4 addresses measures that nations should take to implement the intent of the declaration. Article 5 requires that "due regard for the legitimate interests of persons belonging to minorities" be taken into consideration in national policies and programs; and articles 6 and 7 urge nations to cooperate with respect to the interests of persons belonging to minorities, among other things, in "exchanging information and experiences" and "to promote respect for the rights set forth" in the declaration.

Under article 8, nations are required to fulfill their international obligations in good faith; no prejudice is to result from the exercise of rights in the declaration; measures taken by states to implement the declaration "shall not *prima facie* be considered contrary to the principle of equality contained in the Universal Declaration of Human Rights [1948]"; and nothing in the declaration "may be construed as permitting any activity contrary to the purposes and principles of the United Nations, including sovereign equality, territorial integrity and political independence of States." Article 9, the last item, requires UN agencies and organizations to "contribute to the full realization of the rights and principles set forth in the present Declaration, within their respective fields of competence."

United Nations High Commissioner for Human Rights, 8–14 avenue de la Paix, 1211 Geneva 10, Switzerland. (41-22-917-9000. 🖳 41-22-917-9016. 🖳 webadmin.hchr@unog.ch. 🖳 www.unhchr.ch.

☞

Commission on Human Rights; Cultural Rights; Indigenous Peoples; International Covenant on Civil and Political Rights; Language;

Minorities; Religion; Subcommission on the Promotion and Protection of Human Rights; Race Discrimination; Universal Declaration of Human Rights

Declaration on the Survival, Protection and Development of Children

See World Declaration on the Survival, Protection and Development of Children

Declaration on the Use of Scientific and Technological Progress . . .

On October 11, 1939, a month after Hitler's invasion of Poland and the start of World War II, Albert Einstein, the physicist who gave the world the equation $E=mc^2$ and the theories of relativity, sent an intermediary to President Franklin Roosevelt to warn him of the dangers of atomic energy, especially if it fell into the wrong hands. The warning led Roosevelt to take the initiative and create the Manhattan Project to develop the world's first atomic bomb. In 1955 Einstein joined the nuclear disarmament movement with the British philosopher Bertrand Russell, but the genie could not be put back in the bottle.

Many scientific and technological developments of the twentieth century—from the automobile and aerosol sprays to nuclear energy—have given rise to fears about their possible side effects. After the International Conference on Human Rights in 1968 noted that scientific and technological advances could jeopardize certain human rights, the UN General Assembly conducted its own study of health and environmental rights. On November 10, 1975, it adopted the Declaration on the Use of Scientific and Technological Progress in the Interests of Peace and for the Benefit of Mankind, which urges national governments to prevent or limit scientific and technological progress from infringing on human rights and fundamental freedoms.

The declaration opens by noting that "scientific and technological progress has become one of the most important factors in the development of human society." But, "while scientific and technological developments provide ever increasing opportunities to better the conditions of life of peoples and nations," it adds, "in a number of instances they can give rise to social problems, as well as threaten the human rights and fundamental freedoms of the individual." The preamble concludes by stressing "the urgent need to make full use of scientific and technological developments for the welfare of man and to neutralize the present and possible future harmful consequences of certain scientific and technological achievements."

Paragraph 1 mandates: "All States shall promote international co-operation to ensure that the results of scientific and technological developments are used in the interests of strengthening international peace and security, freedom and independence, and also for the purpose of the economic and social development of peoples and the realization of human rights and freedoms in accordance with the Charter of the United Nations [1945]." According to paragraph 2: "All States shall take appropriate measures to prevent the use of scientific and technological developments, particularly by the State organs, to limit or interfere with the enjoyment of the human rights and fundamental freedoms of the individual as enshrined in the Universal Declaration of Human Rights [1948], the International Covenants on Human Rights [1966] and other relevant international instruments." Paragraph 3 provides that all nations "shall take measures to ensure that scientific and technological achievements satisfy the material and spiritual needs for all sectors of the population."

According to paragraph 4, "All States shall refrain from any acts involving the use of scientific and technological achievements for the purposes of violating the sovereignty and territorial integrity of other States, interfering in their internal affairs, waging aggressive wars, suppressing national liberation movements or pursuing a policy of racial discrimination. Such acts," it adds, "are not only a flagrant violation of the Charter of the United Nations and principles of international law, but constitute an inadmissible distortion of the purposes that should guide scientific and technological developments for the benefit of mankind."

Paragraph 5 urges international cooperation in "accelerating the realization of the social and economic rights of the peoples" in developing countries; paragraph 6 calls for extension of the benefits from and protection against the possible harm of science and technology; and paragraph 7 directs nations to pass legislation ensuring that science and technology promote human rights without discrimination.

Paragraph 8 recommends "effective measures, including legislative measures, to prevent [harm to] human rights . . . and the dignity of the human person." Paragraph 9, the last provision, directs: "All States shall, whenever necessary, take action to ensure compliance with legislation guaranteeing human rights and freedoms in the conditions of scientific and technological developments."

United Nations High Commissioner for Human Rights, 8–14 avenue de la Paix, 1211 Geneva 10, Switzerland. (41-22-917-9000. 🖥 41-22-917-9016. 🖳 webadmin.hchr@unog.ch. 🖳 www.unhchr.ch.

☞

Charter of the United Nations; Declaration on the Prohibition of the Use of Nuclear and Thermo-Nuclear Weapons; International Covenant on Civil and Political Rights; International Covenant on Economic, Social and Cultural Rights; Peace; Universal Declaration of Human Rights

Declarations of Rights

See Bills of Rights; *and specific documents*

Defenders of Human Rights

People who work actively in the field of human rights are variously called defenders, activists, and workers. Among them are not only those who personally stand up for human rights at great risk to themselves, their families, and friends but also politicians who make human rights a part of their agenda; writers who communicate the need for human rights; lawyers who represent victims; doctors who minister to the abused; volunteers who help rights organizations; and anyone who has the opportunity to do something positive for the cause of human rights anywhere in the world.

"The sheer scale and complexity of global poverty can prompt feelings of powerlessness at best, and indifference at worst," says David Bryer, director of Oxfam International, an organization dedicated to overcoming poverty. "Some, however, become energized by the challenge. They have a passion to change the world for the better." A number of representative defenders of human rights are profiled in this book: scholars and philosophers such as St. Thomas Aquinas and John Stuart Mill, national leaders such as Corazon Aquino and Jimmy Carter, political organizers such as Nelson Mandela and Rigoberta Menchú, religious leaders such as the Reverend Martin Luther King Jr. and Archbishop Desmond Tutu, and martyrs such as Archbishop Oscar Romero and Raoul Wallenberg.

Defenders of human rights come from all walks of life, all strata of society, and every corner of the globe—and they speak eloquently about their human rights goals. President Franklin Roosevelt, who helped lead the Allies to victory in World War II, defined the four basic freedoms as freedom of speech, freedom of worship, freedom from want, and freedom from fear, adding in 1941: "Freedom means the supremacy of human rights everywhere. Our support goes to those who struggle to gain those rights and to keep them." One of the late twentieth century's most well known defenders of human rights, Nelson Mandela of South Africa, who was imprisoned from 1964 to 1990 for his fight against apartheid, put his commitment in these terms: "I have cherished the ideal of a democratic and free society.... [I]t is an ideal for which I am prepared to die."

The work of some human rights defenders garners awards, prizes, and international acclaim, but most of those toiling for human rights are largely unsung except by their fellow workers. How well known, for example, is Ngawang Sangdrol, a longtime political prisoner? A Tibetan nun, she was arrested for participating in a political demonstration when she was just ten years old, and later demonstrations again landed her in prison for actions against the repressive Chinese communist regime in Tibet. In 1995 the UN Working Group on Arbitrary Detention concluded that her continued detention was arbitrary because she was being punished for exercising her right to express her opinions. Through her perseverence, Ngawang Sangdrol has set a model for proponents of human rights everywhere.

Those who take part in prodemocracy movements are defenders of human rights alongside those who work against racism, enforced disappearance, torture, and other forms of injustice. Struggles for democracy in places such as Myanmar (Burma) and China are human rights campaigns to allow all citizens an equal opportunity to participate in government, as well as to exercise freedom of speech, the press, conscience, and religion. "We are not myths of the past, ruins in the jungle, or zoos," proclaims Rigoberta Menchú, a Guatemalan of Mayan descent. "We are people and we want to be respected, not to be victims of intolerance and racism."

The ranks of human rights defenders have grown dramatically. Thousands of private, nongovernmental organizations are involved on a day-to-day basis in defending human rights. Amnesty International, for example, was the idea of a British barrister, Peter Benenson, who started a one-year campaign called an Appeal for Amnesty in 1961. Today the organization numbers more than one million supporters in one hundred countries and has offices around the world. Human Rights Watch, another multinational, nongovernmental organization, began in 1978 as Helsinki Watch to help human rights defenders in Moscow, Warsaw, and Prague monitor violations of the Helsinki Final Act (1975).

To defend the defenders, these and other organizations such as the Lawyers Committee for Human Rights send task forces of trained personnel to investigate government harassment of human rights workers, who may be threatened, jailed, tortured, murdered, or victims of disappearance and whose property may be destroyed. Religious groups such as Pax Christi and the World Council of Churches also provide training and support for human rights defenders and activists. Regional and international agencies, from the Council of Europe and the Inter-American Commission on Human Rights to the Commission on Human Rights and its Subcommission on the Promotion and Protection of Human Rights, have sought to set standard rules to protect workers, lawyers, allied experts, and victims' relatives. All human rights defenders, say these organizations, should have immunity for their testimony, be able to communicate freely with investigating agencies, travel without hindrance, be safe from injury, be free from government intimidation or reprisal, and be released from imprisonment if jailed.

Defenders of human rights offer us a number of important lessons. One is that each person's rights are strengthened if the rights of all people are strong. Another is that someone must step forward—If not now, when? If not us, who will extend, promote, defend, protect, and enforce human rights? "It has long been recognized," said the former UN secretary-general Boutros Boutros-Ghali, "that an essential element in protecting human rights was a widespread knowledge among the population of what their rights are and how they can be defended."

Kuklin, Susan. *Irrepressible Spirit: Conversations with Human Rights Activists*. New York: Putnam, 1996.

Shackling the Defenders: Legal Restrictions on Independent Human Rights Advocacy Worldwide. New York: Lawyers Committee for Human Rights, 1994.

Amnesty International; Aquino, Corazon; Carter, James Earl; Declaration on the Right and Responsibility of Individuals, Groups and Organs of Society to Promote and Protect Universally Recognized Human Rights and Fundamental Freedoms; Human Rights Watch; King, Martin Luther, Jr.; Lawyers Committee for Human Rights; Mandela, Nelson; Menchú, Rigoberta; Mill, John Stuart; Oxfam International; Pax Christi; Romero, Oscar; Thomas Aquinas, St.; Tutu, Desmond; Wallenberg, Raoul; Working Groups; World Council of Churches; *and other specific persons and organizations*

Democracy

"No one pretends that democracy is perfect or all-wise," the British statesman Winston Churchill observed in the House of Commons in 1947. "Indeed, it has been said that democracy is the worst form of Government except all those other forms that have been tried from time to time." The philosopher Aristotle was skeptical about the nature of the democratic system even in ancient Greece, the cradle of democracy (from the Greek *demokratia*, meaning rule by the people). Although he believed that granting equality to all free men was unjust, he reasoned that other criteria for determining political rights, such as wealth or birth, were equally unjust. Aristotle's close contemporary Plato concluded that the two major types of governments were monarchy and democracy and that good government was based on a proper mixture.

Direct democracy, in which all citizens vote on the major issues of government, first emerged in the ancient Greek city-states such as Athens. Representative democracy, in which elected representatives vote on citizens' behalf, is the predominant form of government today. It traces its ori-

gins to the Icelandic parliament, the Althing, established in the tenth century, and the English parliamentary form of government, sometimes called the Westminster model.

Democracy has its modern-day critics. In 1996 the UN secretary-general issued an in-depth supplemental report to the General Assembly on the methods by which the United Nations might better support efforts to create and restore democratic governments throughout the world. "[T]he charge is made," said the report, "that there can be no democracy in times of trouble or war, that democracy itself leads to disorder, that democracy diminishes efficiency, that democracy violates minority and community rights, and that democracy must wait until development is fully achieved." However, it continues, "[W]hatever evidence critics of democracy [have] must not be allowed to conceal a deeper truth: democracy contributes to preserving peace and security, securing justice and human rights, and promoting economic and social development."

Democracy, constitutionalism, and the rule of law combined constitute the government structure that best supports the extension, promotion, protection, and enforcement of human rights. No form of government is guaranteed to be perfect, because it must be implemented by imperfect people. Yet democracy as initiated in ancient Greece and as developed in England, the United States, and France has become in one version or another the government of choice among the nations of the world. Other forms of government include monarchy (as in Saudi Arabia, for example); theocracy (Iran); personal dictatorship (Iraq); military dictatorship (Central and South America as well as Myanmar, formerly Burma); and single-party dictatorship (China). Some governments are hybrid types, nominally democratic but dominated by one political party or the military. The difference between democracy and all other types of government lies in democratic rulers' accountability to those ruled.

Most written national constitutions, either expressly or by the nature of the institutions they create, establish some form of democratic representative government. Most regional and international organizations operate under generally democratic principles. The 1996 UN secretary-general's report, paragraphs 104 and 105, states, "By promoting democratization within its own architecture, the United Nations, as the world's largest and most inclusive organization of Governments, can make a major contribution to democratization at the international level. . . . This reform needs to be advanced by reform in the United Nations intergovernmental machinery, for which democratization can also serve as a guiding objective."

Constitution of Sweden, Instrument of Government (1975), chapter 1, The Basic Principles of the Constitution, article 1: "Swedish democracy is founded on freedom of opinion and on universal and equal suffrage. It shall be realized through a representative and parliamentary polity and through local self-government."

Charter of Paris for a New Europe (1990): "Ours is a time for fulfilling the hopes and expectations our peoples have cherished for decades: steadfast commitment to democracy based on human rights and fundamental freedoms; prosperity through economic liberty and social justice; and equal security for all our countries."

Constitutional Court of South Africa (1998): "[A] suspension of a member of the Assembly from Parliament for contempt is not consistent with the requirements of representative democracy."

European Court of Human Rights (1978): "The Court agrees with the [European Commission of Human Rights] that some compromise between the requirements for defending democratic society and individual rights is inherent in the system of the [European Convention for the Protection of Human Rights and Fundamental Freedoms (1950)]."

Hardin, Russell. *Liberalism, Constitutionalism, and Democracy.* Oxford, England: Clarendon Press, Oxford University Press, 1999.

Macpherson, C. B. *The Real World of Democracy.* Concord, Ontario: Anansi, 1992.

Aristotle; Constitutional Rights; Constitutionalism; Equality; International Covenant on Civil and Political Rights; Majority Rule; Plato; Rule of Law; United Nations; Voting

Deportation

International law provides that aliens are subject to the laws of their host country and that, if they transgress those laws, the host nation may expel or deport them. Expulsion connotes removal of an alien to any country that will grant admittance, while deportation (from the Latin *deportare,* meaning to carry off or transport) involves the alien's return to his or her country of origin after a due process hearing.

As punishment for a crime, deportation—called transportation in cases involving a nation's own citizens—is not new. Under ancient Roman law, a citizen could be exiled or an alien deported. In the past Russia, Portugal, France, and Great Britain have all used transportation to outlying areas or colonies—Siberia, South America, Devil's Island, and Australia, respectively—as a means of punishment.

Aliens may be deported for procedural reasons, such as illegally or fraudulently entering the host country, failing to abide by visa or other entry requirements, or holding an improper passport or if their request for asylum is refused. They may also be sent back for subversive activity, any conduct deemed undesirable by the host country, and other serious crimes.

Aliens have no right to remain in a country of which they are not citizens nor to humane treatment by the host state except what it wishes to extend. However, if an alien is treated in a manner below the standard required by international law, his or her native country may have a claim for mistreatment against the host country. Arbitrary deportation, without cause or without sufficient cause, or the use of harsh or violent means can give rise to such a claim.

Deportation proceedings should respect the full spectrum of rights granted to any person accused of a crime. In the United States and many other countries, aliens have some constitutional rights, including the right to due process of law and a fair hearing. At a minimum, persons facing deportation should be informed of the charges against them and an opportunity for rebuttal with the assistance of competent legal counsel and an interpreter, if necessary. Aliens should also have the right to show that return to their native country may result in serious personal danger or harm, in which case they may request *nonrefoulement,* the right to remain in the host country because of likely persecution if returned.

Some international human rights documents that address deportation issues include the International Covenant on Civil and Political Rights (1966), which provides minimum rights for aliens facing expulsion or deportation, and the Declaration on Territorial Asylum (1967), which prohibits the return of aliens to a nation where they may face persecution.

U.K. Commonwealth Immigrants Act (1962), part II, Deportation: "6.—(1) This Part of this Act shall have effect for authorizing the deportation from the United Kingdom of Commonwealth citizens to whom this section applies who are convicted of offenses punishable with imprisonment and recommended by the court for deportation."

International Covenant on Civil and Political Rights (1966), part III, article 13: "An alien lawfully in the territory of a State Party to the present Covenant may be expelled therefrom only in pursuance of a decision reached in accordance with law and shall, except where compelling reasons of national security otherwise require, be allowed to submit the reasons against his expulsion and to have his case reviewed by, and be represented for the purpose before, the competent authority or a person or persons especially designated by the competent authority."

Federal Court of Appeal of Canada (1997): The guarantee of the right to liberty under the Canadian Charter of Rights and Freedoms (1982), section 7, does not protect from deportation permanent residents convicted of serious crimes.

Human Rights Committee (1993): The human rights guaranteed by the International Covenant on Civil and Political Rights (1966) afforded no protection to a citizen of Scotland who had resided in Canada since the age of seven and was being lawfully deported after having been convicted of crimes on forty-two occasions.

United Nations High Commissioner for Human Rights, 8–14 avenue de la Paix, 1211 Geneva 10, Switzerland. (41-22-917-9000. 41-22-917-9016. webadmin.hchr@unog.ch. www.unhchr.ch.

Bash, Tami, et al. Translated by Jessica Bonn. *Deportation of Palestinians from the Occupied Territories and the Mass Deportation of December 1992.* Jerusalem: B'tselem, 1993.

Gilbert, Geoff. *Transnational Fugitive Offenders in International Law: Extradition and Other Mechanisms.* The Hague: Kluwer Academic Publishers, 1998.

Accused; Aliens; Asylum; Declaration on Territorial Asylum; Expulsion; Extradition; Forced Eviction; Immigrants; *Refoulement*

Derogation

Derogation (from the Latin *derogare*, meaning to repeal in part, take away, or diminish) is the partial abrogation or repeal of a law, contract, treaty, or legal or other right. In law *derogation* may also mean the lessening or weakening of a right or a power. Used in this sense in English since the sixteenth century, the term was applied by the English jurist Sir Edward Coke in 1628 when he denounced "[n]ew and subtle 'inventions' in derogation of the Common Law."

Some national constitutions and international human rights documents contain provisions describing the circumstances—such as emergencies, natural disasters, war, or insurrection—under which all or certain provisions guaranteeing or requiring observance of human rights can be suspended and thus when derogation is acceptable. Such documents may also contain provisions that prohibit the derogation of some basic rights under any conditions.

In 1988 the UN General Assembly adopted a resolution emphasizing that national governments should not erode human rights by improperly derogating such rights under the pretext of emergency conditions. The resolution also encouraged nations that are parties to the International Covenant on Civil and Political Rights (1966), which requires governments to justify the conditions for the dero-

gation of rights "through the intermediary of the Secretary-General of the United Nations," to provide the fullest possible information during the declared state of emergency to support the appropriateness of the measures taken.

Constitution of South Africa (1996), chapter 2, Bill of Rights, article 37(4): "Any legislation enacted in consequence of a declaration of a state of emergency may derogate from the Bill of Rights only to the extent that—(a) the derogation is strictly required by the emergency; and (b) the legislation—(i) is consistent with the Republic's obligations under international law applicable to states of emergency...."

International Covenant on Civil and Political Rights (1966), part II, article 4: "1. In time of public emergency which threatens the life of the nation and the existence of which is officially proclaimed, the States Parties to the present Covenant may take measures derogating from their obligations under the present Covenant to the extent strictly required by the exigencies of the situation, provided that such measures are not inconsistent with their other obligations under international law and do not involve discrimination solely on the ground of race, color, sex, language, religion or social origin."

Supreme Court of Ghana (1961): The court held that the writ of habeas corpus could not be used to challenge detentions ordered by the president under a 1958 preventive detention law because the country's constitution vests the president with plenary discretion and its requirement that the leader respect certain fundamental rights "does not represent a legal requirement which can be enforced by the courts."

Inter-American Commission on Human Rights (1991): An attempt by the government of Mexico to rely on *force majeure* (an act of God) as an explanation for changing polling places at the last minute was a violation of the petitioners' right to participate in government as guaranteed by the American Convention on Human Rights (1969), article 23, a nonderogable provision.

Fitzpatrick, Joan. *Human Rights in Crisis: The International System for Protecting Rights during States of Emergency.* Procedural Aspects of International Law series, vol. 19. Philadelphia: University of Pennsylvania Press, 1994.

Maior, George C. *Derogations from Human Rights Treaties.* LL.M. thesis, The George Washington University, 1992.

International Covenant on Civil and Political Rights; Limitations

Detention

The confinement of persons as punishment for crimes or to prevent them from committing additional crimes is probably as old as humanity itself. There is no evidence that the ancient Greeks used imprisonment extensively as a means of punishment, but a person awaiting trial or sentencing could be detained. In *The Laws*, written in the fourth century B.C.E., Plato suggests imprisonment as a punishment for such acts as striking anyone twenty years older or engaging in a retail trade.

Detention (from the Latin *detentus*, meaning kept back) has since come to mean a government's holding a person in custody not as punishment after a fair trial but either pending trial or sentencing or simply administratively. In administrative detention, individuals are detained or interned by a government's administrative authorities without formally being charged or brought to trial. After the French Revolution in 1789, for example, the king and the royal family were said to be "in a state of detention." Such detention constitutes a denial of the detainees' human rights, including the rights of any person accused of a crime as well as the right to be treated with respect and dignity and as a person before the law.

In 1955 the Standard Minimum Rules for the Treatment of Prisoners were adopted by the First United Nations Congress on the Prevention of Crime and the Treatment of Offenders. According to the document's preliminary observations, paragraph 1, the rules attempted to state "the essential elements" of good principles and practices in treating prisoners and managing institutions. The document acknowledged that penal conditions vary greatly from country to country.

To supplement these rules, in 1988 the UN General Assembly adopted the Body of Principles for the Protection of All Persons under Any Form of Detention or Imprisonment, whose purpose was to protect the physical safety of prisoners and detainees. Persons held in custody are to be treated humanely and with respect for their dignity, it states, and the use of torture or other cruel, inhumane, or degrading treatment was prohibited. Unlike the Standard Minimum Rules, however, it did not specify procedures for implementing the principles or reporting violations. In 1994 the Commission on Human Rights called attention to the fact that arbitrary detention was often a result of a government's abuse of emergency powers and vague definitions of offenses against state security. That year the Working Group on Arbitrary Detention received nearly three hundred complaints from persons regarding arbitrary detention, but requests to the accused governments resulted in fewer than one hundred responses. As a result, the working group has made recommendations to improve government concern for persons detained arbitrarily, including members of the UN staff.

Detention is addressed in some national constitutions and a number of international human rights documents. Specific provisions in the European Convention for the Protection of Human Rights and Fundamental Freedoms (1950) may have had a salutary effect on detention practices in some European nations, including Belgium, Greece, and Italy. In addition, in 1987 the Council of Europe established the European Committee for the Prevention of Torture and Inhuman or Degrading Treatment or Punishment, a group of international inspectors that since 1989 has visited police stations, barracks, psychiatric hospitals, detention centers for foreigners, and other places where abuses of detention or imprisonment may occur.

Constitution of Portugal (1976), article 28, paragraph 1: "Preventive custody without judicial charge is subject to the scrutiny of a court within 48 hours, in order to determine the validity of, or to continue, the detention; the court shall hear the reasons for the detention and shall inform the detainee of them, and conduct an examination of and provide him or her with the opportunity to present a defense."

International Covenant on Civil and Political Rights (1966), article 9, paragraph 1: "Everyone has the right to liberty and security of person. No one shall be subjected to arbitrary arrest or detention. No one shall be deprived of his liberty except on such grounds and in accordance with such procedure as are established by law."

High Court of Ireland (1971): "It is . . . sufficient to say that . . . the arrest and detention of an unconvicted person . . . [and] a person duly convicted and properly sentenced is quite different."

Inter-American Commission on Human Rights (1996): In the case of a person held in preventive detention from 1989 to 1993 without being sentenced, Argentina violated the American Convention on Human Rights (1969), article 7(5), which guarantees the right of a detained person to a trial within a reasonable time or to be released without prejudice to the continuation of the proceedings.

Cassese, Antonio. *Inhuman States: Imprisonment, Detention and Torture in Europe Today*. Cambridge, England: Polity, 1996.

Frankowski, Stanislaw, and Dinah Shelton, eds. *Preventive Detention: A Comparative and International Law Perspective*. The Hague: Martinus Nijhoff, Kluwer Law International, 1992.

Body of Principles for the Protection of All Persons under Any Form of Detention or Imprisonment; Commission on Human Rights; European Convention for the Protection of Human Rights and Fundamental Freedoms; Fair Trial; International Covenant on Civil and Political Rights; Liberty; Prisoners; Punishment; Security; Standard Minimum Rules for the Treatment of Prisoners; Working Groups

Development

The notion that a country's potential for economic, social, and cultural growth should be developed has been held for at least as long as humans have formed political communities. Today the right of development (from the Old French *desvolper*, meaning to unwrap or disentangle) is primarily a corollary of economic and collective rights and is linked with the phasing out of European colonial empires. Based on the inherent sovereignty of each nation, development—often considered a third-generation right—is of special significance for the postcolonial countries because it embodies their right to exploit their own resources free from foreign domination or undue influence and to improve their economic, social, and cultural well-being in accordance with their own national policies and priorities.

Many nations have, in addition to national laws and regulations dealing with development policy and rights, a stated national policy on development. Some national constitutions expressly address development objectives, and some countries provide foreign aid to promote other countries' development. Private businesses also offer such assistance and in turn benefit from the increased development opportunities.

International documents such as the International Covenant on Civil and Political Rights (1966) and the International Covenant on Economic, Social and Cultural Rights (1966) illustrate a worldwide interest in the right of all peoples to "dispose of their wealth and resources." In 1986 the UN General Assembly adopted the Declaration on the Right to Development, which proclaimed development to be an inalienable right of each person and peoples and emphasized that humans are the activity's central subject and should actively participate in and benefit from the right to development.

Development has been a continuing concern of the Commission on Human Rights and the UN Committee on Economic, Social and Cultural Rights, which in 1990 sponsored in Geneva a Global Consultation on the Realization of the Right to Development as a Human Right. In addition, in 1995 a commission of experts on sustainable development was created to advise the United Nations. A report addressed, among other issues, the rights to development and a healthy environment, eradication of poverty, equity, sovereignty over natural resources, sustainable use of natural resources, and prevention of environmental harm.

Declaration of the Establishment of the State of Israel (1948): "The State of Israel will be open for Jewish immigration and for the Ingathering of the Exiles; it will foster the development of the country for the benefit of all its inhabitants. . . ."

African Charter on Human and Peoples' Rights (1981), article 22: "1. All peoples shall have the right to their economic, social and cultural development with due regard to their freedom and identity and in the equal enjoyment of the common heritage of mankind. 2. States shall have the duty, individually and collectively, to ensure the exercise of the right to development."

High Court of Australia (1983): The court upheld a statute prohibiting construction of a dam in an area eligible for inclusion on the World Heritage List and therefore for protection under the Convention Concerning the Protection of the World Cultural and Natural Heritage (in force in Australia since 1975), thus saving the Western Tasmanian Wilderness National Parks from government development.

International Court of Justice (1949): In addition to their right to exploit their own resources, nations have the responsibility to ensure that they do not damage the environment of other nations.

UN Development Fund for Women, 304 East 45th Street, 15th Floor, New York, N.Y. 10017. (212-906-6400. 212-906-6705. unifem@undp.org. www.unifem.undp.org.

UN Development Program, Sustainable Development Networking Program, One United Nations Plaza, New York, N.Y. 10017. (212-906-5315. 212-906-5364. hq@undp.org. www.undp.org.

The World Bank, 1818 H Street, N.W., Washington, D.C. 20433. (202-477-1234. 202-522-1500. growth@worldbank.org. www.worldbank.org.

Ginther, Konrad, Erik Denters, and Paul J. I. M. de Waart, eds. *Sustainable Development and Good Governance*. The Hague: Martinus Nijhoff, Kluwer Law International, 1995.

Integrating Human Rights with Sustainable Development. New York: United Nations Development Program, 1998.

Collective Rights; Convention on the Protection of the World Cultural and Natural Heritage; Declaration on Social Progress and Development; Declaration on the Right to Development; Economic Rights; Environment; Natural Resources; Rio Declaration on Environment and Development

Die, Right to

The fact that all human beings must face death has been the source of much moral, religious, social, and artistic comment. Plato, the ancient Greek philosopher, accepted the taking of one's own life under certain circumstances, while his student Aristotle declared that suicide was cowardly and "treats the state unjustly." The Greek and Roman Stoics, on the other hand, viewed suicide at the close of life as the responsible, appropriate act of a wise person. Seneca, the first-century Roman Stoic, playwright, and essayist, declared: "Just as I choose a ship to sail in or a house to live in, so I choose a death for my passage from life."

Even as it becomes more recognized as a human right, the right to die remains extremely controversial, garnering—along with the issues of abortion and capital punishment—vehement proponents and opponents. This act entails each individual's right to decide, whether because of extreme pain, suffering, or terminal illness, to end his or her own life. The right to die is closely related to the concepts of euthanasia and assisted suicide and the more universally recognized right to refuse medical treatment.

Euthanasia (from the Greek *eu*, meaning good, and *thanos*, meaning death) is the act of bringing a painless death, presumably for merciful reasons. Since World War II, however, when it was associated with the Nazis' enforced death of the elderly, sick, and unwanted, the term has had a strongly negative connotation.

Assisted suicide refers to help given by one person, often a physician or other medically trained individual, to another who seeks a voluntary death. Because suicide is considered an act that the state or an individual should try to prevent, the question arises whether a person who facilitates such a death, even if it is the conscious choice of the person assisted, is guilty of a crime. In March 1999 a Michigan jury convicted Jack Kevorkian, a seventy-year-old retired doctor, of second-degree murder for administering a lethal injection at the request of a fifty-year-old man. Oregon as well as Switzerland and the Netherlands, however, have legalized assisted suicide.

The right to refuse medical treatment or to declare that one does not want life-sustaining treatment in the event of extreme disability is now routinely accepted in some countries, including the United Kingdom and the United States. Such a decision grants individuals a measure of control over the conditions of their life and death, but it is far from acknowledging the right to die, which requires a positive act—taking a life—rather than a negative act—terminating life-sustaining treatment. For persons unable to make an informed, rational decision for themselves, the questions continue as to who decides to terminate life support—family members, doctors, or the courts—and on what basis—the patient's chances of recovery, likely quality of life, painfulness of the condition, age, or religious belief.

A person's right to die raises a number of conflicting moral concerns. Many religions and human rights documents proclaim the sanctity of life and the right to life. Doctors are sworn to preserve life and "do no harm." Yet, to be treated with dignity and respect is a basic human right, and right-to-die advocates often describe assisted suicide as exercising "the right to die with dignity." The right to privacy supports individuals' freedom to choose the method of their death without the state's interference, and it also allows family members to make such a decision in consultation with doctors in cases where the individual had previously made a voluntary medical directive or "living will."

Although national constitutions may contain language guaranteeing the right to life in order to deter abortions, none of the written national constitutions of major countries directly addresses the issue of one's right to die. Similarly, international human rights documents have not declared that the right to die is a universal human right. Like abortion and the death penalty, the right-to-die issue will probably remain a polarizing one, unresolved for some time.

Constitution of New Zealand, Bill of Rights (1990), part II, Civil and Political Rights, [article] 11: "Everyone has the right to refuse to undergo any medical treatment."

U.K. Court of Appeals, Criminal Division (1975): The fact that a stabbing victim died after refusing a blood transfusion because of religious beliefs, in effect hastening death, did not in any way vindicate the perpetrator.

Exit, 17 Hart Street, Edinburgh EH1 3RN, Scotland. ☎ 44-131-556-4404. 📠 44-131-557-4403. 🖳 didmsnj@easynet.co.uk. 🖥 www.euthanasia.org.

Hemlock Society U.S.A., P.O. Box 101810, Denver, Colo. 80250. ☎ 303-639-1202. 📠 303-639-1224. 🖳 hemlock@privatei.com. 🖥 www.hemlock.org.

World Federation of Right to Die Societies. 📠 61-2-98092-5340. 🖳 libbydrake@optushome.com.au. 🖥 www.finalexit.org.

Griffiths, John, Alex Bood, and Heleen Weyers. *Euthanasia and Law in the Netherlands*. Amsterdam: Amsterdam University Press, 1999.

Zucker, Marjorie B., ed. *The Right to Die Debate: A Documentary History*. Westport, Conn.: Greenwood, 1999.

Abortion; Aristotle; Capital Punishment; Dignity; Life; Plato; Privacy

Dignity

The pursuit of human rights rests on the concept that each person has worth or dignity (from the Latin *dignus*, meaning worthy or suitable, and *dignatio*, meaning reputation). "[R]ecognition of the inherent dignity and of the equal and inalienable rights of all members of the human family," states the preamble of the Universal Declaration of Human Rights (1948), "is the foundation of freedom, justice, and peace in the world. . . ." Toward this end, government must respect individuals for themselves and not simply as the means by which its policies are executed.

In ancient Greece, *timē* (honor or worth) was highly prized by the citizens of democratically governed Athens. Ambition, or the love of *timē*, drove Greeks to accomplish great deeds, while *atimia* (dishonor) could result in the loss of rights, including disenfranchisement. An official of the Roman Republic called a censor could place a mark *(censure)* by a citizen's name on the census list to indicate great social disgrace. In Magna Carta (1215), the earliest English constitutional document, article 39 provides that "no free man shall . . . in any way be destroyed . . . ," a provision that includes an attack on a person's reputation or honor.

Centuries later, the notion that all people have a right to be treated with equal dignity is far from fully accepted in the world. Even though personal dignity is inherent in most national constitutions and international human rights documents, public officials in many countries fail to observe these provisions and treat numerous individuals with disdain. Slavery, as such, has been banned worldwide, but in many countries the treatment of women, children, the mentally ill, homeless people, and members of religious, ethnic, political, and cultural minorities is an affront to human dignity. Members of minority groups, however, are increasingly focusing on instilling in their youth a sense of cultural identity to raise their self-esteem, which is often difficult to maintain in the face of a pervasive majority culture.

National constitutions and laws generally contain provisions guaranteeing citizens' dignity or reputation, ensuring, for example, that a person whose reputation has been damaged by slander or libel has legal redress. More broadly, the rights of freedom of speech, the press, religion, and assembly are predicated on the assumption that individuals have the right to give personal meaning and expression to their lives without government interference or coercion. Similarly, the rights of persons accused of crimes, such as the presumption that the accused is innocent until proven guilty in accordance with due process of law, is based on a person's presumed worth and dignity.

Constitution of South Africa (1997), chapter 2, Bill of Rights, section 10: "Everyone has inherent dignity and the right to have their dignity respected and protected."

African Charter of Human and Peoples' Rights (1981), chapter I, Human and Peoples' Rights, article 5: "Every individual shall have the right to the respect of the dignity inherent in a human being. . . ."

Constitutional Court of South Africa (Concurring Opinion) (1995): "The importance of dignity as a founding value of the new Constitution cannot be overemphasized. Recognizing a right to dignity is an acknowledgement of the intrinsic worth of human beings: human beings are entitled to be treated as worthy of respect and concern."

Inter-American Commission on Human Rights (1983): A man whose personal and civic honor is insulted in a magazine controlled by the government must be afforded the opportunity to clear his name in a fair trial.

Egonsson, Dan. *Dimensions of Dignity: The Moral Importance of Being Human.* The Hague: Kluwer Law International, 1998.

Stetson, Brad. *Human Dignity and Contemporary Liberalism.* Westport, Conn.: Praeger, 1998.

Accused; Cultural Rights; Due Process; Expression; Magna Carta; Minorities; Names; Personality; The Press; Religion; Speech

Diplomats and Consuls

Throughout history, emissaries or representatives of territorial jurisdictions have journeyed to foreign territories on matters of state. Officials who serve as their country's accredited representatives in a foreign country and are accepted as such by the host government are known as diplomatic officers. *(Diplomatic,* meaning pertaining to the management of international relations, is derived from the Greek word for *diploma,* a certificate conferring a privilege or an honor.)

Diplomatic rights are the privileges and immunities of diplomatic officers in host countries as well as the rights and protections that such officers may afford to fellow citizens who are temporarily in the host country. Consuls (from the Latin *consulo,* meaning to promote interests) are officials from one country sent to another to facilitate commercial transactions between citizens of their country and the host nation and to assist its citizens abroad. They also have certain rights and protections but not to the same extent as diplomatic officers.

The principles of international law governing diplomatic immunity that developed in Europe after the Middle Ages stem from the basic presumption that a country's sovereign was above domestic law and that his or her personal representatives in a foreign country should be accorded the same immunity. When permanent diplomatic missions were established reciprocally, the territory of the mission itself was deemed to be the territory of the foreign sovereign. As such, it might provide sanctuary for persons trying to escape apprehension by the domestic law enforcement forces of the host state.

Most national constitutions provide for the accreditation of diplomatic officers from one state to another. Because diplomatic and consular affairs deal with interstate or international matters, they are generally handled in the executive branch of government through the department or ministry of state or foreign affairs. In addition, because the UN headquarters is located in New York City, the U.S. International Organizations Immunities Act (1945) extends certain protections to both UN representatives from foreign governments and UN employees.

At the international level, a number of customary law provisions and agreements address the rights, duties, and privileges of diplomatic and consular officers and the rights of the citizens they serve. With respect to the right of asylum, for example, the Inter-American Convention on Diplomatic Asylum (1954), article 8, provides that the "diplomatic representative [among others] shall as soon as possible after asylum is granted, report the fact to the Minister of Foreign Affairs of the territorial State, or to the local administrative authority if the case arose outside the capital."

Constitution of Italy (1948), part II, The System of the Republic, title II, President of the Republic: "87. The President of the Republic is the Chief of State and represents the national unity.... He accredits and receives the diplomatic representatives...."

Declaration on the Human Rights of Individuals Who Are Not Nationals of the Country in Which They Live (1985), article 10: "Any alien shall be free at any time to communicate with the consulate or diplomatic mission of the State of which he or she is a national or, in the absence thereof, with the consulate or diplomatic mission of any other State entrusted with the protection of the interests of the State of which he or she is a national in the State where he or she resides."

U.S. Court of Appeals, Ninth Circuit (1999): In setting aside the conviction of a Mexican citizen for possession of marijuana, the court directed that a federal trial judge determine if the fact that the defendant was not notified of his consular rights had harmed his defense.

Permanent Court of International Justice (1939): Because the right to diplomatic protection depends on the nationality of the injured party, in the absence of an agreement between two states waiving the strict application of the rule, the nation asserting the right of protection must establish the nationality of the injured party.

Frey, Linda S., and Marsha L. Frey. *The History of Diplomatic Immunity.* Columbus: Ohio State University Press, 1999.

Ludwik, Dembinski. *Diplomatic and Consular Law: Selected Instruments.* New York: P. Lang, 1992.

Asylum; Declaration on Territorial Asylum; Sovereignty; Territorial Jurisdiction

Disabled Persons

The disabled—physically or mentally handicapped individuals who require special care or accommodation—number some 500 million persons, most of them living in developing countries, and constitute the world's largest minority. Care for the disabled has traditionally fallen to the family or the community, but social changes since World War II, particularly in the world's developed nations, have led to a heightened awareness of the needs, abilities, and rights of disabled persons. Much of the responsibility for assisting them is now shared by local and national governments through direct assistance and special programs.

The rights of the disabled are positive rights in that they require governments and private individuals subject to public laws to make an effort to accommodate them. Such rights require either enforcement of nondiscrimination statutes or the creation of new provisions to take care of the special needs of disabled persons. In this latter category are laws and regulations requiring such changes as architectural considerations (ramps, seating, and restrooms), accessible public transportation, and special equipment for communicating with the deaf and the blind. While many developed nations have laws accommodating the disabled with respect to political participation, employment opportunities, and access to public and commercial spaces and activities, national constitutions generally address only the possible disability of the chief executive.

Little international attention was given to the needs of the disabled until the UN General Assembly in 1971 adopted the Principles for the Protection of Persons with Mental Illness and the Improvement of Mental Health Care and issued the Declaration on the Rights of Mentally Retarded Persons. In 1975 the General Assembly adopted the Declaration on the Rights of Disabled Persons, which in paragraph 1 defines *disabled person* as "any person unable to ensure by himself or herself, wholly or partly, the necessities of a normal individual and/or social life, as a result of a deficiency, either congenital or not, in his or her physical or mental capabilities." (The terms *able* or *able bodied* are now preferred to *normal individual.*) The declaration, which the UN recommends all member states bear in mind when developing their national plans and programs, states in paragraph 3: "Disabled persons have the inherent right to respect for their human dignity . . . [and] the same fundamental rights as their fellow-citizens of the same age, which implies first and foremost the right to enjoy a decent life, as normal and full as possible." Paragraph 8 provides that "disabled persons are entitled to have their special needs taken into consideration at all stages of economic and social planning."

In addition, the General Assembly designated 1981 as the International Year of Disabled Persons, promulgated the World Program of Action concerning Disabled Persons in 1982, proclaimed 1983 to 1992 the Decade of Disabled Persons, and adopted the Standard Rules on Equalization of Opportunity for Persons with Disabilities in 1993. In 1989 an Additional Protocol to the American Convention on Human Rights (1969), article 18, also addressed the handicapped.

The International Meeting on Human Resources in the Field of Disability, held in Tallinn, Estonia, in 1989, adopted the Guidelines for Action on Human Resources Development in the Field of Disability, which the United Nations then recommended be brought to the attention of member states and other concerned organizations. Known as the Tallinn Guidelines, the document's philosophy is stated in paragraph 7: "Through human resources development, disabled persons are able effectively to exercise their rights of full citizenship. As full citizens, they have the same rights and responsibilities as other members of society. . . ."

Disabled Peoples International, a nongovernmental organization founded in 1981, has formal associations with international bodies such as the Economic and Social Council (ECOSOC), International Labor Organization, and United Nations Educational, Scientific and Cultural Organization (UNESCO). Its manifesto calls for equalization of opportunities to ensure full participation for the world's disabled in education, rehabilitation, employment, economic security, and independent living, among other rights.

And yet, according to the former UN secretary-general Javier Perez de Cuellar, for most of the world's disabled "[e]quality of opportunity simply does not exist. . . ." He warned that "the number of disabled persons is likely to increase radically over the next twenty-five years . . . posing major questions on how governments are to square their commitments to introduce equal rights legislation with the fiscal demands this will impose on their budgets." The High Commissioner for Human Rights, however, has stated that "law-makers are beginning to accept that disability is first a human rights issue, and only secondly a medical [matter]."

Canadian Charter of Rights and Freedoms (1982), part I, Equality Rights, [section] 15: "(1) Every individual is equal before and under the law and has the right to the equal protection and equal benefit of the law without discrimination and, in particular, without discrimination based on . . . mental or physical disability. (2) [Section 15(1)] does not preclude any law, program or activity that has as its object the amelioration of conditions of disadvantaged individuals or groups including those that are disadvantaged because of . . . mental or physical disability."

Declaration on the Rights of Mentally Retarded Persons (1971): "1. The mentally retarded person has, to the maximum degree of

feasibility, the same rights as other human beings. 2. The mentally retarded person has a right to proper medical care and physical therapy and to such education, training, rehabilitation and guidance as will enable him to develop his ability and maximum potential."

Ontario (Canada) Board of Inquiry (1993): Lack of visual acuity not resulting "from bodily injury, birth defect or illness" does not constitute a "handicap" under the Human Rights Code (1981).

European Court of Human Rights (1979): The court set forth the minimum conditions required for the "lawful detention of a person of unsound mind [mentally disabled]" in the context of the European Convention for the Protection of Human Rights and Fundamental Freedoms (1950), article 5.1, which guarantees that a person can be deprived of his or her liberty only in accordance with a procedure prescribed by law.

Disabled Peoples International, 101-7 Evergreen Place, Winnipeg, Manitoba, R3L 2T3 Canada. (204-287-8010. 204-453-1367. dpi@dpi.org. www.dpi.org.

Degener, Theresia, and Yolan Koster-Dreese, eds. *Human Rights and Disabled Persons: Essays and Relevant Human Rights Instruments.* The Hague: Martinus Nijhoff, Kluwer Law International, 1995.

Levy, Robert M., and Leonard S. Rubenstein. *The Rights of People with Mental Disabilities.* Carbondale, Ill.: Southern Illinois University Press, 1996.

American Convention on Human Rights; Declaration on the Rights of Disabled Persons; Discrimination; Guidelines for Action on Human Resources Development in the Field of Disability (Tallinn Guidelines); Health; Rehabilitation

Disappearance

Citizens who are illegally removed from society by their government without any warning or explanation are said to be victims of disappearance, enforced disappearance, or involuntary disappearance. Such persons—called "the disappeared"—are held incommunicado and are often tortured, raped, and murdered.

Government authorities have long acted outside the law to commit violations of human rights against their own unsuspecting and undefended citizens. The Nazis used this tactic, as did the dictators of the Soviet Union and other countries. Today the term refers specifically to a repressive practice used in the "Southern Cone" of South America—countries such as Argentina, Chile, and Uruguay, which were under military rule in the 1970s and 1980s. Such measures have generally been rationalized by those in power as necessary for national security, but they become simply a license to torture and murder with impunity.

A 1986 report prepared by the Independent Commission on International Humanitarian Issues in London described a typical disappearance: "Some men arrive. They force their way into a family's home.... They come at any time of the day or night, usually in plain clothes, sometimes in uniform, always carrying weapons. Giving no reasons, producing no arrest warrant, frequently without saying who they are or on whose authority they are acting, they drag off one or more members of the family towards a car, using violence in the process if necessary."

The horrors of disappearance became so great in Argentina that on April 30, 1977, a dozen women who had searched in vain for their disappeared children gathered in the Plaza de Mayo, the main square, of the capital city of Buenos Aires. Soon known as the Mothers of the Plaza de Mayo, they held a weekly vigil there and became symbols of resistance to the Argentine government's repressive nature. Although some of these brave women also disappeared, their numbers grew to nearly five thousand. Similar groups formed throughout Latin America under the name of the Federation of Families of Disappeared Persons and Political Prisoners (FEDEFAM), including the Grandmothers of the Plaza de Mayo, organized in October 1977. Although military rule has ended in the Southern Cone, the matter of the missing victims of these regimes has been handled in various ways, none satisfactory.

In 1980 the Commission on Human Rights established the Working Group on Enforced or Involuntary Disappearances. "There is every reason for the international community to remain alert," the group's 1994 report stated, "for the phenomenon of disappearances is still rampant." In 1992 the UN General Assembly adopted the Declaration on the Protection of All Persons from Enforced Disappearance, which affirmed that any act of involuntary disappearance is "an offense to human dignity," urged countries to take measures to ensure that such acts do not take place in their territory, and provided guidelines for nations on how to deal with the problem. Although enforced disappearance in South America's Southern Cone has abated, this practice as well as even more direct attacks on citizens suspected of disloyalty to the government in power undoubtedly continues to be used by repressive regimes in such countries as Iraq and Serbian Yugoslavia.

Constitution of Argentina (1994), first part, second chapter, New Rights and Guarantees, article 43: "When the right which has been harmed, restricted, altered, or threatened relates to physical liberty or to a case of illegal worsening in the form or condition of deten-

tion, or in the forced disappearances of persons, the writ of habeas corpus may be imposed by the affected person or by someone else to benefit him; the judge is to resolve the issue immediately, even while there is a state of siege."

Declaration on the Protection of All Persons from Enforced Disappearance (1992), preamble: "[E]nforced disappearance undermines the deepest values of any society committed to respect for the rule of law, human rights and fundamental freedoms, and . . . the systematic practice of such acts is of the nature of a crime against humanity."

U.S. District Court, Northern District of California (1988): A complaint against a former Argentine general who helped conduct a war against subversives cited the international tort of "causing disappearance." The complaint was upheld on the basis that disappearance is a universally recognized wrong under the law of nations.

Inter-American Court of Human Rights (1989): In the so-called Honduran disappearance cases, the first international adjudication of enforced disappearance found that Honduras was responsible for the disappearance of two Honduran nationals but that its responsibility for the disappearance of two Costa Ricans had not been established.

Derechos Human Rights, P.O. Box 2516, El Cerrito, Calif. 94530-5516. ☎ 510-483-4005. 📠 603-372-9710. 📧 hr@derechos.org. 🖥 www.derechos.org.

FEDEFAM, 2444 Carmelitas 1010-A, Caracas, Venezuela. ☎ 58-2-564-0503. 📠 58-2-564-2746. 📧 fedefam@true.net. 🖥 www.desaparecidos.org/fedefam.

Enforced or Involuntary Disappearances. Fact Sheet no. 6, rev. 2. Geneva: Center for Human Rights, 1997.

Declaration on the Protection of All Persons from Enforced Disappearance; Detention; Habeas Corpus; Impunity

Discrimination

"Let the very best educational opportunities be provided both races; and add to this an election law that shall be incapable of unjust discrimination," wrote Booker T. Washington, the black American educator and founder of the Tuskegee Institute in Alabama, in 1899. Discrimination (from the Latin *discriminatus,* meaning divided, separated, or distinguished) is the act of making distinctions between things and has been in use in English since the seventeenth century. Its meaning of prejudicial distinctions between people, especially between people of a different color or race, is of more recent origin.

At the core of human rights is the principle that all people should have equal political rights and be treated equally before the law. Freedom and justice for all depend on non-discrimination in the political process and the legal system: although individuals may never become truly tolerant and nondiscriminatory, governments—which are the objects of human rights provisions—should be.

Aristotle, the Greek philosopher of the fourth century B.C.E., points out in *The Politics* that in "the many forms of government which have sprung up there has always been an acknowledgment of justice and proportionate equality, although mankind fail[s] in attaining them. . . . Democracy, for example, arises out of the notion that those who are equal in any respect are equal in all respects; because men are equally free, they claim to be absolutely equal." Of course, only adult male citizens of Greece were considered free and equal (women and slaves were not included in Aristotle's notion of democracy).

Slavery, the caste system, aristocracy, single-party political domination of government, apartheid, segregation, and genocide are all forms of discrimination by one group or type of people against others. Much of history has been a struggle to expand the universe of people who must be considered equal and not discriminated against. An early milestone along this path was Magna Carta (1215), the charter of English rights and liberties that prohibited the English king from denying to any man either justice or right. The Bill of Rights (1791) of the U.S. Constitution and the Universal Declaration of Human Rights (1948) are similar milestones. In times of emergency, however, even such strong guarantees may be ignored. During World War II, for example, the United States, contrary to its own constitutional provisions, treated Asian Americans discriminatorily by interning them in camps.

The experiences of slavery, colonialism, and world war culminated in the prohibition of discrimination in many national constitutions and international treaties drawn up after the war. The Charter of the United Nations (1945) expressly acknowledges the "equal rights of men and women." The Universal Declaration of Human Rights, after declaring in article 1 that "[a]ll human beings are born free and equal in dignity and rights," states in article 2: "Everyone is entitled to all the rights and freedoms set forth in this Declaration, without distinction of any kind, such as race, color, sex, language, religion, political or other opinion, national or social origin, property, birth or other status." Additional international documents that address the evils of discrimination include the International Convention on the Elimination of All Forms of Racial Discrimination (1965) and the Declaration on the Elimination of All Forms of Intolerance and of Discrimination Based on Religion or Belief (1981).

Constitution of Japan (1947), chapter III, Rights and Duties of the People, article 14: "All of the people are equal under the law and there shall be no discrimination in political, economic, or social relations because of race, creed, sex, social status, or family origin."

International Covenant on Civil and Political Rights (1966), part II, article 2: "1. Each State Party to the present Covenant undertakes to respect and to ensure to all individuals within its territory and subject to its jurisdiction the rights recognized in the present Covenant, without distinction of any kind, such as race, color, sex, language, religion, political or other opinion, national or social origin, property, birth or other status."

Supreme Court of Canada (Dissenting Opinion) (1989): "[D]iscrimination may be described as a distinction, whether intentional or not but based on grounds relating to personal characteristics of the individual or group, which has the effect of imposing burdens, obligations, or disadvantages on such individual or group not imposed upon others, or which withholds or limits access to opportunities, benefits, and advantages available to other members of society. Distinctions based on personal characteristics attributed to an individual solely on the basis of association with a group will rarely escape the charge of discrimination, while those based on an individual's merits and capacities will rarely be so classed."

Inter-American Court of Human Rights (Advisory Opinion) (1984): "The notion of equality springs directly from the oneness of the human family and is linked to the essential dignity of the individual. That principle cannot be reconciled with the notion that a given group has the right to privileged treatment because of its perceived superiority. It is equally irreconcilable with that notion to characterize a group as inferior and treat it with hostility or otherwise subject it to discrimination in the enjoyment of rights which are accorded to others not so classified. It is impermissible to subject human beings to differences in treatment that are inconsistent with their unique and congenerous [belonging to the same species] character."

MacEwen, Martin. *Anti-Discrimination Law Enforcement: A Comparative Perspective.* Brookfield, Vt.: Ashgate, 1997.

Svensson-McCarthy, Anna-Lena. *The International Law of Human Rights and States of Exception.* The Hague: Kluwer Law International, 1998.

Apartheid; Aristotle; Charter of the United Nations; Declaration on the Elimination of All Forms of Intolerance and of Discrimination Based on Religion or Belief; Equality; Genocide; International

Convention on the Elimination of All Forms of Racial Discrimination; Magna Carta; Minorities; Race Discrimination; Religion; Sex Discrimination; Slavery; Tolerance; Universal Declaration of Human Rights

Displaced Persons

See Expulsion; Refugees; Statelessness

Divorce

See Marriage

Doctors without Borders

Medical treatment can be considered part of the right to basic health care guaranteed in many national constitutions and international human rights documents. Begun in 1971 by young French doctors as Médecins sans Frontières, Doctors without Borders (as it is known in English) established an international presence over two decades and in 1999 was awarded the Nobel Peace Prize. Although the organization's major emphasis is to provide medical relief to populations in crisis, it also speaks out against human rights abuses and violations when medical assistance alone is not enough to save lives. A private, nonprofit, nongovernmental humanitarian organization with offices in eighteen countries, Doctors without Borders relies on volunteer health professionals and charitable contributions to fulfill its mission.

The organization's basic principles are found in its charter. Doctors without Borders offers assistance to victims of natural or human disasters, including armed conflicts, without discrimination by race, religion, creed, or political affiliation. It pledges to maintain strict neutrality and impartiality in the name of universal medical ethics as well as complete independence from political, economic, and religious influence. Its volunteers are aware of the risks and dangers of their missions and agree to accept only whatever compensation or benefits the organization may be able to provide for their support.

Since its founding Doctors without Borders has provided medical assistance to victims of earthquakes in Nicaragua, El Salvador, and Armenia; war in Lebanon, Somalia, Sudan, Kenya, and Rwanda; the Soviet invasion of Afghanistan; famine in Ethiopia; the Kurdish refugee crisis in northern Iraq; a meningitis outbreak in Nigeria, and the temporary disruption of medical services in Eastern Europe after the collapse of communism. More recently, its volunteers assisted with refugee camps in Albania, Macedonia, and Montenegro in the wake of the Serbian government's attempt at

ethnic cleansing in Kosovo in 1998–99; they also continued to provide services to the refugees when they returned to Kosovo after the military intervention by the forces of the North Atlantic Treaty Organization (NATO). Other areas of the world in which the organization has provided urgently needed medical assistance include Sierra Leone, Angola, Congo, and Sri Lanka.

Doctors without Borders USA, Six East 39th Street, Eighth Floor, New York, N.Y. 10016. (212-679-6800. 🖳 212-679-7016. 🖳 doctors@newyork.msf.org. 🖳 www.doctorswithoutborders.org.

Médecins sans Frontières International, 39 rue de la Tourelle, 1040 Brussels, Belgium. (32-2-280-1881. 🖳 32-2-280-0173. 🖳 office-intnl@brussels.msf.org. 🖳 www.doctorswithoutborders.org.

Leyton, Elliott. *Touched by Fire: Doctors without Borders in a Third World Crisis.* Toronto: McClelland and Stewart, 1998.

Health; Physicians for Human Rights; World Health Organization

Domestic Violence

Domestic violence is as old as the human family. Households and extended families have long been headed by a man and subject to his will. In ancient Greece, although all Athenian men of legal age were citizens with rights to vote and participate in governing the city-state, women were considered akin to children, under the control of a male family member. In ancient Rome, by law no woman could head a household or exercise the legal authority given to the head of the family.

Violence between members of a household constitutes unwarranted and unlawful physical force with the intent to do harm. Typically it pits a man against a woman with whom he is living, whether in marriage or not. Such violence may take the form of beatings, rape, or verbal attacks. When directed against children, it may include incest, extreme physical punishment, and even torture. Elderly parents or other relatives living in the same household may also be subject to domestic violence.

Because violence in the family is often unreported—or, if reported, treated by the police as a matter to be settled domestically—it is difficult to know its true extent. The Center for Health and Gender Equity recently released figures indicating that about one in three women around the world reported battering and abuse by their husbands and partners. In countries such as Turkey, Bangladesh, and Ethiopia, about half of women reported such abuse. Twenty-two percent of U.S. women said that they suffered from violence at home, while in Britain the figure was 30 percent, in Canada 29 percent, in the Netherlands 21 percent, and in South Africa 13 percent. Continuing physical and emotional abuse by family members has led to identification of such problems as the "battered-woman" and "battered-child" syndromes. In 1996 three million children in the United States were reported to be victims of domestic violence, and annual costs for intervention services resulting from the maltreatment of children are conservatively estimated at a half billion dollars.

To a great extent, women, children, and elderly family members have relied on chivalry, religion, and social constraints to protect them from the head of the household's near absolute right to treat them in any manner he pleases. The emergence of legal systems and the equal application of human rights laws have offered vulnerable persons greater protection from abuse at the hands of stronger or more aggressive family members. But debate still continues over the point at which private violence is an abuse of human rights and which national and international responses are required to effectively deal with it. Awareness by law enforcement officials, social workers, and judges of the physical and mental trauma as well as the criminal behavior involved is therefore an important step in protecting the human rights of victims of family abuse.

Western constitutional democracies are leading the effort to develop social and legal policies to deal with domestic violence. In many countries, however, the problem is exacerbated by both culture and religion, which tend to reinforce the unequal rights of male members of households and thus vindicate their acts of violence against weaker family members. Some international human rights documents—for example, the Declaration on the Elimination of Violence against Women (1993) and the Declaration on Social and Legal Principles Relating to the Protection and Welfare of Children, with Special Reference to Foster Placement and Adoption Nationally and Internationally (1986)—address issues associated with domestic violence. But the generally accepted notion of the sanctity of the family and many countries' cultural support for a male-dominated family unit make it more difficult to raise freedom from domestic violence to the level of a universal human right.

Prevention of Family Violence Act 133 (South Africa) (1993): "The promise of equal protection may require the state to foster equality by protecting vulnerable persons and groups from domination by more powerful individuals and groups, whether within the public or the private domain."

United Nations Resolution 40/36 (1985): UN member states are called on "(a) [t]o introduce . . . civil and criminal legislation in order to deal with particular problems of domestic violence, and to enact and enforce such laws in order to protect battered family members

and punish the offender and to offer alternative ways of treatment for offenders. . . . (b) to respect, in all instances of the criminal proceeding, starting with the police investigation, the special and sometimes delicate position of the victim. . . . (f) to provide, as a temporary solution, shelters and other facilities and services for the safety of victims of domestic violence. . . ."

U.S. District Court, Eastern District of Pennsylvania (1985): "Expert testimony on battered woman syndrome is distinctly related to a psychological evaluation beyond the comprehension of the average lay person, and thus assists the jury to understand the evidence."

European Court of Human Rights (1995): In holding that the conviction of a husband for the rape of his wife did not violate the European Convention for the Protection of Human Rights and Fundamental Freedoms (1950), article 7, the court noted: "[T]he abandonment of the unacceptable idea of a husband being immune from prosecution for rape of his wife was in conformity with a civilized concept of marriage, but also, and above all, with the fundamental objectives of the Convention, the very essence of which is respect for human dignity and human freedom."

MacLeod, Linda, and Dianne Kinnon. *Taking the Next Step to Stop Woman Abuse: From Violence Prevention to Individual, Family, Community and Societal Health.* Ottawa: National Clearinghouse on Family Violence, Health Promotion and Programs Branch, Health Canada, 1996.

UN Center for Social Development and Humanitarian Affairs. *Strategies for Confronting Domestic Violence: A Resource Manual.* New York: United Nations, 1993.

Declaration on Social and Legal Principles Relating to the Protection and Welfare of Children, with Special Reference to Foster Placement and Adoption Nationally and Internationally; Declaration on the Elimination of Violence against Women; Families; Inter-American Convention on the Prevention, Punishment and Eradication of Violence against Women

Drugs

Drug use and trafficking in illegal substances have posed major threats to individuals and nations for several centuries, but in the last half of the twentieth century the problems reached epidemic proportions in many countries. Greater freedom of movement internationally, the technology to synthesize new drugs, and the involvement of international drug cartels and criminal organizations have exacerbated the drug problem. The debilitating effect of drugs on families and especially on children and young adults has driven many countries to demand extreme measures to prevent their use and abuse. As a result, a number of rights issues can be identified: the right to use drugs, the production and distribution of drugs, drug abuse, treatment and rehabilitation of drug abusers and addicts, punishment of personal users and dealers, and drug experimentation on human subjects.

Long before modern drugs and narcotics such as morphine, cocaine, and heroin were manufactured, coca leaves, peyote, and the juice of opium poppies were used for religious and recreational purposes. Many plants from which drugs derive grew wild and were undoubtedly taken by early humans to alter their mental state. "Pharmacology antedated agriculture," contended Aldous Huxley, the British author of *Brave New World* (1932). Derived from Scandinavian and Middle English, the word *drug* to mean a medicinal substance has been in use in English since at least the fourteenth century. Only recently, beginning about the late nineteenth century, has it denoted narcotics, opiates, and hallucinogens used for personal enjoyment.

Drugs, like fire, have both beneficial and harmful uses, so the addiction to some drugs—like the addiction to alcohol, gambling, and tobacco—presents a public policy dilemma. National drug policies consequently vary from country to country. One solution, enforced in many nations today, is to declare all narcotic or recreational drugs illegal and enforce criminal sanctions against users. An alternative policy is to decriminalize their use but maintain government control of drug distribution and sale, the rationale being that recreational drugs—again like alcohol, gambling, and tobacco—should be a matter of personal choice and privacy: those who can afford them and are willing to risk using them may do so. The Netherlands allows the use of some drugs, particularly so-called soft drugs such as hashish and marijuana. Other nations, including Bolivia, Colombia, and Peru, either overtly or tacitly allow the production and sale of hard drugs such as cocaine and heroin. A complicating factor is that a large part of the drug trade today is an international criminal activity operating outside all laws, leaving death and devastation in its wake.

The first international conference on the problem of narcotic drugs was held in Shanghai, China, in 1909. Narcotic drugs were a focus of the League of Nations in 1920 and have been a concern of the United Nations almost since its inception in 1945. After World War II the World Health Organization addressed narcotic drugs through a series of international treaties that restricted the flow of opium, cocaine, and marijuana. The Single Convention on Narcotic Drugs (1961), dealing with synthetic narcotics, cannabis (marijuana), and cocaine, was followed by the Convention on Psychotropic Substances (1971); this document was amended in 1972 to highlight treatment and rehabilitation of drug addicts.

Noting "the urgency of preventing and punishing the illicit demand for . . . and illicit . . . traffic in drugs," the UN General Assembly in 1984 issued a Declaration on the Control of Drug Trafficking and Drug Abuse and then in 1988 adopted the Convention against Illicit Traffic in Narcotic Drugs and Psychotropic Substances. The drug problem was still acute in 1993, when the General Assembly acknowledged in a resolution its profound alarm at the "magnitude of the rising trend in drug abuse, illicit production and trafficking in narcotics and psychotropic substances that threaten the health and well-being of millions of persons, in particular the youth, in all the countries of the world."

Constitution of Singapore (1963), part IV, article 9: "(6): Nothing in this Article shall invalidate any law—. . . (b) relating to the misuse of drugs or intoxicating substances which authorizes the arrest and detention of any person for the purpose of treatment and rehabilitation."

Declaration on the Control of Drug Trafficking and Drug Abuse (1984): "1. Drug trafficking and drug abuse are extremely serious problems which, owing to their magnitude, scope and widespread pernicious effects, have become an international criminal activity demanding urgent attention and maximum priority. 2. The illegal production of, illicit demand for, abuse of and illicit trafficking in drugs impede economic and social progress, constitute a grave threat to the security and development of many countries and peoples and should be combated by all moral, legal and institutional means, at the national, regional and international levels."

Constitutional Court of Germany (1994): While sustaining the existing national drug laws, the court nevertheless advised the parliament to decriminalize the possession and use of small amounts of soft drugs such as hashish and marijuana.

European Court of Human Rights (1996): In the case of a Moroccan national deported from Belgium after being sentenced to seven years' imprisonment for drug possession and conspiracy, the court stated: "In the light of the ravages of drugs among the population, and especially among young people, it is not surprising that the authorities show great firmness with regard to those who actively contribute to the spread of this scourge."

Drug Watch International, P.O. Box 45218, Omaha, Neb. 86145-0218. (402-384-9212. 402-397-9924. DrugWatch6@aol.com. www.drugwatch.org.

Gaines, Larry K., and Peter B. Kraska, eds. *Drugs, Crime, and Justice: Contemporary Perspectives.* Prospect Heights, Ill.: Waveland, 1997.

Jayasuriya, D. C., R. K. Nayak, and A. Wells, eds. *Global Drugs Law: Selected Papers Presented at the Indian Law Institute.* UNDCP, International Law Association, Regional Branch, India, International Conference on Global Drugs Law. New Delhi, February 28–March 3, 1997. New Delhi: Har-Anand Publications, 1997.

Declaration on the Control of Drug Trafficking and Drug Abuse; Privacy; World Health Organization

Due Process of Law

Due process of law is defined in the United States as law in its regular course of administration through courts of law. Derived from a form of the Latin word *debitus* (something owed) as well as from Middle English and Old French, the concept is equivalent to "the law of the land" mentioned in the Great Charter of Liberties of England (1215), known as Magna Carta. Due process, as it is usually termed, is one of the basic elements of the rule of law and is recognized in most legal systems, if not specifically in the same words. It is the opposite of special laws or courts and arbitrary administrative actions that do not apply to all persons equally, thus precluding equal rights.

Due process has been used by the U.S. Supreme Court to analyze and decide cases in a number of legal rights areas, including criminal prosecution, the application of state laws, subversive activity, zoning laws, education, employment, and property rights, to name just a few. U.S. courts employ substantive due process to invalidate legislation and acts of the executive branch that are deemed arbitrary or unconstitutional. Procedural due process was described by Daniel Webster, the nineteenth-century U.S. statesman and orator, as procedure that hears before it condemns, proceeds on inquiry, and renders judgment only after a trial.

The concept of due process has also found its way into the European courts and is reflected in decisions that require fair procedures in the administration of state social programs, including a hearing and the right to appeal.

Constitution of Japan (1947), chapter III, Rights and Duties of the People, article 31: "No person shall be deprived of life or liberty, nor shall any other criminal penalty be imposed, except according to procedure established by law."

International Covenant on Civil and Political Rights (1996), part III, article 14: "1. All persons shall be equal before the courts and tribunals. In the determination of any criminal charge against him, or of his rights and obligations in a suit at law, everyone shall be entitled to a fair and public hearing by a competent, independent and impartial tribunal established by law. . . . 5. Everyone convicted of a crime shall have the right to his conviction and sentence being reviewed by a higher tribunal according to law."

U.S. Supreme Court (1937): "The power to regulate or prohibit the sale of cosmetics containing poisonous, injurious, or harmful ingredients is not a violation of any provision of the federal Constitution. The requirement of due process is sufficiently guarded by an appeal to the superior court of the county."

European Court of Human Rights (1986): "Framed as they were in such restrictive terms, the conditions of access to the two Boards prevented [the applicant] from challenging the merits of the decision by the President of the Appeals Board. . . . Accordingly, the shortcoming found to exist in respect of the procedure before this judicial officer was not capable of being cured at a later stage."

Galligan, D. J. *Due Process and Fair Procedures: A Study of Administrative Procedures.* New York: Oxford University Press, 1996.

Ramcharan, B. G. *The Principle of Legality in International Human Rights Institutions: Selected Legal Opinions.* The Hague: Martinus Nijhoff, Kluwer Law International, 1997.

Accused; Appeals; Equality; Fair Trial; Magna Carta; Rule of Law

Education is recognized as a right in many national constitutions and international human rights documents and is a primary concern of the United Nations Educational, Scientific and Cultural Organization (UNESCO). To help Palestinian refugee children continue their education, a UN relief agency established schools in places such as Jordan, Lebanon, Syria, and the West Bank of Israel.
[M. Nasr, United Nations]

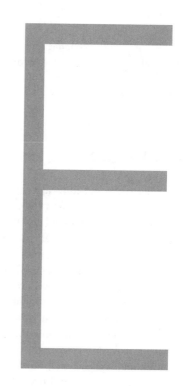

Economic and Social Council (ECOSOC)

A central forum for discussion of international economic and social policy, the Economic and Social Council (ECOSOC) was created by the UN charter (1945) to serve as the principal UN agency on the subject. It promotes higher standards of living, full employment, and economic and social progress; seeks solutions for international economic, social, health, and related problems; furthers international cultural and educational cooperation; and encourages universal respect for human rights. ECOSOC also facilitates discussion, formulates policy recommendations, makes studies and recommendations, convenes international conferences, and prepares draft conventions for submission to the UN General Assembly on matters within its competence.

A number of "functional" ECOSOC commissions work on human rights issues, including the Commission on Human Rights and its Subcommission on the Promotion and Protection of Human Rights, Commission on the Status of Women, and Commission on Crime Prevention and Criminal Justice. In addition, ECOSOC administers a number of regional commissions for areas such as Africa, Asia and the Pacific, Western Asia, and Latin America and the Caribbean, which monitor economic and social development and seek to strengthen the economic relations among the regions' nations. Standing committees address topics such as human settlements, nongovernmental organizations, and natural resources.

Fifteen specialized agencies, including the International Labor Organization, United Nations Educational, Scientific and Cultural Organization (UNESCO), Food and Agriculture Organization, International Atomic Energy Agency, World Bank, and World Health Organization, report annually to ECOSOC. A number of nongovernmental organizations also have consultative status with the council, which may consult as well with the UN secretariat on matters of mutual concern.

Originally ECOSOC had eighteen members, but amendments to the UN charter enlarged its membership to twenty-seven in 1965 and to its current total of fifty-four in 1973. Eighteen members are elected each year by the General Assembly for three-year terms and are eligible for reelection. ECOSOC usually holds one five-week substantive session each year, alternating between New York City and Geneva, where ministers and other senior government officials deliberate over economic and social issues. At least two organizational sessions are held in New York. Commissions and committees meet throughout the year at various locations and report to the council.

Economic and Social Council (ECOSOC) One United Nations Plaza, Room s-2963, New York, N.Y. 10017. (212-963-4640. 🖶 212-963-5935. 🖳 esa@un.org. 🖳 www.ecosoc.org.

Commission on Human Rights; Economic Rights; Social Rights; Subcommission on the Promotion and Protection of Human Rights; United Nations Educational, Scientific and Cultural Organization (UNESCO)

Economic Rights

Economic rights, like social and cultural rights, are generally considered second-generation human rights, on a tier beneath fundamental freedoms and civil and political rights. Included among national economic rights are such issues as legalization of unions (the right to organize workers and to strike for better wages or working conditions), social security and medical insurance entitlements, welfare for the needy, minority business subsidies, protection against monopolies and unfair trade practices, and consumer protection.

Early gatherer-hunter groups who husbanded their scarce resources—practicing *economy* (from the Greek *oikonomia*, meaning household management)—had a better chance of survival than those who did not. Provisioning arrangements among primitive humans, preserving and doling out food supplies within a family or small band, may also have played a key role in the development of politics and government. In later centuries slavery, forced labor, and feudalism were significant elements of the economy of most societies; only the powerful and the wealthy had what might be called economic human rights. The increase in trade and the establishment of large commercial centers after the Middle Ages, especially in Europe, resulted in an increase in wealth and its dispersal among a greater number of people than ever before.

In 1776 the Scottish economist Adam Smith published *The Wealth of Nations,* in which he argued that modern political economic theory was based on the free working of individual enterprise and the necessity of free trade. Such enterprise, however, favors the capitalist—the person who contracts for the labor of another—over the individual worker. A master and a slave, for example, do not bargain from the same position of strength as to the value of the slave's labor to the master. Similarly, poor laborers, while not technically slaves, have traditionally been at a disadvantage in bargaining with wealthy capitalists for their services. A wealthy person who is under no legal restraint in a time when an abundance of people are willing to sell their labor, may basically set his or her own price for the competing laborers. For the economically dependent worker, the only alternative to accepting a low wage may be starvation.

The industrial revolution, which began in England in the mid-eighteenth century, brought with it new economic and social problems. During the nineteenth century, industrial nations began to grapple with the health and safety of workers and their families, many of whom lived near polluting factories, as well as the workers' ability to bargain fairly for their wages. Riots, strikes, and revolutions erupted out of the growing frustration and degradation of the workers in their confrontations with the capitalist owners. Union and collective bargaining laws gave workers the legal backing they needed to negotiate fairly with owners to protect their economic rights.

During the late nineteenth and early twentieth centuries, the writings of Karl Marx, who urged workers to take control of the means of production, were a primary impetus for the rise of the Communist Party and revolutions in many countries, the most significant of which was the 1917 Russian Revolution. Since the fall of communist rule in the Soviet Union and Eastern Europe in 1989, the problem of economic rights is no longer one of absolute capitalism versus absolute communism—that is, private rather than state control of a nation's economy—but one of the proper mix of government and private involvement in each country's economic life.

In the language of economics the term *economic freedom* has a narrow technical meaning. The nineteenth-century English philosopher John Stuart Mill defined it, as taken up by political libertarians, as the essence of an economic system in which individuals are free to make as many choices about their own economic activities as possible with a minimum of government interference, which would be justified only if the system resulted in harm to others.

Today each nation has to define the economic rights of its citizens in ways that are appropriate culturally, politically, and fiscally. The German economy is often described as a "social market economy," a recognition of the free-market system acting within a socially conscious state. The amount of national resources that can be dedicated to social problems, such as public welfare and old-age pension guarantees, is a constant source of political confrontation in many developed nations. Developing nations, on the other hand, generally have fewer options available for expanding and protecting economic rights. There is no perfect balance between private incentive, which should increase economic growth, and the distribution of the wealth created by such growth to those members of society who have not or cannot contribute to the economy.

The International Covenant on Economic, Social and Cultural Rights (1966) provides guidance to nations seeking to promote and enforce individual economic rights. In 1974 the UN General Assembly adopted by resolution the Charter of Economic Rights and Duties of States, which promotes "the establishment of a new international economic order based on equity, sovereign equality, interdependence, common interest, and cooperation" among all nations regardless of their economic and social systems. It also encourages the "acceleration of the economic growth of developing countries with a view to bridging the gap between developing and developed countries." Other documents that recognize economic rights include the Charter of the Organization of American States (1948), European Social Charter (1961), American Convention on Human Rights (1969), and African Charter on Human and Peoples' Rights (1981).

A number of specific international agreements were entered into after World War II by countries wishing to stabilize international economic activity as much as possible. The Bretton Woods Conference, for example, provided for the creation of the International Monetary Fund and the International Bank for Reconstruction and Development, known as the World Bank.

Constitution of Ireland (1937), Fundamental Rights, Directive Principles of Social Policy, article 45: "4.1. The State pledges itself to safeguard with especial care the economic interests of the weaker sections of the community, and, where necessary, to contribute to the support of the infirm, the widow, the orphan, and the aged."

International Covenant on Economic, Social and Cultural Rights (1966), part II, article 2: "3. Developing countries, with due regard to human rights and their national economy, may determine to what extent they would guarantee the economic rights recognized in the present Covenant to non-nationals."

Constitutional Court of Germany (1961): "In a modern liberal state different views will always exist as to what broad economic and social policy and what specific measures serve the public interest.... [The proposed sale of a publicly owned enterprise] lies within the discretion of the federation's political organs, as long as implementation does not violate constitutional law and, in particular, basic rights...."

Court of Justice of the European Communities (1996): Fundamental economic rights such as the freedom to pursue a commercial activity may be subject to restrictions in the general interest of the community; and, therefore, an airplane of a Turkish company acquired from the Republic of Yugoslavia, against which sanctions had been implemented, could be impounded by the Irish Ministry for Transport.

International Monetary Fund, 700 19th Street, N.W., Washington, D.C. 20431. (202-623-7000. 🖶 202-623-4661. 🖳 publicaffairs@imf.org. 🖳 www.imf.org.

The World Bank, 1818 H Street, N.W., Washington, D.C. 20433. (202-477-1234. 🖶 202-522-1500. 🖳 growth@worldbank.org. 🖳 www.worldbank.org.

Compa, Lance A., and Stephen F. Diamond, eds. *Human Rights, Labor Rights, International Trade.* Philadelphia: University of Pennsylvania Press, 1996.

Taylor, Annie, and Caroline Thomas, eds. *Global Trade and Social Issues.* New York: Routledge, 1999.

African Charter on Human and Peoples' Rights; American Convention on Human Rights; Cultural Rights; Development; European Social Charter; Forced Labor; International Covenant on Economic, Social and Cultural Rights; International Labor Organization; Limburg Principles on the Implementation of the International Covenant on Economic, Social and Cultural Rights; Property; Slavery; Social Rights; Workers

Education

To develop self-sufficiency, human beings require a long period of maturation, much longer comparatively than for other animals. During this time we learn not only about the surrounding physical world but also about the culture into which we are born: its language, manners, history, science, arts, and even sports. To prosper as well as survive, young people must be educated (from the Latin *educare*, meaning to rear or educate). "It much concerneth every parent to see their children to have the best education and instruction," wrote an English commentator in 1616.

The ancient Greek philosophers Plato and Aristotle both placed great importance on education. In *The Laws*, Plato includes a section entitled "The Arts in the Service of Education." The Renaissance that began in Europe in the fourteenth century represented the institution of a broader, wider base of learning than had been allowed monastic scholars of the Middle Ages. The Enlightenment that followed in the eighteenth century was marked by an explosion of knowledge and creativity in science, technology, politics, and government. Simply put, better education generally translates into a better world.

Thomas Jefferson, the author of several influential human rights documents, including the U.S. Declaration of Independence (1776), believed that free public education is the key to an informed electorate in a democracy. A basic distinction between a totalitarian government and a democracy is that under totalitarianism the goal of education is to inculcate obedience to the state, whereas in a democracy its aim is to improve and enhance citizens' personal life, one aspect of which is helping them understand and contribute to the political process of which they are an integral part. In modern society education has come to represent the avenue for obtaining status and wealth in addition to intellectual enjoyment. The right to have an opportunity to obtain the best possible education is therefore of vital concern to both parents and children. Education is also a continuing process: people can and often do seek to continue some form of education throughout their lives.

The Universal Declaration of Human Rights (1948), adopted by the UN General Assembly, declares in article 26, paragraph 1: "Everyone has the right to education. Education shall be free, at least in the elementary and fundamental stages. Elementary education shall be compulsory. Technical and professional education shall be made generally available and higher education shall be equally accessible to all on the basis of merit." A number of other human rights documents address education, among them the International Convention on the Elimination of All Forms of Racial Discrimination (1965), International Covenant on Economic, Social and Cultural Rights (1966), and African Charter on Human and Peoples' Rights (1981).

National constitutions from Belgium (1831) to Panama (1972) include provisions regarding rights to education. As contained in constitutions and human rights documents, generally agreed-on education rights include the right to free public education for children and freedom from discrimination in education. In addition to public education facilities, voluntary religious, linguistic, and private alternatives to public education are acceptable, and separate institutions for the sexes may not be discriminatory as long as they are otherwise equal. Other rights include equality of opportunity and treatment in matters relating to education; respect for the rights of teachers, students, and parents; and the rights of national minorities to conduct their own educational activities. Finally, there is growing awareness of a right to an education that promotes human rights, international understanding, and world peace.

Most nations today have compulsory elementary education, and many provide free education up to the age of eighteen. Some governments may subsidize higher education, but generally it is provided by private institutions. The ability to pay thus becomes a factor in determining access to and the quality of higher education and in some ways tends to perpetuate economic class divisions. To correct this imbalance a nation's higher education policy may provide scholarships and special programs, often through the military. The G.I. Bill, enacted by Congress following World War II, provided tuition for college and higher-level study to American war veterans.

Some human rights issues related to education include segregation of students on the basis of race, which until 1954 was constitutionally upheld in the United States; public financing of private and religious schools; the rights of teachers, parents, and students; bilingual education and similar minority cultural and religious rights in public schools; sex education programs; and the extent to which vocational education and training should be supported by the state or required for students unqualified for higher education.

The United Nations Educational, Scientific and Cultural Organization (UNESCO) has special responsibilities for promoting and protecting the right to education. In 1960 it adopted the Convention against Discrimination in Education, and two years later it added a protocol creating a conciliation commission to settle disputes among parties to the convention. Education is the major field of activity for UNESCO, which works to achieve basic education for all people; develop higher education; promote training for

teachers, education planners, and administrators; and obtain better buildings and equipment for schools.

Education is also key to promoting and enforcing human rights, preventing violations, and meting out punishment for abuses. Mindful of the importance of education in this respect, the UNESCO General Conference, meeting in Paris in 1974, adopted a Recommendation Concerning Education for International Understanding, Co-operation and Peace and Education Relating to Human Rights and Fundamental Freedoms. Its underlying idea is that all education should further the principles of the Universal Declaration of Human Rights. "Education should be infused with the aims and purposes set forth in the Charter of the United Nations [1945], the Constitution of [UNESCO] [1946] and the Universal Declaration of Human Rights," states the recommendation. It then cites article 26, paragraph 2, of the declaration, noting that education "shall promote understanding, tolerance and friendship among all nations, racial and social groups, and shall further the activities of the United Nations for the maintenance of peace." In 1994 the UN General Assembly designated 1995–2005 as the United Nations Decade for Human Rights Education.

Constitution of Belgium (1831), heading II, Concerning the Belgians and Rights, article 17: "Education is free; any preventive measure is forbidden. . . . Public education provided at the expense of the state is . . . regulated by law."

European Social Charter (1961), part II, article 10: "With the view to ensuring effective exercise of the right to vocational training, the Contracting Parties undertake: 1. To provide or promote, as necessary, the technical and vocational training of all persons, including the handicapped, in consultation with employers' and workers' organizations, and to grant facilities for access to higher technical and university education, based solely on individual aptitude. . . ."

U.S. Supreme Court (1954): Segregation of children in public schools solely on the basis of race deprives minority students of equal educational opportunities and is unconstitutional as a violation of equal protection of the laws as guaranteed by the Fourteenth Amendment (1868) to the U.S. Constitution.

European Court of Human Rights (1976): Legislation in Denmark that required compulsory sex education in state schools was challenged by some parents who claimed that it violated their right not to have their children instructed in a manner contrary to their religious and philosophical beliefs as guaranteed by Protocol I, article 2 (1952), of the European Convention for the Protection of Human Rights and Fundamental Freedoms (1950). The court held, however, that article 2 did not prevent the state from imparting information, even of a religious or philosophical nature, as long as such information was presented in an objective, critical, and pluralistic manner and not in the form of indoctrination.

United Nations Educational, Scientific and Cultural Organization (UNESCO), 7 place de Fontenoy, 75352 Paris 07 SP, France. (31-1-45-68-10-00. 🖨 31-1-45-67-16-90. 🖳 webmaster@unesco.org. 🖳 www.unesco.org.

Hodgson, Douglas. *The Human Right to Education*. Brookfield, Vt.: Ashgate, 1998.

Spring, Joel H. *The Universal Right to Education: Justification, Definition, and Guidelines*. Mahwah, N.J.: Lawrence Erlbaum, 2000.

African Charter on Human and Peoples' Rights; Aristotle; Convention against Discrimination in Education; International Convention on the Elimination of All Forms of Racial Discrimination; International Covenant on Economic, Social and Cultural Rights; Jefferson, Thomas; Plato; United Nations Educational, Scientific and Cultural Organization (UNESCO)

Elderly

See Aged

Elections

See Voting

Emigration

See Immigrants; Movement; Refugees

Employees

See Association; International Labor Organization; Workers

Enforcement

Enforcement is the linchpin of any effective system of human rights protection. More than just giving effect to decisions of courts and other bodies, enforcement (from the Vulgar Latin *infortiare*, meaning to make strong, and the Middle English *enforcen*) entails developing policies and institutions that foster human rights as well as basic principles of good governance, such as constitutional democracy, separation of government powers, and strict adherence to the rule of law. "Is it consistent with the divine wisdom to prescribe rules to us," asked Edmund Burke, the British politician and theorist, in 1756, "and leave the enforcement of them to the folly of human institutions?"

Because there is no international legislature to enact laws and no international police force to enforce them, international human rights provisions are sometimes perceived as unenforceable. International institutions' lack of inherent sovereignty and police power means that up until recently enforcement has been left primarily to individual nations or sovereign governments, where the ability—but not always the motivation—to enforce human rights is far superior than at the regional or the international level.

If a nation wants to enforce human rights provisions in its own constitution or laws, as well as in international declarations, treaties, guidelines, principles, and standards, it can use its police power to implement such policies. Historically rebellion against an abusive government has been an effective if drastic method of change, but more peaceful enforcement mechanisms include executive departments charged with enforcing laws, human rights institutions such as commissions and ombudsmen, the courts, nongovernmental organizations, political organizations focused on changing discriminatory laws or removing recalcitrant public officials, and public media.

International human rights conventions require the ratifying nations to domestically enforce their principles. In addition to indirect enforcement through these national mechanisms, enforcement measures at the international level include public exposure, economic sanctions, diplomatic pressure, and military action. To enforce international human rights norms, the North Atlantic Treaty Organization (NATO), for example, closed out the twentieth century by sending in troops to prevent further ethnic cleansing in the Yugoslavian province of Kosovo. Thus, despite the absence of international sovereignty, international human rights documents and principles are enforceable, even if not as simply and effectively as national laws.

The Nuremberg trials of Nazi war criminals following World War II represented international enforcement of judicial findings that human rights had been violated by genocide and other crimes against humanity. These trials were unique in that the victorious Allied forces were in a position to enforce the tribunal's decisions because of the collapse of the German state. More recent experiments in internationally enforcing gross human rights violations include the ad hoc criminal tribunals established under the UN Security Council for Rwanda and the former territory of Yugoslavia. The new International Criminal Court, once it becomes fully operational, offers a more permanent solution to enforcement of international human rights principles.

No system of enforcement is perfect, however, and enforcement of human rights varies greatly throughout the world. In many countries, domestic as well as internationally recognized human rights are consistently being violated with impunity. Enforcement depends on more than just the capability for enforcement: it requires the commitment of each nation's political leaders, institutions, and citizens.

Canadian Charter of Rights and Freedoms (1982), Enforcement, 24(1): "Anyone whose rights or freedoms, as guaranteed by this Charter, have been infringed or denied may apply to a court of competent jurisdiction to obtain such remedy as the court considers appropriate and just in the circumstances."

Kampala Declaration on Human Rights (1993), paragraph 11: "The primary responsibility for implementing and giving effect to human rights is at the national level. . . . There is no single universally valid system, prescription or model."

U.S. Supreme Court (1943): "Government of limited power need not be anemic government. Assurance that rights are secure tends to diminish fear and jealousy of strong government, and by making us feel safe to live under it makes for its better support. . . . To enforce these rights today is not to choose weak government over strong government."

International Court of Justice (1986): "[W]hile the United States might form its own appraisal of the situation as to respect for human rights in Nicaragua, the use of force could not be the appropriate method to monitor or ensure such respect."

Lawyers Committee for Human Rights, 100 Maryland Avenue, N.E., Washington, D.C. 20002. ☎ 202-547-5692. 🖷 202-543-5999. 🖳 wdc@lchr.org. 🖳 www.lchr.org.

United Nations Security Council, One United Nations Plaza, Room S-3520A, New York, N.Y. 10017. ☎ 212-963-1234. 🖷 212-758-2718. 🖳 inquiries@un.org. 🖳 www.un.org.

Conforti, Benedetto, and Francesco Francioni, eds. *Enforcing International Human Rights in Domestic Courts.* The Hague: Kluwer Law International, 1997.

Gibney, Mark, and Stanislaw Frankowski, eds. *Judicial Protection of Human Rights: Myth or Reality?* Westport, Conn.: Praeger, 1999.

Impunity; International Criminal Court; International Law; Law Enforcement; Monitoring Compliance; North Atlantic Treaty Organization (NATO); Ombudsmen; Remedies; Reporting Violations; Resolution 1503 Procedure; Violations

Environment

The right to a healthy environment—clean air and water, uncontaminated and fertile soil, healthy plants and animals—is primarily a physical requirement but one that also has aesthetic and spiritual dimensions. As used in international law, however, the term *environment* refers strictly to the physical bases for human life. Derived from the French *environs* (vicinity or neighborhood), *environment* means the conditions under which a person lives or develops or all the influences that modify and determine the development of life and character. This sense of the term has been in use since the early nineteenth century.

Environmental rights, as they have evolved, represent a subset of collective human rights, which are third-generation rights, following first-generation individual human rights, such as the personal freedoms of speech, religion, and assembly, and second-generation economic, social, and cultural rights. Like the latter, environmental rights require positive actions on the government's part to limit damage that may be caused by private individuals and businesses and its own actions and thus to ensure the overall well-being of a nation's people and other nations as well. The right to a livable environment encompasses a broad range of problems: industrial and residential waste, nuclear energy, soil erosion, deforestation, commercial uses of chemicals and gases, fossil fuel consumption, mining techniques, water consumption, marine ecology, sites of historic and cultural interest and natural beauty, and harmful substances such as asbestos and tobacco products.

The industrial revolution, which began in England in the mid-eighteenth century, set in motion a chain of events that has led to massive environmental damage. In many industrialized nations factory smoke has polluted the air and toxic waste has poisoned the water and land. Carbon dioxide emissions from the use of fossil fuels have caused a buildup of gases, resulting in a global warming that portends disastrous consequences for life on this planet. Other emissions, such as fluorocarbons used in aerosol sprays, are believed to have weakened the atmosphere's ozone layer, which protects living things from the sun's deadly ultraviolet rays. Half of the world's wetlands have been lost during the past century; half of its forests have disappeared; dams and other diversions have fragmented sixty percent of the world's largest rivers, resulting in the loss of twenty percent of the freshwater fish; and the oceans are being overfished. Pesticides and nuclear wastes, as well as the chemical and biological weapons developed by many countries for military purposes, represent other threats to the right of all people to a clean and safe environment.

Provisions ensuring the right to a healthy environment have recently found their way into some national constitutions and international human rights documents. Among a number of developed nations, especially in Europe and the Americas, the concept of sustainable development (planning for and controlling human activities that significantly affect the environment) has been proposed as a necessary requirement for good government. But because activities in one country can degrade the environment of neighboring nations, environmental protection and environmental rights may require regional and even global cooperation to be effective. One step in this direction has been the Rio Declaration on Environment and Development (1992), the result of a UN Conference on Environment and Development, held in Rio de Janeiro, Brazil. According to this document, human beings, not industrial output or monetary return on investments, must be placed at the center of concerns about sustainable development, and the "special situation and needs of developing countries, particularly the least developed and those most environmentally vulnerable ... should be given special priority."

Reports to the Subcommission on the Promotion and Protection of Human Rights in 1991 and 1993 addressed the relationship between the environment and human rights. "The realization of the global character of environmental problems," the 1993 report stated, "is attested [to] by the progress made in understanding the phenomena that create hazards for the planet, threaten the living conditions of human beings and impair their fundamental rights."

Environmental human rights that are the responsibility of national governments individually and cooperatively include reducing air and water pollution and soil erosion, protecting and promoting biodiversity (the maintenance of a wide variety of species of flora and fauna), promoting sustainable development policies, protecting against major environmental disasters involving chemical, biological, and nuclear products, and enacting laws to assess liability and provide compensation for victims of environmental damage.

Many international documents, including human rights instruments, address environmental concerns—for example, the Convention on Prevention of Marine Pollution by Dumping of Wastes and Other Matter (1972), Basel Convention on the Transboundary Movements of Hazardous Wastes and Their Disposal (1989), and UN Framework Convention on Climate Change (1992). A specific concern of this last document is "that human activities have been substantially increasing the atmospheric concentrations of greenhouse gases, that these increases enhance the natural greenhouse effect, and that this will result on average in an additional warming of the Earth's surface and atmosphere and may adversely affect the natural ecosystems and mankind."

Constitution of Brazil (1988), title VIII, The Social Order, chapter VI, Environment, article 225: "All shall have the right to an ecologically balanced environment, which is an asset of common use and essential to a healthy quality of life, and both the government and the community shall have the duty to defend and preserve it for present and future generations."

Convention on the Prohibition of Military or Any Other Hostile Use of Environmental Modification Techniques (1976): The document asserts that the UN General Assembly is "[d]etermined to avert the potential dangers of military or any other hostile use of environmental modification techniques ... [and intends] to prohibit effectively military or any other hostile use of environmental modification techniques in order to eliminate the dangers to mankind from such use ."

Ontario (Canada) Court, General Division (1995): Judgments rendered in the United States in a case assessing compensation for environmental damage in Michigan are enforceable against defendants in Canada.

International Court of Justice (1996): The court recognized that "the existence of the general obligation of States to ensure that activities within their jurisdiction and control respect the environment of other States or of areas beyond national control is now a part of the corpus of international law relating to the environment."

International Council of Environmental Law, Adenauerallee 214, D-53113, Bonn, Germany. (49-228-2692-240. 📠 49-228-2692-250. 🖳 www. law.pace.edu.

Sierra Club International Program, 408 C Street, N.E., Washington, D.C. 20002. (202-547-1141. 📠 202-547-6009. 🖳 information@sierraclub.org. 🖳 www.sierraclub.org.

Burhenne, Wolfgang E., and Nicholas A. Robinson, eds. *International Protection of the Environment/Conservation in Sustainable Development*. Dobbs Ferry, N.Y.: Oceana, 1995.

Werksman, Jacob, ed. *Greening International Institutions*. London: Earthscan, 1996.

Collective Rights; Convention Concerning the Protection of the World Cultural and Natural Heritage; Cultural Rights; Development; Economic Rights; Natural Resources; Rio Declaration on Environment and Development; Subcommission on the Promotion and Protection of Human Rights

Equality

The motto of the French Revolution, which began in 1789— "Liberty, Equality, Brotherhood"—expresses a striving toward three important elements of the human rights canon. Equality (from the Latin *auquē*, meaning equally or justly) is the principle that all humans, regardless of social or political status, race, ethnic or national origin, sex, age, or disability, are entitled to the same rights. It is the foundation of other more specific rights, including equal protection of the law, equal rights for women and minorities, and equal opportunity in employment. Along with the concepts of individual liberty, the rule of law, and constitutional democracy, equality is a cornerstone of human rights theory.

Although fundamental, the concept of equality is nevertheless complex: how can such individually unique creatures as people be considered equal in any sense? The idea of persons with equal status emerged in the democracies of ancient Greece and England's Magna Carta (1215), with its reference to peers (equals), and is embodied in the U.S. Declaration of Independence (1776), which proclaims that "all Men are created equal." In 1794 Robert Southey, the poet laureate of England, wrote: "Ye are all equal; nature made you so. Equality is your birth-right." Yet even today racial, religious, sexual, age, and ethnic grounds for unequal treatment remain a part of the world's political landscape.

In the civic and political sense, equality requires the government to extend the same rights and privileges to all citizens. Everyone is equal before the law and entitled to equal protection of the laws. In a constitutional democracy no person may have any special privilege or burden, except those conferred temporarily by law. Judges, legislators, and executive branch officials of a democratic government, for example, may have privileges not granted to ordinary citizens so that they can carry out their duties on behalf of the people. Convicted criminals, in contrast, may lose their rights to property, liberty, and even life. Physical differences between men and women can also complicate the goal of equal treatment, especially with respect to pregnancy and maternity. Similarly, indigenous peoples may require seemingly unequal treatment to bring about equality with the majority culture. Such inequality, as long as there is no abuse of power or unjust treatment, does not violate the basic principle that all persons should have equal rights.

Much time and energy have been spent in justifying and enforcing the notion of the inequality, rather than the equality, of people. Religion, language, culture, race, social and economic status, sex and sexual preferences, appearance, age, national origin—all have been used as excuses for one group to treat another as less than equal. The ancient Greek democracies granted equal political status to all adult male citizens but excluded women, slaves, and aliens (sometimes referred to as "barbarians"). The divine right of kings to rule and the feudal economic system that developed in Europe after the fall of the Roman Empire in the West perpetuated acceptance of a hierarchy of human society, with God at the top, then kings, the royal family, the aristocracy, and church leaders, followed by freemen, peasants, serfs, and finally slaves.

Although Magna Carta limited King John, the thirteenth-century English monarch, by making his power less than absolute, it also codified a number of inequalities. The earls and barons who drew it up had privileges that freemen did not, and Jews were blatantly discriminated against: "If a man dies owing money to Jews," it states, "his wife may have her dower and pay nothing towards the debt from it." But the long march toward the Universal Declaration of Human Rights (1948) had begun. Other significant documents in the history of the struggle for equality are the U.S. Constitution (1789) and its Bill of Rights (1791) as well as France's Declaration of the Rights of Man and of the Citizen (1789).

The nineteenth and twentieth centuries, however, witnessed some of the most invidious forms of discrimination, including Nazi Germany's enslavement and murder of "racially inferior" human beings during the Holocaust of the 1930s and 1940s and the Japanese military's brutal treatment of various ethnic groups during World War II in Asia and the western Pacific region. Even the United States violated its own Constitution by resorting to unconstitutional discrimination against Japanese American citizens during World War II.

National constitutions and human rights documents that contain a list of basic rights invariably include some reference to the equality of citizens or individuals. In addition to the Universal Declaration of Human Rights, equality is addressed in the European Convention for the Protection of Human Rights and Fundamental Freedoms (1950), International Covenant on Civil and Political Rights (1966), International Covenant on Economic, Social and Cultural Rights (1966), International Convention on the Elimination of All Forms of Racial Discrimination (1966), American Convention on Human Rights (1969), Convention on the Elimination of All Forms of Discrimination against Women (1979), and African Charter on Human and Peoples' Rights (1981).

Canadian Charter of Rights and Freedoms (1982), Equality Rights, 15(1): "Every individual is equal before and under the law and has the right to equal protection and equal benefit of the law without discrimination...."

Universal Declaration of Human Rights (1948), preamble: "[R]ecognition of the inherent dignity and of the equal and inalienable rights of all members of the human family is the foundation of freedom, justice and peace in the world...."

Supreme Court of Canada (1989): According to the leading judgment in a case involving the guarantee of equality in the Canadian Charter of Rights and Freedoms (1982), "[D]iscrimination may be described as a distinction, whether intentional or not but based on grounds relating to the personal characteristics of the individual or group, which has the effect of imposing burdens, obligations or disadvantages on such individuals or groups not imposed on others, or which withholds or limits access to opportunities, benefits and advantages available to other members of society."

Inter-American Court of Human Rights (1995): Under several provisions of the American Convention on Human Rights (1969), including article 1.1, which requires that the government treat all citizens equally and without discrimination on the basis of "political or other opinion," Argentina violated the rights of one of its citizens who was arrested in 1989 for taking part in a peaceful demonstration.

Kernohan, Andrew W. *Liberalism, Equality, and Cultural Oppression.* New York: Cambridge University Press, 1998.

Pojman, Louis P., and Robert Westmoreland, eds. *Equality: Selected Readings.* New York: Oxford University Press, 1997.

Bills of Rights; Democracy; Discrimination; Equality of Arms; *Erga Omnes;* Minorities; Race Discrimination; Sex Discrimination

Equality of Arms

Used particularly in European courts to refer to the right of all parties, especially individuals, to have equal access to documents and court procedures, equality of arms is a concept promoted to avoid "star chamber" proceedings, in which a person is tried without access to all the evidence available to the prosecution and judges. To guarantee that legal contests are fair, this term of art has been adopted as a metaphor for combatants who have equal (from the Old French word *équalité)* access to weapons.

As applied by the European Commission of Human Rights, the concept of equality of arms implies that each party to a judicial proceeding must be given a full opportunity to present both the facts and the law regarding his or her case. This places a duty on the court or the tribunal to ensure that all parties have equal access to information and to call witnesses, as long as nothing unduly delays the proceedings. In Anglo-American law, the same situation is governed by the right to a fair trial and the prohibition against *ex parte* communication, meaning by one party to the court or the tribunal without the knowledge of the other party.

Standard Minimum Rules for the Administration of Juvenile Justice (Beijing Rules) (1985), part three, Adjudication and Disposition, 14, Competent Authority to Adjudicate, Commentary: "The procedure for dealing with juvenile offenders shall in any case follow the minimum standards that are applied almost universally for any criminal defendant . . . [including] such basic safeguards as . . . the presentation and examination of witnesses, . . . [and] the right to have the last word in a hearing [which precludes the presentation of information to the adjudicating body by the prosecution outside of the defendant's knowledge, an unfair procedure that the principle of equality of arms prohibits]. . . ."

U.K. Kings Bench (1914): "No communication shall be made by one party to a judicial tribunal without the knowledge of the other party."

Human Rights Committee (1992): A ruling by a judge in a murder trial in Jamaica to exclude evidence of a witness for the defendant because it was not a part of the *res gestae* (the circumstances of the case) was not an infringement of the right of equality of arms between the prosecution and the defense, and therefore the International Covenant on Civil and Political Rights (1966), article 14, paragraph 3(e), was not violated.

Dijk, P. van, and G. J. H. van Hoof. *Theory and Practice of the European Convention on Human Rights.* The Hague: Kluwer Law International, 1998.

Accused; European Commission of Human Rights; Fair Trial

Erga Omnes

The Latin phrase *erga omnes* (toward all) is used in international law to identify the obligations that nations owe to all other nations, regardless of whether a treaty between or among them contains any such specific provisions. In the monumental case *Barcelona Traction, Light and Power Company, Limited* (1970), the International Court of Justice held that, among other things, obligations resulting "in contemporary international law, from the outlawing of acts of aggression, and of genocide, as also from the principles and rules concerning the basic rights of the human person, including protection from slavery and racial discrimination," are obligations of nations *erga omnes*—that is, of the international community as a whole.

Although a relatively new term in the context of human rights, *erga omnes*—like *jus cogens*, those principles of international law that are so fundamental they bind all nations without exceptions—is being used to support findings that all countries must conform their actions to the human rights norms declared by the international community in documents such as the Universal Declaration of Human Rights (1948). The term *erga omnes* is a creation of the judicial decision-making process and is thus generally not expressed or referred to in documents concerning human rights.

Constitutional Court of Portugal (1976): The absolute constitutional prohibition against extradition to a requesting nation where such a crime is punishable by death bars extradition *[erga omnes]* even if the requesting nation guarantees that it will refrain from imposing the death penalty.

International Court of Justice (Advisory Opinion) (1971): "[T]he termination of the Mandate [internationally sanctioned territorial administration] and the declaration of the illegality of South Africa's presence in Namibia are opposable to all States in the sense of barring *erga omnes* the legality of a situation which is maintained in violation of international law."

Ragazzi, Maurizio. *The Concept of International Obligations Erga Omnes.* Oxford, England: Clarendon Press, Oxford University Press, 1997.

International Court of Justice; International Law; *Jus Cogens*; Norms; Universal Declaration of Human Rights

European Commission of Human Rights

For more than forty-five years the European Commission of Human Rights, together with the European Court of Human Rights, played a key role in protecting human rights in Europe. Both were established under the European Convention for the Protection of Human Rights and Fundamental Freedoms (1950), adopted by the Council of Europe, an organization formed after World War II to further the development of democracy, human rights, and the rule of law in Western Europe. The commission, however, went out of existence on October 30, 1999, pursuant to the terms of the convention's Protocol no. 11, which entered into force on November 1, 1997. The commission took a year to complete work on cases received before November 1, 1998, when the amended convention became effective. After that date, the European Court of Human Rights assumed its new role as the sole enforcement body for the rights expressed in the convention.

From the time it began operation in 1954, the commission received more than forty-five thousand complaints by people representing a hundred nationalities alleging violations by the European parties to the convention. It produced some 3,700 reports on the merits of cases. The commission's purpose was to screen the complaints and refer only a limited number of cases to the court. However, the number of referrals rose from seven in 1981 to fifty-two

in 1993, and then to 119 in 1997. The increase in the number of cases referred to the court, the backlog of pending complaints, and the average length of time—up to five years—for a case to be resolved by the commission all led to a 1992 recommendation by the Parliamentary Assembly of the Council of Europe to create "a single court as a full-time body in place of the existing Commission and Court."

Under the original convention, any participating nation could "refer to the Commission, through the Secretary General of the Council of Europe, any alleged breaches of the provisions of the Convention" by another party. The commission was further authorized to "receive petitions addressed to the Secretary General ... from any person, non-governmental organization or group of individuals claiming to be the victim of a violation" by one of the parties. Only complaints for which all domestic remedies had been exhausted could be considered, and the commission was precluded from acting on anonymous complaints, duplicates of complaints already acted on, and ones incompatible with the convention's provisions, manifestly ill-founded, or abusing the right of petition.

To handle these complaints, the commission would examine the petitions, ascertain the facts, and if necessary investigate the complaint. Its first objective was to reach a friendly settlement between the accuser and the country concerned. If the matter was not settled or otherwise disposed of, the commission was required to "draw up a Report on the facts and state its opinion as to whether the facts disclose a breach by the State concerned of its obligations under the Convention." These reports were transmitted to the Committee of Ministers and the country concerned, which was prohibited from publishing it.

The commission was also authorized to refer cases to the European Court of Human Rights, but if the matter was not referred within three months after the report on it was sent to the Committee of Ministers, the committee could decide by a two-thirds majority if a violation had occurred. It could then prescribe a period during which the country involved had to take the measures required. The committee also handled those cases that could not be referred to the court because the nation had not accepted the court's jurisdiction.

The Committee of Ministers elected commission members for six-year renewable terms. Membership was equal to the number of nations party to the convention, but no two members could be from the same country.

Council of Europe, Point I, F-67075 Strasbourg Cedex, France. 33-3-88-41-20-00. 33-3-88-41-27-81. webmaster@www.coe.fr. www.coe.fr.

European Court of Human Rights, Council of Europe, F-67075 Strasbourg Cedex, France. 33-3-88-41-20-18. 33-3-88-41-27-30. dhcour@court1.coe.fr. www.dhcour.coe.fr.

☞

European Convention for the Protection of Human Rights and Fundamental Freedoms; European Court of Human Rights; Regional Human Rights Systems

European Convention for the Prevention of Torture and Inhuman or Degrading Treatment or Punishment

"No one shall be subjected to torture or to inhuman or degrading treatment or punishment," state both the Universal Declaration of Human Rights (1948) and the European Convention for the Protection of Human Rights and Fundamental Freedoms (1950). Several decades later the UN General Assembly adopted the Declaration on the Protection of All Persons from Being Subjected to Torture and Other Cruel, Inhuman or Degrading Treatment or Punishment (1975), which was supplemented by the Convention against Torture and Other Cruel, Inhuman or Degrading Treatment or Punishment (1984).

On November 26, 1987, the Committee of Ministers of the Council of Europe concluded the European Convention for the Prevention of Torture and Inhuman or Degrading Treatment or Punishment. It entered into force on February 1, 1989. Like the 1984 UN convention, which established a Committee against Torture to supervise its implementation, the European convention creates a committee that is authorized to visit prisons to ensure humane treatment of prisoners.

Citing the 1950 European human rights convention, the preamble notes that "the protection of persons deprived of their liberty against torture and inhuman or degrading treatment or punishment could be strengthened by nonjudicial means of a preventive character based on visits [to places of detention]."

Section I, article 1, establishes a European Committee for the Prevention of Torture and Inhuman or Degrading Treatment or Punishment. "The Committee shall, by means of visits," it states, "examine the treatment of persons deprived of their liberty with a view to strengthening, if necessary, the protection of such persons from torture and from inhuman or degrading treatment or punishment." According to article 2, "Each Party shall permit visits ... to any place within its jurisdiction where persons are deprived of their liberty by a public authority." Article 3 mandates that "the Committee and the competent national authorities of the Party concerned shall co-operate with each other."

Section II, article 4, provides that the committee membership will equal the number of nations that ratify the con-vention but that members may not be from the same nation. They serve in their individual capacities, rather than as representatives of their countries, to ensure independence and impartiality. Committee members are elected by the Council of Europe's Committee of Ministers for a term of four years and may be reelected only once. According to article 6, the committee "shall meet in camera"; a "quorum shall be equal to a majority of its members"; and it "shall draw up its own rules of procedure."

Section III describes how visits are carried out. Under article 7, the committee is directed to organize visits to places where persons are held in custody. "Apart from periodic visits, the Committee may organize such other visits as appear to it to be required in the circumstances. As a general rule, the visits shall be carried out by at least two members of the Committee ... [and it] may, if it considers it necessary, be assisted by experts and interpreters." Article 8 requires the committee to "notify the Government of the Party concerned of its intention to carry out a visit." The country to be visited is to provide the committee with "the right to travel without restriction"; "full information on the places where persons ... are being held"; "unlimited access ... including the right to move inside such places without restriction"; and "other information ... necessary to the Committee to carry out its task."

Article 9 allows a state party to the convention to prohibit or postpone a visit in "exceptional circumstances," such as on the grounds of national defense or public safety or when there is "serious disorder in places where persons are deprived of their liberty," a prisoner has a medical condition, or an "urgent interrogation relating to a serious crime is in progress." In these cases, the committee may ask that a prisoner whom it intends to visit be transferred to another place.

"After each visit," article 10 provides, "the Committee shall draw up a report on the facts found during the visit" and transmit it to the government concerned along with any recommendations considered necessary. If the country fails to cooperate or to improve the conditions cited, "the Committee may decide, after the Party has had an opportunity to make known its views, by a majority of two-thirds of its members to make a public statement on the matter."

Section IV addresses notification to the committee of the name and address of the government authorities competent to receive notification, extends privileges and immunities to committee members and any accompanying experts, and, among other things, provides that the committee "shall not visit places which representatives or delegates of Protecting Powers or the International Committee of the Red Cross effectively visit on a regular basis by virtue of the Geneva Conventions of 12 August 1949 and the Additional Protocols of 8 June 1977 thereto."

An Annex to the convention provides details on the privileges and immunities to be enjoyed by the committee members.

✉

Council of Europe, Point I, F-67075 Strasbourg Cedex, France.
☎ 33-3-88-41-20-00. 🖷 33-3-88-41-27-81. 🖳 webmaster@
www.coe.fr. 🖳 www.coe.fr.

☞

Basic Principles for the Treatment of Prisoners; Convention against Torture and Other Cruel, Inhuman or Degrading Treatment or Punishment; Declaration on the Protection of All Persons from Being Subjected to Torture and Other Cruel, Inhuman or Degrading Treatment or Punishment; European Convention for the Protection of Human Rights and Fundamental Freedoms; Geneva Conventions; Inter-American Convention to Prevent and Punish Torture; Prisoners; Punishment; Red Cross and Red Crescent; Torture

European Convention for the Protection of Human Rights and Fundamental Freedoms

World War II and the atrocities of Nazi Germany made it abundantly clear that the nations of Europe could not be left on their own to promote and protect human rights. A first step came with the Universal Declaration of Human Rights (1948), which proclaimed human rights but lacked any enforcement procedure. Two years later the European Convention for the Protection of Human Rights and Fundamental Freedoms broke new ground by providing a two-tiered system—a commission and a court—to enforce human rights at the regional level.

Opened for signature in Rome on November 4, 1950, the document entered into force when it was ratified by the tenth nation on September 3, 1953. Eleven protocols have been added to date. As a regional statement of human rights principles, the European convention has proved more effective than similar regional treaties, such as the American Convention on Human Rights (1969) and the African Charter on Human and Peoples' Rights (1981).

The convention was drafted under the direction of the Council of Europe, which was formed in 1949 to rebuild the continent's cultural, social, and political life in the wake of the war's devastation. One of the council's three major bodies, the Committee of Ministers, plays an important role in the human rights procedures under the convention as well as under the European Social Charter (1961), which added economic and social rights to the civil and political rights identified in the earlier convention.

In addition to guaranteeing certain rights, the convention created two agencies to carry out its provisions: the European Commission of Human Rights, which no longer exists, and the European Court of Human Rights. Both were basically judicial organs but could only react to mat-

ters brought to them by the European countries party to the convention and by individual applicants. The court now handles complaints by both individuals and nations and has built up an impressive body of jurisprudence interpreting and applying the convention's provisions, which are implemented by the participating countries.

The convention begins by noting that the European nations "are like-minded and have a common heritage of political traditions, ideals, freedom and the rule of law" and desire to take steps to collectively enforce rights stated in the Universal Declaration of Human Rights. The aim of the Council of Europe, it notes, "is the achievement of greater unity between its Members and . . . one of the methods by which the aim is to be pursued is the maintenance and further realization of Human Rights and Fundamental Freedoms." The introductory text goes on to reaffirm the parties' "profound belief in those Fundamental Freedoms which are the foundation of justice and peace in the world and are best maintained on the one hand by an effective political democracy and on the other by a common understanding and observance of the Human Rights upon which they depend."

"The High Contracting Parties," states article 1, Obligation to Respect Human Rights, "shall secure to everyone within their jurisdiction the rights and freedoms defined in Section 1 of this Convention." As specified in articles 2 through 14, these rights include the right to life, with certain exceptions; freedom from torture, slavery, forced labor, and servitude, except for certain types of labor, such as "any service of a military nature"; the right to personal liberty and security; the right to a fair trial; freedom from retroactive or ex post facto laws; the right to marry and to have a private and family life; freedom of thought, expression, conscience, and religion; freedom of assembly and association; the right to effective remedies for abuses; and freedom from discrimination.

According to article 15, provisions of the convention may be suspended in "time of war or other public emergency threatening the life of the nation," but it upholds the right to life "except in respect of deaths resulting from lawful acts of war" and freedom from torture, slavery, and ex post facto laws. Article 16 permits certain restrictions on the political activities of aliens, while article 17 mandates that "[n]othing in this Convention may be interpreted as implying for any State, group or person any right to engage in any activity or perform any act aimed at the destruction of any of the rights and freedoms set forth herein. . . ." According to article 18, "The restrictions permitted under this Convention to the said rights and freedoms shall not be applied for any purpose other than those for which they have been prescribed."

Sections II and III deal with the establishment and functions of the European Commission of Human Rights, while section IV establishes the European Court of Human Rights. In accordance with the provisions of Protocol no. 11, which was adopted in 1994 and made effective as of November 1, 1998, the commission ceased to function in

1999 as part of the convention's enforcement machinery. Responsibility for enforcement was placed with a newly constituted permanent European Court of Human Rights.

Protocol no. 1 (1952) added several new rights, including the right to education and to free elections, as well as the right of every "natural or legal person . . . to the peaceful enjoyment of his possessions." Protocol no. 2 (1963) gives the European Court of Human Rights authority to issue advisory opinions. Protocol no. 4 (1963) grants freedom of movement and prohibits imprisonment for debt, expulsion of nationals, and the collective expulsion of aliens. Protocol no. 6 (1983) abolishes the death penalty except in time of war. Protocol no. 7 (1984) mandates that aliens can be expelled only "in pursuance of a decision reached in accordance with law"; extends certain rights to those accused of crimes, including the right of appeal and to compensation for wrongful conviction; prohibits a second trial or punishment for the same crime; and provides for equality between spouses.

Council of Europe, Point I, ꜰ-67075 Strasbourg Cedex, France. (33-3-88-41-20-00. 33-3-88-41-27-81. webmaster@ www.coe.fr. www.coe.fr.

African Charter on Human and Peoples' Rights; American Convention on Human Rights; European Commission of Human Rights; European Court of Human Rights; European Social Charter; Regional Human Rights Systems

European Court of Human Rights

Originally established with the European Commission of Human Rights to enforce the provisions of the European Convention for the Protection of Human Rights and Fundamental Freedoms (1950), the European Court of Human Rights became the sole permanent body for adjudicating rights under the convention on October 30, 1999. The ground-breaking regional convention, adopted just two years after the Universal Declaration of Human Rights (1948), authorized a two-tiered enforcement system. The commission and the court were to serve basically as judicial bodies, except that they did not have the full powers of a domestic judicial system. For example, they generally could act only on past violations and could not intervene to prevent potential violations, nor could they issue statements on their own motion. The court and the commission were limited to reacting to matters brought to them by the European countries that ratified the convention and by individual applicants in those countries.

The court, which is administered by the Council of Europe, officially began its work in 1959. The commission's role involved screening complaints, acting on them, or referring them to the court. In the first fifteen years, only eleven cases were brought to the court, but the cases grew to 119 in 1997 alone. That same year, the number of complaints registered with the commission, however, reached nearly five thousand.

The proposal to establish a single judicial body, a full-time, permanent court of human rights for Europe, was endorsed at a 1993 Council of Europe meeting of heads of state and government. To put this proposal into effect, Protocol no. 11 to the European Convention was opened for signature on May 11, 1994. The protocol entered into force on November 1, 1997, and the amended convention became effective on November 1, 1998. The commission took a year to wind up its affairs regarding cases received before November 1, 1998, and then went out of existence on October 30, 1999.

Today the court's jurisdiction encompasses all matters concerning the interpretation and application of the convention and its protocols. A country may bring "any alleged breach" to the court, which now also receives individual applications from any person, nongovernmental organization, or group of individuals claiming to be victims of a violation by one of the states parties to the convention. For a claim to be admissible, however, all domestic remedies must have been exhausted, an applicant must not be anonymous, and the matter must be new and not "manifestly ill-founded, or an abuse of the right of application."

The court sits in committees of three judges, in chambers of seven judges, and in a grand chamber of seventeen judges. Currently forty-one judges represent countries ranging from Russia, France, and Great Britain to Croatia, Liechtenstein, and San Marino. The total number of judges is to remain equal to the number of parties to the convention. Judges are elected by the Parliamentary Assembly of the Council of Europe for six-year terms and must be of high moral character and professional standing. They serve "in their individual capacity" and must retire at age seventy.

Procedures for handling cases include examination of complaints and friendly settlement. A committee of judges may unanimously declare an individual application inadmissible "where such decision can be taken without further examination." Chambers are designated to decide on the admissibility and merits of interstate applications as well as individual applications where no committee action has been taken. A chamber may relinquish jurisdiction to the grand chamber when a case "raises a serious question affecting the interpretation of the Convention or Protocols thereto" or where the matter "might have a result inconsistent with a judgment previously delivered by the Court . . . unless one of the parties to the case objects."

Hearings and documents are generally to be accessible to the public. In cases before the chamber and grand chamber, an ex officio member, either the judge from the country concerned or another person designated by the country to act in the capacity of judge, also participates. "[I]f the

Court finds that there has been a violation . . . , and if the internal laws of the High Contracting Party concerned allow only partial reparation to be made," states the protocol, "the Court shall, if necessary, afford just satisfaction to the injured party."

The court must give reasons "for judgments as well as for decisions declaring applications admissible or inadmissible." Appeals are allowed "in exceptional cases" from a chamber to the court's grand chamber within three months of a judgment. The protocol requires that the states parties "undertake to abide by the final judgment of the Court in any case to which they are parties." Final judgments are transmitted to the Council of Europe's Committee of Ministers, which supervises their execution.

The court is also authorized to furnish advisory opinions on legal questions concerning the interpretation of the convention and its protocols. By a majority vote the Council of Ministers may request such opinions, which may not relate to the content or scope of the basic rights and freedoms set out in the convention.

European Court of Human Rights, Council of Europe, F-67075 Strasbourg Cedex, France. (33-3-88-41-20-18. 🖨 33-3-88-41-27-30. 📧 dhcour@court1.coe.fr. 🖥 www.dhcour.coe.fr.

European Commission of Human Rights; European Convention for the Protection of Human Rights and Fundamental Freedoms; Regional Human Rights Systems

European Social Charter

Because the Council of Europe, an organization formed after World War II to assist in developing democracy, human rights, and the rule of law in Western Europe, considers civil and political rights and social and economic rights to be interdependent, it adopted the European Social Charter on October 18, 1961. Acknowledging more than a dozen fundamental economic and social rights, the charter went into force on February 26, 1965, to complement the civil and political guarantees of the European Convention for the Protection of Human Rights and Fundamental Freedoms (1950). Four additional rights and principles, including the right of workers to take part in determining and improving their working conditions and granting the elderly the right to social protection, were contained in a protocol concluded on May 5, 1988, which went into force on September 4, 1992. Following several protocols adopted to strengthen enforcement, a revised charter was adopted on May 3, 1996, and took effect on July 1, 1999.

The revised charter begins by noting the need "to give the European Social Charter fresh impetus," especially "to take account in particular of the fundamental social changes which have occurred since the text was adopted."

"The Parties," states part I, "accept as the aim of their policy, to be pursued by all appropriate means, both national and international in character, the attainment of conditions in which the following rights and principles may be effectively realized." Following is a list of thirty-one rights and principles, guaranteeing everyone the opportunity to earn a living "in an occupation freely entered upon" and providing workers just as well as safe and healthy working conditions, dignity, fair remuneration, equal opportunity and treatment, freedom of association in workers' organizations, collective bargaining rights, protection on termination of employment, and vocational guidance. "Children and young persons," it adds, "have the right to a special protection against the physical and moral hazards to which they are exposed," while "[e]mployed women, in case of maternity, have the right to a special protection." It notes that all persons "with family responsibilities . . . have a right to [work] without being subject to discrimination and as far as possible without conflict between their employment and family responsibilities."

The charter further recognizes everyone's right "to benefit from any measures enabling [them] to enjoy the highest possible standard of health attainable," as well as social security for workers and their dependents, social and medical assistance for those in need, and social welfare services. "Disabled persons," it observes, "have the right to independence, social integration and participation in the life of the community." Additional groups singled out include the family, children, the elderly, nationals of other states parties, and migrant workers. Part I ends by mandating that everyone has "the right to protection against poverty and social exclusion" and "the right to housing."

Part II addresses each of the thirty-one rights listed in part I. Article 30, for example, provides: "With a view to ensuring the effective exercise of the right to protection against poverty and social exclusions, the Parties undertake: a. to take measures . . . to promote effective access of persons who live or risk living in a situation of social exclusion or poverty, as well as their families, to, in particular, employment, housing, training, education, culture and social and medical assistance; b. to review these measures with a view to their adaptation if necessary." Regarding the right to housing, article 31 suggests measures "1. to promote access to housing of an adequate standard; 2. to prevent and reduce homelessness with a view to its gradual elimination; 3. to make the price of housing accessible to those without adequate resources." Part III concerns the specific undertakings of the parties to the charter.

Part IV details the implementation of the charter, which was originally enforced primarily through the submission of biannual reports by the participating nations. An October 21, 1991, protocol amended this mechanism somewhat. Reports are now reviewed by a committee of independent experts, whose nine members are elected by the Council of Europe's Committee of Ministers. Assisted by an observer from the

International Labor Organization (ILO), the committee examines the reports and provides a legal assessment of how well the nations have fulfilled their responsibilities. Decisions are prepared by a governmental committee, after which the Committee of Ministers issues recommendations to countries that fail to fully comply with the charter's requirements. Policy debates in the council's Parliamentary Assembly may also be initiated on the basis of the findings.

Another mechanism—added by a protocol adopted on June 22, 1995—is used for implementing the charter: collective complaints. Nations, however, must specifically choose to be governed by this process, under which complaints may be made by certain international and national organizations, including nongovernmental organizations and groups representing employers and trade unions. They are empowered to submit to the council's secretary-general complaints in writing that relate to provisions of the charter, indicating "in what respect the [country] has not ensured the satisfactory application of this provision." These complaints are handled by the same committee of independent experts that receives the country reports. The committee, after considering information from the complaints, the countries involved, and other relevant sources, then makes a report to the council's Committee of Ministers. If the committee finds that "the Charter has not been applied in a satisfactory manner," the committee may adopt by a two-thirds vote a recommendation to the country concerned. That nation then must indicate in its next report "the measures it has taken to give effect" to the recommendation.

Part V addresses a number of considerations, including nondiscrimination on the basis of "race, color, sex, language, religion, political or other opinion, national extraction or social origin, health, association with a national minority, birth or other status" and derogations from the charter's provisions in times of war, threats of war, or public emergencies. An Appendix addresses the charter's scope in terms of persons protected, such as foreigners, refugees, and stateless persons.

Council of Europe, Point I, F-67075 Strasbourg Cedex, France. (33-3-88-41-20-00. 🖷 33-3-88-41-27-81. 🖳 webmaster @www.coe.fr. 🖳 www.coe.fr.

Economic Rights; European Convention for the Protection of Human Rights and Fundamental Freedoms; Housing; International Covenant on Economic, Social and Cultural Rights; International Labor Organization; Social Rights; Welfare; Workers

Euthanasia

See Die, Right to

Eviction

See Forced Eviction

Exhaustion of Remedies

A common legal doctrine asserts that if an administrative remedy is provided by statute, a person seeking judicial relief must first determine whether such relief is available administratively before the courts will hear the matter. Because administrative authorities are more likely to have relevant expertise, this policy requiring the exhaustion of remedies (from the Latin *exhaurio,* meaning to exhaust or empty, and *exhaustus,* meaning drained or worn out) gives them a chance to act before the courts are burdened with the matter.

In a federal system of government such as in the United States, a similar doctrine applies to cases in which the party seeking a remedy must obtain a decision from the state court system before going to a federal court. A state prisoner in the United States, for example, must first seek and be denied relief in the state before the federal courts will entertain a petition for a writ of habeas corpus. In Mexico, under the process of *amparo* (an action against governmental infringement of a citizen's civil rights), other remedies must be exhausted before a trial will be granted.

Under international law, when a citizen of one country seeks to have his or her government present a claim to another government, the citizen must generally show that he or she has exhausted the possibility of all remedies in the other country. The availability of such a local or domestic remedy, through a court or an administrative process, thus bars a claim under international law. This same reasoning has been used to determine the admissibility of petitions and complaints regarding human rights violations presented to international and regional human rights tribunals, such as those established under the European Convention for the Protection of Human Rights and Fundamental Freedoms (1950), International Covenant on Civil and Political Rights (1966), and American Convention on Human Rights (1969).

The exhaustion of remedies doctrine, however, presents a formidable obstacle to complainants and petitioners who seek relief for human rights violations, especially where the accused country unreasonably delays the domestic relief procedures or unfairly handles the pursuit of a domestic remedy.

Constitution of Mexico (1917), title III, article 107, III: "In judicial, administrative or labor matters a writ of amparo shall be granted only: . . . (b) Against acts at the trial, the execution of which would be irreparable out of court, or at the conclusion of the trial once all available recourses have been exhausted. . . ."

American Convention on Human Rights (1969), part II, Means of Protection, chapter VII, Inter-American Commission on Human Rights, section 3, Competence, article 46: "1. Admission by the Commission of a petition or communication . . . shall be subject to the following requirements: a. that the remedies under domestic law have been pursued and exhausted in accordance with generally recognized principles of international law."

U.S. Supreme Court (1982): "In determining whether exhaustion of state administrative remedies is required [under the Civil Rights Act of 1871], [the] initial question should be answered by reference to congressional intent and courts should not defer the exercise of jurisdiction under a federal statute unless it is consistent with that intent."

Committee against Torture (1997): "Article 22, paragraph 5(b), of the Convention [against Torture and Other Cruel, Inhuman or Degrading Treatment or Punishment (1984)] precludes the Committee from considering any communication unless it has ascertained that all available domestic remedies have been exhausted. The Committee notes that the ill-treatment inflicted on the complainants is currently the subject of a judicial review in [the country against which the complaint is made and] that the information before [the Committee] does not suggest that the recourse procedure is being unreasonably delayed or that it is unlikely to bring the complainants effective relief."

Clements, L. J., Nuala Mole, and Alan Simmons. *European Human Rights: Taking a Case under the Convention.* London: Sweet and Maxwell, 1999.

American Convention on Human Rights; *Amparo;* European Convention for the Protection of Human Rights and Fundamental Freedoms; Habeas Corpus; International Covenant on Civil and Political Rights; Remedies; Reporting Violations; Violations

Exile

See Deportation; Expulsion; Forced Eviction

Expression

Freedom of expression, like freedom of speech and the press, bars government infringement of an individual's right to state ideas, whether political, artistic, cultural, or religious. In a pluralistic society all members should be free to express themselves, as long as such expression (from the Latin *ex,* meaning out, and *pressare,* meaning to press) does not transgress the bounds of decency or contain falsehoods that materially injure others. Freedom of expression is often paired with freedom of information, which is needed to ensure the flow of data necessary for individuals to make informed decisions, especially political ones.

Freedom of expression is a broader term for freedom of speech. In fact, the U.S. Supreme Court on occasion has had to interpret nonverbal expressions, such as public burnings of the American flag, as symbolic speech covered by the freedom of speech guarantee in the Bill of Rights (1791). Freedom of expression is also often linked with freedom of opinion and the press, because opinions are generally expressed in speech or some other medium such as the press. Freedom of expression and speech are rights intended to encourage political discourse; for the same reason legislators are generally immune from suits for slander.

For most of history, the right to express oneself freely was limited, generally depending on one's position in society. The ancient Greek democracies permitted some degree of free speech but prohibited swearing falsely, treasonous words, and blasphemy; slaves, women, children, and aliens were further restricted in what they could express and how it could be expressed. In ancient Rome, citizenship entailed duties to the state more than individual rights. After the decline of the Greek democracies, freedom of expression was strictly controlled by cultural forces, including religion, social mores, law, and the authorities in power. William Blackstone, the eighteenth-century commentator on the laws of England, indicated that it was questionable as to "[h]ow far mere words, spoken by an individual, and not relative to any treasonable act or design then in agitation, shall amount to treason," but he does cite two persons who were executed for treason in the reign of Edward IV for such infractions.

The European Declaration on Freedom of Expression and Information (1982), adopted by the Council of Europe, notes that "the freedom of expression and information is a fundamental element" of "the principles of genuine democracy, the rule of law and respect for human rights," declaring that "in the field of information and mass media" council members seek to protect "the right of everyone, regardless of frontiers, to express himself. . . ." The average citizen's right to do so is not absolute, however, and there is much disagreement as to which justifications are sufficient to restrain or punish expression, with the arguments often turning on the same considerations as with the issue of freedom of speech—whether, for example, such freedom permits obscenity or incitement to criminal acts.

Constitution of Sweden, Instrument of Government (1974), chapter 2, Fundamental Rights and Freedoms, article 1: "All citizens shall be guaranteed the following in their relations with the public administration: 1. freedom of expression: the freedom to communicate information and to express ideas, opinions and emotions, whether orally, in writing, in pictorial representations, or in any other way. . . ."

Universal Declaration of Human Rights (1948), article 19: "Everyone has the right to freedom of opinion and expression; this right includes freedom to hold opinions without interference and to seek, receive and impart information and ideas through any media and regardless of frontiers."

Supreme Court of Japan (1987): The Constitution of Japan (1947), article 21, does not provide "grounds [for] the right to reply or to have a refuting article placed in publication . . . [e]ven when one of the parties [in a private dispute] publishes or sells a national newspaper with an extremely strong influence in gathering, controlling and dealing with information."

European Commission of Human Rights (1978): "The concept of 'expression' concerns mainly the expression of opinions and receiving and imparting information and ideas, but not the notion of physical expression of feelings in homosexual relations."

Kennedy, Shelia S., ed. *Free Expression in America: A Documentary History*. Westport, Conn.: Greenwood, 1999.

Trager, Robert, and Donna L. Dickerson. *Freedom of Expression in the Twenty-first Century*. Thousand Oaks, Calif.: Pine Forge, 1999.

Information; Opinion; The Press; Speech; Thought

Expulsion

The international law principle of sovereignty allows a nation to treat its citizens as it wishes without interference from other countries. As punishment for crimes as well as for arbitrary reasons, such as political differences, nations have long exiled or banished their own citizens or subjects—unwanted people who are unable to protect themselves, including minorities. They also maintain the right to deport aliens for administrative and criminal transgressions.

The concept of expulsion, involving the exile of a citizen or the deportation of an alien to his or her native country or another place, was recognized in ancient Greece and Rome. The Greeks would ostracize leaders of political factions for up to ten years. As punishment for serious crimes, Roman citizens also could be sent into exile. The procedure of *deportatio*, consisting of banishment and loss of Roman citizenship, was begun by Augustus Caesar, who acquired full power in 27 B.C.E., and was used until the reign of the Emperor Justinian in the fifth century C.E. Deportation, however, today generally refers to the involuntary return of aliens to their country of origin.

Mass expulsions coerced by violence, often deadly force, have become of great concern because they violate human rights on a large scale and the expelled people have an impact on neighboring nations. During World War II Joseph Stalin, the communist leader of the Soviet Union, forcibly transported, or "resettled," 1.5 million non-Russian peoples, including Bulgarians, Greeks, and Armenians. One recent example of mass expulsion is the 1999 ethnic cleansing of the Kosovar Albanians by the Serbian government of Yugoslavia, which caused several hundred thousand refugees to flee Kosovo.

A drastic measure, the forcible removal of a citizen or an alien requires substantial justification under international law. Countries have given various reasons for expelling people, including to create internal order and to root out "bad weeds" and people who defy the "call for racial harmony." In time of war or internal unrest, nations often expel suspected enemy or rebel sympathizers. Arbitrary expulsions that are not reasonably justified, that are contrary to a treaty or a domestic law, or that are carried out by unnecessarily harsh or violent means violate international legal norms. As such, they may be the subject of an international claim by an alien's home country for damages against the expelling country.

In 1986 the Human Rights Committee clarified its position on the expulsion of aliens under its governing treaty, the International Covenant on Civil and Political Rights (1966). The provisions of article 13 regarding expulsion, it stated in General Comment 15, "would not be satisfied by laws or decisions providing for collective or mass expulsions." In other words, each expellee must be treated individually and provided a due process hearing to challenge the basis for expulsion.

Magna Carta (1297 version), chapter 29, Imprisonment, etc. Contrary to Law: "No freeman shall be taken or imprisoned, or be disseised [dispossessed] of his freehold, or liberties, or free customs, or be outlawed, or exiled, or any other wise destroyed; nor will we [the sovereign] pass upon him, nor [condemn him] but by lawful judgment of his peers, or by the law of the land."

International Covenant on Civil and Political Rights (1966), part III, article 13: "An alien lawfully in the territory of a State Party to the present Covenant may be expelled therefrom only in pursuance of a decision reached in accordance with law and shall, except where compelling reasons of national security otherwise require, be allowed to submit the reasons against his expulsion. . . ."

U.S. Supreme Court (1896): In addition to expulsion, Congress may provide for detention or confinement of aliens as punishment for illegal entry into the United States, but it may not subject such aliens to punishment at hard labor or confiscate their property without a trial to establish their guilt.

Arbitration under U.S.A.–Mexico Convention (1863): Mere suspicion is not sufficient grounds for expulsion from Mexico even where the expellee is notorious and suffers no monetary loss by being expelled.

United Nations High Commissioner for Human Rights, 8–14 avenue de la Paix, 1211 Geneva 10, Switzerland. ☎ 41-22-917-9000. 🖷 41-22-917-9016. ✉ webadmin.hchr@unog.ch. 🖳 www.unhchr.ch.

United Nations High Commissioner for Refugees, C.P. 2500, 1211 Geneva 2, Switzerland. ☎ 41-22-739-8111. 🖷 41-22-739-7377. ✉ hqpioo@unhcr.ch. 🖳 www.unhcr.ch.

Henckaerts, Jean-Marie. *Mass Expulsion in Modern International Law and Practice.* The Hague: Martinus Nijhoff, Kluwer Law International, 1995.

Pohl, J. Otto. *Ethnic Cleansing in the USSR, 1937–1949.* Westport, Conn.: Greenwood, 1999.

Aliens; Asylum; Deportation; Forced Eviction; *Refoulement;* Refugees; Statelessness

Extradition

Extradition (from the Latin *ex,* meaning out, and *tradere,* meaning to deliver up) refers to a state or a country's surrender to another jurisdiction of a person accused of committing a crime in the latter state. Such action is usually taken pursuant to a specific treaty provision to ensure reciprocity in such matters.

The concept of extradition contrasts with that of asylum, whereby a person is protected from being delivered up to another jurisdiction. The notion of asylum, based on the sanctity of church grounds, originated in the Middle Ages but gradually gave way to an examination of the reason for which asylum was sought. By the eighteenth century a particular place was no longer deemed a sanctuary for criminals, and states were considered to have a reciprocal obligation to punish criminals. By the beginning of the twentieth century the U.S. Supreme Court legally defined extradition as "the surrender by one nation to another of an individual accused or convicted of an offense outside its own territory, and within the territorial jurisdiction of the other, which, being competent to try and to punish him, demands surrender." In 1933 the Court added: "The principles of international law recognize no right to extradition apart from treaty."

International instruments regarding extradition include the Convention on Extradition (1933), adopted by the Organization of American States (OAS); European Convention on Extradition (1957), adopted by the Council of Europe; and Inter-American Convention on Extradition (1981), drafted by the Inter-American Council of Jurists, approved in 1981 by the Inter-American Juridical Committee, and adopted by the OAS General Assembly. These conventions aim at standardizing extradition treaty provisions and incorporating international norms. For example, they set forth the obligation of states parties to extradite persons who, as determined by the competent authorities of the requesting state, are required for prosecution or trial, are under a sentence of incarceration, or are otherwise legally detained. The conventions also offer a list of extraditable offenses, such as those in which the punishment requires a deprivation of liberty for a certain period of time or a more severe penalty, as well as certain exceptions, such as cases of political offenses and the legitimate exercise of the right of asylum.

In 1990 the UN General Assembly, on the recommendation of the Eighth United Nations Congress on the Prevention of Crime and the Treatment of Offenders, adopted a Model Treaty on Extradition to encourage and assist countries to enter into treaties for extradition and mutual legal assistance in order to improve international cooperation against organized crime.

Constitution of Jordan (1952), chapter two, Rights and Duties of Jordanians, article 21: "(i) Political refugees shall not be extradited on account of their political beliefs or for their defense of liberty. (ii) Extradition of ordinary criminals shall be regulated by international agreements and laws."

European Convention on Extradition (1957), article 2, Extraditable Offenses: "1. Extradition shall be granted in respect of offenses punishable under the laws of the requesting Party and of the requested Party by deprivation of liberty or under a detention order for a maximum period of at least one year or by a more severe penalty. Where a conviction and prison sentence have occurred or a detention order has been made in the territory of the requesting Party, the punishment awarded must have been for a period of at least four months."

U.K. Court of Appeals (Opinion of Lord Denning) (1962): "[T]he law of extradition is one thing; the law of deportation is another. . . . As I understand it, by the common law of England . . . every person coming from abroad, as soon as he sets foot lawfully in this country, is free; and so long as he commits no offense here, he is not to be arrested or detained for any offense that he may have committed in some other country. If any attempt were made to arrest him in order to surrender him to that other country, he would at once be entitled to be set free. The writ of habeas corpus is available to him for the purpose. In the absence of an extradition treaty, it is no answer for . . . any officer of the Crown, to say that he wishes to send him off to another country to meet a charge there."

Human Rights Committee (1993): Canada's extradition of a British subject to California, where, if convicted, he could be punished by death in the gas chamber, violated its obligations under the International Covenant on Civil and Political Rights (1966), article 7, which deems the death penalty a "cruel and unusual punishment."

Council of Europe, Point I, F-67075 Strasbourg Cedex, France. (33-3-88-41-20-00. 🖥 33-3-88-41-27-81. 🖳 webmaster@www.coe.fr. 🖳 www.coe.fr.

Lawyers Committee for Human Rights, 100 Maryland Avenue, N.E., Washington, D.C. 20002. (202-547-5692. 🖥 202-543-5999. 🖳 wdc@lchr.org. 🖳 www.lchr.org.

Organization of American States, 17th Street and Constitution Avenue, N.W., Washington, D.C. 20006. (202-458-3000. 🖥 202-458-3967. 🖳 pi@oas.org. 🖳 www.oas.org.

Gilbert, Geoff. *Transnational Fugitive Offenders in International Law: Extradition and Other Mechanisms*. The Hague: Martinus Nijhoff, Kluwer Law International, 1998.

Plachta, Michal. *Transfer of Prisoners under International Instruments and Domestic Legislation: A Comparative Study*. Freiburg im Breisgau, Germany: Max Planck Institute for Foreign and International Criminal Law, 1993.

Asylum; Prisoners; Punishment; Treaties

The family is recognized nationally and internationally as the basic unit of society, one deserving of special rights and assistance by government. Hard times may place a strain on families, but they also often bring them closer together. The face of this poverty-stricken American mother during the Great Depression indelibly captures the stress her family suffers. [Dorothea Lange, Library of Congress/Corbis]

Fair Trial

"In the ordinary trialls of Right, Twelve men of the common People, are the Judges," wrote Thomas Hobbes, the English political philosopher, in *Leviathan* (1651). A trial (derived from both Scandinavian and French words) is the legal examination of an accused person or of a controversy between parties and the determination of guilt or innocence or of fault. As such, the term has been in use in English since at least the sixteenth century.

A fair trial is a major component of the rights of the accused in a criminal proceeding and is a part of the broader concept of due process of law. The potential impact of a trial's outcome—the loss of property, freedom, and possibly even life—makes the requirement of a fair trial an important human right as well. Trials in ancient Athens were held before jurors, but the modern concept of proper legal procedures had not yet been developed. The accused had no lawyers to represent them, and when Socrates was on trial for his life in Athens, according to Plato, he had to appeal to the jurors not to drown out his defense speech with their shouts.

Trial procedures could be far worse than those Socrates faced. William Blackstone, in his *Commentaries on the Laws of England* (1769), describes "the most ancient species of trial"—trial by ordeal, either by fire or water. Other English methods included trial by combat, by morsel (the assumption was that the guilty party would choke on a piece of cheese or bread), by Parliament, and by jury.

Many national constitutions today require a fair trial or specify the requirements for a fair trial, such as the presumption of innocence, the right to face accusers and cross-examine witnesses, an impartial judge, and a jury of one's peers. The Universal Declaration of Human Rights (1948), articles 10 and 11, and the International Covenant on Civil and Political Rights (1966), article 14, address the elements of a fair trial. The Safeguards Guaranteeing Protection of the Rights of Those Facing the Death Penalty (1984), paragraph 5, requires "a final judgment rendered by a competent court after legal process which gives all possible safeguards to ensure a fair trial, at least equal to those contained in article 14 of the International Covenant on Civil and Human Rights. . . ."

At the request of the Subcommission on the Promotion and Protection of Human Rights, a study entitled *The Right to a Fair Trial: Current Recognition and Measures Necessary for Its Strengthening* was prepared by special rapporteurs (experts) and presented in 1994. The rapporteurs reviewed international human rights instruments guaranteeing a fair trial and remedies for violations of that right, as well as decisions of such human rights bodies as the Human Rights Committee and regional agencies. Some of the violations of the right to a fair trial noted included deviations from standard legal procedures in emergency situations or through the use of military courts. In their conclusion the rapporteurs stated: "Governments should recognize that judicial and administrative structures necessary to guarantee the right to a fair trial and a remedy are indispensable for the protection of all other human rights."

Constitution of Colombia (1991), title VIII, Concerning the Judiciary Branch, article 230: "In their decisions, the judges are bound exclusively by the rule of law. Fairness, jurisprudence, and the general principles of law and doctrine are auxiliary criteria of judicial proceedings."

Standard Minimum Rules for the Administration of Juvenile Justice (Beijing Rules) (1985), part three, Adjudication and Disposition, 14, Competent Authority to Adjudicate: 14.1: "Where the case of a juvenile offender has not been diverted [to an informal procedure], he or she shall be dealt with by the competent authority . . . according to the principles of a fair and just trial."

Supreme Court of Japan (1972): "In a criminal case, if the trial is delayed for an unduly long period, the accused left for that period without a verdict, suffers not only tangible and intangible disadvantages in society, but also from various impediments in his trial, such as the decrease or loss of his own memory, or that of his witnesses, the death of persons involved, and the loss of evidence."

African Commission on Human and Peoples' Rights (1996): "[D]uring the trials defense counsel for the complainants was harassed and intimidated to the extent of being forced to withdraw from the proceedings. In spite of this . . . the tribunal proceeded to give judgment [and sentence] the accused to death. The Commission finds that [the] defendants were deprived of their right to [a] defense, including the right to be defended by counsel of their choice, a violation of Article 7.1(c) [of the African Charter on Human and Peoples' Rights]."

International Commission of Jurists, 26 chemin de Joinville, P.O. Box 160, 1216 Geneva, Switzerland. (41-22-788-4747. 🖷 41-22-788-4880. 🖳 info@icj.org. 🖳 www.icj.org.

Lawyers Committee for Human Rights, 100 Maryland Avenue, N.E., Washington, D.C. 20002. (202-547-5692. 🖷 202-543-5999. 🖳 wdc@lchr.org. 🖳 www.lchr.org.

Galligan, D. J. *Due Process and Fair Procedures: A Study of Administrative Procedures.* Oxford, England: Clarendon Press, Oxford University Press, 1996.

Stavros, Stephanos. *The Guarantees for Accused Persons under Article 6 of the European Convention on Human Rights: An Analysis of the Application of the Convention and a Comparison with Other Instruments.* The Hague: Martinus Nijhoff, Kluwer Law International, 1993.

☞

Accused; Counsel; Due Process of Law; International Commission of Jurists; International Covenant on Civil and Political Rights; Judicial Independence; Justice; Limitations; Rule of Law; Safeguards Guaranteeing Protection of the Rights of Those Facing the Death Penalty; Standard Minimum Rules for the Administration of Juvenile Justice (Beijing Rules); Universal Declaration of Human Rights

Families

"The family is the natural and fundamental group unit of society and is entitled to protection by society and the State," asserts the International Covenant on Civil and Political Rights (1966). National governments vary in the extent to which they provide specific family rights and guarantees, but the need to maintain strong, viable families is generally an important human rights goal at the national and international levels. Family rights fall into the category of economic and social rights—second-generation rights.

The concept of the family (from the Latin *familia*, meaning a family or a household) is universal and, according to anthropologists, has been the basic unit of social organization for both humans and our ancestors. The nuclear family—a mother, a father, and their offspring or adopted children—as well as the extended family of more distant relations has undoubtedly contributed to the survival of humanity and the development of human civilization. The ancient Greek philosopher Aristotle described the family of his day in *The Politics*, but some later scholars have argued that the family is separate and outside the scope of political theory rather than a unit of political organization.

A number of rights are associated with the family, such as the right to marry, the rights of spouses in marriage, the rights of children, privacy and security in the home, and maternity rights. Welfare rights include family, spousal, and child assistance. In addition, the question of the nationality of children and spouses typically arises in the context of the family. Some countries, including the United States, relax the laws requiring citizenship for spouses and children of U.S. citizens. Immigration is also generally made easier for immediate family members of citizens.

Tangential family rights issues may concern religion; ownership and inheritance of property; child custody, support, and division of property in the event of separation or divorce; and even the rights of grandparents with respect to the children of failed marriages. The rights of the family, however, do not include the right to physically or mentally abuse family members or to deny members their fundamental human rights, such as taking part in political, economic, and social activities.

Especially in many developed countries, the nuclear family created by marriage is being replaced by partnerships, both heterosexual and homosexual. Such nontraditional families raise issues from the right of homosexual partners to marry and to obtain government or employment benefits for partners to the right to raise children in such partnerships.

"Marriage and family shall enjoy the special protection of the state," asserts article 6(1) of Germany's constitution (1949). Bulgaria, Ireland, Italy, and Spain are among the many other countries whose constitutions expressly provide for family rights. Most national laws address traditional bases for the family, including prescriptions of what constitutes a marriage, itemizations of the rights of parties to a marriage and those of other family members, and the rights of married persons in the event of divorce or separation. Some countries grant male spouses legal control of all property, including the wife's, and support primogeniture, under which property rights go to the oldest male child, effectively disinheriting other family members on the death of the father. Social and religious rules—the biblical injunction to honor one's father and mother is the most well known—also affect marriage and family rights.

The first international document to assert the rights of the family was the Universal Declaration of Human Rights (1948), although long and difficult negotiations were required to reach agreement on the language. Nearly two decades later, the International Covenant on Civil and Political Rights stated that the "right of men and women of marriageable age to marry and to found a family shall be recognized" and that "[n]o marriage shall be entered into without the free and full consent of the intending spouses." This important document urges all signatory countries to "take appropriate steps to ensure equality of rights and responsibilities of spouses as to marriage, during marriage and at its dissolution. In the case of dissolution, provisions shall be made for the necessary protection of any children." The covenant extends certain rights to each child, including protection required "by his status as a minor, on the part of his family, society and the State."

Following on the rights expressed in the 1966 covenant and its companion covenant on Economic, Social and Cultural Rights (1966), a Declaration of Family Rights was adopted by the General Council of the International Union of Family Organizations on February 5, 1994. It notes that families are founded "on the universal values of love, solidarity, liberty and responsibility" and extends to them such rights as "to have at [their] disposal economic and social conditions and means . . . adapted to the reality of situations and needs" as well as "access to all the means of communication in so far as elements of education, information, culture, development of interpersonal relationships and spare time."

Constitution of Italy (1948), title I, article 29: "The republic acknowledges the rights of the family as a natural society founded on marriage. Marriage is based on the moral and juridical equality of the spouses, within limits provided for by law for ensuring the unity of the family."

European Convention for the Protection of Human Rights and Fundamental Freedoms (1950), section 1, article 8: "Everyone has the right to respect for his private and family life, his home and his correspondence."

Constitutional Court of Turkey (1995): Under Turkey's constitution (1982), the family is acknowledged as the foundation of Turkish society, and the state is required to ensure its peace and welfare. Family life referred to in the constitution, however, is based on marriage and does not include "family ties" of persons living outside marriage.

European Court of Human Rights (1979): "Article 8 [of the European Convention for the Protection of Human Rights and Fundamental Freedoms (1950)] thus applies to the 'family life' of the 'illegitimate' family as it does to that of the 'legitimate' family."

American Civil Liberties Union, 125 Broad Street, New York, N.Y. 10004. (212-549-2500. 212-549-2648. aclu@aclu.org. www.aclu.org.

International Union of Family Organizations, 28 place Saint-Georges, F-75009 Paris, France. (33-1-48-78-07-59. 33-1-42-82-95-24.

United Nations High Commissioner for Human Rights, 8–14 avenue de la Paix, 1211 Geneva 10, Switzerland. (41-22-917-9000. 41-22-917-9016. webadmin.hchr@unog.ch. www.unhchr.ch.

Belembaogo, Akila. *The Family in International and Regional Human Rights Instruments.* New York: United Nations, 1999.

Guggenheim, Martin, Alexandra Dylan Lowe, and Diane Curtis. American Civil Liberties Union. *The Rights of Families: The Authoritative ACLU Guide to the Rights of Family Members Today.* Carbondale, Ill.: Southern Illinois University Press, 1996.

Adoption; Children; Convention on Consent to Marriage, Minimum Age for Marriage and Registration of Marriages; Declaration of the Rights of the Child; Declaration on Social and Legal Principles Relating to the Protection and Welfare of Children, with Special Reference to Foster Placement and Adoption Nationally and Internationally; Economic Rights; Homosexuals; Marriage; Maternity; Nationality; Privacy; Social Rights; Welfare; Women

Fang Lizhi

A professor of physics in communist China, Fang Lizhi (b. 1936) was publicly rebuked for criticizing the Marxist influence on physics in China and urging reform of the educational system in 1957. After later being restored to his teaching position and made a vice president of a branch of Beijing's University of Science and Technology, he was held responsible by the Chinese government for encouraging student demonstrations in the 1980s, including those in Tiananmen Square in 1989.

Born in Beijing on February 12, 1936, Fang Lizhi was thirteen years old when Mao Zedong's communist army drove out Generalissimo Chiang Kai-shek's Chinese Nationalists and created the People's Republic of China in 1949. Fang, a brilliant student, entered Beijing University in 1952, where he studied physics, earning an appointment to the Chinese Academy of Sciences' Institute of Modern Physics Research. His outspoken attack on the influence of Marxism on the teaching of physics got him expelled from the Communist Party in 1957.

A promising scientist, he continued to teach and conduct research and helped set up the Department of Physics at the University of Science and Technology. Arrested in 1966 during the cultural revolution instigated by Mao, Fang spent a year in jail and then was forced to live and work on a communal farm for two years to complete his communist "reeducation." His membership in the party was restored in 1978, and several years later he was named a university vice president. Bent on continuing educational reforms to remove political influence from the teaching of science, he encouraged his students to participate in public demonstrations supporting democracy. Fang became well known for his concern for human rights, as well as for his advocacy of democratic reforms in China. "Human rights aren't the property of a particular race or nationality," he said. "Every human being has from birth the right to live, to think, to speak, [and] to find a mate. These are the most fundamental freedoms a human being has."

Fang was held responsible for the public demonstrations, transferred, and again expelled from the Chinese Communist Party in 1987, and his travel abroad was restricted. When he was charged with inciting the April 1989 student demonstrations in Tiananmen Square, he was forced to seek asylum in the U.S. Embassy in Beijing. The Chinese government finally allowed him to leave the country in 1990. Since then Fang, who was awarded the Robert F. Kennedy Human Rights Award in 1989, has continued his mission in Great Britain and the United States to bring pressure on the Chinese communist regime, urging President Clinton in 1994 to punish China by revoking its most-favored-nation status in retaliation for products made or sold by government-controlled enterprises. In 1995 he became a professor of physics at the University of Arizona.

Fang Li-chih and James H. Williams. *Bringing Down the Great Wall: Writings on Science, Culture, and Democracy in China.* New York: Knopf, 1991.

Federalism

Derived from the Latin *foedus* (treaty or contract), *federal* refers to a system of government in which two or more constituent states form a nation and yet retain a certain amount of sovereignty over their own internal affairs. Since at least the late eighteenth century, the term *federalism* has denoted the principle of the federal system of government or its advocacy. In *The Federalist Papers,* a compilation of essays drafted in 1787 to support adoption of the U.S. Constitution (1789), James Madison wrote: "The difference between a federal government and a national government, as it relates to the *operation of the government,* is ... that in the former the powers operate on the political bodies composing the Confederacy in their political capacities; in the latter, on the individual citizens composing the nation in their individual capacities."

History provides many examples of independent polities that combine, either temporarily or permanently, to form leagues or confederations. The peace alliance of Swiss cantons in 1219 led to the formation of the Swiss Confederation, known today as Switzerland. Modern-day federal republics include Argentina, Brazil, and the United States. Canada and Australia, although technically federations of provinces and states, respectively, are not republics, because the English monarch or his or her representative, the governor-general, is the constitutional head of state, although only in title.

Federalism's double layer of constitutional government—at the state level and at the national level—gives citizens more options for obtaining greater human rights and This two-level system also ensures greater accountability of political authorities because the states or provinces themselves are not totally under the control of a unitary (nonfederal) national government; second-tier elected officials in the states or provinces are directly responsible to their own constituents. In a unitary system of government, local administrators would be accountable to nationally elected officials. Federalism provides additional opportunities for the extension of rights and freedoms from constituent states to the entire nation: as Louis Brandeis, an associate justice of the U.S. Supreme Court from 1916 to 1939, expressed it, the states function as "laboratories in democracy," with the more successful of their experiments carrying the potential for adoption at the national level. In 1869, for example, the territory of Wyoming, before it joined the Union, became the first jurisdiction in the world to grant women the right to vote; fifty-one years later women's suffrage was finally attained at the national level.

A nation's particular form of government in and of itself does not determine its stand on human rights; thus, the issues of federal government and federalism are not often addressed in international human rights documents. Although the dispersal of power on national and state levels has some obvious advantages for human rights, a number of nonfederal governments, such as France and the United Kingdom, have maintained excellent human rights records.

Constitution of Germany (1949), II, The Federation and the States (*Länder*), article 20: "(1) The Federal Republic of Germany shall be a democratic and social federal state."

American Convention on Human Rights (1969), part I, State Obligations and Rights Protected, chapter IV, Suspension of Guarantees, Interpretation, and Application, article 28, Federal Clause: "1. Where a State Party is constituted as a federal state, the national government of such State Party shall implement all the provisions of the Convention over whose subject matter it exercises legislative and judicial jurisdiction."

Supreme Court of the State of Texas (1992): A "gag order" (a judicial prohibition against talking about a case) issued by a Texas court was overturned on the grounds that the state constitution provides greater rights with respect to freedom of expression than the U.S. Constitution.

European Court of Human Rights (1981): The court held that the United Kingdom, a member of the European Community, could not act with respect to fishery conservation measures even though the European Community had taken no action to indicate its intention to "occupy the field" in this area. (In a federal system, the national government may constitutionally manifest its intention to govern an area where it has discretionary authority. The national government's action to "occupy the field," therefore, preempts, or voids, any state or provincial action in this area.)

Cohen, Martin B., ed. *Federalism: The Legacy of George Mason.* Fairfax, Va.: George Mason University Press, 1988.

King, Preston. *Federalism and Federation.* Baltimore: Johns Hopkins University Press, 1982.

Constitutionalism; Mason, George

Firearms

See Basic Principles on the Use of Force and Firearms by Law Enforcement Officers; Law Enforcement; Weapons

Food

Like air and water, food is a prime necessity of human life. The need to provision for the family, extended family, clan, and larger groups formed the basis of economic and political development in early human societies. Anthropologists have established that the excess of food produced by early agricultural technology made possible human civilization and culture. Yet food, as a source of life and wealth, has also been the cause of strife among people.

In some international human rights documents, the right to food is considered a fundamental right. The Universal Declaration of Human Rights (1948), Declaration on Social Progress and Development (1969), and Universal Declaration on the Eradication of Hunger and Malnutrition (1974), adopted by the World Food Conference, contain language supporting the right to food, as do the UN Food and Agricultural Organization's 1943 constitution and the UN General Assembly's 1974 mandate for the World Food Council. In 1996, when a World Food Summit met in Rome in response to a UN appeal to address the issue of the right to food, the report of a UN special rapporteur (expert) estimated that at least 1.1 billion people in the world were living in extreme poverty.

At the regional and national levels, however, the absolute right to adequate food is generally considered a social or welfare right, not an individual human right equivalent to civil and political rights. This philosophical distinction is based partly on the fear that if everyone is entitled to adequate food, housing, and medicine, many citizens would have no incentive to work. However, starvation and malnutrition in a country or region with enough food to feed everyone adequately ranks alongside torture and inhuman treatment as an affront to human dignity; it is also an abdication of the government's responsibility to treat all citizens equally.

Constitution of India (1950), part IV, Directive Principles of State Policy, article 47, Duty of the State to Raise the Level of Nutrition: "The State shall regard the raising of the level of nutrition . . . as among its primary duties. . . ." **Article 48, Organization of Agriculture and Animal Husbandry:** "The State shall endeavor to organize agriculture and animal husbandry on modern and scientific lines. . . ."

International Covenant on Economic, Social and Cultural Rights (1966), part III, article 11(1): "The States Parties to the present Covenant recognize the right of everyone to an adequate standard of living for himself and his family, including adequate food. . . ."

Supreme Court of Canada (1989): "Lower courts have found that the rubric of 'economic rights' embraces a broad spectrum of

interests, ranging from such rights, included in various international covenants, as rights to social security, equal pay for equal work, adequate food, clothing and shelter.... To exclude all of these at this early moment in the history of interpretation [of the Canadian Charter of Rights and Freedoms (1982)] seems to us to be precipitous."

Human Rights Committee (1994): "[I]n view of the lack of information from the State party," allegations by a prisoner in Jamaica—including charges that he was "subjected for two weeks to a special regime of detention (only one or two meals per day . . .)" and that "the ordinary prisoners . . . began to protest for food, water, and better treatment"—amounted to "cruel and inhuman treatment" within the meaning of the International Covenant on Civil and Political Rights (1966), article 7, and also violated article 10, paragraph 1.

Food and Agriculture Organization of the United Nations, Viale delle Terme di Caracalla, 00100 Rome, Italy. (39-6-57051. 📠 39-6-57053152. 🖳 webmaster@fao.org. 🖳 www.fao.org.

International Fund for Agricultural Development, 107 Via del Serafico, 00142 Rome, Italy. (39-6-54591. 📠 39-6-5043463. 🖳 ifad@ifad.org. 🖳 www.ifad.org.

World Food Program, Via Cesare Giulio Viola, 68 Parco de Medici, Rome 00148, Italy. (39-6-65131. 📠 39-6-6590632. 🖳 webadministrator@wfp.org. 🖳 www.wfp.org.

Riches, Graham, ed. *First World Hunger: Food Security and Welfare Politics.* New York: St. Martin's, 1997.

Robson, John R. K., ed. *Famine: Its Causes, Effects, and Management.* New York: Gordon and Breach, 1981.

Declaration on Social Progress and Development; Economic Rights; Fundamental Rights; International Covenant on Economic, Social and Cultural Rights; Social Rights; Standard of Living; Universal Declaration of Human Rights; Universal Declaration on the Eradication of Hunger and Malnutrition; Welfare

Forced Eviction

Throughout history individuals, families, and whole communities have been removed against their will from their homes, lands, or neighborhoods by direct or indirect state action or by a conquering force. *Eviction* (from the Latin words *evince* and *evictus,* meaning to conquer or overcome) has been used since the sixteenth century to mean recovering or taking possession of lands by a legal process. At common law the term refers to the act of depriving a person of the possession of property pursuant to a court judgment.

All nations have laws that determine an individual's right to own or reside on property within their territorial jurisdiction, although a government's ability to dispossess people living lawfully on its property is generally subject to constitutional protections. Sovereign governments have an inherent right of eminent domain (the power to take private property for public use), but implementation of this authority should be governed by law and a dispossessed person is entitled at least to just and prompt compensation for the loss. Governments may also use their police power to remove people living illegally on public land and may evict people who attempt to remain on private property without authorization. Residents may additionally be legally removed from their own property for reasons such as natural disasters or health emergencies.

National policies such as the Soviet Union's collectivization of farms in the late 1920s and early 1930s during Stalin's reign and China's cultural revolution, which began in 1966 during Mao Zedong's rule, resulted in forced eviction of people from their traditional homes and lands without compensation or any legal recourse and generally with unwarranted force and violence. In 1990, according to calculations by the United Nations, some 300,000 people in one large West African city were evicted from their homes by the government and deprived of their possessions in a matter of hours; they received no compensation, were not given space in which to resettle, and were not allowed any form of legal redress. In 1999, at the government's direction, the Serbian military in Yugoslavia forced hundreds of thousands of Kosovars from their homes, creating a flood of refugees in southeastern Europe.

A 1993 UN report pointed out that "the issue of forced removals and forced evictions has in recent years reached the international human rights agenda because it is considered a practice that does grave and disastrous harm to the basic civil, political, economic, social and cultural rights of large numbers of people...." The UN human rights bodies have declared forced evictions to be "gross violations of human rights," and the governments responsible have been requested to cease such action.

Forced evictions differ from other types of displacement—mass exodus, refugee flows, internal displacement, and population transfers—in several important ways. Forced evictions are always the result of specific policy decisions by a government or its failure to intervene to stop such evictions by third parties. Coercion is always involved, the evictions are generally planned and announced before being put into effect, and they often involve identifiable individuals and discrete groups. When a forced eviction conforms to human rights standards, it is called legal eviction, as opposed to illegal, unfair, or arbitrary eviction.

Constitution of Paraguay (1992), part I, About Basic Principles, Rights, Duties, and Guarantees, title II, Rights, Duties, and Guarantees, chapter V, About Indian People, article 64, About Property Owned by the Community: "The removal or transfer of Indian groups from their habitat, without their express consent, is hereby prohibited."

Geneva Convention Relative to the Protection of Civilian Persons in Time of War (1949), part III, Status and Treatment of Protected Persons, section III, Occupied Territories, article 49: "Individual or mass forcible transfers, as well as deportations of protected persons from occupied territory to the territory of the Occupying Power or to that of any other country, occupied or not, are prohibited, regardless of their motive."

Constitutional Court of Croatia (1996): Eviction proceedings are unconstitutional where the occupant of a property has a claim to its use. The validity of such a claim must be tested in the courts before a person may be evicted.

UN Committee on Economic, Social and Cultural Rights, General Comment no. 4 (1991): "[A]ll persons should possess a degree of security of tenure which guarantees legal protection against forced eviction, harassment and other threats."

Forced Evictions and Human Rights. Fact Sheet no. 25. Geneva: Center for Human Rights, 1996.

Deportation; Expulsion; Geneva Conventions; Property; Refugees

Forced Labor

From the pyramids of ancient Egypt to the Great Wall of China, many monumental government projects have been built by people required to work against their will and under inhumane conditions. Other instances of forced labor or involuntary servitude extended into the twentieth century at the hands of Germany's Nazi regime and Japan's occupying forces during World War II. As late as 1960 *The Guardian Weekly*, an English publication, noted: "Lord Altrincham's call for conscription seems to be for both military service and civil jobs such as road making. The latter is ordinarily termed forced labor." Even today in many countries women and children are especially vulnerable to forced labor practices.

In civilized nations, however, forced labor, like slavery, has been outlawed. There is no acceptable basis on which one individual or the government should have the power to force other people to work. Governments have a duty to proscribe forced labor and enforce such prohibitions in the private sector. Legally incarcerated prisoners, an exception, may be compelled to perform services for the state for little or no remuneration. Military duty or true volunteer work for private parties, whether or not any payment is received, is not considered forced labor.

A number of national constitutions—that of Honduras (1982), for example—expressly prohibit forced labor, while others—such as that of Italy (1948)—require fair compensation and other protection for workers. Forced labor is generally banned when it is used for political coercion ("education") or as punishment for expressing an opinion; for economic development projects; for disciplining workers or punishing them for strikes; or as a tool for carrying out racial, social, national, or religious discrimination policies. Child labor and prostitution are other examples of forced labor practices that violate human rights.

Since 1922 the International Labor Organization (ILO) has studied the problem of forced labor. In 1929 it released a survey listing three reasons for forced labor: for general public purposes such as public works projects, for local public needs such as refuse disposal, and for private employers where such labor could be required by law or custom. The ILO's Forced Labor Convention (1930) did not ban several types of forced labor practices, including any service that is "exacted in virtue of compulsory military service laws for work of a purely military character"; that "forms part of the normal civic obligations of citizens of a fully self-governing country"; that results "as a consequence of a conviction in a court of law"; and that is "exacted in cases of emergency . . . and in general any circumstance that would endanger the existence or well-being of the whole or part of the population." Also exempted are "minor communal services of a kind which, being performed by members of the community in the direct interest of the said community, can therefore be considered as normal civic obligations. . . ."

The Protection of Wages Convention (1929) required that "wages shall be paid regularly" and prohibited "methods of payment which deprive the worker of a genuine possibility of terminating his employment." Forced labor and slavery are also prohibited in international documents such as the ILO's Convention Concerning the Abolition of Forced Labor (1957) as well as the European Convention for the Protection of Human Rights and Fundamental Freedoms (1950), International Covenant on Civil and Political Rights (1966), and American Convention on Human Rights (1969).

Constitution of Honduras (1982), title III, Declarations, Rights, and Guarantees, chapter II, Individual Rights, article 70: "No personal service may be exacted, nor must it be rendered gratuitously, except by virtue of the law or by a sentence based on the law."

Convention Concerning the Abolition of Forced Labor (1957), article 2: "Each member of the [ILO] which ratifies this convention undertakes to take effective measures to secure the immediate and complete abolition of forced or compulsory labor...."

Belgian Court of Arbitration (1995): The European Convention for the Protection of Human Rights and Fundamental Freedoms (1950), articles 4.2 and 4.3, as interpreted by the European Commission of Human Rights, excludes military service from the "forced or compulsive labor" prohibited therein without distinguishing between "voluntary engagement" and "compulsory service." However, because of the special nature of a military career and the limited nature of constraints, temporary measures requiring some soldiers to serve about three weeks per year at most in a reserve status after their active service does not constitute forced labor or involuntary servitude.

European Court of Human Rights (1982): The Belgian Recidivists Board denied the release of a prisoner who had been sentenced to two years and "placed at the Government's disposal" for ten years until he performed work in prison long enough to save sufficient funds to be able to have a chance to survive outside prison. Such action by the board did not violate the provisions of the European Convention for the Protection of Human Rights and Fundamental Freedoms (1950), which prohibits slavery and forced labor, because it came under the exception set forth in article 4.3(a), as "work required to be done under ordinary detention . . . or during conditional release from such detention."

International Labor Organization, 4 route des Morillons, 1211 Geneva 22, Switzerland. (41-22-799-6111. 🖷 41-22-798-8685. 🖳 somavia.ilo.org. 🖳 www.ilo.org.

Child Labor and the New Global Marketplace: Reaping Profits at the Expense of Children? Hearing before the U.S. Senate Subcommittee on Labor, Committee on Labor and Human Resources. Washington, D.C.: U.S. Government Printing Office, 1994.

Ferencz, Benjamin B. *Less than Slaves: Jewish Forced Labor and the Quest for Compensation.* Cambridge, Mass.: Harvard University Press, 1979.

American Convention on Human Rights; European Convention for the Protection of Human Rights and Fundamental Freedoms; International Covenant on Civil and Political Rights; International Labor Organization; Military Personnel; Slavery; Workers

Forefront

Forefront is a global network of young human rights advocates in nearly thirty countries who strive to end practices such as ethnic and domestic violence, abusive treatment of children and laborers, and environmental injustice. The nonprofit group was established in 1993 to link recipients of the Reebok Human Rights Award, an annual prize honoring young people who, often under extreme conditions and at great personal risk, have made significant contributions to human rights around the world. Many of these activists work in isolation, without peer support or connections to the international community and other human rights organizations.

Forefront's mission is to encourage and assist young human rights advocates who bring innovative ideas and energy to the human rights challenges where they live. Ranging in age from seventeen to forty and representing nearly fifty nongovernmental organizations, Forefront's members provide assistance through technological resources, information and activity development, and advocacy support. Technological aid includes e-mail access, equipment to enhance communications with the media and the international community, and a Web site for posting reports, press releases, and other information about how to support these human rights advocates. Research and information include a biweekly publication, *Action Brief;* assistance with publications and briefings; and information sharing among the members. Advocacy operations include support for activists in emergencies through an Urgent Action Network to generate correspondence campaigns; funds in emergency life-or-death situations; campaigns for members who are prisoners of conscience; promotion of adequate protection for young human rights workers; and a Partnership Project to connect members with schools and community groups in wealthy countries to raise awareness about human rights needs as well as funds to support young activists.

Some of the organization's accomplishments include grants for e-mail accounts given to young human rights workers in Cambodia, Liberia, Nigeria, and Eritrea; a $2,000 matching grant to install the first telephone line in an activist's community in Guatemala; and the creation of a $10,000 "lifeline" fund to provide quick transfers of money to members caught in life-threatening situations. Its activists have run health clinics in Haiti, advocated peace in Northern Ireland, taught literacy to bonded laborers in Nepal, criticized violence against women in Jordan, advocated on behalf of street children in Guatemala, and worked to eliminate racial bias in the judicial system of rural Alabama.

One of Forefront's key long-term goals is creation of a broad international community of young human rights leaders whose skills and leadership qualities can be maximized for their mutual benefit and the benefit of human rights around the world.

Forefront, 333 Seventh Avenue, 13th Floor, New York, N.Y. 10001-5004. (212-845-5273. 212-253-4244. forefront@fore-frontleaders.org. www.forefrontleaders.org.

Defenders of Human Rights; Nongovernmental Organizations; Youth

Freedom

See Liberty

Freedom House

A nonprofit, nonpartisan organization established in 1941, Freedom House conducts programs to promote an engaged U.S. foreign policy and monitor human rights and elections around the world. It also sponsors public education campaigns, offers training and technical assistance to promote democracy and free-market economic reforms, and supports the rule of law, free media, and effective local governance. The organization publishes *Freedom in the World*, an annual international survey.

Founded by Eleanor Roosevelt, Wendell Willkie (a lawyer and U.S. Republican presidential candidate in 1940), and others, Freedom House in the 1940s advocated the Marshall Plan for the restoration of war-torn Europe along with the North Atlantic Treaty Organization (NATO). During the 1950s and 1960s, it supported the civil rights movement in the United States. Vietnamese refugees—the "boat people"—who fled after the fall of Saigon to the North Vietnamese captured the organization's attention in the 1970s. In the 1980s Freedom House supported the Polish Solidarity Movement and the democratic opposition to Ferdinand Marcos's dictatorship in the Philippines, and in 1997 it incorporated the democratization training programs of the National Forum Foundation. Recent activities include international programs for democracy, reports on religious persecution and journalism and corruption in Eastern Europe, and a World Forum on Democracy.

In addition to opposing dictatorships, apartheid, genocide, and other brutal human rights violations, Freedom House has championed the rights of democratic activists, religious believers, trade unionists, journalists, and free-market proponents. According to Freedom House's research, democracy had recorded dramatic gains near the end of the twentieth century. By late 1998 eighty-eight of the world's 191 nations were rated as being "free," meaning that they meet a number of criteria for political rights and civil liberties. This represents a gain of seven countries over

the previous year. Newly added "free" countries included India, Nicaragua, Slovakia, and Thailand. Fifty-three countries were rated "partly free," enjoying more limited political rights and civil liberties. Although democracies have a good record overall on human rights, new democracies often lack strong civic institutions and support for the rule of law, generally resulting in weaker human rights records.

Freedom House's board of trustees includes Zbigniew Brzezinski, national security adviser to President Jimmy Carter, and Andrew Young, the former ambassador to the United Nations. Among its funding sources are the Ford Foundation, Grace Foundation, Sarah Scaife Foundation, Soros Foundation, U.S. Agency for International Development, and U.S. Information Agency.

Freedom House, 1319 18th Street, N.W., Washington, D.C. 20036. (202-296-5101. 202-296-5078. fh@freedomhouse.org. www.freedomhouse.org.

Carter, James Earl; Democracy; Education; Monitoring Compliance; North Atlantic Treaty Organization (NATO); Roosevelt, Eleanor; Rule of Law; Violations

Fundamental Rights

Fundamental rights and *fundamental liberties* are common terms in the field of human rights but have often been used without great precision or consistency. In a general sense, all human rights are fundamental in that they are necessary for the protection and development of every human being, but not all human rights have similar stature. Should the right to participate in the cultural life of the community, for example, be of equal weight to the right to life, liberty, and property? Like inviolable and absolute rights, fundamental rights generally refer to the most basic and important rights rather than rights of a more temporary or conditional nature, such as collective or group rights or the rights of airline passengers or consumers. Fundamental rights are generally considered to include civil and political rights, sometimes called first-generation rights. Second-generation rights encompass economic, social, and cultural rights, while third-generation rights involve collective or community rights.

Fundamental human rights and freedoms generally include the right to life (although capital punishment and abortion may be considered exceptions in some countries); liberty and security of the person; recognition as a person; freedom of opinion, expression, the press, and religion; freedom of assembly and association; privacy; equality before the law; equal participation in government; freedom of movement; rights of persons accused of crimes; due process of law; freedom from torture and cruel or inhuman treatment; and freedom from slavery. Gross violations, such as genocide, ethnic cleansing, summary executions, and disappearances, represent extreme denials of fundamental human rights and freedoms.

Fundamental rights are expressly guaranteed in a number of national constitutions. The constitutions of Ireland (1937), Mozambique (1990), and Slovakia (1993), for example, place protection of individual rights under a specific heading of fundamental rights, while the constitutions of other nations, South Korea (1948) and Hungary (1949) among them, refer generally to fundamental rights or fundamental human rights under headings stating citizen rights and duties.

Several international human rights documents use the terms *fundamental rights* or *fundamental freedoms* in their titles—for example, the European Convention for the Protection of Fundamental Rights and Freedoms (1950) and the Declaration on the Right and Responsibility of Individuals, Groups and Organs of Society to Promote and Protect Universally Recognized Human Rights and Fundamental Freedoms (1998).

Constitution of Ireland (1937), Fundamental Rights, Personal Rights, article 40: "All citizens shall, as human persons, be held equal before the law. This shall not be held to mean that the State shall not in its enactments have due regard to differences of capacity, physical and moral, and of social function."

European Convention for the Protection of Human Rights and Fundamental Freedoms (1950): The members of the Council of Europe reaffirm "their profound belief in those Fundamental Freedoms which are the foundation of justice and peace in the world and are best maintained on the one hand by an effective political democracy and on the other by a common understanding and observance of the Human Rights on which they depend...."

U.S. Supreme Court (1937): The rights encompassed by the Fourteenth Amendment (1868) to the U.S. Constitution, such as freedom of thought and speech, are so fundamental that "neither liberty nor justice would exist if they were sacrificed.... Fundamental too in the concept of due process, and so in that of liberty, is the thought that condemnation shall be rendered only after trial. The hearing, moreover, must be a real one, not a sham or pretense...."

International Court of Justice (1993): "Amongst the Purposes set out in Article 1(3) of the Charter [of the United Nations (1945)] is that of achieving international co-operation 'in promoting and encouraging respect for human rights and for fundamental freedoms for all without distinction as to race, sex, language or religion.'"

Shue, Henry. *Basic Rights: Subsistence, Affluence, and U.S. Foreign Policy*. Princeton, N.J.: Princeton University Press, 1980.

Bills of Rights; Civil Rights; European Convention for the Protection of Fundamental Rights and Freedoms; Declaration on the Right and Responsibility of Individuals, Groups and Organs of Society to Promote and Protect Universally Recognized Human Rights and Fundamental Freedoms; Human Rights; Inviolable Rights; Political Rights; Rights; Violations; *and other specific rights*

Mahatma Gandhi, the spiritual leader of India's struggle for independence from Great Britain, preached the doctrine of nonviolent protests to achieve human rights objectives. In their struggles for equality and justice, other human rights leaders such as the American civil rights advocate Martin Luther King Jr. were influenced by Gandhi's successful example of peaceful change.
[Library of Congress]

Gandhi, Mohandas K.

Called Mahatma, meaning "Great Soul," Mohandas Karamchand Gandhi (1869–1948) dedicated most of his life to freeing India from British colonial domination and to obtaining equality for all people. His emphasis on revolution and political change through nonviolent protests influenced other human rights efforts such as the 1960s civil rights movement in the United States. "That we should obey laws whether good or bad is a newfangled notion," said Gandhi in 1909 about his doctrine of passive resistance. "Such teaching is opposed to religion and means slavery."

Mohandas Gandhi was born on October 2, 1869, in Probandar, north of Bombay. He was a small, quiet, and average child of a wealthy merchant-class family. Gandhi left to study in London in 1888 and became a barrister there in 1891. While traveling on business for a client in South Africa, he was asked by a white passenger to leave his first-class train compartment. After meditating overnight in the train station, Gandhi decided to dedicate himself to fighting against race discrimination and began a campaign to improve the status of Indians living in South Africa, where both Indians and blacks suffered discrimination.

On returning home in 1896 to bring his wife, to whom he had been married by his family when he was thirteen years old, to South Africa with him, Gandhi began speaking out on the plight of his fellow countrymen in South Africa. When he returned there, he was stoned and barely escaped being lynched by the Afrikaners, the white descendants of the country's Dutch settlers. Undaunted, he stayed, and in 1907 he was jailed for urging Indians to resist being registered and fingerprinted as required under South African law.

Gandhi returned to India in 1915 and, continuing the techniques of passive resistance he had developed in South Africa, started a campaign to boycott British-made goods and encourage Indians to make their own clothes at home. In 1930, to protest a British tax on salt, Gandhi led a march of thousands 241 miles to the seacoast, where he symbolically picked up a handful of salt in defiance of the law. Later in the 1930s he worked closely with Indian political leaders to achieve independence from Britain. Imprisoned by the British during World War II because he urged noncooperation with Britain during the war, Gandhi was released in 1944 and lived to see India obtain independence in 1947.

While leading the nonviolent disobedience campaign against British colonial rule, Gandhi also fought against the Indian caste system, under which a large segment of society known as the Untouchables was treated as less than human. The designation came from the belief that by touching a member of the caste, a person could be polluted spiritually. Gandhi, however, referred to them as "Children of God." As a result of a fast by Gandhi begun on September 20, 1932, some lower castes were allowed in Hindu temples, from which they had always been barred. The 1950 constitution of the new Republic of India prohibited discrimination based on caste, stating: "'Untouchability' is abolished and its practice in any form is forbidden."

The life he chose to lead brought many hardships. Beaten and jailed often during his struggle for freedom and human dignity, Mahatma Gandhi died in 1948 at the hands of an assassin, a Hindu nationalist, during violence that erupted after the Muslim area of Pakistan separated from India.

Chakrabarti, Mohit. *Gandhian Humanism*. New Delhi: Concept, 1992.

Parekh, Bhikhu C. *Gandhi*. New York: Oxford University Press, 1997.

Gays

See Homosexuals

Geneva Conventions

The first multilateral humanitarian treaty was the Geneva Convention of 1864. Based on the recommendations of the Geneva International Conference held in 1863, the treaty was drafted to provide that "in time of war the belligerent nations should proclaim the neutrality of ambulances and military hospitals, and that neutrality should be recognized, fully and absolutely, in respect of official medical personnel, voluntary medical personnel [and] inhabitants of the country who go to the relief of the wounded, and the wounded themselves." The importance of this International Convention for the Amelioration of the Condition of Soldiers Wounded in Armies in the Field is underscored by the fact that it officially recognized the role of the predecessor of the International Committee of the Red Cross, the first international nongovernmental human rights organization, in bringing relief to those wounded in battle. Supplementary agreements in 1906 and 1907 modified the convention and extended protection to maritime warfare.

In 1929 a third Geneva Convention Relating to the Treatment of Prisoners of War was adopted. At the Nuremberg trials of war criminals after World War II, the tribunal held that this convention was, in its principal aspects, a part of international law and thus was binding on all nations, including those that had not ratified it.

In an attempt to prevent more war crimes like those of World War II, four new and stronger Geneva Conventions were adopted on August 12, 1949, and entered into force on October 21, 1950. The first agreement is the Geneva Convention for the Amelioration of the Condition of the Wounded and Sick in Armed Forces in the Field, the second is the Geneva Convention for the Amelioration of the Condition of Wounded, Sick and Shipwrecked Members of Armed Forces at Sea, the third is the Geneva Convention Relative to the Treatment of Prisoners of War, and the fourth is the Geneva Convention Relative to the Protection of Civilian Persons in Time of War. Almost all nations are parties to the Geneva Conventions, whose humanitarian rules for international armed conflicts are considered to be a part of customary international law, which means that all countries are bound by them.

Each of the four conventions contains an article 2, which provides that "[i]n addition to the provisions which shall be implemented in peacetime, the present Convention shall apply to all cases of declared war or of any other armed conflict which may arise between two or more of the High Contracting Parties, even if the state of war is not recognized by one of them. The Convention shall also apply," it adds, "to all cases of partial or total occupation of the territory of a High Contracting Party, even if the said occupation meets with no armed resistance. Although one of the Powers in conflict may not be a party to the present Convention, the Powers who are parties thereto shall remain bound by it in their mutual relations. They shall furthermore be bound by the Convention in relation to the said Power, if the latter accepts and applies the provisions thereof."

The first of the 1949 conventions, for the Amelioration of the Condition of the Wounded and Sick in Armed Forces in the Field, provides in part in article 3 that "[i]n the case of armed conflict not of an international character occurring in the territory of one of the High Contracting Parties," each party is bound to treat persons no longer fighting in a humane manner, "without any adverse distinction founded on race, color, religion or faith, sex, birth or wealth, or any similar criteria." Certain acts are specifically prohibited, among them violence leading to murder, mutilation, cruel treatment, and torture; the taking of hostages; personal humiliation; and sentencing and executions outside regularly constituted courts and without due process.

The convention also requires that the wounded and sick be cared for and provides that an "impartial humanitarian body, such as the International Committee of the Red Cross, may offer its services to the Parties to the conflict." An Annex to the agreement specifies the treatment of hospital zones, calling for their strict segregation from military operations and protection from attack.

The second convention, for the Amelioration of the Condition of Wounded, Sick and Shipwrecked Members of Armed Forces at Sea, has similar provisions. "In case of hostilities between land and naval forces of Parties to the conflict," states article 4, "the provisions of the present Convention shall apply only to forces on board ship. Forces put ashore shall immediately become subject to the provisions of the [first convention]."

In the third convention, Relative to the Treatment of Prisoners of War, article 4 provides in part: "Prisoners of war, in the sense of the present Convention, are persons belonging to one of the following categories, who have fallen into the power of the enemy: 1. Members of the armed forces of a Party to the conflict as well as members of militias or volunteer corps forming part of such armed forces. 2. Members of other militias and members of other volunteer corps, including those of organized resistance movements [meeting certain listed requirements]. . . . 3. Members of regular armed forces who profess allegiance to a government or an authority not recognized by the Detaining Power. 4. Persons who accompany the armed forces without actually being members thereof, such as [civilian workers, war correspondents, and supply contractors]. . . . 5. Members of crews [of ships and aircraft] who do not benefit by more favorable treatment under any other provisions of international law. 6. Inhabitants of a non-occupied territory, who on the approach of the enemy spontaneously take up arms to resist the invading forces, without having had time to form themselves into regular armed units, provided they carry arms openly and respect the laws and customs of war." The first of several annexes presents a model agreement concerning direct repatriation and accommodation of wounded and sick prisoners of war in neutral countries.

The fourth convention, Relative to the Protection of Civilian Persons in Time of War, article 3, mandates similar humane treatment for noncombatants in armed conflicts that are not international in scope. "Persons protected by the Convention," article 4 states in part, "are those who, at a given moment and in any manner whatsoever, find themselves, in case of a conflict or occupation, in the hands of a Party to the conflict or Occupying Power of which they are not nationals. Nationals of a State which is not bound by the Convention are not protected by it." Article 32 prohibits "not only murder, torture, corporeal punishment, mutilation . . . of a protected person, but also any other measures of brutality whether applied by civilian or military agents." Annexes address hospital and safety zones, collective relief shipments, internment cards, and correspondence.

The four conventions were supplemented on June 8, 1977, by two protocols that became effective on December 7, 1978. Protocol I and Protocol II, respectively, address victims of international and noninternational armed conflicts. These protocols have not been ratified to the same extent as the conventions themselves.

Protocol I provides extensive definitions of terms used in the earlier documents, adds issues such as spies and mercenaries, and, in its Annex, details identification procedures to protect humanitarian workers. Protocol II notes that "in cases not covered by the law in force, the human person remains under the protection of the principles of humanity and the dictates of the public conscience."

International Committee of the Red Cross, 19 avenue de la Paix, 1202 Geneva, Switzerland. (41-22-734-6001. 🖨 41-22-733-2082. 🖳 press.gva@icrc.org. 🖳 www.icrc.org.

United Nations High Commissioner for Human Rights, 8–14 avenue de la Paix, 1211 Geneva 10, Switzerland. (41-22-917-9000. 🖨 41-22-917-9016. 🖳 webadmin.hchr@unog.ch. 🖳 www.unhchr.ch.

Convention on Prohibitions or Restrictions on the Use of Certain Conventional Weapons Which May Be Deemed to Be Excessively Injurious or to Have Indiscriminate Effects; Crimes against Humanity; Declaration on the Protection of Women and Children in Emergency and Armed Conflict; Hostages; International Law; Military Personnel; Prisoners; Red Cross and Red Crescent; Summary Executions; Terrorism; War; War Crimes

Genocide

"The United Nations' indictment of the 24 Nazi leaders," reported the New York *Times* on October 7, 1945, "has brought a new word into the language—genocide . . . namely, the extermination of racial or national groups." Derived from the Greek word for genus (birth, race, or kind) and the Latin *caedere* (to kill), *genocide* was first used in 1944 by Raphael Lemkin, a Holocaust survivor in Nazi Germany, to describe the destruction of a nation or an ethnic group.

Acts of genocide are probably as old as war and interracial hatred. Genocide may simply be the unintended consequence of the expansion of one group of people and the conquest of another, as was the case with the European settlement of the New World after 1492. However, the extermination of Armenians by the Ottoman Empire between 1915 and 1918 as well as the Soviet Union's decimation of millions of landowners (Kulaks) in the 1930s were intended consequences of a policy of genocide.

The Holocaust—the extermination of some six million Jews and large numbers of other ethnic and racial minorities in Nazi Germany before and during World War II—led to world outrage and efforts to criminalize this form of mass murder. The Nuremberg war crimes trials in Germany after World War II resulted in the conviction of many Nazi leaders for crimes against humanity, including genocide. More recent examples of genocide are the communist leader Pol Pot's attempt at restructuring Cambodian society in the 1970s, which by some estimates exterminated nearly one-third of the Cambodian population, and Sadam Hussein's military actions against the Kurdish population in northern Iraq since his rise to power in 1977.

In 1946 the UN General Assembly declared that genocide is a crime under international law and that those guilty of it are punishable. Two years later it adopted the Convention on the Prevention and Punishment of the Crime of Genocide (1948). Because the convention outlawed the destruction of national, ethnic, racial, and religious groups, the right of such groups to exist has been recognized in international law. Unlike most other human rights, which are rights of the individual, the right to be protected from genocide recognizes group rights, of both minorities and majorities.

A 1978 report on genocide by the Subcommission on the Promotion and Protection of Human Rights indicated that, although a number of allegations of genocide had been made since the convention's adoption, because of a lack of prompt and impartial investigations it was not possible to verify them. The report also noted that the lack of any international criminal court made the possibility of punishment for violations problematic. It was not until 1993 that the International Tribunal for the Prosecution of Persons Responsible for Serious Violations of International Humanitarian Law Committed in the Territory of the Former Yugoslavia was created by the UN Security Council. Since then a similar tribunal for Rwanda has been established and a statute to set up the International Criminal Court adopted. In 1998 the Rwanda tribunal issued the first conviction for genocide by an international court. The following year the Yugoslavia tribunal convicted a Bosnian Serb who had been commander of a detention camp for Muslims and Croats (and who had taken the name Adolf in tribute to Adolf Hitler) on thirty-one counts of crimes against humanity and war crimes; however, it found him not guilty of the charge of genocide.

Convention on the Prevention and Punishment of the Crime of Genocide (1948), article 1: The acts constituting genocide include "(a) killing members of the group; (b) causing serious bodily or mental harm to members of the group; (c) deliberately inflicting on the group conditions of life calculated to bring about its physical destruction in whole or in part; (d) imposing measures intended to prevent births within the group; and (e) forcibly transferring children of the group to another group."

Report on Genocide for the Economic and Social Council (ECOSOC) (1985): "Genocide is the ultimate crime and the gravest violation of human rights it is possible to commit. Consequently, it is difficult to conceive of a heavier responsibility for the international community and the Human Rights bodies of the United Nations than to undertake any effective steps possible to prevent and punish genocide in order to deter its recurrence."

District Court of Jerusalem (1961): In the trial of Adolf Eichmann, an Austrian Nazi who ordered the murder of thousands of Jews during World War II, the court concluded that the Convention on the Prevention and Punishment of the Crime of Genocide (1948), article 6, which states that "[p]ersons charged with genocide . . . shall be tried by a competent tribunal of the States in the territory of which the act was committed, or by such international penal tribunal as may have jurisdiction . . . ," did not prevent Eichmann from being tried in Israel for this crime.

International Court of Justice (Advisory Opinion) (1951): "The origins of the [Convention on the Prevention and Punishment of the Crime of Genocide (1948)] show that it was the intention of the United Nations to condemn and punish genocide as 'a crime under international law' involving a denial of the right of existence of entire human groups, a denial which shocks the conscience of mankind and results in great losses to humanity, and which is contrary to moral law and to the spirit and aims of the United Nations. . . ."

Andreopoulos, George J. *Genocide: Conceptual and Historical Dimensions.* Philadelphia: University of Pennsylvania Press, 1994.

Convention on the Prevention and Punishment of the Crime of Genocide; Crimes against Humanity; International Criminal Court; Minorities; Race Discrimination; War Crimes

Grotius, Hugo

Hugo Grotius (1583–1645), called the "jurist of humanity" by the Italian philosopher Jean-Baptist Vico, played a key role in the transition from medieval concepts of sovereignty and natural law to the modern era of international law. His legal works, principally *De Jure Belli ac Pacis (The Laws of War and Peace)* (1625), laid the groundwork for modern international law and, by extension, international human rights.

Huigh de Groot, as he was known in his native Dutch tongue, was born in Delft, Holland, in 1583 (Grotius is the Latin form of his Dutch name). An infant prodigy, he became a precocious student of Latin and the law, studying first at Leiden University and then obtaining a doctorate of laws at Orléans in France. At the age of sixteen he began practicing law in The Hague, becoming a state's attorney of the Court of Holland eight years later. A historian, poet, theologian, and diplomat (he served as Sweden's ambassador to France), he has been honored as the "father of international law" for his work as a legal scholar and jurist.

In his most significant work, *De Jure Belli ac Pacis,* Grotius wrote: "The law which is broader in scope than municipal law [the law of each individual sovereign state] is the law of nations, or of many nations. I added 'of many nations' for the reason that, outside of the sphere of the law of nature [natural law], which is also frequently called the law of nations, there is hardly any law common to all nations. . . ."

For Grotius, natural law, or the law of reason, supplemented customary law resulting from the consent of nation-states. At the center of his concept of human law is the dignity of human beings and the conclusion that justice is simply a reflection of respect for this dignity.

These principles constitute the foundation even of modern human rights documents such as the Universal Declaration of Human Rights (1948), adopted by the UN General Assembly after World War II.

Grotius's development of international law principles led to the adoption of rules of warfare and, much later, principles of human rights that he could not have possibly foreseen. Whether or not his proposal for periodic conferences of Christian rulers to avert warfare prefigured the rise of international institutions such as the League of Nations and the United Nations is a matter of speculation. But his work led directly to the eventual incorporation into international law of principles aimed at ameliorating the suffering of the subjects of sovereign authority.

Bull, Hedley, Benedict Kingsbury, and Adam Roberts, eds. *Hugo Grotius and International Relations.* New York: Oxford University Press, 1990.

Dunn, John, and Ian Harris, eds. *Grotius.* Great Political Thinkers series. Northampton, Mass.: Edward Elgar, 1997.

Dignity; International Law; Natural Rights; Sovereignty; Universal Declaration of Human Rights; War

Guidelines for Action on Human Resources Development in the Field of Disability (Tallinn Guidelines)

Beginning with its adoption of the Declaration on the Rights of Disabled Persons in 1975, the UN General Assembly went on in 1982 to promote a World Program of Action Concerning Disabled Persons and then designated 1983–92 as the UN Decade of Disabled Persons. Continuing the emphasis on the rights of the disabled, the International Meeting on Human Resources in the Field of Disability, held in Tallinn, Estonia, in August 1989, adopted the Guidelines for Action on Human Resources Development in the Field of Disability, known as the Tallinn Guidelines.

In December 1989 the General Assembly asked the UN secretary-general to make the guidelines available to member UN nations and to international and national organizations concerned with the disabled. Emphasizing equal opportunity and development of all individuals' full potential and capabilities, the guidelines state the basic philosophy regarding human rights for disabled persons as well as strategies for implementing them.

The Introduction, paragraph 1, observes that "reinforcement of existing as well as new and innovative action is required to promote the further development and continued progress of disabled persons." It goes on to recall in paragraph 3 that the World Program of Action's main objectives "are to promote effective measures for the prevention of disability, for rehabilitation and for the realization of the goals of full participation and equality for persons with disabilities. To accomplish these goals, due regard must be paid to education, training and work opportunities." In paragraph 4 it urges special attention to the disabled in developing countries.

"Human resources development is a human-centered process that seeks to realize the full potential and capabilities of human beings," states Guiding Philosophy, paragraph 6. "This process is fundamental to the concept of equalization of opportunities, in keeping with the goals of the World Program of Action." Paragraph 7 provides that "[t]hrough human resources development, disabled persons are able effectively to exercise their rights of full citizenship. As full citizens, they have the same rights and responsibilities as other members of society, including the right to life, as declared in international human rights instruments. They also have the same choices as other citizens in the social, cultural, economic and political life of their communities." Paragraphs 8 and 9, respectively, recommend involving disabled persons in government decision making "as equal partners" and point out the need for government and nongovernmental, community-based supplementary services for disabled persons.

Strategies, paragraph 10, suggests laws "to enable disabled persons to participate as full citizens in decision-making at all levels of the planning, implementation, and monitoring and evaluation of policies and programs." Other goals for disabled persons include improved information about rights (presented in Braille, large print, sign language, and other accessible forms), physical access to buildings and places, and employment opportunities. The guidelines also encourage grass-roots organizations and education and training opportunities. "The early years are critical in the overall development of a disabled child and in fostering positive attitudes toward the child," observes paragraph 22. "Disabled persons have the right to be trained for and to work on equal terms in the regular labor force," states paragraph 33, while paragraph 37 adds that "[p]olicies for affirmative action should be formulated and implemented to increase the employment of disabled women."

In discussing funding provisions, paragraph 38 proposes that a "national rehabilitation fund may be established to facilitate the employment or self-employment of disabled persons." To help promote community awareness of the rights and needs of the disabled, paragraph 40 suggests that "collaborative efforts with disabled persons and their organizations are required to develop and promote a flow of information using mass media, especially film, television, radio and print media. In particular, information for disabled persons and their families on all aspects of living with a disability should be as clear and uncomplicated as possible." Noting that those with mental and multiple disabilities "are among the most stigmatized groups of citizens," paragraph 42 underscores their "right to make choices, take risks, control their own lives, and live in the community."

The guidelines also address ways to improve methods of human resources development and to encourage international cooperation. "Implementation of these Guidelines," declares paragraph 56, the last item, "relies on effective action at the national level. This action should be supplemented by concerted efforts at the international level, particularly on the part of the United Nations and its focal point for the implementation of the World Program of Action Concerning Disabled Persons, as well as its relevant organizations and specialized agencies. National and international non-governmental organizations, in particular organizations of disabled persons, should be fully involved."

United Nations High Commissioner for Human Rights, 8–14 avenue de la Paix, 1211 Geneva 10, Switzerland. (41-22-917-9000. 🖳 41-22-917-9016. 🖳 webadmin.hchr@unog.ch. 🖳 www.unhchr.ch.

Declaration on the Rights of Disabled Persons; Disabled Persons; Equality; Health

Guidelines for the Prevention of Juvenile Delinquency (Riyadh Guidelines)

Juveniles who are older than children and younger than adults represent a transitional age but may be treated as one or the other by government authorities, especially when they get into trouble with the law. Children generally are not held responsible for illegal acts because they lack an ability to distinguish right from wrong and cannot be held to the adult standard of knowledge of the law. Given that juvenile delinquency is a serious problem in many countries and large cities, an important strategy for developing law-abiding citizens is to prevent young people from becoming criminal offenders in the first place

Recognizing that young people can suffer irreparable harm in the juvenile justice system, the UN General Assembly in 1985 adopted its Standard Minimum Rules for the Administration of Juvenile Justice (Beijing Rules). These were followed in 1990 by the Rules for the Protection of Juveniles Deprived of Their Liberty, and on the same day, December 14, 1990, the General Assembly adopted its Guidelines for the Prevention of Juvenile Delinquency

(Riyadh Guidelines). The guidelines state that preventing juvenile delinquency "requires efforts on the part of the entire society to ensure the harmonious development of adolescents, with respect for and promotion of their personality from early childhood."

"The prevention of juvenile delinquency is an essential part of crime prevention in society," observes part I, Fundamental Principles, paragraph 1. "By engaging in lawful, socially useful activities and adopting a humanistic orientation towards society and outlook on life, young persons can develop non-criminogenic attitudes." Paragraph 3 adds that "a child-centered orientation should be pursued. Young persons should have an active role and partnership within society and should not be considered as mere objects of socialization or control." Labeling an adolescent as deviant, delinquent, or predelinquent, notes paragraph 5, "often contributes to the development of a consistent pattern of undesirable behavior by young persons."

According to part II, Scope of the Guidelines, paragraph 7, present guidelines "should be interpreted and implemented within the broad framework" of a number of important international human rights documents, including the Universal Declaration of Human Rights (1948), Declaration of the Rights of the Child (1959), International Covenant on Civil and Political Rights (1966), International Covenant on Economic, Social and Cultural Rights (1966), Convention on the Rights of the Child (1989), and Standard Minimum Rules for the Administration of Juvenile Justice (Beijing Rules), "as well as other instruments and norms relating to the rights, interest and well-being of all children and young persons." Paragraph 8 suggests that the guidelines "be implemented in the context of the economic, social and cultural conditions prevailing in each Member State."

Part III, General Prevention, paragraph 9, recommends that prevention plans be instituted at every government level. Each should include "(a) In-depth analyses of the problem and inventories of programs, services, facilities and resources available; (b) Well-defined responsibilities for the qualified agencies, institutions and personnel involved in preventive efforts; (c) Mechanisms for the appropriate coordination of prevention efforts between governmental and non-governmental agencies." Plans should also allow for monitoring and evaluation of progress, effective methods for "reducing the opportunity to commit delinquent acts," community involvement, interdisciplinary cooperation among governments, participation by young people, and specialized personnel at all levels.

Suggesting that young people "should be accepted as full and equal partners in socialization and integration processes," part IV, Socialization Processes, focuses on "the family, the community, peer groups, schools, vocational training and the world of work, as well as voluntary organizations," including detailed suggestions for each. Governments, states paragraph 13, "should establish policies that are conducive to the bringing up of children in stable and settled family environments. Families in need of assistance in the resolution of conditions of instability or conflict should be provided with requisite services." Special attention should be given, adds paragraph 15, to children affected by rapid and uneven economic, social, and cultural change, particularly children of indigenous, migrant, and refugee families.

In addition, in paragraphs 40 and 41, respectively, the document calls on the mass media to provide diversified information to each nation's youth and encourages them "to portray the positive contribution of young persons to society." The media are asked in paragraph 43 to minimize their coverage of pornography, drug and alcohol abuse, and violence.

Part V, Social Policy, paragraph 45, directs government agencies to "give high priority to plans and programs for young persons and . . . provide sufficient funds and other resources . . . for adequate medical and mental health care, nutrition, housing and other relevant services, including drug and alcohol abuse prevention and treatment, ensuring that such resources reach and actually benefit young persons." Participation in plans should be voluntary, according to paragraph 50, and young people should be involved in formulating, developing, and implementing them.

Governments should ensure that young persons are treated differently from adults in the criminal justice system, states part VI, Legislation and Juvenile Justice Administration, and that an ombudsman or other special agency be designated to supervise implementation of the Riyadh Guidelines, Beijing Rules, and Rules for the Protection of Juveniles Deprived of Their Liberty. "No child or young person should be subjected to harsh or degrading correction or punishment measures at home, in schools or in any

other institutions," mandates paragraph 54. This part also urges special training to enable law enforcement personnel to respond to young people's needs and, in paragraph 59, recommends that legislation "be enacted and strictly enforced to protect children and young persons from drug abuse and drug traffickers."

In addition to other recommendations, the last section, part VII, Research, Policy Development and Co-ordination, paragraph 62, calls for an exchange of information about youth crime, delinquency prevention, and juvenile justice on the national, regional, and international levels. In conclusion, it asks the UN secretary-general to cooperate with interested institutions and "play an active role in the conduct of research, scientific collaboration, the formulation of policy options and the review and monitoring of [the] implementation of [the guidelines]."

United Nations High Commissioner for Human Rights, 8–14 avenue de la Paix, 1211 Geneva 10, Switzerland. (41-22-917-9000. 🖥 41-22-917-9016. 🖳 webadmin.hchr@unog.ch. 🖳 www.unhchr.ch.

Youth Unit, United Nations, One United Nations Plaza, Room DC 2-1318, New York, N.Y. 10017. (212-963-1380. 🖥 212-963-3062. 🖳 youth@un.org. 🖳 www.un.org/esa/socdev/unyin.

Drugs; Rules for the Protection of Juveniles Deprived of Their Liberty; Standard Minimum Rules for the Administration of Juvenile Justice (Beijing Rules); Youth

Taking and holding a person hostage violates a number of basic human rights, including the right to liberty and security of the person as well as freedom of movement. Americans taken hostage in 1979 on the first day of the occupation of the U.S. Embassy in Tehran were paraded blindfolded by their captors, who were militant Iranian students, and then held for fourteen months. [UPI/Corbis-Bettmann]

Habeas Corpus

"The great and efficacious writ, in all manner of illegal confinement, is that of *habeas corpus ad subjiciendum*," observed William Blackstone, the noted commentator on the laws of England, in 1768. *Habeas corpus* (from the Latin *habeo*, meaning to have, and *corpus*, meaning body) is strictly translated as "thou shalt have the body." In Anglo-American law the term refers to a prerogative writ issued by a judicial officer requiring that "the body"—a living person—be presented in court or before a judge for the purposes shown in the writ, principally to allow the reason for the person's detention to be ascertained; if the allegation is not proven, the person must be released from custody.

The phrase has been in use in England since at least the thirteenth century and perhaps even before Magna Carta (1215). In 1679 Parliament passed the Habeas Corpus Act, which greatly facilitated use and enforcement of the writ. The U.S. Constitution (1789), section 9, paragraph 2, which specifically refers to "the privilege of the writ of *habeas corpus*," considers it so important to liberty that Congress may not suspend it "unless when in the case of rebellion or invasion the public safety may require it."

For people held by the government, habeas corpus provides a way to use an impartial court of law to test the reasons why they are being denied their liberty. It can be used by people who are being held but are not charged with any crime, who are being held under improper charges, or who have been convicted but want to challenge the convic-

tion's legality. Similar procedures, such as *amparo* in Latin America, have developed around the world to challenge a government's authority to deprive a person of freedom.

Constitution of India (1950), part III, Fundamental Rights, article 32, Remedies for Enforcement of Rights Conferred by this Part: "(2) The supreme court shall have power to issue directions or orders or writs, including writs in the nature of *habeas corpus*. . . ."

American Convention on Human Rights (1969), part I, State Obligations and Rights Protected, chapter II, Civil and Political Rights, article 7, Right to Personal Liberty: "6. Anyone who is deprived of his liberty shall be entitled to recourse to a competent court, in order that the court may decide without delay on the lawfulness of his arrest or detention and order his release if the arrest or detention is unlawful."

U.K. Court of Appeals, King's Bench Division (1941): "On an application for habeas corpus by a person detained under [a regulation conditioning detention on the secretary of state's determination of "reasonable cause"], the gaoler or other officer detaining the applicant must justify the detention by producing a valid order of the Home Secretary issued pursuant to the Order in Council. If he produces an order which on its face is valid and so issued, the onus of showing that the order is invalid then rests on the applicant. . . ."

Inter-American Commission on Human Rights (Advisory Opinion) (1987): "From what has been said before, it follows that writs of habeas corpus and of 'amparo' are among those judicial remedies that are essential for the protection of various rights whose derogation is prohibited by Article 27(2) [of the American Convention on Human Rights (1969)] and that serve, moreover, to preserve legality in a democratic society."

Antieau, Chester J. *The Practice of Extraordinary Remedies: Habeas Corpus and the Other Common Law Writs.* Dobbs Ferry, N.Y.: Oceana, 1987.

Kutner, Luis, ed. *The Human Right to Individual Freedom: A Symposium on World Habeas Corpus.* Foreword by Arthur J. Goldberg. Introduction by Roscoe Pound. Coral Gables, Fla.: University of Miami Press, 1970.

Amparo; Detention; Due Process of Law; Fair Trial

Habitats

See Housing; Vancouver Declaration on Human Settlements

Handicapped Persons

See Disabled Persons

Havel, Václav

The Russian invasion of Czechoslovakia in August 1968 impelled the Czech playwright and poet Václav Havel (b. 1936) to begin a campaign to condemn and harass the communist regime in his homeland, regardless of the personal consequences. Later a leader of the Charter 77 activists in 1977, Havel became the first elected president of the free and democratic nation of Czechoslovakia in 1989 and then of the newly formed Czech Republic in 1993.

Born in Prague on October 5, 1936, Havel is the son of a wealthy businessman whose property was confiscated when the communists came to power in 1948. After finishing high school and taking some college courses, he served in the army from 1957 to 1959. Following his army service, when he helped form a regimental theater group, he joined a theater company in Prague as a stagehand. Havel, a talented writer, had become a successful playwright by 1968, when Russian troops attempted to crush the cultural

flowering known as the Prague Spring. As a spokesman for an underground radio station, he incurred the wrath of the communist leadership, which banned publication and performance of his works and revoked his passport. Taking a job in a brewery, he continued to write, and his works were clandestinely distributed in Czechoslovakia and abroad.

In 1977 Havel—unable to "live within a lie"—wrote a lengthy open letter to the head of the Czechoslovakian government condemning the state of his country. In the letter he excoriated the lack of dissent concerning government policy, pinpointing it as a byproduct of the people's fear of the government, and concluded that government programming was destroying the ability to hold differing opinions and thus the basis of culture itself. That same year he became a key figure in the Charter 77 movement, which protested the failure of the Czechoslovakian government to live up to the human rights pledges made in the Helsinki Final Act (1975). Freedom of expression, for example, was blocked by government control of the media and cultural facilities, and freedom of thought, conscience, and religion were arbitrarily suppressed by government officials. For these objections he was sentenced to four and a half years' imprisonment at hard labor.

After the fall of the Berlin Wall on November 19, 1989, Havel helped create the Civic Forum, a coalition of Czechoslovakian activist groups, to implement a drive to topple the communist regime. One week later the government fell, the communist leadership resigned, and Havel was unanimously elected by the existing parliament as the interim president of a free Czechoslovakia. Havel ran unopposed for president in 1990, when he was reelected by the new democratically elected parliament. When Slovakia's parliament voted in 1992 to separate from Czechoslovakia, he was elected president of the newly formed Czech Republic.

Havel's successful fight for truth, freedom, democracy, and human rights has proved the effectiveness of what he called "the power of the powerless." For Havel, the recipient of many awards and honors, the Czech Republic's invitation in 1997 to join the democratic nations of the North Atlantic Treaty Organization (NATO) along with Hungary and Poland was "the crowning achievement of enormous efforts by these countries to shed their communist pasts."

Havel, Václav. *Disturbing the Peace: A Conversation with Karel Hvizdale.* New York: Knopf, 1990.

Kriseova, Eda. *Václav Havel: The Authorized Biography.* New York: St. Martin's, 1993.

Charter 77 (Czechoslovakia); Helsinki Final Act; North Atlantic Treaty Organization (NATO)

Health

"Everyone has the right to a standard of living adequate for the health and well-being of himself and of his family, including ... medical care," stated the Universal Declaration of Human Rights (1948). Nearly two decades later, the International Covenant on Economic, Social and Cultural Rights (1966) recognized "the right of everyone to the enjoyment of the highest attainable standard of physical and mental health." Countries that ratify the covenant are urged to take steps "to achieve the full realization of this right," including reducing infant mortality; helping children develop; improving "environmental and industrial hygiene"; preventing, treating, and controlling "epidemic, endemic, occupational, and other diseases"; and creating "conditions which would assure to all medical service and medical attention in the event of sickness."

Health (from Old English and High German words meaning hale and whole) is viewed as a basic right of all people, one on which the full exercise of other human rights depends. John Stuart Mill concluded in the nineteenth century that the desire for health follows from people's general desire for happiness, a quest that the U.S. Declaration of Independence (1776) placed among our inalienable rights. Receiving adequate health care without cost, however, is considered a second-generation social right, a step removed from first-generation civil and political rights such as freedom of speech and religion. As with other social rights from adequate housing to freedom from hunger, the right to health represents a desirable goal rather than a prohibition against government actions that infringe personal freedom.

Some national constitutions, including those of the Netherlands (1814), Italy (1948), and Poland (1997), expressly address health rights. "Citizens," provides the Polish constitution, "shall have the right to health protection and to assistance in the event of sickness or the inability to work." Canada and the United Kingdom are among the countries that already provide government-sponsored health care at little or no cost to their citizens. The United States offers government health care benefits only to some citizens, such as the elderly and the poor, so that most Americans must rely on private health care insurance and providers. The American Declaration of the Rights and Duties of Man (1948), European Social Charter (1966), Declaration on Social Progress and Development (1969), African Charter on Human and Peoples' Rights (Banjul Charter) (1981), and Cairo Declaration on Human Rights in Islam (1990) all call for nations in their regions to ensure that citizens receive adequate health care.

Many issues impact health rights, including family planning to help alleviate overpopulation, abortion, women's health and maternity needs, and sickness that results from toxic wastes and other environmental pollution. The current AIDS epidemic is a major health concern for many countries and the world at large, affecting individual rights to medical treatment without discrimination, privacy rights in the matter of testing, and access to adequate medicine, experimental drugs, and nursing care.

The World Health Organization (WHO) seeks to help its member nations lead their citizens to the best possible health care. On its own and in cooperation with others, including the United Nations, WHO has sponsored a number of international documents dealing with specific health issues, for example, Marketing of Breast-Milk Substitutes (1981), Improving the Health of Women and Girls (1987), and Reducing the Risk of Transmission of HIV by Blood Transfusion (1989).

Constitution of Italy (1948), part one, Duties and Rights of the Citizens, title II, Ethical and Social Problems, article 32: "The Republic protects health as a fundamental right of the individual and as an interest of the community. It assures free treatments for the needy."

African Charter on Human and Peoples' Rights (Banjul Charter) (1981), article 16: "1. Every individual shall have the right to enjoy the best attainable state of physical and mental health. 2. States parties to the present Charter shall take the necessary measures to protect the health of their people and to ensure that they receive medical attention when they are sick."

Czech Republic Constitutional Court (1996): How citizens assert their right to free health care must be defined by law, and the legislature has a duty to enact such laws rather than delegate authority to an executive agency that would simply issue regulations on the subject.

African Commission on Human and Peoples' Rights (1997): Denial of basic services such as safe drinking water, electricity, and medicine to Jehovah's Witnesses arbitrarily arrested, detained, and tortured by authorities in Zaire constituted "serious and massive violations" of the African Charter on Human and Peoples' Rights.

World Health Organization, 20 avenue Appia, 1211 Geneva 27, Switzerland. (41-22-791-2111. 📠 41-22-791-3111. 📧 info@ who.int. 🖥 www.who.int.

Alfredsson, Gudmundur, and Katarina Tomaševski, eds. *A Thematic Guide to Documents on Health and Human Rights: Global and Regional Standards Adopted by Intergovernmental Organizations, International Non-Governmental Organizations and Professional Associations.* Raoul Wallenberg Institute Human Rights Guides, vol. 2. The Hague: Martinus Nijhoff, Kluwer Law International, 1998.

Economic and Social Rights and the Right to Health: An Inter-disciplinary Discussion Held at Harvard Law School in September, 1993. Cambridge, Mass.: Harvard Law School Human Rights Program, 1995.

Abortion; African Charter on Human and Peoples' Rights; AIDS; American Declaration of the Rights and Duties of Man; Cairo Declaration on Human Rights in Islam; Declaration on Social Progress and Development; Disabled Persons; Doctors without Borders; European Social Charter; Guidelines for Action on Human Resources Development in the Field of Disability (Tallinn Guidelines); International Covenant on Economic, Social and Cultural Rights; Maternity; Physicians for Human Rights; Social Rights; Universal Declaration of Human Rights; World Health Organization

Helsinki Accords

See Helsinki Final Act

Helsinki Final Act

The Final Act of the Helsinki Conference on Security and Co-operation in Europe, signed on August 2, 1975, was a diplomatic compromise between Western nations and the Soviet Union on political and military issues and economic and humanitarian relations. The document's human rights provisions, however, became the foundation of political movements in Eastern European countries, notably Poland and Czechoslovakia, that helped bring down communist governments in the Soviet Union and its satellites.

The Helsinki Final Act grew out of the Conference on Security and Co-operation in Europe (CSCE), now called the Organization for Security and Cooperation in Europe (OSCE), which met in Helsinki in 1975. The Soviet Union saw the CSCE, created in 1973 to improve East-West relations, as an opportunity to enhance its access to Western trade and technology and so acceded to the inclusion of limited human rights language in the act, signed by delegates from Eastern and Western European nations, including the Soviet Union, Poland, Czechoslovakia, France, Germany, and the United Kingdom, as well as the United States and Canada. The significant section dealing with human rights, among other issues, is principle VII, which mandates "[r]espect for human rights and fundamental freedoms, including the freedom of thought, conscience, religion or belief...." In the years following the act's signing, the human rights system described in the act was viewed narrowly by the Soviets, while the Western nations and nongovernmental human rights organizations promoted a more expansive interpretation.

Follow-up conferences were held in Belgrade in 1977–78,

in Madrid in 1980–83, and in Vienna in 1986–89. The last conference concluded with a document that greatly expanded freedom of religion and treatment of detainees as well as new CSCE procedures for consultation among nations regarding alleged human rights violations.

The Helsinki Final Act of 1975 begins by noting that the participating countries, "[m]otivated by the political will, in the interest of peoples, to improve and intensify their relations and to contribute in Europe to peace, security, justice and co-operation as well as to rapprochement among themselves and with other States of the world," recognize "the close link between peace and security in Europe and in the world as a whole and ... the need for each of them to make its contribution to the strengthening of world peace and security and to the promotion of fundamental rights, economic and social progress and well-being for all peoples...."

Principle I deals with sovereign equality and respect for the rights inherent in sovereignty. Principles II, III, and IV, respectively, address the use of force, the inviolability of frontiers, and territorial integrity, all principles consistent with the Soviets' desire for recognition of the territorial and ideological division of Europe during this period. Principles V and VI provide for the peaceful settlement of disputes and nonintervention in the internal affairs of the participating states.

Principle VII declares in part that signatory nations "will respect human rights and fundamental freedoms, including the freedom of thought, conscience, religion, or belief, for all without distinction as to race, sex, language or religion. They will promote and encourage the effective exercise of civil, political, economic, social, cultural and other rights and freedoms all of which derive from the inherent dignity of the human person and are essential for his free and full development." These rights are encompassed in the two international covenants included in the International Bill of Rights: the International Covenant on Civil and Political Rights (1966) and the International Covenant on Economic, Social and Cultural Rights (1966). Principle VII also affirms respect for "the right of persons belonging to [national] minorities to equality before the law"; recognition of "the universal significance of human rights and fundamental freedoms," language echoing that of the Universal Declaration of Human Rights (1948) and the European Convention for the Protection of Human Rights and Fundamental Freedoms (1950); and respect for "the right of the individual to know and act upon his rights and duties in this field." It also calls for national action "in conformity with the purposes and principles of the Charter of the United Nations [1945] and with the Universal Declaration of Human Rights."

Principle VIII covers equal rights and self-determination of people; principle IX provides for cooperation among the nations; and principle X addresses fulfillment in good faith of obligations under international law. The remainder of the act contains details on "giving effect to certain of the above principles," "[c]o-operation in the

Field of Economics, of Science and Technology and of the Environment," and other matters.

The regional human rights system delineated in the Helsinki Final Act and the activities of nongovernmental organizations such as Helsinki Watch and other Helsinki rights monitoring groups are often collectively referred to as the Helsinki process.

Atlantic Council of the United States, 910 17th Street, N.W., Suite 1000, Washington, D.C. 20006. (202-463-7226. 202-463-7241. info@acus.org. www.acus.org.

International Helsinki Federation for Human Rights, Wickenburg, 14/7, A-1080 Vienna, Austria. (43-1-408-88-22. 43-1-408-88-22-50. office@ihf-hr.org. www.ihf-hr.org.

North Atlantic Treaty Organization (NATO), boulevard Leopold III, 1110 Brussels, Belgium. (32-2-707-41-11. 32-2-707-12-52. natodoc@hq.nato.int. www.nato.int.

European Convention for the Protection of Human Rights and Fundamental Freedoms; Human Rights Watch; International Covenant on Civil and Political Rights; International Covenant on Economic, Social and Cultural Rights; North Atlantic Treaty Organization (NATO); Organization for Security and Cooperation in Europe; Regional Human Rights Systems; Universal Declaration of Human Rights

High Commissioner for Human Rights

On December 20, 1993, the UN General Assembly adopted Resolution 48/141, creating the Office of the United Nations High Commissioner for Human Rights and vesting it with primary responsibility for coordinating the organization's human rights activities. In creating this position with the rank of undersecretary-general, the UN strengthened its ability to accomplish the human rights mission of its charter (1945) by adding an executive officer to complement other UN agencies responsible for human rights, such as the General Assembly, Economic and Social Council (ECOSOC), Commission on Human Rights, and High Commissioner for Refugees.

Among the office's goals are promoting the universal enjoyment of all human rights and international cooperation in achieving this end; emphasizing the importance of human rights at the national and international levels; encouraging and coordinating UN efforts to achieve human rights; promoting universal ratification of human rights agreements and implementation of international

human rights standards by individual nations; and assisting in the development of new human rights norms or standards.

The high commissioner's specific duties include promoting and protecting all civil, political, economic, social, and cultural rights; engaging in dialogue with all governments to secure respect for human rights; carrying out tasks assigned by the UN human rights agencies, such as the General Assembly, ECOSOC, and Commission on Human Rights; and making recommendations for improving the promotion and protection of all human rights. Other activities include preventing or alleviating serious human rights abuses; assisting in establishing and maintaining national human rights institutions; and working in the field to provide education programs, advisory services, and technical assistance for human rights activities.

Special emphasis is placed on strengthening support within the UN for the right to development, which is furthered through a Research and Right to Development Branch within the office. The high commissioner is also required to play an active role in realizing the goals of the Vienna Declaration and Program of Action (1993), an ambitious contemporary statement of human rights goals. The high commissioner submits annual reports of the office's activities to the Commission on Human Rights and, through ECOSOC, to the General Assembly.

The office also provides support capabilities for the bodies charged with implementing UN human rights treaties, among them the Human Rights Committee set up under the International Covenant on Civil and Political Rights (1966). Other human rights agencies serviced by the high commissioner's office are the Subcommission on the Promotion and Protection of Human Rights and its working groups and special rapporteurs (experts); Committee against Torture; Committee on the Elimination of Racial Discrimination; Committee on the Rights of the Child; and Committee on Economic, Social and Cultural Rights.

The office holder is required to be "a person of high moral standing and personal integrity" and must have relevant expertise. He or she is appointed by the UN secretary-general and approved by the General Assembly "with due regard to geographical rotation, and for a fixed term of four years with a possibility of one renewal...." The first high commissioner was José Ayala-Lasso of Ecuador. Mary Robinson, the former president of Ireland, succeeded him on September 12, 1997, and began to reorganize the UN's human rights activities to make them more efficient and effective. For example, on September 15, 1997, its Center for Human Rights was merged into the high commissioner's office. Its work is implemented with a deputy, several branches, and an office in New York City.

In debates in Canada's House of Commons on April 23, 1996, the parliamentary secretary of the ministry of foreign affairs praised the role of the high commissioner, noting that "[a]lthough severely underfunded, the creation of the post has already had a salutary effect," particularly with respect to the famine in Rwanda.

United Nations High Commissioner for Human Rights, 8–14 avenue de la Paix, 1211 Geneva 10, Switzerland. (41-22-917-9000. 📠 41-22-917-9016. 🖳 webadmin.hchr@unog.ch 🖳 www.unhchr.ch.

United Nations High Commissioner for Human Rights, One United Nations Plaza, New York, N.Y. 10017. (212-963-4475. 📠 212-963-0071. 🖳 inquiries@un.org 🖳 www.un.org.

Clark, Roger S. *A United Nations High Commissioner for Human Rights.* The Hague: Martinus Nijhoff, Kluwer Law International, 1972.

The High Commissioner for Human Rights: An Introduction. Making Human Rights a Reality. Notes of the United Nations High Commissioner for Human Rights, no. 1. Geneva: Center for Human Rights, 1996.

Center for Human Rights; Commission on Human Rights; Committee on the Elimination of Racial Discrimination; Development; Economic and Social Council (ECOSOC); High Commissioner for Refugees; Human Rights Committee; United Nations; Vienna Declaration and Program of Action

High Commissioner for Refugees

The Office of the United Nations High Commissioner for Refugees seeks to protect refugees and provide long-term solutions to their problems. Established in 1951 under a statute adopted by the UN General Assembly on December 14, 1950, the office succeeded the High Commissioner for Refugees created in 1921 by the League of Nations; the UN Relief and Rehabilitation Administration, set up in 1943; and the International Refugee Organization, created in 1946. Recognizing the UN's continuing responsibility for protecting refugees, the General Assembly appointed the first High Commissioner for Refugees on December 3, 1949, a year before the governing statute was adopted. Since then the office has helped tens of millions of refugees start a new life, and for its efforts it received the Nobel Peace Prize in both 1954 and 1981.

In 1995 the office assisted some 27 million persons, including 14.5 million refugees who had crossed international borders as well as 12.5 million internally displaced persons and others returned to their country of origin. Its major operations at the beginning of the twenty-first century include assisting the more than 26,000 persons who have fled war-ravaged Angola for Zambia, citizens of

East Timor returning to their homeland after the withdrawal of Indonesian military forces, and refugees from the numerous conflicts in the Balkans.

Under the 1950 statute, the high commissioner is to aid refugees "by assisting governments and, subject to the approval of the governments concerned, private organizations to facilitate the voluntary repatriation of such refugees, or their assimilation within new communities." The office's work is to be of an "entirely non-political character," and the high commissioner is to "follow policy directives given him by the General Assembly or the Economic and Social Council [ECOSOC]."

Guided by strictly humanitarian considerations, the high commissioner promotes ratification and implementation of international agreements dealing with refugee problems, as well as special agreements with governments to alleviate specific refugee problems and the admission of refugees into host countries. The office also assists government and private efforts to repatriate or assimilate refugees, transfer refugee assets necessary for resettlement, obtain information on refugee laws and regulations in the host countries, and generally coordinate government and nongovernmental efforts to handle refugee problems. The high commissioner also administers public and private funds and reports annually to the General Assembly through ECOSOC.

The high commissioner is elected for a term of three years by the General Assembly on the nomination of the secretary-general; a deputy is appointed by the high commissioner for the same term. An executive committee helps administer the refugee programs. Although some of the administrative costs of the office are included in the UN budget, its refugee assistance programs are based on voluntary contributions.

The status of refugees is addressed in a number of international instruments, including the Convention Relating to the Status of Refugees (1951) and its 1967 protocol, as well as the Convention Governing the Specific Aspects of Refugee Problems in Africa (1969), adopted by the Organization of African Unity.

United Nations High Commissioner for Refugees, C.P. 2500, 1211 Geneva 2, Switzerland. (41-22-739-8111. 📠 41-22-739-7377. 🖳 hqpioo@unhcr.ch. 🖳 www.unhcr.ch.

Convention Relating to the Status of Refugees; Refugees; Statelessness

Holocaust

See Genocide

Homosexuals

Human homosexuality has probably existed since the beginning of the species. As the American researcher Alfred Kinsey concluded in his ground-breaking work *The Sexual Behavior of the Human Male* (1948): "A considerable portion of the population . . . has had at least some homosexual experience between adolescence and old age." The prefix *homo* is derived from the Greek word meaning the same, not the Latin word *homo*, meaning human being. The word *homosexual,* as an adjective, came into use in English at least as early as 1892, and since 1912, as a noun, it has referred to a person who has a sexual propensity or desire for persons of the same sex. *Gays* refers to male homosexuals and *lesbians* to female homosexuals.

The expression of homosexuality has been accepted in some cultures and criminalized in others. In ancient Athens, homosexuality between an older male and a young man was generally sanctioned, but an Athenian male could be deprived of his citizenship if convicted of prostitution. Other societies have tolerated homosexuality in the upper classes but not in the lower ones. This ambivalence both within and between cultures has complicated the question of homosexuals' rights.

In some countries, particularly Islamic nations, homosexual behavior is still considered criminal or immoral. Homosexuals in Afghanistan, Iran, and Saudi Arabia have been subjected to the death penalty, according to the International Gay and Lesbian Association. An attempt in 1995 to have the African Commission on Human and Peoples' Rights look into the laws of Zimbabwe regarding discrimination against homosexuals had to be withdrawn for fear of reprisals. That year the president of Zimbabwe denounced homosexuals, saying that homosexuality had no place in African culture. In Finland, the violation of "sexual morality" carries a sentence of up to six months' imprisonment.

A number of countries, particularly in the Western world, however, have relaxed legal prohibitions against homosexuality. In 1977 the Canadian province of Quebec became the first jurisdiction in North America to ban discrimination on the basis of sexual orientation. The state of Vermont in 2000 decided to legally recognize same-sex civil unions, even as other U.S. states moved with alacrity to ban homosexual marriages. Similar civil unions are allowed in other nations, among them France, the Netherlands, Hungary, and Scandinavian countries. South Africa's temporary 1994 constitution extended protection to homosexuals, a provision retained in the 1997 permanent constitution, and same-sex partnerships are allowed partial rights elsewhere, for example, in England, Spain, Canada, Brazil, Argentina, New Zealand, and New South Wales. A number of these jurisdictions have also moved to ban discrimination against homosexuals. The European Court of Human Rights found in 1981 that an Irish law requiring ten-year and life sentences for certain homosexual acts violated the European Convention for the Protection of Human Rights and Fundamental Freedoms (1950). In 1994 courts in Colombia and Japan also held, respectively, that "the condition of homosexuality, by itself, cannot be a reason for exclusion from the armed forces" and that barring a gay and lesbian group from a youth center "violated the spirit of human rights enshrined in the constitution."

Social acceptability, however, has not always kept pace even with the slow pace of the law. Religious strictures and some people's fears that homosexuals are improper role models for children continue to impede unconditional toleration. Homosexuals face discrimination in many areas of life: in such activities as employment, military service, marriage, child custody, adoption, medical care, insurance and social benefits, and inheritance. From discrimination to homophobia and homophobic violence, private actions may not be the state's fault, but if a government condones such treatment or inappropriate actions by the police, prosecutors, or courts, it is guilty of violating the right to equality before the law and denying due process of law.

In 1988 a report to the Subcommission on the Promotion and Protection of Human Rights addressed the questions of whether sexual minorities—homosexuals as well as transsexuals and transvestites—are subjected to legal and social discrimination and, if so, whether valid grounds exist for such discrimination. During a 1992 subcommission session, a homosexual nonetheless noted that gays and lesbians remained unrepresented in the UN itself. The following year homosexual organizations were accredited for the first time for a UN meeting—the World Conference on Human Rights, held in Vienna—and the International Gay and Lesbian Association was granted consultative status with the Economic and Social Council (ECOSOC), although the council's vote was not unanimous.

Whether homosexual behavior is learned or genetically based continues to incur scientific and social debate; if it is inborn, then clearly heterosexual societies lack the right to require that homosexuals conform to heterosexual behavior. However, like other divisive human rights issues—notably abortion, capital punishment, and the right to die—it may be a long time before there is universal agreement on the rights of homosexuals in a heterosexual world.

Constitution of South Africa (1997), chapter 2, Bill of Rights, Equality, 9(3): "The state may not unfairly discriminate directly or indirectly against anyone on one or more grounds, including race, gender, sex, pregnancy, marital status, ethnic or social origin, sexual orientation, age, disability, religion, conscience, belief, language and birth."

International Labor Organization Convention no. 111 (1958): Although the convention does not expressly prohibit discrimination on the basis of sexual orientation, Australia has declared that such discrimination is grounds for invoking the document's provisions regarding prohibited discrimination.

British Columbia (Canada) Supreme Court (1996): The refusal of a doctor to provide artificial insemination to a lesbian couple constitutes discrimination on the basis of sexual orientation.

Human Rights Committee (1982): A state-controlled broadcasting company's refusal to air balanced information on homosexuals was only partly subject to examination under the International Covenant on Civil and Political Rights (1966), article 19, as it relates to freedom of expression and respect of the rights and reputations of others.

International Gay and Lesbian Human Rights Commission, 1360 Mission Street, Suite 200, San Francisco, Calif. 94103. (415-255-8680. 🖳 415-255-8662. 🖳 iglhrc@iglhrc.org. 🖳 www.iglhrc.org.

International Lesbian and Gay Association, 81 Kolenmarkt, B 1000, Brussels, Belgium. (32-2-502-24-71. 🖳 32-2-502-24-71. 🖳 ilga@ilga.org. 🖳 www.ilga.org.

Gerstman, Evan. *The Constitutional Underclass: Gays, Lesbians, and the Failure of Class-based Equal Protection.* Chicago: University of Chicago Press, 1999.

Medhurst, Andy, and Sally R. Munt, eds. *Lesbian and Gay Studies: A Critical Introduction.* London: Cassell, 1997.

Wintermute, Robert. *Sexual Orientation and Human Rights: The United States Constitution, the European Convention, and the Canadian Charter.* Oxford, England: Clarendon Press, Oxford University Press, 1995.

Discrimination; Equality; Minorities; Tolerance

Hostages

The taking of hostages (from the Old French *ostage*) as security for some cause infringes a number of human rights, including the right of security of the person, freedom of movement, and the right of communication, not to mention the right of human dignity. To protect these rights, governments are obliged to deter hostage taking, deny any assistance to those responsible, and comply with international law governing the capture, treatment, and punishment of perpetrators.

Long ago hostages were given by one ruler to another as security for a pledge, and a prominent person might be captured in battle and held hostage in return for payment of a ransom for his release. England's Richard I (The Lionheart), for example, was captured while returning from the Crusades and held hostage by the Holy Roman emperor Henry VI until a large ransom was paid. Sometimes hostages are abducted to be used in exchange for other detainees.

In 1979 militant student followers of the Iranian revolutionary leader Ayatollah Khomeini took some ninety persons, including sixty-three Americans, hostage in Tehran. The failure to gain their release crippled the presidency of Jimmy Carter, and he was overwhelmingly defeated in his 1980 bid for reelection, in part because of the hostage crisis that lasted until minutes after the inauguration of his successor on January 20, 1981. While there is little if any support for a hostage's right to be rescued when held in a foreign country (and an effort to free the Iranian hostages failed), an executive order implementing the agreement for the release of the Iranian hostages created a presidential commission that paid them $12.50 for each day of their detention.

The rights of families and associates aggrieved by a hostage situation also have not been firmly established, although the parents and family of an American hostage in Iran filed suit for "emotional distress." In rejecting one such case, even though the injury to the parents clearly occurred in the United States as the result of an action condoned by Iran, a U.S. Court of Appeals held that there was a "constitutional requirement that minimum contact [between the victim and the state responsible for the injury] must exist for the assertion of jurisdiction against a foreign sovereign."

When hostage taking occurs within a nation, it is generally treated as abduction or kidnapping under the country's domestic criminal laws. Hostage taking on an international basis, whether during an armed conflict or in peacetime, is recognized as a serious and flagrant violation of human rights, one that often entails great hardship and deprivation for the hostages as well as anguish and suffering by their families and friends. The practice is banned under the Geneva Convention Relative to the Protection of Civilian Persons in Time of War (1949) and other international instruments, including a 1970 UN resolution condemning the hijacking of airplanes and interfering with civil aviation.

Under the International Convention against the Taking of Hostages (1979), adopted by the UN General Assembly, hostage takers are defined and each state party is required to "make the offenses … punishable by appropriate penalties which take into account the grave nature of those offenses." A country in which a hostage is held must "take all measures it considers appropriate to ease the situation of the hostage, in particular, to secure his release and, after his release, to facilitate, when relevant, his departure." The convention also requires participating nations to return "any object which the offender has obtained as a result of the taking of hostages" if it comes into its custody.

The UN Security Council followed this document in 1985 by unanimously adopting a resolution condemning the taking of hostages and affirming the obligation of all nations in which hostages or abducted persons are held to secure their safe release and to take steps to prevent such acts in the future.

U.S. Army Basic Field Manual (1956), article 497, Reprisals: "g. Hostages. The taking of hostages is forbidden. . . ."

International Convention against the Taking of Hostages (1979), article 1: "1. Any person who seizes or detains and threatens to kill, to injure or to continue to detain another person (hereinafter referred to as the "hostage") in order to compel a third party, namely a State, an international intergovernmental organization, a natural or juridical person, or a group of persons, to do or abstain from doing any act as an explicit or implicit condition for the release of the hostage commits the offense of taking hostages ("hostage-taking") within the meaning of this Convention."

Constitutional Court of Germany (1977): Whether the German federation should negotiate for the release of a hostage out of respect for the right to life secured by article 2(2) of the Basic Law (Germany's constitution [1949]) or resort to other actions in dealing with terrorists is wholly a matter within the discretion of the politically responsible agencies of government.

International Court of Justice (Iranian hostages case) (1980): "Wrongfully to deprive human beings of their freedom and to subject them to physical constraint in conditions of hardship is in itself manifestly incompatible with the principles of the Charter of the United Nations [1945], as well as with the fundamental principles enunciated in the Universal Declaration of Human Rights [1948]."

Antokol, Norman, and Mayer Nudell. *No One a Neutral: Political Hostage-taking in the Modern World.* Medina, Ohio: Alpha, 1990.

Lambert, Joseph J. *Terrorism and Hostages in International Law: A Commentary on the Hostage Convention, 1979.* Research Center for International Law, University of Cambridge. Cambridge, England: Grotius, 1990.

Poland, James M., and Michael J. McCrystle. *Practical, Tactical, and Legal Perspectives of Terrorism and Hostage-Taking.* Lewiston, N.Y.: Edwin Mellon, 1999.

Carter, James Earl; Compensation; Dignity; Disappearance; Geneva Conventions; Movement; Security; Terrorism; Victims

Housing

National governments approach the problem of providing adequate housing for their citizens—a social and economic right related to having an adequate standard of living—in different ways. A strictly capitalist approach is to rely on the private sector to build sufficient housing to meet the demand and require that individuals and families, according to their financial ability, rent or buy available housing units. Under this approach, however, many citizens are unable to afford private housing and a large homeless population may result.

In many societies the provision of housing has instead been a community or a government concern. The ancient Greek philosophers Plato and Aristotle wrote of the government's interest in housing, agreeing that it should be built for security in the event of war. Today more socially oriented countries, such as many in Europe, allocate government funds to people who cannot afford housing and also supply housing units to meet the demand, although they still rely on the private sector to handle the bulk of the nation's housing needs. In communist countries like China, Cuba, and Vietnam, housing is often guaranteed to all citizens and is almost exclusively provided for and managed by the state.

Since World War II a number of national governments in Europe have taken steps to alleviate housing shortages by subsidizing construction of private housing. In addition to the former communist countries, nations like Finland and Spain have provided significant government housing subsidies. Because of the importance of adequate housing to a country's economic progress, not just to the health and security of its citizens, some national constitutions, such as those of Finland (1919) and Portugal (1976), treat it as a fundamental right. Others, such as that of Nicaragua (1987), proclaim the right to housing to be a national goal.

The Universal Declaration of Human Rights (1948) confirmed the right to adequate housing, as have documents such as the Declaration of the Rights of the Child (1959), International Convention on the Elimination of All Forms of Racial Discrimination (1965), and International Covenant on Economic, Social and Cultural Rights (1966), among others. In 1976 the United Nations Conference on Human Settlements (called Habitat) met in Vancouver, Canada, and produced the Vancouver Declaration on Human Settlements. At a second conference, Habitat II, held in 1996 in Istanbul, Turkey, the right to housing as a basic human right was affirmed.

Habitat II produced the Istanbul Declaration on Human Settlements, which endorsed the Habitat Agenda, a statement reflecting the international community's program for addressing the world's housing needs. The participating nations stated in chapter II, Goals and Principles, paragraph 25, that they are "committed to a political, economic, environmental, ethical and spiritual vision of human settlements based on the principles of equality, solidarity, partnership, human dignity, respect and cooperation." To provide adequate housing for all people, the declaration recommended several strategies: partnerships with local communities within the framework of each country's laws; cooperation with lawmakers, the private sector, unions, and nongovernmental organizations; facilitation of funding and transfer of appropriate technology; and strengthening the UN Center for Human Settlements.

Constitution of Portugal (1976), part I, Fundamental Rights and Duties, section II, Rights, Freedoms, and Safeguards, chapter II, Social Rights and Duties, article 65, Housing: "1. Everyone shall have the right for himself and his family to a dwelling of adequate size satisfying standards of hygiene and comfort and preserving personal and family privacy."

Universal Declaration of Human Rights (1948), article 25: "(1) Everyone has the right to a standard of living adequate for the health and well-being of himself and his family, including food, clothing, housing. . . ."

Constitutional Council of France (1995): Safeguarding the dignity of human beings against all forms of degrading treatment is a principle that ranks as constitutional law such that the nation must guarantee "individuals and families the conditions needed for them to develop"; therefore, the objective of ensuring that everyone has a decent home is constitutionally sound.

UN Committee on Economic, Social and Cultural Rights (1991): "Pursuant to article 11(1) of the [International Covenant on Economic, Social and Cultural Rights (1966)] States parties 'recognize the right of everyone to an adequate standard of living for himself and his family, including adequate food, clothing and housing, and to the continuous improvement of living conditions.' The human right to adequate housing, which is thus derived from the right to an adequate standard of living, is of central importance for the enjoyment of all economic, social and cultural rights."

UN Center for Human Settlements (Habitat), P.O. Box 30030, Nairobi, Kenya. (254-2-621234. 🖳 254-2-624266. 🖳 habitat@unchs.org. 🖳 www.unchs.org.

UN Commission on Human Settlements, P.O. Box 30030, Nairobi, Kenya. (254-2-623149. 🖳 254-2-624040. 🖳 habitat@unchs.org. 🖳 www.unchs.org.

Forrest, Ray, and Alan Murie, eds. *Housing and Family Wealth: Comparative International Perspectives.* New York: Routledge, 1995.

The Human Right to Adequate Housing. Fact Sheet no. 21. Geneva: Center for Human Rights, 1993.

Declaration of the Rights of the Child; Economic Rights; International Covenant on Economic, Social and Cultural Rights; Standard of Living; Vancouver Declaration on Human Settlements

Human Rights

Human rights, as Boutros Boutros-Ghali, former secretary-general of the United Nations, declared at the World Conference on Human Rights held in Vienna, Austria, in June 1993, "are the quintessential values through which we affirm together that we are a single community." This noble sentiment emphasizes the global importance to which human rights have been elevated at the beginning of the twenty-first century. Throughout history communities have been founded on the basis of family, neighbors, shared cultural, linguistic, and religious values, or political jurisdiction. Now, for the first time, it may be possible to create a global community of individuals and groups of peoples linked by the "quintessential values" of human rights.

Human rights have been defined as those rights that an individual acquires solely by reason of being human (from the Latin words *homo*, meaning man, and *humanus*, meaning belonging to man). Within the arc of human rights three categories have evolved: first-, second-, and third-generation rights. First-generation rights—human rights that are basic and necessary to a free and democratic society—encompass civil and political rights, such as freedom of speech and the right to vote and hold public office, for example. Second-generation rights include economic, social, and cultural rights, such as the right to work, the right to an adequate standard of living, and the right to take part in cultural activity. Third-generation rights cover collective or peoples' rights, such as the right to self-determination and the right to development.

The advancement of human rights has proceeded at different rates and in different ways throughout the world. Civil and political rights have been more highly developed in Britain, Europe, and the Americas, whereas peoples' rights have received more attention in Africa in response to the history of colonialism in most countries there. Regional systems for promoting and protecting human rights have been established in Europe, the Americas, and Africa, while none has yet been formally adopted by the Asia-Pacific region.

The inchoate notion of human rights may be nearly as old as humanity itself. The Code of Hammurabi in the eighteenth century B.C.E. and the Ten Commandments of the Israelites some centuries later are written evidence of an early concern that individuals be accorded certain rights and respect and that injurious behavior be punished.

Citizens of some ancient Greek cities, including Athens, were granted certain rights called *isogoria* (equal freedom of speech) and *isonomia* (equality before the law). Greek Stoic philosophers concluded that natural rights existed and belonged to all men all the time, although such rights were not extended to women, slaves, or aliens. Male Roman citizens had certain rights, including *patria potestas* (rights of the father as head of the family or household), but individual rights were generally subordinated to the rights of the Roman state.

After the ancient Greek democracies fell, the concept of human rights all but disappeared for a long period. A resurgence came with the rise and domination of the Christian Church in Europe during and after the decline of the Roman Empire. Renewed interest in the works of the ancient Greeks led St. Thomas Aquinas in the thirteenth century to formulate a theory of natural law that could be used to judge the justice of human laws. In the same century bold English barons forced King John to confirm some of their basic rights in Magna Carta (1215), which became the first document of England's unwritten constitution.

Seventeenth-century scholars and philosophers, including Hugo Grotius of Holland and John Locke of England, further developed the concepts of natural law and natural rights, which became the basis of modern individual human rights. Later critics including David Hume and Jeremy Bentham of Britain and the Hegelian Idealists of Germany disputed the idea of thinking of oneself as an individual with separate inalienable rights. In the eighteenth century the United States was founded to preserve natural rights—the first country so conceived. The U.S. Declaration of Independence (1776), Constitution (1789), and Bill of Rights (1791) unalterably changed history by setting in black and white the ideal of human rights for all, even though, as in the ancient Greek democracies, women and slaves were denied such rights, as were Native Americans. "[I]gnorance, neglect, or contempt of human rights, are the sole causes of public misfortunes," wrote Thomas Paine in *The Rights of Man* (1791), going on to applaud the French people for proclaiming what he called "these natural, imprescriptible, and unalienable rights" through the Declaration of the Rights of Man and of the Citizen (1789).

During the nineteenth century the rights of ethnic and religious minorities began to receive more attention and were embodied in several treaties, including the Treaty of Paris (1856); Treaty of Berlin (1878), which required Romania to grant religious tolerance to minorities in its jurisdiction; and Treaty of Paris (1898). Human rights developed further under the League of Nations, established in 1920 after World War I. Among other things, the League required countries to promote the welfare of the people in their colonial territories and to cease abuses such as the slave trade. In 1926 the Slavery Convention, developed under the League's auspices, entered into force. In addition, the League became concerned with fair and humane conditions of labor for men, women, and children, as called for by article 23 of its covenant. In 1919, in accordance with the Versailles Peace Treaty ending World War I, the International Labor Office was established. Between 1921 and 1932 a number of international conventions on labor sponsored by the ILO entered into force.

The atrocities of World War II, particularly the genocide practiced in Nazi Germany, impelled what the British wartime prime minister Winston Churchill called "the enthronement of human rights" internationally. The newly created United Nations (1945) took a significant step in that direction in 1948, when it promulgated the Universal Declaration of Human Rights. This document, along with the International Covenant on Civil and Political Rights (1966) and the International Covenant on Economic, Social and Cultural Rights (1966) and two optional protocols, make up what is called the International Bill of Human Rights.

In theory there are now two types of human rights: those enforceable under the laws of a nation and those acknowledged by nations in regional and international agreements. Not all human rights mandated by national constitutions are enforced, however, and not all international human rights are unenforceable. In both cases, however, the machinery of the nation-state is generally necessary for enforcement. There is no police force at the disposal of international and regional human rights bodies such as the Commission on Human Rights and the Inter-American Court of Human Rights. The U.S. Constitution's Bill of Rights mandates freedom of speech, for example, and the machinery of the government, legislature, courts, and law enforcement are available to enforce this right. The provision of the Universal Declaration of Human Rights that asserts a right to an adequate standard of living can be enforced only to the extent that a particular nation feels required and able to do so. A person going to court in the United States to demand rights set forth in the Universal Declaration will not be successful unless it can be established that such rights constitute norms of international law that bind the United States, but the U.S. courts will enforce American constitutional rights using the nation's police power if necessary.

A consensus is growing under international law that where a country or its leaders encourage or condone such flagrant violations of human rights as slavery, genocide, or the disappearance of individuals, other nations may hold them accountable whether or not the nation is a party to any relevant international human rights document. This move from the strict principle of national sovereignty is supported by the precedent of the Nuremberg trials, in which the victorious Allies tried Nazi leaders for crimes against humanity during World War II. A case in point is Spain's 1998 request that Chile's former military ruler Augusto Pinochet, temporarily in the United Kingdom, be turned over to Spain for trial on charges of flagrant human rights violations during his rule between 1973 and 1988. Although Pinochet was subsequently allowed to return to Chile, he may yet be held accountable for gross human rights violations there. Other developments in international human rights enforcement include establishment of ad hoc tribunals under the auspices of the United Nations to try war crimes in Rwanda and the former territory of Yugoslavia and the adoption of the Rome Statute for the creation of the International Criminal Court, a permanent body to prosecute and punish gross violations of human rights.

A list of basic human rights acceptable, at least in theory, to most of the world's major countries can be found in the Universal Declaration of Human Rights. These rights include nondiscrimination on the basis of race, color, sex, language, religion, political or other opinion, national origin, property, birth, or other status; the rights to life, liberty, and security of the person; freedom from torture and cruel, inhuman, or degrading treatment or punishment; the rights to recognition as a person before the law, equal protection of the law, and an effective remedy for violations of fundamental, constitutional, and other legal rights; freedom from arbitrary arrest, the right to a fair and public hearing by an independent and impartial tribunal on any criminal charges, and the right to presumption of innocence; punishment only for acts that were crimes at the time they were committed; freedom from arbitrary interference with privacy, family, home, correspondence, honor, and reputation; freedom of movement; the right to seek asylum from persecution; the rights to a nationality, to marry, and to own property; freedom of thought, conscience, and religion; freedom of opinion and expression; the rights to peaceful assembly and association; the right to take part in government; the rights to work, to receive equal pay for equal work, to social security, and to form trade unions; the rights to rest and leisure, reasonable working hours, and periodic holidays with pay; the right to an adequate standard of living; the right to education; and the right to freely participate in the cultural life of the community.

These basic human rights may be phrased slightly differently in other human rights documents and in national constitutions. Additional rights may have been added, such as rights of the disabled, while others are still being debated—the right to an abortion, the right to die, and freedom from discrimination on the grounds of sexual orientation, for example. Undoubtedly the list of human rights, which has grown so extensively in the recent past, will continue to grow in the future.

U.S. Declaration of Independence (1776): "We hold these Truths to be self-evident, that all Men are created equal, that they are endowed by their Creator with certain unalienable Rights, that among these are Life, Liberty, and the Pursuit of Happiness. . . ."

Constitution of Portugal (1976), article 7, International Relations: "1. In international relations, Portugal is governed by the principles of national independence, respect for human rights, the right of peoples to self-determination and independence, equality between States, the peaceful settlement of international disputes, non-interference in the internal affairs of other states and cooperation with all other peoples for the emancipation and progress of humanity."

Universal Declaration of Human Rights (1948), preamble: "[D]isregard and contempt for human rights have resulted in barbarous acts which have outraged the conscience of mankind, and the advent of a world in which human beings shall enjoy freedom of speech and belief and freedom from fear and want has been proclaimed as the highest aspiration of the common people."

U.S. District Court, Kansas (1980): "Perpetuating a state of affairs which results in the violation of an alien's fundamental human rights is clearly an abuse of discretion on the part of the responsible agency officials. This Court is bound to declare such an abuse and to order its cessation."

European Court of Human Rights (1969): When provisions are ambiguous in the text of an application for benefits, preference will be given to the version least "capable of prejudicing the fundamental human rights enshrined in the general principles of [European] Community law and protected by the Court."

Donnelly, Jack. *International Human Rights*. Boulder, Colo.: Westview, 1998.

Gearty, C. A., and Adam Tomkins. *Understanding Human Rights*. London: Mansell, 1996.

Lawson, Edward. *Encyclopedia of Human Rights*. Washington, D.C.: Taylor and Francis, 1996.

Shute, Stephen, and Susan Hurley, eds. *On Human Rights: The Oxford Amnesty Lectures*. New York: Basic Books, 1993.

Aristotle; Bills of Rights; Civil Rights; Collective Rights; Cultural Rights; Declaration of Independence (United States); Declaration of the Rights of Man and of the Citizen (France); Economic Rights; Enforcement; Grotius, Hugo; International Bill of Human Rights; International Criminal Court; Locke, John; Magna Carta; Natural Rights; Norms; Paine, Thomas; Plato; Regional Human Rights Systems; Social Rights; Thomas Aquinas, St.; Universal Declaration of Human Rights

Human Rights Commission

See Commission on Human Rights

Human Rights Committee

The Human Rights Committee was created under part IV of the International Covenant on Civil and Political Rights (1966), which entered into force on March 23, 1976. The committee was established to monitor implementation of the covenant and compliance with its provisions by those countries that have ratified it. Some of the basic rights included in the covenant are the right to life; prohibitions against torture, cruel, inhuman, or degrading treatment or punishment, and slavery; the right to liberty and security of person; freedom of movement; equality before courts and tribunals; the right to recognition as a person before the law; the right to privacy; freedom of thought, conscience, and religion; freedom of opinion and expression; and freedom of association. Other important rights include the right to participate in the conduct of public affairs, to vote, and to have equal access to public services.

The Human Rights Committee is distinct from the Commission on Human Rights, a separate body created by the Economic and Social Council (ECOSOC). The committee is therefore a "treaty body" under the covenant, while the commission is a "charter body," established under the authority of the Charter of the United Nations (1945). The commission is responsible for submitting proposals, recommendations, and investigative reports on human rights issues through ECOSOC to the General Assembly for its consideration and action and, under ECOSOC resolutions, for considering complaints concerning violations of human rights. The committee, on the other hand, has four separate functions under the covenant and its two optional protocols.

The Human Rights Committee receives and studies reports that states parties to the covenant are required to make on measures they have adopted to promote and enforce rights recognized in the document. It then forwards these reports, with comments, to the states parties and may also submit them to ECOSOC.

The committee also receives complaints by one state party against another, as long as the criticized nation has agreed to recognize the committee's right to do so. A procedure established under the covenant provides for such complaints to be processed and solved as far as possible.

In addition, under the covenant's First Optional Protocol, adopted by the General Assembly in 1966, the committee receives and considers communications or complaints from individuals who claim that rights set forth in the covenant have been violated. Between July 14 and November 4, 1997, for example, the Human Rights Committee reported acting on twenty-six individual complaints. Ten were determined to be inadmissible for various reasons, but of the sixteen admissible communications twelve were found to constitute violations of various provisions of the covenant.

Pursuant to the Second Optional Protocol, Aiming at the Abolition of the Death Penalty, adopted by the General Assembly in 1989, the right of individuals to file complaints is extended to include nations that have already recognized the committee's competence in this regard under the First Optional Protocol.

The committee numbers eighteen members who are nationals of the covenant's signatory countries and "persons of high moral character and recognized competence in the field of human rights, consideration being given to the usefulness of participation of some persons having legal experience." Members are elected by secret ballot for a term of four years by the states parties; no two may be from the same country. The committee usually meets at UN headquarters in New York City but is authorized to meet also in Geneva. Officers are elected for two years. Twelve members constitute a quorum for doing business, and decisions are made by a majority vote of the members present.

United Nations High Commissioner for Human Rights, 8–14 avenue de la Paix, 1211 Geneva 10, Switzerland. ☎ 41-22-917-9000. 🖨 41-22-917-9016. 💻 webadmin.hchr@unog.ch. 🖥 www.unhchr.ch.

Commission on Human Rights; Economic and Social Council (ECOSOC); International Covenant on Civil and Political Rights; International Covenant on Civil and Political Rights, First Optional Protocol; International Covenant on Civil and Political Rights, Second Optional Protocol, Aiming at the Abolition of the Death Penalty

Human Rights Internet

The Human Rights Internet, a nongovernmental organization based in Canada, facilitates information exchange within the worldwide human rights community. The main objective of the organization, which communicates with more than five thousand groups and individuals around the world, is supporting the work of the global private community in its struggle to obtain human rights for all. Founded in 1976 in the United States, the organization promotes human rights education, research, information sharing, and solidarity among those committed to the principles of the International Bill of Human Rights.

The databases of the Human Rights Internet are available to help scholars, activists, lawyers, and members of human rights organizations. These databases contain information on thousands of human rights organizations, funding sources, human rights awards, education programs, and children's rights, as well as bibliographies of human rights literature. Online resources include an Internet directory of human rights organizations that may be searched by the name of the organization, acronym, Web site, type of organization, country, geographic focus, key words, and issues. Entries in the HRI directory contains direct links to each organization's Web site.

The Human Rights Internet also provides training programs and internships for Canadian youth. With the Canadian government's Department of Foreign Affairs and International Trade, it sponsors a Youth International Internship Program. Another program, jointly sponsored by NetCorps Canada and managed by a coalition of nine Canadian development agencies and nongovernmental organizations, offers six-month information and communications technology internships in developing countries.

The organization publishes books and periodicals, including *Human Rights Tribune*, a quarterly publication, and *HRI Reporter*, which contains abstracts and indexes of publications on human rights. Other publications include *Do It Right!! Who's Doing What on Child and Youth Rights in Canada; African Directory: Human Rights Organizations in Africa; Funding Human Rights: An International Directory of Funding Organizations and Human Rights Awards*, and *The Masterlist: A Listing of Organizations Concerned with Human Rights and Social Justice Worldwide.*

Human Rights Internet, 8 York Street, Suite 302, Ottawa, Ontario K1N 5S6, Canada. (613-789-7407. 🖨 613-789-7414. 🖳 hri@hri.ca. 🖳 www.hri.ca.

Communication; Information; International Bill of Human Rights; Internet; Nongovernmental Organizations

Human Rights Watch

A nongovernmental organization, Human Rights Watch works to stop human rights abuses through its monitoring, reporting, and advocacy efforts. The organization, the largest U.S.-based human rights group, relies on a staff of more than one hundred regional experts, including lawyers and linguists, to analyze the causes of human rights abuses and how to stop them. It is privately funded and takes no contributions from any government in order to maintain its neutrality and ability to criticize human rights activities of any government.

Human Rights Watch began in 1978 as Helsinki Watch (now Human Rights Watch/Helsinki) to help embattled groups in Moscow, Warsaw, and Prague that were set up to monitor compliance with the human rights provisions of the Helsinki Final Act (1975). Americas Watch (now Human Rights Watch/Americas) was created in 1981 to counter the Reagan Administration's policy of condoning human rights abuses by right-wing authoritarian governments, such as those in Chile and Argentina, while condemning similar abuses by communist governments in the Soviet Union, China, and Cuba. "Those who defend human rights look to Human Rights Watch when their own rights are threatened," said Jacobo Timerman, a former Argentine political prisoner and author of *Prisoner without a Name, Cell without a Number* (1981).

The avowed goal of Human Rights Watch is to defend freedom of thought and expression, due process of law, equal protection of the law, and a vigorous civil society by holding governments accountable if they infringe on the rights of their citizens. The organization specifically attempts to influence the U.S. government's policy toward countries that violate human rights; to accomplish this, it publishes a critical review of the U.S. Department of State's annual report on human rights in other countries.

Today Human Rights Watch focuses on a number of regions including sub-Saharan Africa, Asia, Latin America, the Caribbean, and the Middle East and conducts projects related to weapons, children's rights, and women's rights. To monitor and report on human rights activities, missions are sent to countries in which abuses are alleged to have occurred. Mission members meet with government officials, opposition politicians, and community and religious leaders to document the allegations, interview victims and witnesses, and research official and unofficial records. This process may be effective at least indirectly by making the abuses known publicly to the country's citizens and the international community, including centers of influence such as the United States and the European Union.

The organization also sponsors fellowships and internships and publishes numerous documents on human rights in countries around the world. The Human Rights Watch International Film Festival presents films and videos that incorporate human rights themes. The 1999 festival focused on land mines and collaborated with the New York Lesbian and Gay Film Festival to copresent *The Man Who Drove with Mandela*. Recent special initiatives have focused on academic freedom, drugs, free expression, prison conditions, and corporations and human rights.

"We seek to curb abuses," notes a Human Rights Watch publication, "regardless of whether the victims are well-known political activists or those of lesser visibility such as factory workers, peasant farmers, undocumented migrants, women forced into prostitution, street children, or domestic workers. We also address such war-related abuses as indiscriminate shelling or the use of rape or starvation as weapons of war—no matter which side in a conflict is responsible."

Human Rights Watch, 350 Fifth Avenue, 34th Floor, New York, N.Y. 10118-3299. (212-290-4700. 🖨 212-736-1300. 🖳 hrwnyc@hrw.org. 🖳 www.hrw.org.

Human Rights Watch, 1630 Connecticut Avenue, N.W., Suite 500, Washington, D.C. 20009. (202-612-4321. ▤ 202-612-4333. ▤ hrwdc@hrw.org. ▤ www.hrw.org.

Human Rights Watch, 333 South Grand Avenue, Suite 430, Los Angeles, Calif. 90071-1508. (213-680-9906. ▤ 213-680-9924. ▤ hrwla@hrw.org. ▤ www.hrw.org.

Human Rights Watch, 33 Islington High Street, N1 9LH London, England. (44-207-713-1995. ▤ 44-207-713-1800. ▤ hrwatchuk@ gn.apc.org. ▤ www.hrw.org.

Human Rights Watch, 15 rue Van Campenhout, 1000 Brussels, Belgium. (3-22-732-20-09. ▤ 3-22-732-04-71. ▤ hrwatcheu@ gn.apc.org. ▤ www.hrw.org.

☞

Defenders of Human Rights; Helsinki Final Act; Monitoring Compliance; Reporting Violations; Timerman, Jacobo

Humane Treatment

See Prisoners; Punishment

Humanitarian Law

See Geneva Conventions

More than fourteen thousand
immigrants to the United
States became naturalized
American citizens en masse
in a Florida football stadium
in 1986. The rights of
immigrants like these are
determined by the domestic
law of their host country,
but to ensure that immi-
grants' basic human rights
are protected, international
standards also govern
the treatment of aliens.
[UPI/Bettmann News Photo]

Immigrants

Immigration (from the Latin *immigro)* is the purposeful movement of a person from one country to another, generally with the intention of becoming a permanent resident or a citizen of the host country. Rules for admission are made by the receiving nation on the basis of national policy and often require some connection with the new country, such as a spouse who is a citizen or an offer of employment.

In part because of the ease of modern transportation and the relaxation of restrictions on travel, immigration has become an important human rights issue in recent years. Between 1821 and 1830, for example, immigration into the United States totaled 143,439, whereas between 1981 and 1990 it mushroomed to 7.3 million, rising even higher in the next decade. During 1997 immigrants accounted for some forty-three percent of the population growth of Australia, another popular destination.

Under international law immigration is not considered a right but rather a matter of policy for the host country. Some nations have strict immigration laws, others more liberal ones. Germany, Ireland, and Israel are among the countries with a discriminatory policy favoring immigrants of their own heritage. The United States and some other nations promote liberal immigration but impose quotas for immigrants from various parts of the world. Even so, the United States faces an influx of illegal immigrants, especially from Mexico, with whom it shares an extensive border, and from Central America to its south.

Human rights issues relating to immigration range from the fairness of admission determinations to the treatment of immigrants, both legal and illegal, and the equity of requirements for citizenship and deportation. A key concern is to what extent legal aliens (those lawfully residing in a host country and perhaps intending to become citizens) enjoy the basic rights extended to citizens. Although the rights to vote and hold office are generally restricted to citizens, governments typically grant legal aliens access to the courts, due process of law, public education, and even welfare and health care benefits. Another concern is that provisions for acquiring citizenship be non-discriminatory; some nations give preference to immigrants with cultural or linguistic ties to the host country, or they may permit corrupt practices such as bribery to favor certain applicants.

People will continue to migrate legally and illegally, seeking a better life for themselves and their families. Ensuring human rights while dealing with the demands of an uninvited population in particular—and in some cases handling the return of such aliens—places an extra burden on governments. Due process of law must be observed in determining immigration status, and humane conditions must be provided during processing or before deportation. To avoid subjecting illegal political refugees to harm if returned to their country of origin, governments also must take into consideration the issue of *refoulement.* For these reasons, many countries have established special agencies to assist aliens, including migrant laborers, temporary workers, and other immigrants.

Constitution of Austria (1920), The Federal Constitution, chapter I, General Provisions, article 10: "1. The *Bund* [federation] has powers of legislation and execution in the following matters: . . . 3. regulation and control of entry into and exit from the federal territory; immigration and emigration. . . ."

Declaration on the Human Rights of Individuals Who Are Not Nationals of the Country in Which They Live (1985), preamble: "[T]he protection of human rights and fundamental freedoms provided for in international instruments should also be ensured for individuals who are not nationals of the country in which they live. . . ."

U.S. Supreme Court (1999): In a key victory for immigrants' rights, the Court refused to review lower-court rulings that permit immigrants convicted of crimes to appeal to federal courts for review of their cases and intervention in their deportation orders.

Human Rights Committee (1991): After the pension of an elderly British citizen living as an immigrant in New Zealand was reduced, he filed a discrimination claim under the International Covenant on Civil and Political Rights (1966), First Optional Protocol, article 2. The claim was denied on the basis that the New Zealand law requiring the reduction of pensions applied equally to citizens and to foreigners alike.

Center for Immigration and Multicultural Studies, Research School of Social Sciences, The Australian National University, Canberra ACT 0200, Australia. ☏ 61-2-6249-2006. 🖷 61-2-6249-0771. 🖳 jupp@coombs.anu.edu.au. 🖳 cims.anu.edu.au.

International Immigrants Foundation, 1435 Broadway, Second Floor, New York, N.Y. 10018. ☏ 212-221-7255. 🖷 212-221-7206. 🖳 ejuarez@10.org. 🖳 www.10.org.

National Immigration Forum, 220 I Street, N.E., Suite 220, Washington, D.C. 20002-4362. ☏ 202-544-0004. 🖷 202-544-1905. 🖳 www.immigrationforum.org.

Plender, Richard. *International Migration Law.* Rev. 2nd ed. The Hague: Martinus Nijhoff, Kluwer Law International, 1988.

Vincenzi, Christopher, and David Marrington. *Immigration Law: The Rules Explained.* London: Sweet and Maxwell, 1992.

Aliens; Asylum; Deportation; Movement; Nationality; *Refoulement;* Refugees

Impartiality

See Judicial Independence

Impunity

For much of human history, rulers have acted to a large extent with impunity, meaning without any possibility of punishment for the manner in which they deal with their subjects. "This unlimited power of doing anything with impunity," wrote R. Coke in *Power and Subject* (1660), "will only beget a confidence in kings of doing what they [please]." Like sovereign immunity, impunity (from the Latin *impunitus,* meaning unpunished) is an attribute of those with absolute power or authority over others, although impunity implies a flagrant disregard for any constraints on one's actions.

The legal concept of sovereign immunity historically protected a monarch from being accountable or punished for acts committed as head of state. In the first civilizations, such as those in the Fertile Crescent of Mesopotamia, governments were hierarchical and sacral kings or divine rulers made the laws. They were unaccountable to anyone. In medieval Europe it was accepted that the secular rulers—emperors, kings, queens, and princes—had a divine right to rule. Rulers were thus by definition above the law, because they made the laws, although they were theoretically accountable to God for their acts.

A similar sovereign immunity now insulates constitutional monarchs, heads of state, and government officials, unless the privilege is waived by law. But how far should such a concept be honored where gross violations of human rights have been carried out or condoned by a head of state or those acting under his authority? The constitutional concept of accountability is intended to act as a check on the illegal or unconstitutional acts of government officials who have been delegated powers by the people. Such accountability may be enforced by impeachment, regular elections, or an election to recall an elected official before completion of a term, as well as by judicial review and constitutional review of executive and legislative actions.

When governments initiate or condone murder, torture, or disappearance of citizens, they ignore the inviolable right of human integrity and protections in international agreements such as the Universal Declaration of Human Rights (1948), European Convention for the Protection of Human Rights and Fundamental Freedoms (1950), International Covenant on Civil and Political Rights (1966), and American Convention on Human Rights (1969). Such governmental impunity has taken on special relevance in Latin American countries including Argentina, Brazil, and Chile as a result of gross human rights violations during recent military dictatorships. Now the question is how to hold dictators and military juntas accountable for abuses after they leave office, assuming that it is not possible to hold them accountable while they are in power. Transitional justice, as it is called, addresses means to investigate and prosecute these violators and negate their assertion of immunity, even if they were granted immunity as a condition for being ousted.

While victims of gross human rights violations may focus more on retribution, redress, and compensation, the nation as a whole has to find a way of expeditiously removing rulers who have violated rights with impunity. If this means that the state must grant such rulers immunity after they leave office, the price may be worth it although the rights of some individuals are thereby sacrificed for the protection of the rights of others. The international community is nonetheless finding ways to hold such persons accountable. In 1998 Spain sought extradition of the former Chilean dictator Augusto Pinochet from the United Kingdom to stand trial for human rights abuses. The House of Lords voted to extradite Pinochet, who had stepped down as head of state in return for a grant of immunity, but he was later returned to Chile on the basis that he was too infirm for trial; he may yet face charges in Chile. Other national rulers and military leaders have been tried in international tribunals set up under the UN Security Council for crimes committed in the former Yugoslavia and in Rwanda, and the Rome Statute of the International Criminal Court (1998) was drafted to provide an international forum for trying and punishing leaders like Pinochet who have violated citizen rights with impunity.

Chapultepec Agreement (1992), article 5: "The Parties recognize the need to clarify and put an end to any indication of impunity on the part of officers of the armed forces, particularly in cases where respect for human rights is jeopardized."

Geneva Convention for the Amelioration of the Condition of the Wounded and Sick in Armed Forces in the Field (1949), chapter VIII, Execution of the Convention, article 49: "Each High Contracting Party shall be under obligation to search for persons alleged to have committed, or to have ordered to be committed, such grave breaches [of human rights], and shall bring such persons, regardless of their nationality, before its own courts . . . [or] hand such persons over for trial to another High Contracting Party. . . ." **Article 50:** "Grave breaches . . . [include] willful killing, torture or inhumane treatment, including biological experiments. . . ."

House of Lords, United Kingdom (Opinion of Lord Steyn) (1998): "[T]he development of international law since the second world war justifies the conclusion that by the time of the 1973 coup d'etat [by Chilean General Augusto Pinochet], and certainly ever since, international law condemned genocide, torture, hostage-taking and crimes against humanity (during an armed conflict or in

peace time) as international crimes deserving of punishment. Given this state of international law, it seems to me difficult to maintain that the commission of such high crimes may amount to acts performed in the exercise of the functions of a head of state."

Inter-American Court of Human Rights (1988): Honduras violated the rights of a student arrested, tortured, and executed by its military specifically with respect to the American Convention on Human Rights (1969), article 1(1), which mandates that governments "undertake to . . . ensure" the rights set forth therein. This means that "[t]he State has a legal duty to take reasonable steps to prevent human rights violations and to use the means at its disposal to carry out a serious investigation of violations committed within its jurisdiction, to identify those responsible, impose the appropriate punishment and ensure the victim adequate compensation."

Derechos Human Rights, P.O. Box 2516, El Cerrito, Calif. 94530-5516. (510-483-4005. 📠 603-372-9710. ▣ hr@derechos.org. ▣ www.derechos.org.

International Center for Human Rights and Democratic Development, 63 rue de Bresoles, Montreal, Quebec, Canada **H2Y 1V7.** (514-283-6073. 📠 514-283-3792. ▣ ichrdd@ichrdd.ca. ▣ www.ichrdd.ca.

Harper, Charles, ed. *Impunity: An Ethical Perspective. Six Case Studies from Latin America.* Geneva: World Council of Churches, 1996.

Jones, John R.W.D. *The Practice of the International Criminal Tribunals for the Former Yugoslavia and Rwanda.* Irvington-on-Hudson, N.Y.: Transnational, 1997.

Roht-Arriaza, Naomi, ed. *Impunity and Human Rights in International Law and Practice.* New York: Oxford University Press, 1995.

Crimes against Humanity; Disappearance; International Criminal Court; Inviolable Rights; Judicial Review; Justice; Rome Statute of the International Criminal Court; Sovereignty; War Crimes

Inalienable Rights

See Inviolable Rights; Natural Rights

Independent Judiciary

See Judicial Independence

Indigenous and Tribal Peoples Convention

The General Conference of the International Labor Organization (ILO) on June 27, 1989, adopted the Indigenous and Tribal Peoples Convention, which emphasizes respect for the culture of indigenous and tribal peoples and their right to exist alongside more dominant national cultures without discrimination or exploitation. The convention, no. 169, revises ILO Convention no. 107 (1957), which addressed the no-longer acceptable policy of integration and assimilation of indigenous peoples.

"The developments which have taken place in international law since 1957, as well as developments in the situation of indigenous and tribal peoples in all regions of the world," notes the preamble, "have made it appropriate to adopt new international standards on the subject with a view to removing the assimilationist orientation of the earlier standards." The document goes on to note that the ILO recognizes "the aspirations of these peoples to exercise control over their own institutions, ways of life and economic development and to maintain and develop their identities, languages and religions, within the framework of the States in which they live."

Part I, General Policy, article 1, declares: "1. This Convention applies to: (a) tribal peoples in independent countries whose social, cultural and economic conditions distinguish them from other sections of the national community, and whose status is regulated wholly or partially by their own customs or traditions or by special laws or regulations; (b) peoples in independent countries who are regarded as indigenous on account of their descent from the populations which inhabited the country, or a geographical region to which the country belongs, at the time of conquest or colonization or the establishment of the present state boundaries and who, irrespective of their legal status, retain some or all of their own social, economic, cultural and political institutions."

"Self-identification as indigenous or tribal," specifies article 1, paragraph 2, "shall be regarded as a fundamental criterion for determining the groups to which the provisions of this Convention apply." Paragraph 3 adds: "The use of the term 'peoples' in this Convention shall not be construed as having any implications as regards the rights which may attach to the term under international law." Article 2, among other things, directs that governments, "with the participation of the peoples concerned," are responsible for developing "coordinated and systematic action to protect the rights of these peoples and to guarantee respect for their integrity."

"Indigenous and tribal peoples shall enjoy the full measure of human rights and fundamental freedoms without hindrance or discrimination," mandates article 3, adding that "[n]o form of force or coercion shall be used in violation of [such rights and freedoms], including the rights contained in this Convention." Under article 5, their "social, cultural, religious and spiritual values and practices ... shall be recognized and protected ...; the integrity of the values, practices and institutions of these peoples shall be respected; policies aimed at mitigating the difficulties experienced by these peoples in facing new conditions of life and work shall be adopted, with the participation and cooperation of the peoples affected."

According to articles 6, 7, and 8, respectively, the peoples concerned are to be consulted with respect to government actions affecting them, have the right to decide their own priorities, and in "applying national laws and regulations ... due regard shall be had to their customs or customary laws." Articles 9 through 12 address special methods for dealing with offenses committed by indigenous and tribal peoples and preventing abuse of their rights.

Part II, Land, article 13, requires respect for "the special importance for the cultures and spiritual values of the peoples concerned of their relationship with the lands or territories ... , which they occupy or otherwise use...." Article 15 directs that the "rights of the peoples concerned to the natural resources pertaining to their lands shall be specially safeguarded."

Part III addresses recruitment and conditions of employment; part IV vocational training and handicrafts and rural industries; part V social security and health; part VI education and means of communications; and part VII contacts and cooperation across borders. Pursuant to part VIII, Administration, article 33, governments are urged to "ensure that agencies or other appropriate mechanisms exist to administer programs" for indigenous peoples, including planning, coordinating, executing, and evaluating programs addressing the goals identified in the convention as well as taking legislative or other measures to implement them, all conducted "in cooperation with the peoples concerned."

✉

Center for World Indigenous Studies, PMB 214, 1001 Cooper Point Road S.W., Suite 140, Olympia, Wash. 98502-1107. ☏ 888-286-2947. 🖷 360-786-5034. 🖳 usaoffice@cwis.org. 🖳 www.cwis.org.

Cultural Survival, 96 Mount Alban Street, Cambridge, Mass. 02138. ☏ 617-441-5400. 🖷 617-441-5417. 🖳 csinc@cs.org. 🖳 www.cs.org.

International Labor Organization, 4 route des Morillons, 1211 Geneva 22, Switzerland. ☏ 41-22-799-6111. 🖷 41-22-798-8685. 🖳 somavia.ilo.org. 🖳 www.ilo.org.

☞

Collective Rights; Cultural Rights; Declaration on the Rights of Persons Belonging to National or Ethnic, Religious and Linguistic Minorities; Development; Discrimination; Indigenous Peoples; International Labor Organization; Language; Minorities; Peoples' Rights; Self-Determination

Indigenous Peoples

Estimated to number about 300 million persons, or five percent of the world's population, indigenous peoples inhabit a large portion of the Earth's surface. They are the natives of lands that were colonized by people of vastly different cultures and levels of technical development: peoples such as the Indians of Central and South America, Native Americans, the Inuit (derogatorily referred to as Eskimos, meaning fisheaters) in North America's circumpolar region, the Saami (Lapplanders) of northern Europe, the Aborigines and Torres Strait Islanders of Australia, and the Maori of New Zealand. Aggressive colonization and development have threatened the existence of indigenous peoples (from the Latin word *indigena,* meaning native) as they seek to preserve their cultures and ways of life. In many instances they have been relegated to territory that is the least able to support life comfortably.

Indigenous, or aboriginal, peoples constitute a special class of minority. They have historically been among the poorest of the poor, living in remote areas far from health care, schools, and employment opportunities. Their fundamental rights have been violated by removal from their ancestral lands and acts of genocide and forced assimilation. They may be exploited economically, excluded socially, deprived of strong political representation, and subjected to armed conflicts. Special problems they face today include poverty, a lack of health services, substandard education, unemployment, and violation of cultural and intellectual property rights. Other key issues include protection of resources, land development, self-determination, and basic human rights. In addition, according to the International Labor Organization (ILO), "a wealth of accumulated knowledge adapted to local conditions is being lost with the extinction of indigenous societies."

Despite great cultural diversity among indigenous peoples, the similarities of their plight have brought them together to present their concerns to the world community. American Indians first approached the League of Nations in the 1920s, and in 1948 the Bolivian government urged the United Nations to create a subcommission to study the social problems of aboriginal populations—to no avail. The ILO recognized indigenous peoples' problems in 1921, and in 1957 and 1989 it adopted conventions promoting their human and national cultural rights.

In 1971 the Economic and Social Council (ECOSOC), on the recommendation of its Subcommission on the Promotion and Protection of Human Rights, began to focus on the problem of discrimination against indigenous peoples. A report requested by the subcommission in 1971 and completed in 1985 addresses a number of issues, including the right "of indigenous peoples themselves to define what and who is indigenous," their historical rights to land, and their right to retain their cultural identity. "Governments which have not yet done so," suggests the report, "should consider establishing institutions, machinery and special-ized administrative procedures, since entities with specific and clearly defined mandates are in a better position to accord due attention to solving the difficult and complex problems currently facing indigenous populations in the countries in which they live."

The World Conference on Human Rights held in Vienna in 1993 proposed that the UN General Assembly establish a permanent forum for indigenous peoples. An international declaration on the subject has also been drafted, emphasizing the rights of indigenous peoples to be free and equal; to achieve self-determination; to pursue economic, social, and cultural development; to preserve their traditions; to control their educational systems; to participate in decision making that affects their lives; and to preserve their lands and resources.

To draw further attention to the plight of indigenous peoples, the UN designated 1993 as the International Year of the World's Indigenous People and 1995–2004 as the International Decade of the World's Indigenous People. "An objective of the Decade," said the General Assembly, "is the promotion and protection of the rights of indigenous people and their empowerment to make choices which enable them to retain their cultural identity while participating in political, economic and social life, with full respect for their cultural values, languages, traditions and forms of social organization." The Voluntary Fund for the International Decade of the World's Indigenous People was established by the General Assembly at the same time to support programs during the decade.

"The effective protection of indigenous peoples' heritage," states a 1994 report to the UN subcommission entitled Protection of the Heritage of the Indigenous Peoples, "will be of long-term benefit to all humanity [because] [c]ultural diversity contributes to the adaptability and creativity of the human species as a whole."

Canadian Charter of Rights and Freedoms (1982), part I, section 25: "The guarantee of this Charter of certain rights and freedoms shall not be construed so as to abrogate or derogate from any aboriginal treaty or other rights or freedoms that pertain to the aboriginal peoples of Canada. . . ."

Vienna Declaration and Program of Action, part I, paragraph 20: "The World Conference on Human Rights recognizes the inherent dignity and the unique contribution of indigenous people to the development and plurality of society and strongly reaffirms the commitment of the international community to their economic, social and cultural well-being and their enjoyment of the fruits of sustainable development."

Manitoba (Canada) Court of Appeals (1996): An indigenous peoples' bylaw banning intoxicants does not contravene the Canadian Charter of Rights and Freedoms (1982).

Economic and Social Council (ECOSOC) Report (1986): "No State may take, by legislation, regulations or other means, measures that interfere with the power of indigenous nations or groups to determine who are their members."

Center for World Indigenous Studies, PMB 214, 1001 Cooper Point Road S.W., Suite 140, Olympia, Wash. 98502-1107. (888-286-2947. 🖨 360-786-5034. 🖳 usaoffice@cwis.org. 🖵 www.cwis.org.

Cultural Survival, 96 Mount Alban Street, Cambridge, Mass. 02138. (617-441-5400. 🖨 617-441-5417. 🖳 csinc@cs.org. 🖵 www.cs.org.

International Work Group for Indigenous Peoples, Classensgade 11E, DK 2100 Copenhagen, Denmark. (45-35-27-05-00. 🖨 45-35-27-05-07. 🖳 iwgia@iwgia.org. 🖵 hem.passagen.se/iwgia.reading.

United Nations High Commissioner for Human Rights, 8–14 avenue de la Paix, 1211 Geneva 10, Switzerland. (41-22-917-9000. 🖨 41-22-917-9016. 🖳 webadmin.hchr@unog.ch. 🖵 www.unhchr.ch.

Buchi, Silvia, ed. *Indigenous Peoples, Environment, and Development: Proceedings of the Conference, Zurich, May 15–18, 1995.* With Department of Social Anthropology, University of Zurich. Copenhagen: International Work Group for Indigenous Affairs, 1997.

The Rights of Indigenous Peoples. Fact Sheet no. 9. Geneva: Center for Human Rights, 1997.

Simpson, Tony. *Indigenous Heritage and Self-Determination: The Cultural and Intellectual Property Rights of Indigenous Peoples.* Copenhagen: International Work Group for Indigenous Affairs, 1997.

Collective Rights; Cultural Rights; Declaration on the Rights of Persons Belonging to National or Ethnic, Religious and Linguistic Minorities; Development; Discrimination; Economic and Social Council (ECOSOC); Indigenous and Tribal Peoples Convention; International Labor Organization; Language; Minorities; Peoples' Rights; Self-Determination

Information

The right to timely and accurate information—closely related to freedom of speech, the press, and communication—is a weapon for citizens in the battle with governments to ensure observance of all human rights. The biblical promise "You shall know the truth, and the truth shall make you free" (John 8:32) was never truer than today. In some countries governments try to withhold information from their own citizens and from the world at large to cover up mistakes, ill treatment of citizens, and even crimes against humanity. But satellite communications, mass media, and the Internet are making it more difficult for governments to misuse or hide information (from the Latin *informo*, meaning to shape or educate).

How information is gathered, interpreted, and disseminated has been important since humans first developed language. The ancient Greek philosopher Socrates was sentenced to death for imparting information deemed impious and a corrupting influence on the youth of Athens. To protect their liberty and exercise their rights, citizens must have access to independent sources of information, otherwise their decisions and actions are based on propaganda rather than accurate news.

According to a draft declaration on freedom of information prepared in 1960, information rights include the right "to know and freely seek the truth ... [and] individually and collectively, to seek, receive, and impart information." These guidelines urge governments to "pursue policies under which the free flow of information, within countries and across frontiers, will be protected." It also asserts that the "right to seek and transmit information should be assured in order to enable the public to ascertain facts and appraise events." The declaration also notes that the "exercise of these rights and freedoms entails special responsibilities and duties. Those [especially in the media] who disseminate information must strive in good faith to ensure the accuracy of the facts reported. ..." Furthermore, it suggests, rights and freedoms relating to information should be subject only "to such limitations as are determined solely for the purpose of securing due recognition and respect for the rights and freedoms of others and of meeting the just requirements of national security, public order, morality and the general welfare in a democratic society."

Information is the lifeblood of any government, particularly a democracy. Under totalitarian systems all political information is managed by the government. Even open, democratic societies, however, cannot reveal everything but must carefully determine which information should be kept secret for national security reasons and which should be made publicly available. Too much information, on the other hand, may pose a threat to privacy rights: modern technology makes financial, medical, and other personal information readily available to the government, private organizations, and other individuals.

Some national constitutions and laws detail the issues of citizens' rights to information, privacy, and security. Brazil's constitution (1988), for example, provides for "habeas data," derived from the concept of habeas corpus, which "shall be granted ... for the correction of data" in government files. Sweden's constitution provides in its Freedom of the Press Act (amended in 1992) that "[a]ny official document which may be made accessible to the public shall be produced forthwith, or as quickly as possible, at the place where it is kept, and free of charge, to any person who desires to have access to it. . . ." American citizens are likewise entitled to certain government documents under the Freedom of Information Act (1967).

In 1948 a UN Conference on Freedom of Information drafted language for the Universal Declaration of Human Rights (1948) and adopted general principles for promoting and protecting freedom of information, as stated in the declaration's article 19, paragraph 1: "[E]veryone shall have the right to freedom of thought and expression: this shall include freedom to hold opinions without interference; and to seek, receive and impart information and ideas by any means and regardless of frontiers."

Constitution of South Africa (1997), chapter 2, Bill of Rights, article 32: "(1) Everyone has the right of access to—(a) any information held by the state; and (b) any information that is held by another person and that is required for the exercise or protection of any rights."

Convention on the International Right of Correction (1953), preamble: "[T]he maintenance of friendly relations between peoples and the preservation of peace, [is endangered by] the publication of inaccurate reports. . . . [T]o prevent the publication of reports of this nature or to reduce their pernicious effects, it is above all necessary to promote wide circulation of news and to heighten the sense of responsibility of those regularly engaged in the dissemination of news."

Constitutional Court of Hungary (1994): "The right to informational self-determination [established by Hungary's constitution (1989), article 59] "means in effect that all individuals who enjoy protection of the Constitution have control over the disclosure and use of their personal records. . . . All individuals on whom records were kept [by the state] or are mentioned at all in the reports at issue enjoy the constitutional right to access this information and control its use."

European Court of Human Rights (1987): "[T]he right to freedom to receive information basically prohibits a Government from restricting a person from receiving information that others wish or may be willing to impart to him." But the European Convention for the Protection of Human Rights and Fundamental Freedoms (1950), article 10, which guarantees freedom of information, among other things, does not require that the Swedish government turn over to the complainant information in a secret police register that was a part of the record relied on to reject his application for a position at the naval museum.

Coliver, Sandra, Paul Hoffman, Joan Fitzpatrick, and Stephen Bowen, eds. *Security and Liberty: National Security, Freedom of Ex-*

pression and Access to Information. The Hague: Martinus Nijhoff, Kluwer Law International, 1999.

Maherzi, Lotfi. *World Communication Report: The Media and the Challenge of the New Technologies.* Paris: United Nations Educational, Scientific and Cultural Organization (UNESCO), 1997.

Williams, Frederick, and John Vernon Pavlik, eds. *The People's Right to Know: Media, Democracy, and the Information Highway.* Hillsdale, N.J.: Erlbaum, 1994.

Communication; Convention on the International Right of Correction; Declaration on Fundamental Principles Concerning the Contribution of the Mass Media to Strengthening Peace and International Understanding, to the Promotion of Human Rights and to Countering Racialism, Apartheid and Incitement to War; Expression; Opinion; The Press; Privacy; Speech

Institute for Global Communications

A nonprofit, nongovernmental organization, the Institute for Global Communications provides alternative sources of information, online access, and comprehensive Internet services. The group's mission is "to advance and inform movements for peace, economic and social justice, human rights and environmental sustainability around the world by promoting strategic use of appropriate computer networking technology."

The institute was founded in 1987 to manage PeaceNet and EcoNet, the world's first computer network dedicated to environmental sustainability. It has since extended its Internet and online capabilities to organizations and activists working for peace, economic and social justice, human rights, environmental protection, labor issues, and conflict resolution. With a national membership of more than fifteen thousand, the organization says that it represents "the nation's only nonprofit, unionized, full-service Internet service provider."

In 1990 the institute cofounded the Association for Progressive Communications, which has twenty-five autonomous but affiliated members and forty partners and provides communications and information-sharing facilities to nongovernmental organizations and individuals working for social change in some 130 countries. Both the institute and the association have been the primary information and communications service providers at major world conferences of the United Nations.

Other information and communications services of the organization include ConflictNet; LaborNet; and WomensNet. Its Web site also provides links to various types of human rights information, such as action alerts, news and recent developments, documents and clearinghouses, and organizations including children's rights groups.

Institute for Global Communications, P.O. Box 29904, San Francisco, Calif. 94129-0904. (415-561-6100. 🖨 415-561-6101. 🖳 support@igc.org. 🖳 www.igc.org.

Environment; Internet Resources; Project Diana

Intellectual Property

See Artists; Universal Copyright Convention

Inter-American Charter of Social Guarantees

In 1948, the year in which it was established, the Organization of American States (OAS) sponsored several key regional human rights documents. Among them were the American Declaration of the Rights and Duties of Man, Inter-American Convention on the Granting of Civil Rights to Women, Inter-American Convention on the Granting of Political Rights to Women, and Inter-American Charter of Social Guarantees. Addressing the rights and protection of workers, the charter was adopted on May 2, 1948, to improve standards of living through economic development and cooperation between workers and employers. Two months later, the International Labor Organization adopted the Freedom of Association and Protection of the Right to Organize Convention, which covers many of the same issues at the international, rather than the regional, level.

The charter opens with General Principles, article 1 of which declares: "It is the aim of the present Charter of Social Guarantees to proclaim the fundamental principles that must protect workers of all kinds, and it sets forth the minimum rights they must enjoy in the American States, without prejudice to the fact that the laws of each State may extend such rights or recognize others that are more favorable. This Charter of Social Guarantees," it continues, "gives equal protection to men and women. It is recognized that the supremacy of these rights and the progressive raising of the standard of living of the community in general depend to a large degree upon the development of economic activities, upon increased productivity, and upon co-operation between workers and employers, expressed in harmonious relations and in mutual respect for and fulfillment of their rights and duties."

Article 2 sets out five basic principles "fundamental in the social legislation of the American countries: (a) Labor is a social function; it enjoys the special protection of the State and must not be considered as a commodity. (b) Every worker must have the opportunity for a decent existence and the right to fair working conditions. (c) Intellectual, as well as technical and manual labor, must enjoy the guarantees established in labor laws, with the distinctions arising from the application of the law under the different circumstances. (d) There should be equal compensation for equal work, regardless of the sex, race, creed or nationality of the worker. (e) The rights established in favor of workers may not be renounced, and the laws that recognize such rights are binding on and benefit all the inhabitants of the territory, whether nationals or aliens."

Every worker "has the right to engage in his occupation and to devote himself to whatever activity suits him. He is likewise free to change employment," mandates article 3. Article 4 addresses vocational and technical training, while article 5 proclaims that workers "have the right to share in the equitable distribution of the national well-being, by obtaining the necessary food, clothing, and housing at reasonable prices." The charter suggests that nations sponsor farms and restaurants as well as consumer and credit cooperatives, organizing institutions to finance them, and supply "low-cost, comfortable, hygienic housing for laborers, salaried employees and rural workers."

Articles 6 through 25 deal with individual labor contracts, collective labor contracts and agreements, wages, work periods, rest and vacations, child labor, women's work, tenure, apprentice contracts, work at home, domestic work, merchant marine and aviation service, public employees, and intellectual workers.

"Workers and employers, without distinction as to sex, race, creed or political ideas," states The Right of Association, article 26, "have the right freely to form associations for the protection of their respective interests, by forming trade associations or unions, which in turn may form federations among themselves." Articles 27 through 39, the last items of the charter, address the right to strike, social security and welfare, supervision of labor conditions, labor courts, conciliation and arbitration of labor problems, and rural work.

Derechos Human Rights, P.O. Box 2516, El Cerrito, Calif. 94530-5516. (510-483-4005. 🖨 603-372-9710. 🖳 hr@derechos.org. 🖳 www.derechos.org.

Inter-American Institute of Human Rights, A.P. 10.081-1000, San José, Costa Rica. (506-234-0404. 🖨 506-234-0955. 🖳 instituto@iidh.ed.cr. 🖳 www.iidh.ed.cr.

Organization of American States, 17th Street and Constitution Avenue, N.W., Washington, D.C. 20006. (202-458-3000. 🖨 202-458-3967. 🖳 pi@oas.org. 🖳 www.oas.org.

Inter-American Commission of Women

The Fifth International Conference of American States, which met in Santiago, Chile, in 1923, adopted a resolution entitled On the Rights of Women and called on the Pan American Union, the predecessor of the Organization of American States (OAS), to investigate methods of securing equal civil and political rights for women. At the sixth such conference, which met in Havana, Cuba, in 1928, paid maternity leave was recommended and the Inter-American Commission of Women—the first intergovernmental agency established to ensure women's civil and political rights—was created. Today the commission's mission is to "promote and protect women's rights, and to support the member states [of the OAS] in their efforts to ensure full exercise of civil, political, economic, social and cultural rights that will make possible equal participation by women and men in all aspects of society, so that women and men will share, fully and equally, both the benefits of development and the responsibility for the future."

Originally the commission consisted of seven women appointed by the Pan American Union's governing board. Meeting at its seventh conference in Montevideo, Uruguay, in 1933, the commission was successful in gaining adoption of the first international instrument on women's rights: the Convention on the Nationality of Women, which allowed women to retain their own nationality when marrying a man of another nationality. Despite its success with this convention, the commission's draft treaty on equal civil and political rights was deemed "unwise" because of "deeply rooted customs" in the Latin American countries; four of them—Cuba, Ecuador, Paraguay, and Uruguay—nonetheless signed it. The commission continued its work, which resulted in the adoption in 1948 of the Inter-American Convention on the Granting of Political Rights to Women and its companion Convention on the Granting of Civil Rights to Women.

An organic statute for governing the commission was adopted in 1976 and amended in 1986. Under a 1978 agreement with the OAS, it became a specialized organization within the OAS. The commission's basic functions include harmonizing the roles of men and women in family life, promoting laws to aid working mothers, increasing the participation of women in development programs, and promoting the education of women, with emphasis on women workers in deprived areas. Other activities include acting as an advisory body for the OAS, establishing ties to other public and private women's organizations, and providing status reports on women to the governments of the American countries and the OAS General Assembly.

The commission is now made up of thirty-four permanent delegates, all of them women, appointed by each member government of the OAS. It meets every two years and addresses such issues as violence against women; removal of barriers to women's full and equal participation in civic, economic, social, cultural, and political activities; and adoption or adaptation of national laws to eliminate all forms of discrimination against women. One of its most important recent activities was preparation of the Inter-American Convention on the Prevention, Punishment and Eradication of Violence against Women (1994).

Derechos Human Rights, P.O. Box 2516, El Cerrito, Calif. 94530-5516. (510-483-4005. 🖷 603-372-9710. 🖳 hr@derechos.org. 🖳 www.derechos.org.

Inter-American Commission of Women, 1889 F Street, N.W., Washington, D.C. 20006. (202-458-6084. 🖷 202-458-6094. 🖳 cim@oas.org. 🖳 www.oas.org.

Inter-American Commission on Human Rights

The inter-American system of human rights began with the American Declaration of the Rights and Duties of Man (1948), which was adopted by an international conference of American nations and became the first general international human rights instrument. A decade later the Inter-American Commission on Human Rights was established by a resolution of the Fifth Meeting of the Consultation of Foreign Ministers in 1959. The commission held its first session in 1960, after the Organization of American States (OAS) adopted a statute in which the body was designated an autonomous entity of the OAS intended "to promote respect for human rights."

"[F]or the purpose of this Statute," declares article 2, "human rights are understood to be those set forth in the American Declaration of the Rights and Duties of Man." Under article 9, the commission was given authority to promote human rights, including the power to prepare studies and reports and "to make recommendations to the governments of the member states in general ... for the adoption of progressive measures in favor of human rights within the framework of their domestic legislation. ..." Based on this language, the commission began making country studies regarding the status of human rights. These studies involved on-site investigations and recommendations for an end to practices that violate human rights. At the same time the commission accepted petitions from individuals about specific human rights violations to aid in determining individual countries' compliance.

In 1965 the commission was specifically authorized by the Second Special Inter-American Conference to act on individual petitions and to charge OAS members with violations of certain human rights, including the rights to life, liberty, and personal security; the right to equality before the law; freedom of religion and expression; freedom from arbitrary arrest; and the right to due process of law. This petition system derived its authority from the implied powers of the OAS charter (1948), as amended, rather than from any regional human rights document.

By 1970 the commission was conducting investigations in various countries of Latin America (with the nations' permission), hearing petitioners, meeting with government officials, and visiting jails. During the same year, the Protocol of Buenos Aires, which amended the OAS charter, made the commission a formal OAS agency "to promote the observance and protection of human rights and to serve as a consultative organ of the [OAS] in these matters." The amendments also left the commission's "structure, competence and procedures" to be determined by a new American Convention on Human Rights adopted in 1969. Until the new convention entered into force, the current commission was to "keep vigilance over the observance" of human rights.

When the American Convention on Human Rights finally became effective in 1978, it provided for both the commission's existing functions and new responsibility for accepting petitions alleging individual abuses in countries party to the convention—two dozen nations including Argentina, Chile, Colombia, Guatemala, Haiti, Mexico, Nicaragua, Paraguay, Peru, Uruguay, and Venezuela. Article 12 of the commission's new statute, adopted by the OAS General Assembly in 1979, states that "human rights are understood to be: (a) The rights set forth in the American Convention on Human Rights, in relation to the States Parties thereto; (b) The rights set forth in the American Declaration of the Rights and Duties of Man, in relation to the other [OAS] Member States." Seven commission members are elected in their personal capacities for four-year terms by the OAS General Assembly. Membership is not full time, but there is a small permanent staff.

The commission's work consists of examining individual petitions and interstate communications, or complaints, about human rights violations; observing and publishing reports on member countries' human rights' records; making visits to the member countries; promoting public awareness of human rights; recommending measures to further human rights; requesting the adoption of specific precautionary measures in urgent cases; submitting cases to the Inter-American Court of Human Rights; requesting from the court advisory opinions regarding interpretations of the American Convention; and organizing conferences. Since its inception the commission has considered more than twelve thousand cases, and its workload currently includes more than eight hundred cases.

While petitions can be filed by any person or group and some nongovernmental organizations, to be admissible, among other things, local remedies must have been exhausted and the complaint must state a *prima facie* case under the American Convention and not be "manifestly groundless or obviously out of order." The commission then investigates a complaint, holding hearings if necessary. A friendly settlement must be explored, but if that fails the commission transmits its recommendations to the nation concerned, which has three months to comply or respond. During this period, the commission may refer the matter to the Inter-American Court of Human Rights. Otherwise, if a case is not settled, the commission must make its recommendation, if any, "and prescribe a period within which the state is to take the measures [necessary] to remedy the situation examined." Finally, the commission may include its recommendations and findings in its annual report to the OAS General Assembly, thereby placing the matter on the agenda so that a country's failure to remedy human rights violations can be discussed by the full assembly.

Derechos Human Rights, P.O. Box 2516, El Cerrito, Calif. 94530-5516. (510-483-4005. ☏ 603-372-9710. ✉ hr@derechos.org. ☐ www.derechos.org.

Inter-American Commission on Human Rights, 1889 F Street, N.W., Washington, D.C. 20006. (202-458-6002. ☏ 202-458-3992. ✉ cidhoea@oas.org. ☐ cidh.oas.org.

Davidson, Scott. *The Inter-American Human Rights System.* Aldershot, Hants, England: Dartmouth, 1997.

American Convention on Human Rights; American Declaration of the Rights and Duties of Man; Inter-American Court of Human Rights; Regional Human Rights Systems

Inter-American Convention on the Granting of Civil Rights to Women

Although the Charter of the United Nations (1945) proclaimed the principle of equality for women and men and the Universal Declaration of Human Rights (1948) asserted that all persons have basic civil and political rights, including universal and equal suffrage, not until 1966 did the UN General Assembly adopt an international human rights instrument—the International Covenant on Civil and Political Rights—guaranteeing civil and political rights for all people around the world.

Before this important agreement was adopted, and two years before the European Convention for the Protection of Human Rights and Fundamental Freedoms (1950) guaranteed basic rights and freedoms for "everyone" in the participating European countries, the Inter-American Commission of Women drafted an Inter-American Convention on the Granting of Civil Rights to Women. This became the first regional document underscoring women's right to the same civil rights enjoyed by men. It was adopted by the Ninth International Conference of American States on May 2, 1948, along with the Inter-American Convention on the Granting of Political Rights to Women, American Declaration of the Rights and Duties of Man, and Inter-American Charter of Social Guarantees. The convention entered into force on April 22, 1949.

The use of the term *granting* to guarantee women's rights may seem condescending today, but the intention to acknowledge the equality of women and men with respect to civil rights was an important step at the time. More than a half century later, traditions in many of the countries of the Americas, however, still effectively preclude many women from being able to fully enjoy the civil rights to which they are entitled.

The Inter-American Convention on the Granting of Civil Rights to Women begins by observing that "the majority of the American Republics, inspired by lofty principles of justice, have granted civil rights to women," adding that "it has been a constant aspiration of the American Community of nations to equalize the status of men and women in the enjoyment and exercise of civil rights." The document also takes note of a resolution passed by the previous International Conference of American States declaring that "women have the right to the enjoyment of equality as to civil status." The preamble concludes by stating that "long before the women of America demanded their rights they were able to carry out nobly all their responsibilities side by side with men" and recalling that "the principle of equality of human rights for men and women is contained in the Charter of the United Nations."

Under article 1, the convention provides simply that "the American States agree to grant to women the same civil rights that men enjoy."

The second of the document's two articles, article 2, sets out procedural details, indicating that the governments represented are to ratify the convention "in accordance with their respective constitutional procedures." It also provides that the "instruments of ratification shall be deposited with the General Secretariat of the Organization of American States, which shall notify the signatory Governments of the said deposit. Such notification shall serve as an exchange of ratifications."

Inter-American Commission on Human Rights, 1889 F Street, N.W., Washington, D.C. 20006. (202-458-6002. 202-458-3992. cidhoea@oas.org. cidh.oas.org.

Organization of American States, 17th Street and Constitution Avenue, N.W., Washington, D.C. 20006. (202-458-3000. 202-458-3967. pi@oas.org. www.oas.org.

American Declaration of the Rights and Duties of Man; Civil Rights; Inter-American Charter of Social Guarantees; Inter-American Commission of Women; Inter-American Commission on Human Rights; Inter-American Convention on the Granting of Political Rights to Women; Inter-American Convention on the Prevention, Punishment and Eradication of Violence against Women; International Covenant on Civil and Political Rights; Sex Discrimination; Women

Inter-American Convention on the Granting of Political Rights to Women

Two decades after its creation in 1928, the Inter-American Commission of Women prepared a draft of a regional agreement guaranteeing women civil and political equality with men. During the Ninth International Conference of American States in 1948, at which this document was presented, the proposed convention was divided into two agreements, one representing women's civil rights and the other their political rights.

The Inter-American Convention on the Granting of Political Rights to Women, like its sister Convention on the Granting of Civil Rights to Women, was adopted on May 2, 1948, and entered into force on April 22, 1949, making the pair the first regional documents to declare the equality of women and men.

The Inter-American Convention on the Granting of Political Rights to Women begins by stating that "the majority of the American Republics, inspired by lofty principles of justice, have granted political rights to women," adding that "it has been a constant aspiration of the American community of nations to equalize the status of men and women in the enjoyment and exercise of political rights." The document also takes note of a resolution passed by the previous International Conference of American States declaring that "women have the right to political treatment on the basis of equality with men." Like its sister civil convention, the document also asserts that "long before the women of America demanded their rights they were able to carry out nobly all their responsibilities side by side with men." It similarly concludes by observing that "the principle of equality of human rights for men and women is contained in the Charter of the United Nations [1945]."

Article 1 states briefly: "The High Contracting Parties agree that the right to vote and to be elected to national office shall not be denied or abridged by reason of sex." Article 2, the second of the convention's two articles, indicates that the agreement is to be ratified by the participating nations according to their individual constitutional procedures and that copies of the ratified documents are to be deposited with the Organization of American States.

Inter-American Commission on Human Rights, 1889 F Street, N.W., Washington, D.C. 20006. (202-458-6002. 202-458-3992. cidhoea@oas.org. cidh.oas.org.

Organization of American States, 17th Street and Constitution Avenue, N.W., Washington, D.C. 20006. (202-458-3000. 202-458-3967. pi@oas.org. www.oas.org.

American Declaration of the Rights and Duties of Man; Inter-American Charter of Social Guarantees; Inter-American Commission of Women; Inter-American Commission on Human Rights; Inter-American Convention on the Granting of Civil Rights to Women; Inter-American Convention on the Prevention, Punishment and Eradication of Violence against Women; International Covenant on Civil and Political Rights; Political Rights; Sex Discrimination; Women

Inter-American Convention on the Prevention, Punishment and Eradication of Violence against Women

The Inter-American Convention on the Prevention, Punishment and Eradication of Violence against Women is also known as the Convention of Belém do Pará, because it was adopted by representatives of the Organization of American States in Belém do Pará, Brazil, on June 9, 1994. The Inter-American Commission of Women played a key role in the development of this document, which became effective on March 5, 1995, following ratification by two nations.

The convention grew out of the Latin American women's rights movement and reflects increased international concern with violence against women in various settings, including during armed conflicts and in family disputes. Wife beating is one of the most common forms of violence against women. The Center for Health and Gender Equity recently found that a high percentage of adult women in Latin America reported that they had been physically assaulted by their husbands or intimate partners: 28 percent in Nicaragua (17 percent of whom reported the assaults to police), 27 percent in Mexico, 19 percent in Colombia, and 10 percent in Paraguay.

Like the Declaration on the Elimination of Violence against Women (1993), this regional convention affirms that "violence against women constitutes a violation of their human rights and fundamental freedoms, and impairs or nullifies the observance, enjoyment and exercise of such rights and freedoms." Its preamble goes on to state that such violence "is an offense against human dignity and a manifestation of the historically unequal power relations between women and men." It concludes that "the elimination of violence against women is essential for their individual and social development and their full and equal participation in all walks of life."

"For the purposes of this Convention," states chapter I, Definition and Scope of Application, article I, "violence against women shall be understood as any act or conduct, based on gender, which causes death or physical, sexual or psychological harm or suffering to women, whether in the public or the private sphere." According to article 2, "Violence against women shall be understood to include physical, sexual and psychological violence: a. that occurs within the family or domestic unit or within any other interpersonal relationship, whether or not the perpetrator shares or has shared the same residence with the woman, including, among others, rape, battery and sexual abuse; b. that occurs in the community and is perpetrated by any person, including, among others, rape, sexual abuse, torture, trafficking in persons, forced prostitution, kidnapping and sexual harassment in the workplace, as well as in educational institutions, health facilities or any other place; and c. that is perpetuated or condoned by the state or its agents regardless of where it occurs."

Pursuant to chapter II, Rights Protected, article 3, "Every woman has the right to be free from violence in both the public and private spheres." Article 4 guarantees to each woman the right to have her life and physical, mental, and moral integrity respected; personal liberty and security; freedom from torture; and respect for the inherent dignity of her person and protection for her family. Other rights guaranteed under article 4 include the rights to equal protection before the law and of the law; to prompt recourse to a competent court for protection against abuses; to associate freely with others; to profess her religion and beliefs within the law; to have equal access to the public service of her country and to take part in the conduct of public affairs, "including decision making."

Article 5 guarantees "civil, political, economic, social and cultural rights," while article 6 provides that women have a right "to be free from all forms of discrimination; and . . . to be valued and educated free of stereotyped patterns of behavior and social and cultural practices based on concepts of inferiority or subordination."

Nations that ratify the convention are called on, under chapter III, Duties of States, article 7, to, among other things, "condemn all forms of violence against women . . . , refrain from engaging in any act or practice of violence against women . . . , [and] apply due diligence to prevent, investigate and impose penalties for violence against women." They are also required to use domestic legislation and other legal measures to achieve the convention's aims and to "establish fair and effective legal procedures for women who have been subjected to violence" as well as "the necessary legal and administrative mechanisms to ensure that women subjected to violence have effective access to restitution, reparations or other just and effective remedies."

Article 8 requires the states parties to "undertake progressively specific measures" to promote awareness and observance of the right of women to be free from violence, modify social and cultural patterns of conduct of men and women that legitimize or exacerbate violence against women, and take other measures including providing specialized services for women who have been subjected to violence, encouraging the development of media guidelines to enhance respect for women, ensuring the gathering of relevant statistics concerning violence against women, and fostering international cooperation.

Under Chapter IV, Inter-American Mechanisms of Protection, states parties are asked to report to the Inter-American Commission of Women on measures taken as well as on "difficulties they observe in applying those measures, and the factors that contribute to violence against women." Both the relevant nations and the women's commission are authorized to seek advisory opinions on the convention from the Inter-American Court of Human Rights. Most important, the convention encourages individuals, groups, and nongovernmental organizations to "lodge petitions" with the Inter-American Commission on Human Rights alleging violations of rights specified in article 7 of the document.

Organization of American States, 17th Street and Constitution Avenue, N.W., Washington, D.C. 20006. (202-458-3000. 202-458-3967. pi@oas.org. www.oas.org.

Convention on the Elimination of All Forms of Discrimination against Women; Declaration on the Elimination of Discrimination against Women; Declaration on the Elimination of Violence against Women; Declaration on the Protection of Women and Children in Emergency and Armed Conflict; Domestic Violence; Inter-American Commission of Women; Inter-American Commission on Human Rights; Inter-American Court of Human Rights; Sex Discrimination; Women

Inter-American Convention to Prevent and Punish Torture

"No one shall be subjected to torture or to cruel, inhuman or degrading punishment," states the Universal Declaration of Human Rights (1948). As an instrument of the state, whether used against innocent people or those guilty of crimes, torture reflects a failure to observe human rights in general as well as the specific rights to dignity and safety and security.

In the 1970s and 1980s the UN General Assembly adopted several instruments on the subject of torture, including the Declaration on the Protection of All Persons from Being Subjected to Torture and Other Cruel, Inhuman or Degrading Treatment or Punishment (1975) and the Convention against Torture and Other Cruel, Inhuman or Degrading Treatment or Punishment (1984). A year later, on December 9, 1985, in the wake of a number of gross violations of human rights in South American countries such as Argentina and Chile, the Organization of American States (OAS) adopted the Inter-American Convention to Prevent and Punish Torture, which entered into force on February 28, 1987.

The convention opens by recalling "the provision of the American Convention on Human Rights [1969] that no one shall be subjected to torture or to cruel, inhuman, or degrading punishment or treatment" and reaffirming "that all acts of torture or any other cruel, inhuman or degrading treatment or punishment constitute an offense against human dignity. . . ."

"The States Parties shall prevent and punish torture in accordance with the terms of this Convention," proclaims article 1. Torture is defined in article 2 as "any act intentionally performed whereby physical or mental pain or suffering is inflicted on a person for purposes of criminal investigation, as a means of intimidation, as personal punishment, as a preventive measure, as a penalty, or for any other purpose. Torture shall also be understood to be the use of methods upon a person intended to obliterate the personality of the victim or to diminish his physical or mental capacities, even if they do not cause physical pain or mental anguish. The concept of torture shall not include physical or mental pain or suffering that is inherent in or solely the consequence of lawful measures, provided that they do not include the performance of acts or use of the methods referred to in this article."

According to article 3, "The following shall be guilty of the crime of torture: (a) A public servant or employee who acting in that capacity orders, instigates or induces the use of torture, or who directly commits it or who, being able to prevent it, fails to do so. (b) A person who at the instigation of a public servant or employee mentioned in subparagraph (a) orders, instigates or induces the use of torture, directly commits it or is an accomplice thereto."

Article 4 bars the excuse of "having acted under the orders of a superior," while article 5 prohibits derogation from the convention's provisions even in the case of war or emergency or because of "the dangerous character of the detainee or prisoner, [or] the lack of security of the prison...." Article 6 mandates that the states party to the convention "shall take effective measures to prevent and punish torture within their jurisdiction" and "shall ensure that all acts of torture and attempts to commit torture are offenses under their criminal law and shall make such acts punishable by severe penalties that take into account their serious nature. [They] likewise shall take effective measures to prevent and punish other cruel, inhuman, or degrading treatment or punishment within their jurisdiction."

Articles 7 through 9, respectively, emphasize "training of police officers and other public officials responsible for the custody of persons"; require that "any person making an accusation of having been subjected to torture within [a state party's jurisdiction] shall have the right to an impartial examination of his case"; and direct that provisions for compensation to victims of torture be incorporated into national laws. According to article 10, statements obtained by torture are not admissible as evidence in a legal proceeding, "except in a legal action taken against a person or persons accused of having elicited it through acts of torture...." Article 11 mandates that persons accused of torture be extradited, if necessary, to be brought to justice.

Under article 17, states parties "undertake to inform the Inter-American Commission on Human Rights of any legislative, judicial, administrative, or other measures they adopt in application of this Convention."

Derechos Human Rights, P.O. Box 2516, El Cerrito, Calif. 94530-5516. (510-483-4005. 🖷 603-372-9710. 🖳 hr@derechos.org. 🖳 www.derechos.org.

Organization of American States, 17th Street and Constitution Avenue, N.W., Washington, D.C. 20006. (202-458-3000. 🖷 202-458-3967. 🖳 pi@oas.org. 🖳 www.oas.org.

American Convention on Human Rights; Beccaria, Cesare; Convention against Torture and Other Cruel, Inhuman or Degrading Treatment or Punishment; Declaration on the Protection of All Persons from Being Subjected to Torture and Other Cruel, Inhuman or Degrading Treatment or Punishment; European Convention for the Prevention of Torture and Inhuman or Degrading Treatment or Punishment; Inter-American Commission on Human Rights; Punishment; Torture; Victims

Inter-American Court of Human Rights

Created by the American Convention on Human Rights, which was opened for signature in 1969 and entered into force in 1978, the Inter-American Court of Human Rights is an autonomous judicial institution and the principal judicial body for promoting and enforcing human rights in Latin America. In addition to its responsibilities under the convention, the court has certain functions relating to the Charter of the Organization of American States (OAS) (1948) and other human rights instruments in the Americas.

Two types of jurisdiction are authorized: contentious and advisory. Contentious cases can be brought before the court either by parties to the convention or by the Inter-American Commission on Human Rights, which may submit a case on behalf of an individual after first ruling on the matter. All OAS agencies as well as the commission may request advisory opinions from the court. Most of the court's work so far has consisted of advisory opinions, such as a recent finding that Mexico's denial of information on consular assistance to a foreign national in custody would make imposition of the death penalty an arbitrary violation of human rights under instruments including the American Convention. Ruling in an actual case, the court found that Peru had not exercised due process of law in prosecuting several Chilean citizens and ordered that relatives be reimbursed for legal fees.

All judgments of the court are final and may not be appealed. While the rulings in contentious cases are binding, if a nation does not act on the decision, the court's only recourse is to the OAS, where the matter may brought up before the General Assembly and the state party declared to be in violation of the convention. By definition, advisory opinions are not binding, although the court's reasoning and public knowledge of the opinion may lend some force of persuasion.

The court consists of seven judges from the nations that constitute the OAS, each of whom must be from a different country. So-called titular judges (as opposed to ad hoc and interim jurists) are elected by secret ballot for one or two terms of six years, under the supervision of the OAS General Assembly, by an absolute majority of the states party to the convention. According to the convention, article 55, if two nations are involved in a case before the court and one of the titular judges is from one of the countries, the other nation may appoint an ad hoc judge. Interim judges may also be appointed as necessary to maintain a quorum of five judges or to replace a judge disqualified from a case. The judges serve on a part-time basis and receive no salary but are provided an honorarium and expenses, along with certain privileges and immunities.

A president and vice president, a permanent commission, and a secretariat carry out the court's work. The president serves full time and, like the vice president, is elected by the titular members of the court for a two-year term and has a number of specific duties and powers. The president represents the court, presides over and determines the agenda for meetings, rules on points of order (unless a judge requests a determination by majority vote), directs and promotes the court's work, presents regular reports on the conduct of the office, and exercises other duties conferred by the court's statute or rules. The vice president acts in the absence of the president or if he or she is disqualified from participating in a matter. The president, vice president, and a third judge make up the permanent commission to assist and advise the president. The chief administrative officer and head of the secretariat is the chief clerk, who is appointed by the court for a renewable five-year term; he or she may be removed by the court.

Although the court is dependent on the nations at fault to implement its decisions, it has nevertheless begun the development of regional case law on human rights in the Americas that can provide a basis for national leaders, organizations, and citizens to promote improved human rights protections in this area of the world.

Derechos Human Rights, P.O. Box 2516, El Cerrito, Calif. 94530-5516. (510-483-4005. ⊞ 603-372-9710. ▣ hr@derechos.org. ▣ www.derechos.org.

Inter-American Court of Human Rights, P.O. Box 6906-1000, San José, Costa Rica. (506-234-0581. ⊞ 506-234-0584. ▣ corteidh@sol.racsa.co.cr. ▣ corteidh-oea.nu.or.cr.

American Convention on Human Rights; American Declaration of the Rights and Duties of Man; Inter-American Commission on Human Rights; Regional Human Rights Systems

International Bill
of Human Rights

The International Bill of Human Rights is the collective term for the Universal Declaration of Human Rights (1948), International Covenant on Civil and Political Rights (1966), including its two optional protocols adopted in 1966 and 1989, and International Covenant on Economic, Social and Cultural Rights (1966). This trio was formally referred to as the International Bill of Human Rights in the Limburg Principles on the Implementation of the International Covenant on Economic, Social and Cultural Rights (1986).

The notion of creating an international bill of rights after World War II was inspired by the first bill of rights, drafted by George Mason for the Virginia constitution (1776), as well as by France's Declaration of the Rights of Man and of the Citizen (1789) and the U.S. Bill of Rights (1791). Inspiration also came from President Franklin Roosevelt's "four freedoms"—freedom of speech and worship and freedom from want and fear—which were included in the text of the Atlantic Charter (1941), a precursor of the United Nations. British Prime Minister Winston Churchill also hoped that the war would end "with the enthronement of human rights."

The Charter of the United Nations (1945) called for "promoting and encouraging respect for human rights and for fundamental freedoms for all without distinction as to race, sex, language or religion." During the San Francisco conference at which the charter was drafted, a proposal was made that a Declaration on the Essential Rights of Man also be drawn up; however, time constraints made this impossible. The idea nonetheless took root that the charter itself implied that an international bill of human rights would be promulgated by the UN.

At its first session in 1946, the UN General Assembly considered a draft Declaration on Fundamental Human Rights and Freedoms and sent it to its human rights agency, the Economic and Social Council (ECOSOC), with a request that it be forwarded to ECOSOC's Commission on Human Rights for consideration "in the preparation of an international bill of rights." The next year the commission decided to apply the concept of an international bill of human rights to several documents being prepared by working groups under its direction, among them a declaration of human rights, a covenant, and an implementing document.

In 1948 the commission produced the Universal Declaration of Human Rights, which, although not binding, was the first comprehensive statement of human rights ever proclaimed on a global level. On the same day that it was adopted by the General Assembly, the UN requested that the commission, as a matter of priority, draft a covenant on human rights and measures for implementing it. It would be eighteen years, however, before these documents were actually adopted.

Although the General Assembly in 1950 resolved that "the enjoyment of civic and political freedoms and of economic, social and cultural rights are interconnected and interdependent," it later decided to draft two separate covenants for these rights. The International Covenant on Civil and Political Rights, together with a protocol that provided for its implementation, and the International Covenant on Economic, Social and Cultural Rights were both adopted by the General Assembly on December 16, 1966. A second protocol to the civil covenant urging abolition of the death penalty was adopted on December 15, 1989.

Although the Universal Declaration of Human Rights was and still is a significant statement, the two covenants that followed added teeth to the international community's lofty goals. By providing that nations had to ratify the covenants and implement their provisions through domestic laws and policies, as well as through bodies such as the Human Rights Committee set up under the civil and political covenant, these instruments made great strides in the enforcement of human rights around the world. The International Bill of Human Rights stands today as a beacon of hope for all victims of human rights abuses. While the provisions of the component documents may not be adequately observed in many countries, they nevertheless represent milestones in how far the ideals of human rights have come and set out the goals yet to be reached.

United Nations High Commissioner for Human Rights, 8–14 avenue de la Paix, 1211 Geneva 10, Switzerland. ℭ 41-22-917-9000. 🖷 41-22-917-9016. 🖳 webadmin.unhchr@unog.ch. 🖳 www.unhchr.ch.

The International Bill of Human Rights. Fact Sheet no. 2, rev. 1. Geneva: Center for Human Rights, 1996.

Bills of Rights; Charter of the United Nations; Commission on Human Rights; Economic and Social Council (ECOSOC); Human Rights Committee; International Covenant on Civil and Political Rights; International Covenant on Civil and Political Rights, First Optional Protocol; International Covenant on Civil and Political Rights, Second Optional Protocol, Aiming at the Abolition of the Death Penalty; International Covenant on Economic, Social and Cultural Rights; Limburg Principles on the Implementation of the International Covenant on Economic, Social and Cultural Rights; United Nations; Universal Declaration of Human Rights

International Commission of Jurists

The International Commission of Jurists, established in Berlin in 1952, is one of the oldest international non-governmental organizations dedicated to human rights. It consists of a maximum of forty-five eminent jurists dedicated to the rule of law and representing the world's various legal systems and traditions. Other individuals and organizations with similar goals may become associates of the commission, which also grants honorary memberships.

In 1978, in response to increasing attacks on judges and lawyers, it created the Center for the Independence of Judges and Lawyers to promote and protect the independence of the judiciary and the legal profession.

The commission operates as a human rights watch group, conducting research, holding seminars and international conferences of jurists, undertaking investigative missions, and publishing reports on violations of legal and human rights. It is particularly alert to the abuse of emergency regulations, arrests of opposition leaders, harassment of judges and lawyers, and attempts to destroy democracy movements. The commission also appeals to military regimes to restore civilian control of government, criticizes governments' failure to implement constitutional provisions, and promotes such basic rights as freedom of the press, movement, and religion; social and economic rights; trade union rights; and judicial independence. Technical assistance in law and human rights is provided in more than thirty countries.

All programs are based on international human rights standards, including the Basic Principles on the Independence of the Judiciary (1985) and Basic Principles on the Role of Lawyers (1990), as well as the African Charter on Human and Peoples' Rights (1981) and the European Convention for the Prevention of Torture and Inhuman or Degrading Treatment or Punishment (1987). The commission has official consultative status with the United Nations, Council of Europe, and Organization of African Unity. National sections and affiliated organizations exist on all five continents.

A secretary-general is aided by legal officers and administrative personnel from the five continents. Commission members meet triennially, at which time they elect an executive committee that convenes twice a year. The first permanent headquarters was in The Hague, but in 1959 the commission was moved to Geneva. In addition to other awards, it received the European Human Rights Prize from the Council of Europe in 1980 and the United Nations Award for Human Rights in 1993.

Center for the Independence of Judges and Lawyers, avenue de Châtelaine 81A, P.O. Box 216, 1219 Châtelaine/Geneva, Switzerland. ℭ 41-22-979-3800. 🖷 41-22-979-3801. 🖳 info@icj.org. 🖳 www.icj.org.

International Commission of Jurists, 26 chemin de Joinville, P.O. Box 160, 1216 Geneva, Switzerland. ℭ 41-22-788-4747. 🖷 41-22-788-4880. 🖳 info@icj.org. 🖳 www.icj.org.

African Charter on Human and Peoples' Rights; Basic Principles on the Role of Lawyers; European Convention for the Prevention of Torture and Inhuman or Degrading Treatment or Punishment; Judicial Independence; Lawyers Committee for Human Rights

International Convention on the Elimination of All Forms of Racial Discrimination

The concept that all individuals, regardless of race or color, are equal members of the human family is a fundamental principle of human rights. "We hold these Truths to be self-evident," the U.S. Declaration of Independence boldly declared in 1776, "that all Men are created equal, that they are endowed by their Creator with certain unalienable Rights, that among these are Life, Liberty, and the Pursuit of Happiness." In 1776, however, slavery—based on rationalizations including racial inferiority—was the rule rather than the exception throughout the world, even in the American colonies that were seeking freedom from Great Britain. Up to and including the period of World War II, racism had been an avowed basis for invading territories and abusing their inhabitants' rights. Even today, more than a half century after the UN General Assembly adopted the Universal Declaration of Human Rights (1948), racism still produces acts of cruelty and the abrogation of human rights around the world.

Many nations have declared in their constitutions the same right to equality proclaimed in the Declaration of Independence, the Universal Declaration of Human Rights, and a multitude of other human rights documents. The UN General Assembly in 1948 adopted the Convention on the Prevention and Punishment of Genocide, which defines *genocide* as "acts committed with the intent to destroy, in whole or in part, a . . . racial . . . group," and it issued a Declaration on the Elimination of All Forms of Racial Discrimination in 1963, but it did not take up a more binding treaty on the subject until December 21, 1965. Its International Convention on the Elimination of All Forms of Racial Discrimination entered into force on January 2, 1969.

The document begins by recalling that the Charter of the United Nations (1945) is based on the principles of dignity and equality and that the Universal Declaration of Human Rights, adopted three years later, "proclaims that all human beings are born free and equal in dignity and rights and that everyone is entitled to all the rights and freedoms set out therein, without distinction of any kind, in particular as to race, color or national origin." It goes on to note that "the United Nations has condemned colonialism and all practices of segregation and discrimination associated therewith" and points out that the 1963 declaration "solemnly affirms the necessity of speedily eliminating racial discrimination throughout the world in all its forms and manifestations. . . ."

"[A]ny doctrine of superiority based on racial differentiation," the convention adds, "is scientifically false, morally condemnable, socially unjust and dangerous. . . ." Racial barriers are "repugnant to the ideals of any human society," it states, noting its alarm at "manifestations of racial dis-

crimination still in evidence in some areas of the world and [at] governmental policies based on racial superiority or hatred, such as policies of *apartheid*, segregation or separation." The preamble concludes by resolving "to adopt all necessary measures for speedily eliminating racial discrimination in all its forms and manifestations, and to prevent and combat racist doctrines and practices in order to promote understanding between races and to build an international community free from all forms of racial segregation and racial discrimination."

Part I, article 1, defines *racial discrimination* as "any distinction, exclusion, restriction or preference based on race, color, descent, or national or ethnic origin which has the purpose or effect of nullifying or impairing the recognition, enjoyment or exercise, on an equal footing, of human rights and fundamental freedoms in the political, economic, social, cultural or any other field of public life." Article 1 adds that the convention is not applicable to "distinctions, exclusions, restrictions or preferences" made by a nation between citizens and noncitizens.

According to article 2: "1. States Parties condemn racial discrimination and undertake to pursue by all appropriate means and without delay a policy of eliminating racial discrimination in all its forms and promoting understanding among all races. . . . 2. States Parties shall, when the circumstances so warrant, take, in the social, economic, cultural and other fields, special and concrete measures to ensure the adequate development and protection of certain racial groups or individuals belonging to them, for the purpose of guaranteeing them full and equal enjoyment of human rights and fundamental freedoms. These measures shall in no case entail as a consequence the maintenance of unequal or separate rights for different racial groups after the objectives for which they were taken have been achieved."

Articles 3 and 4, respectively, announce that the states parties "particularly condemn racial segregation and *apartheid* and undertake to prevent, prohibit and eradicate all practices of this nature in territories under their jurisdiction" and "condemn all propaganda and all organizations which are based on ideas or theories of superiority of one race or group of persons of one color or ethnic origin, or which attempt to justify or promote racial hatred and discrimination in any form. . . ." Among activities to be deemed illegal are dissemination of ideas based on racial superiority or hatred, incitement to racial discrimination, acts of violence, and financing of racist groups.

Part II, article 8, establishes a Committee on the Elimination of Racial Discrimination, whose eighteen members are elected for four-year terms by secret ballot by the states parties from among persons they nominate. Article 9 requires nations that have signed the convention to submit to the UN secretary-general for the committee's consideration "a report on the legislative, judicial, administrative or other measures which they have adopted and which give effect to the provisions of this Convention. . . ." The committee reports annually to the General Assembly, through the secretary-general, on its activities and the national reports received.

Under article 11, the committee is authorized to receive complaints from one state party that another "is not giving effect to the provisions of this Convention.... The Committee shall then transmit the communication to the State Party concerned," which has three months in which to respond. If the committee cannot resolve the matter "to the satisfaction of both parties ... within six months after the receipt by the receiving State of the initial communication, either State shall have the right to refer the matter again to the Committee...." The committee may deal with the matter as before or "may call upon the States Parties concerned [for more] information." After all the information deemed necessary has been collected, the committee chair is to appoint an ad hoc conciliation commission, which, according to article 13, "shall prepare and submit to the Chairman of the Committee a report embodying its findings ... and containing such recommendations as it may think proper for the amicable solution of the dispute."

Under article 14, a state party "may at any time declare that it recognizes the competence of the Committee to receive and consider communications from individuals or groups of individuals within its jurisdiction claiming to be victims of a violation by that State Party of any of the rights set forth in this Convention." In handling such communications, the committee, after considering the matter, "shall forward its suggestions and recommendations, if any, to the State Party concerned and to the petitioner ... [and] shall include in its annual report a summary of such communications and, where appropriate, a summary of the explanations and statements of the States Parties concerned and of its own suggestions and recommendations."

Both article 15 and an Annex to the convention refer to the Declaration on the Granting of Independence to Colonial Countries and Peoples (1960), asking that the UN keep the committee informed of relevant information, petitions, and reports. Administrative aspects of the convention are addressed in part III.

United Nations High Commissioner for Human Rights, 8–14 avenue de la Paix, 1211 Geneva 10, Switzerland. (41-22-917-9000. 🖳 41-22-917-9016. 🖳 webadmin.hchr@unog.ch. 🖳 www.unhchr.ch.

☞

Apartheid; Civil Rights; Committee on the Elimination of Racial Discrimination; Declaration on Fundamental Principles Concerning the Contribution of the Mass Media to Strengthening Peace and International Understanding, to the Promotion of Human Rights and to Countering Racialism, Apartheid and Incitement to War; Declaration on the Elimination of All Forms of Racial Discrimination; Declaration on the Granting of Independence to Colonial Countries and Peoples; Equality; Genocide; King, Martin Luther, Jr.; Minorities; Race Discrimination; Self-Determination; Slavery; Slavery Convention

International Court of Justice (World Court)

The International Court of Justice, sometimes called the World Court, was established in 1946 as the primary UN instrument for the settlement of disputes. The court's role in adjudicating human rights issues is limited by the fact that it has no authority over individuals, only over nations that submit a particular matter to its jurisdiction. A supreme international court was proposed as long ago as the Middle Ages. Ad hoc arbitration of controversies beween or among sovereign nations in the nineteenth century led to the Convention for the Pacific Settlement of International Disputes (1899), which created the Permanent Court of Arbitration in The Hague. With the creation of the League of Nations after World War I, the Permanent Court of International Justice was set up in The Hague in 1922 to adjudicate purely legal disagreements among nations.

Two world wars and numerous other regional conflicts led many countries to conclude that the Permanent International Court of Justice had not played a significant role in maintaining peace. After World War II, however, the founders of the United Nations decided to reconstitute the court as the International Court of Justice and make it an integral part of the UN system. The court was created under the UN charter (1945), chapter XIV, and the statute governing the court is annexed to the charter. All UN member nations are parties to this statute, but any country that is not a UN member may also submit to its jurisdiction on conditions set by the Security Council and the General Assembly.

The court's fifteen judges are elected by the General Assembly and the Security Council from candidates nominated by national committees of experts on international law. In addition to the selection of judges who are recognized authorities in international law, the statute requires that "the main forms of civilization and ... the principal legal systems of the world" be represented on the court. Judges are elected for nine-year terms, three of which end every five years, and they may be reelected. The court elects its own president and vice president for three-year terms.

Much of the court's work has involved boundary disputes, determination of questions of the nationality of legal entities under international law, and interpretation of treaty provisions. Although the World Court has no direct jurisdiction over individual human rights cases, its decisions and advisory opinions have had an impact. Its ruling in *Barcelona Traction* (1970), for example, set important international law precedents for determining nationality and defining *erga omnes* rights—rights and duties of countries under international law regardless of treaty provisions or the lack thereof. The court's 1951 advisory opinion concerning the Convention on the Prevention and Punishment of the Crime of Genocide (1948) influenced this aspect of international law, specifically in the case of the trial of the

Nazi official Adolf Eichmann in 1960. Its 1962 opinion in *Certain Expenses of the United Nations* had an impact on the maintenance of international peace by security and peacekeeping forces. More recently, in the 1999 matter of the bombing by the North Atlantic Treaty Organization (NATO) to stem the Serbian leader Slobodan Milosovic's ethnic cleansing in Kosovo, the government of Yugoslavia asked the court to declare the attacks to be violations of the UN charter's prohibition against the use of force; the request was dismissed for lack of jurisdiction.

Other international and regional tribunals that deal more directly with human rights issues include the ad hoc international war crimes tribunals for the former territory of Yugoslavia and Rwanda, Inter-American Court of Human Rights, and European Court of Human Rights. In 1998 representatives from many countries met in Rome and began the process of setting up the International Criminal Court, which, when it becomes operational, will have international jurisdiction over a number of crimes involving gross violations of human rights.

International Court of Justice, Peace Palace, 2517 KJ The Hague, Netherlands. (31-070-302-23-23. 📠 31-070-364-99-28. 📧 information@icj-cij.org. 🖥 icj-cij.org.

Lowe, Vaughan, and Malgosia Fitzmaurice, eds. *Fifty Years of the International Court of Justice: Essays in Honour of Sir Robert Jennings.* New York: Cambridge University Press, 1996.

Rosenne, Shabtai. *The World Court: What It Is and How It Works.* The Hague: Martinus Nijhoff, Kluwer Law International, 1995.

Charter of the United Nations; Convention on the Prevention and Punishment of the Crime of Genocide; *Erga Omnes;* European Court of Human Rights; Genocide; Inter-American Court of Human Rights; International Criminal Court; Nationality; Rome Statute of the International Criminal Court; War Crimes

International Covenant on Civil and Political Rights

The International Covenant on Civil and Political Rights, like the International Covenant on Economic, Social and Cultural Rights—a companion adopted at the same time on December 16, 1966—was written to give legal effect to the principles set forth in the Universal Declaration of Human Rights (1948); having been adopted merely by resolution of the UN General Assembly, the declaration was not considered binding under international law. Today the three documents, together with two protocols to the civil and political covenant, constitute what is known as the International Bill of Human Rights.

On the same day in 1948 that the General Assembly adopted the Universal Declaration of Human Rights, it had requested the Commission on Human Rights to draft a covenant to implement the declaration. The Cold War hampered the efforts to extend human rights worldwide, but the commission persevered in its work. In 1950 the General Assembly declared that "the enjoyment of civil and political freedoms and of economic, social and cultural rights are interconnected and interdependent." After many debates ending in 1952, however, the commission was asked to draft two covenants on human rights, one to describe civil and political rights and the other economic, social, and cultural rights. Civil and political rights are sometimes referred to as first-generation rights, encompassing individual rights necessary to establish and maintain a democratic, constitutional government, whereas economic, social, and cultural rights are seen as second-generation rights.

Little progress was made on the covenants until the early 1960s, when the decolonization that had been taking place since the end of World War II began to have an impact around the world. Many newly independent nations that had emerged from former colonies were seeking normative human rights standards that the two proposed covenants could provide. The International Covenant on Civil and Political Rights, which finally entered into force on March 23, 1976, after the thirty-fifth nation agreed to its terms, addresses such rights as freedom of movement; equality before the law; the right to a fair trial and the presumption of innocence; freedom of thought, conscience, and religion; freedom of expression and opinion; the right of peaceful assembly; freedom of association; the right to participate in public affairs and elections; and protection of minority rights. The covenant prohibits arbitrary deprivation of life, torture and cruel or degrading treatment or punishment, slavery and forced labor, arbitrary arrest and detention, and arbitrary interference with privacy. War propaganda and the advocacy of racial or religious hatred are also proscribed.

The covenant creates the Human Rights Committee to receive reports from signatory nations on measures taken to implement its provisions and to consider communications from them regarding the failure of other countries to carry out their obligations under the document. One of two optional protocols to the covenant, entitled the First Optional Protocol and adopted at the same time as the covenant itself, provides a procedure for individuals to file complaints about violations of their rights under the covenant. The Second Optional Protocol, Aiming at the Abolition of the Death Penalty, was adopted by the General Assembly on December 15, 1989.

The preamble of the covenant observes that "in accordance with the principles proclaimed in the Charter of the

United Nations [1945], recognition of the inherent dignity and of the equal and inalienable rights of all members of the human family is the foundation of freedom, justice and peace in the world." It adds that "in accordance with the Universal Declaration of Human Rights, the ideal of free human beings enjoying civil and political freedom and freedom from fear and want can only be achieved if conditions are created whereby everyone may enjoy his civil and political rights, as well as his economic, social and cultural rights."

Part I, article 1, declares: "1. All peoples have the right of self-determination. By virtue of that right they freely determine their political status and freely pursue their economic, social and cultural development. 2. All peoples may, for their own ends, dispose of their natural wealth and resources.... In no case may a people be deprived of its own means of subsistence. 3. The States Parties to the present Covenant ... shall promote the realization of the right of self-determination...."

According to part II, article 2, the states parties to the covenant agree to ensure the enumerated rights "without distinction of any kind, such as race, color, sex, language, religion, political or other opinion, national or social origin, property, birth or other status." The nations must adopt "legislative or other measures as may be necessary to give effect to the rights recognized...." Article 2 also provides that each nation "undertakes: (a) To ensure that any person whose rights or freedoms as herein recognized are violated shall have an effective remedy, notwithstanding that the violation has been committed by persons acting in an official capacity; (b) To ensure that any person claiming such a remedy shall have his right thereto determined by competent judicial, administrative or legislative authorities, or by any other competent authority provided for by the legal system of the State, and to develop the possibilities of judicial remedy; (c) To ensure that the competent authorities shall enforce such remedies when granted."

Article 3 mandates equal civil and political rights for women and men. Article 4 addresses emergency situations and derogation of the rights in the covenant. No derogation is permitted from the guarantees of the right to life, to be recognized as a person before the law, and to freedom of thought, conscience, and religion, or with respect to the prohibitions against torture or cruel, inhumane, or degrading treatment or punishment; slavery or servitude; imprisonment for the "inability to fulfill a contractual obligation"; or ex post facto laws.

The list of rights to be protected and acts that are prohibited are contained in part III, articles 6 through 27. Protected rights include the right to life, although in the covenant the death penalty is permitted in some cases; liberty or treatment with humanity and dignity when such liberty is deprived in accordance with the law; freedom of movement and residence; equality before courts and tribunals, together with specific rights of those accused of crimes; and recognition everywhere as a person before the law. Other protected rights include freedom of thought, conscience, and religion; freedom of opinion and expression; the rights of peaceful assembly and association; the rights to marriage and a family; and the right to participate in the political process. Certain children's rights are recognized, as are equality before the law and ethnic, religious, and linguistic minority rights. Acts prohibited include cruel, inhumane, or degrading treatment or punishment; slavery and servitude; ex post facto laws; war propaganda; imprisonment for failure to fulfill a contractual obligation; "arbitrary or unlawful interference with ... privacy, family, home or correspondence"; and unlawful attacks on one's "honor and reputation."

Article 14 addresses legal rights. "All persons shall be equal before the courts and tribunals," it states. Those charged with a crime are "entitled to a fair and public hearing by a competent, independent and impartial tribunal established by law." Other rights extended to the accused include the presumption of innocence; the right to be fully informed of the charges; and the rights to an adequate defense, a speedy trial at which the accused is present, an opportunity to examine witnesses, the free assistance of an interpreter if necessary, and freedom from being compelled to testify against oneself. The covenant also prescribes that everyone is entitled to the right of appeal from a criminal conviction, to compensation in the event of a miscarriage of justice, to avoid being tried twice for the same offense (double jeopardy), and not to be found guilty of an offense that was not a crime at the time the act was committed (ex post facto or retroactive law).

Part IV establishes a Human Rights Committee, which has authority to receive reports from the states parties to the covenant regarding its implementation and to receive communications from them about the failure of other nations to implement or observe the rights guaranteed. The First Optional Protocol to the covenant provides a mechanism by which individuals can communicate with the committee concerning human rights violations.

"Nothing in the present Covenant," adds part V, article 47, "shall be interpreted as impairing the inherent right of all peoples to enjoy and utilize fully and freely their natural wealth and resources."

United Nations High Commissioner for Human Rights, 8–14 avenue de la Paix, 1211 Geneva 10, Switzerland. (41-22-917-9000. 🖷 41-22-917-9016. 🖳 webadmin.hchr@unog.ch. 🖳 www.unhchr.ch.

☞

Civil Rights; Commission on Human Rights; Human Rights Committee; International Bill of Human Rights; International Covenant on Civil and Political Rights, First Optional Protocol; International Covenant on Civil and Political Rights, Second Optional Protocol, Aiming at the Abolition of the Death Penalty; International Covenant on Economic, Social and Cultural Rights; Political Rights; Self-Determination

International Covenant on Civil and Political Rights, First Optional Protocol

A major step forward in providing remedies for human rights violations at the international level occurred when the First Optional Protocol to the International Covenant on Civil and Political Rights was adopted unanimously by the UN General Assembly on December 16, 1966. A protocol is an international legal instrument that amends or modifies an existing treaty. Protocols to human rights documents can add new rights, change rights, or set up an implementation mechanism. Actually a treaty itself, a protocol must be adopted and ratified before it is binding.

The Commission on Human Rights, created under the Charter of the United Nations (1945), had recognized from its inception that it lacked authority to deal with individual human rights complaints; not until 1967 was the commission allowed to investigate such communications. Under the First Optional Protocol to the 1966 covenant, however, nations could agree to have the Human Rights Committee, created by the covenant, investigate and take action on individual complaints based on the document's guarantees. The covenant itself authorizes the committee to receive complaints from signatory nations that other countries have failed to carry out their human rights obligations under the document. Although the protocol provides no real enforcement power for bringing violators of civil and political rights to justice, it does assert a measure of pressure on states parties to avoid international publicity that they violate the rights of citizens and fail to compensate the victims of proven abuses.

The protocol begins by stating that "in order further to achieve the purposes of the Covenant on Civil and Political Rights ... it would be appropriate to enable the Human Rights Committee ... to receive and consider, as provided in the present Protocol, communications from individuals claiming to be victims of violations of any of the rights set forth in the Covenant."

According to article 1, "A State Party to the Covenant that becomes a party to the present Protocol recognizes the competence of the Committee to receive and consider communications from individuals subject to its jurisdiction who claim to be victims of a violation by that State Party of any of the rights set forth in the Covenant. No communication shall be received by the Committee if it concerns a State Party to the Covenant which is not a party to the present Protocol."

Article 2 provides, however, that only individuals "who have exhausted all available domestic [national or local] remedies may submit a written communication to the Committee. . . ." Also inadmissible, under article 3, are "anonymous" communications or those "which [the committee] considers to be an abuse of the right of sub-

mission . . . or to be incompatible with the provisions of the Covenant."

Procedures prescribed in article 4 call for the committee to "bring any communications submitted . . . to the attention of the State Party . . . alleged to be violating any provision of the Covenant. Within six months, the receiving State shall submit to the Committee written explanations or statements clarifying the matter and the remedy, if any, that may have been taken by that State." Article 5 provides that after considering the state's response, the committee is to "forward its views to the State Party concerned and to the individual." According to article 6, the committee "shall include in its annual report under article 45 of the Covenant a summary of its activities under the present Protocol."

Article 7 declares that the protocol's provisions "shall in no way limit the right of petition granted . . . by the Charter of the United Nations and other international conventions and instruments under the United Nations and its specialized agencies" to colonial countries and peoples. Articles 8 and 9 address procedures for ratification of the protocol and call for it to enter into force three months after ten nations have agreed to it. Article 10 extends the protocol's authority to all jurisdictions [such as states or provinces] within federal states, while article 11 addresses amendments. Article 12 explains procedures for denouncing the protocol, providing, however, that such denunciation "shall be without prejudice to the continued application of the provisions of the . . . Protocol to any communication [received] before the effective date of denunciation."

United Nations High Commissioner for Human Rights, 8–14 avenue de la Paix, 1211 Geneva 10, Switzerland. (41-22-917-9000. 📠 41-22-917-9016. 🖥 webadmin.hchr@unog.ch. 🖥 www.unhchr.ch.

Commission on Human Rights; Complaints; Enforcement; Human Rights Committee; International Covenant on Civil and Political Rights; International Covenant on Economic, Social and Cultural Rights; Remedies; Violations

International Covenant on Civil and Political Rights, Second Optional Protocol

Revisiting the issue of the death penalty raised two decades earlier in the International Covenant on Civil and Political Rights (1966), a Second Optional Protocol, Aiming at the Abolition of the Death Penalty, came out much more strongly in favor of ending this form of punishment. The protocol, which was adopted by the UN General Assembly on December 15, 1989, and entered into force on July 11, 1991, asserts that "abolition of the death penalty contributes to enhancement of human dignity and progressive development of human rights." It goes on to cite both the Universal Declaration of Human Rights (1948) and the 1996 civil covenant's reference in article 6 suggesting that abolition of the death penalty is desirable. "All measures of abolition of the death penalty should be considered as progress in the enjoyment of the right to life," the protocol adds, urging the signatory nations "to undertake hereby an international commitment to abolish the death penalty."

"No one within the jurisdiction of a State Party to the present Protocol shall be executed," says article 1, the first of the instrument's eleven articles. "Each State Party shall take all necessary measures to abolish the death penalty within its jurisdiction." The only exception allowed is "in time of war pursuant to a conviction for a most serious crime of a military nature committed during wartime." Article 2 specifies that to avail itself of such an exception, a nation must state a reservation at the time it ratifies the protocol. Under article 3, states parties are asked to include in their reports to the Human Rights Committee under the covenant information on the measures taken to comply with the protocol.

United Nations High Commissioner for Human Rights, 8–14 avenue de la Paix, 1211 Geneva 10, Switzerland. (41-22-917-9000. 🖶 41-22-917-9016. 🖳 webadmin.hchr@unog.ch. 🖳 www.unhchr.ch.

Capital Punishment; Human Rights Committee; International Covenant on Civil and Political Rights; Punishment

International Covenant on Economic, Social and Cultural Rights

Along with the Universal Declaration of Human Rights (1948) and the International Covenant on Civil and Political Rights (1966) and its two optional protocols (1966 and 1989), the International Covenant on Economic, Social and Cultural Rights is part of the International Bill of Human Rights. This covenant, like its companion civil and political covenant, was prepared to strengthen principles declared in the Universal Declaration of Human Rights by making them binding under international law for nations that ratify the covenant. Both covenants were adopted by the UN General Assembly on December 16, 1966, and this instrument guaranteeing the so-called second-generation

rights went into force on January 3, 1976, after the thirty-fifth nation had ratified it.

The International Covenant on Economic, Social and Cultural Rights seeks to promote and protect the rights to work in just and favorable conditions, social security and insurance, an adequate standard of living, physical and mental health, education, and the benefits of cultural freedom and scientific progress. Representing basic elements of citizens' economic, social, and cultural well-being, these goals are considered second-generation rights because they are ones that nations should strive for at their own pace. As such, they take second place to civil and political rights, known as first-generation rights because they are essential for individual liberty and constitutional democracy.

The covenant's preamble observes that "in accordance with the Universal Declaration of Human Rights, the ideal of free human beings enjoying freedom from fear and want can only be achieved if conditions are created whereby everyone may enjoy his economic, social and cultural rights, as well as his civil and political rights." It goes on to note national obligations under the UN charter (1945) "to promote universal respect for, and observance of, human rights and freedoms," adding that "the individual, having duties to other individuals and to the community to which he belongs, is under a responsibility to strive for the promotion and observance of the rights recognized in the present Covenant."

"All peoples have the right of self-determination," states part I, article I, in language identical to that of the International Covenant on Civil and Political Rights. "By virtue of that right they freely determine their political status and freely pursue their economic, social and cultural development." Article I further provides that all peoples may dispose of their economic wealth and resources "without prejudice to any obligations arising out of international economic cooperation" and that parties to the covenant, including those administering non-self-governing trust territories at the time, should promote self-determination and "shall respect that right, in conformity with the provisions of the Charter of the United Nations."

Part II, article 2, requires that each state party to the covenant "take steps, individually and through international assistance and cooperation ... to the maximum of its available resources, with a view to achieving progressively the full realization of the rights recognized in the present Covenant by all appropriate means, including particularly the adoption of legislative measures." Rights are to be guaranteed without discrimination, but developing countries, "with due regard to human rights and their national economy, may determine to what extent they would guarantee the economic rights recognized in the present Covenant to non-nationals." Article 3 mandates that signatory nations "undertake to ensure the equal right of men and women to the enjoyment of all economic, social and cultural rights set forth...." Article 5, paragraph 2, declares: "No restriction upon or derogation from any of the fundamental human rights recognized or existing in any country in virtue of law, conventions, regulations or custom shall be admitted on the pretext that the present Covenant does not recognize such rights or that it recognizes them to a lesser extent."

Basic economic, social, and cultural rights are set forth in part III. According to articles 6 and 7, such rights include the right to earn a living by freely chosen or accepted employment and the right of just and favorable working conditions. These conditions include "[f]air wages and equal remuneration for work of equal value without distinction of any kind, in particular women being guaranteed conditions of work not inferior to those enjoyed by men, with equal pay for equal work"; "a decent living for [the workers] and their families"; "[s]afe and healthy working conditions"; "[e]qual opportunity for everyone to be promoted"; and "[r]est, leisure and reasonable limitation of working hours," plus paid holidays. Article 8 sanctions the right to form and join trade unions, including the right to strike.

Other rights enumerated include, in article 9, the "right of everyone to social security, including social insurance." Article 10 requires that the "widest possible protection and assistance should be accorded to the family," adding that special protection be given "to mothers during a reasonable period before and after childbirth. During such period working mothers should be accorded paid leave or leave with adequate social security benefits." The article additionally encourages special protection for children "without any discrimination for reasons of parentage or other conditions. Children and young persons should be protected from economic and social exploitation," it states. "Their employment in work harmful to their morals or health or dangerous to life or likely to hamper their normal development should be punishable by law." Child labor is also discouraged.

Under article 11, recognition must be given to "the right of everyone to an adequate standard of living . . . , including adequate food, clothing and housing, and continuous improvement of living conditions." This article also recognizes "the fundamental right of everyone to be free from hunger" and urges national and international programs to improve methods of food production, conservation, and distribution and "to ensure an equitable distribution of world food supplies in relation to need." The right to enjoyment of "the highest attainable standard of physical and mental health" is expressed in article 12, which calls for reducing infant mortality, improving hygiene, preventing diseases, and guaranteeing medical care for all "in the event of sickness."

Articles 13 and 14 address "the right of everyone to education" for personal development as well as to "participate effectively in a free society" and promote tolerance worldwide. The covenant calls for compulsory, free public schooling in the primary years plus secondary and higher education that is "accessible to all." In article 15, the states parties recognize universal rights to take part in cultural life, to enjoy the benefits of scientific progress, and to control intellectual rights in scientific, literary, and artistic work. The covenant underscores respect for "the freedom indispensable for scientific research and creative activity."

Part IV, article 16, calls for reports on measures taken and progress made toward achieving the rights enumerated in the covenant. Signatory nations are to submit these reports to the UN secretary-general, who transmits copies to the Economic and Social Council (ECOSOC) as well as to specialized UN agencies. Under article 17, reports "may indicate factors and difficulties affecting the degree of fulfillment of obligations" under the covenant.

"Nothing in the present Covenant," adds article 47, in language mirroring that of its companion civil and political covenant, "shall be interpreted as impairing the inherent right of all peoples to enjoy and utilize fully and freely their natural wealth and resources."

Two decades later, a group of international experts met in June 1986 and developed a set of principles to guide the implementation of the covenant's principles and to provide a foundation for them under international law. Entitled the Limburg Principles on the Implementation of the International Covenant on Economic, Social and Cultural Rights, they were endorsed by the UN in 1993.

United Nations High Commissioner for Human Rights, 8–14 avenue de la Paix, 1211 Geneva 10, Switzerland. (41-22-917-9000. 🖨 41-22-917-9016. 🖳 webadmin.hchr@unog.ch. 🖳 www.unhchr.ch.

Cultural Rights; Economic and Social Council (ECOSOC); Economic Rights; International Bill of Human Rights; International Covenant on Civil and Political Rights; Limburg Principles on the Implementation of the International Covenant on Economic, Social and Cultural Rights; Self-Determination; Social Rights; Workers

International Criminal Court

"Many thought . . . that the horrors of the Second World War—the camps, the cruelty, the exterminations, the Holocaust—could never happen again. And yet they have. In Cambodia, in Bosnia and Herzegovina, in Rwanda. Our time—this decade even—has shown us that man's capacity for evil knows no limits," declared UN Secretary-General Kofi Annan in introducing the UN's proposal for a permanent international criminal court in 1998. "[The International Criminal Court] promises, at last, to supply what has for so long been the missing link in the international legal system, a permanent court to judge the crimes of the gravest concern to the international community as a whole—genocide, crimes against humanity, and war crimes."

Little logic can be found in a system of justice in which a person responsible for killing one person is more likely to be punished than someone who kills thousands. The International Criminal Court will provide a mechanism by which the world can bring to justice those who have perpetrated gross crimes against humanity and have historically gone unpunished because of the international law principle of sovereign immunity, which prohibits interference in a nation's internal affairs. If it can achieve this objective, the International Criminal Court will represent a significant advancement in enforcing human rights.

On June 15, 1998, representatives from 160 countries met in Rome for the United Nations Diplomatic Conference of Plenipotentiaries on the Establishment of an International Criminal Court. On July 17, 120 of those representatives adopted a treaty called the Rome Statute of the International Criminal Court. Headquartered in The Hague, the International Criminal Court will be the first permanent, independent global tribunal for trying, convicting, and sentencing the perpetrators of the worst human rights abuses. The International Court of Justice, established in 1946 and also headquartered in The Hague, has jurisdiction only over nations, not individuals, and only when they agree to submit a matter to the court. The International Criminal Court, however, will be the first court to have international jurisdiction over individuals, including political leaders. The court will become officially operational only after sixty nations ratify the Rome Statute. Although ninety-five nations signed the document in the first year and a half after it was adopted, only seven had ratified it.

The ideal of a universal law that applies to every person is ancient. Under the empires of Alexander the Great and later the Romans, both of which encompassed much of the known world, universal law virtually prevailed, at least for the citizens of those empires. But during the Middle Ages acceptance of the divine right of rulers—the idea that rulers made laws and were responsible only to God for the wisdom and justice of their actions—led to development of the principle of sovereign immunity. Under this principle, rulers of sovereign states were entitled to absolute immunity from accountability or punishment for mistreatment of their own citizens. Under international law, rulers additionally had the right to conduct war, seen as an acceptable extension of failed diplomacy, and to do so as they wished. Scholars and philosophers such as St. Thomas Aquinas, Franciso Suárez, and Hugo Grotius sought ways through international law to reduce the violence of war. But because of the principle of sovereign immunity, there was no way to enforce such restrictions, except for voluntary restraint. Thus, other nations had no legitimate basis for taking action to punish rulers for even the most gross violations of human rights in time of war or peace.

The idea of a universal criminal tribunal was fueled by citizen outrage at the brutality and viciousness, in both methods and scope, of some of the national governments involved in World War II. The Nuremberg trials in Germany and the trials of Japanese war criminals following the war foreshadowed the creation of an international criminal court to bring to justice those responsible for gross violations of human rights—genocide, ethnic cleansing, disappearances, and torture, rape, and murder condoned or directed by government.

Even before World War II, however, a number of international agreements, including the Geneva Conventions of 1864 and 1929 and the Hague Conventions of 1907 dealing with the conduct of war and the treatment of prisoners and noncombatants, were in place, although the concept of war crimes and crimes against humanity, such as genocide, had not been fully developed. Prosecution was generally left to the discretion of the victors, and often exile was the only punishment for the leaders of conquered states. The monarchs of three nations involved in World War I— England, Germany, and Russia—were all closely related by blood, so the defeated German monarch was merely exiled.

After World War II, except for the ad hoc trials of German and Japanese war criminals, there was little real change in international law relating to the sovereign immunity of heads of state or governments that violated human rights. National sovereignty still meant that Joseph Stalin in the Soviet Union, Mao Zedong in China, Augusto Pinochet in Chile, Ferdinand Marcos in the Philippines, Pol Pot in Cambodia, and Kim Il Sung in North Korea, to name only a few notorious human rights violators, could commit and permit all manner of atrocities against their own citizens. But ad hoc tribunals set up under UN auspices to try leaders in the former Yugoslavia and Rwanda for crimes such as ethnic cleansing after bloody civil wars in the 1990s paved the way for the International Criminal Court.

According to the Rome Statute, the International Criminal Court will become a permanent institution with power "to exercise jurisdiction over persons for the most serious crimes of international concern" and is designed to be "complementary to national criminal jurisdiction." The court's jurisdiction encompasses genocide, crimes against humanity, war crimes, and aggression. It obtains jurisdiction over a matter if a crime is referred to the court prosecutor by a nation that is a party to the statute, by the UN Security Council, or by the prosecutor after an investigation. In addition, the court can rule on the admissibility of a matter brought before it and dismiss it if it is being effectively handled by a country that has jurisdiction over it or if the matter "is not of sufficient priority" to warrant action by the court.

The court will apply several sources of law: its statute; its Elements of Crimes, adopted by the court; its Rules of Procedure and Evidence, adopted by a two-thirds majority of the states party to the Rome Statute; applicable treaties as well as principles and rules of international law; and, in the absence of the preceding, general principles of law derived by the court from national laws worldwide. In enforcing its decisions, the court is authorized to hand down sentences of imprisonment "to be served in a State designated by the Court from a list of States which have indicated to the Court their willingness to accept sentenced persons."

The court will consist of eighteen members, including a president, and is to be organized into a prosecutor's office, trial and pretrial divisions, an appeals division, and a registry office. Candidates for judges may be nominated by any of the states parties, elections are by secret ballot, and candidates must receive a two-thirds majority of the states parties present and voting. The prosecutor is elected by secret ballot by an absolute majority of the states parties.

Some critics of the court fear that it may be used selectively as a political weapon rather than as an impartial institution for justice. Such reservations may discourage a number of countries, including the United States, from ratifying the Rome Statute, thus reducing the likelihood that the court will become operational in the near future.

Coalition for an International Criminal Court, 777 United Nations Plaza, New York, N.Y. 10017. (212-687-2176. 🖨 212-599-1332. 🖳 cicc@igc.org. 🖳 www.igc.org/icc.

International Criminal Court, 777 United Nations Plaza, 12th Floor, New York, N.Y. 10017. (212-599-1320. 🖨 212-599-1332. 🖳 wfm@igc.org. 🖳 www.igc.org/icc.

Report of the Task Force on an International Criminal Court of the American Bar Association. Chicago: American Bar Association, Section of International Law and Practice, 1995.

Crimes against Humanity; Enforcement; Geneva Conventions; Genocide; Grotius, Hugo; Impunity; International Court of Justice; Rome Statute of the International Criminal Court; Sovereignty; Thomas Aquinas, St.; War; War Crimes

International Helsinki Federation for Human Rights

The International Helsinki Federation for Human Rights consists of a number of self-governing nongovernmental human rights organizations for Europe, North America, and the Central Asian republics formed from the territories of the former Soviet Union. Its primary mission is to monitor compliance with the human rights provisions of the Helsinki Final Act (1975) and its subsequent documents.

In 1976 the Moscow Helsinki Group was founded by, among others, Anatoly Shcharansky and Yelena Bonner, the wife of Andrei Sakharov, to ensure that the Soviet Union complied with the Helsinki Final Act. Similar "Helsinki committees" were founded in Czechoslovakia and Poland, for

example, as well as in Western Europe, Canada, and the United States. The groups in communist countries were for the most part harassed and sometimes forced by the government to disband.

Inspired by Sakharov's call for the creation of a "unified international committee to defend all Helsinki Watch Group members," an International Citizens Watch Conference was held in 1982 and an international secretariat set up in Vienna. The International Helsinki Federation subsequently worked to support human rights efforts behind the Iron Curtain and has documented the lack of human rights implementation for the Conference on Security and Cooperation in Europe (renamed the Organization for Security and Cooperation in Europe in 1994). The federation now supports thirty-nine "Helsinki committees" and associated human rights groups and represents them internationally.

Among its programs are transnational human rights projects and fact-finding missions, such as a program with local organizations in Belarus, Moldova, and Ukraine to overcome human rights problems. The federation, which has consultative status with the Council of Europe and the United Nations, also assists in monitoring human rights compliance and reporting violations, sponsors training, monitors trials and elections, and briefs international organizations and the media. Individual countries and foundations, including the European Human Rights Foundation and the Ford Foundation, provide major funding for the federation, which is administered by a president, an advisory board, and an executive committee.

International Helsinki Federation for Human Rights, Rummelhardtg. 2/18, A-1090, Vienna, Austria. (43-1-408-88-22. 🖨 43-1-408-88-22-50. 🖳 office@ihf-hr.org. 🖳 www.ihf-hr.org.

Defenders of Human Rights; Helsinki Final Act; Human Rights Watch; Organization for Security and Cooperation in Europe; Sakharov, Andrei; Shcharansky, Anatoly

International Human Rights Instruments

Human rights instruments are any written documents that in an authoritative or a legal manner declare, guarantee, or prescribe human rights principles or relate in some way to human rights. At the national level, human rights instruments may include historic documents such as England's Magna Carta (1215), provisions in written national constitutions such as the U.S. Bill of Rights (1791), statutory laws of countries or their political subdivisions, common law, or government regulations. At the international and regional levels, there are literally hundreds of human rights instruments. They range from declarations of international bodies such as the United Nations, which are often adopted by the UN General Assembly in the form of resolutions, to international treaties or agreements ratified by individual nations, some of which grow out of these declarations, to guidelines, principles, and recommendations adopted by international groups and ad hoc conferences on specific rights issues.

The term *instrument* (from the Latin *instrumentum*) to mean a formal legal document creating or confirming a right has been in use since at least the fifteenth century. In Anglo-American law, an instrument may be any written or formal legal document. At the national level, the term may refer to a written document or a law, even a constitutional document. Sweden's constitution, for example, consists of several written documents, including the Instrument of Government (1975).

Declarations, one of four general kinds of international human rights instruments, attempt to define significant principles on the basis of a consensus or a majority of the representatives to an organization such as the UN General Assembly or another international or regional body. Such declarations set standards for all the nations within the organization's scope. By merely declaring principles without requiring countries to formally sign and ratify them, declarations are less forceful than international agreements. However, through acceptance over time by national governments and adjudicative bodies, they may evolve into principles of international law. Some of the most significant international human rights declarations, such as the Universal Declaration of Human Rights (1948), are featured as individual entries in this book, but many others have been adopted.

A number of UN human rights declarations have been followed several years later by more binding international agreements or treaties, typically called conventions, on the same subject. The Declaration on the Protection of All Persons from Being Subjected to Torture and Other Cruel, Inhuman or Degrading Treatment or Punishment (1975), for example, was followed in 1984 by the Convention against Torture and Other Cruel, Inhuman or Degrading Treatment or Punishment. As treaties among nations, international agreements like this convention are significant human rights instruments because they bind countries—to the extent that any government permits itself to be bound in accordance with the international law principle of sovereignty—to abide by the treaty's terms. Much depends, of course, on how effective enforcement is within individual countries that ratify an agreement. Conversely, the fact that some countries do not ratify such human rights conventions does not necessarily mean that they do not vigorously support and enforce the rights embodied in the instrument.

International human rights agreements sometimes contain language that allows nations to opt out of or avoid certain provisions simply by acknowledging reservations at the time of ratification. The American Convention on Human Rights (1969) permits reservations by ratifying parties "only in conformity with the provisions of the Vienna Convention on the Law of Treaties [1969]" and further provides that state parties "may denounce [the convention] at the expiration of [a] five-year period starting from the date of its entry into force...." Protocols are amendments to international agreements that must be ratified separately from the main instrument.

Other international human rights instruments that are generally more limited in scope than declarations or conventions include guidelines, principles, and rules. These instruments are usually drawn up to set general standards for certain behavior in areas of human rights, often for particular professions such as law enforcement personnel, prosecutors, doctors, and lawyers. Many of the significant international guidelines, principles, and rules are featured or discussed in this book.

Recommendations are similar in function to guidelines, principles, and rules, except that they are often intended not as final documents but as catalysts for more permanent instruments such as declarations or conventions. Examples of recommendations include the Recommendation Concerning Education for International Understanding, Cooperation and Peace and Education Relating to Human Rights and Fundamental Freedoms (1974), issued by the United Nations Educational, Scientific and Cultural Organization (UNESCO), and the Recommendation on Consent to Marriage, Minimum Age for Marriage and Registration of Marriages (1965), issued by the UN.

Most international human rights instruments emanate from the UN. Other international organizations that promulgate or sponsor the development and adoption of these instruments usually represent the regional human rights systems: the Council of Europe, Organization of African Unity, and Organization of American States. International conventions also originate with the World Health Organization and the International Labor Organization, whose international conventions concerning workers' rights include, in addition to those presented in individual entries in this book, the Forced Labor Convention (1930), Equal Remuneration Convention (1951), and Employment Policy Convention (1964).

Commission of the European Communities. *Legal Instruments to Combat Racism and Xenophobia: Comparative Assessment of the Legal Instruments Implemented in the Various Member States to Combat All Forms of Discrimination, Racism and Xenophobia and Incitement to Hatred and Racial Violence.* Lanham, Md.: UNIPUB, 1993.

Lillich, Richard B. ed. *International Human Rights Instruments: A Compilation of Treaties, Agreements, and Declarations of Special Interest to the United States.* Buffalo, N.Y.: W. S. Hein, 1990–.

Enforcement; International Labor Organization; Regional Human Rights Systems; Treaties; United Nations; World Health Organization; *and specific international human rights instruments*

International Labor Organization

Founded in 1919, the International Labor Organization (ILO) is an autonomous intergovernmental organization that promotes the rights and interests of workers around the world. Its mission encompasses protection of specific groups listed in the Declaration of Philadelphia (1944), which is annexed to the ILO's constitution; these include workers and employers exercising freedom of association as well as women, children, and migrant workers. In addition to promoting the right of association, the ILO supports the elimination of discrimination in employment and occupation, including against women; protection of migrant workers; and accommodation of disabled workers.

International labor conventions in England, France, and Belgium in the nineteenth century began seeking to mitigate many of the pernicious effects of the industrial revolution. In 1890 the Swiss government, in consultation with other European governments, proposed convening a conference on labor matters in Bern. Instead, Kaiser Wilhelm of Germany called a similar conference in Berlin, which made some recommendations. A congress for workers was held in Zurich and another for scholars and administrators in Brussels in 1897. These were followed by the creation of the International Association of the Legal Protection of Workers, headquartered in Basel, Switzerland.

The international labor movement was interrupted by World War I, but its importance was recognized by world leaders. The Treaty of Versailles (1919), which ended the war, included language addressing the subject and providing for the establishment of an International Labor Organization. Later that year the International Labor Conference convened in Washington, D.C.; it adopted the first labor conventions and established a governing body, the ILO. Thereafter the conference met regularly except during World War II, adopting international conventions and working to have them ratified by various countries—its principal method for promoting the rights of workers.

The earliest ILO convention in 1921 concerned the right of association in agriculture. More than one hundred other ILO conventions have since addressed such issues as forced labor (1930), freedom of association and the right of workers to organize (1948), night work by women (1948), collective bargaining (1949), discrimination in employment (1958), medical care and sickness benefits (1969), rural and migrant workers' rights (1975), the working environment, specifically air pollution and noise and vibration (1977), and indigenous and tribal peoples (1989). Conven-

tions such as these have helped advance working conditions for men and women around the world.

The ILO's fifty-six-member governing body includes twenty-eight members who represent governments and fourteen who represent employees and employers. Components include a Committee of Experts on the Application of Conventions and Recommendations as well as offices that handle complaints that trade union rights have been infringed: the Freedom of Association Committee and the Freedom of Association Fact-Finding and Conciliation Commission. Its International Labor Office, with a staff of more than three thousand, collects and disseminates information regarding changes in the industrial and labor movements. When warranted, such information is brought to the attention of the ILO's governing body for possible action, which may take the form of an investigation or preparation of an international convention.

International Labor Organization, 4 route des Morillons, 1211 Geneva 22, Switzerland. (41-22-799-6111. 🖨 41-22-798-8685. 🖳 somavia@ilo.org. 🖳 www.ilo.org.

Bartolomei de la Cruz, Hector G. *The International Labor Organization: The International Standards System and Basic Human Rights.* Boulder, Colo.: Westview, 1996.

Valticos, Nicholas. *International Labor Law.* The Hague: Kluwer Law International, 1995.

Association; Convention Concerning Freedom of Association and Protection of the Right to Organize; Forced Labor; Indigenous and Tribal Peoples Convention; Slavery; Workers

International Law

Classically defined as a body of rules governing relations among nations, international law today includes the laws and instruments under which nations are treated as individual entities with rights and responsibilities vis-à-vis one another and the community of nations as a whole. It is built on the concept of *jus gentium* (law of nations), which as developed by the ancient Romans meant the rules common to the law of all nations.

Unlike national laws, there is neither an international legislature to enact international laws nor an international police force, at least not a permanent one, to enforce them. The main sources of international law traditionally have been the customs and accepted practices of nations in dealing with one another, together with any treaties they might ratify. Because international tribunals have limited jurisdiction, conferred only by consent of the states parties to agreements, much of the international decisional law comes from the application of international law principles by domestic courts within individual nations. Other traditional sources of international law principles are the works of scholars and legal codifiers.

International law has evolved beyond its historic definition, however, to include documents subscribed to by a relatively large number of countries: declarations of international and regional organizations of nations as well as treaties, including covenants and conventions. Even when a country does not legally bind itself to observe the provisions of an international treaty, it may nevertheless act in such a manner, giving more stature in international law to the principles embodied in the document.

Both international and national laws provide the foundation for human rights law. International law is broader in scope and, in the last half of the twentieth century, has greatly extended guarantees of human rights. It encompasses not only the rights of nations but also those of individuals. For example, self-determination—a country's right to choose its own form of government—is a right of the state, whereas the right "to recognition everywhere as a person before the law," proclaimed in the Universal Declaration of Human Rights (1948), is an individual right. The inclusion of individual human rights has expanded international law's scope.

National governments predominantly retain the authority to enforce the rights proclaimed in both domestic laws, including national constitutions, and international and regional instruments. International human rights provisions and principles may be enforced by national tribunals as well as international tribunals such as the European Court of Human Rights and the Human Rights Committee. Nongovernmental human rights organizations also play an important role in protecting and enforcing human rights by bringing pressure to bear on national and local governments to conform to international law norms regarding human rights as well as to a nation's own constitutional and statutory human rights guarantees. As more human rights principles become part of the customary and treaty law among nations and of public international law, the enforcement of international human rights law will undoubtedly become more effective.

Constitution of Portugal (1976), Fundamental Principles, article 8, International Law: "1. The rules and principles of general or ordinary international law shall be an integral part of Portuguese law."

Declaration on Principles of International Law Concerning Friendly Relations and Co-operation among States in Accordance with the Charter of the United Nations (1970), preamble: "[T]he faithful observance of the principles of international law concerning friendly relations and co-operation among States and the fulfillment in good faith of obligations assumed by States, in accordance

with the Charter [1945], is of the greatest importance for the maintenance of international peace and security and for the implementation of the other purposes of the United Nations."

U.S. Supreme Court (1900): "International law is part of our law, and must be ascertained and administered by the courts of justice of appropriate jurisdiction, as often as questions of right depending upon it are duly presented for their determination."

International Court of Justice (1950): "International law has recruited and continues to recruit many of its rules and institutions from private systems of law. Article 38(1)(c) of the Statute of the Court . . . authorizes the Court to 'apply . . . the general principles of law recognized in civilized nations'."

Center for Justice and International Law, 1522 K Street, N.W., Suite 1034, Washington, D.C. 20005-1202. ☎ 202-842-8630. 🖷 202-371-8032. 🖳 cejil@igc.apc.org. 🖥 www.derechos.org.cejil.

Sieghart, Paul. *The International Law of Human Rights*. Oxford, England: Clarendon Press, Oxford University Press, 1983.

Svensson-McCarthy, Anna-Lena. *The International Law of Human Rights and States of Exception: With Special Reference to the Travaux Preparatoires and Case-Law of the International Monitoring Organs*. The Hague: Martinus Nijhoff, Kluwer Law International, 1998.

Declaration on Principles of International Law Concerning Friendly Relations and Co-operation among States in Accordance with the Charter of the United Nations; Enforcement; European Court of Human Rights; Human Rights Committee; International Court of Justice (World Court); International Criminal Court; International Human Rights Instruments; Nongovernmental Organizations; Norms; Remedies; Treaties

International League for Human Rights

Founded in New York City in 1941 as the International League for the Rights of Man, the International League for Human Rights has focused on defending the defenders of human rights by assisting those on the front lines of the international struggle for human rights. Establishment of the league was spearheaded by Roger Baldwin, also a founder of the American Civil Liberties Union. The league's current mission includes promoting the realization of human rights and fundamental freedoms set forth in the Universal Declaration of Human Rights (1948) and other international human rights documents. It is a nongovernmental organization with special consultative status with the United Nations, International Labor Organization, and Council of Europe.

The league monitors the implementation of human rights in countries around the world, investigates violations, contacts governments directly, and assists its partners worldwide in reporting on human rights issues before the UN and other international bodies. The organization also conducts human rights research and education programs, publishes reports on human rights conditions, assists victims of abuse, sends observers to political trials, and sponsors missions to investigate specific alleged violations to obtain redress for the victims. Other activities include helping establish national human rights groups and standards.

An example of the league's activities is the successful defense of the Korean political prisoner Kim Dae Jung, whose release the league ultimately obtained after sending a fact-finding mission. The group has also helped defend human rights activists from persecution in Afghanistan, China, Tibet, Belarus, Nigeria, and elsewhere. It presents a human rights award each year to those who have made an outstanding contribution to the promotion and protection of international human rights. Past recipients of the award have included Fang Lizhi, Andrei Sakharov, Helen Suzman, and Elie Wiesel.

International League for Human Rights, 432 Park Avenue South, New York, N.Y. 10016. (212-684-1221. 212-684-1696. ilhr@perfekt.net. www.ilhr.org.

Defenders of Human Rights; Fang Lizhi; Monitoring Compliance; Reporting Violations; Sakharov, Andrei; Suzman, Helen; Wiesel, Elie

International Peace Bureau

The International Peace Bureau was created more than a century ago as a permanent office to coordinate the activities of national peace societies formed in Europe and North America after the Napoleonic Wars of 1815. Its primary objective is to develop nonviolent solutions to potential or active conflicts, and over the years this nongovernmental organization and its officers have garnered more than a dozen Nobel Peace Prizes for their efforts on behalf of world peace; the bureau's was awarded in 1910.

The organization was founded as the Permanent International Peace Bureau by the Third Universal Peace Congress, held in Rome in 1891. Bern, in neutral Switzerland,

was chosen as the first site for its headquarters, which were later moved to Geneva. Disarmament, peaceful settlement of conflicts, and the development of international law have been its primary focuses. The bureau was instrumental in persuading Nicholas II of Russia to establish the International Peace Conference, first held in The Hague in 1899, and it encouraged the wealthy Swedish inventor Alfred Nobel to establish the international peace prize now named for him. It also supported the League of Nations and the Women's International League for Peace and Freedom, as well as the idea of an international court.

In the 1960s the organization's efforts centered on opposition to the Vietnam War and support of the rights of conscientious objectors. Dwindling membership in the following decades was offset by its merger in 1984 with the International Confederation for Disarmament and Peace, bringing recent membership to some 170 organizations in forty countries and expanding concerns to include foreign military bases, the arms trade, militarism and the environment, women and peace, and abolition of nuclear weapons. In the 1990s the bureau celebrated its centenary and participated in the World Court Project and presentation of the Lawyers' Appeal against Nuclear Weapons to the United Nations. It also serves as a consultant to the Economic and Social Council (ECOSOC) and the United Nations Educational, Scientific and Cultural Organization (UNESCO).

International Peace Bureau, rue de Zurich 41, 1201 Geneva, Switzerland. (41-22-731-6429. 41-22-738-9419. webmaster@ipb.org. www.ipb.org.

International Court of Justice (World Court); International Law; Peace; Weapons

Internet Resources

Called Arpanet when it began officially in 1969, the Internet (from the Latin *inter*, meaning among or between) links millions of computers to create a global communications system. It was born when computers at the University of California at Los Angeles, Stanford Research Institute, University of California at Santa Barbara, and University of Utah were successfully linked. Academic researchers were interested in the Internet's informational capabilities, while the U.S. Department of Defense wanted access to a decentralized computer network that could continue to function even if part of it were destroyed. Managing the growing Internet thus became a shared function, and soon private companies began providing commercial online services.

Human rights information on the Internet has proliferated and is still expanding. Resources available include declarations and conventions, reports on violations in specific countries, decisions and reports by international tribunals, national legislation and court decisions, news, bibliographies, lists of activist organizations, and references to specific issues such as women, children, and indigenous peoples. Although the Internet is one of many sources of such information, its advantages as a research tool include the potential for up-to-date data, quick access to information overviews, direct links to related Web sites, the ability to download and print material, and the opportunity to correspond directly with the sources via e-mail.

Listed below are a number of helpful Internet sites relating to human rights. For additional sites of international and regional human rights agencies and nongovernmental organizations, see entries in this book on specific topics and organizations.

Concise Guide to Human Rights on the Internet: ⌨ www.derechos.org/human–rights/manual.

Council of Europe: ⌨ www.coe.fr.

Directory of Human Rights Resources on the Internet: ⌨ www.shr.aaas.org/dhr.

Guide to Electronic Resources for International Law: Human Rights: ⌨ www.asil.org/resource/humrts1.

Human Rights Internet: ⌨ www.hri.ca.

Human Rights Today: A United Nations Priority: ⌨www.un.org/rights/HRToday.

International Criminal Court: ⌨ www.igc.org/icc.

International Labor Organization: ⌨ www.ilo.org.

Internet Directory: A Database of Human Rights Web Sites: ⌨ www.hri.ca/coldfusion/cfidir.

Organization of African Unity: ⌨ www.oau-oua.org.

Organization of American States: www.oas.org.

United Nations: ⌨ www.un.org.

United Nations High Commissioner for Human Rights: ⌨ www.unhchr.ch.

University of Minnesota Human Rights Center: ⌨ www.umn.edu/humanrts.

U.S. Department of State, Country Reports on Human Rights Practices: ⌨ www.state.gov/www/global/human rights/hrreports mainhp.

Human Rights Internet; Institute for Global Communications; Project Diana

Inviolable Rights

Inviolable rights are absolute and inalienable rights that cannot be diminished, withdrawn, abrogated, or derogated from. They differ from fundamental or basic rights, which are rights that other rights depend on. The fundamental right to have a court of law determine if a person is being held or detained lawfully by the government, which in Anglo-American law may be secured through the issuance of a writ of habeas corpus, may be suspended under certain circumstances, such as those set forth in the U.S. Constitution (1789). The right to life and freedom from torture, on the other hand, are inviolable rights and freedoms that may not be suspended for any reason.

The responsibility for deciding which human rights are truly inviolable (from the Latin *inviolatus,* meaning unharmed) in all situations often devolves on national courts charged with interpreting a country's constitution or on international tribunals or courts whose role is to interpret international and regional human rights agreements. Universal agreement does not exist as to which rights are inviolable or inalienable, but freedom from slavery and discrimination, equality before the law, and the right to be treated as a person and with dignity are usually included. There are times, however, when citizens' obligations—for example, to serve in the military—result in restrictions on their inviolable rights. In many countries military personnel do not have the same inviolable rights, such as freedom of speech, assembly, and conscience, as they would have if they were civilians. Moreover, at times absolute rights themselves may be in conflict.

The inviolability of certain rights simply recognizes that if the standards for these rights are ever relaxed, some important human rights may become so diluted that they no longer have the moral or authoritative force necessary to protect citizens from government injustice. The fourth-century B.C.E. Greek philosopher Plato cautioned in *The Laws* that "[w]here the law is subject to some other authority and has none of its own, the collapse of the state, in my view, is not far off; but if law is the master of the government and the government is its slave, then the situation is full of promise and men enjoy all the blessings that the gods shower on a state."

Constitution Act of Finland (1919), section 1, as amended: "Finland is a sovereign Republic, the constitution of which shall

guarantee the inviolability of human dignity and the freedom and rights of the individual as well as promoting justice in society."

International Covenant on Civil and Political Rights (1966), preamble: "[I]n accordance with the principles proclaimed in the Charter of the United Nations [1945], recognition of the inherent dignity and of the equal and inalienable rights of all members of the human family is the foundation of freedom, justice and peace in the world. . . ."

Constitutional Court of Germany (Dissenting Opinions) (1970): On the basis of the concept of "the unconstitutional constitutional amendment," found by the court in 1953 to be encompassed in Germany's constitution (1949), article 117, a minority of the justices were willing to invalidate an amendment to the German constitution because it would limit the "inviolable" right "of privacy of posts and telecommunications."

European Court of Human Rights (1994): The European Convention for the Protection of Human Rights and Fundamental Freedoms (1950), article 10, which guarantees freedom of expression, "should not be interpreted in such a way as to limit, derogate from or destroy the right to protection against racial discrimination under the [International Convention on the Elimination of All Forms of Racial Discrimination (1965)]."

Inalienable Rights, Fundamental Freedoms: A U.N. Agenda for Advancing Human Rights in the World Community. New York: United Nations Association of the United States of America, 1996.

Bills of Rights; Fundamental Rights; Habeas Corpus; Human Rights; Natural Rights; Military Personnel; Plato; Rights; *and specific rights*

In 1776 Thomas Jefferson, the third president of the United States, wrote one of the world's seminal human rights documents: the U.S. Declaration of Independence. Proclaiming that "all Men are created equal" and declaring the "unalienable Rights . . . of Life, Liberty, and the Pursuit of Happiness," Jefferson laid the groundwork for many significant human rights documents to come. [Library of Congress]

Jefferson, Thomas

The author of the U.S. Declaration of Independence (1776), Thomas Jefferson (1743–1826) gave the world an elegantly worded and enduring rationale for establishing governments founded on the observation of human rights. As the third president of the fledgling United States of America, Jefferson was committed to the ideals he expressed in the declaration and to the manifest destiny of America.

Born on April 13, 1743, in colonial Virginia, the uncommonly talented Jefferson attended William and Mary College in Williamsburg and studied for the law. Admitted to the bar in 1767, he was elected two years later to the lower house of the Virginia legislature, and in 1775 he was appointed by that body to represent the colony at the Second Continental Congress held in Philadelphia.

Along with Benjamin Franklin of Pennsylvania, John Adams of Massachusetts, and two others, Jefferson was assigned to the committee responsible for drafting a document declaring the American colonies' independence from Great Britain; the committee members, acknowledging Jefferson's ability with words, allowed him to be the principal author. The opening words of the declaration's second paragraph—"We hold these Truths to be self-evident, that all Men are created equal, that they are endowed by their Creator with certain unalienable Rights, that among these are Life, Liberty, and the Pursuit of Happiness—That to secure these Rights, Governments are instituted among Men, deriving their just Powers from the Consent of the Governed"—have since been quoted repeatedly in documents and speeches around the world in support of human rights and freedoms.

During the Revolutionary War, Jefferson served from 1779 to 1781 as governor of Virginia, succeeded Benjamin Franklin as the American minister to France in 1784, and then, as a representative to the Continental Congress, helped draft the Northwest Ordinance(1787), a law guaranteeing political liberties and eventual statehood for those who settled in the Northwest Territories.

Jefferson did not directly participate in the Constitutional Convention in Philadelphia in 1787, which produced the U.S. Constitution, but his words and ideas informed that historic body. Like George Washington and other members of the convention, Jefferson was a Deist, believing that God created the universe but plays no further role in how it functions or how human beings live their lives. The Constitution consequently lacks religious overtones (it contains only a single reference to a "Creator") and includes a freedom of religion provision in the U.S. Bill of Rights, added to the Constitution in 1791. Jefferson had drafted the Statute of Religious Freedom for Virginia, which after much controversy was adopted in 1786, a year before the convention.

In later years, adding a constitutional concept that has endured for more than two centuries, he stated his own views on religion in a letter to a religious association dated January 1, 1802: "Believing with you that religion is a matter which lies solely between man and his God, that he owes account to none other for his faith or his worship, . . .

I contemplate with sovereign reverence that act of the whole American people which declared that their legislature should 'make no law respecting an establishment of religion, or prohibiting the free exercise thereof,' thus building a wall of separation between Church and State.' Adhering to this expression of the supreme will of the nation in behalf of the rights of conscience," he concluded, "I shall see with sincere satisfaction the progress of those sentiments which tend to restore to man all his natural rights, convinced he has no natural right in opposition to his social duties."

Jefferson became the first secretary of state under the new constitution in 1789, vice president of the United States in 1797, and president in 1801, serving two terms. A product of his times, he maintained slaves despite his heroic language of equality in the Declaration of Independence. Similarly, it will be some time before every person is guaranteed the inalienable rights that he so eloquently articulated in 1776.

A prolific writer, Jefferson often commented on rights, not just religious freedom but individual and minority rights, among others. Writing to James Madison from Paris on September 6, 1789, Jefferson declared his belief in the universality and equality of all rights. "What is true of every member of society, individually," he wrote, "is true of them all collectively; since the rights of the whole can be no more than the sum of the rights of the individuals."

In his first inaugural address, given on March 4, 1801, Jefferson observed: "All, too, will bear in mind this sacred principle, that though the will of the majority is in all cases to prevail, that will, to be rightful, must be reasonable; that the minority possess their equal rights, which equal laws must protect, and to violate which would be oppression."

Thomas Jefferson Papers, Manuscript Division, Library of Congress, 101 Independence Avenue, S.E., Washington, D.C. 20540. (202-707-5387. 202-707-6336. lcweb@loc.gov. www.loc.gov.

Lerner, Max, and Robert Schmuhl. *Thomas Jefferson: America's Philosopher-King*. New Brunswick, N.J.: Transaction, 1996.

Malone, Dumas. *Jefferson and the Rights of Man*. Boston: Little, Brown, 1951.

Mayer, David N. *The Constitutional Thought of Thomas Jefferson*. Charlottesville: University Press of Virginia, 1994.

Bills of Rights; Conscience; Declaration of Independence (United States); Inviolable Rights; Majority Rule; Minorities; Natural Rights; Religion; Separation of Church and State

Judicial Independence

An independent judiciary—courts and judges collectively, forming the judicial branch of government—is one that is coequal with and separate from a government's other branches. Judicial independence ensures freedom from control by or subordination to the executive power of the state and is necessary to protect individual and group rights from government infringement. (Judicial independence differs from impartiality, which is a decision maker's lack of personal interest in the outcome of a case or an activity.) Together with the broader concept of the separation of powers, an independent judiciary is a basic component of the rule of law and of constitutionalism, which ensures a government of limited, as opposed to absolute, power. The term *judiciary* (from the Latin words *judicium*, meaning trial or verdict, and *judiciarius*) was recorded in English as early as the seventeenth century.

The Greek philosopher Plato wrote in the fourth century B.C.E. that unchecked political power in the hands of one person was dangerous, commenting in *The Laws* that a balance of power was needed among a state's ruling elements. More than two thousand years later, the French legal theorist Montesquieu advanced the principle of the separation of powers in his work *The Spirit of the Laws* (1748). In 1787 this seminal concept informed the drafters of the world's first written constitution, the U.S. Constitution, although it is not expressly stated in the document.

Early in the new American republic, the U.S. Supreme Court asserted in 1803 in the case of *Marbury v. Madison* that, as a coequal branch of the federal government, it had the authority to declare null and void a law passed by Congress and approved by the president if, in its opinion, such a law was not permitted by the Constitution. This declaration by the chief justice of the United States, John Marshall, became the basis for the concept of judicial review—the authority of the courts to determine, in cases brought before them, if laws enacted by the legislature or actions by government officials are constitutional or unconstitutional. By this move, the judiciary affirmed itself to be a wholly independent branch of government. Countries with parliamentary-type governments, especially in Europe—for example, Germany and France—have created constitutional courts or constitutional councils to supervise adherence to the national constitution. These courts or councils, which are independent of the executive and legislative branches, also determine the constitutionality of government actions and laws.

Ways in which judicial independence can be furthered include insulating judges from arbitrary dismissal; promoting respect for the judiciary by selecting competent, well-trained people of the highest integrity for judicial positions; and encouraging constitutionalism and the rule of law. Judges are not infallible, but honest judges whose salaries are protected from being decreased while in office and who have sufficiently long tenures have little to gain by ruling arbitrarily in favor of the government against the rights of the people.

In 1985 the United Nations adopted the Basic Principles on the Independence of the Judiciary, mandating that judicial independence be "enshrined in the Constitution or the law of the country" and that "judicial proceedings are conducted fairly," as a standard for countries in drafting constitutional provisions or legislation. This document was followed by the Basic Principles on the Role of Lawyers (1990) and Guidelines on the Role of Prosecutors (1990).

The Commission on Human Rights in 1994 authorized a special rapporteur (expert) on the independence of judges and lawyers, whose mandate was renewed in 1997 for an additional three years. Its 1997 report addressed, among other problems, disregard of court decisions by governments, dismissal of judges from cases, and actions by military personnel to contravene judicial orders. While noting an increase in the attacks on the independence of judges, lawyers, and court officers, the commission affirmed at its 1997 session that an independent and impartial judiciary and legal profession are prerequisites for protecting human rights and eliminating discrimination in the administration of justice.

Constitution of Bulgaria (1991), chapter 6, The Judicial Branch, article 117: "(2) The judicial branch is independent. Judges, court assessors, prosecutors, and investigators are guided strictly by law in the exercise of their functions."

Universal Declaration of Human Rights (1948), article 10: "Everyone is entitled in full equality to a fair and public hearing by an independent and impartial tribunal, in the determination of his rights and obligations and of any criminal charge against him."

U.K. House of Lords (1985): Although the judiciary has no power of judicial review with respect to Parliament or the officers on which it confers power, it can review their decisions on the grounds of illegality, irrationality, and procedural impropriety.

European Commission of Human Rights (1978 and 1979): In two separate matters the commission determined that the independence of a tribunal or a court is secured under the European Convention on the Protection of Human Rights and Fundamental Freedoms (1950) if in the performance of their duties members are not "answerable at any stage to anyone in the hierarchy of government" and "enjoy irremovability during the exercise of their functions."

American Bar Association, Standing Committee on Judicial Independence, 541 North Fairbanks Court, Chicago, Ill. 60611. (312-988-5522. ☎ 312-988-5709. ✉ abasvcctr@abanet.org. 🖥 www. abanet.org/judind/home.

Center for the Independence of Judges and Lawyers, avenue de Châtelaine 81A, P.O. Box 216, 1219 Châtelaine/Geneva, Switzerland. (41-22-979-3800. ☎ 41-22-979-3801. ✉ info@icj.org. 🖥 www.icj.org.

International Commission of Jurists, 26 chemin de Joinville, P.O. Box 160, 1216 Geneva, Switzerland. (41-22-788-4747. ☎ 41-22-788-4880. ✉ info@icj.org. 🖥 www.icj.org.

Dakolias, Maria. *Court Performance around the World: A Comparative Perspective.* Washington, D.C.: The World Bank, 1999.

Independence of the Judiciary: A Human Rights Priority. UN Backgrounder. New York: UN Department of Public Information, 1996.

Basic Principles on the Role of Lawyers; Commission on Human Rights; Constitutionalism; Fair Trial; International Commission of Jurists; Judicial Review; Rule of Law

Judicial Review

A basic tenet of constitutionalism is that constitutional government and the rights of individual citizens are best protected when power is divided among the three basic functions of government—the executive, legislative, and judicial—rather than being concentrated in one or two branches of government. Such separation of powers is designed to give each branch checks and balances on the authority of the others. One of the judicial branch's important powers is judicial review, through which it may void as unconstitutional the actions of the legislative and executive branches, thus protecting the national constitution's integrity and the rights it guarantees.

Urging adoption of the U.S. Constitution, which was drafted in 1787 and became effective in 1789, Alexander Hamilton wrote in *The Federalist*, essay no. 78: "Limitations [on legislative authority] can be preserved in practice no other way than through the medium of courts of justice, whose duty it must be to declare all acts contrary to the manifest tenor of the Constitution void." The Constitution itself, however, makes no reference to judicial review, which simply grew out of the document's reliance on the separation of government powers.

The concept of judicial review (from the Latin words *judicialis,* meaning judicial, and *revidere,* meaning to review or see again) was not new to the American colonial governments, and there was some precedent for it even earlier in England. In *Dr. Bonham's case* (1607), an English court invalidated a law of Parliament. Sir Edward Coke, chief justice of the common pleas court, declared: "[I]t appears in our books, that in many cases, the common law will control Acts of Parliament, and sometimes adjudge them to be utterly void: for when an Act of Parliament is against common right and reason, or repugnant, or impossible to be performed, the common law will control it, and adjudge such Act to be void." Although this strong statement never led to true coequal status for the English judiciary, it laid the groundwork for the development of judicial review in other countries.

In 1803 the U.S. Supreme Court declared in the case of *Marbury v. Madison* that the courts, as a coequal branch of government, had the inherent authority under the Constitution to determine if laws or executive acts were valid. Such a determination could be made only in a case brought before the courts, because the Court has no authority to extend its own jurisdiction or issue advisory opinions. As judicial review was developed by the U.S. courts, they might refuse to decide a question of constitutionality where the cases before them could be resolved without such a determination or where the Constitution clearly left resolution of constitutionality to the other two branches.

By using the power of judicial review, independent and impartial courts are able to enforce rights against the government itself. If a national constitution guarantees, for example, freedom of assembly to protest government action or inaction, and citizens exercising that right are arrested, the courts can declare such arrests unconstitutional. Other types of judicial review include the use of special constitutional courts that can void laws deemed unconstitutional, a practice followed in Austria, Germany, Hungary, Italy, and South Korea, for instance. France's constitution (1958) creates a constitutional council that in certain circumstances can negate unconstitutional acts of the legislature. In nations where no judicial review is authorized, the government may be able to act unconstitutionally with impunity and the democratic process of majority rule may diminish or violate individual rights.

Although judicial review occurs only under national governments, the principle has also been applied at the international level. For example, on the question of the authority of UN agencies, the International Court of Justice makes determinations based on provisions of the UN charter (1945). Judicial review in the more narrow sense of an individual's right to have an administrative decision reviewed by a court may also be considered in matters before regional human rights tribunals. Although not empowered to void national legislation or actions that contravene human rights provisions of international treaties, tribunals such as the European Court of Human Rights may declare that such laws or actions violate those treaty provisions.

Constitution of Honduras (1982), chapter XII, The Judicial Branch, article 319: "The supreme court of justice shall have the following powers and duties: . . . 12. To declare laws to be unconstitutional in the manner and in the cases provided for in this constitution. . . ."

Constitution of Brazil (1988), title IV, Organization of the Powers, chapter III, The Judicial Power, section II, The Supreme Federal Court, article 102: "The Supreme Federal Court is responsible, essentially, for safeguarding the Constitution, and it is within its competence: I—to institute legal proceeding and judgment, in the first instance, of: a) direct actions of unconstitutionality of a federal or state law or normative act. . . ."

Constitutional Court of Germany (1958): The Basic Law (Germany's 1949 constitution), article 2, which guarantees each person's right to free development of his or her personality, is not a special right like those listed in article 1 but a general right protecting many types of human activity. This holding confirmed the court's power of judicial review for the protection of individual human rights.

European Court of Human Rights (1991): The lack of judicial review of a county administrative board's revocation of a permit constituted a violation of the European Convention for the Protection of Human Rights and Fundamental Freedoms (1950), article 6, which declares that "[in] the determination of his civil rights and obligations . . . everyone is entitled to a fair and public hearing . . . by an independent and impartial tribunal established by law."

Beatty, David M., ed. *Human Rights and Judicial Review: A Comparative Perspective.* The Hague: Martinus Nijhoff, Kluwer Law International, 1994.

Zhang, Yong, ed. *Comparative Studies on the Judicial Review System in East and Southeast Asia.* The Hague: Kluwer Law International, 1997.

Constitutionalism; European Court of Human Rights; International Court of Justice; Judicial Independence

Jus Cogens

Derived from an ancient legal principle, the concept of *jus cogens* (coercive law) holds that there is a higher order of legal norms that cannot be abrogated or derogated from by the laws of nations or humankind. This higher order is so fundamental that it binds all states and allows for no exceptions. Scholars have traced *jus cogens* (from the Latin *jus* or *ius*, meaning law or right, and *cogo*, meaning coerce) to ancient Roman law. The concept has been compared to certain overriding civil and common law precepts—for example, that contracts are void if by their very nature they are injurious to the public good (*contra bonos mores*).

Jus cogens used in the context of human rights refers to the principle that rights acknowledged in international documents such as the Charter of the United Nations (1945), particularly in its preamble, may not be unilaterally abandoned by any nation. International law prohibitions against slavery, genocide, and piracy are examples of *jus cogens* rules. Piracy, for instance, has long been held to be a crime under international and domestic law. In an 1820 decision the U.S. Supreme Court noted: "The general practice of all nations in punishing all persons, whether natives or foreigners, who have committed this offense [piracy] . . . is conclusive proof that the offense is supposed to depend, not upon the particular provisions of any municipal code, but upon the law of nations, both for its definition and punishment." Moreover, the American Law Institute's Restatement of the Foreign Relations Law of the United States (1987) provides: "It is generally accepted that the principles of the [UN] Charter prohibiting the use of force [for example, article 2(4)] . . . have the character of *jus cogens.*"

Once such norms have been accepted by the international community, either in treaties or in custom, they are considered bases for protecting the interests of nations and upholding recognized standards of public morality. The fact that a country had not ratified the Convention on the Prevention and Punishment of the Crime of Genocide (1948) at the time that any of its nationals committed genocidal acts, for example, would not preclude other nations from punishing the perpetrators because such a crime is a violation of a *jus cogens* norm against genocide.

Restatement of the Law, The Foreign Relations Law of the United States, vol. 1 (1986), section 102, Sources of International Law, comment K: "Peremptory norms of international law *(jus cogens).* Some rules of international law are recognized by the international community of states as peremptory, permitting no derogation."

Vienna Convention on the Law of Treaties (1969), article 53: "A treaty is void if, at the time of its conclusion, it conflicts with a pre-emptory norm of general international law *[jus cogens].*"

U.S. Court of Appeals, Fifth Circuit (1993): "'Jus cogens' describes preemptory norms of law which are nonderogable and form the highest level of international law."

Permanent Court of International Justice (1934): "[It is hard to] believe that the League of Nations would have already embarked on the codification of international law if it were not possible, even today, to create a *jus cogens*, the effect of which would be that, once States have agreed on certain rules of law, and have also given an undertaking that these rules may not be altered by some only of their number, any act adopted in contravention of that undertaking would be automatically void."

Kasto, Jalil. *Jus Cogens and Humanitarian Law*. London: Author, 1994.

Sunga, Lyal S. "Advent of Normative Hierarchy in International Law and Its Relation to Individual Criminal Responsibility." In *The Emerging System of International Criminal Law: Developments in Codification and Implementation*. The Hague: Kluwer Law International, 1997.

Charter of the United Nations; Derogation; International Law; Norms

Justice

In law, justice (from the Latin *jus* or *ius*, meaning law, legal status, right, or authority) is the constant and perpetual disposition to render every person his or her due. As an abstract concept, justice is a noble ideal toward which all systems of law and human rights enforcement must strive. In its broadest sense, *justice* is similar in meaning to *virtue* or *proper conduct.*

The ancient Greek philosophers Plato and Aristotle both sought to understand what justice means and how a system of government could ensure justice for its citizens. James Madison, the "father of the U.S. Constitution," wrote in essay no. 51 of *The Federalist*, a 1788 compilation of essays endorsing adoption of the Constitution, that justice is the end sought by government and civil society. However, in essay no. 17 of the same work, Alexander Hamilton pointed out that the administration of justice, the "great cement of society," left to the constituent states of the United States by the Constitution protects them from excessive encroachment by the national government. Here Hamilton is referring to the independent state court systems that cannot be the subject of control by the national government.

Everyone can agree that justice in the abstract is a desirable end of government activity, but determining justice for whom and at what cost is more difficult. In the context of human rights, justice has many dimensions. Time is one. For instance, how far back in time must justice reach? Are the Native Americans in the United States entitled to the return of the lands taken from them by the European colonizers? Are the Christian Serbs in Yugoslavia entitled to punish Muslim Kosovars for centuries-old wrongs? Justice also has an economic dimension. The cost of compensating people for wrongs, even if acknowledged, may be prohibitive. And, in a time of complex legal systems and complicated laws, are the wealthy, who can afford to hire better lawyers, entitled to better justice than the average citizen?

To complicate the issue, justice generally takes a number of forms. Commutative justice refers to honoring contracts, regardless of the personal merits of the parties involved. Distributive justice, on the other hand, entails the distribution of rewards and punishments based on personal merit. For example, one party to a contract may not unilaterally abrogate it on the grounds of the other party's gender, race, or national origin. And an employer may not pay a man a higher wage for doing the same job as a woman; the value or merit of the service rendered, not the sex of the person performing the work, should determine the amount of wages.

A new term, *transitional justice*, refers to the justice meted out to rulers responsible for gross violations of human rights. Bolivia, for example, suffered under military rule from 1964 to 1982, a particularly violent episode of which was García Meza's bloody coup in July 1981. After his ouster the general was tried for his crimes, which included assassination and genocide. On April 21, 1993, declared a "day of national dignity" by the government, the Bolivian supreme court sentenced Meza and his principal collaborators to thirty years' imprisonment without parole, the severest penalty permitted under Bolivia's constitution.

A major flaw with transitional justice occurs when a violator avoids or obtains reduced punishment in return for turning power over to a democratic successor government. In 1990 Augusto Pinochet escaped prosecution in Chile for gross human rights violations, including enforced disappearances, in exchange for agreeing to relinquish his dictatorial power. In some cases transitional justice foregoes punishment in favor of a healing process, a solution tried in South Africa after the end of apartheid, where a Truth and Reconciliation Commission was established to investigate violations of human rights rather than to exact legal sanctions.

Constitution of Spain (1978), preamble: "The Spanish nation, desirous of establishing justice, liberty, and security and promoting the good of its members. . . ," proclaims this constitution.

Charter of Paris for a New Europe (1990), Human Rights, Democracy and Rule of Law: "Democracy, with its representative and pluralistic character, entails accountability to the electorate, the obligation of public authorities to comply with the law and justice administered impartially."

Commission on Human Rights, Resolution 1993/32, The Administration of Justice and Human Rights (1993): "The Commission on Human Rights . . . 7. Appeals to Governments to include in their national development plans the administration of justice as an integral part of the development process and to allocate adequate resources for the provision of legal aid services with a view to the promotion and protection of human rights."

Nuremberg International Military Tribunal (1945–46): "The privilege of opening the first trial in history for crimes against the peace of the world imposes a grave responsibility," said Associate Justice Robert H. Jackson of the U.S. Supreme Court, trial prosecutor before the world's first international transitional justice tribunal. "The wrongs we seek to condemn and punish have been so calculated, so malignant, and so devastating, that civilization cannot tolerate their being ignored, because it cannot survive their being repeated."

U.K. Court of Appeals, Criminal Division (1981): "An act could not have a tendency to pervert the course of justice unless proceedings of some kind were in being or imminent or an investigation was in progress which might bring about proceedings, so that a course of justice had been embarked on."

Coalition for International Justice, 740 15th Street, N.W., Eighth Floor, Washington, D.C. 20005-1009. (202-662-1595. 🖨 202-662-1597. 🖥 coalition@cij.org. 🖥 www.cij.org.

Coalition for International Justice, Javastraat 119, 2585 AH, The Hague, Netherlands. (31-70-363-9721. 🖨 31-70-363-9721. 🖥 coalition@cij.org. 🖥 www.cij.org.

Solomon, Robert C., and Mark C. Murphy, eds. *What Is Justice? Classic and Contemporary Readings*. New York: Oxford University Press, 1999.

Teitel, Ruti. *Transitional Justice*. New York: Oxford University Press, 1999.

Aristotle; Enforcement; Equality; Impunity; International Criminal Court; Plato

Juveniles

See Guidelines for the Prevention of Juvenile Delinquency (Riyadh Guidelines); Rules for the Protection of Juveniles Deprived of Their Liberty; Standard Minimum Rules for the Administration of Juvenile Justice (Beijing Rules); Youth

The 1960s civil rights movement in the United States spearheaded a world-wide assault on racism that eventually brought about the end of racist apartheid policies in South Africa in the 1990s. Martin Luther King Jr., the assassinated leader of the U.S. movement, has become a symbol of the struggle for racial equality and nonviolent protest against unjust government policies. [Library of Congress]

Kampala Declaration on Human Rights

Lacking the cohesiveness of other world regions, Asia and the Pacific area have not advanced to the same level as Western regions in addressing human rights activities on a regional basis, nor has Africa. An African Charter on Human and Peoples' Rights, adopted by the Organization of African Unity in 1981, created a commission to act on human rights complaints. Africa's regional system, however, has yet to prove as effective as Europe's, which has developed an impressive record of decisions by the commission and court (since combined) established under the European Convention for the Protection of Human Rights and Fundamental Freedoms (1950).

A small step toward developing an African-Asian inter-regional human rights system similar to those in Europe and the Americas was taken when the Asian-African Legal Consultative Committee, with representatives from forty-three African and Asian countries, met in Kampala, Uganda, and adopted the Kampala Declaration on Human Rights on February 6, 1993. In 1992 the UN General Assembly had recognized the committee for its efforts in support of UN goals and programs.

The declaration begins by recalling the provisions of the Charter of the United Nations (1945), the Universal Declaration of Human Rights (1948), and other international human rights instruments. "The Universal Decla-ration of Human Rights," states paragraph 1, "proclaims a common understanding of all the peoples of the world in the field of human rights and gives help, guidance, and inspiration to humanity in the promotion of human rights and fundamental freedoms." Paragraph 2 recognizes that the UN, through various international instruments, has "made much progress in defining standards for the promotion, enjoyment, and protection of human rights and fundamental freedoms. It is the obligation of the members of the international community to ensure the observance of these rights and freedoms," notes the declaration.

Paragraph 4 calls on all states to ratify the International Covenant on Civil and Political Rights (1966) and the International Covenant on Economic, Social and Cultural Rights (1966), while paragraph 5 declares: "It is the oblig-ation of all members of the international community to ensure [enforcement of] the principles enshrined in the Charter of the United Nations and in other international human rights instruments." According to paragraph 6, "Peace and security are a prerequisite for the full realiza-tion of all inalienable and indivisible human rights." Para-graph 7 notes that "all governments have a special duty to ensure that the constitutions and laws of their States that relate to human rights are in compliance with interna-tional human rights standards and are observed and respected."

The right to development and the importance of economic and social progress "to the full enjoyment of human rights" are recognized in paragraph 8, which adds: "It is undoubted that the existence of widespread poverty is a main reason resulting in the insufficient enjoyment of human rights by the majority of humanity. Therefore, all States should cooperate in the essential task of eradicating poverty as an indispensable requirement for the universal realization of human rights." Paragraph 9 emphasizes "the human right to a clean and salubrious environment" and urges the promotion of sustainable development. Paragraph 10 acknowledges that the "principle of the indivisibility and interdependence of human rights . . . must be given effect in policy formulation and implementation."

"The primary responsibility for implementing and giving effect to human rights," notes paragraph 11, "is at the national level. Consequently, the most effective system or method of promoting and protecting these rights has to take into account the nation's history, culture, traditions, norms, and values." Special attention, observes paragraph 12, should be given to "the rights of vulnerable groups such as women, children, refugees, disabled, migrant workers, and minorities." Paragraph 13 calls on the international community to "devise effective action plans and concrete measures to overcome the current obstacles to the full realization of human rights, namely, threats to peace and security, foreign aggression and occupation, colonization, racism, racial discrimination, apartheid, terrorism, xenophobia, ethnic and religious intolerance . . . , denial of justice, torture, unfair and unjust international economic order, widespread poverty and illiteracy, worsening economic situation of developing countries, and heavy burden of external debts."

Paragraphs 14, 15, and 16 focus on the rule of law and the administration of justice, while paragraph 17 addresses standards for law enforcement officials. Cooperation among "national, regional, and international organizations in the field of human rights," the importance of the role of nongovernmental organizations to human rights, and enhancement of public awareness and concerns for human rights are covered in paragraphs 18, 19, and 20, respectively.

The last item of the declaration, paragraph 21, urges the "United Nations system in the field of human rights . . . to use existing mechanisms and resources effectively and efficiently. . . . All members of the international community," it adds, "are called upon to contribute additional financial and other resources for human rights activities."

Asian-African Legal Consultative Committee, 27 Ring Road, Lajpat Nagar-IV, New Delhi 110024, India. (91-11-641-5280. 🖶 91-11-622-1344.

United Nations High Commissioner for Human Rights, 8–14 avenue de la Paix, 1211 Geneva 10, Switzerland. (41-22-917-9000. 🖶 41-22-917-9016. 🖳 webadmin.hchr@unog.ch. 🖳 www.unhchr.ch.

Bauer, Joanne R., and Daniel A. Bell, eds. *The East Asian Challenge for Human Rights.* New York: Cambridge University Press, 1999.

Woodiwiss, Anthony. *Globalisation, Human Rights and Labour Law in Pacific Asia.* New York: Cambridge University Press, 1998.

African Charter on Human and Peoples' Rights; Development; Environment; International Covenant on Civil and Political Rights; International Covenant on Economic, Social and Cultural Rights; Regional Human Rights Systems; Self-Determination

King, Martin Luther, Jr.

Adopting the nonviolent strategy of the Indian human rights leader Mohandas Gandhi, the Reverend Martin Luther King Jr. (1929–68) led the campaign in the 1960s to ensure that black Americans could exercise their civil rights throughout the nation. For his efforts he became an international symbol of the struggle for civil rights, won the Nobel Peace Prize in 1964, and died at the hands of an assassin.

Michael King Jr. was born on January 15, 1929, in Atlanta. He and his father would later take the name Martin Luther, after the leader of the Protestant movement and founder of the Lutheran denomination. Educated at Morehouse College in Georgia and Crozer Theological Seminary, King received a Ph.D. in theology from Boston University in 1955. From 1947 until his death he was a Baptist minister.

Rosa Parks, a black woman, was arrested in 1955 in Montgomery, Alabama, for refusing to sit at the back of a public bus. King, an active member in the National Association for the Advancement of Colored People (NAACP) and the Alabama Council for Human Relations, organized a bus boycott with other black leaders in Alabama that led to the abandonment of the discriminatory seating policy and the hiring of black drivers. The U.S. Supreme Court subsequently held that bus segregation laws were unconstitutional. As a result, King gained national prominence in the movement to ensure civil rights for blacks in America.

With some sixty other black ministers, King helped form the Southern Christian Leadership Conference (SCLC) and was elected its first president. The SCLC sponsored a number of nonviolent protests to further their cause. In one type of protest, the "sit-in," black civil rights activists sat in seats reserved for whites at segregated lunch counters in urban stores, forcing well-publicized encounters with local police. In another form of protest, the "freedom rides," white and black activists boarded interstate buses to test a new federal law prohibiting segregated accommodations in bus stations.

In 1959 King, an admirer and emulator of Gandhi and his

philosophy of nonviolence, was invited by Prime Minister Jawaharlal Nehru to visit India, which in large part through Gandhi's efforts had won its independence from Britain a decade earlier. But on King's return to the United States, the white opposition to the nonviolent civil rights movement took a more violent turn. Although his home had been bombed earlier and he lived under constant threats to his and his family's safety, King renewed his campaign for civil rights. On August 28, 1963, at the end of a protest march for civil rights, King delivered his now-famous "I have a dream" speech at the Lincoln Memorial in Washington, D.C. King's efforts culminated in Congress's enactment of civil rights laws in 1964 to promote and protect the rights of blacks.

In 1964 King was awarded the Nobel Peace Prize for his nonviolent human rights crusade. Continuing his fight, he began speaking out against the Vietnam War and in 1967 began planning a "poor peoples' march" to unite the poor of all races. On April 4, 1968, however, a bullet from an assassin's rifle cut short his life and work. King has become a worldwide symbol of equal rights for all persons. Today his birthday is a national and state holiday throughout the United States.

Martin Luther King Jr. Center for Nonviolent Social Change, 449 Auburn Avenue, N.E., Atlanta, Ga. 30312. (404-526-8900. 404-526-8969. mlkctr@aol.com. www.thekingcenter.com.

Martin Luther King Jr. National Historic Site, 450 Auburn Avenue, N.E., Atlanta, Ga. 30312-1525. (404-331-5190. 404-730-3112. malu_superintendent@nps.gov. www.nps.gov.

Pyatt, Sherman E. *Martin Luther King, Jr.* New York: Greenwood, 1986.

Tucker, Deborah J. *Unstoppable Man*. Detroit: Wayne State University Press, 1994.

Apartheid; Civil Rights; Equality; Gandhi, Mohandas K.; Minorities; Race Discrimination

Modeled on the Statue of Liberty in New York Harbor, the *Goddess of Democracy* carried by Chinese student protesters in Tiananmen Square in Beijing on May 30, 1989, symbolized basic yearnings for freedom. Liberty for all citizens requires constitutional democracy to translate the will of the people into effective and accountable government. [Reuters/Bettmann News Photo]

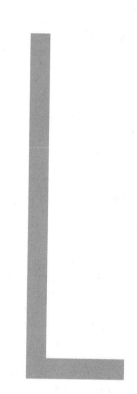

Labor Unions

See Association; International Labor Organization; Workers

Language

"The tie of language is, perhaps, the strongest and most durable that can unite mankind," observed Alexis de Tocqueville, the French jurist and commentator on early American government, in his book *Democracy in America* (1835). From another perspective, however, language can be a barrier between peoples. Without the freedom to speak one's language, the human rights of linguistic minorities have lesser value than those of the majority. Because a person's first language, like his or her culture and religion, is nearly always an accident of birth, language *(lingua* in Latin) is beginning to be shown the same respect as cultures and religions that do not infringe on others' rights.

The ancient Greeks, who contributed heavily to the development of democracy and human rights, saw language as the defining boundary between themselves—free, self-governing citizens—and the *barbaroi* (barbarians). The Greeks were proud of their language and its role in arguing for and maintaining their freedom and democracy. During the long period of the Roman Empire, Latin became the *lingua franca*, or universal language, of Europe, North Africa, and Asia Minor.

Human rights guarantees depend on language, particularly access to information about rights and procedures for asserting them. Language determines how human rights are described, promoted, and enforced. A nation that includes a number of linguistic minorities but officially records its laws in only one language may diminish those minorities' employment opportunities, for example, or access to the courts for redress of grievances. Today a number of nations confront the problem of accommodating more than one language. In Canada, both English and French are official languages. In Belgium, national legislation affecting the Flemish-speaking and French-speaking regions must be passed by a majority vote of each linguistic group in both houses of the legislature. Some countries—for example, Ethiopia, Finland, Israel, and South Africa, which has nine official languages in addition to Afrikaans and English—designate a national or an official language or languages in their constitutions. The constitutions of a number of states in the United States, including Arizona, Colorado, Florida, and North Carolina, expressly make English the official language, while Hawaii designates both English and Hawaiian as official languages. Even so, there is much debate over bilingual education in many states with large minority populations of recent immigrants.

For citizens who do not speak their country's principal or official language, language rights that are becoming recognized include the use of translators or interpreters when dealing with the government, especially in civil and criminal proceedings, and, to some extent, bilingual education. The

Declaration on the Rights of Persons Belonging to National or Ethnic, Religious and Linguistic Minorities (1992) mandates, among other things, that nations "take appropriate measures so that, wherever possible, persons belonging to minorities have adequate opportunities to learn their mother tongue or to have instruction in their mother tongue." The document further directs countries to "consider appropriate measures so that persons belonging to minorities [including linguistic minorities] may participate fully in the economic progress and development of their country." Ethnic, cultural, and linguistic minorities also seek to preserve and pass along to their children their own language as part of their cultural heritage, their way of knowing and describing the world.

Why should linguistic differences be preserved if within a generation everyone could speak the same language if only they were taught to do so? One argument is that cultural diversity, including linguistic diversity, is as beneficial to society as species diversity is in nature. Lockstep language, like lockstep thought, is a counterproductive survival technique, at least for our particularly linguistic species. On the other hand, the modern world is becoming more competitive, and people with only minority language skills are at a relative disadvantage with respect to opportunities for education, work, and travel compared with those who speak more widely used languages. As the ability to travel and communicate worldwide increases, it may be more difficult for minority languages to survive.

A number of nations address language rights in their constitutions or national laws, among them Cambodia, Colombia, Ecuador, Egypt, Greece, Italy, India, and Spain. Some international human rights documents also guarantee a measure of language rights or at least acknowledge the potential conflicts in national policies concerning language. In 1992 the Council of Europe promulgated the European Charter for Regional or Minority Languages, which contains a detailed program for addressing issues relating to linguistic minorities.

Constitution of Belgium (1831), heading II, Concerning the Belgians and Their Rights, article 23: "The use of languages spoken in Belgium is optional: it may only be regulated by law and only in the case of acts by the public authorities and legal matters."

European Charter for Regional or Minority Languages (1992), part III, Measures to Promote the Use of Regional or Minority Languages in Public Life . . . , article 8, Education: "1. With regard to education, the Parties undertake, within the territory in which such languages are used, according to the situation of each of these languages, and without prejudice to the teaching of the official language(s) of the State: a. i. to make available pre-school education in the relevant regional or minority languages; or ii. to make available a substantial part of pre-school education in the relevant regional or minority languages; or iii. to apply one of those measures

. . . above at least to those pupils whose families so request and whose number is considered sufficient; or iv. if the public authorities have no direct competence in the field of pre-school education, to favor and/or encourage the application of the measures referred to . . . above. . . ."

Supreme Court of Canada (1986): Although Canada's constitution (1982), article 16, recognizes two official languages, French and English, this provision alone does not guarantee a right to any particular service in either official language.

European Court of Human Rights (1978): The European Convention for the Protection of Human Rights and Fundamental Freedoms (1950), article 6(3)(e), provides as a minimum right that a person accused of a crime is "to have the free assistance of an interpreter if he cannot understand or speak the language used in court." It also prohibits assessment of costs for such an interpreter, even if the person is convicted.

Terralingua, P.O. Box 122, Hancock, Mich. 49930-0122. dharmon@georgewright.org. cougar.ucdavis.edu/nas/terralin/learn.

Varennes, Fernand de. *Language, Minorities and Human Rights*. The Hague: Kluwer Law International, 1996.

Cultural Rights; Declaration on the Rights of Persons Belonging to National or Ethnic, Religious and Linguistic Minorities; Information; Minorities

Las Casas, Bartolomé de

A Spanish missionary to the New World, Bartolomé de Las Casas (1474–1566) denounced the Spaniards' cruelty and acts of barbarism against the native peoples of the West Indies and Central and South America. Called "the Apostle of the Indies," he spent much of his life defending and seeking justice for the persecuted inhabitants of lands conquered by the Spanish.

Born in Seville, Spain, in 1474, Las Casas was a young adult when Christopher Columbus returned from his first voyage to the New World in 1493. His father, a merchant, sailed with Columbus on his second trip, while Bartolomé, serving in the Spanish militia, fought off rebellious Moors in Granada. In 1502, as both a Christian lay teacher and a member of a Spanish military contingent, he sailed for America to the island of Hispanola, where he participated in the military suppression of the indigenous peoples, seemingly with little remorse. For his services he received from the Spanish Crown an *encomienda*, a tract of land with the right to use the natives living on it as slaves.

Las Casas became an ordained priest in Rome in 1506 and in 1512 returned to the New World, where, as chaplain to the Spanish troops conquering Cuba, he was granted another *encomienda*. Increasingly sickened by the cruelty suffered by the native peoples, he renounced the grant two years later. Experiencing a moral conversion, Las Casas wrote graphically of the horrors inflicted by the Spanish *conquistadors:* "The Spaniards with their Horses, their Speares and Lances, began to commit murders, and strange cruelties: they entered into Townes, Borowes, and Villages, sparing neither children nor old men, neither women with childe, neither them that lay in, but that they ripped their bellies, and cut them in peeces.... They made certaine grates of pearches laid on pickforkes, and made a little fire underneath, to the intent, that by little and little yelling and despairing in these torments, they might give up the Ghost." For the rest of his life, through his writings and advocacy, he worked to end the *encomienda* system and bring dignity and justice to the indigenous peoples in the Spanish colonies.

Las Casas's efforts were rewarded in 1542 by the passage of Spain's New Laws, which proposed to phase out the *encomienda* system and ban slavery and forced labor. A revolt in Peru and a threatened revolt elsewhere in Spain's colonies forced some scaling back of these laws, however. At Vallodolid, Spain, in 1550, Las Casas debated the status of the indigenous peoples of the Americas with Juan Ginés de Sepúlveda, a defender of Spain's colonial policy. Sepúlveda cited the ancient Greek philosopher Aristotle's comment to the effect that some men are slaves by nature, but Las Casas countered that all people are equal because of the oneness of humankind. His impassioned arguments resulted in further measures to eliminate slavery and curtail future conquests.

Las Casas died at the age of ninety-two in a Dominican monastery in Madrid. His writings, including his *Very Brief Account of the Destruction of the Indies* (1552) and *History of the Indies* (not published until 1875–76), believed by some to exaggerate the cruelty of the Spanish *conquistadores,* are still important for understanding the development of Spain's colonial empire in the New World. His stand against wanton cruelty and slavery and for the human rights of all peoples was an important step on the long road to the modern-day human rights movement.

Gonzálas-Casanovas, Roberto J. *Imperial Histories from Alfonso X to Inca Garcilaso: Revisionist Myths of Reconquest and Conquest.* Potomac, Md.: Scripta Humanistica, 1997.

Keen, Benjamin. *Essays in the Intellectual History of Colonial Latin America.* Boulder, Colo.: Westview, 1998.

Aristotle; Forced Labor; Indigenous Peoples; Slavery

Law Enforcement

Law enforcement—a nation's first line of internal security—presents many opportunities for an agent acting on behalf of the government, knowingly or unknowingly, to violate the rights of citizens. While police and other law enforcement officers are protecting citizens from those who would violate the law, they must also carry out their work in a manner that respects the rights of both the victims and the accused. At the same time as they are acting to protect others, typically under extreme conditions and provocation, law enforcement officers often also risk their own lives.

Because law enforcement (from the Vulgar Latin *infortiare,* meaning to make strong, and the Middle English *enforcen*) is an important aspect of national sovereignty, national constitutions invariably charge the head of the executive branch with seeing that the nation's laws are executed. A chief executive's failure to see that law enforcement officials live up to human rights principles leads to an erosion of public confidence in law enforcement, creates civil unrest, hampers effective prosecutions in court, and results in freedom for the guilty and punishment of the innocent. "[I]t is essential, if man is not to be compelled to have recourse, as a last resort, to rebellion against tyranny and oppression," states the preamble to the Universal Declaration of Human Rights (1948), "that human rights should be protected by the rule of law."

Basic human rights principles for law enforcement require that police officers respect and obey the law at all times, protect human dignity and uphold the rights of all people without discrimination, be responsible and accountable to the community as a whole, and report violations of laws, codes, and principles that protect human rights. Unnecessary force or violence should not be used in making an arrest to avoid injury to suspects as well as to innocent bystanders. Persons detained should be treated with respect, and the principle of the presumption of innocence should apply. During investigations, the police should not use force or intimidation to coerce testimony. In accordance with the principles of the rule of law and due process of law, exculpatory evidence should be made available to the court.

"Police officers and law enforcement agencies that respect human rights thus reap benefits which advance the very objectives of law enforcement, while at the same time building a law enforcement structure that does not rely on fear and raw power, but rather on honor, professionalism and legality," states the UN publication *Human Rights and Law Enforcement: A Manual on Human Rights Training for the Police* (1966), a guide for law enforcement officials based on the principles of the Universal Declaration of Human Rights. A more recent primer, *International Human Rights*

Standards for Law Enforcement: A Pocket Book on Human Rights for the Police (1996), contains detailed instructions on investigations, arrests, detention, and the use of force and firearms, including during times of civil disorder, states of emergency, and armed conflict. Specifically addressed are the rights of women, juveniles, refugees, nonnationals, and victims.

Significant international human rights documents relating to law enforcement include the Code of Conduct for Law Enforcement Officials (1979); its Guidelines for Implementation, adopted by the UN General Assembly (1989); and Basic Principles on the Use of Force and Firearms by Law Enforcement Officials (1990), developed by the Eighth United Nations Congress on Prevention of Crime and the Treatment of Offenders. Among other things, these documents call for police to use a high degree of personal responsibility as they serve the community and protect all persons against illegal acts, exercise restraint in using force and firearms, and obtain proper training, supervision, and counseling.

Constitution of the Philippines (1987), article VII, Executive Department, section 17: "The president shall have control of all the executive departments, bureaus, and offices. He shall ensure that the laws are faithfully executed."

Kampala Declaration on Human Rights (1993), paragraph 17: "The international community calls upon States to ensure that law enforcement officials shall, in the performance of their duties, respect and protect human dignity and maintain and uphold human rights of all persons in accordance with international standards. . . ."

European Court of Human Rights (1995): An Austrian national alleged that he had been beaten and kicked while in custody after being arrested for drug trafficking and interrogated by the Austrian police. Such treatment, confirmed by a doctor's examination, constituted a breach by Austria of the European Convention for the Protection of Human Rights and Fundamental Freedoms (1950), article 3, which prohibits torture, and entitled the victim to 100,000 Austrian shillings for nonpecuniary damages and 200,000 shillings for costs and expenses.

Inter-American Commission on Human Rights (1994): The Government of El Salvador is responsible in the death of a victim by agents of the National Police and "has violated the rights to life, humane treatment, a fair trial and judicial protection, upheld in . . . the American Convention on Human Rights [1969]. . . ."

Alliance of NGOs on Crime Prevention and Criminal Justice, P.O. Box 81826, Lincoln, Neb. 68501-1826. (402-464-0602. 🖶 402-464-5931. 🖳 garyhill@cega.com.

International Police Association, One Fox Road, West Bridgford, Nottingham NG2 6AJ, England. (44-115-945-5985. 🖶 44-115-982-2578. 🖳 wendy@ipa-iac.demoon.co.uk. 🖳 www.ipa-iac.org.

Crawshaw, Ralph, Barry Devlin, and Tom Williamson. *Human Rights and Policing: Standards for Good Behavior and a Strategy for Change.* The Hague: Kluwer Law International, 1998.

International Human Rights Standards for Law Enforcement: A Pocket Book on Human Rights for the Police. New York: United Nations, 1996.

Accused; Basic Principles on the Use of Force and Firearms by Law Enforcement Officials; Civil Rights; Code of Conduct for Law Enforcement Officials; Due Process of Law; Fair Trial; Prisoners; Punishment; Torture

Lawyers Committee for Human Rights

The Lawyers Committee for Human Rights was founded in 1978 to promote and protect human rights through the rule of law at both the international and national levels. Using the services of prominent lawyers, judges, law professors, and bar associations worldwide, it provides an urgent response system, an asylum program, and a lawyer-to-lawyer network. The committee played a significant role in helping establish the International Criminal Court in 1998.

Through its urgent response system, the group assists human rights advocates and other nongovernmental organizations by protesting specific human rights violations, exposing underlying systemic defects, and providing casework assistance, such as fact-finding missions, diplomatic visits, legal briefs, and trial observations. The committee aids asylum seekers and other refugees and promotes humane immigration laws and regulations by providing legal assistance to individuals and presenting their cases before various government branches. In 1998 the committee's asylum program represented some eight hundred fifty clients in sixty countries and provided legal training and support to their volunteer attorneys.

An important program of the Lawyers Committee is its lawyer-to-lawyer network, which provides assistance and support for lawyers involved in human rights around the world. In December 1999 a lawyer from Kosovo was abducted while representing Albanian political prisoners being held in Serbia, held incommunicado for almost two weeks, and released only after a ransom was paid. The Lawyers Committee questioned the Serbian government's commitment to the Basic Principles on the Role of Lawyers (1990), particularly the provision that requires the government to permit lawyers to perform their professional duties without "intimidation, hindrance, harassment or improper interference." The network also made available online addresses of Serbian government officials to whom protests about the lawyer could be sent.

In addition, the committee works to hold governments accountable to the standards of the International Bill of Human Rights, to support human rights advocacy at the local level, and to urge greater emphasis on human rights by international organizations. It provides legal reform aid to various countries, video equipment and guidance in using communications technology, training and workshops, and technical assistance to international organizations and publishes books on human rights and a quarterly newsletter, *The Advisor*. Every two years, alternating with the American Civil Liberties Union (ACLU), it awards the Roger Baldwin Medal of Liberty, named for the founder of the ACLU and the International League for Human Rights. The Lawyers Committee's work is administered by a national council, a Washington, D.C., council, an international rule of law council, and a board of directors.

Lawyers Committee for Human Rights, 100 Maryland Avenue, N.E., Washington, D.C. 20002. (202-547-5692. 202-543-5999. wdc@lchr.org. www.lchr.org.

☞

Basic Principles on the Role of Lawyers; Counsel; International Criminal Court; International League for Human Rights

Legal Aid

See Counsel

Lesbians

See Homosexuals

Liberty

"The Idea of Liberty," wrote the English philosopher John Locke in 1690, "is the Idea of a Power in any Agent to do or forbear any particular Action." Today the terms *liberty* and *freedom*, taken literally, suggest exemption from extraneous control. Denials of individual liberties by government generally take the form of arrest and detention. Gross vio-

lations of human rights include forced labor, slavery, disappearance, hostage taking, incommunicado detention, and placement in concentration or death camps.

"The basis of a democratic state is liberty, which, according to the common opinion of men, can only be enjoyed in such a state....," concluded the ancient Greek philosopher Aristotle in *The Politics*. In his time, however, the Greeks practiced slavery—the denial of liberty to an entire class of people—but a person wrongly enslaved could be freed by a friend. In ancient Rome, a freed slave acquired the status of *libertas* (Latin for freedom).

In 1215 Magna Carta asserted that "men in our kingdom shall have and keep all these liberties, rights, and concessions." The creation of the United States of America and the framing of its constitution in 1787—using concepts derived from English districts outside the sheriff's jurisdiction called liberties—were in essence attempts to secure certain freedoms and liberties from the encroachment of government. The Declaration of Independence (1776) emphasized individuals' "unalienable" rights of "Life, Liberty, and the Pursuit of Happiness." A weak government, however, is not necessarily better for guaranteeing liberty. In the first essay of *The Federalist* (1788), a collection of articles promoting ratification of the U.S. Constitution (1789), Alexander Hamilton wrote that "the noble enthusiasm of liberty is apt to be infected with a spirit of narrow and illiberal distrust ... [and] the vigor of government is essential to the security of liberty...."

The right to liberty has remained a fundamental component of human rights instruments ever since. The French Declaration of the Rights of Man and of the Citizen (1789) proclaimed that "the natural and inalienable rights of man ... are liberty, property, security and resistance to oppression." The Universal Declaration of Human Rights (1948) declared that "[e]veryone has the right to life, liberty and security of person." As recently as 1969, the nations of the Americas stated in the American Convention on Human Rights that their goal is "to consolidate in this hemisphere ... a system of personal liberty and social justice based on respect for the essential rights of man."

In the modern civil state, liberty theoretically includes the relinquishment of certain natural rights such as personal vengeance or vigilante justice in exchange for the equal protection and opportunity afforded by the political community. Every government has to decide where to draw the line between the liberty of citizens and the authority of the state and how much to circumscribe that liberty for the common good. Rather than an absolute right, liberty is perhaps more an ideal state in which all citizens must forego some freedom in order to share in a number of rights afforded by government.

Constitution of Italy (1948), part one, The Duties and Rights of the Citizens, title I, Civil Relations, article 13: "Personal freedom is inviolable."

African Charter on Human and Peoples' Rights (1981), part I, Rights and Duties, chapter I, Human and Peoples' Rights, article 6: "Every individual shall have the right to liberty and to the security of his person."

U.K. House of Lords (1987): The courts attach great weight to the right to personal liberty, and any infringement will attract intense scrutiny.

European Commission of Human Rights (1978): "The word 'liberty' means freedom from arrest and detention."

Cole, Phillip. *The Free, the Unfree, and the Excluded: A Treatise on the Conditions of Liberty.* Aldershot, Hants, England: Ashgate, 1998.

Epstein, Richard A. *Principles for a Free Society: Reconciling Individual Liberty with the Common Good.* Reading, Mass.: Perseus Books, 1998.

Aristotle; Detention; Fundamental Rights; Locke, John; Natural Rights; Security; Slavery

Life

The right to life is the most basic of all human rights, because the enjoyment of all other rights depends on it. "While there is life, there's hope . . . ," the British poet and dramatist John Gay wrote in 1727. Life alone, however, is not enough for a full human existence; it is the quality of life that gives meaning to our time on Earth.

In its simplest form, the right to life (derived from Teutonic, German, and Old English words) requires that no person's life be taken without procedural safeguards. Although many governments are now prohibited from exercising capital punishment, for most of human history the state's power to put people to death was widely accepted. The question was not whether to do so but for which reasons and by which legal procedures.

Even in relatively enlightened ancient Greek city-states such as Athens, death sentences were meted out for serious crimes, but trials and appeals served as legal safeguards. Later political and religious leaders often found ways to justify killing pagans, heretics, and other innocent people when their agendas called for it. While the state may put citizens' lives at risk during military service to maintain national security, the right to life continues to be violated with every act of genocide, every summary execution, and every disappearance that ends in the murder of the victim.

Many national constitutions—those of Ireland (1937), Ecuador (1979), and Brazil (1988), for example—declare the right to life to be inviolable, and various national institutions and procedures ensure that a person's life is not taken arbitrarily by the state. These include constitutional guarantees embodied in bills of rights, the observance of the rule of law, strict adherence to due process of law, an independent and impartial judiciary, access to independent and professional legal counsel, rights of appeal, separation of government powers, and effective checks and balances in the system of government.

The right to life is also acknowledged in the major international human rights documents, including the Universal Declaration of Human Rights (1948), European Convention for the Protection of Human Rights and Fundamental Freedoms (1950), and American Convention on Human Rights (1969). "Every human being has the inherent right to life," declares the International Covenant on Civil and Political Rights (1966), article 6. "This right shall be protected by law. No one shall be arbitrarily deprived of his life." The concept is underscored by the document's Second Optional Protocol, Aiming at the Abolition of the Death Penalty (1989).

However, as court cases and treatises with widely differing interpretations continue to indicate, there may never be universal agreement on the extent of the right to life. The U.S. Supreme Court has declared both abortion and capital punishment constitutional within certain limits, whereas in Ireland abortion is illegal while the death penalty is constitutional and in South Africa abortion is legal while the death penalty is unconstitutional. Opponents of abortion, particularly in the United States, have adopted the term *right to life* for their movement, engendering philosophical and legal arguments as to what constitutes human life—whether a reproductive cell, a fertilized egg cell, or a fetus, and, if the latter, at what stage in the gestation period human life begins and requires the state to protect it. By concluding that life begins at conception, such adherents argue that the right to life attaches at the moment of conception.

U.S. Declaration of Independence (1776): "We hold these Truths to be self-evident, that all Men are created equal, that they are endowed by their Creator with certain unalienable Rights, that among these are Life, Liberty, and the Pursuit of Happiness. . . ."

Guidelines for Action on Human Resources Development in the Field of Disability (Tallinn Guidelines) (1989), Guiding Philosophy: "7. As full citizens, [disabled persons] have the same rights and responsibilities as other members of society, including the right to life, as declared in international human rights instruments."

Constitutional Court of Germany (1975): "Human life represents a supreme value within the constitutional order that needs no further

justification; it is the vital basis of . . . human dignity and the pre-requisite of all other basic rights."

European Court of Human Rights (1992): "The Government [of Ireland] maintained that [an] injunction [against providing information to women in Ireland on how to obtain a legal abortion in Great Britain] was necessary in a democratic society for the protection of the right to life of the unborn. . . . The Court observes at the outset that in the present case it is not called upon to examine whether a right to abortion is guaranteed under the [European Convention for the Protection of Human Rights and Fundamental Freedoms (1950)] or whether the fetus is encompassed by the right to life as contained in Article 2 [thereof]."

Agamben, Giorgio. *Homo Sacer: Sovereign Power and Bare Life.* Translated by Daniel Heller-Roazen. Stanford, Calif.: Stanford University Press, 1998.

Ibegbu, Jude. *Rights of the Unborn Child in International Law.* Lewiston, N.Y.: Edwin Mellen, 2000.

Abortion; Capital Punishment; Disappearance; Genocide; International Covenant on Civil and Political Rights, Second Optional Protocol, Aiming at the Abolition of the Death Penalty; Inviolable Rights; Summary Executions

Limburg Principles on the Implementation of the International Covenant on Economic, Social and Cultural Rights

The International Covenant on Economic, Social and Cultural Rights, adopted by the UN General Assembly in 1966, sets forth goals for nations to achieve in developing citizens' so-called second-generation human rights. Unlike the International Covenant on Civil and Political Rights (1966), which mandates first-generation rights—ones governments can immediately put into practice to ensure individual freedom, the rule of law, and constitutional democracy—the rights in the economic covenant require long-term governmental policy and resource commitments. Included are such goals as an adequate standard of living, physical and mental health, education, cultural freedom, scientific progress, and just and favorable conditions for work. The international community is not in complete agreement about either the need for governments to guarantee these economic, social, and cultural rights or the urgency of implementing them.

To provide a foundation in international law as well as guidance for carrying out the covenant's provisions, a group of independent experts in international law met in June 1986 in Maastricht, the Netherlands. The meeting, which was sponsored by the International Commission of Jurists, the law faculty of the University of Limburg in Maastricht, and the Urban Morgan Institute for Human Rights of the University of Cincinnati, unanimously adopted the Limburg Principles. The twenty-nine experts who participated were from Australia, the Federal Republic of Germany, Hungary, Ireland, Mexico, the Netherlands, Norway, Senegal, Spain, the United Kingdom, the United States, and Yugoslavia, as well as from the UN Center for Human Rights, International Labor Organization, and other international groups, including the sponsors. The significance of the principles, which represented the extent of international law at the time, was confirmed in 1993 by a resolution of the Commission on Human Rights.

"Economic, social and cultural rights are an integral part of international human rights law," observes part I, The Nature and Scope of States Parties' Obligations, section A, General Considerations, paragraph 1. "They are the subject of specific treaty obligations in various international instruments, notably the International Covenant on Economic, Social and Cultural Rights." Referring to both of the 1966 international covenants and the Universal Declaration of Human Rights (1948), paragraphs 2 and 3 note that because "human rights and fundamental freedoms are indivisible and interdependent, equal attention and urgent consideration should be given to the implementation, promotion and protection of both civil and political, and economic, social and cultural rights."

Paragraphs 4 and 5, respectively, urge that the International Covenant on Economic, Social and Cultural Rights "be interpreted in good faith, taking into account the object and purpose, the ordinary meaning, the preparatory work and the relevant practice" and that the experience of UN agencies, intergovernmental organizations, working groups, and special rapporteurs (experts) on human rights be considered in implementing and monitoring the covenant.

"The achievement of economic, social and cultural rights may be realized in a variety of political settings," notes paragraph 6. "There is no single road to their full realization. Successes and failures have been registered in both market and non-market [government-directed] economies, in both centralized and decentralized structures."

Paragraph 7 addresses the need to act in good faith, while paragraph 8 raises the possibility of making some rights "justiciable [subject to court enforcement] immediately while others can become justiciable over time." According to paragraph 9, the role of nongovernmental organizations should be "facilitated at the national as well as the international level." Paragraph 10 reminds the states parties to the covenant that they "are accountable both to the international community and to their own people" for compliance with its obligations.

"Given the significance for development of the progressive realization of the rights set forth in the Covenant," states paragraph 14, "particular attention should be given to measures to improve the standard of living of the poor and other disadvantaged groups, taking into account that special measures may be required to protect cultural rights of indigenous peoples and minorities." Paragraph 15, the last item under section A, urges that "[t]rends in international economic relations should be taken into account in assessing the efforts of the international community to achieve the Covenant's objectives."

Section B, Interpretative Principles Specifically Relating to Part II of the Covenant, urges the covenant's signatory nations to implement its provisions. "All States parties have an obligation to begin immediately to take steps towards full realization of the rights contained in the Covenant," directs paragraph 16. "At the national level," adds paragraph 17, "States parties shall use all appropriate means, including legislative, administrative, judicial, economic, social and educational measures, consistent with the nature of the rights in order to fulfill their obligations under the Covenant." The principles stress in article 25 that "States parties are obligated, regardless of the level of economic development, to ensure respect for minimum subsistence rights for all."

Other provisions of the document are set forth in detail, including sections dealing with discrimination, equal rights for women, and nonnationals. For example, in articles 37 and 38, respectively, countries are urged to eliminate "without delay" *de jure* discrimination affecting economic, social, and cultural rights and to end *de facto* discrimination "as speedily as possible." Article 42 notes that "[a]s a general rule the Covenant applies equally to nationals and nonnationals." Article 49 mandates that any limitations on these rights "not be arbitrary or unreasonable or discriminatory."

Section C, Interpretative Principles Specifically Relating to Part III of the Covenant, addresses provisions in article 8, particularly the terms *prescribed by law, necessary in a democratic society, national security, public order,* and *rights and freedoms of others.* For example, paragraph 60 notes that the covenant "imposes a greater restraint upon a State party which is exercising limitations on trade union rights," adding: "It requires that such a limitation is indeed necessary. The term 'necessary' implies that the limitation: (a) responds to a pressing public or social need; (b) pursues a legitimate aim; and (c) is proportional to that aim."

Under section D, Violations of Economic, Social and Cultural Rights, paragraph 70 provides that a nation's failure "to comply with an obligation contained in the Covenant is, under international law, a violation of the Covenant." But, states paragraph 71, "In determining what amounts to a failure to comply, it must be borne in mind that the Covenant affords to a State party a margin of discretion in selecting the means for carrying out its objects, and that factors beyond its reasonable control may adversely affect its capacity to implement particular rights." Paragraph 72 suggests that a signatory nation violates the covenant if it fails to take

a required step, to promptly remove obstacles to rights, to implement a right, to meet generally accepted minimum standards of achievement within its powers, or to submit required reports or if it unfairly limits a right.

Part II, Consideration of States Parties' Reports and International Cooperation under Part IV of the Covenant, addresses countries' submission of reports measuring their achievements. "The effectiveness of the supervisory machinery provided in Part IV of the Covenant," observes section A, Preparation and Submission of Reports by States Parties, paragraph 74, "depends largely upon the quality and timeliness of reports by States parties." Paragraph 76 suggests that individual nations "should view their reporting obligations as an opportunity for broad public discussion on goals and policies designed to realize economic, social and cultural rights."

Section B, Role of the Committee on Economic, Social and Cultural Rights, devotes nine paragraphs to the work of the Committee on Economic, Social and Cultural Rights, which has been assigned the task of assisting the Economic and Social Council (ECOSOC) in carrying out the substantive duties designated by the covenant, including reviewing national reports and making recommendations on compliance.

The final section of the Limburg Principles, encompassing paragraphs 92 through 103, is Section C, Relations between the Committee and Specialized Agencies, and Other International Organizations. Among other recommendations for greater international cooperation, this section, in paragraph 102, suggests "an agreed system for recording, storing and making accessible case law and other interpretative material relating to international instruments on economic, social and cultural rights."

United Nations High Commissioner for Human Rights, 8–14 avenue de la Paix, 1211 Geneva 10, Switzerland. ☎ 41-22-917-9000. 🖨 41-22-917-9016. 🖳 webadmin.hchr@unog.ch. 🖳 www.unhchr.ch.

Cultural Rights; Economic and Social Council (ECOSOC); Economic Rights; International Commission of Jurists; International Covenant on Economic, Social and Cultural Rights; Social Rights

Limitations

So-called absolute rights are not always absolute. There is, however, no simple formula for determining just when and to what degree human rights guaranteed in national and international instruments may be limited (from the Latin word *limes,* meaning boundary). For example, the European Convention for the Protection of Human Rights and Fundamental Freedoms (1950), Protocol no. 1 (1952), article 1,

Protection of Property, states in part: "No one shall be deprived of his possessions except in the public interest and subject to conditions provided for by law and by general principles of international law." Some questions arise from this statement: What is the public interest? Who decides what is in the public interest? Are national laws and principles of international law clear and unambiguous as to these questions? Because the world has witnessed many government rationalizations for restricting citizen rights, the more precise the definition of terms such as *the public interest*, the more secure an individual's rights will be.

Many legitimate—as well as illegitimate—limitations are used by governments to moderate or deny rights proclaimed as absolute. The nature of a sovereign state lends itself to placing the rights or privileges of government officials or the state above those of individual citizens or groups, even when such rights are guaranteed in constitutions or treaties. For example, article 11 of the African Charter of Human and Peoples' Rights provides that the exercise of the "right to assemble freely with others . . . shall be subject only to necessary restrictions . . . , in particular [laws] enacted in the interest of national security, the safety, health, ethics and rights and freedoms of others."

In addition to *the public interest*, mentioned earlier, some of the terms and concepts that governments often use to limit rights include the following justifications: *sovereign immunity, national security, health, safety, morals, public order*, and *public* or *national emergency*. Human rights that often suffer under these limitations, which may or may not be legitimate, include freedom of movement, freedom of the press, and the right to peaceful assembly, not to mention access to the courts and a fair trial. Some courts, particularly in Europe, use a concept known as the "margin of appreciation" to support government determinations of when emergency conditions apply and, therefore, when rights may be limited; these courts allow wide or narrow margins, or flexibility, depending on the nature of the limitation and the importance of the right being limited.

Because public emergencies, real or alleged, may be abused to limit human rights, the European Commission of Human Rights determined that certain conditions are required to establish the legitimacy of a public crisis: the emergency must be actual or imminent; its effects must involve the whole nation; the continuance of community life must be threatened; and the danger must be exceptional in that normal measures or restrictions to maintain public safety, health, and order, as permitted by the European Convention for the Protection of Human Rights and Fundamental Freedoms (1950), are plainly inadequate.

At times rights may also conflict with each other, requiring courts to decide which right prevails. Such a conflict may arise, for instance, when a group attempts to exercise its right of peaceful assembly on private property without permission of the owner, thus infringing the owner's right to the private use of his or her property. Some basis is needed to determine which rights take precedence over others, and the standard for settling disputes over which rights prevail in these situations should also be clear and unambiguous.

National constitutions in some cases set out the nature of limitations on guaranteed rights, and in others they leave it to the courts to determine on a case-by-case basis. Germany's constitution (1949), for example, provides in article 4, Freedom of Faith, of Conscience and of Creed: "(2) The undisturbed practice of religion shall be guaranteed" and "(3) No one may be compelled against his conscience to render war service involving the use of arms. Details shall be regulated by a federal statute." In the first example, the practice of religion is guaranteed and unrestricted, but in the second the constitution itself provides for statutory limits on the right to conscientious objection. For different matters Germany's constitution and others spell out the nature of the limitations in the constitution itself, rather than leaving it to the legislative process.

Among the international human rights documents that address limitations or restrictions on certain noninviolable rights (ones that may be derogated from or limited legitimately in certain emergency situations) are the European Convention for the Protection of Human Rights and Fundamental Freedoms (1950), International Covenant on Civil and Political Rights (1966), and American Convention on Human Rights (1969).

Constitution of Italy (1948), part one, The Duties and Rights of the Citizens, title I, Civil Relations: "15. Freedom and secrecy of correspondence and any other form of communication are inviolable. They may be subject to limitations only under a justified act issued by the judicial authorities and with the guarantees provided for by law."

International Covenant on Civil and Political Rights (1966), article 4: "(1) In time of public emergency which threatens the life of the nation and the existence of which is officially proclaimed, the States Parties to the present Covenant may take measures derogating from their obligations under the present Covenant to the extent strictly required by the exigencies of the situation, provided that such measures are not inconsistent with their other obligations under international law and do not involve discrimination solely on the ground of race, color, sex, language, religion or social origin."

Constitutional Court of Spain (1995): The Constitution of Spain places limits on the right of assembly, as in the case of any other right, when the exercise of this right on a public thoroughfare may cause "public order disturbances which could endanger persons and property."

European Commission of Human Rights (1978): The requirement to wear a helmet when riding a motorcycle as a safety or health precaution is justified even though it may interfere with tenets of the Sikh religion.

Etzioni, Amitai. *Rights and the Common Good: The Communitarian Perspective*. New York: St. Martin's, 1995.

Fitzpatrick, Joan. *Human Rights in Crisis: The International System for Protecting Human Rights during States of Emergency*. Philadelphia: University of Pennsylvania Press, 1994.

American Convention on Human Rights; Derogation; European Commission of Human Rights; European Convention for the Protection of Human Rights and Fundamental Freedoms; International Covenant on Civil and Political Rights; Inviolable Rights

Locke, John

The ideas of the seventeenth-century philosopher John Locke (1632–1704) have contributed significantly to the development of civil liberties and constitutional democracy. His basic principle of human rights—the right to life, liberty, and property—had a profound impact on the framers of the U.S. Constitution in 1787 and is reflected in aspects of the French Revolution and France's Declaration of the Rights of Man and of the Citizen (1789).

Born in 1632 in Wrington, Somerset, England, Locke was educated at Westminster School and Christ Church, Oxford, where he became a friend of Lord Ashley, earl of Shaftesbury. When Shaftesbury became involved with the English colony of Carolina in America, Locke helped him draft a constitution for it. Although it never became effective, some of its provisions—for example, the guarantee of trial by jury and the prohibition against double jeopardy—found their way into South Carolina's constitutions.

Locke's most influential work, *Two Treatises of Government* (1690), published anonymously, justified insurrection against the growing absolutism of the English monarch Charles II. The second of these treatises, on civil government, contains an argument in support of the collective right to revolution. His *Letters on Toleration*, published between 1689 and 1692, call for absolute religious tolerance, except in the case of atheism.

For Locke, the right to property is a natural right that predates the development of human political organization; therefore, no government should be able to take away that right or a person's property without the consent of the governed or of the owners. "The great and *chief end*, therefore, of Mens uniting into Commonwealths, and putting themselves under Government," he said, *"is the preservation of their Property."*

Locke also conditioned the legitimacy of government on the consent of the governed and the law of nature, from which modern human rights laws developed. He championed other rights, including education for women and better education for children, and argued that liberty of conscience was also a natural right and could not be infringed by any political authority, including representative democracy.

Through his insistence on fundamental rights such as his doctrine of implied consent of the governed, Locke contributed significantly to the intellectual struggle to create a rational basis for human rights in a world governed to a large extent by absolute monarchies.

Goldies, Mark, ed. *Locke: Political Essays*. New York: Cambridge University Press, 1997.

Milton, J. R. *Locke's Moral, Political and Legal Philosophy*. Brookfield, Vt.: Ashgate, 1999.

Declaration of the Rights of Man and of the Citizen (France); Fundamental Rights; Natural Rights; Property

A·D·1215.
MAGNA CARTA
Regis Johannis.

With the Seals of the King's Securities to Magna Charta and Shields of ye Barons in Arms.

Fac-simile by EXPRESS PERMISSION from the original Document in the British Museum.

Magna Carta, the Great
Charter of English Liberties
that King John's barons
forced him to confirm at
Runnymede in 1215, is the
first in a long line of written
instruments limiting the
absolute power of rulers.
Constitutional documents
such as this make manifest
the power of the people
to harness government to
ensure their own rights
rather than the power of
rulers. [Corbis-Bettmann]

Magna Carta

Magna Carta (or Charta) is the charter of personal and political liberty sealed by King John of England at Runnymede in 1215 at the insistence of English barons. It is the oldest known document protecting rights, although a similar instrument, the Golden Bull, was forced on Andrew II of Hungary by nobles in 1222.

Acknowledged as the foundation of constitutional liberty in the United Kingdom, Magna Carta (from the medieval Latin *magna chartae*, meaning great document) was based on a charter of liberties originally granted by Henry I on August 6, 1100, his coronation day. His successors, however, failed to abide by the terms of the charter. In 1214 King John attempted to mount a military campaign to reclaim Normandy for the English crown. He had previously lost out in a clash with Pope Innocent III over the choice of a new archbishop of Canterbury. The pope won, and John was forced to pay an annual tribute to the Holy See so that he could remain king—an arrangement that alienated him from his subjects. The English clergy and powerful feudal lords refused to support the Normandy venture unless the king promised to grant concessions based on those set forth in the earlier charter. The barons formed a confederacy, vowing war if John did not meet their demands. On June 15, 1215, having been abandoned by most of his supporters, the king reluctantly placed his royal seal on the document entitled the Great Charter of the Liberties of England and of the Liberties of the Forest.

Magna Carta contained a preamble and sixty-three clauses. In it the king declared the church to be free and inviolate and granted all freemen certain rights, including the right to trial by a jury of peers and distribution of an intestate inheritance to one's nearest kin. Other rights and concessions were granted to nobles, widows, and the city of London.

A document of constitutional stature in England and subsequently in Great Britain and the United Kingdom, Magna Carta provided guarantees to subjects of the crown, albeit mostly for members of the nobility, and hastened the development of the royal courts at the expense of the local courts and sheriffs. Although much of the original document has been superseded and repealed, Magna Carta was an early harbinger of constitutional government and more inclusive and extensive documents guaranteeing individual rights, including human rights, from infringement by the government.

Holt, James Clarke. *Magna Carta*. New York: Cambridge University Press, 1992.

Howard, A. E. Dick. *Magna Carta: Text and Commentary*. Charlottesville: University Press of Virginia, 1998.

Bills of Rights; Constitutionalism

Majority Rule

Majority rule—the process whereby public officials are elected and laws enacted through votes by the greatest number of persons voting—is the basis of all democratic governments. A clear historical correlation exists between constitutional democratic government based on majority rule and the expansion and protection of human rights. Two of the world's greatest human rights documents—France's Declaration of the Rights of Man and of the Citizen (1789) and the U.S. Bill of Rights (1791)—emerged in the wake of revolutions against monarchies, which along with dictatorial regimes have had poor human rights records. "When . . . deep and permanent cleavages are absent," suggested a 1959 encyclopedia, "majority rule seems more likely to secure more equal freedom than any other, at least if free discussion and airing of grievances are presupposed."

Nearly all national constitutions embrace the principle of majority rule, although it may not always be expressly stated, whereas exceptions or limitations are generally spelled out. Voting for public officials, for example, may require an absolute majority rather than simply a plurality of the votes, while passage of legislation may require a majority vote of members present or a majority of all the members elected to the legislative body.

At the international level, various human rights bodies, including the UN General Assembly and regional groups such as the Organization of American States, follow procedural rules based on the principle of majority rule with some variations in details. Decisions by the UN Security Council, however, require supermajorities or even agreement by all of the permanent members.

Majority rule can, however, become a tyranny of the majority—as detrimental to human rights as the tyranny of any absolute dictatorship or monarchy. A majority of voters or legislators always carries the potential to destroy the minority. In constitutional democracies, therefore, majority rule is tempered with a number of limitations and exceptions known as checks and balances to maintain the democratic system and protect minorities. Such checks and balances include judicial review by an independent court system and bills or declarations of rights that place certain rights beyond the scope of elected officials to abrogate or infringe. National constitutions often even require supermajorities and multistep procedures for amending constitutional guarantees of rights.

Constitution of Sweden, Instrument of Government (1975), chapter 4, The Business of the Riksdag [parliament], article 5: "When a vote is taken in the Riksdag, the opinion in which more than half of those present and voting concur shall constitute the decision of the Riksdag, unless otherwise specifically provided in the present Instrument of Government or, in the case of matters relating to Riksdag procedure, in the main provision of the Riksdag Act [(1974) another constitutional document]. Provisions regarding the procedure to be followed in the case of a tied vote are laid down in the Riksdag Act."

Charter of the United Nations (1945), chapter IV, The General Assembly, article 18, Voting: "2. Decisions of the General Assembly on important questions shall be made by a two-thirds majority of the members present and voting. . . . 3. Decisions on other questions, including the determination of additional categories of questions to be decided by a two-thirds majority, shall be made by a majority of the members present and voting."

Constitutional Court of Germany (1978): "If the right of the minority—and thus the parliamentary right to control—is not to be weakened unduly, then the minority must not be left at the mercy of the majority. This could prevent [the minority] from unqualifiedly investigating circumstances embarrassing to the existing majority. Thus parliamentary opposition would be deprived of an instrument with which it was entrusted not just in its own interest but rather in the interest of the democratic state. . . ."

European Court of Human Rights (1981): "Although individual interests must on occasion be subordinated to those of a group, democracy does not simply mean that the views of the majority must always prevail: a balance must be achieved which insures the fair and proper treatment of minorities and avoids any abuse of a dominant position."

Bridwell, R. Randall. *The Power: Government by Consent and Majority Rule in America.* San Francisco: Austin and Windfield, 1999.

Döring, Herbert, ed. *Parliaments and Majority Rule in Western Europe.* New York: St. Martin's, 1995.

Spaeth, Harold J. *Majority Rule or Minority Will: Adherence to Precedence on the U.S. Supreme Court.* New York: Cambridge University Press, 1999.

Bills of Rights; Constitutionalism; Declaration of the Rights of Man and of the Citizen (France); Democracy; Derogation; Judicial Review; Minorities; Voting

Malnutrition

See Food

Mandela, Nelson

The life of Nelson Mandela (b. 1918) has mirrored the long suffering of the South Africans and their ultimate triumph in the struggle for human rights. Jailed in 1964 for his anti-apartheid activities in his homeland and not released until February 11, 1990, he became South Africa's first president chosen in an election in which all the citizens were allowed to participate.

Born on July 18, 1918, Nelson Rolihlahla Mandela grew up in the Transkei district of Umata in South Africa. For organizing a boycott of the student council at Fort Hare University in 1940, he was expelled. In 1944 Mandela joined the African National Congress (ANC), a basically nonviolent political organization opposed to South Africa's policy of racial segregation known as apartheid, and emerged as one of its leaders. In 1951 he was elected president of the ANC Youth League, founded in 1943 by more militant activists.

After the ANC was banned in 1960, Mandela endorsed and participated in acts of sabotage to fight apartheid. Although arrested, he managed to escape and continued to promote the anti-apartheid cause outside South Africa. He was arrested again in 1962 and sentenced to five years' imprisonment. While standing trial, Mandela declared in court: "I am prepared to die for what I believe." Sentenced to life imprisonment, he was incarcerated until 1990, after the collapse of the political regime that had enforced the apartheid policies.

Upon his release Mandela again became the dominant voice of the ANC as he worked to create a new, truly democratic transitional constitution for the country. The constitution, adopted on January 25, 1994, became effective in April, and Mandela was elected president under the new document that same month. He served out his term as president of South Africa, relinquishing power constitutionally to his elected successor in 1999. For his leadership in the dismantling of apartheid, Mandela was awarded the 1993 Nobel Peace Prize, sharing it with F. W. de Klerk, the leader of the racist opposition who had finally authorized his release from prison.

DeLuca, Anthony R. *Gandhi, Mao, Mandela, and Gorbachev: Studies in Personality, Power, and Politics.* Westport, Conn.: Praeger, 2000.

Mandela, Nathan. *Mandela: An Illustrated Autobiography.* New York: Little, Brown, 1996.

Sampson, Anthony. *Mandela: The Authorized Biography.* New York: Knopf, 1999.

Apartheid; Race Discrimination; Suzman, Helen; Tutu, Desmond

Marriage

The marriage contract has been characterized as having three parties: the bride, the groom, and the state. The laws of society and the laws of the state have traditionally regulated aspects of both marriage and divorce, such as the age of consent to marry, the respective rights of spouses within marriage, the allocation of property, the status of children, and the rights of each partner and the children in the event of divorce. The English word *marriage* to signify the condition of being husband and wife is probably derived from the French words *mariage* and *mari* (meaning husband) and dates from the thirteenth century. Under English common law the general rule was that a husband and wife were one—and it has been presumed for most of subsequent history that the husband was the one.

In *The Laws*, Plato's attempt to write a constitution for a new colony, the ancient Greek philosopher comments in his discussion of marriage laws that "when a man of twenty-five has observed others and been observed by them and is confident that he has found a family offering someone to his taste who would make a suitable partner for the procreation of children, he should get married, and in any case before he reaches thirty." In the Roman Republic, marriage was a highly regarded estate, although it was more a social than a legal institution.

Among the rights issues that arise in the context of marriage are equal rights for spouses, especially to guarantee equality for the wife; freedom from abuse, with respect to both spouses and children; the age of consent; the right to choose one's spouse rather than have one chosen by parents; access to family planning; choice of a family name; property ownership; and discrimination resulting from marriage, for example, by unequal tax laws.

The rights of spouses in marriage are set forth in the Convention on the Elimination of All Forms of Discrimination against Women (1979). These include, for both "the same right to enter into marriage [and] freely to choose a spouse and to enter into marriage only with their free and full consent" and "the same rights and responsibilities during marriage." Other provisions grant both partners in marriage "the same rights and responsibilities as parents," including the right to decide on "the number and spacing of their children"; the right to choose "a family name, a profession, and an occupation"; and equal rights with respect to "ownership, acquisition, management, administration and disposition of property." The betrothal and marriage of a child are made illegal.

Regarding divorce, the Universal Declaration of Human Rights (1948) provides that because men and women are entitled to "equal rights as to marriage [and] during marriage," they are entitled to equal rights "at its dissolution." The Convention on the Elimination of All Forms of Discrimination against Women and the European Convention for the Protection of Human Rights and Fundamental Freedoms (1950), Protocol no. 7 (1984), also proclaim the equality of spouses in divorce as well as in marriage. However, each spouse's rights in the event of a divorce are determined by domestic law. Divorce can be both emotionally traumatic and legally complicated, and the ability of spouses to assert their rights depends on many factors, including the grounds for the dissolution of the marriage, assets of the spouses, access to competent legal representation, religious requirements, and concern for the well-being of children of the marriage. Many developed countries have greatly enhanced women's ability to enforce their equal rights during divorce, but in most other countries, many factors, especially religious rules and customs, conspire to keep women from asserting their equal rights in this important area of human relations.

The traditional understanding of marriage is that of a man and a woman being joined together legally to form a family and, in most cases, to have and raise children. However, this view is being challenged today by some homosexual couples who want to solemnize and legalize their commitment to each other in the same manner as heterosexuals. Homosexual couples also seek to benefit from certain spousal marriage rights such as employer-provided insurance and retirement benefits.

Some national constitutions, including those of Italy (1948), South Korea (1948), and Honduras (1982), address marriage rights, as do a number of international human rights documents. In addition to the Universal Declaration of Human Rights and European Convention for the Protection of Human Rights and Fundamental Freedoms, among these are the International Convention on the Elimination of All Forms of Racial Discrimination (1965), International Covenant on Economic, Social and Cultural Rights (1966), and Convention on the Elimination of All Forms of Discrimination against Women (1979).

Constitution of Italy (1948), part one, The Duties and Rights of the Citizens, title I, Civil Relations, article 29: "The republic acknowledges the rights of the family as a natural society founded on marriage. Marriage is based on the moral and juridical equality of the spouses, within the limits provided for by law for ensuring the unity of the family."

Universal Declaration of Human Rights (1948), article 16: "1. Men and women of full age, without any limitation due to race, nationality or religion, have the right to marry and to found a family. They are entitled to equal rights as to marriage, during marriage and at its dissolution. 2. Marriage shall be entered into only with the free and full consent of the intending spouses."

Supreme Court of Ireland (1980): "The right of privacy of a spouse in his or her marital affairs . . . is not violated by the State in compelling one spouse to disclose particulars of his or her income [relative to income tax liability] to the other, in as much as such

right of privacy relates solely to purely personal elements of their relationship with each other, and not to the elements of that relationship which form a part of their joint relationship with society."

European Court of Human Rights (1986): "In any society espousing the principle of monogamy, it is inconceivable that [a person] should be able to marry as long as his marriage . . . has not been dissolved."

Eriksson, Maja Kirilova. *The Right to Marry and to Found a Family: A World-Wide Human Right.* Uppsala, Sweden: Iustus, 1990.

Waite, Linda J., Christine Bachrach, et al. *The Ties that Bind: Perspectives on Marriage and Cohabitation.* New York: Aldine de Gruyter, 2000.

Children; Convention on Consent to Marriage, Minimum Age for Marriage and Registration of Marriages; Convention on the Elimination of All Forms of Discrimination against Women; Convention on the Rights of the Child; European Convention for the Protection of Human Rights and Fundamental Freedoms; Families; Homosexuals; International Convention on the Elimination of All Forms of Racial Discrimination; International Covenant on Economic, Social and Cultural Rights; Plato; Universal Declaration of Human Rights; Women

Mason, George

An American patriot and statesman from Virginia, George Mason (1725–92) drafted the Virginia Declaration of Rights (1776), the first written constitutional guarantee by any government of the rights of citizens, including freedom of religion, speech, and the press and the rights of persons accused of crimes. A link between England's Magna Carta (1215) and the U.S. Bill of Rights (1791), the document influenced the U.S. Declaration of Independence (1776) and the many national and international declarations and bills of rights that followed.

Born in 1725 in Dogue's Neck along the Potomac River, where his ancestors had lived for nearly 150 years, George Mason became a neighbor and mentor of George Washington. Even before American independence was declared on July 4, 1776, the thirteen British colonies along the Atlantic coast from Massachusetts to Georgia made important decisions that would lead to revolution and self-government. Mason, a widower with nine children, wrote the widely published Virginia Resolves of August 1774, which contained revolutionary slogans to inspire the colonists in their confrontations with Great Britain. When Washington was appointed commander of the Continental armies in 1775, Mason took Washington's place in the Virginia legislature.

In 1776 Mason wrote the committee draft of the Virginia Declaration of Rights, which was adopted with only minor changes on June 12. Praised as one of the most influential documents of freedom in Anglo-American history, alongside Magna Carta and England's Bill of Rights (1689), the declaration proclaimed that "all men are born equally free and independent, and have certain inherent natural rights, of which they cannot, by any compact, deprive or divest their posterity; among which are the enjoyment of life and liberty, with the means of acquiring and possessing property, and pursuing and obtaining happiness and safety." Much of this language is similar to the moving wording of the Declaration of Independence, which was then being drafted by Thomas Jefferson in Philadelphia, where a copy of Mason's declaration was available to him. Mason soon set his hand to writing Virginia's first constitution, adopted on July 5, 1776, which had a significant influence on other colonial and state constitutions and constitutional documents around the world.

In 1787 Mason served as a delegate to the constitutional convention for the new nation in Philadelphia, and his input is evident in a number of the final provisions. His concern for human rights transcended his loyalty to his own state: an opponent of slavery, he spoke against the slave trade during the convention and refused to sign the draft constitution. However, with the ratification in 1791 of the first ten amendments—the Bill of Rights—he commented that he could now "chearfully put [his] hand and heart to the new government."

Cohen, Martin B., ed. *Federalism: The Legacy of George Mason.* Fairfax, Va.: George Mason University Press, 1988.

Rutland, Robert A. *George Mason: Reluctant Statesman.* Baton Rouge: Louisiana State University Press, 1961.

Bills of Rights; Declaration of Independence (United States); Federalism; Jefferson, Thomas; Magna Carta; Slavery

Maternity

"Motherhood and childhood are entitled to special care and assistance," asserts the Universal Declaration of Human Rights (1948), recognizing that although everyone is born with equal human rights, women's biologically different reproductive role requires special consideration. Motherhood is a particularly vulnerable condition for women and their children and a time when society must balance the need to foster maternal care with the general social, economic, and political structure of the state and the policies of employers.

Maternity rights are extended in national laws and international human rights documents to women who are pregnant or have recently given birth; Italy and India are two nations that also address the issue in their constitutions (1948 and 1950, respectively). Rights for motherhood are most frequently addressed in the context of workers' rights, which may grant pregnant women maternity leave to give birth as well as to return to their former job after some reasonable period; they may also be assured of safe working environments and responsibilities that will not harm their fetuses. mothers are sometimes afforded the right to prenatal care, medical coverage for delivery, and postnatal care. Rights related to maternity include family planning, access to abortion, equality for women, the rights of the child and the family, marriage rights, and health and environmental protection.

Two national models of maternity rights have emerged: one that favors equal treatment and another that allows for biological difference. The United States tends to follow the equal treatment approach, although the U.S. Constitution (1789) does not expressly grant equal rights to women. The Family and Medical Leave Act of 1993 guarantees some working women a period of twelve weeks of unpaid leave for childbirth or adoption and requires that employers continue health insurance coverage for employees on family leave, including fathers and other male workers. Germany's constitution (1949), on the other hand, explicitly provides protection for "marriage and family," guaranteeing that "[e]very mother shall be entitled to the protection and care of the community." An example of the difference model, German laws cover many aspects of motherhood to protect the pregnant woman, the unborn child, and breast-feeding mothers, including paid maternity leave and parental leave allowances.

Expectant mothers' basic rights may also be abused because of their condition. On the grounds that pregnant women were illegally "distributing" drugs to their children, some hospitals in the United States recently began to test them for drug use and provide the results to the police. This clash of rights has been styled as one involving the constitutional prohibition of unreasonable searches for evidence versus possible child abuse resulting from the mother's taking harmful drugs. A federal appeals court ruling upheld the procedure, citing "special governmental needs" that exempt such testing from the requirement under the Fourth Amendment (1791) to the U.S. Constitution that a search warrant be obtained before evidence of a crime is sought.

Maternity rights are addressed in a number of international human rights documents, especially those involving discrimination against women. The International Labor Organization in 1919 adopted a maternity rights treaty, which was updated in 1952 as the Convention Concerning Maternity Protection. Under it, working women are guaranteed maternity leave of at least twelve weeks, including "a period of compulsory leave after confinement . . . [to] be prescribed by national laws or regulations."

"Special protection should be accorded to mothers during a reasonable period before and after childbirth," added the International Covenant on Economic, Social and Cultural Rights (1966). "During such period working mothers should be accorded paid leave or leave with adequate social security benefits." The African Charter on the Rights and Welfare of the Child (1990) calls for special treatment for "expectant mothers and mothers of infants and young children who have been accused or found guilty" of a crime. The European Social Charter (1996) and the Convention on the Elimination of All Forms of Discrimination against Women (1979) also address maternity rights. The charter, for example, provides that employed women, "in the case of maternity, have the right to special protection," while the convention urges the signatory nations to take appropriate measures "to prevent discrimination against women on the grounds of marriage or maternity and to ensure their effective right to work...."

Constitution of India (1949), part IV, Directive Principles of State Policy, article 42: "The State shall make provisions for securing just and humane conditions of work and for maternity relief."

Convention on the Elimination of All Forms of Discrimination against Women (1979), part III, article 11: "2. In order to prevent discrimination against women on the grounds of marriage or maternity and to ensure their effective right to work, States Parties shall take appropriate measures. . . ."

U.S. Supreme Court (1977): An employer's policy of denying accumulated seniority to female employees returning from pregnancy leave imposed a substantial burden that men do not suffer; such a policy, absent proof of any business necessity for it, is thus an unlawful employment practice under the Civil Rights Act of 1964.

European Court of Human Rights (1979): A Belgian law was found to violate the European Convention for the Protection of Human Rights and Fundamental Freedoms (1950), article 8, Right to Respect for Private and Family life, because it required an unmarried mother to affirmatively recognize her illegitimate child, whereas a birth certificate was sufficient to prove a married mother's relationship to her child. The law reduced the illegitimate child's rights of inheritance compared with those of a child born in wedlock.

International Labor Organization, 4 route des Morillons, 1211 Geneva 22, Switzerland. (41-22-799-6111. 🖳 41-22-798-8685. 🖳 somavia.ilo.org. 🖳 www.ilo.org.

UN Development Fund for Women, 304 East 45th Street, 15th Floor, New York, N.Y. 10017. (212-906-6400. 🖳 212-906-6705. 🖳 unifem@undp.org. 🖳 www.unifem.undp.org.

Humber, James M., and Robert F. Almeder, eds. *Reproduction, Technology, and Rights*. Totowa, N.J.: Humana, 1996.

Rights in Marriage. St. Paul, Minn.: Legislative Commission on the Economic Status of Women, 1998.

Weisberg, Anne Cicero. *Everything a Working Mother Needs to Know about Pregnancy Rights, Maternity Leave, and Making Her Career Work for Her*. New York: Doubleday, 1994.

Abortion; Children; Convention on the Elimination of All Forms of Discrimination against Women; European Social Charter; Families; Health; International Covenant on Economic, Social and Cultural Rights; International Labor Organization; Social Rights; Women; Workers

Menchú, Rigoberta

A Guatemalan human rights activist whose younger brother was kidnapped, tortured, and burned to death by a military death squad, Rigoberta Menchú (b. 1959) was awarded the Nobel Peace Prize in 1992 for her efforts to stop the Guatemalan government's brutal treatment of Indian peasants.

Menchú was born in the northwest highlands of Guatemala into an indigenous group called the Quiché Maya. As a child she accompanied her parents to the southern coastal plantations, where they picked cotton and coffee for part of the year. When she was eight years old, she began working on the plantations and at home, where she helped collect wicker in the mountains and grow food for the family. She spoke only her native language until she was nineteen, although at thirteen she began working as a maid for a wealthy family in Guatemala City, where she first encountered people of Spanish culture as well as discrimination.

The Guatemala in which Menchú grew up was ruled by authoritarian military governments. The revolutionary opposition, organized in 1962, was met with violence, and those perceived as the movement's supporters were dealt with summarily. In the early 1960s Menchú's father, who was active in the Peasants Unity Committee, was arrested for trying to prevent a takeover of land by large landowners. Not long after she joined the committee in 1979, her sixteen-year-old brother was tortured and killed by the military, her father was killed in a protest at the Spanish embassy in Guatemala City, and her mother was kidnapped, tortured, and killed by the army.

In 1981 Menchú escaped to Mexico and began an international crusade to publicize the plight of the Guatemalan Indians, serving as a member of the UN Working Group on Indigenous Populations. Afraid to return to Guatemala, she continued her crusade on behalf of her people by traveling around the world and writing about her experiences and the need to bring peace and harmony to her country. Her book *I, Rigoberta Menchú: An Indian Woman in Guatemala* (1983) drew some criticism for alleged inaccuracies but increased international attention to her cause. In 1988, when she tried to return to Guatemala, she was briefly jailed by the government but courageously continues to make visits to her homeland.

In 1992, at the age of thirty-three, Menchú received the Nobel Peace Prize "in recognition of her work for social justice and ethno-cultural reconciliation based on the rights of indigenous peoples," the first indigenous person and the youngest person ever to receive this prestigious award. Continuing her mission, she has received other awards for her efforts. She witnessed the cease-fire agreement between the Guatemalan government and rebels, signed in Norway in 1996. Summarizing her philosophy, she has said: "I believe that in Guatemala the solution is not confrontation between indigenous people and the [people of Spanish descent]. Rather we need a country where we can live together with mutual respect."

Menchú, Rigoberta. *Crossing Borders*. Translated and edited by Ann Wright. New York: Verso, 1998.

Stoll, David. *Rigoberta Menchú and the Story of All Poor Guatemalans*. Boulder, Colo.: Westview, 1999.

Disappearance; Indigenous Peoples

Migrant Workers

See Immigrants; Workers

Military Personnel

Like law enforcement officials, military personnel—members of a nation's armed forces, including the national guard and militia—have a special duty to observe and respect international humanitarian rules of warfare and the human rights of noncombatants, particularly women and children. Because of the nature of their occupation, however, their own rights are restricted. Without rigorous checks and balances, the sheer power of a trained, armed body of men and women at the disposal of the head of state or government would be a constant threat to civilian peace and security. "The Army raised by

the Crown, officered by the Crown, commanded by the Crown," said William Blackstone, the eighteenth-century commentator on the laws of England, "puts at its disposal a force which is more than equivalent to a thousand little prerogatives."

To maintain discipline in the armed forces, many rights and freedoms that civilians take for granted are either denied or greatly curtailed. Freedom of speech and movement and the rights of workers in general are greatly restricted for both recruited and conscripted service people, more so for enlisted personnel than for officers. The duty to obey a superior officer's order, however, is not without limits, and soldiers are within their rights not to follow an order that is clearly a gross violation of so-called humanitarian warfare.

Some rights issues that arise in civilian life—discrimination on the basis of sex or sexual orientation, for example—also affect military personnel. Discrimination in the armed forces has long been rationalized for military reasons. The picture of women sharing a foxhole with male soldiers or being captured and subjected to harassment and torture has been conjured up to limit the combat roles of women. The need to live and sleep in close quarters has also been used to discriminate against both women and homosexuals in the military. It is now increasingly believed in many parts of the world that discrimination is not the way to deal with such fears.

One area where civilian and military rights diverge is protection for military personnel accused of crimes and breaches of military discipline. Basic rights in such cases are usually spelled out by a code of military justice, such as the U.S. Uniform Code of Military Justice. This federal law outlines crimes and the types of courts and procedures for handling criminal cases in the military. Minor offenses may be punished nonjudicially by a commanding officer, while more serious crimes are tried by a court-martial.

Freedom of conscience issues occur frequently in the military with respect to service members' refusal to perform certain duties such as killing enemy soldiers, not to mention civilians in the vicinity of military targets. In many countries, including the United States and Germany, conscientious objection to hurting or killing a human being has been an acceptable excuse for avoiding military service, at least in a combat capacity.

Provisions of international humanitarian law found in documents such as the Geneva Conventions and the rules of warfare both restrict what military personnel can do during war and impose obligations on them regarding treatment of a number of categories of people. The Geneva Convention Relative to the Protection of Civilian Persons in Time of War (1949) and the Geneva Convention Relative to the Treatment of Prisoners of War (1949), for example, prohibit the military from passing sentences and carrying out executions without a judgment pronounced by a regularly constituted court and require that the sick and wounded be collected and cared for.

Constitution of Brazil (1988), title III, The Organization of the State, chapter VII, section III, Military Public Servants, article 42, paragraphs 5 and 6: "Servicemen are forbidden to join unions and to strike. While in actual service, servicemen are forbidden to belong to political parties."

Geneva Convention Relative to the Treatment of Prisoners of War (1949), article 88: "A woman prisoner of war shall not be awarded or sentenced to a punishment more severe, or treated whilst undergoing punishment more severely, than a woman member of the armed forces of the Detaining Power dealt with for a similar offense."

Constitutional Court of Lithuania (1998): "The peculiarities of the voluntary service for protection of the country condition the social guarantees for the volunteers. One of such guarantees is benefits for the family of the volunteer who died while performing his duties. . . . [T]he right to the said compensation [has] only one condition: 'provided a volunteer died while performing official assignments.'"

European Court of Human Rights (1976): Where penalties were meted out to conscripted soldiers for offenses against military discipline that were of the same type as penalties for criminal offenses, the soldiers were entitled to the benefit of provisions of the European Convention for the Protection of Human Rights and Fundamental Freedoms (1950), article 6, Right to a Fair Trial.

Bluhm, Raymond K., Jr., and James B. Motley. *The Soldier's Guidebook*. Washington, D.C.: Brassey's, 1995.

Eccles, Henry E. *Military Power in a Free Society*. Naval War College. Washington, D.C.: U.S. Government Printing Office, 1979.

Conscience; Discrimination; Geneva Conventions; Homosexuals; Law Enforcement; Prisoners of War; War; War Crimes

Mill, John Stuart

In *On Liberty* (1859), John Stuart Mill (1806–73) presented the classic defense of liberalism and the right of individuals to think and act for themselves. An early champion of suffrage for women, he urged limits on government interference with respect to an individual's liberty and freedom.

Born in London on May 20, 1806, Mill was a precocious child. Under the tutelage of his father, James Mill, he learned Greek at the age of three, Latin and arithmetic at twelve, and political economy at thirteen. He began studying law but in 1823 went to work for the British East India Company. When the company went out of business in 1858, Mill pursued his interests in philosophy and politics.

Mill's father and a friend, the English jurist and philosopher Jeremy Bentham, had pioneered the concept of utilitarianism, which declared that the government's role was creating the "greatest happiness for the greatest number" of people. Building on this philosophy, Mill underscored in his works the concepts of individual freedom and liberty exemplified in the U.S. Constitution (1789). In 1865 Mill was elected to the British Parliament from Westminster and served a three-year term, during which he introduced a motion calling for extending the right to vote to women. He was not reelected and later moved to France, where he died on May 7, 1873.

In addition to *On Liberty*, Mill's works include *A System of Logic* (1843), *Considerations on Representative Government* (1861), and *On the Subjection of Women* (1869). Concerning the idea of individual liberty, Mill wrote: "[T]he sole end for which [human beings] are warranted, individually or collectively, in interfering with the liberty of action of any of their number, is self-protection." He also held that a person "cannot rightfully be compelled to do or forebear because . . . in the opinions of others, to do so would be wise, or even right."

August, Eugene. *John Stuart Mill: A Mind at Large*. New York: Scribner, 1975.

Ryan, Alan. *Mill: Texts, Commentaries*. New York: Norton, 1997.

Expression; Liberty; Opinion; Voting; Women

Minorities

"Our best hope," wrote the anthropologist Margaret Mead in *Some Personal Views* (1979), "is that we can come to care positively about the diversity of human beings and ally ourselves with many different groups, all of whom we think of as 'we.'" Because human rights are predicated on the dignity and equality of every person, those peoples who are not culturally, racially, linguistically, or religiously the same as the majority of a country's citizens are nevertheless entitled to equal political and civil rights and to equality before the law. The English word *minority*, meaning the condition of being smaller, inferior, or subordinate, is derived from similar words in French (*minorité*) and Latin (*minor, minoritas*) and has been used in English since at least the sixteenth century.

Biblical stories of the captive Hebrews in Babylon and Egypt exemplify the difficulty minorities may have when forced to live within a more dominant culture. Centuries later, the issue of minorities was recognized in treaties ending World War I that provided for "the protection of racial, linguistic, or religious minorities included within the boundaries of the specified States." The late-twentieth-century plight of the ethnic and religious minorities in the former Yugoslavia attests to the fact that such problems have not decreased even after thousands of years.

Because democracy is based on majority rule, the members of the majority in any voting process are by definition the winners and the members of a minority are the losers. And, just as an absolute monarchy is capable of excesses that threaten human rights, an absolute democracy may diminish the rights of minorities. Constitutionalism requires that checks on governments be put in place to prevent such discrimination or at least to ameliorate its effect. Therefore, any democratic government that supports human rights must protect minorities from the possible excesses of the majority. Such protections include constitutional guarantees of religious tolerance and freedom, separation of church and state, allowances for the use of one or more official languages, and protections for minorities' cultural identity and heritage. Other minority rights issues include intermarriage, adoption, official holidays, education, employment, special laws and courts, and the right of autonomy and self-determination.

The protection of minority rights does not always involve merely starting at a moment in time and guaranteeing an end to discrimination. Quite often, a history of discrimination condoned by the government or former rulers has created a historical inequality that requires positive redress in addition to prospective guarantees. In the United States, for example, a policy of affirmative action in education and business was adopted by the government after passage of the Civil Rights Act of 1964 to help correct the centuries of discrimination against minorities, including African American descendants of slaves. In India, the nation's 1950 constitution singles out the Untouchable caste for protection because of longtime discrimination. Groups identified as minorities for purposes of a national human rights policy—such as women—may in fact be a majority of the population.

After World War I the protection of minorities became an important part of the international mission of the League of Nations. Colonialism was being eradicated in much of the world, and in the process of preparing former colonies for self-governance, minorities needed special attention. After World War II, however, the United Nations did not make protection of minorities within their own countries a high priority, faced as it was with the aftermath of the Holocaust and the large-scale movement of refugees throughout Europe, although its Universal Declaration of Human Rights (1948) did prohibit discrimination on the basis of national origin, race, and language and extended cultural rights to everyone. Other international documents addressing minority rights include the Convention no. 107 (1957) and Convention no. 169 (1989) of the International Labor Organization, Declaration on the Elimination of All Forms of Intolerance and of Discrimination Based on Religion or Belief (1981), Convention on the Rights of the Child (1989), and Declaration on the Rights of Persons Belonging to National or Ethnic, Religious and Linguistic Minorities (1992).

The Minority Rights Group, an international nongovernmental organization, was founded in 1970 to perform impartial and independent research and publish information to secure justice for groups suffering from discrimination; it also helps prevent destructive conflicts triggered by human rights violations and promotes research into the causes of prejudices and tensions relating to minority groups. In addition to publishing a newsletter (*Outsider*), the group has produced a number of reports on minorities in Japan, Europe, South America, and Ethiopia.

Constitution of Finland, Parliament Act (1928), chapter 4, Preparation of Matters, section 52a (added in 1991): "The Sámi [Lapplanders] shall be heard in a matter of special consequence to them, as further provided in the procedure of parliament."

Convention against Discrimination in Education (1960), article 5(1): "(c) It is essential to recognize the right of members of national minorities to carry on their own educational activities . . . provided however: (i) That the right is not exercised in a manner which prevents the members of these minorities from understanding the culture and language of the community as a whole . . . ; (ii) That the standard of education is not lower than the general standard . . . ; and (iii) That attendance at such schools is optional."

Israeli High Court of Justice (1956): The court will not interfere with the discretion of the minister of defense in determining which ethnic minorities may be drafted into the armed forces.

Permanent Court of International Justice (1930): A minority is "[b]y tradition . . . a group of persons living within a given country or locality, having race, religion, language and traditions of their own and united by this identity of race, religion, language and traditions in a sentiment of solidarity, with a view to preserving their traditions, maintaining their form of worship, ensuring the instruction and upbringing of their children in accordance with the spirit and traditions of their race and rendering mutual assistance to each other."

Minorities at Risk Project, Center for International Development and Conflict Management, 0145 Tydings Hall, University of Maryland, College Park, Md. 20742-7231. (301-314-7706. 📠 301-314-9256. 📧 minpro@cidcm.umd.edu. 🖥 www.bsos.umd.edu/cidcm/mar.

Minority Rights Group, 379 Brixton Road, London SW9 7DE, England. (44-207-978-9498. 🖨 44-207-738-6265. 🖳 minority. rights@mrgmail.org. 🖳 www.minorityrights.org.

Alfredsson, Gudmundur, and Peter Macalister-Smith, eds. *The Living Law of Nations: Essays on Refugees, Minorities, Indigenous Peoples, and the Human Rights of Vulnerable Groups.* Arlington, Va.: Engel, 1996.

Brölmann, Catherine, René Lefeber, and Marjoleine Zieck, eds. *Peoples and Minorities in International Law.* The Hague: Martinus Nijhoff, Kluwer Law International, 1993.

☞

Convention on the Rights of the Child; Cultural Rights; Declaration on the Elimination of All Forms of Intolerance and of Discrimination Based on Religion or Belief; Declaration on the Rights of Persons Belonging to National or Ethnic, Religious and Linguistic Minorities; Discrimination; Indigenous Peoples; Language; Majority Rule; Race Discrimination; Religion; Self-Determination; Women

Minors

See Children; Youth

Monitoring Compliance

If the price of liberty is eternal vigilance, the price of protecting human rights is constant and pervasive monitoring of government actions. The more individuals, organizations, and agencies that watch all aspects of government activity at the national, regional, and local levels, the more difficult it is for government officials to escape accountability for ignoring human rights. Investigating, documenting, and reporting on government compliance with human rights standards is an important aspect of enforcing rights, particularly under international treaties and conventions. The term *monitor* (from the Latin *monitor*, meaning adviser or instructor, and *monitio*, meaning warning) signifies one who gives advice or warns, a usage dating from the sixteenth century; its definition of observing, supervising, or keeping under review is relatively recent.

The concept of monitoring government activities is not new, however. In *The Laws*, the ancient Greek philosopher Plato creates a "nocturnal" council to keep track of government procedures under his proposed constitution for the fictitious colony of Magnesia. Plato would have had the council continually compare information about foreign legal codes with activities in the colony to decide if changes were needed.

Monitoring is related to government accountability, the idea that a government should be acting in the best interests of its citizens or in accordance with its constitution or international obligations. In a democracy there are many "watchdogs"—interested individuals, opposing political parties, the press, an independent judiciary, ombudsmen, inspectors general, and nongovernmental organizations, among others—who monitor and provide feedback on government action or inaction. Democratic checks and balances written into national constitutions are often supplemented by public-interest groups that help observe government activity.

International human rights agreements often expressly endorse monitoring by establishing human rights commissions, committees, or courts authorized to keep tabs on and enforce human rights obligations of countries that are parties to the agreements. These treaty-monitoring bodies include the Inter-American Commission on Human Rights, Inter-American Court on Human Rights, and European Court of Human Rights, as well as human rights committees set up under the International Covenant on Civil and Political Rights and other international agreements relating to torture, race discrimination, the rights of the child, and discrimination against women.

The United Nations also has organs that can investigate, report on, and recommend solutions to human rights problems. Its Office of the High Commissioner for Human Rights, Commission on Human Rights, and Subcommission on the Promotion and Protection of Human Rights are general human rights monitoring bodies. Its *Manual on Human Rights Reporting* (1997) states that "a precondition for effective reporting is the existence of an adequate system for monitoring the situation [in the particular country] with respect to each of the rights [it is obliged to observe] on a regular basis. It cannot safely be asserted that torture never occurs in prisons unless regular monitoring of the situation occurs."

Nongovernmental human rights organizations such as Amnesty International, Human Rights Watch, the International League for Human Rights, and the Lawyers Committe for Human Rights are important elements in the international process of monitoring human rights. Their role may involve investigating charges of human rights abuses, observing trials and elections, and publicizing human rights violations.

Constitution of Portugal (1997), part III, Organization of the Political Power, title III, Assembly of the Republic, chapter II, Competence, article 163, Competencies in Relation to Other Organs: "The Assembly of the Republic [parliament] has the following competencies in relation to other organs: . . . f. [t]o monitor and to evaluate, in accordance with the law, the participation of Portugal in the process for implementing the European Union; . . . j. [t]o monitor, in accordance with the law and Standing Orders, the involvement of Portuguese military contingents abroad."

Standard Rules on Equalization of Opportunity (1992), IV, Monitoring Mechanism: "1. The purpose of a monitoring mechanism is to further the effective implementation of the Standard Rules. . . . The monitoring should identify obstacles and suggest suitable measures which would contribute to the successful implementation of the Rules. The monitoring mechanism will recognize the economic, social, and cultural features existing in individual States."

U.S. Court of Appeals, Third Circuit (1990): The district court found the Commonwealth of Pennsylvania "in substantial non-compliance with its monitoring obligations because it never took any enforcement steps, beyond persuasion, to correct the large number of problems its on-site, and other, inspection visits . . . revealed."

Inter-American Commission on Human Rights (1997): In considering charges against the United States for alleged violations of the American Declaration of the Rights and Duties of Man (1948) with regard to the treatment of Haitian "boat people" seeking asylum in the United States, the commission included the following prior statement by the United States in the record of its proceedings: "It [the declaration] is a solemn moral and political statement of the [member states of the Organization of American States], against which each member state's respect for human rights is to be evaluated and monitored, including the policies and practices of the United States. . . ."

Human Rights Watch, 350 Fifth Avenue, 34th Floor, New York, N.Y. 10118-3299. Tel: 212-290-4700. 📠 212-736-1300. 📧 hrwnyc@hrw.org. 🖥 www.hrw.org.

United Nations High Commissioner for Human Rights, 8–14 avenue de la Paix, 1211 Geneva 10, Switzerland. Telephone 41-22-917-9000. 📠 41-22-917-9016. 📧 webadmin.hchr@unog.ch 🖥 www.unhchr.ch.

United Nations High Commissioner for Human Rights, United Nations, New York, N.Y. 10017. 📞 212-963-4475. 📠 212-963-0071. 📧 inquiries@un.org 🖥 www.un.org.

Bloed, Arie, et al., eds. *Monitoring Human Rights in Europe: Comparing International Procedures and Mechanisms*. The Hague: Martinus Nijhoff, Kluwer Law International, 1993.

Light, Paul C. *Monitoring Government: Inspectors General and the Search for Accountability*. Washington, D.C.: Brookings Institution, 1993.

Amnesty International; Commission on Human Rights; Enforcement; European Court of Human Rights; High Commissioner for Human Rights; Human Rights Watch; Inter-American Commission on Human Rights; Inter-American Court of Human Rights; International Covenant on Civil and Political Rights; International League for Human Rights; Lawyers Committee for Human Rights; Reporting Violations; Subcommission on the Promotion and Protection of Human Rights

Movement

The ability to move freely from place to place is a basic human right. Freedom of movement, like freedom of communication, permits people to develop themselves as individuals by giving them access to the widest possible range of opportunities and thus to knowledge. The freedom to move about the country in which one lives and to travel throughout the world in general is linked to the right to educational and employment opportunities, the rights of families to be together, freedom of commerce, and freedom of scientific inquiry, among other rights.

In addition to physical, cultural, and economic barriers, however, individuals and groups have often encountered governmental restrictions on the right to move freely. Some nations, especially those with nondemocratic governments, continue to limit access to their territory and to prohibit their own citizens from going abroad or traveling or relocating internally without government permission.

Even if a country allows foreigners to enter, it generally has a number of procedural requirements for entry. A person coming into a foreign country may be required to have a valid passport issued by his or her country of origin and a visa issued by an official of the host country. Time limits may be placed on the length of stay. Certain parts of the host country may be off limits to foreigners, and persons planning an extended stay may have to register and obtain identity papers. Returning to the country of origin, a traveler may be required to present a valid passport or other identification to be readmitted. People seeking to permanently reside in a new country may have to meet certain criteria or be sponsored by a resident citizen, as well as comply with quotas for immigrants from their country or region.

Some national constitutions provide for freedom of movement. Italy's constitution (1948), for example, states: "Every citizen may freely circulate and stay in any part of the national territory, except [for] the limitations generally established by law for sanitary [health] and safety reasons." According to Japan's constitution (1947), "Every person shall have freedom to choose and change his residence," and Sweden's (1975) provides that "[n]o citizen may be deported or refused entry to Sweden."

International human rights documents that expressly provide for freedom of movement include the Universal Declaration of Human Rights (1948), European Convention for the Protection of Human Rights and Fundamental Freedoms (1950), International Covenant on Civil and

Political Rights (1966), American Convention on Human Rights (1969), and African Charter on Human and Peoples' Rights (1981).

Canadian Charter of Rights and Freedoms (1982), Mobility Rights: "6(1). Every citizen of Canada has the right to enter, remain in and leave Canada. (2) Every citizen of Canada and every person who has the status of a permanent resident of Canada has the right (a) to move to and take up residence in any province; and (b) to pursue the gaining of a livelihood in any province."

International Covenant on Civil and Political Rights (1966), article 12: "1. Everyone lawfully within the territory of a State shall, within that territory, have the right to liberty of movement and freedom to choose his residence. 2. Everyone shall be free to leave any country, including his own."

U.K. High Court, London (1982): While member states of the European Community may not discriminate on the basis of nationality, they may nevertheless require nationals of other member states to obtain driving permits if they establish permanent residence.

European Court of Human Rights (1994): The Italian government's confiscation of real property designed to block the movement of suspect capital connected with organized crime activities, particularly drug trafficking, was not a violation of Protocol no. 2 (1952), article 2, Freedom of Movement, of the European Convention for the Protection of Human Rights and Fundamental Freedoms (1950) "in view of the threat posed by the mafia to 'democratic society'" and because "the measure was necessary 'for the maintenance of *public ordre'* and "for the prevention of crime.'"

Bauman, Zygmunt. *Globalization: The Human Consequences*. New York: Columbia University Press, 1998.

Freedman, Warren. *The International Right to Travel, Trade, and Commerce*. Buffalo, N.Y.: W. S. Hein, 1993.

☞

African Charter on Human and Peoples' Rights; American Convention on Human Rights; European Convention for the Protection of Human Rights and Fundamental Freedoms; Immigrants; International Covenant on Civil and Political Rights; Universal Declaration of Human Rights

Earth's natural resources are not infinite, but they are renewable to a large extent. Proper management of scarce resources ensures that present and future generations can survive and prosper. Although the international principle of sovereignty gives nations the right to exploit their own natural resources, the people hold a concomitant human right to expect protective stewardship of those resources. [Corbis]

Names

"Who steals my purse steals trash . . . ," says Iago in William Shakespeare's *Othello* (1602). "But he that filches from me my good name robs me of that which not enriches him and makes me poor indeed." While Iago may have been worrying over his reputation, Shakespeare well knew the significance of one's name.

Humans need to name things as well as each other because they are dependent on language to understand the world. The power to name things has always carried importance. Usually given at birth, a name becomes an integral part of each person's character and makes him or her unique. One's identity and existence are confirmed by having a name, which provides information about a person's family, his or her ethnic or national origin, and, as Iago articulated, one's reputation. The right to a name is so fundamental that most national constitutions do not even refer to it.

Being denied a name or having one's name arbitrarily changed is degrading and violates the right to dignity of the person as well as the right to a personality before the law and in one's community. Under the Nazi regime in Germany and territories conquered by Hitler's military forces in the 1930s and 1940s, Jews were stripped of their citizenship, put in concentration and work camps, and identified merely by numbers tattooed on their skin. This dehumanizing process led to inclusion of the right to both a name and a nationality in the International Covenant on Civil and Political Rights, adopted by the UN General Assembly in 1966.

"Every person has a right to a given name and to the surnames of his parents or that of one of them," reaffirms the American Convention on Human Rights (1969), article 18. "The law shall regulate the manner in which this right shall be ensured for all, by the use of assumed names if necessary." Other international human rights documents that guarantee the right to a name include the Convention on the Rights of the Child (1989) and the African Charter on the Rights and Welfare of the Child (1990).

Constitution of Ethiopia (1995), chapter three, Fundamental Rights and Freedoms, part two, Democratic Rights, article 36, Rights of Children: "1. Every child has the right: . . . (b) To a name and nationality. . . ."

International Covenant on Civil and Political Rights (1966), part III, article 24: "2. Every child shall be registered immediately after birth and shall have a name."

Constitutional Court of Italy (1996): "[N]ames have special protection as being essential to personal identity, and as such they are fundamental to personality . . . ; the right to one's name is one of the fundamental and absolute rights of the individual and cannot be renounced."

European Court of Human Rights (1994): "[F]orenames constitute a means of identifying persons within their families and the community. . . . Furthermore, the choice of a child's forename by its parents is a personal, emotional matter and therefore comes within their private sphere."

Dignity; Personality

National Origin

See Cultural Rights; Minorities; Nationality

Nationality

The idea of nationalism emanates from the human urge to belong to a social and political group larger than the family but smaller than all of mankind. Nationality (from the Latin *natio*, meaning race or breed, via the Old English *nacioun* and the Old French *nacion)* binds a person to a sovereign jurisdiction with reciprocal obligations for the citizen and the government. For example, the government has the obligation to provide police and military forces to protect the citizen or national, who has the reciprocal obligation to pay taxes and serve in the military when required. Citizens and nationals have rights such as voting and holding public office that are generally denied to nonnationals. Other rights of citizens and nationals generally include the right to diplomatic assistance and protection abroad, the right of reentry into the country of one's nationality, rights of preference to jobs over nonnationals or aliens, and the right to some government benefits, such as social security, that may be denied to aliens.

A distinction is made between a national and a citizen, although the term *national* is often used to refer generally to citizens and nationals alike. A citizen is always a national of his or her native country, while a national may or may not enjoy all the rights and privileges of a citizen. Legal entities, such as corporations, are never referred to as citizens, but they do possess nationality under international law.

Isocrates, an Athenian orator of the fourth century B.C.E., defined being Greek as sharing the Greek culture but not necessarily Greek blood. As the Roman Empire began expanding in the first century B.C.E., the conquered peoples were allowed to retain their culture although not their nationality; they were required to owe their political allegiance to Rome. The concept of the modern nation, sometimes called the nation-state, began in Europe and developed out of the German concept of *Volkgeist*, the cohesive forces of a common literature, folklore, language, and history—a common culture. But some nations developed from several cultures, as in the case of Belgium, which has two major linguistic groups, the Flemish and the French, as well as a small German-speaking minority.

Problems related to dual nationality, the loss of nationality or citizenship, and the treatment of one country's nationals in another country all have human rights implications. National laws determine how a person acquires nationality. Some countries, including Austria and Japan, require that one or both parents be nationals; in others, such as Thailand and the United States, nationality is determined by where a person is born. Because of this variance, some persons may obtain dual nationality or have to elect their nationality. "The more important states," an 1880 international law treatise observed, "recognize . . . that the child of a foreigner ought to be allowed to be himself a foreigner unless he manifests a wish to assume or retain the nationality of the state in which he has been born." Most nations have laws prescribing how citizens may lose their citizenship or nationality and how citizenship or nationality may be obtained by the process of naturalization.

Most nations also maintain some kind of representation in foreign countries, so that citizens or nationals can take advantage of their country's embassy or consular services when they travel. Nationality is important for various rights in one's home country, but because of the international rule that sovereigns—and therefore nations—deal only with each other and not with individual citizens of other countries, the rights of any person in a foreign country or the right to do business in a foreign country depend to a large extent on the reciprocity between a national's homeland and other foreign countries. Citizens of one country who find themselves in another country that is at war with or has no diplomatic relations with their own have no protected rights. Stateless persons, those who have no nationality, face this problem in any country.

A number of international human rights documents address problems that arise from nationality and related issues, particularly the problems of refugees, foreign-born spouses of citizens, and stateless persons. In 1985 the UN General Assembly adopted the Declaration on the Human Rights of Individuals Who Are Not Nationals of the Country in Which They Live (1985). This document, citing the Universal Declaration of Human Rights (1948), prohibits discrimination on the basis of national origin, among other things, and sets forth certain minimum rights for nonnationals and aliens.

Constitution of Israel, Law of Return (1950, as amended), section 4A: "The rights of a Jew under this law and the rights of an *oleh* [a Jew immigrating into Israel] under the Nationality Law . . . [of 1952], as well as the rights of an *oleh* under any other enactment, are also vested in a child and a grandchild of a Jew and the spouse of a child of a Jew, and the spouse of a grandchild of a Jew, except for a person who has been a Jew and has voluntarily changed his religion."

Universal Declaration of Human Rights (1948), article 15: "(1) Everyone has the right to a nationality. (2) No one shall be arbitrarily deprived of his nationality nor denied the right to change his nationality."

U.S. Court of Appeals, Second Circuit (1943): "In our view an invader cannot under international law impose its nationality upon non-residents of the subjugated country without their consent, express or tacit. . . ."

Italian–United States Conciliation Commission (1955): "In order to establish the prevalence of the United States nationality in individual cases [involving dual Italian and American nationality before the commission], habitual residence can be one of the criteria of evaluation, but not the only one. The conduct of the individual in his economic, social, political, civic and family life as well as the closer and more effective bond with one of the two States must be considered."

Flournoy, Richard W., Jr., and Manley O. Hudson, eds. *A Collection of Nationality Laws of Various Countries, as Contained in Constitutions, Statutes, and Treaties.* Littleton, Colo.: Rothman, 1983.

Grugel, Jean, ed. *Democracy without Borders: Transnationalization and Conditionality in New Democracies.* New York: Routledge, 1999.

Aliens; Declaration on the Human Rights of Individuals Who Are Not Nationals of the Country in Which They Live; Diplomats and Consuls; Refugees; Statelessness; Universal Declaration of Human Rights

Native Peoples

See Indigenous Peoples

Natural Resources

A nation's wealth depends heavily on the exploitation of its natural resources—its land, forests, minerals, bodies of water, and air, as well as places of historical and cultural significance to its people and the world. Who owns these resources, who can develop them, and how they should be managed and conserved are all issues of vital concern both within a nation's borders and beyond. The right to use natural resources is a collective or peoples' right, not an individual human right, although ultimately it is individual citizens who either benefit or lose from the proper or improper exercise of dominion over a nation's scarce resources.

Natural resources have always been an important element in the growth, development, and survival of human societies. It is thought that the exceptional fertility of the Mesopotamian floodplains called the Fertile Crescent made possible the great leap forward in human civilization that began about nine thousand years ago. A similar natural resource, the annual flooding of the Nile River, contributed significantly to the size and stability of the Egyptian state and culture that began some four thousand years later. The opportunity to own and exploit virgin natural resources spurred the colonization of the New World after Columbus's famous voyage in 1492.

Tragic legacies of this rush to appropriate natural resources in all parts of the world, especially by European nations, included colonialism and slavery. The right of political self-determination and freedom from servitude have thus become linked with control of natural resources, the right to development, economic growth, and environmental protection. Natural resource and economic development is vital to implementation of social rights, from providing job opportunities as well as adequate housing, health care, and welfare benefits for citizens.

Many aspects of national and international policy now touch on natural resources. Fresh water rights and marine rights, for example, can be a cause of friction or cooperation among nations. The need to allow foreign investment and technology to maximize the potential of certain natural resources such as oil and mineral deposits can create both benefits and exploitation. Destructive mining methods, oil spills, and nuclear waste can bring negative environmental impacts. National treasures and historic sites create commercial opportunities such as tourism, which may also produce economic disparities and environmental degradation.

A number of national constitutions address natural resources. Bulgaria's constitution (1991), for one, provides that the "land is a basic national resource and benefits from special protection of the state and society." Germany's constitution (1949) states that "[l]and, natural resources and means of production may for the purposes of socialization be transferred to public ownership. . . ." Ireland's constitution (1937) declares that "[a]ll natural resources, including the air and all forms of potential energy . . . belong to the State subject to . . . interest therein for the time being lawfully vested in any person or body."

The first article of both the International Covenant on Civil and Political Rights (1966) and the International Covenant on Economic, Social and Cultural Rights (1966) provides that "[a]ll peoples may, for their own ends, freely dispose of their natural wealth and resources. . . ." The Charter of Economic Rights and Duties of States (1974) and the African Charter of Human and Peoples' Rights (1981) also sanction the right of governments and citizens to use or freely dispose of their resources. "This right," adds the African charter, "shall be exercised in the exclusive interest of the people. In no case shall a people be deprived of it. In case of spoliation the dispossessed people shall have the right to the lawful recovery of its property as well as to an adequate compensation."

Areas over which no nation has sovereignty, such as the oceans beyond the states' territorial limits and places like Antarctica, are governed by treaties as well. The Law of the Sea Treaty (1982) extended sovereign territorial waters to twelve nautical miles beyond a nation's coast but granted exclusive fishing rights up to 200 nautical miles out. Minerals on the ocean floor beneath the high seas were deemed "the common heritage of mankind." Some 117 coastal nations signed the treaty, not including the United States, United Kingdom, West Germany, Italy, or Israel, which claimed that the seabed mining provisions would inhibit free enterprise. The Antarctic Treaty (1959), signed by countries including Argentina, Australia, Belgium, Chile, France, Japan, New Zealand, Norway, South Africa, the Soviet Union, the United Kingdom, and the United States, authorized joint scientific research and a sharing of results but prohibited any one nation from exploiting or damaging the continent's natural resources.

Constitution of Mexico (1917), title I, chapter I, Individual Guarantees, article 27: "The Nation shall at all times have the right to impose on private property such limitations as the public interest may demand, as well as the right to regulate the utilization of natural resources . . . in order to conserve them to ensure a more equitable distribution of public wealth. . . ."

Declaration on the Granting of Independence to Colonial Countries and Peoples (1960), preamble: "[P]eoples may, for their own ends, freely dispose of their natural wealth and resources without prejudice to any obligations arising out of international economic co-operation, based upon the principle of mutual benefit, and international law."

Slovenian Constitutional Court (1995): The Slovenian government assumed the ownership of certain natural resources that previously had been owned by the predecessor socialist state. A consequence of the transfer is that a license is required for a business or individual to use or exploit these resources.

Lac Lanoux Arbitration Tribunal (1957): Spain objected to a French project to use the waters of Lake Lanoux, which was in French territory but flowed across the border into Spain. The arbitrators held that "the upstream State has, procedurally, a right of initiative; it is not obliged to associate the downstream State in the elaboration of its [plans]. If, in the course of discussions, the downstream State submits [its own plans], the upstream State must examine them, but it has the right to give preference to the solution contained in

its own [plans] provided that it takes into consideration in a reasonable manner the interests of the downstream State."

Natural Resources Institute, Central Avenue, Chatham Maritime, Chatham ME4 4TB, England. (44-163-488-0088. 🖶 44-163-488-0066. 🖳 nri@ukc.ac.uk. 🖳 www.nri.org.

United Nations Committee on Energy and Natural Resources for Development, Department of Economic and Social Affairs, Division for Sustainable Development, United Nations, Room DC2-2220, New York, N.Y. 10017. (212-963-1234. 🖶 212-963-4260. 🖳 dsd@un.org 🖳 www.un.org.esa.

Cooper, Richard N. *Environment and Resource Policies for the World Economy*. Washington, D.C.: Brookings, 1994.

Cutter, Susan L., Hilary Lambert Renwick, and William H. Renwick. *Exploitation, Conservation, Preservation: A Geographic Perspective on Natural Resource Use*. 2nd ed. New York: Wiley, 1991.

Collective Rights; Convention Concerning the Protection of the World Cultural and Natural Heritage; Declaration on the Right to Development; Development; Economic Rights; Environment; Property; Rio Declaration on Environment and Development; Social Rights; Sovereignty

Natural Rights

"The end of all political associations," wrote Thomas Paine in *The Rights of Man* (1791), "is the preservation of the natural and imprescriptible rights of man; and these rights are liberty, property, security, and resistance of oppression." The philosophical antecedents of modern human rights, natural rights place the individual at the center of legal and political systems and relegate the state to serving all people equally in their quest for personal self-fulfillment and happiness. They are inherent individual rights that existed, at least in theory, before human civilization created social rights and duties.

Derived from the law of nature (*naturalis* in Latin means by birth or nature), natural rights are inalienable and supposedly beyond the power of the state. Accordingly, they may not be surrendered by an individual even through an express contract with the government. Because personal liberty, for example, is considered a natural and inalienable right, a person may not be made a slave even if he or she agrees to enter into such a condition.

The modern concept of natural rights was explored and developed in the seventeenth century by the English philosopher Thomas Hobbes and the Dutch philosopher Benedict Spinoza and expanded further in the eighteenth century by the French philosopher Jean-Jacques Rousseau, among others. The essence of their work is this: in a state of nature all persons have natural rights, but in a social or political context these rights may be surrendered or transformed so that the individual may reap the benefits of living in an organized state. Natural law theorists before the American and French Revolutions also tried to extend this rationale to require that all social institutions be subordinate to the development of the individual.

The concept of natural rights, as described by Thomas Jefferson in the U.S. Declaration of Independence (1776), eventually came to refer to an individual's inherent rights except for those surrendered to the state—such as the right to personally punish those who commit a crime or to maintain an army for one's own self-defense—for the sole purpose of protecting the remaining individual rights—such as the right to life, liberty, property, and "the Pursuit of Happiness." As the German scholar Otto Gierke, who died in 1921, described the evolution of the theory of natural rights: "In the heart of social life itself the individual had now a sphere reserved for him which was itself immune from society; and this Sovereignty of the Individual was obviously more original, and more sacrosanct, than any possible Sovereignty of Society, which could only be derived from *him*, and could only serve *him* as a means."

Today the broad concept of natural rights is encompassed by other terms. National constitutions and major international human rights documents generally avoid the term *natural rights*, perhaps because of its broad and somewhat amorphous scope or its association with revolutionary causes, referring instead to *inalienable rights, fundamental rights, constitutional rights,* or *human rights.*

Declaration of the Rights of Man and of the Citizen (France) (1789): "The representatives of the French people . . . have resolved to set forth in a solemn declaration the natural, inalienable and sacred rights of man, in order that this declaration, continually before all members of the body politic, may be a perpetual reminder of their rights and duties. . . ."

Constitution of Ireland (1937), Fundamental Rights, Education, article 42: "5. In exceptional cases . . . the State as guardian of the common good . . . shall endeavor to supply the place of parents, but always with due regard for the natural and imprescriptible rights of the child."

Supreme Court of Ireland (1974): Ireland's constitution (1937), articles 41, 42, and 43, respectively, regarding family, education, and private property, "emphatically reject the theory that there are no rights without laws, no rights contrary to the law and no rights

anterior to the law. They indicate that justice is placed above the law and acknowledge that natural rights, or human rights, are not created by law but that the Constitution confirms their existence and gives them protection."

International Court of Justice (1986): Regarding the use of force by sovereign nations, a distinction may be drawn between the rules of customary international law and the provisions of the Charter of the United Nations (1945). The court noted that the charter "refers to pre-existing customary international law" [by mentioning in article 51] the 'natural' or 'inherent' right of individual or collective self-defense, which 'nothing in the present Charter shall impair,' and which applies in the event of an armed attack against a member state.

Meyers, Diana T. *Inalienable Rights: A Defense.* New York: Columbia University Press, 1985.

Veatch, Henry B. *Human Rights: Fact or Fancy?* Baton Rouge: Louisiana State University Press, 1985.

Declaration of Independence (United States); Fundamental Rights; Inviolable Rights; Jefferson, Thomas; Paine, Thomas; Spinoza, Benedict

Ngugi wa Thiong'o

A leading East African author, Ngugi wa Thiong'o (b. 1938) has movingly expressed Africans' struggle against colonialism, racism, religious hypocrisy, corruption, and related social and moral issues. Through his writings he has articulated the longings and desires of Africans subjected to colonial and postcolonial repression—proving that in fighting for human rights, the pen is equally as mighty as the sword and certainly more humane.

Born on January 5, 1938, in Limuru, Kenya, James Thiong'o Ngugi eventually dropped his English name and became known as Ngugi. His elementary education in Kenya was interrupted by a Mau Mau uprising, but he went on to earn a degree from Makerere University in Kampala, Uganda, in 1963, and another from Leeds University in Yorkshire, England, in 1964. After a six-month stint as a reporter for a Nairobi newspaper, he continued his studies at Leeds.

In 1967 Ngugi began teaching at Nairobi University College, but two years later he resigned in protest during a student strike. After lecturing in the United States, he returned to teach at Nairobi only to be arrested and imprisoned for a year without being charged, apparently for his efforts to increase the political awareness of peasants and workers in his hometown. Thereafter he chose to live in exile in London and New York City.

Ngugi's writing expresses his sympathy for the oppression of his fellow Africans. *Weep Not, Child* (1964), *The River Between* (1965), and *A Grain of Wheat* (1967) dealt with problems such as the struggle for Kenyan independence and conflicts between traditional culture and Western values. Ngugi vowed to restrict his future novels and plays to Gikuyu, his native tongue, and in *Decolonizing the Mind: The Politics of Language in African Literature* (1986), he promoted African languages as the only true means of communication for Africans.

Always sympathizing with the oppressed and underprivileged, Ngugi used his gift for writing to criticize all forms of repression, whether Kenya's colonial administration or its neocolonial government after independence was obtained. He was especially active in the adult literacy campaign in his hometown of Limuru, even writing musicals to educate through the use of allegory. His accomplishments garnered many awards, including the East Africa Novel Prize in 1962, UNESCO's first prize in 1963, the Lotus Prize for Afro-Asian literature in 1973, and the New York African Studies Association's Distinguished African Award in 1996.

Ogude, James. *Ngugi's Novels and African History*. Sterling, Va.: Pluto, 1999.

Ngugi wa Thiong'o. *Detained: A Writer's Prison Diary*. Nairobi: Heineman, 1981.

Race Discrimination; Self-Determination

Noncombatants

See Geneva Conventions; War

Nongovernmental Organizations

Nongovernmental organizations (NGOs) are private, often multinational organizations that engage in political and humanitarian activities. With the exception of the International Committee of the Red Cross, which is chartered internationally, NGOs have no international legal personality or status. Because of their independence from any national government or international treaty committee, nongovernmental organizations are able to unconditionally mobilize support for human rights projects and victims.

NGOs vary according to their avowed mission, their location or areas of interest, and the nature of their membership. One of the most prominent groups involved in human rights activities is Amnesty International, which since its inception in 1961 has investigated more than forty-two thousand cases of prisoners around the world. In 1977 it was awarded the Nobel Peace Prize for its work in human rights. Other NGOs specialize in providing medical and related treatment for soldiers in battle, refugees, and needy women and children; furnishing legal assistance to political prisoners and victims of human rights abuses; lobbying for legislation and other political changes; creating information and support networks for human rights workers; and monitoring compliance with international human rights instruments.

The methods used by NGOs to accomplish their missions also vary. Some investigate and report on allegations of abuses. Often, if the country responsible for the abuses does not respond to such reports, NGOs can mobilize popular opinion both locally and internationally to bring pressure on the guilty governments. They may also monitor the way countries implement human rights provisions of their own laws and international treaties to which they are a party. NGOs created to monitor the human rights provisions of the Helsinki Final Act (1975) helped bring about the fall of the communist regimes in the Soviet Union and Eastern European countries. Although NGOs possess none of the police power of a national or state government, their powers of publicity and persuasion can be just as effective.

Many human rights NGOs maintain an official relationship with international and regional organizations that have human rights responsibilities. Most of the major organizations have been accorded consultative status in some form by the United Nations, Council of Europe, Organization of American States, or United Nations Educational, Scientific and Cultural Organization (UNESCO). Other human rights groups, although lacking official status, nevertheless seek to influence the action of international and regional organizations.

Since the 1970s NGOs have proliferated, and today thousands of them operate nationally and internationally. To remain impartial and independent, most are financed totally by private funding. This allows them to criticize government activities, even in the countries in which they are established. They may also lobby for changes in laws or policies nationally and internationally to improve human rights.

NGOs differ from GANGOs (government-appointed NGOs). GANGOs, unlike NGOs, are not independent of the governments that create them and in certain countries are established to counteract criticism of official acts that violate human rights.

International NGO Training and Research Center, P.O. Box 563, Oxford OX2 6RZ, England. (44-186-520-1851. 🖳 44-186-520-1852. 🖳 intrac@gn.apc.org. 🖳 www.intrac.org.

United Nations Committee on Nongovernmental Organizations, Department of Economic and Social Affairs, United Nations, Room DCI-1070, New York, N.Y. 10017. (212-963-1234. 🖳 212-963-4114. 🖳 esa@un.org. 🖳 www.un.org/esa/coordination/ngo.

Human Rights Internet Reporter Masterlist: A Listing of Organizations Concerned with Human Rights and Social Justice Worldwide. Supplement to Human Rights Internet Reporter, vol. 15. Ottawa: Human Rights Internet, 1994.

Korey, William. *NGOs and the Universal Declaration of Human Rights: "A Curious Grapevine."* New York: St. Martin's, 1998.

Mosse, Gail M. L. "U.S. Constitutional Freedom of Association: Its Potential for Human Rights NGOs at Home and Abroad." *Human Rights Quarterly* 19 (1997): 738–812.

Amnesty International; Helsinki Final Act; Red Cross and Red Crescent; United Nations; United Nations Educational, Scientific and Cultural Organization (UNESCO); *and other specific nongovernmental organizations*

Nonrefoulement

See Deportation; *Refoulement*

Norms

Norms are widely agreed upon and accepted standards of human rights that governments may not derogate from or infringe. In international law, peremptory norms, sometimes referred to as *jus cogens* (coercive rights), are similarly those rules to which other acts must conform. *Norm* is a somewhat technical term not generally found in national constitutions or even international human rights documents, but its meaning is often important in adjudication of human rights issues by courts and tribunals. Derived from the Latin *norma* (meaning a carpenter's or mason's square or rule), *norm* has been in use in English since at least the early nineteenth century.

Family and social groups generally reinforce norms, or standards, of acceptable behavior and punish unacceptable behavior during their offspring's childhood and adolescence. According to *Psychological and Social Problems* (1964), "One particular respect in which a group equilibrium develops is in the formation of norms—shared patterns of behaving, feeling and thinking. All social groups develop norms, particularly about matters connected with the group's main purposes and activities. . . ." When group members deviate

from the norms, various kinds of persuasion, pressure, and sanctions are exerted to make them conform. In domestic and international law, authoritative documents and decisions similarly identify legal norms by which individuals and states will be judged.

In American law, *normal* means according to or not deviating from an established norm, rule, or principle. Normative language—language that sets forth ideals rather than descriptions of factual conditions—is characterized by such words as *ought, must, should, right,* and *wrong.* Hans Kelsen, a professor of law and constitutional court judge who had a significant influence on Austria's 1920 constitution, saw laws as "a pyramid of successive legal norms, extending from municipal ordinances at the bottom to constitutional and even international law at the top."

National human rights norms are generally embodied in a country's constitution. Freedom of religion, for example—the norm that the state should not control a person's beliefs—is set forth in the First Amendment (1791) to the U.S. Constitution: "Congress shall make no law respecting an establishment of religion, or promoting the free exercise thereof." At the international and regional levels, human rights norms are generally expressed first in declarations of human rights, such as the Universal Declaration of Human Rights, adopted by the UN General Assembly in 1948. Such norms may later be embodied in conventions or treaties that individual nations ratify, signifying that they intend to promote and enforce the specified rights within their territorial jurisdictions. The Declaration on the Elimination of Discrimination against Women, adopted by the General Assembly in 1967, was followed by a similarly titled convention in 1979.

Some of the major human rights norms contained in international human rights declarations and treaties include the right to life; the right to equality and nondiscrimination; protection from torture and cruel, inhuman or degrading treatment or punishment; freedom of movement; recognition as a person before the law; freedom of thought, conscience, and religion; freedom of opinion, expression, and information; freedom of assembly; children's rights; and the cultural, religious, and linguistic rights of ethnic, religious, and linguistic minorities.

Constitution of Portugal (1997), Fundamental Principles, article 8, International Law: "1. The norms and principles of general or customary international law are an integral part of Portuguese law."

Vienna Convention (1969), article 53: "A treaty is void if, at the time of its conclusion, it conflicts with a peremptory norm of general international law. For the purposes of the present Convention, a peremptory norm of general international law is a norm accepted and recognized by the international community of states as a whole as a norm from which no derogation is permitted and which can be modified only by a subsequent norm of general international law having the same character."

Constitutional Court of Germany (1975): "According to established precedent of the Federal Constitutional Court, the constitutional norms contain not only an individual's subjective defensive rights against the state. They also represent an objective order of values that serves as a basic constitutional decision for all areas of the law and provide guidelines and impulses for legislative, administrative, and judicial practice. . . ."

European Commission of Human Rights (1981): Referring to the judgment of the European Court of Human Rights in the *National Belgium Police Case*, the commission concluded that the European Convention for the Protection of Human Rights and Fundamental Freedoms (1950), article 14, "safeguards individuals or groups of individuals ... from all discrimination in the enjoyment of the rights and freedoms set forth in the other normative provisions of the Convention."

Brkič, Jovan. *Norm and Order: An Investigation into Logic, Semantics, and the Theory of Law and Morals.* New York: Humanities, 1970.

Hannikainen, Lauri. *Peremptory Norms (Jus Cogens) in International Law: Historical Development, Criteria, Present Status.* Helsinki: Finnish Lawyers' Publishing Company, 1988.

Derogation; European Convention for the Protection of Human Rights and Fundamental Freedoms; Fundamental Rights; International Law; *Jus Cogens*

North Atlantic Treaty Organization (NATO)

Established in 1949 as a defense alliance of democratic nations, the North Atlantic Treaty Organization (NATO) has in addition to its military role defended human rights and freedoms and expanded their scope. NATO, which as of 2000 had nineteen member nations, played a key role in the ultimate dissolution of communist dictatorships in Eastern Europe after the fall of the Berlin Wall in 1989 and more recently has taken action to stop the ethnic cleansing in the Yugoslav province of Kosovo.

NATO was created to serve as a military counterweight to the Soviet military presence in post–World War II Eastern Europe. The alliance was facilitated by the Brussels Treaty of Economic, Social and Cultural Collaboration (1948), entered into by Belgium, France, Luxembourg, the Netherlands, and the United Kingdom. The Vandenberg Resolution, named for U.S. Senator Arthur Vandenberg, a converted pre–World War II isolationist, gave the United States impetus to join in a defense coalition with the Western Europeans. The blockade of Berlin by the Soviet Union in June 1948 also influenced the alliance's formation.

On April 4, 1949, the North Atlantic Treaty was signed by twelve nations—Belgium, Canada, Denmark, France, Iceland, Italy, Luxembourg, the Netherlands, Norway, Portugal, the United Kingdom, and the United States—and entered into force on August 24, 1949. Greece and Turkey joined the NATO alliance in 1952, the Federal Republic of Germany (then West Germany) in 1955, and Spain in 1982. In 1990 the reunification of Germany brought the former territory of East Germany into the Federal Republic of Germany and thus into NATO. In 1999 the Czech Republic, Hungary, and Poland also joined.

Although not its primary purpose, NATO has been effective in protecting and enforcing human rights. It has acted as both a shield for its free and democratic member nations and a protector of human rights in those countries and others. NATO was also a positive force for change in the former communist countries of Europe. By the end of the 1980s, NATO's defense capability, particularly that of the United States, was able to undermine the Soviet Union's alliance of communist satellite countries, called the Warsaw Pact, resulting in freedom from dictatorships for millions of people and access to constitutional governments that can promote and protect human rights. In 1999 NATO waged a bombing campaign against Serbian-dominated Yugoslavia to halt the genocidal killings in Kosovo.

NATO's governing body is the North Atlantic Council, which is composed of representatives of the member nations and meets twice a year. The council's chair, selected by rotation among the member nations, also heads NATO's civilian operations.

Atlantic Council of the United States, 910 17th Street, N.W., Suite 1000, Washington, D.C. 20006. (202-463-7226. 202-463-7241. info@acus.org. www.oac.cd.lib.org/dynaweb/ead.

North Atlantic Treaty Organization (NATO), boulevard Leopold III, 1110 Brussels, Belgium. (32-2-707-41-11. 32-2-707-12-52. natodoc@hq.nato.int. www.nato.int.

Cornish, Paul. *Partnership in Crisis: The U.S., Europe and the Fall and Rise of NATO.* London: Royal Institute of International Affairs, 1997.

The NATO Handbook. Brussels: NATO Office of Information and Press, 1998.

Enforcement; Organization for Security and Cooperation in Europe; Security

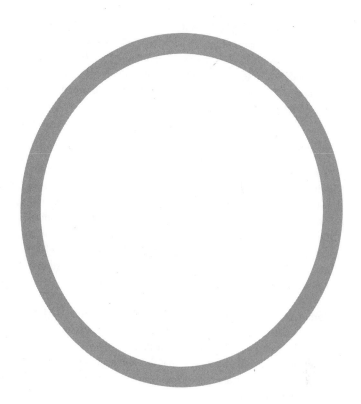

Oxfam International, a non-governmental organization that specializes in providing assistance to those in need around the world, supplied emergency relief to Rwandan refugees in Tanzania. Working with international and national agencies, organizations such as Oxfam help realize the human rights to food, clothing, and other basic necessities of life during times of crisis. [Howard Davies, Panos Pictures]

Ombudsmen

An ombudsman is any person authorized by an institution to investigate complaints against the institution or its agents. The government position of ombudsman was created by the Swedish parliament, but at least eighteen other countries, including Austria, Bangladesh, Colombia, Denmark, Hungary, New Zealand, Nigeria, Norway, Portugal, Russia, South Africa, and Zimbabwe, have established national ombudsmen. This government position is generally instituted by the legislative branch to hear, investigate, report, and take action on complaints of citizens against public officials in the executive branch. *Ombudsman* is derived from the early Germanic word for a person chosen to collect *Wergild,* or blood money, on behalf of those offended by the actions of others.

In 1713 the Swedish monarch appointed a chancellor of justice to investigate complaints against royal officials. When Sweden became a constitutional monarchy in 1809, the parliament appointed its own similar official, the *Justitieombudsman,* to investigate citizens' complaints. A second ombudsman was installed in 1915 to investigate complaints against the military. Since then the number of Sweden's ombudsmen and their purview have increased.

Today an ombudsman generally receives complaints from aggrieved parties and subsequently initiates an investigation if the claim has merit and falls within his or her jurisdiction. Ombudsmen are generally granted access to official records and, on the basis of an investigation, file a report with the complainant and the public office involved. If the matter is not resolved at this stage, an ombudsman has recourse to the legislature for redress of the complaint. In countries such as the United States, legislators generally perform a similar service for their constituents.

In 1978 the International Ombudsman Institute was established at the Law Center of the University of Alberta in Edmonton, Canada, to promote the concept of the ombudsman and research problems facing these officials. Publications of the institute include the *IOI Directory of Ombudsmen and Other Complaint-Handlers,* the *Ombudsman Journal,* issued annually, and *Court Cases of Interest to the Institution of Ombudsman.*

In addition to governments, many private organizations and businesses use ombudsmen to enhance the objectivity of investigations into complaints about their products and services. However, ombudsmen are not generally used beyond the national level—at the international and regional levels—to resolve human rights problems.

Constitution of Portugal (1976), part III, Organization of Political Powers, section III, Assembly of the Republic, chapter II, Powers, article 166 (added in 1992), Powers with Respect to Other Organs: "With respect to other organs, the assembly [parliament] shall have the following powers: . . . i). To elect by a two-thirds majority of the members present where the majority is larger than the absolute majority of the members entitled to vote, ten judges of the constitutional court, the ombudsman, [and other named officials]. . . ."

National Institutions for the Protection and Promotion of Human Rights (1987), Report of the UN Secretary-General: "The ombudsman is an independent mediator—and in some instances, a collegiate body—whose primary role is to protect the rights of the individual who believes he is the victim of unjust acts on the part of the public administration."

U.K. Select Committee on the Parliamentary Commissioner for Administration (1978): "[Although] the experience of the past eleven years has fully justified the value both to the individual citizen and to Parliament of the office of Parliamentary Commissioner [a quasi-ombudsman], . . . the time has come to extend the Commissioner's jurisdiction and powers in a number of ways which are compatible with the premises on which the office is based and which serve to distinguish [it] from Ombudsmen overseas."

European Court of Human Rights (1987): "It is the particular duty of an Ombudsman to ensure that courts of law and administrative authorities observe the provisions of the Constitution regarding objectivity and impartiality and that the fundamental rights and freedoms of citizens are not encroached upon in the processes of public administration."

Government and the Individual: The Citizen's Means of Redress. London: Publishing Services, Central Office of Information, 1996.

Reif, Linda C., ed. *The International Ombudsman Anthology: Selected Writings from the International Ombudsman Institute.* The Hague: Kluwer Law International, 1999.

Third African Regional Ombudsman Conference. Abuja, Nigeria: Public Complaint Commission, 1994.

Complaints; Remedies; Reporting Violations

Opinion

"If all mankind minus one, were of one opinion, and only one person were of the contrary opinion, mankind would be no more justified in silencing that one person, than he, if he had the power, would be justified in silencing mankind," proclaimed the nineteenth-century English philosopher John Stuart Mill. The right to hold opinions and express them is one of the cornerstones of a democracy. Along with freedom of thought, speech, the press, religion, conscience, information, and expression, freedom of opinion (from the Latin *opinio,* meaning supposition or belief) is one of a number of rights relating to an individual's ability to communicate with fellow citizens.

Opinions, like religious beliefs and political philosophy, are highly personal attributes. In an autocracy or a theocracy, an individual's freedom of opinion is limited to the guidelines promulgated by the state. In a democracy, however, freedom of opinion and the right to express opinions are limited by law only when the expression of opinions causes direct harm to others. A person who states an unfounded opinion that damages another person's reputation or business cannot successfully mount a defense in a resulting lawsuit by claiming freedom of opinion.

Public, as opposed to personal, opinion is a manifestation of a consensus among individuals, each of whom holds a similar opinion. Public opinion in a democracy is important because it reflects the will of the people, which democratic government is established to implement as far as reasonable and possible. However, as Mill declared, no amount of public opinion can justify infringing the right of each individual to his or her own, contrary opinion.

A human rights issue arises when one group of citizens must tolerate what seem to be discriminatory or inhumane opinions, such as those held by members of groups like the Ku Klux Klan or neo-Nazis. But as long as a person's opinion, no matter how obnoxious or abhorrent to others, causes no one else harm, the government has no reason to punish that person. All the opinions that provide the foundation for scientific and technological progress, political and economic development, and culture and religion were once held by a single person. Galileo, the sixteenth-century Italian astronomer and physicist, for example, challenged one of the unquestioned principles of his time, derived from the works of the ancient Greek philosopher Aristotle and perpetuated by the Roman Catholic Church through its universities: that the Earth was the center of the universe. Galileo's opinions, based on his observations and calculations published in 1632, were banned by the church because they were contrary to its teachings, and he lived under house arrest during his last years.

The English Bill of Rights (1689) guaranteed freedom of speech for members of Parliament during debates or proceedings, and France's Declaration of the Rights of Man and of the Citizen (1789), article 10, states: "No one is to be importuned because of his opinions, even religious ones, provided their manifestation does not disturb the public order established by law." Article 11 of that document provides in part that "[f]ree communication of ideas and opinions is one of the most precious of the rights of man."

Many national laws and constitutions, including those of Ireland (1937), Germany (1949), and Sweden (1975), guarantee freedom of opinion either expressly or in similar terms. International human rights documents that do so include the Universal Declaration of Human Rights (1948), European Convention for the Protection of Human Rights and Fundamental Freedoms (1950), International Convention on the Elimination of All Forms of Racial Discrimination (1965), International Covenant on Civil and Political Rights (1966), and African Charter on Human and Peoples' Rights (1981).

Constitution of Sweden, Instrument of Government (1975), chapter 1, The Basic Principles of the Constitution, article 1: "Swedish democracy is founded on freedom of opinion and on universal and equal suffrage."

Universal Declaration of Human Rights (1948), article 19: "Everyone has the right to freedom of opinion and expression; this right includes freedom to hold opinions without interference and to seek, receive and impart information and ideas through any media and regardless of frontiers."

Constitutional Court of Germany (1980): "Because value judgments are so much at issue in public discussion, freedom of speech must be allowed in the interest of furthering the formation of public opinion . . . , [b]ut this protection does not extend to false statements of fact. Incorrect information does not merit protection under the rubric of freedom of opinion, because it does not contribute to the constitutionally guaranteed process of forming public opinion."

European Court of Human Rights (1993): Protection of personal opinion is one of the purposes of freedom of association guaranteed by the European Convention for the Protection of Human Rights and Fundamental Freedoms (1950), article 11.

Fishkin, James S. *The Voice of the People: Public Opinion and Democracy.* New Haven, Conn.: Yale University Press, 1995.

Shetreet, Shimon, ed. *Free Speech and National Security.* The Hague: Martinus Nijhoff, Kluwer Law International, 1991.

Aristotle; Association; Communication; Conscience; European Convention for the Protection of Human Rights and Fundamental Freedoms; Declaration of the Rights of Man and of the Citizen (France); Expression; Information; The Press; Religion; Speech; Thought

Organization for Security and Cooperation in Europe

The Organization for Security and Cooperation in Europe (OSCE) was originally established as the Conference on Security and Cooperation in Europe (CSCE). After being formally convened on July 3, 1973, in Helsinki, Finland, the conference produced what turned out to be a significant human rights document: the Helsinki Final Act (1975), known as the Helsinki Accords. This agreement played a key role in the collapse of the communist regimes in the Soviet Union and Eastern Europe as well as the removal of the Berlin Wall in 1989.

The conference involved the foreign ministers of thirty-five countries, including all the European nations (except Albania), Canada, and the United States. In addition to the Final Act, CSCE initiated follow-up meetings to improve mutual relations and security. These were held in Belgrade, Yugoslavia, in 1977 and 1978; in Madrid, Spain, from 1980 to 1983, and in Vienna, Austria, from 1986 to 1989.

A significant achievement of CSCE was its ability to bring together democratic nations and communist blocs in Europe, particularly in the area of human rights. Proceeding on the premise that international relations had to include a human dimension directly beneficial to the individual, CSCE was able to exact commitments to human rights from the Soviet-bloc nations represented. By helping dispel mistrust between the confrontational groups, it helped reduce military tension in Europe.

With the fall of the Berlin Wall and the opening of free passage between East and West Germany on November 9, 1989, CSCE's work came to fruition. On November 21, 1990, at the end of a three-day Paris summit meeting, the Charter of Paris for a New Europe was announced. In addition to democracy, the document emphasizes peace, unity, economic liberty and responsibility, human rights, and the rule of law for all the nations and peoples of Europe. "Human rights and fundamental freedoms," says the charter, "are the birthright of all human beings, are inalienable and are guaranteed by law. Their protection and promotion is the first responsibility of government."

At the Budapest summit on December 5–6, 1994, the decision was made to rename CSCE the Organization for Security and Cooperation in Europe, effective January 1, 1995. The decision-making bodies became the ministerial council, senior council, and permanent council. Today OSCE consists of fifty-five nations and takes an active part in three areas of concern in Europe: human rights, economics, and security. Its human rights responsibilities are addressed specifically by its office for democratic institutions and human rights and its high commissioner for national minorities. In addition to its negotiating and decision-making bodies, OSCE's administration includes a chairman-in-office, a secretary-general, and a secretariat.

Conference on Security and Cooperation in Europe, 234 Ford House Office Building, Washington, D.C. 20515-6460. (202-225-1901. 🖳 csce@mail.house.gov. 🖳 www.house.gov/csce.

Organization for Security and Cooperation in Europe, Kärntner Ring 5-7, A-1010 Vienna, Austria. (43-1-514-36-0. 🖳 43-1-514-36-96. 🖳 pm@osce.org. 🖳 www.osce.org.

Charter of Paris for a New Europe; Helsinki Final Act; North Atlantic Treaty Organization (NATO); Regional Human Rights Systems

Organization of African Unity

See Regional Human Rights Systems

Organization of American States

See Regional Human Rights Systems

Oxfam International

The Oxfam movement had its beginnings in Oxford, England, in 1942, when the Oxford Committee on Famine Relief provided assistance to war-stricken, Nazi-occupied Greece. After World War II the organization helped raise funds for war refugees and opened the organization's first permanent charity shop in Oxford. In the 1960s Oxfam, as it became known from its telegraph address, focused on poverty in Third World countries, working in partnership with local people and organizations.

The organization defines poverty as "a state of powerlessness in which people are unable to exercise their basic human rights or control virtually any aspect of their lives." According to Oxfam, poverty manifests itself in the inadequacy of material goods, lack of access to basic services, and lack of opportunities, which lead to a condition of insecurity. Entrenched inequalities and institu-

tional and economic mechanisms perpetuate the conditions creating poverty.

In 1995 Oxfam International was established to coordinate joint international campaigns against poverty and conduct advocacy and lobbying activities. Oxfam's programs address the underlying causes of poverty and the injustices that result, seek to strengthen local organizations, and assist in developing structures to combat poverty and injustice. The ultimate goal is to enable people to exercise their rights and manage their own lives.

Today Oxfam International consists of eleven autonomous nongovernmental organizations that share its goals. Its structure includes a secretariat based in Oxford, a board of directors made up of delegates from Oxfam affiliates, a council of executive directors, and volunteer board members. Its advocacy office in Washington, D.C., lobbies the World Bank, International Monetary Fund, and United Nations on matters of common concern to the affiliates, which are located in the United Kingdom, United States, Ontario, Quebec, Ireland, Belgium, the Netherlands, Spain, Hong Kong, New Zealand, and Australia.

Oxfam America, 26 West Street, Boston, Mass. 02111-1206. (617-482-1211. 🖨 617-728-2594. 📠 info@oxfamamerica.org. 🖥 www.oxfamamerica.org.

Oxfam International, 267 Banbury Road, Second Floor, Oxford OX2 7HT, England. (44-186-531-3939. 🖨 44-186-531-3935. 📠 administration@oxfaminternational.org. 🖥 www.oxfaminternational.org.

Oxfam International Advocacy, 733 15th Street, N.W., Suite 340, Washington, D.C. 20005. (202-783-3331. 🖨 202-783-5547. 📠 oxfamintdc@igc.apc.org. 🖥 www.oxfaminternational.org.

Economic Rights; Food; Standard of Living

Peace is a basic human right on which all other rights depend. The United Nations, like the North Atlantic Treaty Organization (NATO), increasingly enforces peace around the world by using troops from many member nations. Often asked on short notice to undertake difficult missions, the UN's blue-helmeted peacekeeping forces received the Nobel Peace Price in 1988. [Saw Lwin, United Nations]

Paine, Thomas

A political gadfly, Thomas Paine (1737–1809) wrote *Common Sense* (1776), a pamphlet that sparked the American Revolution; *The Rights of Man* (1791), a defense of the French Revolution of 1789; and *The Age of Reason* (1793), a defense of deism. A man ahead of his time, in 1775 he called for the abolition of slavery and wrote the preamble to an act by the Pennsylvania legislature—the first law in America of its kind—providing for the gradual emancipation of slaves in the commonwealth. In *The Rights of Man,* he argued that it was government's duty to use taxes to pay for public education, old-age pensions, assistance for youth, unemployment insurance, soldiers' benefits, and care of the indigent.

Born in Theford, England, on January 29, 1737, Paine was the son of an Anglican mother and a Quaker father. After serving for a while as a sailor, he came to America in 1774 carrying letters of introduction from Benjamin Franklin, whom he had met in London. He quickly found a job writing and editing the *Pennsylvania Magazine,* a pulpit he used to condemn slavery and the slave trade. Early in 1776 he produced the seventy-nine-page pamphlet *Common Sense,* which argued for American independence from Great Britain and became an instant bestseller among the American colonists. Paine worked on the 1776 constitution of the new commonwealth of Pennsylvania after independence was declared and served in George Washington's army during the American Revolution (1775–81).

Some years later Paine returned to England and wrote *The Rights of Man,* in which he defended French democracy against an attack by Edmund Burke, the British statesman and defender of the British monarchy. In this book Paine outlined "a system of principles as universal as truth and the existence of man . . . : I. Men are born and always continue free and equal in respect to their rights. Civil distinctions, therefore, can be founded only on public utility. II. The end of all political associations is the preservation of the natural and imprescriptible rights of man; and these rights are liberty, property, security, and resistance of oppression. III. The Nation is essentially the source of all Sovereignty; nor can any individual or any body of men, be entitled to any authority which is not expressly derived from it."

The British government banned the popular book as seditious, and Paine fled to France, where he was elected to the national constitutional convention and later appointed as one of nine members to draft the French constitution. His argument against executing the deposed king resulted in his arrest by the French revolutionaries, but he was released after eleven months through American intervention on his behalf.

In his last book, *The Age of Reason,* Paine argued in favor of deism—a religious belief held by some, including Thomas Jefferson and George Washington, that God does not act in the world in which we live—and against all "revealed" religions. Condemned as an atheist, he returned to the United States, where he died on June 8, 1809, shunned by old friends and compatriots.

Ayer, Alfred J. *Thomas Paine*. Chicago: University of Chicago Press, 1990.

Keane, John. *Tom Paine: A Political Life*. Boston: Little, Brown, 1995.

Constitutional Rights; Declaration of the Rights of Man and of the Citizen; Jefferson, Thomas; Natural Rights; Slavery; Sovereignty

Participatory Rights

Women, minorities, and the disabled are some of the people who have traditionally been left out of the political decision-making process. Participatory rights—through which all individuals and groups are allowed or encouraged to participate in making decisions that can affect their rights and interests—empower citizens such as these to join equally with others in their nation's political life. The term also refers to the extension of rights to groups such as workers and unions to enable them to participate in economic and social decision making including management decisions affecting their physical and economic well-being.

Humans are social as well as political animals. Anthropological evidence indicates that from the earliest times *Homo sapiens* has lived and worked in groups—families, bands, clans, and tribes. The right to participate in group activities is linked to recognition of the worth of a person in the social and political structure of the group. The Greek philosopher Plato, in *The Laws*, was far ahead of his time when he discussed the merits of including women in communal meals in his proposed new colony of Magnesia: "So the happiness of the state will be better . . . served if we . . . put things right, by providing that all arrangements apply to men and women alike." From the fourth century B.C.E., when this theoretical proposal was advanced, it was to be well over two millennia before most women attained the constitutional right to participate equally with men in a nation's political life.

The concept of participatory rights, a relatively recent phenomenon whose goal is broad and active participation in all aspects of society, differs from representative democracy, whereby a few represent the many. "Those who really are committed to 'participatory democracy,' and hence insist on participating directly and fully in all forms of social life that can rightly command their allegiance," commented a writer in the *New York Review of Books* in July 1968, "are separated by an ideological abyss from those traditional representatives of 'representative democracy.'"

The right to equal participation in society is sometimes emphasized in countries that have a history of discrimina-

tion against a group or groups of people. Where persons have been excluded from public or private social institutions, an attempt may be made to correct this denial of equal rights or to ensure that private actions do not perpetuate discriminatory behavior. Malaysia's constitution (1963), for example, reserves certain public-service positions and business and trade permits for Malays and other indigenous peoples to encourage their participation in public and economic activities, while Pakistan's constitution (1973) has set aside seats in the lower house of its parliament for religious minorities and women.

At the international level, the International Covenant on Economic, Social and Cultural Rights (1966) recognizes the right of each person "to take part in cultural life"; the American Convention on Human Rights (1969) specifically provides for the right to participate in government, including the right to vote and hold public office; and the Convention on the Rights of the Child (1989) recommends that children's views be heard in official decision-making processes that would affect them.

Constitution of India (1949), part IV, Directive Principles of State Policy, article 43A: "Participation of workers in management of industries.—The State shall take steps, by suitable legislation or in any other way, to secure the participation of workers in the management of undertakings, establishments or other organizations engaged in any industry."

Declaration on the Rights of Disabled Persons (1975): "9. Disabled persons have the right to live with their families or with foster parents and to participate in all social, creative or recreational activities."

U.S. Supreme Court (1939): The Fourteenth Amendment (1868) to the U.S. Constitution protects the right of citizens to participate in political assemblies, including those organized for the purpose of distributing materials promoting trade unionism.

European Court of Human Rights (1993): The freedoms guaranteed by the European Convention for the Protection of Human Rights and Fundamental Freedoms (1950), article 11, which protects freedom of assembly, association, and participation in trade unions, equally protects the right of an individual not to participate in such activities.

Benello, C. George, and Dimitrios Roussopoulos, eds. *The Case for Participatory Democracy: Some Prospects for a Radical Society*. New York: Grossman, 1971.

Dalton, Russell J., ed. *Citizens, Protest, and Democracy*. Newbury Park, Calif.: Sage, 1993.

Assembly; Association; Collective Rights; Declaration on the Rights of Disabled Persons; Disabled Persons; Equality; Minorities; Plato; Political Rights; Social Rights; Suffrage; Women; Workers

Pax Christi International

A Roman Catholic movement based on Christ's gospel of peace, Pax Christi was founded in France after World War II to foster reconciliation between Germany and France. In 1952 it was given international status by Pope Pius XII and authorized for three purposes: prayer, study, and action. Since the end of the Cold War, Pax Christi International, a nongovernmental organization, has focused on implementing the objectives of the Charter of the United Nations (1945), emphasizing education, research, conferences, and grass-roots activities to achieve peace, justice, and human rights.

The movement, which adopted Pope John XXIII's encyclical Pacem in Terris as its charter in 1963, grew and spread throughout Europe during the 1960s. During the next decade, Pax Christi International began working in the United States and Australia and set up groups in Portugal, Puerto Rico, and the Philippines. Today it has sections in nearly twenty countries, including Great Britain, Denmark, France, Germany, Ireland, Italy, New Zealand, Slovakia, and Switzerland, as well as associated groups and affiliated organizations in a dozen others, including Bangladesh, Brazil, Guatamela, Haiti, Hungary, India, Pakistan, Poland, and Thailand.

Pax Christi's mission includes reducing violence, oppression, militarism, and terrorism. Of special concern are personal security, sustainable development, self-determination for small ethnic and cultural minorities, the economic gap between rich and poor and the northern and southern hemispheres, and the widening separation of humans and nature. According to its current mission statement, the organization intends to "develop a greater variety of practical strategies rooted in a vision of a world which revolves on principles of peace with justice."

Since 1991 Pax Christi International has sponsored an annual peace march, held each year in a different country, in which participants walk and pray together. The journey draws young people from all over the world and focuses on themes of peace and justice such as multiethnic and pluralistic societies, overcoming violence, and overcoming religious and ethnic divides. Other activities include regional consultations and a series of international meetings for representatives from all over the world.

The organization has official consultative status with the United Nations and the Council of Europe and is governed by an international council of delegates who are drawn from national sections and meet in different parts of the world every two years.

Pax Christi International, 21 rue du Vieux Marché aux Grains, B-1000 Brussels, Belgium. (32-2-502-55-50. 🖥 32-2-502-46-26. 🖥 office@pci.ngonet.be. 🖥 www.pci.ngonet.be.

Peace

Peace

Peace is perhaps the ultimate human right, a foundation on which all others rest. Without peace, individuals' rights to life, liberty, and the enjoyment of property, among others, are either restricted or jeopardized. Warfare, the opposite state of peace (from *pacem*, a form of the Latin word *pax*, meaning peace), also creates conditions for flagrant violations of basic human rights by members of the armed forces, as recent war crimes in Rwanda, Chechnya, and the former Yugoslavia attest.

In domestic law, peace refers to the right of individuals to enjoy security and tranquillity; as a result, a breach of the peace is a crime. In his eighteenth-century commentaries on English law, William Blackstone devotes an entire chapter to offenses against the public peace.

Declaring peace, like declaring war against other territories, is a prerogative of sovereignty exercised by national governments. "War, peace, and neutrality . . . ," Geoffrey Best states in *War and Law since 1945* (1994), "have . . . lost their earlier, clearer meanings. The eighteenth- and nineteenth-century constructors of modern international law shared the common understanding of their culture that war and peace were contrasted conditions of existence, that peace was morally the more desirable, and that civilization meant a preponderance of peace over war."

The idea of peace through military strength seems to be an oxymoron, and the notion of peace at any price has resulted in untold horrors. Appeasement of aggressors can lead to a loss of basic rights, as unequivocally proven by British Prime Minister Neville Chamberlain's attempt in 1938 to avoid war with Germany by appeasing Adolf Hitler.

Human rights became an issue in more recent peace negotiations concluding episodes of armed aggression in places such as Afghanistan, Cambodia, Central America, and southern Africa. In these cases human rights experts helped ensure that postwar protection of individual rights was not overlooked. Peace agreements initiated by the International Conference on the Former Yugoslavia, convened in 1993, contain some of the most far-reaching human rights provisions.

In 1949 the UN General Assembly, after strong debate over proposals by the Soviet Union on one side and the United Kingdom and United States on the other, adopted the Declaration on the Essentials of Peace, which declares in part: "[T]he Charter of the United Nations [1945], the most solemn pact of peace in history, lays down basic principles necessary for an enduring peace. . . ." The General Assembly followed this in 1965 with the Declaration on the Promotion among Youth of the Ideals of Peace, Mutual Respect and Understanding between Peoples and in 1984 with the Declaration on the Right of Peoples to Peace. In 1992, at the request of the UN Security Council, the UN secretary-general submitted *An Agenda for Peace,* a report to the member states on programs for peace. The report addressed preventive diplomacy and a new concept—preventive deployment, in which in some situations UN troops would be sent to deter hostilities rather than waiting to react until after armed conflict occurs. The report also urged nations to increase their reliance on the International Court of Justice to settle disputes.

Although peace seems to have taken its place in human history as merely a respite between wars, John Keegan, author of *A History of Warfare* (1993), suggests that the day may be coming when governments will realize that war is simply no longer a cost-effective option. Until then, however, humankind will have to determine how to prevent wars, end wars quickly, and mitigate the human toll engendered by warfare. What is needed are government institutions and economic conditions that maintain peace through strength by deterring aggression from without and breaches of the peace within each country.

Constitution of Portugal (1976), part III, Organization of Political Power, section II, President of the Republic, chapter II, Powers, article 138, Powers in International Relations: "The president of the republic shall be competent in international relations to: . . . c. [d]eclare war . . . and make peace. . . ."

Charter of the United Nations (1945), preamble: "We the peoples of the United Nations, determined to save succeeding generations from the scourge of war . . . and . . . to practice tolerance and live together in peace with one another as good neighbors. . . ."

Sapporo District Court, Japan (1973): "[W]e Japanese, realizing the unlimited disaster and untold sadness that war inevitably brings to all people of the world and deeply conscious of the high ideals of human nature, deeply desire and strive positively to realize permanent world peace. This determination lives and will continue to live in the hearts of the Japanese people, present and future; it defends the safety and peace of our country and makes both more secure. Eventually, it will create peace in all the world."

International Court of Justice (Advisory Opinion) (1962): "[U]nder the Charter [of the United Nations] it is the Security Council that determines which States are to participate in carrying out decisions involving the maintenance of international peace and security. . . ."

Carnegie Endowment for International Peace, 1779 Massachusetts Avenue, N.W., Washington, D.C. 20036-2103. (202-483-7600. 202-483-1840. info@ceip.org. ceip.org.

Human Rights Center, University of Minnesota, 229 19th Avenue South, Minneapolis, Minn. 55455. (612-625-5027. 612-625-2011. humanrts@gold.tc.umn.edu. www1.umn.edu/humanrts/hrcenter.

Stockholm International Peace Research Institute, Signalistgatan 9, s-169 70 Solna, Sweden. (46-8-655-97-33. 46-8-655-97-33. sipri@sipri.se. www.sipri.se.

Dorn, A. Walter. *World Order for a New Millennium: Political, Cultural, and Spiritual Approaches to Building Peace.* New York: St. Martin's, 1999.

Forsythe, David P. *Human Rights and Peace: International and National Dimensions.* Lincoln: University of Nebraska Press, 1993.

Kunder, James. *How Can Human Rights Be Better Integrated into Peace Processes?* Conference Report. Washington, D.C.: Fund for Peace, 1998.

Charter of the United Nations; Declaration on the Promotion among Youth of the Ideals of Peace, Mutual Respect and Understanding between Peoples; Declaration on the Right of Peoples to Peace; International Court of Justice; Sovereignty; War

Peace Brigades International

Inspired by the life and work of Mohandas Gandhi, Peace Brigades International was founded on September 4, 1981, as a nonprofit, nonsectarian, nongovernmental network of unpaid volunteers and a small paid staff to help deter violence in areas undergoing political repression and conflict. Using nonviolent action, the organization focuses on protective escorting, education for peace, and the dissemination of information about human rights and the nonviolent struggle for peace and social justice.

In keeping with its "practical philosophy," Peace Brigades International has pioneered the strategy of providing protective escort services on request, sometimes around the clock for several weeks, for local activists threatened with violence. Because death squads and other human rights violators do not want the outside world to witness their actions, the presence of a Peace Brigades International volunteer, armed only with a camera but backed by a well-developed emergency response network, helps deter violence. This strategy was developed in Guatemala beginning in 1983, when Peace Brigades International provided unarmed accompaniment for a mutual support group of relatives of victims of enforced disappearance. After two members of the support group were assassinated, escorting was conducted around the clock.

Since then the organization has provided protective escorts for clergy, union leaders, human rights workers, and returning exiles, including the Guatemalan activist Rigoberta Menchú. Linked to the local diplomatic community, the media, and global human rights networks, Peace Brigades International serves as an international alert network, thus further diminishing the possibility of violence. Other places in which it has worked include El Salvador, Sri Lanka, and Haiti.

Peace Brigades International is associated with country groups in Belgium, Canada, France, Germany, Great Britain, Italy, the Netherlands, New Zealand, Norway, Southeast Asia, Spain, Sweden, Switzerland, and the United States, which support projects such as the emergency response network. They also recruit and train volunteers, raise funds, provide publicity, and safeguard volunteers and the people they accompany. The highest decision-making body is a general assembly, made up of representatives from the core groups and projects; it meets every three years. An international council implements policies set by the assembly.

Peace Brigades International, 5 Caledonian Road, London N1 9DX, England. (44-207-713-0392. 🖨 44-207-837-2290. 🖳 pbiio@gn.apc.org. 🖳 www.igc.org/pbi.

Defenders of Human Rights; Disappearance; Gandhi, Mohandas K.; Menchú, Rigoberta; Peace

Peoples' Rights

Groups of human beings who are related culturally and ethnically have long referred to themselves as "a people"—a community, tribe, race, or nation distinct from other humans. The Hebrews considered themselves a people chosen by God, and in the twentieth century Nazi Germany was declared by Adolf Hitler to be "one people *(volk)*, one empire *(Reich)*, [with] one leader *(führer)*."

In the post–World War II era, the concept of peoples' rights has been linked with the independence and self-determination movements of colonial territories, particularly those in Africa. As used in the African Charter of Human and Peoples' Rights (1981), the term refers to collective rights of African peoples derived from precolonial tribal groups. Today the term is somewhat less distinct

because of the conflict between a nation's sovereign integrity and the aspirations of minorities in some countries for autonomy or independence, which runs counter to the principle of national sovereignty.

The term *peoples' rights* currently refers to the rights asserted by a group that views itself as united by common bonds such as language, culture, religion, or ethnicity and that may also aspire to various degrees of political self-governance. These rights generally include the right to economic, social, and cultural development; the right to control and exploit the resources of the territory belonging to the people; and freedom from external domination by other nations or economic powers. Recognition of peoples' rights, however, may depend on political factors. In 1967 the Ibo people of Nigeria were forcibly denied the right of self-governance as the state of Biafra. At the time the Organization of African Unity did not support the Ibo peoples' efforts, although fourteen years later, in 1981, it sponsored the African Charter on Human and Peoples' Rights, which specifically refers to a peoples' right to self-determination.

As the collective rights of a people or a nation, peoples' rights have an international character and therefore are not generally addressed in national constitutions. Some international documents that set forth peoples' rights include the Cairo Declaration on Human Rights in Islam (1990), which provides that "all States and peoples have the right to preserve their independent identity and exercise control over their wealth and resources," and both the International Covenant on Civil and Political Rights (1966) and the International Covenant on Economic, Social and Cultural Rights (1966).

Constitution of Nicaragua (1987, as amended in 1995), title I, Fundamental Principles, chapter I, article 5: "Liberty, justice, and respect for the dignity of the human person, political, social and ethnic pluralism, the recognition of different forms of property, unhindered international cooperation and respect for the free self-determination of peoples are principles of the Nicaraguan nation."

African Charter on Human and Peoples' Rights (1981), article 19: "All peoples shall be equal; they shall enjoy the same respect and shall have the same rights. Nothing shall justify the domination of a people by another."

Ontario Court of Appeals, Canada (1997): A woman who had lost her status as a member of a band of aboriginal people but had been reinstated after a distribution of land claim settlement funds to the members of the tribe claimed a share of the funds. The court found that she and her children, who also were not members of the tribe at the time the financial distribution was made, were entitled to an equal share.

African Commission on Human and Peoples' Rights (1992): The Katangese Peoples' Congress asked the commission to recognize the right of the Katangese people to sovereign independence so that they could secede from Zaire. The commission denied the request as being not compatible with the African Charter on Human and Peoples' Rights (1981) but noted that such a request might be considered if there was "concrete evidence of violations of human rights" or evidence that the people concerned were being denied the right to participate in the country's government as guaranteed by the charter.

Ankumah, Evelyn A. *The African Commission on Human and Peoples' Rights: Practices and Procedures.* The Hague: Martinus Nijhoff, Kluwer Law International, 1996.

African Charter on Human and Peoples' Rights; African Commission on Human and Peoples' Rights; Collective Rights; Cultural Rights; Development; Equality; Minorities; Self-Determination

Pérez Esquivel, Adolfo

A devout Roman Catholic, Adolfo Pérez Esquivel (b. 1931) has made a significant contribution to human rights on behalf of the *desaparecidos* (the disappeared ones) in Argentina. As a result he was tortured and held without trial for more than a year. In 1980 he won the Nobel Peace Prize.

Pérez Esquivel was born in Argentina on November 26, 1931. The son of a poor Spanish immigrant, he nevertheless attended private schools and became a voracious reader. After studying at the National School of Fine Arts of Buenos Aires and La Plata, he began his career as a sculptor and professor of art.

Influenced by Mohandas Gandhi and St. Augustine, Pérez Esquivel began attending conferences on nonviolent ways to improve living conditions in Latin America. In 1971 he joined a Gandhian group in Argentina and the following year participated in a hunger strike to protest terrorist and police violence there. In 1974 he started the magazine *Paz y Justicia (Peace and Justice)* and was made coordinator of the human rights organization Servicio de Paz y Justicia en Latin America, founded in 1968.

In 1976 the Argentinian military seized control of the government, beginning a reign of terror. Pérez Esquivel's leadership of attempts to enforce the Universal Declaration of Human Rights (1948) and his denouncement of government atrocities brought his arrest and detainment for fifteen months, during which time he was tortured. After his release he insisted that Argentina's approximately twenty thousand disappeared persons be accounted for.

For his efforts on behalf of human rights, Pérez Esquivel was awarded the Pax Christi by Pope John XXIII and was named a "prisoner of conscience" by Amnesty International, which works for the release of political prisoners around the world. In 1980, in awarding him the Nobel Peace Prize, the prize committee said: "The views he represents carry a vital message to many other countries, not the least in Latin America." In accepting the prize, Pérez Esquivel criticized "the old, well-known, and dilapidated structure of injustice" and added that "[t]he rules of this play, which have been laid down by the big powers and have been inflicted upon the rest of the world, also permit the biggest crime of our time, the arms race."

Pérez Esquivel, Adolfo. *Christ in a Poncho: Testimonials of the Nonviolent Struggles in Latin America.* Maryknoll, N.Y.: Orbis, 1983.

Augustine, St.; Amnesty International; Disappearance; Gandhi, Mohandas K.; Universal Declaration of Human Rights

Personality

The right to one's unique personality, the full development of one's potential, and the rewards of one's talents is central to the exercise of individual human rights. At a time when science is on the verge of being able to clone human beings, these personal attributes are being reexamined. The qualities that make each of us human and the commonality of being human determine everyone's entitlement to human rights, but what makes each of us different from one another deserves to be protected in the same way that the right to personal security is intended to protect our physical well-being. Freedom to fully develop one's intellectual capacity and unique personality, for example, is as much a human right as is physical freedom.

Personality derives from the Latin *persona* (a character in a play or simply a person) and today signifies the quality of being one of many individuals in human society as well as the aggregate of the characteristics that make each person unique. The French psychologist and physician Pierre Janet, who died in 1947, defined personality as "the notion of my body, of my capacities, of my name, my social position, of the part I play in the world; it is an ensemble of moral, political, [and] religious thought."

The first principle of the right of personality is that all individuals' separate and distinct personhood beyond their physical being is one they should be allowed to develop without fear or coercion. Although arbitrary detention, torture, and slavery are primarily physical infringements, they also violate the right of personality.

One's personality thus depends on other basic rights: freedom of thought, conscience, expression, and religion;

recognition as a person before the law; and privacy. Germany's constitution (1949), article 2, Rights of Liberty, provides in part: "(1) Everyone shall have the right to the free development of his personality insofar as he does not violate the rights of others or offend against the constitutional order or morality. . . . (2) Everyone shall have the right to life and to physical integrity."

A second principle of the right of personality is that those with unique and valuable talents should be entitled to just rewards. The appropriation of a person's talents or attributes for the profit of another without compensation or the invasion of privacy resulting from the destruction or degradation of a person's character violate that right. Similarly, when the state permits the unauthorized appropriation of a person's name or likeness, the action also infringes personality rights.

Constitution of Portugal (1976), Title II, Rights, Freedoms and Guarantees, chapter I, Personal Rights, Liberties, article 26, Other Personal Rights: "1. All are recognized as having the right to personal identity, personality development, civil capacity, citizenship, good name and reputation, image, the right to speak out and the right to the protection of the privacy of their personal family life and to legal protection against any form of discrimination."

American Declaration of the Rights and Duties of Man (1992): "The American States have on repeated occasions recognized that the essential rights of man are not derived from the fact that he is a national of a certain state, but are based upon attributes of human personality. . . ."

Constitutional Court of Hungary (1992): A local government law that "provides an opportunity for [a local government body] . . . to publicize personal data in a manner which violates the rights of personality" is unconstitutional.

European Court of Human Rights (1981): The European Convention for the Protection of Human Rights and Fundamental Freedoms (1950), article 8, protects "an essentially private manifestation of the human personality," in this case the right to engage in "private homosexual acts between males over the age of 21 capable of valid consent."

Pinckaers, Julius C. S. *From Privacy toward a New Intellectual Property Right in Persona: The Right of Publicity (United States) and Portrait Law (Netherlands) Balanced with Freedoms of Speech and Free Trade Principles.* The Hague: Kluwer Law International, 1996.

Strömholm, Stig. *Right of Privacy and Rights of the Personality: A Comparative Survey.* Nordic Conference on Privacy, International Commission of Jurists. Stockholm: Norstedt, 1967.

Artists; Conscience; Expression; Names; Privacy; Religion; Thought; Universal Copyright Convention

Petition

The ability to petition the government for changes in policies or laws is a fundamental right in democratic societies, which, unlike totalitarian regimes, are accountable to their citizens and thus must be responsive to their concerns. "Petition, peaceable petition, is the course," noted an English writer in 1817. From the French *petition* via the Latin *peto* (meaning to seek), the English word *petition*—to formally ask or humbly request—has been in use since at least the fifteenth century.

Petitioning, or begging a monarch's leave to grant some redress or benefit, has been a time-honored privilege but not always a right. England's Petition of Grievances (1610) was an objection by Parliament to a regulation issued by James I. When he prohibited the making of starch from wheat, the House of Commons objected, noting that the king had not sought Parliament's consent in this matter. When Charles I tried to coerce loans from his subjects by jailing those who refused to pay, the eminent English jurist Edward Coke introduced a bill to bind the king and confirm the provision of Magna Carta (1215) that no freeman could be imprisoned except by lawful judgment of his peers and the concept of due process. This became the Petition of Right of 1627.

The British colonists who established the United States were heirs to the tradition of petitioning the government, having relied on the Petition of Right in demanding "no taxation without representation." As a result, the right to petition was incorporated into the First Amendment to the U.S. Constitution in 1791 along with freedom of religion, speech, assembly, and the press. The right to petition has not always been strictly enforced, however. In 1932 American war veterans and their families—between twelve and fifteen thousand persons—converged on Washington, D.C., set up tents below the U.S. Capitol, and petitioned Congress for a bonus payment for wartime service to alleviate their hardships during the Depression. The bill to meet their requests was defeated, and the petitioners were forcibly dispersed by army tanks and tear gas (Congress subsequently appropriated $100,000 to send the remaining two to five thousand protesters back home).

The process of petitioning the government for redress of grievances has evolved into a number of procedures in democratically governed countries. Citizens, activists, and professional lobbyists contact elected representatives and other government officials in person and through all available means of communication from telephone calls to e-mail to seek changes in laws and regulations affecting them or, in the case of lobbyists, their clients.

To anticipate public expression of grievances or to invite members of the public to comment on problems and proposed government actions, executive officials and legislators may hold meetings and public hearings, including town meetings conducted in person or through mass communication. In a sense, the emphasis in modern democratic politics on polling—asking a representative sample of the public about certain issues—is a form of preemptive action against later expression of grievances by the public. The press and other forms of media, including new electronic means of commuication, also facilitate the transmission of grievances in modern democracies.

Many national constitutions acknowledge the right of citizens to petition their government. Bulgaria's constitution (1991), for one, provides that "[c]itizens have the right to file complaints, suggestions, and petitions with the state authorities"; and Mexico's constitution (1917) directs that "[p]ublic officials and employees respect the exercise of the right of petition, provided it is made in writing and in a peaceful and respectful manner. . . ."

A number of international human rights document recognize the right of peaceful assembly without specifically referring to the purpose of petitioning the government for redress of grievances. These include the Universal Declaration of Human Rights (1948), European Convention for the Protection of Human Rights and Fundamental Freedoms (1950), and International Covenant on Civil and Political Rights (1966).

U.S. Constitution, First Amendment (1791): "Congress shall make no law respecting . . . the right of the people peaceably to assemble, and to petition the Government for a redress of grievances."

American Declaration of the Rights and Duties of Man (1948), chapter one, Rights, article XXIV: "Every person has the right to submit respectful petitions to any competent authority, for reasons of either general or private interest, and the right to obtain a prompt decision thereon."

Supreme Court of Canada (1933): "Apart, however, from such remedies as the subject has by way of petition of right and in some special cases by statute, the rule is a rigorous one that His Majesty cannot be impleaded [made a party to an action in court] in any of His Courts and this rule is just as rigorous . . . when the proceeding is against some property belonging to His Majesty."

Inter-American Commission on Human Rights (1993): A citizen of Trinidad, through a representative, complained that Canada was threatening to deport her or otherwise force her return to Trinidad in violation of her human rights. In its decision the commission set forth part of the complaint in the following language: "II. The Petitioners Request That: 1. In their petition [complaint] to the Commission, that it is hoped that the Commission will apply its powers relative to the American Declaration in a manner consonant with Canada's other human rights treaty obligations." Ultimately the commission concluded that, in light of the domestic remedies available, "the petition is inadmissible."

Jaksha, Edward A. *Of the People: Democracy and the Petition Process.* Omaha, Neb.: Simmons-Boardman, 1988.

Assembly; Communications; Complaints

Physicians for Human Rights

A nongovernmental organization of health professionals, scientists, and concerned citizens founded in 1986, Physicians for Human Rights uses medical and forensic knowledge and skills to prevent and investigate human rights violations and promote humanitarian practices. Basing itself on principles linked to the Universal Declaration of Human Rights (1948) and similar human rights documents, it works to stop torture, disappearances, and political killings; improve health and sanitary conditions in prisons and detention centers; and study the physical and psychological consequences of human rights violations during conflicts. Physicians for Human Rights shared the 1997 Nobel Peace Prize for its involvement in the steering committee of the International Campaign to Ban Landmines.

In 1996 the organization helped provide crucial evidence of genocide to the international criminal tribunals investigating widespread abuses in both Rwanda (1994) and the former territory of Yuogoslavia (1992–95), where it conducted forensic studies of mass graves in the Srebrenica region of Bosnia and Croatia. An antemortem database has also been created in Bosnia in hopes of identifying bodies exhumed from mass graves. The group has additionally revealed the scope of institutional torture in Turkey, documented the suffering of girls and women forced into prostitution in Cambodia, and conducted DNA testing in El Salvador to identify people abducted by the military.

Physicians for Human Rights conducts education and training programs for health professionals, judges, and human rights advocates on how to use medical and forensic methods to investigate human rights violations. Other activities of the organization, which publishes a report on its activities entitled *Physicians for Human Rights Record,* include defending the neutrality of medical personnel, asserting the right of civilians and military personnel to receive medical care during war, assisting health professionals who are victims of human rights violations, and preventing medical complicity in torture and other human rights abuses.

Physicians for Human Rights, 100 Boylston Street, Suite 702, Boston, Mass. 02116. (617-695-0041. 📠 617-695-0307. 🖳 phrusa@igc.apc.org. 🖳 www.phrusa.org.

Convention on Prohibitions or Restrictions on the Use of Certain Conventional Weapons Which May Be Deemed to Be Excessively Injurious or to Have Indiscriminate Effects; Disappearance; Doctors without Borders; Genocide; Principles of Medical Ethics Relevant to the Role of Health Personnel, Particularly Physicians, in the Protection of Prisoners and Detainees against Torture and Other Cruel, Inhuman or Degrading Treatment or Punishment; Prisoners; Torture

Plato

Although he lived and wrote almost 2,500 years ago, Plato (ca. 427–347 B.C.E.), one of the earliest of the significant Greek philosophers, has had a profound influence on proponents of justice, virtue, and constitutional government. His search for the just state and the just citizen began the process of devising methods of making the welfare of citizens the aim of government.

Plato was born into an aristocratic Athenian family about 427 B.C.E. His father died when he was young, and his mother then married a friend of Pericles, who was the leader of democratic Athens. Athens had survived several invasion attempts by the Persians, but its power was beginning to wane while that of Sparta, the neighboring non-democratic Greek city-state, was on the rise.

Influenced by the teachings of the great Athenian moralist and intellectual Socrates, who had been forced to commit suicide as punishment for crimes against Athens, Plato wrote a series of dialogues speaking through the voice of Socrates. In his most famous work, *The Republic*, Plato describes a utopian system of government ruled by philosopher-kings who have unfettered power over the state. The ascendance of undemocratic Sparta and the decline of democratic Athens undoubtedly influenced his abandonment of democracy as the preferred form of government.

In his final work, *The Laws*, however, Plato moderates his earlier position by returning to a mixture of oligarchy and democracy in his attempt to create a constitution for a fictitious colony called Magnesia. In it he sets up the colony's laws as the supreme but acknowledgedly imperfect instrument for both government organization and moral salvation. Anticipating the modern concept of the rule of law, Plato has his Athenian spokesman in *The Laws* comment: "Such people [the holders of high office] are usually referred to as 'rulers,' and if I have called them 'servants of the laws' it is because . . . [w]here the law is subject to some other authority and has none of its own, the collapse of the state, in my view, is not far off. . . ."

Plato, who died in 347 B.C.E. after a long career devoted to politics and philosophy, cannot be considered a great proponent of human rights as understood today. His inquiries into what makes a just society and just citizens, however, began a constructive dialogue that influenced later human rights theorists and continues today in the tangential fields of law and politics.

Buchanan, Scott. *The Portable Plato*. New York: Penguin, 1976.

Kraut, Richard. *The Cambridge Companion to Plato*. New York: Cambridge University Press, 1992.

Augustine, St.; Justice; Rule of Law

Pluralism

Pluralism—the existence or toleration of diverse ethnic, cultural, and other groups within a society—is a basic element of the liberal view of political life in the Western world. A relatively new term in English taken from the Latin *pluralis* (plural or more than one), pluralism encompasses the establishment and maintenance of constitutional institutions and procedures for distributing and sharing government power. The concept helps ensure human rights to the extent that a wide spectrum of political ideas and goals is fostered or at least tolerated. It is the opposite of ideological purity, a single-party system, or lockstep nationalism.

As indicated by the histories of people captured, enslaved, tolerated, or assimilated by major civilizations such as ancient Egypt, diversity within a territorial jurisdiction is not a recent phenomenon. Today few if any nations can claim to be totally homogenous. Because ethnic and cultural pluralism requires toleration of diverse views on religion, morality, and political organization, governments are challenged to ensure that rights within their borders are enforced equally, regardless of ethnic or cultural differences.

Pluralism within a nation can be dealt with in a number of ways. Lebanon, for example, has practiced "confessionalism," the parceling out of government positions on the basis of the relative size of each population confessing one of its major religions. Spain and other countries have made provisions in their constitutions for autonomous regions that have a measure of self-government. In the United States, assimilation of ethnic groups is the unwritten policy, except for Native Americans, who may live in lands especially set aside for them and thus avoid pressure to assimilate into the mainstream of American cultural, social, and political life.

Few national constitutions address pluralism directly, but in international human rights documents pluralism and diversity are generally underlying concepts on which specific provisions, such as equality, tolerance, and cultural rights, are based. "The Universal Declaration of Human Rights enshrines and illuminates global pluralism and diversity," reaffirmed UN Secretary-General Kofi Annan in his December 1997 address at the University of Tehran celebrating the fiftieth anniversary of the Universal Declaration of Human Rights (1948).

Constitution of Brazil (1988), preamble: A goal of this constitution is "to institute a Democratic State destined to assure the exercise of social and individual rights, liberty, security, well-being, development, equality and justice as supreme values of a fraternal, pluralistic and unbiased society. . . ."

Charter of Paris for a New Europe (1990), Human Rights, Democracy and Rule of Law: "Democracy, with its representative and pluralistic character, entails accountability to the electorate, the obligation of public authorities to comply with the law and justice administered impartially. No one will be above the law."

U.S. Supreme Court (1990): "Broadcasting may be regulated in light of rights of [the] viewing and listening audience, and [the] widest possible dissemination of information from diverse and antagonistic sources is essential to [the] welfare of the public."

European Court of Human Rights (1976): "The Court's supervisory functions oblige it to pay the utmost attention to the principles characterizing a 'democratic society.' . . . Such are the demands of . . . pluralism, tolerance and broadmindedness [that without them] there is no 'democratic society.'"

Kane, Robert. *Through the Moral Maze: Searching for Absolute Values in a Pluralistic World.* Armonk, N.Y.: North Castle Books, 1996.

Sarat, Austin, and Thomas R. Kearns, eds. *Cultural Pluralism, Identity Politics, and the Law.* Ann Arbor: University of Michigan Press, 1999.

Democracy; Equality; Minorities; Tolerance

Political Parties

See Democracy; Political Rights

Political Rights

Political rights allow citizens to participate effectively in governing a country or one of its political subdivisions and thus provide individual and collective ability to affect government policy. The notion of political freedom or political rights (from the Latin *politicus,* meaning pertaining to a body of citizens) was first developed by the ancient Greeks. Plato's *Republic* and his lesser-known work, *The Laws,* both attempt to create constitutions balancing the rights of the state with those of citizens. Aristotle's *Politics,* a seminal work of political science, analyzed the nature of governments, including the democracy of Athens. Citizenship in the Roman Republic also bestowed political rights, although patricians (the upper class) generally had a greater share than plebeians (the lower class).

The first stage of political rights is the right to vote and the right to be elected to political office. Other important political rights in a democracy include the rights to petition the government for redress of grievances, to form political parties, and to have access to the courts to enforce such rights. Political parties and interest groups allow citizens to extend, promote, and enforce human rights policies. If these rights are based on the equality of all people, then the equal right of every citizen to participate in the political process and thus in governing helps ensure that everyone's human rights are protected.

National constitutions, including those of Germany (1949) and Sweden (1975), generally specify political rights such as the rights to vote and to hold political office. In countries without written constitutions, including the United Kingdom and New Zealand, many political rights are a matter of convention or tradition, rather than express guarantees. One such tradition in the United Kingdom is the right of political parties, based on an election in which they acquire a majority of parliamentary seats, to form a government and choose a prime minister and cabinet. In the United States, the role of political parties in organizing elections and subsequently the executive and legislative branches of government is also a matter of tradition and not explicitly provided for in the U.S. Constitution (1789).

A number of international human rights documents guarantee political rights. The Universal Declaration of Human Rights (1948), article 21, provides: "1. Everyone has the right to take part in the government of his country, directly or through freely chosen representatives. . . . 3. The will of the people . . . shall be expressed in periodic and genuine elections which shall be by universal and equal suffrage and shall be held by secret vote. . . ." Protocol no. 1 (1952) to the European Convention for the Protection of Human Rights and Fundamental Freedoms (1950) similarly encourages in article 3 "free elections at reasonable intervals by secret ballot, under conditions which will ensure the free expression of opinion of the people in the choice of the legislature." Among other instruments addressing the subject are the Inter-American Convention on the Granting of Political Rights to Women (1949), Convention on the Political Rights of Women (1954), and International Covenant on Civil and Political Rights (1966).

The ideal of popular sovereignty, in which everyone's vote and opportunity to hold political office is theoretically equal, is often diluted by the concentration of economic, religious, and social power in a country. Even in a democracy it is far easier for a wealthy and socially prominent person to attain political office than the average citizen. In constitutional monarchies, furthermore, the monarch and members of the royal family receive large subsidies at taxpayers' expense to carry out the functions of the titular head of state—a station to which they are born rather than elected—and they have other rights and privileges not available to the rest of the citizenry.

Constitution of Argentina (1994), first part, second chapter, New Rights and Guarantees, article 37: "This Constitution guarantees full enjoyment of political rights, in accordance with the principle of popular sovereignty and with laws dictated pursuant thereto."

African Charter on Human and Peoples' Rights (1981), part I, Rights and Duties, chapter 1, Human and Peoples' Rights, article 13: "Every citizen shall have the right to participate freely in the government of his country, either directly or through freely chosen representatives in accordance with the provisions of the law."

U.S. Supreme Court (1962): In deciding whether a matter brought to the Court for judicial review is justiciable—whether it can be decided by the Court under the U.S. Constitution (1789) or must be left to the other branches of government to handle—the mere fact that the suit seeks protection of a political right does not mean that it presents a "political question," which the Court has held would not be justiciable.

Inter-American Commission on Human Rights (1994): "1. [T]he candidacies of president and vice president [of Guatemala] constitute an indissoluble unit, commonly known as the presidential slate. 2. [A]ccordingly, the denial based on [a] lawsuit of one member of the presidential slate can only be interpreted as a violation [under the American Convention on Human Rights (1969)] of the political rights of the other member where the law or the interpretation of it by the electoral organs prohibits or impedes the replacement of the excluded candidate."

Civil and Political Rights in the United States: Initial Report of the United States of America to the U.N. Human Rights Committee under the International Covenant on Civil and Political Rights. Washington, D.C.: U.S. Department of State, 1994.

Martin, Rex. *A System of Rights.* New York: Oxford University Press, 1993.

Aristotle; Convention on the Political Rights of Women; European Convention for the Protection of Human Rights and Fundamental Freedoms; Inter-American Convention on the Granting of Political Rights to Women; International Covenant on Civil and Political Rights; Petition; Plato; Universal Declaration of Human Rights; Voting

Poverty

See Economic Rights; Standard of Living; Welfare

The Press

"The time, it is to be hoped, is gone by, when any defense would be necessary of the 'liberty of the press' as one of the securities against corrupt or tyrannical government," wrote the British philosopher John Stuart Mill in *On Liberty* (1859). The Latin *presso* (to press) and *pressus* (pressure) gave rise to the English word *press,* which since at least the sixteenth century has signified a machine for printing. The term has been used in reference to newspapers, journals, and periodical literature generally since the beginning of the nineteenth century.

Although books were printed in China as early as 600 C.E., the invention of the printing press is credited to Johannes Gutenberg in the fifteenth century. So called because it made impressions from an inked plate or die by pressing it against a sheet of paper, the printing press changed the nature of communication as significantly, if not as quickly, as the telegraph, telephone, and Internet-linked computers have done more recently. The ability to reproduce quickly, cheaply, and accurately many copies of any document meant that knowledge could be disseminated to many people almost simultaneously.

The democratic revolutions in the United States and France at the end of the eighteenth century would not have been possible without the printing press. The idea that the press—now more likely to be called the media—is indispensable to democratic government was enshrined in the First Amendment to the U.S. Constitution in 1791 and is a fundamental right in other democratic governments. Proof of the press's importance to democracy is the fact that among the first actions any dictator takes after assuming control of a country is to curtail freedom of the press.

All truly democratic countries contain guarantees of freedom of the press in their constitutions. One of Sweden's four constitutional documents is the Freedom of the Press Act, first promulgated in 1766. The major international human rights instruments mandate freedom of the press or freedom to disseminate information by various media. "Everyone has the right . . . to seek, receive and impart information and ideas through any media," states the Universal Declaration of Human Rights (1948), article 19. The European Convention for the Protection of Human Rights and Freedoms (1950) includes a similar guarantee, as does the American Convention on Human Rights (1969), which also specifies that "[t]he right of expression may not be restricted by indirect methods or means, such as the abuse of government or private controls over newsprint. . . ." The Declaration on Fundamental Principles Concerning the Contribution of the Mass Media to Strengthening Peace and International Understanding, to the Promotion of Human Rights and to Countering Racialism, Apartheid and Incitement to War (1978) directly addresses freedom of the press, and a 1992 Declaration of Alma Ata promotes an independent and free press in Asia.

A free press is not always perfect, and often some limitations are placed on freedom of the press to ensure that its power to inform does not become the power to destroy. For example, most nations have libel laws that require printed information to meet some standards of truthfulness. The important element of such laws, however, is that they focus on punishment after publication and do not permit government restraint or censorship before publication. Today new media such as television and online journalism are keeping the public informed around the world.

Constitution of Portugal (1976), part I, Fundamental Rights and Duties, section II, Rights, Freedoms, and Safeguards, chapter I, Personal Rights, Freedoms, and Safeguards, article 38, Freedom of the Press and Mass Media: "1. Freedom of the press shall be safeguarded. 2. Freedom of the press shall involve: a. The freedom of expression and creativeness for journalists and literary collaborators as well as a role for the former in giving editorial direction to the concerned mass media, save where the latter belong to the state or have a doctrinal or denominational character. . . ."

African Charter on Human and Peoples' Rights (1981), part I, Rights and Duties, chapter I, Human and Peoples' Rights, article 9: "1. Every individual shall have the right to receive information. 2. Every individual shall have the right to express and disseminate his opinions within the law."

Supreme Court of Japan (1969): "In order to guarantee a fair criminal trial, . . . occasions may arise in which the freedom [of the press] to gather information would have to come under some restriction. . . . However, even in such instances, it is necessary to weigh, on the one hand, the nature of the offense charged at the trial, the manner in which it was committed and its seriousness, the value of the materials accumulated by the press as evidence at the trial and its necessity or indispensability in conducting a fair criminal

trial, and on the other hand, the degree that the production of these materials to the court as evidence by court order would obstruct the freedom to gather information by the press and the extent of the impact it would have upon the freedom of the press and other considerations."

European Commission on Human Rights (1987): "[F]reedom of expression constitutes one of the essential foundations of a democratic society and one of the basic conditions for its progress and for each individual's self-fulfillment. Of particular importance, in this context, is the freedom of the press to impart information and ideas and the right of the public to receive them. . . ."

Committee to Protect Journalists, 330 Seventh Avenue, 12th Floor, New York, N.Y. 10001. (212-465-1004. 212-465-9568. info@cpj.org. www.cpj.org.

International PEN, 9–10 Charterhouse Buildings, Goswell Road, London EC1M 7AT, England. (44-171-253-4308. 44-171-253-5711. intpen@gn.apc.org.

PEN American Center, 568 Broadway, New York, N.Y. 10012-3225. (212-334-1660. 212-334-2181. pen@pen.org. www.pen.org.

PEN Canada, 24 Ryerson Avenue, Suite 401, Toronto, Ontario, M5T 2P3, Canada. (416-703-8448. 416-703-3870. pencan@web.net. www.pencanada.ca.

Reporters Committee for Freedom of the Press, 1815 North Fort Meyer Drive, Suite 900, Arlington, Va. 22209. (703-807-2100; 800-336-4243 (hotline). 703-807-2109. rcfp@rcfp.org. www.rcfp.org.

Reporters sans Frontières, International Secretariat, 5 rue Geoffroy-Marie, 75009 Paris, France. (33-1-44-83-84-84. 33-1-45-23-11-51. rsf@rsf.fr. www.rsf.fr.

World Association of Newspapers, 25 rue d'Astorg, F-75008 Paris, France. (33-1-47-42-85-00. 33-1-47-42-49-48. fiej.nemo@nemo.geis.com. fiej.org.

World Press Freedom Committee, 11690 Sunrise Valley Drive, Reston, Va. 20191. (703-715-9811. 703-620-6790. free-press@wpfc.org. www.wpfc.org.

Inter-American Court of Human Rights. *Licensing of Journalists Violates Human Rights.* Washington, D.C.: World Press Freedom Committee's Rex Rand Fund, 1986.

Ottaway, James H., Jr., et al. *Everyone Has the Right: The Enduring Importance for a Free Press of Article 19, Universal Declaration of Human Rights.* Reston, Va.: World Press Freedom Committee, 1998.

☞

Principles of Medical Ethics Relevant to the Role of Health Personnel ... in the Protection ... against Torture

Government-implemented torture was proscribed as early as 1791 in the U.S. Bill of Rights, which prohibits "cruel and unusual punishments." But in the mid-twentieth century a number of occurrences—torture carried out by the Nazi regime in Germany before and during World War II and by South American countries such as Argentina and Chile in the 1970s and 1980s—together with evidence that medical personnel, including doctors, were participating in such torture, heightened the need for guidelines regarding medical ethics and the treatment of imprisoned persons.

In 1955 the First United Nations Congress on the Prevention of Crime and the Treatment of Offenders adopted the Standard Minimum Rules for the Treatment of Prisoners. Two decades later, the UN General Assembly in 1975 adopted the Declaration on the Protection of All Persons from Being Subjected to Torture and Other Cruel, Inhuman or Degrading Treatment or Punishment. The next year the General Assembly asked the World Heath Organization (WHO) to prepare a draft "code of medical ethics relevant to the protection of persons subjected to any form of detention or imprisonment against torture and other cruel, inhuman, or degrading treatment or punishment." A set of general principles on the subject, prepared by the Council for International Organizations of Medical Sciences, was endorsed by WHO's executive board in 1979.

Finally, in 1982, the General Assembly adopted a version entitled Principles of Medical Ethics Relevant to the Role of Health Personnel, Particularly Physicians, in the Protection of Prisoners and Detainees against Torture and Other Cruel, Inhuman or Degrading Treatment or Punishment. The complete text of the six principles is as follows:

"Principle 1. Health personnel, particularly physicians, charged with the medical care of prisoners and detainees have a duty to provide them with protection of their physical and mental health and treatment of disease of the same quality and standard as is afforded to those who are not imprisoned or detained.

"Principle 2. It is a gross contravention of medical ethics, as well as an offense under applicable international instruments, for health personnel, particularly physicians, to engage, actively or passively, in acts which constitute participation in, complicity in, incitement to or attempts to commit torture or other cruel, inhuman or degrading treatment or punishment.

"Principle 3. It is a contravention of medical ethics for health personnel, particularly physicians, to be involved in any professional relationship with prisoners or detainees the purpose of which is not solely to evaluate, protect or improve their physical and mental health.

"Principle 4. It is a contravention of medical ethics for health personnel, particularly physicians: (a) To apply their knowledge and skills in order to assist in the interrogation of prisoners and detainees in a manner that may adversely affect the physical or mental health or condition of such prisoners or detainees and which is not in accordance with the relevant international instruments; (b) To certify, or to participate in the certification of, the fitness of prisoners or detainees for any form of treatment or punishment that may adversely affect their physical or mental health and which is not in accordance with the relevant international instruments, or to participate in any way in the infliction of any such treatment or punishment which is not in accordance with the relevant international instruments.

"Principle 5. It is a contravention of medical ethics for health personnel, particularly physicians, to participate in any procedure for restraining a prisoner or detainee unless such a procedure is determined in accordance with purely medical criteria as being necessary for the protection of the physical or mental health or the safety of the prisoner or detainee himself, of his fellow prisoners or detainees, or of his guardians, and presents no hazard to his physical or mental health.

"Principle 6. There may be no derogation from the foregoing principles on any grounds whatsoever, including public emergency."

United Nations High Commissioner for Human Rights, 8–14 avenue de la Paix, 1211 Geneva 10, Switzerland. ☎ 41-22-917-9000. 🖷 41-22-917-9016. 🖳 webadmin.hchr@unog.ch. 🖳 www.unhchr.ch.

☞

Principles on the Effective Prevention and Investigation of Extra-Legal, Arbitrary and Summary Executions

In the wake of an upsurge in political executions by military and dictatorial regimes, the Sixth United Nations Congress on the Prevention of Crime and Treatment of Offenders in 1980 condemned "the practice of killing and executing political opponents or suspected offenders carried out by armed forces, law enforcement or governmental agencies or by paramilitary or political groups" under the overt or tacit authority of government officials.

The Economic and Social Council (ECOSOC) subsequently appointed a special rapporteur (expert) in 1982 to investigate and report on allegations of summary executions. An ECOSOC resolution followed on May 24, 1989, recommending that governments follow its Principles on the Effective Prevention and Investigation of Extra-Legal, Arbitrary and Summary Executions.

"Governments shall prohibit by law all extra-legal, arbitrary and summary executions," states Prevention, paragraph 1, "and shall ensure that any such executions are recognized as offenses under their criminal laws, and are punishable by appropriate penalties which take into account the seriousness of such offenses. Exceptional circumstances including a state of war or threat of war, internal political instability or any other public emergency may not be invoked as a justification of such executions. Such executions shall not be carried out under any circumstances including, but not limited to, situations of internal armed conflict, excessive or illegal use of force by a public official or other person acting in an official capacity or by a person acting at the instigation, or with the consent or acquiescence of such person, and situations in which deaths occur in custody."

Paragraph 2 directs that "[g]overnments shall ensure strict control, including a clear chain of command over all officials responsible for apprehension, arrest, detention, custody and imprisonment, as well as those officials authorized by law to use force and firearms." Under paragraph 3, governments are urged to bar "orders from superior officers or public authorities authorizing or inciting other persons to carry out any such extra-legal, arbitrary or summary executions. All persons have the right and the duty to defy such orders. Training of law enforcement officials shall emphasize the above provisions."

Paragraphs 4, 5, and 6, respectively, require protection for threatened individuals and groups; prohibit involuntary return or extradition of persons "to a country where there are substantial grounds for believing that he or she may become a victim"; and mandate that "persons deprived of their liberty [be] held in officially recognized places of custody, and that accurate information on their custody and whereabouts, including transfers, [be] made promptly available to their relatives and lawyer or other persons of confidence." Paragraph 7 emphasizes the need for "[q]ualified inspectors, including medical personnel, or an equivalent independent authority [to] conduct inspections in places of custody," while paragraph 8 calls for government "measures such as diplomatic intercession, improved access of complainants to intergovernmental and judicial bodies, and public denunciation."

Paragraph 9 requires "a thorough, prompt and impartial investigation of all suspected cases of extra-legal, arbitrary and summary executions, including cases where complaints by relatives or other reliable reports suggest unnatural death in the above circumstances." Pursuant to paragraph 15, "Complainants, witnesses, those conducting the investigation and their families shall be protected from violence, threats of violence or any other form of intimidation."

Paragraph 16 mandates that "[f]amilies of the deceased and their legal representatives shall be informed of, and have access to, any hearing as well as to all information relevant to the investigation, and shall be entitled to present other evidence." Under paragraph 17, a "written report shall be made within a reasonable period of time on the methods and findings of such investigations," and it is to "be made public immediately. . . ."

In the last section, Legal Proceedings, paragraphs 18, 19, and 20, respectively, require governments to bring to justice those who participate in summary executions; hold persons in authority responsible for acts committed; and recommend fair, prompt, and adequate compensation to the families and dependents of victims.

United Nations High Commissioner for Human Rights, 8–14 avenue de la Paix, 1211 Geneva 10, Switzerland. (41-22-917-9000. 41-22-917-9016. webadmin.hchr@unog.ch. www.unhchr.ch.

Accused; Capital Punishment; Due Process of Law; Fair Trial; *Refoulement;* Summary Executions; Victims

Prisoners

In the opinion of many, people who have been imprisoned for breaking the law do not deserve any rights. Such rights, they reason, have been forfeited by the offender's own misdeeds. However, a more enlightened view holds that no human being forfeits his or her right to humane treatment, even if imprisoned for the most heinous of crimes.

In his *Commentaries on the Laws of England* (1769), William Blackstone alludes to a fundamental right of prisoners: "The justice before whom such prisoner is brought, is bound immediately to examine the circumstances of the crime alleged."

The concept of a special place to detain and punish those who commit crimes is ancient in origin. In the fifth century B.C.E., the Greek city of Athens had a *desmōtērion*, a prison in which state debtors and people awaiting trial were held. In England imprisonment was just one of many types of punishment that might be handed down by the court, from fines and forfeiture of property to death. A major change in the way prisons and prisoners' rights are viewed occurred in Italy in 1764, with the publication of Cesare Beccaria's *Treatise on Crimes and Punishment*. Beccaria argued for proportionality in punishment of crimes, and his work led to major reforms in criminal law and punishment throughout Western Europe.

The treatment of prisoners (from the Latin *prehendo*, meaning to seize or detain, and the Old French *preson*, meaning prison) has varied depending on the society in which the incarceration takes place and the social class of the prisoner. Prisoners from the lower classes have generally received less humane treatment. Even today in the United States, white-collar criminals are often allowed to serve their terms in minimum-security prisons, while other convicts may be incarcerated in maximum-security prisons where living conditions are harsh and they may be subjected to brutality at the hands of other prisoners.

In addition, the treatment of prisoners is to a large extent a function of the nature of a country's government. Democracies tend to extend greater rights to prisoners and hold officials accountable for inhumane or inappropriate treatment. Details of prisoners' rights are generally spelled out in national laws and regulations, but some national constitutions include general provisions on prisoners. The U.S. Constitution (1789) forbids "cruel and unusual punishments"; Italy's (1948) provides that "[p]unishments cannot consist of treatments against the sense of humanity and must aim at reeducating the convict"; and Germany's (1949) states: "Detained persons may not be subjected to mental or physical ill-treatment."

At the international level, basic rights for prisoners include, according to the Body of Principles for the Protection of All Persons under Any Form of Detention or Imprisonment (1988), treatment "in a humane manner" and "strictly in accordance with the provisions of law by competent officials. . . ." Measures affecting prisoners and detainees also shall be . . . subject to the effective control of . . . a judicial or other authority." Discrimination and torture are prohibited, and acts "contrary to the rights and duties contained in the Principles" are to be prohibited by each country, which should also "make any such act subject to appropriate sanctions and conduct impartial investigations upon complaints." The treatment of detainees not convicted of a crime should be appropriate to that status. Other rights of prisoners, similar to those of persons accused of crimes, relate to medical treatment, communication, and visitation rights and the right to complain about treatment without recriminations.

Of additional concern are such issues as the treatment of juveniles, women, the disabled, and the elderly; forced prison labor; and the purpose of a prison sentence—that is, rehabilitation or temporary removal from society. The extent to which prisoners are entitled to such basic individual rights as privacy of communication, free speech, and freedom of religion are also debated. Human rights relating to prisoners of war are dealt with in the Geneva Convention Relative to the Treatment of Prisoners of War (1949).

On August 30, 1955, the First United Nations Congress on the Prevention of Crime and the Treatment of Offenders adopted the Standard Minimum Rules for the Treatment of Prisoners, which was amended in 1977. Rather than a model penal system, the guidelines "seek only, on the basis of the general consensus of contemporary thought and the essential elements of the most adequate systems of today, to set out what is generally accepted as being good principle and practice in the treatment of prisoners and the management of institutions."

The UN Interregional Crime and Justice Research Institute was established in 1968, and the Economic and Social Council (ECOSOC) established the Commission on Crime Prevention and Criminal Justice in 1992. Important international documents related to the treatment of prisoners include the Declaration on the Protection of All Persons from Being Subjected to Torture and Other Cruel, Inhuman, or Degrading Treatment or Punishment (1975); UN Model Agreement on the Transfer of Foreign Prisoners and recommendations on the treatment of foreign prisoners (1985), which called for strengthening international cooperation in crime prevention and criminal justice; and Body of Principles for the Protection of All Persons under Any Form of Detention or Imprisonment (1988).

Many crimes warrant incarceration, a fact that should not become an excuse for a society to tolerate inhumane and degrading prison conditions. Although it may be difficult to mobilize law-abiding citizens to demand reform of penal systems or elimination of the abuse of prisoners, the real test of morality is how well a society responds to the needs of its most incorrigible members. Proponents for the recognition of prisoners' human rights can point out the need for reform, but ultimately the officials in national and local governments must show moral leadership in responding to their pleas.

Constitution of Nicaragua (1987), title IV, Rights, Duties, and Guarantees of the Nicaraguan People, chapter I, article 39: "In Nicaragua the penitentiary system is humane, and it has as a fundamental objective the transformation of the interned in order to reintegrate him or her into society."

International Covenant on Civil and Political Rights (1966), part III, article 10: "1. All persons deprived of their liberty shall be treated with humanity and with respect for the inherent dignity of the human person."

U.S. Court of Appeals, Second Circuit (1981): In finding that the rights of a prisoner had been violated as a result of overcrowding in the prison where he was being held, the court stated that the Standard Minimum Rules for the Treatment of Prisoners (1955) may be a significant expression of the obligations of the international community and international law concerning human rights.

Human Rights Committee (1988): The beating of a prisoner in Jamaica by his wardens constituted a violation of the International Covenant on Civil and Political Rights (1966), articles 7 and 10, and, therefore, he is entitled to an effective remedy, including appropriate compensation.

Prisoners' Rights Committee, 4826 Papineau, Montreal, Quebec, Canada H2H 1V6. (514-522-5965. 514-597-0486. bernheim@aei.ca. www.aei.ca/~sbrous/liensanglais.

Human Rights and Pre-Trial Detention: A Handbook of International Standards Relating to Pre-Trial Detention. Professional Training Series, no. 3. Geneva: Center for Human Rights, 1994.

Rodley, Nigel S. *The Treatment of Prisoners under International Law.* 2d ed. Oxford, England: Clarendon Press, Oxford University Press, 1998.

Beccaria, Cesare; Basic Principles for the Treatment of Prisoners; Body of Principles for the Protection of All Persons under Any Form of Detention or Imprisonment; Declaration on the Protection of All Persons from Being Subjected to Torture and Other Cruel, Inhuman or Degrading Treatment or Punishment; Detention; Geneva Conventions; International Covenant on Civil and Political Rights; Proportionality; Punishment; Rehabilitation; Rules for the Protection of Juveniles Deprived of Their Liberty; Standard Minimum Rules for the Treatment of Prisoners; Torture

Privacy

Few people have had the luxury of the right to privacy—freedom from disturbance or intrusion—a word originally defined as being withdrawn from the society of others. In *The Laws*, written in the fourth century B.C.E., the Greek philosopher Plato warned against excluding a citizen's private life from legislation. By the nineteenth century, however, the British philosopher John Stuart Mill wrote: "Nobody desires that laws should interfere with the whole detail of private life."

Privacy was recognized implicitly in the Fourth Amend-

ment (1791) to the U.S. Constitution: "The right of the people to be secure in their persons, houses, papers, and effects, against unreasonable searches and seizures, shall not be violated. . . ." The U.S. Supreme Court has held that the Constitution, taken as a whole, supports a constitutionally guaranteed right to privacy. An influential law review article written in 1890 by Samuel D. Warren and Louis D. Brandeis, who served as an associate justice of the Court from 1916 to 1939, referred to "the right to be left alone," which was assumed to be a self-evident right. For Americans the right to privacy has become linked with issues relating to sex, including contraception and abortion. In addition to the more traditional areas of concern, the right to privacy also encompasses personal information lodged in government and corporate records; mail, telephones, and electronic communications; "stalking" behavior; and wiretapping.

A number of national constitutions—those of Ecuador (1979), Brazil (1988), and Bulgaria (1991), for example—contain provisions relating to privacy rights or the right to a private life. Similar provisions can be found in most international human rights documents, including the Universal Declaration of Human Rights (1948), European Convention for the Protection of Human Rights and Fundamental Freedoms (1950), International Covenant on Civil and Political Rights (1966), and American Convention on Human Rights (1969).

Constitution of South Africa (1994), chapter 3, Fundamental Rights, Privacy, article 13: "Every person shall have the right to his or her personal privacy, which shall include the right not to be subject to searches of his or her person, home, or property, the seizure of private possessions or the violation of private communication."

American Convention on Human Rights (1969), part I, State Obligations and Rights Protected, chapter II, Civil and Political Rights, article 11: "1. Everyone has the right to have his honor respected and his dignity recognized. 2. No one may be the object of arbitrary or abusive interference with his private life, his family, his home, or his correspondence, or of unlawful attacks on his honor or reputation. 3. Everyone has the right to the protection of the law against such interference or attacks."

Constitutional Court of South Africa (1996): A section of the Indecent or Obscene Photographic Matter Act (1967), which prohibits possession of indecent or obscene photographs, was found to be unconstitutional as an infringement of the right to privacy as guaranteed by South Africa's constitution (1994), article 13.

European Court of Human Rights (1992): "The Court does not consider it possible or necessary to attempt an exhaustive definition of the notion of 'private life.' However, it would be too restrictive to limit the notion to an 'inner circle' in which the individual may live his own personal life as he chooses and to exclude therefrom entirely the outside world not encompassed within that circle. Respect for private life must also comprise to a certain degree the right to establish relationships with other human beings."

Privacy International, 666 Pennsylvania Avenue, S.E., Suite 301, Washington, D.C. 20003. (202-544-9240. 202-547-5482. pi@privacy.org. www.privacyinternational.org.

Michael, James. *Privacy and Human Rights: An International and Comparative Study, with Special Reference to Developments in Information Technology*. Brookfield, Vt.: Dartmouth, 1994.

Schoeman, Ferdinand D. *Privacy and Social Freedom*. New York: Cambridge University Press, 1992.

Abortion; Communication; Information

Proclamation of Teheran

From April 22 to May 13, 1968, eighty-four representatives of various nations, nongovernmental human rights organizations, and United Nations offices came together in Teheran, Iran, to address a wide range of human rights issues. The most important outcome of the International Conference on Human Rights, convened as an outgrowth of a UN General Assembly resolution, was the Proclamation of Teheran, which was adopted on the last day.

A major focus of the proclamation is racism, including South Africa's apartheid policies then in force. In 1965 the General Assembly had adopted the International Convention on the Elimination of All Forms of Racial Discrimination, but overwhelming evidence remained that racist oppression was causing great suffering and violations of basic civil and political rights for much of South Africa's population. "Gross denials of human rights under the repugnant policy of *apartheid*," the proclamation declares, "[are] a matter of the gravest concern to the international community." The document terms such discrimination "a crime against humanity," one that disturbs international peace and security. More than twenty years passed before the Declaration on Apartheid and Its Destructive Consequences in South Africa (1989) was adopted and the practice of apartheid was finally eliminated.

The proclamation begins by noting that the participants had reviewed the progress made in the twenty years since the Universal Declaration of Human Rights (1948) was adopted, adding that "in an age when conflict and violence prevail in many parts of the world, the fact of human inter-

dependence and the need for human solidarity are more evident than ever before." It goes on to note that "peace is the universal aspiration of mankind and that peace and justice are indispensable to the full realization of human rights and fundamental freedoms."

"It is imperative," proclaims paragraph 1, "that the members of the international community fulfill their solemn obligations to promote and encourage respect for human rights and fundamental freedoms for all without distinctions of any kind such as race, color, sex, language, religion, political or other opinions." Paragraphs 2 and 3 reaffirm the importance of a number of human rights documents, including the Universal Declaration of Human Rights and the International Covenant on Civil and Political Rights (1966) and International Covenant on Economic, Social and Cultural Rights (1966). According to paragraph 4, "[M]uch remains to be done in regard to the implementation of [the] rights and freedoms" set forth in these and other international human rights instruments.

Paragraph 5 calls for every country to embody human rights in its law; paragraph 6 urges them to "reaffirm their determination effectively to enforce the principles enshrined" in the UN charter (1945) and other international documents; and paragraph 7 condemns apartheid. Paragraphs 8 through 11, respectively, are concerned with "the evils of racial discrimination"; "the problems of colonialism"; "[m]assive denials of human rights arising out of aggression or any armed conflict"; and "[g]ross denials of human rights arising from discrimination on grounds of race, religion, belief or expressions of opinion."

Paragraph 12 points to the "widening gap between the economically developed and developing countries," while paragraph 13 calls for "sound and effective national and international policies of economic and social development." According to paragraph 14, there were at the time seven hundred million illerates in the world. "International action aimed at eradicating illiteracy from the face of the earth and promoting education at all levels requires urgent attention," it adds.

Paragraph 15 condemns discrimination against women. The protection of the family and the right to family planning, participation by youth "in shaping the future of mankind," and review of scientific and technological developments for potential evil, respectively, are the subjects of paragraphs 16 through 18. "Disarmament," notes paragraph 19, "would release immense human and material resources now devoted to military purposes. These resources should be used for the promotion of human rights and fundamental freedoms. General and complete disarmament is one of the highest aspirations of all peoples."

The proclamation concludes by urging "all peoples and governments to dedicate themselves to the principles enshrined in the Universal Declaration of Human Rights and to redouble their efforts to provide for all human beings a life consonant with freedom and dignity and conducive to physical, mental, social and spiritual welfare."

United Nations High Commissioner for Human Rights, 8–14 avenue de la Paix, 1211 Geneva 10, Switzerland. (41-22-917-9000. 🖳 41-22-917-9016. 🖳 webadmin.hchr@unog.ch. 🖳 www.unhchr.ch.

☞

Apartheid; Development; International Convention on the Elimination of All Forms of Racial Discrimination; Race Discrimination; Self-Determination

Project Diana

A human rights research tool, Project Diana is the Web site of an international archive of human rights legal documentation named for Diana Vincent-Daviss, the first woman to head the libraries of both the New York University School of Law and Yale Law School. Created after her death in 1993, the archive commemorates her work in preserving library materials on human rights. The project's purpose is to make such materials more accessible and less costly to obtain.

Project Diana archives contain legal briefs, organization charters, texts of treaties, and bibliographies relating to a number of human rights issues. The documents include copies of complaints filed on behalf of human rights victims as well as international human rights instruments, such as the Convention on the Rights of the Child (1989), International Convention on the Protection of the Rights of Migrant Workers and Members of their Families (1990), and Draft Declaration of Principles on Human Rights and the Environment (1994). Diana also maintains Internet links with national and international human rights sites such as Amnesty International; Australian Human Rights Information Center; International Committee of the Red Cross; Women, Law and Development International; and United Nations human rights Web sites. It further lists repositories of reports, documents, and articles as diverse as the U.S. Department of State's annual report on human rights and censored materials contained in the Fileroom site.

The Diana Web site is maintained by the Orville H. Schell Jr. Center for International Human Rights at Yale Law School. Schell was a distinguished lawyer who was active in the human rights organizations Helsinki Watch and Americas Watch, and the Schell Center perpetuates his memory through scholarship and human rights advocacy. Much of the information available through Diana is acquired from the work of the Schell Center and the Allard Lowenstein Clinic, which both participate actively in the improvement of human rights through law. The project has an advisory board consisting of prominent human rights advocates and researchers.

Parallel Diana sites are maintained by other universities, including the University of Cincinnati College of Law, University of Minnesota Human Rights Center, and Bora Laskin Law Library of the University of Toronto, which focuses on women's rights.

Orville H. Schell Jr. Center for International Human Rights, P.O. Box 208215, New Haven, Conn. 06520-8215. (203-432-7480. 🖳 203-432-1040. 🖳 schell@diana.law.yale.edu. 🖳 diana.law.yale.edu.

☞

Human Rights Internet; Institute for Global Communications; Internet Resources

Property

"The third absolute right [after life and liberty], inherent in every Englishman, is that of property: which consists in the free use, enjoyment and disposal of all his acquisitions, without any control or diminution, save only the laws of the land," noted William Blackstone, the eighteenth-century commentator on the laws of England. "So great moreover is the regard of the law for private property that it will not authorize the least violation of it; no, not even for the general good of the whole community," he added. As the failed experiments in communist government during the twentieth century have shown, each person's right to acquire, control, and dispose of property still remains basic to a free and prosperous society, and the ability to check government excesses is enhanced by the balance between private economic power and public political power.

In *The Politics*, Aristotle, the Greek philosopher and scientist of the fourth century B.C.E., noted that "[p]roperty is a part of the household, and the art of acquiring property is a part of the art of managing the household. . . ." *Property*, which appeared in English as early as the fourteenth century, derives from the Latin *proprietas* (property in the sense of a quality or characteristic) and the Middle English *proprete*.

The notion of property and property ownership allows a person to exclude others from the use and enjoyment of his or her possessions. This right not only underlies the field of economics but also plays an important role in the study of political science and the law. Even the concept of government itself may be linked directly to a person's right to control property. In his *Second Treatise of Government* (1690), the English philosopher John Locke proposed: "The great and chief end . . . of men's uniting into commonwealths and putting themselves under government is the preservation of their property."

In the ideological struggle between communism and

capitalism, the past century witnessed one of the greatest challenges to the idea of private ownership of property. According to communist theory, property is the basis of class distinctions and therefore class conflict; by prohibiting private ownership of property, conflict will disappear. Although experiments in communism continue in Cuba, China, and North Korea, the fall of the Soviet Union and its satellite countries has to a large extent proven communal ownership unworkable. "But indeed," as Aristotle had foreseen in *The Politics*, "there is always a difficulty in men living together and having all human relations in common, but especially in their having common property."

The right to private property is implicit in the U.S. Declaration of Independence (1776), which lists the abuses of the English king, including cutting off trade and imposing taxation without representation—both pocketbook issues. In its conclusion the declaration states: "[F]or the support of this declaration . . . we mutually pledge to each our lives, our Fortunes, and our sacred Honor." France's Declaration of the Rights of Man and of the Citizen (1789) is more explicit, including in its list of rights the right of property alongside liberty, security, and resistance to oppression. Today most national constitutions guarantee property owners just compensation for private property taken by the government for public use.

During the Cold War, the Soviet Union's influence on international human rights documents such as the Universal Declaration of Human Rights (1948) precluded strong statements in support of the right of ownership of private property, although article 17 of that document states: "(1) Everyone has the right to own property alone as well as in association with others [and] (2) No one shall be arbitrarily deprived of his property." The International Covenant on Civil and Political Rights and International Covenant on Economic, Social and Cultural Rights (1966), however, address only the rights of ownership and disposition of property by nations or peoples, not by individuals. Individuals' right to own property was also omitted from the European Convention for the Protection of Human Rights and Fundamental Freedoms (1950), although it was included in the convention's first protocol in 1952.

Constitution of Germany (1949), article 14: "(1) Property and the right of inheritance is guaranteed. Their content and limits shall be determined by statute. (2) Property imposes duties. Its use should also serve the public weal. (3) The taking of property shall only be permissible in the public weal. It may be effected only by or pursuant to a statute regulating the nature and extent of the compensation. . . ."

African Charter on Human and Peoples' Rights (1981), part I, Human and Peoples' Rights, article 14: "The right to property shall be guaranteed. It may only be encroached upon in the interest of public need or in the interest of the community and in accordance with the provisions of appropriate laws."

U.S. Supreme Court (1998): A judicial warrant to "arrest" and "detain" a house obtained by the government without notifying the owner of the house is invalid because the due process clause of the U.S. Constitution (1789) requires that owners of real property be given an opportunity to object before their property is taken.

Inter-American Commission on Human Rights, Report on Nicaragua (1993): "Moreover, the interdependence and indivisibility of all human rights is nowadays unquestionable and, in this context, the importance of property ownership, as a contributory factor toward the securing of peace and economic and social development of a State, is assuming growing significance."

Epstein, Richard A., ed. *Classical Foundations of Liberty and Property*. New York: Garland, 2000.

Glendon, Mary Ann. *Rights Talk: The Impoverishment of Political Discourse*. New York: Free Press, 1991.

Pipes, Richard. *Property and Freedom*. New York: Knopf, 1999.

Aristotle; Compensation; Declaration of Independence (United States); Declaration of the Rights of Man and of the Citizen; Development; Economic Rights; Fundamental Rights; Locke, John; Universal Declaration of Human Rights

Proportionality

Proportionality (from the Latin *pro portione*, meaning to compare or estimate in relation to a larger whole) is the concept of balancing or weighing the right of authorities to restrict the rights of the people for good cause. As a legal concept, proportionality has its origins in ancient legal codes that prescribe "an eye for an eye" and in the egalitarian structure of the ancient Greek democracies. Constitutional government, by definition, means that governments and their agents are limited by rules and guarantees of individual rights that circumscribe the extent of their actions. By the nineteenth century the principle of laissez-faire required that the objectives of the government vis-à-vis the individual be restricted or limited.

The principle of proportionality is most often found in continental European legal decisions. Speaking of the European Convention for the Protection of Human Rights and Fundamental Freedoms (1950), a British jurist stated in the House of Lords in 1984: "[A]s construed by the European Court, the interference with freedom of expression must be necessary and proportionate to the damage which the restriction is designed to apply."

More broadly, the general principle of proportionality as applied in the European Community over the last thirty years requires that a public authority, exercising its discretionary power, may place restrictions and obligations on individuals only to the extent that such burdens are absolutely necessary and genuinely related to the objective on which their imposition is based. As another British jurist has commented: "You must not use a steam hammer to crack a nut, if a nutcracker would do."

Proportionality has its counterpart in the British common law system called "reasonableness," which can be traced to an early-sixteenth-century legal decision. In *Rooke's Case*, a court found that a public sewer authority had acted unreasonably by charging only one owner for repairing a riverbank rather than apportioning the charge among all the owners who derived some benefit from the repairs. The reasonableness test, however, is far more deferential to government authority than the proportionality principle, under which a court may question not only the proportional effect of the government action in relation to the objective but also the necessity for the act at all. In France, the courts rely less on the proportionality principle than on the concept of public order, which may be used to justify government acts that infringe on individual rights.

An example of how the proportionality principle may be used today is a case that came before the European Court of Human Rights involving extradition of a German citizen arrested in the United Kingdom to face a possible death sentence in the United States. The court commented that, with respect to the death penalty, "the manner in which it is imposed or executed, the personal circumstances of the condemned person and a disproportionality to the gravity of the crime committed, as well as the conditions of detention awaiting execution" must be considered in determining if the extradition would violate the European Convention for the Protection of Human Rights and Fundamental Freedoms (1950), article 3, Prohibition against Torture.

Canadian Charter of Rights and Freedoms (1982), Guarantee of Rights and Freedoms, section 1: "The Canadian Charter of Rights and Freedoms guarantees the rights and freedoms set out in it subject only to such reasonable limits prescribed by law as can be demonstrably justified in a free and democratic society."

European Convention for the Protection of Human Rights and Fundamental Freedoms (1950), Protocol no. 4, Securing Certain Rights and Freedoms Other Than Those Already Included in the Convention and in the First Protocol Thereto (1963), article 2, Freedom of Movement: "3. No restrictions shall be placed on the exercise of these rights other than such as are in accordance with law and are necessary in a democratic society in the interests of national security or public safety, for the maintenance of *ordre public* [public order]...."

Inter-American Court of Human Rights (Dissenting Advisory Opinion) (1984): A proposed amendment to the constitution of Costa Rica that would require a longer period of time for some persons to become naturalized citizens than others was found to be discriminatory under the American Convention on Human Rights (1969), article 24, because the distinction proposed was "disproportionate and not reasonably related to the governmental objective sought to be accomplished by it."

European Court of Justice (1979): "In order to establish whether a provision of Community law is consonant with the principle of proportionality it is necessary to establish, in the first place, whether the means it employs to achieve its aim correspond to the importance of the aim and, in the second place, whether they are necessary for its achievement."

Emiliou, Nicholas. *The Principle of Proportionality in European Law: A Comparative Study*. The Hague: Kluwer Law International, 1996.

Gydal, Cecilia. *The Principle of Proportionality*. Stockholm: Institute of European Law at Stockholm University, 1996.

Canadian Charter of Rights and Freedoms; Constitutionalism; European Convention for the Protection of Human Rights and Fundamental Freedoms; Limitations

Prostitution

See Convention for the Suppression of the Traffic in Persons and of the Exploitation of the Prostitution of Others; Slavery

Protocols

See European Convention for the Protection of Human Rights and Fundamental Freedoms; International Covenant on Civil and Political Rights, First Optional Protocol; International Covenant on Civil and Political Rights, Second Optional Protocol, Aiming at the Abolition of the Death Penalty; Treaties

Public Order

See Law Enforcement; Proportionality

Punishment

Causing an offender to suffer for wrongdoing is one of the most basic impulses of the human psyche. Punishment (from the Latin *punio*, meaning to punish) has long been the prerogative of those in authority, whether parents or government officials. In analyzing any punishment to be meted out, two basic questions generally arise: Is it necessary, and, if so, is it just? The Greek philosopher Aristotle comments in *The Ethics:* "Take the case of just actions; just punishments and chastisements do indeed spring from a good principle, but they are good only because we cannot do without them—it would be better that neither individuals nor states should need anything of the sort. . . ."

In ancient Athens types of punishment ranged from fines to execution (in such rare cases as the murder of an Athenian by a foreigner). During the time of the Roman Empire, military punishment included flogging as well as execution. William Blackstone, the eighteenth-century commentator on the laws of England, tells of a woman convicted of treason who was burned alive and a man who was disemboweled for the same offense.

The publication of *Treatise on Crimes and Punishment* (1764), by the eighteenth-century Italian jurist and economist Cesare Beccaria, represents an important milestone in the development of a theory of just, proportional, and humane punishment. Becarria contended that a penalty should be based on the extent to which the crime endangers society and that any punishment more severe than necessary to deter a crime is tyrannical and self-defeating.

Today the human rights implications of punishment for crimes, which is the state's responsibility, are still the subject of much debate. Specific issues include whether a punishment is proportional to the offense committed; whether prisoners' conditions of confinement must be humane; what constitutes cruel and unusual punishment; whether heinous crimes committed during authoritarian regimes should be punished; and whether capital punishment is a violation of the right to life.

The severity of punishment meted out around the world varies greatly, although an international consensus on standards for punishment is beginning to develop. Many national constitutions and laws put limits on punishment, especially imposition of the death penalty. "In Nicaragua," asserts its constitution (1987), "the penitentiary system is humane." Mozambique's constitution (1990) mandates that "there shall be no death penalty," while Brazil's constitution (1988) makes one exception: "[T]here shall be no punishment: a) of death, save in the case of declared war. . . ."

A number of international human rights documents also proscribe capital punishment or any treatment that is cruel, inhuman, or degrading. These include the Standard Minimum Rules for the Treatment of Prisoners (1955); Declaration on the Protection of All Persons from Being Subjected to Torture and Other Cruel, Inhuman or Degrading Treatment or Punishment (1975); and International Covenant on Civil and Political Rights, Second Optional Protocol (1989), Aiming at the Abolition of the Death Penalty.

U.S. Constitution, Eighth Amendment (1791): "Excessive bail shall not be required, nor excessive fines imposed, nor cruel and unusual punishments inflicted."

Declaration on the Protection of All Persons from Being Subjected to Torture and Other Cruel, Inhuman or Degrading Treatment or Punishment (1975), article 2: "Any act of torture or other cruel, inhuman or degrading treatment or punishment is an offense to human dignity and shall be condemned as a denial of the purposes of the Charter of the United Nations [1945] and as a violation of the human rights and fundamental freedoms proclaimed in the Universal Declaration of Human Rights [1948]."

Constitutional Court of South Africa (1995): In deciding a case under South Africa's constitution (1994), the court analyzed the provision in the Canadian Charter of Rights and Freedoms (1982) prohibiting cruel and unusual punishment, commenting that it "has been interpreted as outlawing both punishments which are inherently contrary to human dignity and punishments which are grossly disproportionate to the gravity of the offense. There is of course a link between the two, as a disproportionately heavy punishment may be seen as denying the human dignity of the offender."

European Court of Human Rights (1978): The court found that a sentence of "three strokes of the 'birch'" given to a fifteen-year-old boy on the Isle of Man in the United Kingdom constituted degrading punishment and as such was contrary to the European Convention for the Protection of Human Rights and Fundamental Freedoms (1950), article 3, which states: "No one shall be subjected to torture or to inhuman or degrading treatment or punishment."

Newman, Graeme R. *Just and Painful: A Case for the Corporal Punishment of Criminals.* New York: Harrow and Heston, 1995.

Simmons, John A., et al., eds. *Punishment.* Princeton, N.J.: Princeton University Press, 1995.

Aristotle; Beccaria, Cesare; Capital Punishment; Convention against Torture and Other Cruel, Inhuman or Degrading Treatment or Punishment; Declaration on the Protection of All Persons from Being Subjected to Torture and Other Cruel, Inhuman or Degrading Treatment or Punishment; Forced Labor; International Covenant on Civil and Political Rights, Second Optional Protocol, Aiming at the Abolition of the Death Penalty; Prisoners; Standard Minimum Rules for the Treatment of Prisoners; Torture

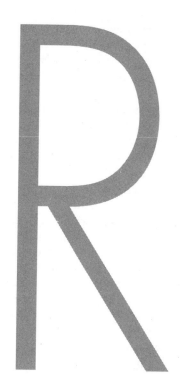

Thousands of civilians are often uprooted and forced to flee their homes during war. Passing a sign saying "We are defending Croatia in Vukovar right now," an elderly Croatian couple from Vukovar arrive at a refugee center in Zagreb, Yugoslavia, during the 1992–95 war. The United Nations High Commissioner for Refugees was established to assist with such refugee problems. [Reuters/Corbis-Bettmann]

Race Discrimination

The perceived ability to distinguish or catalogue people on the basis of racial characteristics has done far more harm than good for mankind. Only by focusing on the similarities among people of all races can the equality and dignity of all individuals and respect for them be realized. Although South Africa's systematic government-enforced policy of race discrimination known as apartheid was finally abandoned in the early 1990s, race discrimination by governments as well as individuals still occurs all over the world.

According to Felix M. Keesing, professor of anthropology at Stanford University and coauthor of *New Perspectives in Cultural Anthropology* (1971), "[I]n popular usage [the term *race]* is emotionally charged and imprecise [but] it has a straightforward and important meaning in evolutionary biology. A race is a geographically separated, hence genetically somewhat distinctive, population within a species." The origin of the word *race,* meaning a group of people connected by common descent or origin, is obscure but may be related to the Spanish *raza* and the Italian *razza.* The word has been in use in English since at least the sixteenth century.

Race discrimination, like discrimination on the basis of religion, national origin, and sex, has been accepted for most of human history. The notion of inferior and superior races and racial characteristics culminated during World War II in the ideologies of both Germany's Nazis and Japan's military leaders, who treated people of different races and cultural backgrounds inhumanely on the assumption that they were inferior.

Equality of treatment for all persons, regardless of race, was enshrined as a goal in both the U.S. Declaration of Independence (1776) and France's Declaration of the Rights of Man and of the Citizen (1789), but translating theory into practice is taking a long time. Not until 1954, almost a century after the Civil War was fought and slaves in the United States were emancipated, did the U.S. Supreme Court declare segregation in the public schools a form of discrimination prohibited by the U.S. Constitution (1789), and another decade passed before the civil rights of African Americans were adequately addressed in national laws.

In 1950 and again in 1951, 1964, and 1967, groups of experts were convened under the auspices of the United Nations Educational, Scientific and Cultural Organization (UNESCO) to present facts to combat racism. "The biological fact of race and the myth of 'race' should be distinguished," concluded the 1950 statement. "For all practical social purposes, 'race' is not so much a biological phenomenon as a social myth . . . [that] has created an enormous amount of human and social damage." These scientific inquiries have reached the same conclusion: all human beings, regardless of how they may be classified into races, are members of the same species, and efforts to promote and extend human rights will be much better served by concentrating on similarities rather than on superficial differences.

U.S. government programs to assist minorities, particularly African Americans, in obtaining educational, business, and employment opportunities to make up for past race discrimination is known as affirmative action. Such treatment has been criticized as reverse discrimination or a denial of the U.S. Constitution's color blindness. Proponents argue, on the other hand, that to ensure equality in American society, the government must compensate minorities for being handicapped by two centuries of past discrimination. The scope and length of affirmative-action policies are still debated.

Most national constitutions contain some language prohibiting discrimination on the basis of race, as do international human rights instruments. The Universal Declaration of Human Rights (1948) proclaims that the rights and freedoms it enumerates are available to all, "without distinction of any kind, such as race. . . ." In 1963 the UN General Assembly adopted the Declaration on the Elimination of All Forms of Racial Discrimination, which it followed in 1965 with the International Convention on the Elimination of All Forms of Racial Discrimination; the latter established an eighteen-member Committee on the Elimination of Racial Discrimination. In 1973, 1983, and 1993 the UN General Assembly declared a Decade for Action to Combat Racism and Racial Discrimination.

"All human beings," stated a 1978 UNESCO Declaration on Race and Racial Prejudice, "belong to a single species and are descended from a common stock. They are born equal in dignity and rights and all form an integral part of humanity."

Constitution of Japan (1947), chapter III, Rights and Duties of the People, article 14: "All of the people are equal under the law and there shall be no discrimination in political, economic, or social relations because of race, creed, sex, social status, or family origin."

International Covenant on Civil and Political Rights (1966), part II, article 2: "1. Each State Party to the present Covenant undertakes to respect and ensure to all individuals within its territory and subject to its jurisdiction the rights recognized in the present Covenant, without distinction of any kind, such as race. . . ."

U.S. Supreme Court (1954): The segregation of schoolchildren on the basis of race, even though the physical facilities and other "tangible" factors may be equal, is discriminatory because it deprives children of the minority group of equal educational opportunities.

Committee on the Elimination of Racial Discrimination (1991): The intimidation of a Moroccan citizen by a number of citizens of the Netherlands when he attempted to lease a house in their neighborhood in Utrecht constituted discrimination and requires that the government "investigate with due diligence and expedition."

Committee on the Elimination of Racial Discrimination, Office of the High Commissioner for Human Rights, United Nations, 8–14 avenue de la Paix, 1211 Geneva 10, Switzerland. (41-22-917-3456. 🖷 41-22-917-0213. 🖳 webadmin.hchr@unog.ch. 🖳 www.unhchr.ch.

Banton, Michael P. *International Action against Racial Discrimination.* Oxford, England: Clarendon Press, Oxford University Press, 1996.

Cohen, Carl. *Naked Racial Preference.* Lanham, Md.: Madison Books, 1995.

Apartheid; Committee on the Elimination of Racial Discrimination; Declaration of Independence (United States); Declaration of the Rights of Man and of the Citizen (France); Declaration on the Elimination of All Forms of Racial Discrimination; Discrimination; Equality; International Convention on the Elimination of All Forms of Racial Discrimination; Minorities; Proclamation of Teheran; United Nations Educational, Scientific and Cultural Organization (UNESCO); Universal Declaration of Human Rights

Ramos-Horta, José

José Ramos-Horta (b. 1949) shared the 1996 Nobel Peace Prize for his efforts to bring about a peaceful, just solution to Indonesia's systematic infringement of the rights of the citizens of East Timor. A resistance leader and supporter of independence, Ramos-Horta has become an international spokesman for his people, an estimated one-third of whom have died of starvation, epidemics, war, and a campaign of terror waged by the Indonesian army.

Ramos-Horta was born on December 26, 1949, in Dili, East Timor. East Timor makes up roughly half of the island of Timor, which lies just north of Australia in the southeast corner of the Indonesian archipelago, and was a Portuguese colony until 1975, when it was occupied and then unlawfully annexed by Indonesia. The son of a Timorese mother whose family was decimated by Japanese soldiers during World War II and a Portuguese father who fought with the revolutionaries against the Franco dictatorship in Spain, Ramos-Horta was educated at the Catholic mission in Soibada. He became a journalist in East Timor and eventually a radio and television correspondent.

On the eve of the Indonesian invasion in 1975, the East Timorese sent Ramos-Horta to the United Nations, where he addressed the UN Security Council to try to deter the attack through international condemnation. A founding member of East Timor's Social Democratic Party, which supported independence for the former Portuguese colony,

Ramos-Horta has worked for independence and the withdrawal of Indonesian troops from his homeland ever since. Over more than two decades his activities have included representing the national resistance movement inside and outside East Timor, presenting the case against Indonesia before various UN bodies and the European Parliament, and speaking at human rights events around the world, such as the 1999 Peace Conference in The Hague. In addition to the Nobel Peace Prize, which he shared with Bishop Carlos Filipe Ximenes Belo, Ramos-Horta has received honorary degrees from universities in Brazil, the United States, and Australia in recognition of his efforts to secure full rights for the people of East Timor.

Following bloody reprisals by Indonesia in 1999 after the East Timorese voted for independence, the Commission on Human Rights and a separate panel both recommended that an international tribunal like those set up for Rwanda and the former territory of Yugoslavia be created to try war crimes perpetrators in East Timor. The Indonesian government finally withdrew its military from East Timor on October 31, 1999, and it apologized to the people of East Timor for its violent actions.

During the conflict Ramos-Horta, who had been exiled to the Philippines, had called on the United States as well as the UN to "exert considerable pressure on Indonesia . . . to withdraw from East Timor, to stop torture, stop the killings, and allow the people . . . to exercise the right to self-determination." As he declared, "For us, it is sacred, the right of self-determination, to make a choice freely by the people of East Timor."

Ramos-Horta, José. *Funu [War]*. Trenton, N.J.: Red Sea, 1987.

Self-Determination

Ramphal, Shridath

Shridath Surendranath ("Sonny") Ramphal (b. 1928) has worked for cooperation between developing and developed countries as well as for stronger ties between the Caribbean countries and Latin America. A member of the International Commission of Jurists with a strong commitment to human rights, he has helped promote international economic reform and global environmental protection. Perhaps his greatest legacy is his professed goal: that all human beings consider the entire planet their home.

A descendant of Indians who had immigrated in the 1880s to British Guiana (now Guyana), on the northeast coast of South America, Ramphal was born there on October 3, 1928. He received a private school education and attended the Modern Educational Institute, headed by his father, in the capital city of Georgetown. After college he studied law in London and was admitted to the British bar in 1951.

Returning home, he began working in the attorney general's office and became interested in constitutional law. He helped create a federation of West Indian countries and in 1958 joined the West Indies federal government, serving as solicitor general the following year and then assistant attorney general. When the federation dissolved, he attended Harvard Law School on a fellowship and began private practice in Kingston, Jamaica, in 1962.

At the request of the prime minister, Ramphal rejoined the British Guiana government as attorney general with the specific task of drafting the nation's independence constitution. After independence was achieved in 1966, he guided the country's nonalignment foreign policy and worked to improve relations between Latin America and the Caribbean countries. He became an active promoter of the interests of Third World countries and an outspoken opponent of apartheid in South Africa.

From 1975 to 1990 he served as secretary-general of the British Commonwealth and later as a member of five international commissions on global development and the environment. As head of the World Conservation Union, both he and his book *Our Country, the Planet* (1992) played a vital role in the Earth Summit held in 1992. The recipient of many awards and honors for his work on such human rights issues as economic justice and environmental protection, Ramphal was knighted in 1970.

Ramphal, Shridath Surendranath. *Our Country, the Planet: Forging a Partnership for Survival*. Washington, D.C.: Island Press, 1992.

Sandars, Ron, ed. *Inseparable Humanity: An Anthology of Reflections of Shridath Ramphal*. New Delhi: Vikas, 1989.

Apartheid; Economic Rights; Environment; International Commission of Jurists; Self-Determination

Rapporteurs

See Working Groups

Ratification

Ratification, also called acceptance or accession, is the act of confirming or approving an agreement or a treaty between sovereign jurisdictions. Rights, duties, and obligations pledged in or imposed by such an international agreement (and sometimes reneged on) have determined the fate of many political entities. The harsh terms of the Treaty of Versailles ending World War I, for example, have been considered a primary cause of World War II.

Under international law, a treaty's formal ratification (from the Latin *ratificare*, a combination of *ratus*, meaning established, and *facio*, meaning to make) is necessary before a nation can be bound by its terms. The process is complicated because countries have different procedures for accomplishing ratification. In the days of absolute monarchs, the signature of a nation's sovereign, properly proven or attested to and often accompanied by the appropriate seals, confirmed the binding agreement. Since the advent of democratic governments, the proper role of each government authority must be taken into account.

In the United States, according to its Constitution (1789), a treaty must be ratified by the president "with the Advice and Consent of the Senate . . . provided two thirds of the Senators present concur." Other international agreements called executive agreements can be ratified either by the president acting alone or together with Congress through a majority vote in each of the two houses.

A country is bound by the terms of treaties, conventions, covenants, and other types of international human rights instruments only through ratification. Some of these agreements specifically allow a ratifying country to make exceptions to provisions of the document, however, and ratification of an agreement does not always ensure that a government will take its obligations seriously. An international human rights agreement may also be signed by a nation's authorized representative but may never be formally ratified by that country; under such circumstances formal approval has not been given, and the country is therefore not bound by the terms of the agreement. The American Convention on Human Rights (1969) was signed on behalf of the United States, but three decades after President Jimmy Carter requested its ratification, the U.S. Senate had not yet given its advice and consent.

Information on the current status of signatories and parties to international human rights agreements can be obtained from the United Nations and a number of human rights monitoring organizations, which are listed in the U.S. State Department's annual report to Congress on human rights issues.

Constitution of Italy (1948), part II, The System of the Republic, title II, The President of the Republic, article 87: "The President of the Republic is the Chief of State and represents the national unity. . . . [H]e ratifies the international treaties upon authorization of the chambers [of parliament] (when such authorization is necessary)."

International Covenant on Economic, Social and Cultural Rights (1966), part V, article 26: "2. The present Covenant is subject to ratification. Instruments of ratification shall be deposited with the Secretary-General of the United Nations."

U.S. Supreme Court (1932): "The ratification of a treaty relates back to its date [when signed by] the two governments and the rights of either [government] under it, but as respects individual rights, the [effective] date of ratification is the date of the treaty."

Permanent Court of International Justice (1929): "[U]nless the contrary be shown . . . , it must be considered that reference was made to a Convention made effective in accordance with the ordinary rules of international law amongst which is the rule that conventions, save in certain exceptional cases, are binding only by virtue of their ratification."

LeBlanc, Lawrence J. *The United States and the Genocide Convention.* Durham, N.C.: Duke University Press, 1991.

Ruda, José María. *The Final Acceptance of International Conventions.* Muscatine, Iowa: Stanley Foundation, 1976.

American Convention on Human Rights; International Human Rights Instruments; Treaties

Reasonableness

See Proportionality

Red Cross and Red Crescent

To bring assistance without discrimination to the wounded on the world's battlefields, the International Red Cross Committee was formed in 1863. Its inspiration was the heroic service performed in the 1840s and 1850s in the field and in military hospitals by medical personnel such as Florence Nightingale. The organization was officially recognized by the Geneva Convention of 1864 and continues its work today.

In 1919 five national Red Cross societies also formed the League of Red Cross Societies, with its headquarters in Geneva. By the following year the league had thirty-one member national societies. Its avowed mission, in addition to developing a national Red Cross organization in every country, included promoting the welfare of mankind and providing a medium for coordinating relief work during great national or international calamities. In 1983 the organization's name was changed to the League of International Red Cross and Red Crescent Societies to recognize Islamic as well as Christian countries, and in 1991 it was changed again to the International Federation of Red Cross and Red

Crescent Societies. Today federation members represent more than 175 countries.

The International Federation of Red Cross and Red Crescent Societies promotes and facilitates the humanitarian activities of it member national societies. In addition to battlefield medical assistance, members offer help and services to large numbers of refugees, including managing refugee camps and aiding internally displaced people; assist areas devastated by natural disasters affecting millions of persons annually; conduct first-aid training; and provide emergency telecommunications.

Its seven governing principles are to "prevent and alleviate human suffering wherever it may be found [and to] protect life and health and to ensure respect for the human being"; "make no discrimination as to nationality, race, religious beliefs, class or political opinion"; maintain neutrality in hostilities or controversies; preserve its autonomy; act only in a voluntary capacity without any "desire for gain"; promote a single Red Cross or Red Crescent society in each country; and stress the universality of the movement.

The International Committee of the Red Cross, the federation's progenitor, directs and coordinates the international relief activities of the national societies and also promotes the strengthening of humanitarian laws and universal human rights. Currently active in some fifty countries, the committee has focused recently on problems such as missing persons in Bosnia and Herzegovina, land mines, blinding weapons, water, and war.

International Committee of the Red Cross, 19 avenue de la Paix, 1202 Geneva, Switzerland. (41-22-734-6001. 🖨 41-22-733-2082. 🖳 press.gva@icrc.org. 🖳 www.icrc.org.

International Federation of Red Cross and Red Crescent Societies, P.O. Box 372, 1211 Geneva 19, Switzerland. (41-22-730-4222. 🖨 41-22-733-0395. 🖳 secretariat@ifrc.org. 🖳 www.ifrc.org.

Haug, Hans, et al. *Humanity for All: The International Red Cross and Red Crescent Movement.* Bern, Switzerland: P. Haupt, 1993.

International Committee of the Red Cross. *Handbook of the International Red Cross and Red Crescent Movement.* Geneva: International Federation of Red Cross and Red Crescent Societies, 1994.

Reid, Daphne A., and Patrick F. Gilbo. *Beyond Conflict: The International Federation of Red Cross and Red Crescent Societies, 1919–1994.* Geneva: International Federation of Red Cross and Red Crescent Societies, 1997.

Doctors without Borders; Geneva Conventions

Refoulement

The right of emigration—to leave a country where one is a citizen and settle in another country—is not an inherent freedom. Each nation sets its own immigration policy and quotas, and each country, for various reasons, may refuse refugees, asylum seekers, and other aliens permission to stay. *Refoulement,* a French term meaning to turn back, refers to the act of returning a refugee or an alien to his or her country of origin. It applies specifically to instances in which the returnee is likely to be subjected to discriminatory mistreatment or serious harm.

The return of refugees has created problems since biblical times. As a result, the principle of *nonrefoulement* is a general policy of civilized nations today and is considered a norm of international law. Some authorities even suggest that it has become *jus cogens,* a higher order of international legal norm that may not be abrogated or derogated from.

Because they refer to international situations, the terms *refoulement* and *nonrefoulement* generally do not appear in national constitutions. The concept is recognized in national laws, however, and in several international human rights instruments, including the American Convention on Human Rights (1969) and the Convention Governing the Specific Aspects of Refugee Problems in Africa (1969).

U.S. Refugee Act (1988), section 243(h)(1): "The Attorney General shall not deport or return any alien . . . to a country if the Attorney General determines that such alien's life or freedom would be threatened in such country on account of race, religion, nationality, membership in a particular social group, or political opinion."

Convention Relating to the Status of Refugees (1951), chapter V, Administrative Measures, article 33, Prohibition of Expulsion or Return ("Refoulement"): "1. No Contracting State shall expel or return ("refouler") a refugee in any manner whatsoever to the frontiers of territories where his life or freedom would be threatened on account of his race, religion, nationality, membership of a particular social group or political opinion."

U.S. Supreme Court (1987): The standard for granting asylum to an alien is a "well-founded fear" of persecution, which is lower than the standard for *refoulement,* which is a showing of a "clear probability" of persecution.

European Court of Human Rights (1991): The extradition of a fugitive may give rise to an issue under the European Convention for the Protection of Human Rights and Fundamental Freedoms (1950), article 3, prohibiting torture or inhuman or degrading treatment or punishment, "where substantial grounds have been shown for believing that the person concerned, if extradited, faces a real risk of being subjected to torture or to inhuman or degrading treatment or punishment in the requesting country."

Bassiouni, M. Cherif. *International Extradition: United States Law and Practice.* 3d rev. ed. Dobbs Ferry, N.Y.: Oceana, 1996.

Aliens; American Convention on Human Rights; Asylum; Convention Relating to the Status of Refugees; Deportation; Expulsion; Immigrants; *Jus Cogens;* Refugees

Refugees

People who flee their native countries because of war, religious or political persecution, ethnic cleansing, or natural disaster are refugees. They believe that they cannot rely on the assistance or protection of their own country or even on the usual aid of diplomatic missions in foreign nations. Often, because of their large numbers, poverty, or ill health, refugees may tax the resources of or jeopardize the population in the receiving country. In some cases refugees are stateless, having lost their nationality because of persecution or the dissolution of their home country.

The plight of refugees is as old as human history. After the Trojan War, according to Virgil's account in *The Aeneid,* Aeneas of Troy led a band of refugees from the war first to Carthage and then to the Italian peninsula, where they finally settled more than four hundred years before the traditional date of the founding of Rome in 751 B.C.E. Many of the settlers in the New World after 1492 were refugees. The term *refugee,* derived from the French *réfugié,* has been used in English since the late seventeenth century, when it was applied to the French Huguenots who came to England to escape religious persecution.

In 1921, following World War I, the League of Nations created the Office of the High Commissioner for Refugees to help cope with the large number of postwar refugees, especially those from Russia, Greece, and Armenia. The League also provided a kind of international passport for refugees that allowed them to cross national borders to seek asylum. During World War II refugees from the Nazi regime in Germany emigrated to the United States and other receptive countries. The International Committee of the Red Cross, assuming some of the duties of the former League of Nations, assisted and protected many refugees.

In the year after it was founded, the United Nations in 1946 created the International Refugee Organization, replacing it in 1950 with the Office of the United Nations High Commissioner for Refugees. According to the statute authorizing that office, a refugee is "any . . . person who is outside the country of his nationality or, if he has no nationality, the country of his former habitual residence, because he has or had well-founded fear of persecution by reason of race, religion, nationality or political opinion and is . . . unwilling to avail himself of the protection of the government of the country of his nationality, or, if he has no nationality, to return to the country of his former habitual residence." The Convention Relating to the Status of Refugees (1951) also contains an extended definition of refugees. Most national constitutions, however, do not directly refer to them.

According to the Convention Relating to the Status of Refugees, the rights of refugees include being treated by the host countries party to the convention "without discrimination as to race, religion or country of origin." Refugees are to be given treatment "at least as favorable as that accorded to their nationals with respect to freedom to their religion and freedom as regards the religious education of their children." Other rights provided to refugees by the convention include the rights of property ownership, association, access to the courts and gainful employment, and certain welfare rights. The duties of refugees, as specified by the convention, include conforming to the host country's "laws and regulations as well as to measures taken for the maintenance of public order."

Declaration of the Establishment of the State of Israel (1948): "The State of Israel will be open for Jewish immigration and the Ingathering of the Exiles [Jewish refugees]. . . ."

Convention Relating to the Status of Refugees (1951), preamble: "[T]he United Nations has, on various occasions, manifested its profound concern for refugees and endeavored to assure refugees the widest possible exercise of these fundamental rights and freedoms. . . ."

Supreme Court of Canada (1985): Any person inside the borders of the country, no matter how briefly and even if illegally, is entitled to due process.

Inter-American Commission on Human Rights (1993): By resolution, the United States was requested to review its practice of stopping vessels containing people fleeing Haiti bound for the United States and returning them to Haiti without the opportunity to establish whether they qualified as refugees.

Amnesty International USA, 322 Eighth Avenue, New York, N.Y. 10001. (212-807-8400. 212-627-1451. admin-us@aiusa.org. www.amnesty-usa.org.

International Rescue Committee, 122 East 42nd Street, New York, N.Y. 10168-1289. (212-551-3000. 212-551-3180. irc@intrescom.org. www.intrescom.org.

Lawyers Committee for Human Rights, 100 Maryland Avenue, N.E., Suite 500, Washington, D.C. 20002-5625. (202-547-5692. 📠 202-543-5999. ✉ comm@lchr.org. 🖥 www.lchr.org.

Refugees International, 1705 N Street, N.W., Washington, D.C. 20036. (202-828-0110, 800-**REFUGEE**. 📠 202-828-0819. ✉ ri@refintl.org. 🖥 www.refintl.org.

United Nations High Commissioner for Refugees, **C.P.** 2500, 1211 Geneva 2, Switzerland. (41-22-739-8111. 📠 41-22-739-7377. ✉ hqpioo@unhcr.ch. 🖥 www.unhcr.ch.

U.S. Committee for Refugees, 1717 Massachusetts Avenue, N.W., Suite 200, Washington, D.C. 20036. (202-347-3507. 📠 202-347-3418. ✉ uscr@irsa-uscr.org. 🖥 www.refugees.org.

USA for UNHCR, 1775 K Street, N.W., Suite 300, Washington, D.C. 20006. (202-296-1115, 800-770-1100. 📠 202-296-1081. ✉ usaforunhcr@usaforunhcr.org. 🖥 www.usaforunhcr.org.

Forum on Refugee Issues and Concerns. *The Rights of Refugees and Asylum-Seekers*. Quezon City, Philippines: Diliman, 1996.

Goodwin-Gill, Guy S. *The Refugee in International Law*. 2d ed. New York: Oxford University Press, 1998.

International Journal of Refugee Law. New York: Oxford University Press, 1996.

Aliens; Asylum; Convention Relating to the Status of Refugees; Declaration on Territorial Asylum; Geneva Conventions; High Commissioner for Refugees; Immigrants; Nationality; Red Cross and Red Crescent; *Refoulement;* Statelessness

Regional Human Rights Systems

All human rights guarantees, including those contained in regional and international instruments, depend on the commitment of sovereign nations, which must enforce them domestically through constitutional and other legal guarantees as well as strict adherence to the rule of law. Regional systems of human rights protections and enforcement mechanisms are international systems based on documents and organizations whose scope extends only to the nations within geographically defined boundaries, such as Africa, the Americas, Europe, and Asia and the Pacific.

Addressing areas between national priorities and international concerns—the latter under the general direction of the United Nations, supported by other global bodies such as the World Health Organization and the International Labor Organization—regional human rights sys-

tems serve a valuable function. They represent a way of recognizing legal and cultural differences that some nations often use as arguments for not accepting international human rights norms, especially those of the developed Western countries. Regional systems that diverge significantly from international norms or that are only window dressing for human rights abuses, however, have the potential of doing far more harm than good.

Of the three active regional systems for promoting and enforcing human rights—the European, inter-American, and African (Asia's is still in developmental stages)—the European model has been the most successful. This no doubt is due in great part to the horrors of the human rights violations of the Nazi regime beginning in the 1930s and of World War II. The European system also owes its strength to the continent's development of humanitarian legal norms and institutions committed to the rule of law.

The European Convention for the Protection of Human Rights and Fundamental Freedoms (1950), adopted by the Council of Europe, launched the European system of human rights. The convention created two bodies, the European Commission of Human Rights and the European Court of Human Rights. The commission, which ceased to exist in 1999, had authority to handle individual cases involving alleged human rights violations and to refer cases with significant issues to the court. Over four decades it received more than forty-five thousand complaints and referred 119 to the court. Protocol no. 11 (1994), however, replaced the two-tiered system in 1999 with a single permanent court to handle all complaints involving the human rights guaranteed in the convention.

Formed in 1949 to rebuild the continent's cultural, social, and political life in the wake of World War II's devastation, the Council of Europe's goals now include to protect human rights and pluralistic democracy; promote awareness of a European cultural identity and encourage its development; seek solutions to problems involving minorities, intolerance, and the environment; and assist Europe's new democracies. The Committee of Ministers, one of the council's three key components, plays an important role in the human rights procedures under both the 1950 convention and the European Social Charter (1961), revised in 1996, which added economic and social rights to the earlier convention's civil and political rights. Enforcement mechanisms under the charter include provisions for receiving reports and complaints by organizations.

The Organization of American States (OAS) has responsibility for the American or inter-American system of human rights, which began with the American Declaration of the Rights and Duties of Man (1948), adopted several days after the OAS charter went into effect. Also adopted in the same year were the Inter-American Charter of Social Guarantees, Inter-American Convention on the Granting of Civil Rights to Women, and Inter-American Convention on the Granting of Political Rights to Women.

In 1959 the Inter-American Commission on Human Rights was created to promote the rights set forth in the

American Declaration, and the following year the OAS adopted the commission's statute of operation. Its human rights functions include analyzing and investigating individual petitions of alleged abuses; by the end of 1999, more than twelve thousand cases had been processed and some eight hundred cases were pending. The commission also submits cases to the Inter-American Court of Human Rights, which was established in 1969 to decide cases involving human rights violations brought by the commission on behalf of individuals or by the states that are parties to the convention.

The African system is under the general aegis of the Organization of African Unity (OAU), a body whose members include the African heads of state and government and their foreign affairs ministers. Among Africa's major human rights documents are the African Charter on Human and Peoples' Rights (1981), also known as the Banjul Charter, and the African Charter on the Rights and Welfare of the Child (1990). Enforcement is the responsibility of the African Commission on Human and Peoples' Rights, created by the Banjul Charter within the OAU "to promote human and peoples' rights and ensure their protection in Africa." The commission began operation in 1986 and a decade later had received twenty-two admissible cases (those not withdrawn or resolved by a friendly settlement), twelve of which involved governmental violations.

The European Court of Human Rights, the Inter-American Court of Human Rights, and the African Commission on Human and Peoples' Rights are the courts of last resort for people whose rights have been violated in their own countries, because complainants must have exhausted all possible domestic remedies. More than a hundred nations now recognize the jurisdiction of these tribunals, making them increasingly significant venues for adjudication of human rights cases.

Although ad hoc groups, with the UN's support, are working to create a regional human rights system in Asia and the Pacific, there is as yet no such system nor any enforcement mechanism or regional group comparable to the Council of Europe, OAS, or OAU. The Kampala Declaration on Human Rights (1993), adopted by representatives of forty-three African and Asian countries, is a nonbinding human rights document, declaring simply that "human rights, whether civil, political, economic, social, or cultural [are] indispensable and . . . must be protected, upheld, and promoted by all."

One nongovernmental organization that is encouraging a more formal system is named the Asian Human Rights Commission. Pressing for civil and political rights as well as social and economic rights and the right to development, the group in 1998 convened a conference in Kwangju, South Korea, and issued an Asian Human Rights Charter. "Asians have in recent decades suffered from various forms of conflict and violence, arising from ultra-nationalism, perverted ideologies, ethnic differences, and fundamentalism of all religions," it states. "Violence emanates from both the state and sections of civil society. For large masses, there is little security of person, property or community. There is massive displacement of communities and there are an increasing number of refugees." The document's sixteen parts emphasize the rights to life, peace, democracy, social justice, and cultural identity; freedom of conscience; the right to development; and protection of vulnerable groups such as women, children, disabled persons, workers, students, prisoners, and political detainees.

Asian Human Rights Commission, 16 Argyle Street, Seventh Floor, Unit D, Mongkok Commercial Centre, Kowloon, Hong Kong. ☎ 85-2-2698-6339. 🖷 85-2-2698-6367. 🖳 ahrchk@ahrchk.org. 🖳 www. ahrchk.net; www.cambodia-hr.org; www.disappearances.org.

Council of Europe, Point I, F-67075 Strasbourg Cedex, France. ☎ 33-3-88-41-2000. 🖷 33-3-88-41-2781. 🖳 webmaster@www. coe.fr. 🖳 www.coe.fr.

Organization of African Unity, P.O. Box 3243, Addis Ababa, Ethiopia. ☎ 251-1-51-7700. 🖷 251-1-51-2622. 🖳 y.afanou@telecom. net. 🖳 www.oau-oua.org.

Organization of American States, 17th Street and Constitution Avenue, N.W., Washington, D.C. 20006. ☎ 202-458-3000. 🖷 202-458-3967. 🖳 pi@oas.org. 🖳 www.oas.org.

Davidson, J. S. *The Inter-American Human Rights System*. Brookfield, Vt.: Dartmouth, 1997.

Fourth Workshop on Regional Human Rights Arrangements in the Asian and Pacific Region: Report. Kathmandu, 26–28 February 1996. Geneva: Center for Human Rights, 1996.

Mower, A. Glenn, Jr. *Regional Human Rights: A Comparative Study of the West European and Inter-American Systems*. Westport, Conn.: Greenwood, 1991.

Peter, Chris Maina. *Human Rights in Africa: A Comparative Study of the African Human and Peoples' Rights Charter and the New Tanzanian Bill of Rights*. Westport, Conn.: Greenwood, 1990.

African Charter on Human and Peoples' Rights; African Commission on Human and Peoples' Rights; American Convention on Human Rights; American Declaration of the Rights and Duties of Man; Complaints; Enforcement; European Convention for the Protection of Human Rights and Fundamental Freedoms; European Court of Human Rights; European Social Charter; Human Rights Watch; Inter-American Commission on Human Rights; Inter-American Court of Human Rights; Kampala Declaration on Human Rights; North Atlantic Treaty Organization (NATO); Organization for Security and Cooperation in Europe; Remedies

Rehabilitation

Rehabilitation is a person's restoration, to the fullest possible extent, to a previous state or condition. In ancient Rome a formerly free person who had been enslaved could be freed and regain the status of a freeborn person; if the pardon was accompanied by a publicly decreed legal reinstatement (restitutio), all of the person's former rights would be restored as well. In the sixteenth century rehabilitation was the act of restoring a person's rank and legal rights. The term can also describe the restoration of position, status, or property to people who have lost these as a result of violations of their human rights. More recently, rehabilitation has come to refer to the process by which a criminal offender is returned to society as a law-abiding and productive citizen.

In medicine, rehabilitation refers to the long period of therapy and retraining required for injured or disabled people to regain some previous abilities and thus some degree of normal life. A speech on soldiers wounded during World War II, included in the 1940 records of the British House of Commons, mentions "the secret of the maximum cure possible for the patient . . . the process known as rehabilitation."

At the state and national levels, provisions for health rights and victims' rights may include rehabilitation and compensation for persons who have suffered injuries. Sweden's Riksdag Act (1974), part of its constitution, assigns rehabilitation relating to health to the parliament's committee on health and welfare, while Ecuador's constitution (1979) provides that when a guilty verdict is reversed, the person "who has suffered punishment as a result of that verdict will be rehabilitated and indemnified by the State in accordance with the law." The concept of an executive pardon or clemency for convicted persons generally includes restoration of rights.

Discriminatory acts and denials of human rights may also violate international and regional agreements. After an exhaustion of domestic remedies, such cases may be brought to the attention of tribunals such as the European Court of Human Rights, Inter-American Court of Human Rights, and Commission on Human Rights, as well as the Human Rights Committee, created under the International Covenant on Civil and Political Rights (1966). These bodies, in adjudicating complaints by people whose human rights have been denied, abused, or violated, may recommend that such victims be rehabilitated or restored to their former position or status by the offending government. If victims have suffered severe mental or physical injuries, appropriate medical rehabilitation may also be required.

Constitution of Singapore (1963), part 4, Fundamental Liberties, article 9: "(6) Nothing in this Article shall invalidate any law—. . . (b) relating to the misuse of drugs or intoxicating substances which

authorizes the arrest and detention of any person for the purpose of treatment and rehabilitation. . . ."

Declaration on the Protection of All Persons from Enforced Disappearance (1992), article 19: "The victims of acts of enforced disappearance and their family shall obtain redress and shall have the right to adequate compensation, including the means for as complete a rehabilitation as possible."

U.K. Chancery Division (1984): A person who has committed various criminal offenses but has become a "rehabilitated person" under the Rehabilitation of Offenders Act (1974) is entitled "to be treated for all purposes in law as a person who had not committed or been . . . convicted of" the offenses in question.

Human Rights Committee (1995): A Czech Republic law endorsing the "rehabilitation of Czech citizens who had left the country under communist pressure" that required such persons to be not only Czech or Slovak citizens but also "permanent residents in its territory" constitutes a violation of the International Covenant on Civil and Political Rights (1996), article 26, which prohibits any discrimination, including that based on national origin, that would infringe the right of equal protection of the law.

Kilbourn, Phyllis, and Marjorie McDermid, eds. *Sexually Exploited Children: Working to Protect and Heal.* Monrovia, Calif.: MARC, 1998.

Smith, Kathleen E. *Remembering Stalin's Victims: Popular Memory and the End of the USSR.* Ithaca, N.Y.: Cornell University Press, 1996.

Amnesty; Compensation; Disabled Persons; Health; Social Rights; Victims

Religion

Even before recorded history, human beings undoubtedly searched for the source of the fundamental forces in their lives and believed in the spirit of things unseen. Religion—belief in a divine power or being—has motivated humans to both great achievements and extreme violations of human rights, fostering salutary principles such as love of neighbor and honor of parents while sanctioning holy wars and inhumane acts in the name of religious purity. The proliferation of religions in the world today makes toleration of others' beliefs, as long as they do not cause injury, of paramount importance to maintaining peace and mutual respect.

The world's various religions and religious sects have generally been a positive force for human rights, but their moral precepts are not uniform and are often counterproductive to the promotion of human rights. The rights of women and homosexuals to full participation in community life, the rights of families to control reproduction, and the rights of women to have abortions are a few of the human rights norms that organized religions may actively disparage and subvert. Some religions maintain that women and children must be subservient to the male head of the family, thus denying their human rights and facilitating their abuse.

The quest for religious freedom that began in England in the early seventeenth century led to the European colonization of the North American continent. The citizens of the thirteen British colonies that a century and a half later formed the United States of America devised a written constitution and a bill of rights to ensure government of the people, for the people, and by the people. Since then, the notion that the rights of individuals, including to their own religious beliefs, should be protected against government authority has been enshrined in constitutional and international human rights documents around the world.

The U.S. Bill of Rights (1791) does not specifically declare freedom of religion but mandates in its first words that "Congress shall make no law respecting an establishment of religion, or prohibiting the free exercise thereof." On the other hand, some national constitutions dictate a state religion. Greece's constitution (1975), part one, Fundamental Provisions, proclaims: "The text of the Holy Scripture shall be maintained. Official translation of the text into any other form of language, without the prior sanction by the Autocaphalous Church of Greece and the Great Church of Christ in Constantinople, is prohibited." Although many constitutional democracies do not emulate America's strict separation of church and state, religious freedom is guaranteed through a policy of religious tolerance.

International and regional documents, however, reflect more uniformity in their provisions regarding freedom of religion, although nuances are still recognized. The International Covenant on Civil and Political Rights (1966), article 18, states: "1. Everyone shall have the right to freedom of thought, conscience and religion. This right shall include freedom to have or to adopt a religion or belief of his choice, and freedom, either individually or in community with others and in public or private, to manifest his religion or belief in worship, observance, practice and teaching." The article continues: "2. No one shall be subject to coercion which would impair his freedom to have or to adopt a religion or belief of his choice. 3. Freedom to manifest one's religion or beliefs may be subject only to such limitations as are prescribed by law and are necessary to protect public safety, order, health, or morals or the fundamental rights and freedoms of others. 4. The States Parties to the present Covenant undertake to have respect for the liberty of parents and, when applicable, legal guardians to ensure the religious and moral education of their children in conformity with their own convictions."

Freedom of religion is often referred to in the same context as freedom of thought and freedom of conscience. In 1981 the UN General Assembly adopted the Declaration on the Elimination of All Forms of Intolerance and of Discrimination Based on Religion or Belief. Its preamble takes note of the fact that "the disregard and infringement of human rights and fundamental freedoms, in particular of the right to freedom of thought, conscience, religion or whatever belief, have brought, directly and indirectly, wars and great suffering to mankind, especially where they serve as a means of foreign interference in the internal affairs of other States and amount to kindling hatred between peoples and nations. . . ." A 1990 report to the Commission on Human Rights regarding this declaration pointed out: "In addition to conflicts between entire religious communities, there are situations in which the activities of extremist or fanatical factions are the main cause of discriminatory practices or of violent outbursts of a religious nature. In fact, the intransigence of extremist elements and their demand for literal interpretation, without consideration of the context of certain religious precepts, is at the root of many of the current manifestations of religious conflicts in the world."

Constitution of Russia (1993), part one, chapter 1, Principles of the Constitutional System, article 14: "1. The Russian Federation shall be a secular state. No religion shall be declared an official or compulsory religion. 2. All religious associations shall be separate from the state and shall be equal before the law."

Universal Declaration of Human Rights (1948), article 18: "Everyone has the right to freedom of thought, conscience and religion; this right includes freedom to change his religion or belief, and freedom, either alone or in community with others and in public or private, to manifest his religion or belief in teaching, practice, worship and observance."

U.K. Queen's Bench Division (1990): The common law of England protects the Christian religion from blasphemy, but such protection does not extend to Islam. The absence of a law protecting religions other than Christianity, however, was not a violation under the European Convention for the Protection of Human Rights and Fundamental Freedoms (1950), because the convention does not require a domestic law for blasphemy, which would be contrary to the right of freedom of expression under the convention's article 10.

African Commission on Human and Peoples' Rights (1997): Persecution, including arbitrary arrest, detention, and torture, of members of the religious sect known as the Jehovah's Witnesses in Zaire constituted a violation of the African Charter on Human and Peoples' Rights (1981), article 8, which guarantees freedom of conscience and the profession and free practice of religion.

International Coalition for Religious Freedom, 7777 Leesburg Pike, Suite 307N-A, Falls Church, Va. 22043. (703-790-1500. 🖷 703-790-5562. 🖳 icrf@aol.com. 🖳 www.religiousfreedom.com.

United States Institute of Peace, 1500 M Street, N.W., Suite 700, Washington, D.C. 20005-1708. (202-457-1700. 🖷 202-429-6063. 🖳 info@usip.org. 🖳 www.usip.org.

Boyle, Kevin, and Juliet Sheen. *Freedom of Religion and Belief: A World Report*. New York: Routledge, 1997.

Religious Intolerance in Europe Today. Hearing before the Commission on Security and Cooperation in Europe, 105th Congress, First Session, September 18, 1997. Washington, D.C.: U.S. Government Printing Office, 1997.

Commission on Human Rights; Conscience; Declaration on the Elimination of All Forms of Intolerance and of Discrimination Based on Religion or Belief; International Covenant on Civil and Political Rights; Pax Christi; Separation of Church and State; Thought; Tolerance; World Council of Churches

Remedies

Once a country has undertaken to guarantee its citizens certain human rights, procedures to ensure avoidance of infringements and abuses and to provide remedies for failure to live up to those guarantees must be instituted. Remedies (from the Latin *remedium*, meaning cure or relief) for violations of human rights are primarily a part of the enforcement process. Not surprisingly, because democracy and human rights flourish in tandem, democratic governments are more likely to provide means for remedying violations of human rights.

Reparations for human rights violations can take a number of forms. Traditional remedies include seeking redress directly from the offending national or local government through the executive, legislative, or judicial branch of government. An individual or a group of citizens who believe that some government policy or officials have violated their rights may petition the ministry or department of justice; contact their elected legislators or an ombudsman; or, in those countries with some form of judicial or constitutional review and an independent judiciary, bring legal action for a court determination.

Other forms of remedies at the national level include public prosecution of the offenders, changes to government policies or personnel, and rehabilitation of victims or their families through restitution and compensation.

Using judicial or constitutional review powers, courts may declare that acts of government officials or public laws are unconstitutional infringements of a citizen's rights, while in some cases domestic courts may apply international human rights norms to provide remedies. The executive branch of government may change the offending policy or discipline the offending officials. In addition, elected legislators may enact remedial legislation.

After World War II new remedies for human rights violations were introduced. At the global level, major human rights institutions were created by the United Nations, including the Commission on Human Rights, Office of the High Commissioner for Human Rights, and Human Rights Committee, the latter established under the International Covenant on Civil and Political Rights (1966). The commission and the committee act on complaints of human rights violations after all domestic remedies have been exhausted and attempt to compel offending nations to grant remedies to complainants found to be the victims of abuse. The Office of the High Commissioner for Human Rights, in addition to providing support for other UN human rights bodies, provides technical assistance to help countries improve their human rights policies and institutions and coordinates much of the international human rights support and assistance effort. A special aspect of the office is the "urgent action" procedure for intervention in the case of imminent serious violations of human rights.

At the regional level, certain bodies now exist in Europe, Africa, and the Americas for facilitating remedies of human rights violations: the European Court of Human Rights, African Commission on Human and Peoples' Rights, and Inter-American Commission on Human Rights and Inter-American Court of Human Rights. These bodies were established after World War II under regional human rights agreements and the auspices of major intergovernmental organizations: the Council of Europe, Organization of African Unity, and Organization of American States. These regional commissions and courts act on complaints regarding violations of human rights by governments that have ratified their enabling agreements, although the commissions, unlike the courts, also have responsibility for promoting human rights in those nations. Although these remedies still depend ultimately on encouraging the countries charged with violating human rights to accept their obligations under the relevant treaty, cease such violations, and compensate victims or their families, they do add some new weapons to the arsenal for protecting and enforcing human rights.

In many cases remedies for human rights violations are also provided by private nongovernmental organizations. These organizations, which include groups such as Amnesty International, Human Rights Watch, and Peace Brigades International, can often act to remedy human rights violations—for example, by obtaining the release of political prisoners or prisoners of conscience, investigating abuses and recommending and mediating remedial action by the offending governments, providing support and publicity for human rights activists in countries with repressive regimes, and bringing human rights violations to the attention of national and international officials and the public at large.

The effectiveness of remedies for human rights violations depends to some degree on whether a country has a well-established constitutional democracy and has endorsed constitutional and international guarantees of human rights. The rule of law, for example, creates the basis of equality before the law and the impartiality of those charged with determining violations and fashioning remedies. In addition, an aggressive, professional, and independent legal profession can make an important difference in how successful victims of human rights abuses will be in obtaining remedies. Finally, creating awareness of the importance of human rights among the citizenry, especially those in positions of authority in the government, helps support those institutions and policies that establish and maintain effective procedures for remedying human rights violations.

Constitution of India (1950), part II, Fundamental Rights, Right to Constitutional Remedies, 32, Remedies for Enforcement of Rights Conferred by the Part: "(1) The right to move the Supreme Court by appropriate proceedings for the enforcement of the rights conferred by this Part is guaranteed."

Declaration of Basic Principles of Justice for Victims of Crime and Abuse of Power (1985), B, Victims of Abuse of Power: "19. States should consider incorporating into national law norms proscribing abuses of power and providing remedies to victims of such abuses. In particular, such remedies should include restitution, and/or compensation, and necessary material, medical, psychological and social assistance and support."

Constitutional Court of South Africa (1997): "Appropriate relief will in essence be relief that is required to protect and enforce [South Africa's constitution (1994)]. Depending on the circumstances of each particular case the relief may be a declaration of rights, an interdict, a mandamus or such other relief as may be required to ensure that the rights enshrined in the Constitution are protected and enforced. If it is necessary to do so, the courts may even have to fashion new remedies to secure the protection and enforcement of these all important rights."

Human Rights Committee (1988): A Jamaican citizen awaiting execution who did not receive a timely reply to his appeal based on violations of the International Covenant on Civil and Political Rights (1966), articles 7 and 10, was found to be entitled "to an effective remedy, including appropriate compensation," and the Jamaican government "is under an obligation to investigate [his] allegations."

African Commission on Human and Peoples' Rights, P.O. Box 673, Banjul, Gambia. (220-39-2962. 220-39-0764. umn.edu/humanrts/Africa/Commission.

European Court of Human Rights, Council of Europe, F-67075 Strasbourg Cedex, France. (33-3-88-41-2018. 33-3-88-41-2730. dhcourt@court1.coe.int. www.ei-ie.org.

Human Rights Committee, Communications Branch, 8–14 avenue de la Paix, 1211 Geneva 10, Switzerland. (41-22-917-1234. 41-22-917-0123. webadmin.hchr@un.org.ch. www.unhchr.ch/htm/menu2/6/hrd.

Inter-American Commission on Human Rights, 1889 F Street, N.W., Washington, D.C. 20006. (202-458-6002. 202-458-3992. cidhoea@oas.org. cidh.oas.org.

Inter-American Court of Human Rights, P.O. Box 6906-1000, San José, Costa Rica. (506-234-0581. 506-234-0584. corteidh@sol.racsa.co.cr. corteidh-oea.nu.or.cr/ci/home_ing.

International (Criminal) Tribunal for Rwanda, P.O. Box 6016, Arusha, Tanzania. (255-57-4369 (via satellite link at 212-963-2850). 255-57-4000 (via satellite link at 212-963-2848). codrington@un.org. www.un.org/ictr.

International (Criminal) Tribunal for Yugoslavia, P.O. Box 13888, 2501 EW The Hague, Netherlands. (31-70-416-5000. 31-70-416-5345. www.un.org/icty.

United Nations High Commissioner for Human Rights, 8–14 avenue de la Paix, 1211 Geneva 10, Switzerland. (41-22-917-9000. 41-22-917-9016. webadmin.hchr@unog.ch. www.unhchr.ch.

Bassiouni, M. Cherif, and Alfred De Zayas. *The Protection of Human Rights in the Administration of Justice: A Compendium of United Nations Norms and Standards.* Geneva: Center for Human Rights, 1994.

Evans, Malcolm D., ed. *Remedies in International Law: The Institutional Dilemma.* Oxford, England: Hart, 1998.

African Commission on Human and Peoples' Rights; *Amparo;* Commission on Human Rights; Compensation; Complaints; Enforcement; European Court of Human Rights; Exhaustion of Remedies; Habeas Corpus; High Commissioner for Human Rights; Human Rights Committee; Inter-American Commission on Human Rights; Inter-American Court of Human Rights; Nongovernmental Organizations; Ombudsmen; Regional Human Rights Systems; Rehabilitation; Reporting Violations; Resolution 1503 Procedure; Victims; Violations

Reporting Violations

Human rights declared in national and international documents are of little value if they cannot be enforced. When denials, abuses, and violations occur, various systems are in place for making reports (from the French word *rapport*, meaning an account, information, or communication) to the proper authorities.

Reporting human rights violations has two aspects. First, individuals or groups may report allegations to national, regional, or international authorities to stop a harmful action by a government agent or to seek redress. Through this means, human rights provisions in national laws and international agreements are enforced. Second, national governments may be required to report to international bodies on steps taken to implement human rights or to make amends for human rights violations under international agreements to which they are parties.

In a constitutional democracy that requires accountability of public officials and separation of powers, national governments have the ability to protect citizens from violations of their rights as well as the power to punish perpetrators. A violation can be reported to a number of government institutions, from the police, public prosecutor, and attorney general to a commission charged with enforcing human rights violations, an ombudsman, or even an elected representative. Nongovernmental organizations, legal practitioners, and the media are other entities to which violations can be made known. The ease and effectiveness of reporting violations, however, vary greatly among the countries of the world. Freedom House, a nongovernmental organization based in Washington, D.C., annually ranks nations on the basis of their record of political rights and civil liberties, including how well they respond to reports of human rights violations.

At the regional and international levels, after exhaustion of domestic remedies, a person or group wishing to report a violation of human rights has a narrower range of options. Moreover, regional and international systems depend on voluntary enforcement by the countries involved. Enforcement at all levels depends on the willingness and in some cases the ability of national officials and institutions to act appropriately. Unfortunately, many reports of human rights denials, abuses, and violations are ignored or covered up by governments hostile to implementing human rights provisions of national or international documents.

Three regional systems of human rights reporting—European, inter-American, and African—exist, respectively, under the European Convention for the Protection of Human Rights and Fundamental Freedoms (1950), American Convention on Human Rights (1969), and African Charter on Human and Peoples' Rights (1981). Each of these systems has a commission or a court charged with receiving communications or complaints about human rights violations.

Under the European system, the European Court of Human Rights has, since the European Commission of Human Rights was abolished in 1999, gained authority to receive petitions directly from individuals and organizations as well as from parties to the European convention. The inter-American system has both a commission and a court, while under the African charter there is the African Commission on Human and Peoples' Rights. Among other functions, these bodies have the authority to receive and act on communications reporting human rights violations, but only after all national or domestic remedies have been exhausted by those persons making the reports. The European court procedures have been far more encompassing and effective than the other two systems. No regional human rights reporting system now exists for Asia and the Pacific, although the United Nations has sponsored preliminary discussions on the subject.

Two types of human rights systems exist at the international level: UN bodies and convention- or treaty-based bodies. The UN institutions, based on authority found in the UN charter (1945), include the General Assembly, Office of the High Commissioner for Human Rights, Economic and Social Council (ECOSOC), Commission on Human Rights and its Subcommission on the Promotion and Protection of Human Rights (formerly the Subcommission on the Prevention of Discrimination and the Protection of Minorities), working groups that assist the commission and subcommission in receiving and considering human rights violations, and Commission on the Status of Women. In the mid-1990s, to enable the UN to monitor and react quickly to developing emergencies, the High Commissioner for Human Rights set up a twenty-four-hour facsimile hotline for victims, relatives, and nongovernmental organizations to use in reporting abuses.

The UN *Manual on Human Rights Reporting* (1997) states that "the reporting process assumes that there is a need for a *constructive dialogue* between the State concerned, on the one hand, and an independent international group of experts on the other." This reporting serves a number of functions: it spurs a review of national policies and laws before a treaty or a convention is signed, creates a monitoring process, gives rise to new administrative practices and legislation, invites public scrutiny of a nation's human rights record, allows periodic evaluation of goals, uncovers human rights problems, and promotes information exchange among nations.

Also at the global level are convention- or treaty-based bodies responsible for receiving reports from countries that are parties to certain international human rights agreements; in some cases they also receive complaints from individuals regarding human rights violations. These bodies include the Committee on the Elimination of Racial Discrimination, created by the International Convention on the Elimination of All Forms of Racial Discrimination (1965); Human Rights Committee, established under the International Covenant on Civil and Political Rights (1966), with responsibilities also under its two optional protocols (1966 and 1989); Committee on the Elimination of Discrimination against Women, created by the Convention on the Elimination of All Forms of Discrimination against Women (1979); and Committee against Torture, created by the Convention against Torture and Other Cruel, Inhuman and Degrading Treatment or Punishment (1984).

Reporting alleged human rights violations to the proper authorities in a country is the first step in halting abuses and punishing offenders. In making such reports, individuals often need assistance, which can be obtained from government officials who have oversight responsibilities for those officials accused of wrongdoing; private nongovernmental organizations that act as watchdogs for the type of abuses alleged; and legal professionals. Victims can also take allegations of human rights violations to the media; journalists' stories may then bring charges to the attention of the government and the public. Depending on the country and the validity of the complaints, such reports may lead to justice for the victim.

At the regional and international levels, reports by individuals and groups are increasingly making a difference in the way countries implement human rights. The UN's charter-based system and the regional and global treaty-based systems are far from perfect, but the more they are used, the more familiar they become to the public and the better they will be. As the importance of human rights protection increases, new means for acting on reports of violations of human rights may also be developed.

African Commission on Human and Peoples' Rights, P.O. Box 673, Banjul, Gambia. (220-39-2962. 🖳 220-39-0764. 🖳 umn.edu/humanrts/Africa/Commission.

European Court of Human Rights, Council of Europe, F-67075 Strasbourg Cedex, France. (33-3-88-41-2018. 🖳 33-3-88-41-2730. 🖳 point_i@coe.int. 🖳 www.dhcour.coe.fr.

Human Rights Committee, Communications Branch, 8–14 avenue de la Paix, 1211 Geneva 10, Switzerland. (41-22-917-1234. 🖳 41-22-917-0123. 🖳 webadmin.hchr@un.org.ch. 🖳 www.unhchr.ch/htm/menu2/6/hrd.

Inter-American Commission on Human Rights, 1889 F Street, N.W., Washington, D.C. 20006. (202-458-6002. 🖳 202-458-3992. 🖳 cidhoea@oas.org. 🖳 cidh.oas.org.

Inter-American Court of Human Rights, P.O. Box 6906-1000, San José, Costa Rica. (506-234-0581. 🖳 506-234-0584. 🖳 corteidh@sol.racsa.co.cr. 🖳 corteidh-oea.nu.or.cr/ci/home_ing.

United Nations High Commissioner for Human Rights, 8–14 avenue de la Paix, 1211 Geneva 10, Switzerland. (41-22-917-9000. 🖳 41-22-917-9016. 🖳 webadmin.hchr@unog.ch. 🖳 www.unhchr.ch.

Kalichman, Seth C. *Mandated Reporting of Suspected Child Abuse: Ethics, Law, and Policy*. Washington, D.C.: American Psychological Association, 1993.

Manual on Human Rights Reporting: Under Six International Human Rights Instruments. Geneva: Office of the High Commissioner for Human Rights, 1997.

African Commission on Human and Peoples' Rights; Commission on Human Rights; Committee on the Elimination of Discrimination against Women; Committee on the Elimination of Racial Discrimination; Complaints; Convention against Torture and Other Cruel, Inhuman or Degrading Treatment or Punishment; Convention on the Elimination of All Forms of Discrimination against Women; Economic and Social Council (ECOSOC); European Court of Human Rights; Exhaustion of Remedies; Freedom House; High Commissioner for Human Rights; High Commissioner for Refugees; Human Rights Committee; International Convention on the Elimination of All Forms of Racial Discrimination; International Covenant on Civil and Political Rights; International Covenant on Civil and Political Rights, First Optional Protocol; Monitoring Compliance; Ombudsmen; Regional Human Rights Systems; Resolution 1503 Procedure; Subcommission on the Promotion and Protection of Human Rights; Violations; Victims

Reproduction

See Abortion; Maternity

Resolution 1503 Procedure

In 1970 the Economic and Social Council (ECOSOC) adopted Resolution 1503 to enable the Commission on Human Rights to investigate communications, or complaints, that "appear to reveal a consistent pattern of gross and reliably attested violations of human rights and fundamental freedoms." Informally known as the Resolution 1503 Procedure, the document and prior commission procedures represent an important process for bringing human rights violations to the attention of the nations involved as well as the world at large.

ECOSOC, which had established the commission in 1947, recognized that it had no authority to deal with specific complaints. Through Resolution 728F (1959), ECOSOC asked the UN secretary-general to compile a list of complaints for commission members to consult, although the body "had no power to take any action [on] any complaint concerning human rights." The secretary-general was also requested to "furnish each Member State concerned with a copy of any [such] communication . . . which refers explicitly to that State or to territories under its jurisdiction, without divulging the identity of the author [unless the author waived the right of confidentiality]." Governments that responded were asked "whether they wished their replies to be presented to the Commission in summary form or in full."

This procedure still applies to communications regarding human rights violations, but in 1967 ECOSOC took another step to extend the commission's power by passing Resolution 1235, which allows examination of allegations contained in the Resolution 728F complaints. Paragraph 2 of the new resolution expressly authorized the commission and its Subcommission on the Promotion and Protection of Human Rights "to examine information relevant to gross violations of human rights and fundamental freedoms, as exemplified by the policy of *apartheid* . . . , and to racial discrimination. . . ." Resolution 1235 also authorized the commission "in appropriate cases" to "make a thorough study of situations that reveal a consistent pattern of violations of human rights . . . and report, with recommendations thereon, to [ECOSOC]." Originally, countries specifically charged with human rights violations maintained that they could not be referred to by name in discussions, but by the 1970s both government and nongovernmental organization representatives were engaging in heated debate over such allegations and naming names.

The procedures established under Resolutions 728F and 1235, however, did not provide a way to analyze complaints in detail. In 1968 the subcommission thus suggested a three-step screening process involving a working group of the subcommission, the entire subcommission, and the commission. Resolution 1503, adopted in 1970, authorized this procedure. The combination of the procedures established under Resolutions 728F, 1235, and 1503 is now known as the 1503 Procedure.

According to paragraph 1 of Resolution 1503, the subcommission is granted authority by ECOSOC "to appoint a working group consisting of not more than five of its members, with due regard to geographical distribution. . . ." The group is "to meet once a year in private meetings . . . before the [subcommission's] sessions . . . to consider all communications . . ." and bring to the subcommission's attention those showing a pattern of "gross and reliably attested" human rights abuses.

Paragraph 2 directs the subcommission to devise "appropriate procedures for dealing with the question of the admissibility of [such] communications. . . ." Paragraph 4 requests that the secretary-general furnish subcommission members with monthly lists of complaints as authorized by Resolution 728F, together with brief descriptions and any government replies. Originals of the complaints are also to be made available to the working group and the subcommission as requested, without "divulging . . . the identity of the authors of communications."

Paragraph 5 charges the subcommission with considering in private meetings "the communications brought

before it in accordance with the decision of a majority of the members of the working group and any replies of Governments relating . . . thereto and other relevant information, with a view to determining whether to refer to the Commission on Human Rights particular situations which appear to reveal . . . violations of human rights. . . ."

Under paragraph 6, the Commission on Human Rights is requested to determine whether the matter "(a) . . . requires a thorough study by the Commission and a report and recommendations thereon to [ECOSOC] . . ." or "(b) . . . may be the subject of an investigation by an *ad hoc* committee. . . ." If the latter, the investigation is to be undertaken "only if: (i) [a]ll available means at the national level have been . . . exhausted; (ii) [t]he situation does not relate to a matter which is being dealt with under other procedures. . . ." Paragraph 7 deals with the composition, rules of procedure, and actions to be taken by the ad hoc investigating committee.

Paragraph 8 provides that all actions under the resolution are to "remain confidential until such time as the Commission may decide to make recommendations to [ECOSOC]." Paragraph 9 directs the secretary-general "to provide all facilities which may be required to carry out the present resolution . . . ," while paragraph 10 authorizes a review of the resolution's procedures in the event that "any new organ entitled to deal with such communications should be established within the United Nations or by international agreement."

In practice, the 1503 process takes at least a year to bring a matter to the commission's attention. The working group, whose five members represent different geographical regions, meets in secret session with UN support staff two weeks before the subcommission's session in August each year. The group must first sift through the previous year's more than twenty thousand communications, or as many as three hundred fifty thousand if there has been a postcard write-in campaign. Each member takes responsibility for one type of violation alleged, for example, personal abuse such as torture and arbitrary killing or race discrimination. A majority of the group must then vote on whether to recommend a complaint to the subcommission.

The complaints chosen are translated and sent to the subcommission with the working group's confidential report. The subcommission deliberates over them for two or three days and then decides by a majority vote which cases to forward to the commission, which also has its own working group of five members from different regions of the world. This group meets to prepare recommendations on how the communications selected should be handled by the commission.

At the full commission's session, each complaint is presented by the chair of the commission's working group or a special rapporteur (expert) appointed at the previous session to handle specific case types. The government against which the allegations are made is then permitted to respond, after which the commission votes on the working group's recommendation. Although it may decide to make a thorough study of a situation or to create an ad hoc fact-finding body to investigate allegations, either is rarely done. Instead, the commission directs written questions to the government concerned, sends a member or a UN staff person to make direct contact with the government, or takes the matter to the public-procedure stage; it may also postpone action or dismiss a complaint. At its public session the commission chair announces the status of its considerations, including whether a country's alleged violations are no longer under active consideration. Those situations still being actively reviewed are continued until the next year's session, at which time the commission follows up on them even if no new communications concerning the violations are received.

Using the 1503 Procedure, the commission so far has handled human rights violations in more than fifty countries. Although its ability to deal with these abuses is highly inefficient—given the difficulty of controlling sovereign governments and the international stigma of serious human rights violations—it is remarkable that the process spurred in 1959 by ECOSOC's Resolution 728F works at all.

United Nations High Commissioner for Human Rights, 8–14 avenue de la Paix, 1211 Geneva 10, Switzerland. ☎ 41-22-917-9000. 🖨 41-22-917-9016. 🖳 webadmin.hchr@unog.ch. 🖳 www.unhchr.ch.

Flood, Patrick James. *The Effectiveness of UN Human Rights Institutions*. Westport, Conn.: Praeger, 1998.

Commission on Human Rights; Complaints; Economic and Social Council (ECOSOC); Remedies; Reporting Violations; Subcommission on the Promotion and Protection of Human Rights; Working Groups

Retroactive Laws

The inherent unfairness of holding a person criminally responsible for an act not proscribed by law at the time it was committed seems obvious today. Because people have a duty to conform their behavior to existing law, punishing past legal behavior is unjust. But the absolute and arbitrary power of governments has often led to this clear infringement of the right to be treated only in accordance with due process of law.

Unjust retroactive laws or acts (from the Latin *retro*, meaning backwards or behind) punish or increase punishment for a crime. The basic legal rule regarding retroactive laws is expressed as *nullum poena sine lege* (Latin for

no punishment without a law). A 1668 report concerning religious persecutions in France noted: "They have given it a Retroactive Power (as they call it) by putting it in Execution against persons who returned to us a long time before the Declaration was in being."

In Anglo-American law, unjust retroactive laws are called ex post facto laws, meaning statutes enacted after the fact or after the occurrence of the proscribed behavior. Most national constitutions and many international human rights documents prohibit such laws. "No Bill of Attainder or ex post facto Law shall be passed," states the U.S. Constitution (1789), article I, section 9, paragraph 3. As upheld by the U.S. Supreme Court in 1798, the prohibition applies only to criminal laws and only to four basic types of law: ones that punish actions that were legal when they occurred, that increase the gravity of a crime, that increase the punishment for a crime, and that reduce the standards for admission of evidence against the accused.

In other areas of the world, such laws are called retroactive laws. The two terms are not identical. *Retroactive* has a wider scope and includes ex post facto laws. According to the European Court of Human Rights, the European Convention for the Protection of Human Rights and Fundamental Freedoms (1950) "is not confined to prohibiting the retrospective application of the criminal law to an accused's disadvantage; it also embodies, more generally, the principle that only the law can define a crime and prescribe a penalty . . . and the principle that the criminal law must not be extensively construed to the accused's detriment."

An ex post facto law, by definition, is detrimental to the accused, whereas a retroactive law can be beneficial—for example, one that decriminalizes an activity or reduces the penalty for a crime. Justice requires that any person who committed a crime should be entitled to any reduction in the penalty for such an offense while not being subject to any penalty increase enacted after the act was committed.

Constitution of Sweden, Instrument of Government (1975), chapter 2, Fundamental Rights and Freedoms, article 10: "No penalty or other penal sanction may be imposed in respect of an act which was not subject to any penal sanction at the time it was committed. Neither may a more severe penal sanction be imposed than that which was prescribed when the act was committed. The provisions thus laid down with respect to penal sanctions apply likewise with respect to confiscation or any other special legal effects attaching to criminal offenses."

American Convention on Human Rights (1969), article 9: "No one shall be convicted of any act or omission that did not constitute a criminal offense, under the applicable law, at the time it was committed. A heavier penalty shall not be imposed than the one that was applicable at the time the criminal offense was committed. If subsequent to the commission of the offense the law provides for the imposition of a lighter punishment, the guilty person shall benefit therefrom."

U.S. Supreme Court (1810): Holding that valid contracts cannot subsequently be rescinded by a legislative act, the Court stated that "if an act be done under a law, a succeeding legislature cannot undo it. . . . When, then, a law is in its nature a contract, when absolute rights have vested under that contract, a repeal of the law [on which those rights are based] cannot divest those rights. . . ."

Human Rights Committee (1994): A widower in the Netherlands retroactively sought benefits when it was determined that under the International Covenant on Civil and Political Rights (1966) the nation could not restrict such benefits to widows. "[A]rticle 26 does not of itself require States parties either to provide social security benefits or to provide them retroactively in respect of the date of application," said the committee. "However, when such beneifts are regulated by law, then such law must comply with article 26 of the Covenant [mandating equality]."

Teitel, Ruti. *Transitional Justice*. New York: Oxford University Press, 1999.

Troy, Daniel E. *Retroactive Legislation*. Washington, D.C.: American Enterprise Institute, 1998.

Accused; Due Process of Law; Fair Trial; Punishment

Rights

The term *right* is legally defined as something a person is entitled to have, to do, or to receive from others within the limits prescribed by law. In the abstract, *right* means justice, ethical correctness, or consonance with the rules of law or moral principles. More concretely, a right connotes one person's power, privilege, faculty, or demand that depends on or requires recognition or action on the part of another. The English word *right* is derived from Old English; in French it is *droit*; in German, *Recht*; and in Spanish, *derecho*.

Although people on occasion may resort to the principle that "might makes right," in a social or a political context one person's physical strength does not guarantee him or her any more rights than another. Rights are generally determined by laws, moral codes, and custom and tradition. Perhaps the first right any person should have is information about legal and societal laws so that he or she can determine his or her other rights. The laws of Solon, the sixth-century B.C.E. Athenian leader, were carved in stone and set in a prominent place to make them accessible to all Athenians.

Civil, political, and property rights have been recognized to some degree in all human civilizations, but in most cases only a select few had them. Rights were often accorded on the basis of a hierarchical social and political order, with a ruler and an aristocracy at the top and male commoners further down. Women and slaves were at the bottom or completely excluded from the rights pyramid. Partly as a result of Christianity's position that all souls are equal before God, the notion that all human beings are equal, at least in the political and legal sense, began to develop in Europe in the Middle Ages. Thereafter, the theory of natural law (law that transcends the will of the rulers of nations), the principle of national sovereignty, and, by extension, the principle of popular sovereignty (the will of the people), as espoused by the eighteenth-century French philosopher Jean-Jacques Rousseau, created an intellectual basis for rights of the people in addition to their traditional duties as subjects or citizens. This concept of peoples' rights and individual rights found expression in such documents as the U.S. Declaration of Independence (1776) and France's Declaration of the Rights of Man and of the Citizen (1789), promulgated during the French Revolution.

A human right is one a person has by virtue of being born, regardless of race, color, sex, national origin, property ownership, social status, or any other consideration. Such rights are inherent in individuals' relationship to their government; they are not rights vis-à-vis other individuals, except to the extent that another individual tries to deny a person the ability to exercise those rights. Rights may be substantive, such as freedom of speech or the right to social security benefits, or they may be procedural, concerned with the mechanisms for enforcing other rights, such as obtaining a writ of habeas corpus from a court to enforce a person's right to liberty.

Other rights in addition to human rights include property rights, which determine who is entitled to have possession of a piece of real or personal property. Development rights grant the authority to exploit certain property and economic interests, among them mining rights, concessions, and franchise rights. Contractual rights are terms that people voluntarily decide to observe through a binding agreement. Legal rights may stem from common usage or written laws and give people a means of protecting themselves or of recovering damages for wrongs done to them. Classical definitions of rights and human rights are being stretched ever further almost daily, as new rights—victims' rights, taxpayers' rights, patients' rights, grandparents' rights, airline passengers' rights, and even animal rights—are being demanded, especially in the United States.

Rights may be established in a number of ways: by contract, by custom and tradition, by law or regulation, and by sufferance, that is, by allowing a person or a group to assert a right without challenge. Correlative duties often accompany rights. For example, a buyer's right under a contract for delivery of goods carries with it the buyer's duty to pay on delivery the price bargained for.

Rights may be positive or negative. A negative right requires the government, an individual, or a legal entity such as a corporation to refrain from doing something. Freedom of religion, for one, requires the state not to interfere beyond some minimal level with a person's peaceful religious observances. A positive right requires the government, a person, or a legal entity to take action permitting the right holder to obtain some objective. The right of citizens to obtain social security requires the government to collect money and establish a bureaucracy to pay benefits to those who are entitled to it.

A government may violate the rights of citizens by failing to guarantee or enforce their rights as established by law. In addition, a person may abuse a right by using it to the detriment of others. The right of peaceful assembly, for instance, does not permit those exercising it to trespass on private property or harass other citizens in the process. In any case, the fact that a right is declared does not necessarily mean that there is an effective remedy for its denial.

Constitution of Poland (1997), chapter two, Freedoms, Rights and Duties of Man and Citizens, General Principles, article 30: "The natural and inalienable dignity of the human being constitutes the source of the freedoms and rights of man and citizen."

Charter 77 (Czechoslovakia) (1977), [paragraph 2]: "The rights and freedoms of everyone, which are guaranteed by [the International Covenant on Civil and Political Rights (1966) and the International Covenant on Economic, Social and Cultural Rights (1966)] are important values for civilization for which the efforts of many progressive forces have been directed in history, and their statement in law can significantly assist human development in our society."

U.S. Supreme Court (1883): A federal civil rights law based on the Fourteenth Amendment (1868) made no mention of individual persons who might infringe on individual rights. Therefore, if a state of the United States "does not assist the discrimination of an individual against another individual, it is purely a matter between the two individuals."

European Court of Human Rights (1994): "The issue before the Court involves weighing . . . the conflicting interests of the exercise of . . . the right of the applicant association to impart to the public controversial views and, by implication, the right of interested persons to take cognizance of such views, on the one hand, and the right of other persons to proper respect for their freedom of thought, conscience and religion, on the other hand."

Jones, Peter. *Rights*. New York: St. Martin's, 1994.

Nino, Carlos S., ed. *Rights*. New York: New York University Press, 1992.

Civil Rights; Collective Rights; Cultural Rights; Declaration of Independence (United States); Declaration of the Rights of Man and of the Citizen (France); Economic Rights; Human Rights; Limitations; Natural Rights; Political Rights; Property; Remedies; Rousseau, Jean-Jacques; Social Rights; Violations; *and other specific rights*

Rights International

Rights International is a nonprofit organization that sues foreign governments before international tribunals on behalf of people throughout the world whose rights have been violated by their governments. The organization's goals include protecting its clients' rights and advancing the development of case law on human rights under international instruments such as the Universal Declaration of Human Rights (1948).

Founded in 1994 by its president, Francisco Forrest Martin, and other lawyers and policy analysts, Rights International carries out its mission by bringing actions for injunctive relief and money damages in response to abuses such as torture, censorship, police mistreatment, disappearances, and discrimination based on race, sex, sexual orientation, and religion. Its actions are brought in forums including the African Commission on Human and Peoples' Rights, European Court of Human Rights, Human Rights Committee, Inter-American Commission on Human Rights, and Inter-American Court of Human Rights. These forums are the courts of last resort for people whose rights have been violated in their own countries, because complainants must have exhausted all possible domestic remedies. More than a hundred nations now recognize the jurisdiction of these tribunals, making them increasingly significant venues for adjudication of human rights cases.

To promote training for lawyers and law students, Rights International has published several books on the law of human rights practice and established a law school consortium program and legal directors committee so that law students can participate in human rights cases. Faculty members of law schools, including American University, New York University, Rutgers University, and the University of Miami, have joined the program. The organization also collaborates with and assists human rights advocates by providing legal help and continuing legal education programs in international human rights law. Model human rights briefs and a research guide to resources are available for human rights litigators at its Web site.

Rights International, Center for International Human Rights Law, 600 Biltmore Way, No.1117, Coral Gables, Fla. 33134. (305-446-7334. 🖷 305-446-7334. 🖳 ricenter@rightsinternational.org. 🖳 www.rightsinternational.org.

Rights International, Center for International Human Rights Law. *International Human Rights Law and Practice*. 2 vols. The Hague: Kluwer Law International, 1997.

African Commission on Human and Peoples' Rights; Counsel; European Court of Human Rights; Exhaustion of Remedies; Human Rights Committee; Inter-American Commission on Human Rights; Inter-American Court of Human Rights; Lawyers Committee for Human Rights; Regional Human Rights Systems; Remedies; Reporting Violations; Victims; Violations

Rio Declaration on Environment and Development

The UN Conference on Environment and Development, which was held from June 3 to June 14, 1992, in Rio de Janeiro, Brazil, was one of the major international events of the 1990s. Although not everyone was satisfied with the outcome, the conference highlighted the urgent need for scientific and political strategies to avert global environmental disasters. An important concern was the "greenhouse effect," the atmospheric buildup of heat-retaining gases such as carbon dioxide that could raise regional and global temperatures and cause extreme or disastrous consequences for the world's environment.

The Rio Declaration on Environment and Development, adopted at the conference, encompasses twenty-six principles for promoting sustainable development and a healthy environment. Sustainable development is growth that avoids destruction of the Earth's vital nonrenewable elements and thus protects the life-sustaining environment needed for present and future generations. Because such environmentally sensitive development can add restrictions and costs, it raises different issues in developing and developed countries.

In principle 1, the declaration observes: "Human beings are at the center of concerns for sustainable development. They are entitled to a healthy and productive life in harmony with nature." Principle 2 notes that the nations of the world "have, in accordance with the Charter of the United Nations [1945] and the principles of international law, the sovereign right to exploit their own resources pursuant to their own environmental and developmental policies, and the responsibility to ensure that activities within their jurisdiction or control do not cause damage to the environment of other States or of areas beyond the limits of national jurisdiction."

"The right to development must be fulfilled so as to equitably meet developmental and environmental needs of present and future generations," states principle 3. According to principle 4, "In order to achieve sustainable development, environmental protection shall constitute an integral part of the development process and cannot be considered in isolation from it. All States and all people," adds principle 5, "shall cooperate in the essential task of eradicating poverty as an indispensable requirement for sustainable development, in order to decrease the disparities in standards of living and better meet the needs of the majority of the people of the world." Principle 6 refers to "[t]he special situation and needs of developing countries, particularly the least developed and those most environmentally vulnerable," urging special priority for these areas.

Principle 7 requires that "States shall cooperate in a spirit of global partnership to conserve, protect and restore the health and integrity of the Earth's ecosystem"; and principle 8 declares: "To achieve sustainable development and a higher quality of life for all people, States should reduce and eliminate unsustainable patterns of production and consumption and promote appropriate demographic policies." Principles 9, 10, and 11, respectively, address the use of science and technology; the importance of the "participation of all concerned citizens, at the relevant [national and community] level" in the handling of environmental issues; and the role of environmental laws, standards, management objectives, and priorities. "States shall enact effective environmental legislation," demands principle 11.

The remaining principles deal with, among other things, cooperation by the states "to promote a supportive and open international economic system"; the use of "environmental impact assessment" for proposed activities; notification regarding natural disasters; the vital role of women, youth, and indigenous peoples "in environmental management and development"; and the peaceful resolution of environmental disputes "by appropriate means in accordance with the Charter of the United Nations." The declaration also observes, in principle 24, that "[w]arfare is inherently destructive of sustainable development. States shall therefore respect international law providing protection for the environment in times of armed conflict and cooperate in its further development, as necessary."

United Nations Environment Program, P.O. Box 30552, Nairobi, Kenya. ☎ 254-2-62-3074. 🖨 254-2-62-3927. ✉ eisin@unep.org. 🖥 www.unep.org.

Convention Concerning the Protection of the World Cultural and Natural Heritage; Development; Environment

Riyadh Guidelines

See Guidelines for the Prevention of Juvenile Delinquency

Rome Statute of the International Criminal Court

The Rome Statute of the International Criminal Court was adopted by 120 nations on July 17, 1998. The most recent in a long line of international treaties attempting to deal with crimes against the law of nations, such as genocide, the statute creates a permanent international court to prosecute gross violations of human rights. The International Criminal Court will be formally established, however, only after sixty countries ratify the statute. By 2000 ninety-five nations had signed the document, but only seven had ratified it.

The UN General Assembly first recognized the need for an international criminal court in a resolution adopted in 1948 and invited the International Law Commission "to study the desirability and possibility of establishing an international judicial organ for the trial of persons charged with genocide. . . ." The commission endorsed the idea, and a committee created by the General Assembly produced drafts of a statute creating such a court in 1951 and 1953. However, no action was taken on the proposal, although the matter was considered periodically.

In 1989 the General Assembly requested that the International Law Commission renew its efforts to establish the proposed court, with jurisdiction over crimes of drug trafficking as well. In 1993, when the conflict in Yugoslavia resulted in charges of war crimes and crimes against humanity, including genocide in the form of ethnic cleansing, the UN Security Council created an ad hoc International Criminal Tribunal to deal with such matters. The following year the law commission submitted its draft statute to the General Assembly, which assigned a committee the task of preparing a consolidated draft for submission to the Diplomatic Conference of Plenipotentiaries on the Establishment of an International Criminal Court. This conference, which met in Rome from June 15 to July 17, 1998, adopted the draft, from then on known as the Rome Statute.

The preamble to the statute, acknowledging "that all peoples are united by common bonds, their cultures pieced together in a shared heritage, . . . that this delicate mosaic may be shattered at any time, . . . [and] that during this century millions of children, women and men have been victims of unimaginable atrocities that deeply shock the conscience of humanity . . . ," expresses a determination "to put an end to impunity for the perpetrators of these crimes and thus to contribute to the prevention of such crimes. . . ."

Part 1, Establishment of the Court, article 1, creates an International Criminal Court, which "shall be a permanent institution and shall have the power to exercise its jurisdiction over persons for the most serious crimes of international concern, as referred to in this Statute, and shall be complementary to national criminal jurisdictions. The jurisdiction and functioning of the Court shall be governed by the provisions of this Statute." Article 2 deals with the court's relationship to the United Nations, while article 3 stipulates that "[t]he seat of the Court shall be established at The Hague in the Netherlands ('the host State')." According to article 4, "The Court shall have international legal personality . . . [and] may exercise its functions and powers . . . on the territory of any State Party and, by special agreement, on the territory of any other State."

Part 2, Jurisdiction, Admissibility and Applicable Law, article 5, establishes the court's jurisdiction with respect to "(a) [t]he crime of genocide; (b) [c]rimes against humanity; (c) [w]ar crimes; [and] (d) [t]he crime of aggression." Articles 6, 7, and 8, respectively, define genocide, crimes against humanity, and war crimes. According to article 9, guidelines called Elements of Crimes to assist the court "shall be adopted by a two-thirds majority of the members of the Assembly of States Parties." Amendments to the Elements of Crimes may be proposed by any state party, the judges "acting by an absolute majority," or the prosecutor. Article 11 restricts the court's jurisdiction to crimes committed "after entry into force of this Statute" or later for a state that becomes a party after the statute's entry into force, unless the state makes a declaration otherwise, as provided in article 12.

Article 13 states that the court "may exercise its jurisdiction with respect to a crime referred to in article 5 in accordance with the provisions of this Statute" if the alleged crimes are referred to the prosecutor by a state party or by the UN Security Council or if the prosecutor has initiated "an investigation in respect of such crime in accordance with article 15." Pursuant to article 14, a state party to the statute can refer crimes to be tried by the court. Article 15 specifies that the court prosecutor "may initiate investigations [on his or her own motion] on the basis of information on crimes within the jurisdiction of the Court."

Articles 17, 18, and 19 address issues of admissibility of a case before the court. A case may be declared inadmissible if it is "being investigated or prosecuted by a State which has jurisdiction over it, unless the State is unwilling or unable genuinely to carry out the investigation or prosecution" or if it is "not of sufficient gravity to justify further action by the Court."

Article 20 prohibits double jeopardy, or a second trial for the same crime. According to article 21, "The Court shall apply: (a) In the first place, this Statute, Elements of Crimes and its Rules of Procedure and Evidence; (b) In the second place, where appropriate, applicable treaties and principles and rules of international law, including the established principles of the international law of armed conflict"; and "(c) . . . other general principles of law. . . ."

Part 3, which begins with article 22, sets forth the general principles of criminal law applicable to the court, while part 4 describes the composition and administration of the court. Part 10, article 103, delineates the role of the states in enforcing sentences of imprisonment, and article 111 deals with the escape of convicted persons from the custody and jurisdiction of the "State of enforcement."

Coalition for an International Criminal Court, 777 United Nations Plaza, New York, N.Y. 10017. (212-678-2176. 📠 212-599-1332. 🖳 cicc@igc.org. 🖳 www.igc.org/icc.

Bassiouni, M. Cherif. *The Statute of the International Criminal Court: A Documentary History.* Ardsley, N.Y.: Transnational, 1998.

Lee, Roy S., ed. *The International Criminal Court: The Making of the Rome Statute—Issues, Negotiations, Results.* The Hague: Kluwer Law International, 1999.

Crimes against Humanity; Genocide; Impunity; International Criminal Court; International Law; Violations; War Crimes

Romero, Oscar

Considered a conservative early in his vocation as a Roman Catholic priest, Oscar Romero (1917–80) experienced a change of heart after working with the poor and landless people of El Salvador. Later an archbishop, he became known as the "Voice of the Voiceless" as a result of his preaching and radio broadcasts against violence, abuse, and injustice. For his efforts on behalf of human rights in Latin America, he was nominated for the Nobel Peace Prize, but opponents soon silenced him by assassination.

Oscar Arnulfo Romero y Galdámez, born on August 15, 1917, in El Salvador, was apprenticed to a carpenter at the age of thirteen. A year later, however, he decided to become a priest, leaving home to study in his country and later in Rome. Ordained in 1942, he was first assigned to a parish in San Miguel, El Salvador.

During the 1960s the Roman Catholic Church in Latin America came to a crossroads. Many regional bishops began to abandon the Church's traditional role in maintaining the extreme inequality of life between the small number of rich landowners and the masses of poor people striving for social and economic justice. In 1970 Romero was elevated to the Church hierarchy as an auxiliary bishop and four years later was posted to the poor rural diocese of Santiago de María. While serving there he began to question his own leanings.

Romero's appointment as archbishop in 1977 was probably based on his reputation as one who would not challenge the status quo, but to the surprise of many he grew into a champion of the poor and oppressed. After the assassination of a close Jesuit friend, Romero became more outspoken, attracting throngs to the cathedral and many thousands more to their radios to hear him preach. He denounced the violence of El Salvador's civil war and the injustice being done to the poor. As archbishop, Romero was able to get his message out even though the government tried to label all dissent as treasonous.

The repressive Salvadoran government was overthrown by a military junta in 1979, but the plight of the oppressed continued. Early in 1980 Romero sent a letter to President Jimmy Carter, begging him to cease arming the military regime. On March 24, while conducting mass in a small chapel in San Salvador, Romero was gunned down by soldiers. "As a Christian, I do not believe in death without resurrection," he once remarked in anticipation that his human rights crusade might bring his death. "If they kill me, I shall arise in the Salvadoran people."

Eaton, Helen May. *Authority and the Role of Archbishop Oscar A. Romero in the Struggle for the Liberation of the Salvadoran People.* San Salvador: Editorial Guayampopo, 1994.

Marie, Dennis. *A Retreat with Oscar Romero and Dorothy Day: Walking with the Poor.* Cincinnati: St. Anthony Messenger, 1997.

Carter, James Earl; Economic Rights

Roosevelt, Eleanor

The niece of Theodore Roosevelt and the wife of Franklin D. Roosevelt, both presidents of the United States, Anna Eleanor Roosevelt (1884–1962) championed human rights causes throughout her life. As chair of the Commission on Human Rights from 1946 to 1952, she played a key role in drafting the ground-breaking Universal Declaration of Human Rights (1948).

Born in New York City on October 11, 1884, Roosevelt was sent to live with her maternal grandmother at the age of eight, when her mother died. At fifteen she entered a finishing school in South Fields, England, where she was inspired by the ideal of social service and responsibility. A shy and insecure girl, she worked for social agencies in New York City until her marriage to her cousin Franklin D. Roosevelt in 1905.

The mother of five children, Roosevelt helped rehabilitate her husband when he lost the use of his legs after contracting polio in 1921. A former state senator and an assistant secretary of the navy in President Woodrow Wilson's cabinet, Franklin pursued his political career, while Eleanor began working, in her disabled husband's behalf, with the League of Women Voters, National Consumers' League, Women's Trade Union League, and New York State Democratic Party. With Eleanor's help, Franklin was elected governor of New York in 1929.

When her husband won the presidency in 1932, Eleanor

continued to act as his eyes and ears, traveling extensively around the country. She also began writing syndicated newspaper columns and giving radio broadcasts, donating the income to charity. An outspoken critic of the rising tide of fascism, she was appointed by her husband deputy director of the Office of Civilian Defense during World War II. Later she traveled overseas to boost troop morale and inspect Red Cross operations.

After Franklin Roosevelt's death in 1945, President Harry S. Truman appointed Eleanor as the U.S. representative to the Commission on Human Rights, which made her its chair the following year. Her personal stature and America's victorious role in World War II undoubtedly influenced the sweeping and progressive language of the Universal Declaration of Human Rights, which was drafted, after much deliberation, under her leadership in 1948. At a crucial juncture in the drafting process, urging delegates "not to let words interfere with getting as much agreement as possible," she endorsed the use of the phrase *are born free and equal* rather than *are created* in article 1 of the declaration to placate the communist representatives. She also served as U.S. ambassador to the United Nations, adviser to the Peace Corps, and chair of the President's Commission on the Status of Women before her death in 1962.

Overcoming many obstacles, not the least of which was being the wife of one of America's greatest politicians, Eleanor Roosevelt was a major force for international human rights. She was nominated for the Nobel Peace Prize—President John F. Kennedy wrote on her behalf to the Nobel committee that she was "a living symbol of world understanding and peace" and her efforts "a vital part of the historical fabric of this century"—and was posthumously awarded the first Human Rights Prize by the UN. In her last speech at the United Nations (she resigned in 1953), Eleanor Roosevelt made an impassioned plea for expanding women's rights: "What I am talking about is whether women are sharing in the direction of the policy-making in their countries; whether they have the opportunities to serve as chairmen of important committees, and as cabinet members and delegates to the UN."

In 1998, in recognition of the fiftieth anniversary of the Universal Declaration of Human Rights, the Franklin and Eleanor Roosevelt Institute began an initiative to urge all countries to ratify UN human rights treaties and improve the protection of fundamental rights and freedoms for every person around the world.

Black, Allida M., ed. *Courage in a Dangerous World: The Political Writings of Eleanor Roosevelt.* New York: Columbia University Press, 1999.

Sears, John F., ed. *Eleanor Roosevelt and the Universal Declaration of Human Rights: An Agenda for Action in 1988.* Hyde Park, N.Y.: Franklin and Eleanor Roosevelt Institute, 1988.

Franklin and Eleanor Roosevelt Institute, 4079 Albany Post Road, Hyde Park, N.Y. 11238. (914-229-5321. 914-229-9046. emurphy@idsi.net. www.feri.org.

Commission on Human Rights; Red Cross and Red Crescent; Universal Declaration of Human Rights

Rousseau, Jean-Jacques

The impact on political thought of Jean-Jacques Rousseau (1712–78), one of the most influential political philosophers in history, has been felt around the world. Rousseau's simple but profound concept of a social contract between rulers and the ruled based on the inherent sovereignty of the people, rather than monarchs, has greatly contributed to the development of constitutional democracies and individual human rights and fundamental freedoms. His progressive ideals have formed the foundations of many national constitutions and theories of human rights.

Born on June 28, 1712, in Geneva (his mother died nine days later), Rousseau was raised by his father, who believed that Geneva was a republic as fine as ancient Sparta or Rome. When his father was forced to leave Geneva to avoid imprisonment for brandishing a sword, Rousseau went to live with his mother's family. At sixteen he too left Geneva to seek his fortune in Sardinia and later in France.

With the baronne de Warens, in the province of Savoy, as his benefactor, Rousseau began a wide-ranging education. A man of paradoxical genius, he wrote operas, novels, and entries for Denis Diderot's famous *Encyclopédie* in the 1750s in addition to works of philosophy. A consistent theme throughout his writings was that a social order based on the ownership of private property produced inequality and unhappiness.

In *Emile: Or, On Education* (1762), Rousseau set out his progressive ideas about education. The same year he published his most influential work, *The Social Contract,* in which he developed the concepts of popular, as opposed to monarchial, sovereignty and the people's will. Citizens should create the laws as well as follow them, he argued, and government should be an instrument for translating the people's will into action.

Other philosophers and writers, including Immanuel Kant and Leo Tolstoy, and political activists such as the French revolutionary Maximilien François Marie Isidore de Robespierre were particularly influenced by Rousseau's ideas. His thoughts later shaped much of the democratic movement that swept through Europe after the French Revolution of 1789 and are reflected in the 1814 Norwegian and 1831 Belgium constitutions, both of which remain in force today. Although Rousseau's broad view of democratic government was not universally adopted, his enlightened ideas on fundamental rights and equality are enshrined in many democratic constitutional documents. Rousseau died on July 2, 1778, in a hospital near Paris, eleven years before the French Revolution began.

Cranston, Maurice W. *The Solitary Self: Jean-Jacques Rousseau in Exile and Adversity*. Chicago: University of Chicago Press, 1997.

Orwin, Clifford, and Nathan Tarcov. *The Legacy of Rousseau*. Chicago: University of Chicago Press, 1997.

Civil Rights; Constitutional Rights; Constitutionalism; Democracy; Equality; Fundamental Rights; Political Rights; Property; Sovereignty

Rule of Law

"When we say that the supremacy or the rule of law is a characteristic of the English constitution," wrote the British constitutional scholar A.V. Dicey in *Law of Constitution* (1885), ". . . [w]e mean, in the first place, that no man is punishable . . . except for a distinct breach of law established in the ordinary legal manner before the ordinary courts of the land." A key element of constitutional democracy, the rule of law (from the Latin *regula,* meaning a rule for measuring) has important implications for human rights because it ensures fairness and equality before the law for all persons.

A distinction is made between *a rule of law* (a valid legal principle) and *the rule of law* (the concept that the exercise of executive political power must conform to general principles as administered by the courts). The rule of law, as opposed to a rule of law, is therefore a term of art in constitutional law, encompassing the concept of constitutionalism that underlies modern democratic government. Some elements of the rule of law, however, may be found in nondemocratic societies and in past history.

The *law of the state* and *a state of laws* should also be distinguished. The United States before the Civil War and Nazi Germany in the 1930s and 1940s legally condoned slavery, inhumane treatment, and torture of people within their jurisdiction as the law of the state. However, a state of laws (a nation under the rule of law) restricts what the government may or may not legalize. Civil and political rights may not be denied to anyone in a state of laws, except when an impartial and independent judicial system finds a breach of a law that applies to all persons equally.

Often considered an Anglo-American concept, the rule of law most likely originated in medieval times when the law of God was believed to rule the world. Later, the no-tion became embodied in the theory of natural law, which was thought to be so fundamental and unalterable that even sovereign governments were subject to it. By providing a stable system of protection for some individual rights against a monarch's arbitrary power, including impartial courts that took the place of personal revenge, English common law gave rise to the rule of law. The early-eighteenth-century French jurist Montesquieu furthered the concept in Europe by insisting on a constitutional system that proscribes government control of individual rights, such as religious beliefs and the expression of public opinion. Government, he reasoned, must be limited, subject to the law, and treat everyone within its jurisdiction justly and fairly.

A constitution establishing a constitutional democracy is of little value in a society where the rule of law is not observed. Human rights are furthered where the rule of law creates a consensus that persons will be governed by constitutionally enacted law and not by individuals; where the law applies to all persons equally, including those who govern; where the laws are enforced swiftly and without discrimination; where justice is dispensed by objective officials who base decisions only on existing laws that are publicly known; and where those charged with enforcing and applying the law are accountable for their actions.

The rule of law is also essential in those areas where rights conflict. Limitations on rights should be kept to a minimum and not expanded in a way that erodes the core of those rights—free speech, for example, is not truly free if someone who is offended can silence another speaker. The rule of law additionally implies that existing legal concepts will be used to interpret new laws. Predictability, stability, accountability, fairness, competence, impartiality, equality, due process of law, and giving the benefit of the doubt to the individual over the state are all hallmarks of the rule of law.

Constitution of Bulgaria (1991), chapter I, Fundamental Principles, article 4(1): "The Republic of Bulgaria is a state based on the rule of law."

European Convention for the Protection of Human Rights and Fundamental Freedoms (1950): "[T]he Governments of European countries which are like-minded and have a common heritage of political traditions, ideals, freedom and the rule of law, [are resolved] to take the first steps for the collective enforcement of certain of the rights stated in the Universal Declaration [of Human Rights (1948)]."

Council of Europe, Report on Russia's Request for Membership (1996): "[T]he Chairman of the President's Human Rights Commission . . . explained the general lack of respect for the rule of law as follows: '. . . The cause lies not only, or not so much, in ill will from the part of the authorities, whether local or federal. Nor does the problem lie merely in unsatisfactory laws. It is rooted [above] all in the extremely low level of legal awareness both of authorities and of the people. . . . What purpose is served by good laws if the people are incapable of ascertaining them and unaccustomed to doing so?"

Supreme Court of Canada (1985): The constitution of the province of Manitoba required all legislation to be enacted in both French and English, but since 1890 legislation had been enacted only in English. The supreme court, rather than invalidate all the laws of Manitoba enacted since 1890, found that "the rule of law requires the creation and maintenance of an actual order of positive laws which preserves and embodies the more general principle of normative order. Law and order are indispensable elements of civilized life. . . . The rule of law simply cannot be fulfilled in a province that has no positive law." Therefore, the laws of Manitoba enacted unconstitutionally since 1890 were not invalid.

European Court of Justice (1991): "[T]he EEC [European Economic Community] Treaty, albeit concluded in the form of an international agreement, none the less constitutes the constitutional charter of a Community based on the rule of law."

Center for the Independence of Judges and Lawyers, avenue de Châtelaine 81A, P.O. Box 216, 1219 Châtelaine/Geneva, Switzerland. (41-22-979-3800. 🖷 41-22-979-3801. 🖳 info@icj.org. 🖳 www.icj.org.

International Commission of Jurists, 26 chemin de Joinville, P.O. Box 160, 1216 Geneva, Switzerland. (41-22-788-4747. 🖷 41-22-788-4880. 🖳 info@icj.org. 🖳 www.icj.org.

International Rule of Law Center, The George Washington University Law School, 720 20th Street, N.W., Washington, D.C. 20052. (202-994-7242. 🖷 202-994-9446. 🖳 sjoshi@main.nic.gwu.edu. 🖳 www.law.gwu/edu/acad/irlc.

Brownlie, Ian. *The Rule of Law in International Affairs: International Law at the Fiftieth Anniversary of the United Nations.* The Hague: Martinus Nijhoff, Kluwer Law International, 1998.

Tremblay, Luc B. *The Rule of Law, Justice, and Interpretation.* Montreal: McGill-Queen's University Press, 1997.

Walker, Geoffrey de Q. *The Rule of Law: Foundation of Constitutional Democracy.* Carlton, Victoria, Australia: Melbourne University Press, 1988.

Constitutionalism; Due Process of Law; International Commission of Jurists; Judicial Independence; Justice; Limitations

Rules for the Protection of Juveniles Deprived of Their Liberty

The rights of adults accused, prosecuted, and convicted of crimes and subsequently imprisoned have been protected for centuries in national constitutions and laws as well as international and regional human rights documents. Magna Carta (1215), for example, provided that every "free man" in England would not be arrested or imprisoned "except by the lawful judgment of his peers or by the law of the land." With the expansion of human rights since the end of World War II, children and young people have also benefited. Recent requirements that juvenile offenders be afforded special treatment are rooted in the fact that young people are still developing morally and socially, so that every effort should be made to give them a chance to become law-abiding adult citizens despite mistakes made during adolescence.

On the recommendation of the Seventh United Nations Congress on the Prevention of Crime and the Treatment of Offenders, the UN General Assembly in 1985 adopted the Standard Minimum Rules for the Administration of Juvenile Justice (Beijing Rules). On the recommendation of the eighth congress on the subject, the General Assembly adopted two related documents on the same day, December 14, 1990: Rules for the Protection of Juveniles Deprived of Their Liberty, which "are designed to serve as convenient standards of reference and to provide encouragement and guidance to professionals involved in the management of the juvenile justice system," as well as Guidelines for the Prevention of Juvenile Delinquency (Riyadh Guidelines), which encourage governments to keep young people from being imprisoned for crimes in the first place.

"The juvenile justice system should uphold the rights and safety and promote the physical and mental well-being of juveniles," declares part I, Fundamental Perspectives, paragraph 1. "Imprisonment should be used as a last resort." Paragraph 2 recommends that juveniles be deprived of their liberty only in accordance with the principles and procedures set forth in these rules and the Standard Minimum Rules for the Administration of Juvenile Justice. "Deprivation of the liberty of a juvenile should be a disposition of last resort and for the minimum necessary period and should be limited to exceptional cases," it states. "The length of the sanction should be determined by the judicial authority, without precluding the possibility of his or her early release."

"The Rules," notes paragraph 3, "are intended to establish minimum standards accepted by the United Nations for the protection of juveniles deprived of their liberty. . . ." Paragraph 4 requires that the rules "be applied impartially, without discrimination of any kind as to race, color, sex, age, language, religion, nationality, political or other opinion, cultural beliefs or practices, property, birth or family status, ethnic or social origin, and disability." Paragraph 6 provides that young people "who are not fluent in the language spoken by the personnel of the detention facility should have the right to the services of an interpreter free of charge whenever necessary, in particular during medical examinations and disciplinary proceedings."

More administrative items address, among other things, translation of the rules into national languages for juvenile justice personnel, incorporation of the rules into national legislation, remedies for breach of the rules, increasing public awareness of the rules, the relevancy of other human rights instruments, and the primacy of the requirements of this section over the remainder of the rules.

Under part II, Scope and Application of the Rules, paragraph 11 defines *juveniles* as "every person under the age of 18" and states that the "age limit below which it should not be permitted to deprive a child of his or her liberty should be determined by law." Deprivation of liberty is defined as "any form of detention or imprisonment or the placement of a person in a public or private custodial setting, from which this person is not permitted to leave at will, by order of any judicial, administrative or other authority." According to paragraph 15, the rules "apply to all types and forms of detention facilities in which juveniles are deprived of their liberty."

Part III, Juveniles under Arrest or Awaiting Trial, paragraph 17, extends the right of the presumption of innocence to juveniles "who are detained under arrest or awaiting trial ('untried')," adding that detention before trial "shall be avoided to the extent possible and limited to exceptional circumstances." Paragraph 18 specifies that detainees should have a right to legal counsel, including free legal aid; opportunities to work or continue their education or training; and receive "materials for their leisure and recreation as are compatible with the interests of the administration of justice."

Part IV, The Management of Juvenile Facilities, paragraph 19, requires juvenile records to be kept confidential, and upon a juvenile offender's release "the records . . . shall be sealed, and, at an appropriate time, expunged." Information that should be maintained on detained juveniles, according to paragraph 21, includes his or her identity; the fact of and reasons for commitment; the day and hour of admission, transfer, and release; details regarding notification of parents and guardians; and information on known physical and mental health problems, including drug and alcohol abuse.

Detailed guidelines are also provided for classification and placement of offenders, the physical environment and accommodations, education, training and work, recreation, religion, medical care, notification of illness or death, contacts with the community, physical restraint and the use of force, disciplinary procedures, inspections and complaints, and return to the community. Some of the rights enumerated include the right of separation from adults in detention facilities, unless they are members of the same family; health and human dignity; privacy; clean sleeping accommodations; use of detainees' own clothing and personal effects; and "food that is suitably prepared and presented at normal meal times and of a quality and quantity to satisfy the standards of dietetics, hygiene and health." During confinement, juveniles should also have the right to education, a suitable amount of recreation, a religious and spiritual life, and "adequate medical care, both preventive and remedial, including dental, ophthalmological and mental health care, as well as pharmaceutical products and special diets as medically indicated."

Addressing physical restraint and the use of force, paragraphs 63 and 64 prohibit instruments of restraint and force except "in exceptional cases, where all other control methods have been exhausted and failed. . . ." According to paragraph 65, "The carrying and use of weapons by personnel should be prohibited in any facility where juveniles are detained." Part IV concludes by noting in paragraph 79 that all juvenile offenders "should benefit from arrangements designed to assist them in returning to society, family life, education or employment after release."

Part V, Personnel, paragraph 81, specifies that all personnel of juvenile facilities "should be qualified and include a sufficient number of specialists such as educators, vocational instructors, counselors, social workers, psychiatrists and psychologists." Paragraph 82 urges "careful selection and recruitment of every grade and type of personnel, since the proper management of detention facilities depends on their integrity, ability and professional capacity to deal with juveniles, as well as personal suitability for the work." According to paragraph 87, the last item, "In the performance of their duties, personnel of detention facilities should respect and protect the human dignity and fundamental human rights of all juveniles," particularly freedom from torture and corruption; respect the Rules for the Protection of Juveniles Deprived of Their Liberty and their charges' physical and mental health, including protection from physical, sexual, and emotional abuse and exploitation; and strive to minimize "any differences between life inside and outside the detention facility which tend to lessen due respect for the dignity of juveniles as human beings."

United Nations High Commissioner for Human Rights, 8–14 avenue de la Paix, 1211 Geneva 10, Switzerland. (41-22-917-9000. 41-22-917-9016. webadmin.hchr@unog.ch. www.unhchr.ch.

United Nations Youth Unit, United Nations Plaza, Room DC2-1318, New York, N.Y. 10017. (212-963-1380. 212-963-3062. youth@un.org. www.un.org/esa/socdev/unyin/yth-unit.

Detention; Guidelines for the Prevention of Juvenile Delinquency (Riyadh Guidelines); Standard Minimum Rules for the Administration of Juvenile Justice; Prisoners; Punishment; Youth

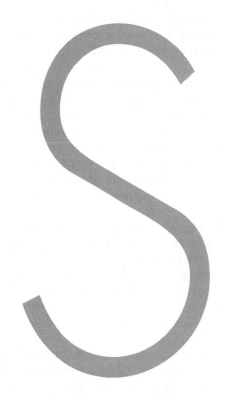

Elizabeth Cady Stanton
(seated), author of the
Seneca Falls Declaration
(1848), and her colleague
Susan B. Anthony were the
driving forces behind the
women's rights movement in
the United States. Neither
lived to see the ratification of
the Nineteenth Amendment
(1920) to the U.S. Constitution, which gave women
the right to vote—a right for
which the pair worked tire-
lessly. [Library of Congress]

Safeguards Guaranteeing Protection of the Rights of Those Facing the Death Penalty

Although the death penalty is denounced or prohibited in some international and regional human rights documents as well as in some national constitutions and laws, ninety countries, including the United States and China, still do not consider capital punishment to violate human rights. Its use may be limited to certain types of crimes involving heinous offenses or the murder of law enforcement officers, as is the case in the United States. The severity and finality of the death penalty, which make it impossible to correct a judicial error once a sentence of death has been carried out, have led to efforts to ensure that capital punishment is restricted to extreme crimes and that those accused of capital offenses receive a fair trial.

While clearly supporting abolition of capital punishment, the International Covenant on Civil and Political Rights (1966), article 6, sets out criteria for protecting the rights of persons sentenced to death for crimes in countries that still use this form of punishment. Stipulations include the right to due process and to seek a pardon or a commutation of the sentence as well as a prohibition on capital punishment for pregnant women and anyone under eighteen years of age. On May 25, 1984, on the recommendation of the Committee on Crime Prevention and Control, the Economic

and Social Council (ECOSOC) approved the Safeguards Guaranteeing Protection of the Rights of Those Facing the Death Penalty. Five years later, the UN General Assembly in 1989 took a firmer stand on capital punishment, adopting the Second Optional Protocol to the International Covenant on Civil and Political Rights, Aiming at the Abolition of the Death Penalty.

The complete text of the 1984 safeguards is as follows:

"1. In countries which have not abolished the death penalty, capital punishment may be imposed only for the most serious crimes, it being understood that their scope should not go beyond intentional crimes with lethal or other extremely grave consequences.

"2. Capital punishment may be imposed only for a crime for which the death penalty is prescribed by law at the time of its commission, it being understood that if, subsequent to the commission of the crime, provision is made by law for the imposition of a lighter penalty, the offender shall benefit thereby.

"3. Persons below 18 years of age at the time of the commission of the crime shall not be sentenced to death, nor shall the death sentence be carried out on pregnant women, or on new mothers, or on persons who have become insane.

"4. Capital punishment may be imposed only when the guilt of the person charged is based upon clear and convincing evidence leaving no room for an alternative explanation of the facts.

"5. Capital punishment may only be carried out pursuant to a final judgment rendered by a competent court after legal process which gives all possible safeguards to ensure a fair trial, at least equal to those contained in article 14 of the International Covenant on Civil and Political Rights, including the right of anyone suspected of or charged with a crime for which capital punishment may be imposed to adequate legal assistance at all stages of the proceedings.

"6. Anyone sentenced to death shall have the right to appeal to a court of higher jurisdiction, and steps should be taken to ensure that such appeals shall become mandatory.

"7. Anyone sentenced to death shall have the right to seek pardon, or commutation of sentence; pardon or commutation of sentence may be granted in all cases of capital punishment.

"8. Capital punishment shall not be carried out pending any appeal or other recourse procedure or other proceeding relating to pardon or commutation of the sentence.

"9. Where capital punishment occurs, it shall be carried out so as to inflict the minimum possible suffering."

Amnesty International, Program to Abolish the Death Penalty, 600 Pennsylvania Avenue, S.E., Fifth Floor, Washington, D.C. 20003. (202-544-0200. 🖨 202-546-7142. 🖳 dppprogram@aiusa.org. 🖳 www.amnesty-usa.org/abolish.

United Nations High Commissioner for Human Rights, 8–14 avenue de la Paix, 1211 Geneva 10, Switzerland. (41-22-917-9000. 🖨 41-22-917-9016. 🖳 webadmin.hchr@unog.ch. 🖳 www.unhchr.ch.

Accused; Capital Punishment; Due Process of Law; Fair Trial; International Covenant on Civil and Political Rights; International Covenant on Civil and Political Rights, Second Optional Protocol, Aiming at the Abolition of the Death Penalty; Life; Prisoners; Punishment; Summary Executions

Sakharov, Andrei

Honored in the Soviet Union for his significant contributions as a nuclear physicist, Andrei Dmitriyevich Sakharov (1921–89) was a constant critic of his country's totalitarian government. With the assistance of his wife, Yelena Bonner, he wrote and protested against the suppression of civil rights as well as the proliferation of nuclear weapons. For his efforts to achieve a peaceful and just world, he was awarded the Nobel Peace Prize in 1975.

Sakharov was born in Moscow on May 21, 1921. The brilliant son of a physics teacher, he studied at Moscow University and served as a munitions factory engineer during World War II. After the war he worked with the Nobel Prize–winning physicist Igor Tamm at the Physics Institute of the Academy of Sciences to develop and produce the Soviet Union's first hydrogen bomb. As a preeminent

Soviet scientist—he was admitted to the Soviet Academy of Sciences at the age of thirty-two—he was accorded honors and luxuries.

In 1961 Sakharov publicly criticized Soviet Premier Nikita Khrushchev's order to test a 100-megaton hydrogen bomb in the atmosphere, and in 1964 he spearheaded an attack on the theories of T. D. Lysenko, a Stalinist biologist who held that acquired characteristics such as social indoctrination could be inherited. Four years later he wrote an essay calling for reductions in nuclear arms and criticizing the repressive treatment of dissidents in the Soviet Union. In 1971 he married Yelena Bonner, a human rights activist, and together they continued their outspoken struggle.

After denouncing his country's invasion of Afghanistan in 1979 and calling for a boycott of the 1980 Olympic Games to be held in Moscow, Sakharov was stripped of his honors and exiled internally to Gorky. In 1984 Bonner was exiled with him for her human rights activities. In 1985 the European Parliament created the Sakharov Award to celebrate freedom of thought and began making awards four years later to activists such as, in 1990, Aung San Suu Kyi of Burma (now Myanmar). Sakharov was released from exile by the U.S.S.R. Chairman Mikhail Gorbachev in 1986, his honors were restored, and in 1989 he was elected to the Congress of People's Deputies of the Soviet Union. He died that year of a heart attack.

With the dismantling of the Soviet regime and the adoption of a democratic constitutional government for the Russian Republic, many reforms Sakharov fought for were realized. "The ideology of human rights [can] serve as a foothold for those . . . who had tired of the abundance of ideologies, none of which have brought . . . simple human happiness," he wrote during his exile. "The defense of human rights is a clear path towards the unification of people in our turbulent world, and a path toward the relief of suffering."

Juviler, Peter H., ed. *Human Rights for the 21st Century. Foundations for Responsible Hope: A U.S.–Post-Soviet Dialogue.* Armonk, N.Y.: M. E. Sharpe, 1993.

Sakharov, Andrei. *Memoirs.* New York: Knopf, 1990.

————. *Reflections on Progress, Peaceful Coexistence, and Intellectual Freedom.* New York: Norton, 1968.

Aung San Suu Kyi; Declaration on the Prohibition of the Use of Nuclear and Thermo-Nuclear Weapons; Expulsion; Weapons

Searches and Seizures

See Privacy

Security

Security (from the Latin *securitas,* meaning freedom from care) is both an individual and a collective human goal. Society needs peace to allow fulfillment of the promise of individual human rights, while people have the right to be secure in their own persons, free from abuse or injury.

The right not to have one's bodily integrity violated, an aspect of personal dignity, precludes such government acts as deprivation of liberty without due process of law, detention without trial, violence, torture, and cruel, inhuman, or degrading treatment. Poland's constitution (1992), for example, provides that "[p]ersonal inviolability and security are assured to everyone," and the American Convention on Human Rights (1969) states: "Every person has the right to personal liberty and security." Security of the person also entails the right to have control over one's body, the freedom to make personal decisions about reproduction, and the right not to be subjected to medical or scientific experiments without informed consent. Bulgaria's constitution (1991) specifies that "[n]o one may be subjected to medical, scientific, or other experiments without a voluntary written agreement on his part."

A nation's external security is the responsibility of the armed forces, whereas its internal security is handled by the police and other law enforcement officials. Both the military and the police are instruments of the state for the protection of the citizenry, but the claim of national security has occasionally been used to rationalize the abrogation or infringement of human rights. During the 1970s and 1980s, governments in the "Southern Cone" of South America condoned enforced disappearances, torture, and mass murders under the pretext of taking security measures against political enemies of the state—meaning enemies of the rulers then in power. Armed personnel trained to obey commands of superiors can become a tool of political and military leaders, such that the very forces created for protection become instruments for violations of human rights with impunity.

Collective security for a group of countries may substitute for or provide coordination for a nation's military forces. The UN Security Council and its peacekeeping forces, for example, are components of the international security system, as is the North Atlantic Treaty Organization (NATO). Both the Security Council and NATO can request military troops from member countries and use them to prevent or counter attempts to disrupt world or regional security or the security of any member nation. International documents that address international and national security include the UN charter (1945), which declares that one of its goals is "to unite our strength to maintain international peace and security"; the North Atlantic Treaty (1949), which provides that the parties thereto "will consult together whenever . . . the territorial integrity, political independence or security of any [member] is threatened"; and the Charter of Paris for a New Europe (1990), which addresses improved mutual security for the nations of Europe.

Constitution of South Africa (1997), chapter 2, Bill of Rights, Freedom and Security of the Person: "12(1) Everyone has the right to freedom and security of the person, which includes the right— . . . (c) to be free from all forms of violence from either public or private sources. . . . (2) Everyone has the right to bodily and psychological integrity, which includes the right— . . . (b) to security in and control over their body; and (c) not to be subjected to medical or scientific experiments without their informed consent."

Basic Principles on the Use of Force and Firearms by Law Enforcement Officials (1990), preamble: "[I]t is appropriate that . . . consideration be given to the role of law enforcement officials in relation to the administration of justice, to the protection of the right to life, liberty and security of the person. . . ."

Supreme Court of Ireland (Opinion of Justice Kenny) (1965): The plaintiff complained that children's bodily integrity was violated because about ten percent of them who drank fluoridated water had mildly discolored teeth. "I understand the right to bodily integrity to mean that no mutilation of the body or of any of its members may be carried out on any citizen under authority of the law except for the good of the whole body and that no process which is or may, as a matter of probability, be dangerous or harmful to the life or health of the citizens or any of them may be imposed . . . by an Act of [parliament]."

Human Rights Committee (1993): On the basis of the International Covenant on Civil and Political Rights (1966), article 9, paragraph 1, which guarantees everyone the right to liberty and security of the person, "the Committee has held that this right may be invoked not only in the context of arrest and detention, [but also] that an interpretation which would allow States parties to tolerate, condone or ignore threats made by persons in authority to the personal liberty and security of non-detained individuals within the State party's jurisdiction would render ineffective the guarantees of the Covenant."

Department for Disarmament Affairs. *Concepts of Security.* Report of the Secretary-General. New York: United Nations, 1986.

Terriff, Terry, et al. *Security Studies Today.* Malden, Mass.: Polity, 1999.

Accused; Charter of Paris for a New Europe; Charter of the United Nations; Dignity; Law Enforcement; Liberty; Limitations; North Atlantic Treaty Organization (NATO); Peace; Privacy; Punishment; Regional Human Rights Systems; Torture

Self-Determination

The right of self-determination is the notion that any group of people who consider themselves a separate national entity on the basis of shared characteristics or history is uniquely and exclusively qualified to determine its own political status. If they desire, the group members have the right to form their own state, because their common heritage is the ultimate standard for political legitimacy. This right has received strong support from the United Nations, to the point that the obstruction of a people's right to self-determination, according to the UN's International Law Commission, is now considered a state crime on a par with genocide and trading in slaves. "Although the expression 'Self-determination' will rightly be forever connected with the name of Woodrow Wilson," wrote Winston Churchill in 1929, "the idea was neither original or new."

Self-determination, like autonomy and self-government, reflects the aspirations of groups of people related culturally, religiously, or linguistically. When one group of people conquered another, the conquered people either assimilated or retained a separate identity under the conquerors' jurisdiction. The Romans often allowed conquered peoples to maintain their cultural identity while under their administration; other conquerors, however, such as the Normans in the eleventh century, themselves became absorbed into the conquered peoples, the Anglo-Saxons.

Following World War I the people in the colonies of the defeated powers such as Germany and the Ottoman Empire were placed under the administration of some of the members of the League of Nations, a procedure accomplished formally through the League's mandate system. The Micronesian islands in the northern Pacific, for example, were awarded to Japan, while Palestine went to Great Britain. The administering nations were given mandates that included the duty to prepare the former colonies for independence and self-government, a process that was continued under the UN by means of trusteeships. The last of the trusteeships, the Pacific island territory of Palau (Belau), then administered by the United States, was not terminated until October 1, 1994.

"[E]qual rights and self-determination of peoples" was first officially recognized in the UN charter (1945), which was followed fifteen years later by the UN General Assembly's adoption of the Declaration on the Granting of Independence to Colonial Countries and Peoples (1960). In 1970 the assembly adopted the Declaration on Principles of International Law Concerning Friendly Relations and Cooperation among States in Accordance with the Charter of the United Nations, which proclaimed certain "principles of equal rights and self-determination of peoples."

The concept of the right of self-determination has expanded since World War II. Self-determination originally referred to the right of colonial peoples to gain their independence. Later, as colonialism was phased out, it came to stand for the right of existing states to determine their own political and economic affairs and to be left alone by other states and the international community. Today it has assumed another dimension, with the focus on protecting the collective and individual rights of peoples, particularly their right to democratic government.

Movements by peoples for more self-government within an established nation, rather than complete independence, represent another facet of self-determination. In recent years a number of unitary, as opposed to federal, nations, including Belgium and the United Kingdom, have been decentralizing or devolving power from the central government to historically separate regional and cultural groups. In Belgium, the French communities in the south and the Flemish communities in the north have been granted broad powers to deal with local matters, and the United Kingdom, through the process of "devolution," has extended more local control to Scotland and Wales, resulting in the establishment of self-governing parliaments for both in 1999.

In federal systems of government, such as in the United States and Russia, self-determination for semisovereign constituent states or provinces is generally not accepted as a right. In the United States, the attempt by the Southern states to secede from the national union led to the Civil War (1861–65) and their ultimate defeat. More recently, the Russian province of Chechnya's attempt to separate from the Russian Federation in the late 1990s has been repulsed by the Russian Army.

Constitution of Spain (1978), title VIII, Concerning Territorial Organization, chapter III, Concerning the Autonomous Communities, article 143: "1. In the exercise of the right of autonomy . . . bordering provinces with common historical, cultural and economic characteristics [such as Catalonia and the Basque Provinces], the island territories and the provinces with a historical regional entity may accede to self-government and constitute themselves into autonomous communities in accordance with the provisions of that Title and respective Statutes."

African Charter on Human and Peoples' Rights (1981), article 20: "1. All peoples shall have the right to existence. They shall have the unquestionable and inalienable right to self-determination. They shall freely determine their political status and shall pursue their economic and social development according to the policy they have freely chosen."

U.K. Privy Council (1969): A unilateral declaration of independence by the legislature and government of Southern Rhodesia was invalid and did not terminate the sovereignty of Great Britain, because it could not be said with certainty that the revolutionary government was in effective control of the territory over which it asserted the right of self-government.

Human Rights Committee (1984): A member of the Mikmaq tribal society alleged that the government of Canada had denied his people the right of self-determination as guaranteed by the International Covenant on Civil and Political Rights (1966), article 1, but the complaint was found to be inadmissible because, among other things, the person making the complaint failed to prove his authority to represent the society.

Cassese, Antonio. *Self-Determination of Peoples: A Legal Reappraisal.* New York: Cambridge University Press, 1995.

Steinhardt, Ralph G. *International Law and Self-Determination.* Washington, D.C.: Atlantic Council of the United States, 1994.

Charter of the United Nations; Collective Rights; Declaration on Principles of International Law Concerning Friendly Relations and Co-operation among States in Accordance with the Charter of the United Nations; Declaration on the Granting of Independence to Colonial Countries and Peoples; Development; Economic Rights; Natural Resources; Peoples' Rights

Seneca Falls Declaration of Sentiments and Resolutions

When political scientists extol the virtues of democracy in the ancient Greek city-states, the equality enshrined in France's Declaration of the Rights of Man and of the Citizen (1789), or the leap forward for human rights embodied in the U.S. Bill of Rights (1791), they tend to overlook the fact that more than half the world's adult population did not share these vaunted rights on a par with males and until relatively recently even had no right to vote.

The advent of the industrial revolution in the mid-eighteenth century began a process by which women were integrated into the work force, and during the first half of the nineteenth century, women in England and the United States also became politically active, especially in the movement to abolish slavery. At an international anti-slavery congress in 1840, English abolitionists and suffragists energized the American women over the need to crusade for, among other rights denied them, votes for women.

Injected with new fervor, American women held a convention in Seneca Falls, New York, in 1848 and issued the Seneca Falls Declaration of Sentiments and Resolutions on July 19, 1848. This revolutionary declaration, drafted by Elizabeth Cady Stanton, forecast the direction of the women's rights movement. It contains a series of "resolves," among them the following:

"That all laws which prevent woman from occupying such a station in society as her conscience shall dictate, or which place her in a position inferior to that of man, are contrary to the great precept of nature, and therefore of no force or authority.

"That woman is man's equal—was intended to be so by the Creator, and the highest good of the race demands that she should be recognized as such. . . .

"That woman has too long rested satisfied in the circumscribed limits which corrupt customs and a perverted application of the Scriptures have marked out for her, and that it is time she should move in the enlarged sphere to which her great Creator has assigned her.

"That it is the duty of the women of this country to secure to themselves their sacred right to the elective franchise.

"That the equality of human rights results necessarily from the fact of the identity of the race in capabilities and responsibilities.

"That the speedy success of our cause depends upon the zealous and untiring efforts of both men and women . . . for the securing to women an equal participation with men in the various trades, professions, and commerce.

"That . . . it is demonstrably the right and duty of woman, equally with man, to promote every righteous cause by every righteous means; and especially in regard to the great subjects of morals and religion, it is self-evidently her right to participate with her brother in teaching them, both in private and in public . . . and this being a self-evident truth growing out of the divinely implanted principles of human nature, any custom or authority adverse to it . . . is to be regarded as a self-evident falsehood, and at war with mankind."

American women did not obtain their "elective franchise" until the Nineteenth Amendment to the U.S. Constitution was ratified in 1920. The women of New Zealand preceded them by more than two decades, gaining their right to vote in 1893.

National Organization for Women (NOW) Legal Defense Fund, 395 Hudson Street, New York, N.Y. 10014. (212-925-6635. 212-226-1066. lir@nowldef.org. www.nowldef.org.

Women's Rights National Historical Park, 136 Fall Street, Seneca Falls, N.Y. 13148. (315-568-2991. 315-568-2141. www.nps.gov/wori.

Convention on the Elimination of All Forms of Discrimination against Women; Convention on the Political Rights of Women; Declaration on the Elimination of Discrimination against Women; Equality; Inter-American Convention on the Granting of Political Rights to Women; Political Rights; Sex Discrimination; Slavery; Stanton, Elizabeth Cady; Voting; Wollstonecraft, Mary; Women

Separation of Church and State

The idea of placing a "wall" between church and state—a particularly American contribution to the protection of human rights penned by Thomas Jefferson—has roots in the religious pluralism that developed in Europe after the sixteenth-century Reformation. Before this time, monarchs were looked on as defenders of the faith—if not gods themselves—and their divine right to rule over their subjects required a fusion of church and state. The ancient Greek philosophers Plato and Aristotle would have rejected out of hand the notion of separating religion and government. Plato, in fact, prescribed harsh punishment for anyone who showed impiety, and Aristotle even suggested that the expense of religious worship should be charged to the public rolls.

The proliferation of Christian religious sects in the seventeenth century and the persecution that ensued motivated many Europeans to settle in the New World. The Puritans, an English sect whose members landed at Plymouth Rock, Massachusetts, in 1620, are credited with establishing the first viable permanent colony in what became the United States of America. They ended up persecuting members of other religious sects who settled in their political jurisdiction, however, and Massachusetts became the last state to disestablish its state-sponsored religion in 1833, more than forty years after the Bill of Rights (1791) enshrined freedom of religion.

The framers of the U.S. Constitution (1789) were not irreligious; they were of different religions and feared the consequences of giving any one church the federal government's imprimatur. Thomas Jefferson, author of the Declaration of Independence (1776), argued that the integrity of the new government of the United States could be maintained only by erecting "a wall of separation" between church and state. The Constitution thus barred any religious test for political office and, in the First Amendment, prohibited the government from making any "law respecting an establishment of religion" as well as standing in the way of "the free exercise thereof."

The rationale for the separation (from the Latin *seperatus*, meaning separate) of church and state lies in the logical difficulty of assuming that other religions or religious practices can be tolerated in a country that sanctions an official religion. Although the English poet William Wordsworth wrote in 1805 that "[t]he mind Learns . . . to keep In wholesome separation [its] two natures," one difficulty with the principle is where to draw the line when certain religious and government activities meet. The U.S. courts have analyzed specific cases on the basis of whether a government action promotes or harms a religion. For example, the use of public school facilities for religious education, even if attendance is voluntary, has been prohibited. The early release of students for religious instruction has been deemed acceptable, however, as have certain religious displays on public property.

Other divisive issues that come under the rubric of separation of church and state, particularly in the United States, include prayer in public schools; public subsidies for families that send their children to church-affiliated schools rather than to public schools; and, in the wake of recent gun violence in public schools, a proposal by some national lawmakers to require the Ten Commandments, a Judeo-Christian document, to be posted in a prominent place in public schools. Despite the U.S. Constitution's requirement that church and state be separated, however, both houses of Congress have their own chaplains, who begin every legislative session with a prayer.

Many constitutional democracies, such as Denmark and the United Kingdom, acknowledge a state-established religion or religious sect. The constitutions of other nations—those of Greece (1975), Iran (1979), and Israel (unwritten), for example—incorporate a specific religion or religious sect. The constitutions of Ireland (1937) and Spain (1978) stop short of merging church and state but acknowledge the leading role of the Roman Catholic Church. On the other hand, Turkey's constitution (1982) expressly states that the Republic of Turkey, a predominantly Islamic nation, is nonetheless a "secular" state.

Most international human rights documents declare freedom of religion, and often the freedoms of thought, conscience, and expression, but they do not require the strict separation of church and state that is found in the U.S. Constitution.

Constitution of Bulgaria (1991), chapter 1, Fundamental Principles, article 13: "(1) There is freedom of religion. (2) Religious institutions are separate from the state. (3) The Eastern Orthodox religion is the traditional religion of the Republic of Bulgaria. (4) Religious communities and institutions or religious convictions may not be used in the pursuit of political objectives."

Declaration on the Elimination of All Forms of Intolerance and of Discrimination Based on Religion or Belief (1981), article 2: "1. No one shall be subject to discrimination by any State, institution, group of persons or person on the grounds of religion or belief."

U.S. Supreme Court (1952): "We are a religious people. . . . When the state encourages religious instruction or cooperates with religious authorities by adjusting the schedule of public events to sectarian needs, it follows the best of our traditions."

European Court of Human Rights (1994): "The Court cannot disregard the fact that the Roman Catholic religion is the religion of the overwhelming majority [87 percent] of [Tyrolean Austrians]. In seizing the film [at the request of the Roman Catholic diocese] the Austrian authorities acted to ensure religious peace in that region and to prevent [some people from feeling] the object of attacks on their religious beliefs in an unwarranted and offensive manner."

Feldman, Stephen M. *Please Don't Wish Me a Merry Christmas: A Critical History of the Separation of Church and State.* New York: New York University Press, 1997.

Wood, James E., Jr. *Separation of Church and State Defended: Selected Writings of James E. Wood, Jr.* Waco, Tex.: J. M. Dawson Institute of Church-State Studies, Baylor University, 1995.

Americans United for Separation of Church and State, 518 C Street, N.E., Washington, D.C. 20002. (202-466-3234. 🖷 202-466-2587. 🖳 americansunited@au.org. 🖳 www.au.org.

International Coalition for Religious Freedom, 7777 Leesburg Pike, Suite 307N-A, Falls Church, Va. 22043. (703-790-1500. 🖷 703-790-5562. 🖳 icrf@aol.com. 🖳 www.religiousfreedom.com.

Conscience; Declaration on the Elimination of All Forms of Intolerance and of Discrimination Based on Religion or Belief; Expression; Jefferson, Thomas; Religion; Thought; Tolerance

Sex Discrimination

Throughout history the biological distinction between males and females has created a number of barriers for females. Women have often been considered the property of men, either their father, their husband, or their lord or master during times of feudalism and slavery. Females have been, and in many societies still are, considered as and treated like children. The biological fact that women bear children and thus devote their energies to caring for and raising their offspring has led to widespread paternalistic treatment throughout history. Yet women were once used in political negotiations by ruling families to make alliances or prevent wars, and in many places they are still treated as objects of commerce, being bought and sold in marriage or for prostitution.

Although the word *sex* (from the Latin *sexus,* meaning sex) may refer to males or females—as in "the male sex" or "the female sex"—in the context of human rights the term generally refers to females. Thus, sex discrimination and sexual harassment usually involve a female as the victim of the discriminatory act, while sexual abuse may refer to both female and male victims, typically young boys in the latter case. Until recently the word *gender* was reserved primarily for sexual distinctions in words or grammar, but now it is often used as a euphemism for a person's sex and has become synonymous with sexual differences in some human rights contexts; controversy exists over whether it has the same meaning, however.

Although most postindustrial Western nations have now adopted the equality of men and women as their human rights norm, abuses based on sexual differences are still rampant on a global scale. The relatively unequal physical strength of men compared to women, together with the social and legal inequality of women, has resulted in discrimination based on sex. Sex discrimination can occur in a number of ways—some overt and obvious, others subtle and not so easily recognized.

A major arena for sex discrimination is the workplace. Equal pay for equal work is a human right that attempts to ensure that women are compensated on the same basis as men and not paid less simply because they are women and thus presumably not heads of households. Sex discrimination may be directed against married women, pregnant women, and mothers. It can occur in the hiring process, when a woman may be excluded from consideration for positions traditionally held by men or stereotyped for jobs that involve menial tasks along with regular work duties that a man in the same position would not be required to do, such as making coffee. Sex discrimination can also hinder a woman's chances for promotion, especially into the managerial ranks. While discrimination by a private employer is not strictly a violation of anyone's human rights, if a nation's laws guarantee equality of treatment for both men and women in employment, then failure to enforce such laws or denial of legitimate claims of discrimination are human rights violations. Sex discrimination also includes sexual harassment of women by male supervisors and employees. Women are sometimes pressured to provide sexual favors in return for keeping their jobs or being promoted.

Another area of sex discrimination involves dealings with government officials, especially the police. Male law enforcement officials—and at times the legal system as a whole—often do not treat as seriously as they should specific complaints by women alleging such problems as spousal abuse and rape. Many other traditional notions of women's status as second-class citizens continue to pervade bureaucratic systems. Even in a country like the United States, in which women have had the right to vote and hold elective office since 1920, no woman has been nominated for the office of president by either of the two major political parties, let alone been elected.

Some national constitutions, including those of Canada (1867), Germany (1949), and Sweden (1975), expressly ban sex discrimination. The Canadian Charter of Rights and Freedoms (1982) grants everyone the equal protection and benefit of the law "without discrimination based on race, national or ethnic origin, color, religion, sex" and further provides that this language "does not preclude any law, program or activity that has as its object the amelioration of conditions of disadvantaged individuals or groups including those that are disadvantaged because of [those same characteristics]." The English translation of Germany's constitution provides: "No one may be disadvantaged or favored because of *his* sex, *his* parentage, *his* race, *his* language. . . [emphasis added]." However, in the United States, a proposed amendment granting women equal rights failed to obtain the necessary state ratifications during the period 1972 to 1982 set by Congress.

At the international level, in addition to the Universal Declaration of Human Rights (1948), a number of other significant human rights documents prohibit discrimination on the basis of sex, including the International Covenant on Civil and Political Rights (1966), International Covenant on Economic, Social and Cultural Rights (1966), and Convention on the Elimination of All Forms of Discrimination against Women (1979). Regional human rights documents such as the European Convention for the Protection of Human Rights and Fundamental Freedoms (1950), American Convention on Human Rights (1969), and African Charter on Human and Peoples' Rights (1981) contain similar language prohibiting discrimination on the basis of sex, among other arbitrary distinctions that continue to be made.

Although laws in each country differ, some types of sex discrimination are generally accepted—for example, where a certain level of strength is a legitimate requirement for a job, such as firefighter, and where affirmative action programs are instituted to correct past discrimination. Obviously, most maternity benefits are limited to women, although some male employees receive parental leave related to the birth or adoption of children. Reverse sex discrimination can also occur, such as when a position for a secretary or a typist is listed as open to women only.

The lines regarding what constitutes sex discrimination cannot always be clearly drawn, but the adverse impact of certain government and business practices that exclude members of either sex from being hired, promoted, or eligible for benefits are suspect. More and more the burden of proving that discrimination is absolutely necessary to the performance of a particular job is being shifted onto those who attempt to discriminate.

Constitution of Sweden, Instrument of Government (1975), chapter 2, Fundamental Rights and Freedoms, article 16: "No Act of law or other statutory instrument may entail the discrimination of any citizen on grounds of sex, unless the relevant provision forms part of efforts to bring about equality between men and women or relates to compulsory military service or any corresponding compulsory national service."

Convention on the Elimination of All Forms of Discrimination against Women (1979), part I, article 1: "For the purposes of the present Convention, the term 'discrimination against women' shall mean any distinction, exclusion or restriction made on the basis of sex which has the effect or purpose of impairing or nullifying the recognition, enjoyment or exercise by women, irrespective of their marital status, on a basis of equality of men and women, of human rights and fundamental freedoms in the political, economic, social, cultural, civil or any other field."

Constitutional Court of Germany (1992): A statute forbidding the employment of women as blue-collar workers during the night was unconstitutional because it violated, among other provisions, article 3(3) of the German Constitution or Basic Law (1949), which provides that "no one may be disadvantaged or favored on the basis of sex."

European Court of Human Rights (1985): On the grounds that they had violated the European Convention for the Protection of Human Rights and Fundamental Freedoms (1950), article 8 (right to respect for private and family life), authorities in the Netherlands were held responsible for failing to prosecute a sexual abuse complaint involving a mentally handicapped sixteen-year-old girl who lived in a home for handicapped children.

Commission on the Status of Women, United Nations, Two United Nations Plaza, DC2-12th Floor, New York, N.Y. 10017. (212-963-9750. ▤ 212-963-3463. ▣ daw@un.org. ▣ www.un.org/womenwatch/daw.

National Organization for Women (NOW) Legal Defense Fund, 395 Hudson Street, New York, N.Y. 10014. (212-925-6635. ▤ 212-226-1066. ▣ lir@nowldef.org. ▣ www.nowldef.org.

UN Development Fund for Women, 304 East 45th Street, 15th Floor, New York, N.Y. 10017. (212-906-6400. ▤ 212-906-6705. ▣ unifem@undp.org. ▣ www.unifem.undp.org.

Babcock, Barbara A. *Sex Discrimination and the Law: History, Practice, and Theory.* Boston: Little, Brown, 1996.

Stychin, Carl F. *Law's Desire: Sexuality and the Limits of Justice.* New York: Routledge, 1995.

Wetzel, Janice Wood. *The World of Women: In Pursuit of Human Rights.* New York: New York University Press, 1993.

Convention on the Elimination of All Forms of Discrimination against Women; Declaration on the Elimination of Discrimination against Women; Discrimination; Domestic Violence; Equality; Homosexuals; Inter-American Convention on the Granting of Civil Rights to Women; Inter-American Convention on the Granting of Political Rights to Women; Seneca Falls Declaration of Sentiments and Resolutions; Women

Sexual Orientation

See Homosexuals

Shcharansky, Anatoly

A dissident and human rights advocate in the Soviet Union, Anatoly Borisovich Shcharansky (b. 1948) was sentenced to hard labor for his active promotion of the right of Jews to emigrate from the Soviet Union. While in prison he became a symbol for the struggle of others similarly oppressed. In 1986, in an exchange of prisoners with the West, he was released and allowed to settle in Israel with his wife and family.

Shcharansky was born in Donetsk, Ukraine, on January 20, 1948, the son of a journalist for a Communist Party newspaper. A student of mathematics and computer sciences, Shcharansky was also a member of the Komsomol communist youth organization. After graduating from the Moscow Physical Technical Institute in 1972, he went to work as a computer specialist for the Oil and Gas Research Institute.

In 1973 Shcharansky and his fiancée, Natalia Stieglitz, both Jews, applied for permission to emigrate to Israel. Her request was granted shortly after they were married, but his was denied, most likely because of his professional training and political activism. Shcharansky was harassed by the KGB, the Soviet secret police, and eventually was fired from his job. Fluent in English, he became a leading spokesman for other "refuseniks," as Jews who were denied permission to leave the Soviet Union were called. In 1977, while walking with Western reporters, he was arrested and tried nonpublicly for treason and espionage.

The trial was widely covered in the world press, however. The solitary vigil of Shcharansky's mother outside the closed courtroom in Moscow touched millions of people and helped publicize her son's plight. His wife championed his cause from Israel. However, Shcharansky was sentenced to thirteen years in hard-labor camps. His health began to deteriorate, but his courage and moral resolve did not, and he became the symbol of all persecuted Jews.

The first meeting of President Ronald Reagan and U.S.S.R. Chairman Mikhail Gorbachev in Geneva in 1985 produced a gesture to improved relations between the two nations: release of Shcharansky in exchange for Soviet spies held in the West. Freed on February 11, 1986, after nine years' imprisonment, he immigrated to Israel and took the name Natan Sharansky. In 1989 he was named the Israeli ambassador to the United Nations. Later, as the Israeli cabinet minister for industry and trade, he returned to Russia in 1997 to sign an economic cooperation agreement with the mayor of Moscow—next door to the building where he had been arrested twenty years earlier.

Shcharansky, Anatoly. *Fear No Evil*. New York: Random House, 1988.

Shcharansky, Avital [Natalia Stieglitz]. *Next Year in Jerusalem*. New York: Morrow, 1979.

☞

Fair Trial; Immigrants; Movement; Punishment

Shelter

See Housing; Vancouver Declaration on Human Settlements

Slavery

In the ancient world, slavery—the practice of owning a person as property—was generally accepted and even condoned by religions and philosophers. Plato, the Greek philosopher, comments in *The Laws* that "we should certainly punish slaves if they deserve it, and not spoil them by simply giving them a warning, as we would free men. Virtually everything you say to a slave should be an order, and you should never become at all familiar with them— neither the women nor the men." In ancient Rome slaves were at the bottom of the social ranks, and Tacitus, the second-century Roman historian, despised even freed slaves as base newcomers who were trying to live above their station.

Slavery continued for many centuries throughout the world. Not until 1807 was the slave trade abolished in the British Empire, and not until late 1865, after the Civil War, was the U.S. Constitution (1789) amended to prohibit the practice. Delegates to a conference held in Brussels in 1889–90 declared their intention to suppress slavery in all its forms. Then in 1926 the Slavery Convention, which undertook to prevent the slave trade and bring about, progressively but as soon as possible, the abolition of slavery in all its forms, was finalized in Geneva. A protocol transferring conventions of the defunct League of Nations, including this one, to the United Nations was adopted in 1953. A supplementary Convention on the Abolition of Slavery, the Slave Trade, and Institutions and Practices Similar to Slavery was drafted in 1956 and entered into force in 1957.

Some forms of slavery still exist, such as the "white slave" trade, or prostitution, in which women are held in bondage for commercial sexual exploitation. Forced labor is practiced in Brazil, the Dominican Republic, and Burma, among other countries, and child labor is allowed in Bangladesh, India, and Pakistan, among others. Institutions and practices similar to slavery include debt bondage, in which a debtor pledges his or her personal services, or those of someone else whom he or she has control over, as security for a debt; serfdom, under which a person is bound by an agreement to live and labor on the land of another person; transfers of family members without their consent, in marriage or otherwise; and transfers of a person under the age of eighteen to another for the purpose of exploiting that person or his or her labor. Migrant workers are another group of people sometimes subjected to conditions approaching serfdom.

Today many national constitutions, including those of the United States (as amended in 1865), Ecuador (1979), and Liberia (1986), specifically prohibit slavery. A number of international human rights documents, in addition to those that directly address slavery, also condemn the practice. Anti-Slavery International, a nongovernmental organization founded in 1839 as the British and Foreign Anti-Slavery Society, has been involved in the development and adoption of international conventions on slavery and the creation of the UN Working Group on Contemporary Forms of Slavery.

Constitution of Singapore (1959), part IV, Fundamental Liberties, article 10: "(1) No person shall be held in slavery."

American Convention on Human Rights (1969), part I, State Obligations and Rights Protected, chapter II, Civil and Political Rights, article 6: "1. No one shall be subject to slavery or to involuntary servitude, which are prohibited in all their forms, as are the slave trade and traffic in women."

U.S. Supreme Court (1825): Chief Justice John Marshall, in a decision returning slaves seized by an American vessel to their Spanish owner, commented: "However abhorrent this traffic may be to a mind whose original feelings are not blunted by familiarity with the practice, it has been sanctioned in modern times by the laws of all nations who possess distant colonies . . . [and that] trade could not be considered as contrary to the law of nations. . . ."

U.S. Supreme Court (1857): A federal law prohibiting involuntary servitude in the Northern states of the United States was declared unconstitutional because, without due process of law, it deprived a slave owner of his "property," a slave named Dred Scott and his family, who had escaped from a Southern state.

European Court of Human Rights (1982): A Belgian recidivists board's retention of an inmate in prison until he had saved enough money from his work there to be reintegrated into society did not constitute slavery or servitude as proscribed by the European Convention for the Protection of Human Rights and Fundamental Freedoms (1950), article 4, section 1.

American Anti-Slavery Group, 198 Tremont Street, Suite 421, Boston, Mass. 02116. ☎ 800-884-0719. 🖨 617-507-8257. 💻 info@anti-slavery.org. 🖥 www.anti-slavery.org.

Anti-Slavery International, Unit 4, Stableyard, Broomgrove Road, London SW9 9TL, England. ☎ 44-207-924-9555. 🖨 44-207-738-4110. 💻 admin@antislavery.org. 🖥 www.antislavery.org.

Frey, Sylvia R., and Betty Wood. *From Slavery to Emancipation in the Atlantic World*. Portland, Ore.: Frank Cass, 1999.

Rodriguez, Junius P. *Chronology of World Slavery*. Santa Barbara, Calif.: ABC-CLIO, 1999.

Convention for the Suppression of the Traffic in Persons and of the Exploitation of the Prostitution of Others; Forced Labor; Liberty; Plato; Slavery Convention; Workers

Slavery Convention

Pervasive throughout much of human history, the invidious practices of slavery and the slave trade were abolished in the British Empire in 1807 and ended in the United States with the Civil War (1861–65). A conference in Brussels in 1889–90 sought to prohibit all forms of slavery, but not until September 25, 1926, was a Slavery Convention finally concluded in Geneva. This convention, which entered into force on March 9, 1927, was amended by a 1953 protocol transferring the convention's assigned functions to the United Nations from the defunct League of Nations. The amended convention became effective on July 7, 1955.

The Slavery Convention begins by recalling that the 1889–90 Brussels conferees "declared that they were animated by the firm intention of putting an end to the traffifc in African slaves" and notes the desire "to complete and extend [the work of the Brussels conference] and to find a means of giving practical effect throughout the world to such intentions as were expressed in regard to [the] slave trade and slavery. . . ." The preamble goes on to observe that "it is necessary to prevent forced labor from developing into conditions analogous to slavery."

Article 1 defines *slavery* as "the status or condition of a person over whom any or all of the powers attaching to the right of ownership are exercised" and *the slave trade* as "all acts involved in the capture, acquisition or disposal of a person with intent to reduce him to slavery; all acts involved in the acquisition of a slave with a view to selling or exchanging him; all acts of disposal by sale or exchange of a slave acquired with a view to being sold or exchanged, and, in general, every act of trade or transport in slaves." In article 2, the signatory nations agree to undertake the necessary steps in their own territories to "prevent and suppress the slave trade" and to "bring about, progressively and as soon as possible, the complete abolition of slavery in all its forms." Article 3 pledges the nations to take measures to suppress the transport of slaves "in their territorial waters and upon vessels flying their respective flags."

Article 4 requires that the parties assist one another in "securing the abolition of slavery and the slave trade." Article 5 addresses compulsory or forced labor, banning it except for public purposes; and article 6 requires that those nations whose laws are inadequate "for the punishment of infractions" relating to the convention's provisions "adopt the necessary measures in order that severe penalties may be imposed in respect of such infractions." Under article 7, the parties agree to notify one another and the League of Nations of laws and regulations enacted.

Article 8 concerns procedures for settling disputes in the interpretation or application of the convention, referring parties to the Permanent Court of International Justice if matters cannot be settled by direct negotiation. Article 12, the last item, provides that the convention "will come into operation for each State on the date of the deposit of its ratification or of its accession."

A Supplementary Convention on the Abolition of Slavery, the Slave Trade, and Institutions and Practices Similar to Slavery was adopted in Geneva on September 7, 1956, by a conference of plenipotentiaries convened by the Economic and Social Council (ECOSOC). This document, which entered into force on April 30, 1957, calls for the abolition or abandonment of such slavery-like practices as debt bondage; serfdom; the sale of a woman into marriage or her transfer to another person by her husband, family, or clan; the inheritance of a woman on the death of her husband; and the delivery of a person under the age of eighteen years "to another person . . . with a view to the exploitation of the child or young person or of his [or her] labor." The supplementary convention also criminalized the slave trade in the signatory nations, stating that any slave "who takes refuge on board any vessel of a State Party to this Convention shall *ipso facto* be free."

Anti-Slavery International, Unit 4, Stableyard, Broomgrove Road, London SW9 9TL, England. ☎ 44-207-924-9555. 🖷 44-207-738-4110. ✉ admin@antislavery.org. 🖥 www.antislavery.org.

United Nations High Commissioner for Human Rights, 8–14 avenue de la Paix, 1211 Geneva 10, Switzerland. ☎ 41-22-917-9000. 🖷 41-22-917-9016. ✉ webadmin.hchr@unog.ch. 🖥 www.unhchr.ch.

Convention for the Suppression of the Traffic in Persons and of the Exploitation of the Prostitution of Others; Forced Labor; Liberty; Slavery

Social Justice

See Social Rights

Social Rights

Government actions to improve individual living and working conditions are known as social programs (from the Latin *socialis,* meaning allied), and from these has come the concept of social rights, which aim to ensure some minimal economic security for each citizen and provide a basis for independence and freedom. Often considered second-generation rights—of lesser importance than fundamental human rights—they nevertheless represent a goal for nations to strive for in fulfilling the promise that all citizens can share in a nation's economic fortune.

The idea that social programs should be implemented by the state is of ancient origin. Whether motivated by altruism or simply the need to placate citizens, many governments have undertaken projects to improve the living and working conditions of people as a whole, such as public baths, houses of worship, and recreation facilities. Ancient Greek officials promoted athletic, choral, dramatic, and musical competitions to enrich people's lives. Ancient Rome is famous for the "bread and circuses" provided for its citizenry. The notion that citizens had any inherent right to such benefits from the government, however, came much later.

The cornerstone of social rights is the right to an adequate standard of living. This means that the government should provide subsistence living as a minimum for each citizen, including sufficient food, housing, health care, and education. Social rights are related to economic rights because the rights to work, to organize and join trade unions, and to receive a living wage contribute to the attainment of an adequate standard of living. Social rights are also closely related to welfare rights. Programs such as social security (protection by the government in case of disability, unemployment, retirement, and old age), free medical care during maternity, and family assistance when necessary are key elements of social and welfare rights now available in most developed countries.

Social and economic rights came to the fore during the Cold War between the Western and Soviet bloc countries, which lasted until the fall of the Berlin Wall in 1989. The extensive social and economic benefits provided by communist countries to their citizens were viewed by many, particularly in the United States, as a threat to free enterprise, capitalism, and democracy itself because of the total control governments gained over the lives of citizens. Many other democratic nations, including Western European countries, however, embarked on extensive programs for providing their citizens with social and economic benefits, such as those encompassed in the 1996 revision of the European Social Charter (1961).

Some national constitutions refer to social rights or the general welfare, but many do not, regarding them instead as the subject of legislation that can be altered as the economic and political conditions allow. At the international level, where the hard choices often required by cost-benefit analysis do not have to be made, a number of human rights instruments promote social rights, along with economic and cultural rights, as goals to be attained as soon as practical. Among the documents that contain provisions regarding social rights are the American Declaration of the Rights and Duties of Man (1948), Inter-American Charter of Social Guarantees (1948), European Social Charter (1961), Declaration on Social Progress and Development (1969), and African Charter on Human and Peoples' Rights (1981).

These documents contain various social rights expressed in various ways. The African Charter on Human and Peoples' Rights, for example, provides that nations that ratify the charter "shall take the necessary measures to protect the health of their people and to ensure that they receive medical attention when they are sick." The European Social Charter, part I, paragraph 13, states: "Anyone without adequate resources has the right to social and medical assistance."

The International Covenant on Economic, Social and Cultural Rights (1966), part of the International Bill of Human Rights, contains specific provisions in part III, article 10, regarding social rights, calling for recognition of the need to provide "the widest possible protection and assistance . . . to the family, which is the natural and fundamental group unit of society," to mothers "during a reasonable period before and after childbirth," and to "all children and young persons," as well as the right of everyone to "an adequate standard of living." In addition, a proposed draft protocol to the covenant creates a mechanism for bringing complaints against states not abiding by its provisions.

Constitution of India (1950), part IV, Directive Principles of State Policy, article 38 (1): "The State shall strive to promote the welfare of the people by securing and protecting as effectively as it may a social order in which justice, social, economic and political, shall inform all institutions of the national life."

International Covenant on Economic, Social and Cultural Rights (1966), preamble: The states parties recognize that, "in accordance with the Universal Declaration of Human Rights [1948], the ideal of free human beings enjoying freedom from fear and want can only be achieved if conditions are created whereby everyone may enjoy his economic, social and cultural rights, as well as his civil and political rights. . . ."

U.S. Supreme Court (1937): Taxation by the national government pursuant to the Social Security Act is not unconstitutional or an invasion of the rights retained by the states under the Tenth Amendment (1791) to the U.S. Constitution. Consequently, when money is spent to promote the general welfare, the concept of general welfare is shaped by Congress and not the states.

European Court of Human Rights (1979): "The court is aware that the further realization of social and economic rights is largely dependent on the situation—notably financial—reigning in the State in question. . . . [T]he mere fact that an interpretation of the [European Convention for the Protection of Human Rights and Fundamental Freedoms (1950)] may extend into the sphere of social and economic rights should not be a decisive factor against such an interpretation; there is no water-tight division separating that sphere from the field covered by the Convention."

Fundamental Social Rights: Case Law of the European Social Charter. Strasbourg, France: Council of Europe, 1997.

Jacobs, Lesley A. *Rights and Deprivation.* New York: Oxford University Press, 1993.

African Charter on Human and Peoples' Rights; American Declaration of the Rights and Duties of Man; Cultural Rights; Declaration on Social Progress and Development; Economic Rights; European Social Charter; Inter-American Charter of Social Guarantees; International Covenant on Economic, Social and Cultural Rights; International Bill of Human Rights; Limburg Principles on the Implementation of the International Covenant on Economic, Social and Cultural Rights; Standard of Living; Welfare; Workers

Social Security

See Economic Rights; Social Rights; Welfare

Sovereignty

According to the English political philosopher Thomas Hobbes, writing in 1670, sovereignty is rooted in ancient common law. The idea that a defined territory had a right to rule supremely and absolutely within its borders without interference from any outside authority dovetailed nicely with the concept of the divine right of kings, by which monarchs were absolute rulers within their territorial jurisdictions, answerable only to God and equal and unbounded in international relationships, except as they chose to be.

Sovereign states are not themselves subject to any other nation, and their citizens or subjects are required by tradition and law to be obedient to those who hold legitimate national political authority. The right of sovereignty (from the Old French *souverainete*), however, has often depended on the ability of a territory's citizens to protect themselves from intervention, generally by force of arms.

Jean Bodin, the sixteenth-century French philosopher, was the first to comprehensively define sovereignty. His definition, based on Roman law and the French monarchy, was "the absolute and perpetual power of a republic, that is to say the active form and personification of the great body of a modern state." The Dutch jurist Hugo Grotius in the seventeenth century and the Swiss jurist Emerich de Vattel in the eighteenth century elaborated on the concept. Grotius linked the idea of sovereignty with certain principles of natural law; Vattel, building on Grotius's work, based his concept on positive law, as reflected in international treaties and the practices of nations, rather than on natural law. Sovereignty as the basis of international law was established by the Treaty of Augsburg in 1555 and confirmed by the Peace of Westphalia in 1648, following religious wars in Europe. The so-called Westphalian system of international relations replaced the dominion that the pope and the Holy Roman Emperor had held over Europe's individual states.

With the spread of constitutional democracy, sovereignty has evolved from being the right of a single person—the monarch—to a right distributed among all the citizens—that is, popular sovereignty. Elected officials in democracies, who are constitutionally responsible to the citizens, now exercise the rights of sovereignty on the public's behalf in the international arena.

Sovereignty is the basis of all national constitutions, and, as it relates to international relations and the obligations of nations, it is expressly referred to in several human rights instruments, including the Universal Declaration of Human Rights (1948) and the Declaration on Principles of International Law Concerning Friendly Relations and Cooperation among States in Accordance with the Charter of the United Nations (1970).

Sovereignty can work against protection of human rights in that it preserves the right of rulers to treat their subjects or citizens in any way they wish without checks or restraints. Cases brought against a government for damages to private interests, for example, are precluded because under the doctrine of sovereign immunity the state may be sued only with its express consent. Sovereignty also prevents enforcement of international human rights norms within a nation without the permission of the government itself. By various means including treaties, however, a sovereign state may limit its sovereignty in certain respects.

Since the end of World War II, the strict rules of sovereignty have been redefined with respect to some nations to accommodate international human rights law. One recent example is NATO's 1999 military intervention in the affairs of the former territory of Yugoslavia, an action intended to stop a gross violation of international human rights by the country's Serbian ruler: ethnic cleansing in the province of Kosovo. Another example is the 1999 finding by the United Kingdom that under international law Augusto Pinochet, the retired leader of a military junta in Chile who was temporarily residing in England for medical treatment, could be held and extradited to Spain to stand trial for human rights violations during his rule in Chile. Pinochet was subsequently allowed to return to Chile, where he may yet be held accountable for gross violations of human rights.

Constitution of Turkey (1982), part one, General Principles, Sovereignty, article 6: "Sovereignty is vested in the nation without reservation or condition. The Turkish nation shall exercise its sovereignty through the authorized organs as prescribed by the principles laid down in the constitution. The right to exercise sovereignty shall not be delegated to any individual, group, or class. No person or agency shall exercise any state authority which does not emanate from the constitution."

Universal Declaration of Human Rights (1948), article 2: "Furthermore, no distinction shall be made on the basis of political, jurisdictional or international status of the country or territory to which the person belongs, whether it be independent, trust, non-self-governing or under any other limitation of sovereignty."

Supreme Court of Canada (1987): The court confirmed a decision finding that claims to lands in Newfoundland based on a 1697 grant by the Dutch sovereign were negated by subsequent treaties transferring sovereignty from France to England.

International Court of Justice (1992): "Territorial sovereignty also connotes obligations and, in the first place, the obligation to maintain and protect it by observing a vigilant conduct towards possible inroads by other States."

Hannum, Hurst. *Autonomy, Sovereignty, and Self-Determination: The Accommodation of Conflicting Rights.* Philadelphia: University of Pennsylvania Press, 1996.

Mills, Kurt. *Human Rights in the Emerging Global Order: A New Sovereignty?* New York: St. Martin's, 1998.

Charter of the United Nations; Constitutionalism; Grotius, Hugo; International Law; Territorial Jurisdiction; Treaties; Self-Determination; Universal Declaration of Human Rights; War

Speech

"Speech, even more than reason, distinguishes man from the brute," observed an 1878 book on English literature. Language, of which speech is one form and writing is another, is used solely by the human species. Other animals make sounds, and many of them have a repertoire of sounds for different situations. But none of them learns a structured language on its own. Even intensively trained and coached primates such as chimpanzees skilled in sign language never approach the fluency of the average three-year-old child.

The earliest form of language, speech (from the same roots as the German word *sprache*) is often credited as the last development in human evolution, facilitating the great leap forward to culture. This in turn led to advances in science, technology, art, religion, and politics. Without being able to share complex ideas about the world around them, people could not have developed cultural concepts.

Speech was once the primary means of conveying important cultural and political messages. Demosthenes of ancient Greece and Marcus Tullius Cicero of ancient Rome were honored as great orators. The philosopher Plato, a contemporary of Demosthenes in Greece, was not an advocate of free speech, however, and Rome used officials called censors (from which the English word *censorship* is derived) to police citizens' morals and manners.

The rise of absolute monarchies eclipsed the idea of freedom of speech. But Magna Carta (1215), the first English charter of liberties, challenged the monarch's right to arbitrarily void rights established by custom although it did not grant the right of free speech to all English subjects. Once the government could be challenged on the basis of law and tradition, the right of free speech became more important. The English Bill of Rights (1688) guaranteed free speech—but only for speech and debate in Parliament—a right adopted in the debate clause of the U.S. Constitution (1789), article I, section 6, which guarantees that members of Congress "for any Speech or Debate in either House [of Congress] . . . shall not be questioned in any other Place." Similar immunity for speech by elected legislators has been adopted in most national constitutions.

The U.S. Bill of Rights (1791) became the world's first national constitutional document to grant freedom of speech to ordinary individuals. At nearly the same time France offered a similar right in the Declaration of the Rights of Man and of the Citizen (1789). Article 11 states: "Free communication of ideas and opinions is one of the most precious of the rights of man. Consequently, every citizen may speak, write and print freely; yet he may have to answer for the abuse of that liberty in the cases determined by law." Today almost all national constitutions that include a bill or a declaration of rights include a provision guaranteeing freedom of speech or expression, as do most international documents that address basic individual rights and freedoms; some of these may be couched in terms of freedom of expression.

Although freedom of speech is designed to further the exchange of ideas, particularly political ideas, the government may permissibly regulate free speech in a number of areas. The laws of slander and libel impose penalties for damaging another person by making misleading, false, or malicious utterances or printed statements. Speech that incites violence or causes injury, such as shouting "Fire!" in a crowded theater and thereby unleashing a stampede of people for the exits, may result in criminal liability. Perjury (lying under oath) and infringing copyrights of published works are not protected speech.

Speech in a public forum may be regulated to a greater degree than the same speech in a private setting. In the United States, at least, the courts have generally required such regulation to be "content neutral" rather than attempt to limit the expression of a particular subject or ideology. Public obscenity and pornography may also be restricted for being beyond the protection of free speech. The use of speech over loudspeakers that produce "loud and raucous noises" may also be limited as a disturbance of the peace.

Freedom of speech or expression is closely related to freedom of association and the right to peacefully assembly and petition the government for redress of grievances. Similar types of protected speech include "speech plus" actions—for example, picketing to protest government or private actions, carrying placards, or distributing leaflets to promote a cause or air a grievance—and symbolic speech, such as burning the national flag to protest a government policy or action.

Commercial activities may also be protected under the right to free speech but are generally subject to greater government restrictions than political speech. The limited number of broadcast bands has led most governments to set standards for radio and television broadcasting rights, thus limiting free speech in this area. Cable television and the Internet have added a new dimension to the conflict between freedom of speech and the government's concern with limiting dangerous or offensive speech. Internet issues include anti-abortionists' posting of lists of doctors who perform abortions, with the implied intent of encouraging viewers to harass them or worse, and the accessibility of pornography to children, which epitomizes the government's concern about balancing the rights of free speech and the public's right to keep such material away from minors.

Constitution of Japan (1947), chapter III, Rights and Duties of the People, article 21: "Freedom of assembly and association as well as speech, press, and all other forms of expression are guaranteed. No censorship shall be maintained, nor shall secrecy of any means of communication be violated."

International Covenant on Civil and Political Rights (1966), part III, article 20: "1. Any propaganda for war shall be prohibited by law. 2. Any advocacy of national, racial, or religious hatred that constitutes incitement to discrimination, hostility or violence shall be prohibited by law."

U.S. Court of Appeals, Fifth Circuit (1992): The right to refrain from speech is violated when the government compels a person to endorse beliefs that she finds repugnant.

European Court of Human Rights (1996): The European Commission of Human Rights found that the British Board of Film Classification had violated the European Convention for the Protection of Human Rights and Fundamental Freedoms (1950), article 10 ("... freedom ... to impart information and ideas without interference by public authority ..."), by rejecting a film on the grounds that it would cause an outrage and that a reasonable jury would find that it infringed the criminal law of blasphemy. When the court reviewed the case, it held that article 10 was not violated, because the imprecise legal definition of *blasphemy* meant that national authorities had to be afforded a degree of flexibility in assessing the facts in each case.

American Civil Liberties Union (ACLU), 125 Broad Street, 18th Floor, New York, N.Y. 10004-2400. (212-549-2500. ⊟ 212-549-2648. ▣ aclu@aclu.org. ▣ www.aclu.org.

Committee to Protect Journalists, 330 7th Avenue, 12th Floor, New York, N.Y. 10001. (212-465-1004. ⊟ 212-465-9568. ▣ info@cpj.org. ▣ www.cpj.org.

Haworth, Alan. *Free Speech*. London: Routledge, 1998.

Ingelhart, Louis E., comp. *Press and Speech Freedoms in the World, from Antiquity until 1998: A Chronology*. Westport, Conn.: Greenwood, 1998.

Assembly; Association; Bills of Rights; Communication; Declaration of the Rights of Man and of the Citizen (France); Expression; Information; Opinion; The Press; Thought

Spinoza, Benedict

A rationalist philosopher, Benedict Spinoza (1632–77) believed that mind and matter are two aspects of an infinite substance that he variously called nature, substance, or God, with good and evil being relative. His classic five-volume work *Ethics* (1675), which concluded that human freedom results from the virtue of the intellect, paved the way for the logical formulation of morality on which human rights are based.

The noted philosopher was born Baruch Spinoza on November 24, 1632, into a prominent Jewish family in Amsterdam, where his family had settled after fleeing religious persecution in Portugal. He studied at the synagogue school and showed an affinity for languages, eventually mastering Spanish, Dutch, Portuguese, Hebrew, Latin, Greek, and German. Although his grandfather had been the leader of the Jewish community, Spinoza developed heretical, atheistic views and was expelled from his congregation in 1656. He reacted by Christianizing his name to Benedict.

After teaching for four years at a private academy in Amsterdam, he joined a free religious sect outside Leiden and began writing and conducting a large correspondence with various scientists and philosophers. During this time he completed the first volume of his *Ethics*, which was eventually finished by 1675. To maintain his intellectual integrity, he later turned down a professorship at the University of Heidelberg, supporting himself as a lens grinder. He died of consumption in The Hague on February 21, 1677.

Spinoza's reasoning in *Ethics* has been called difficult to follow. He concluded that a person has an identity that strives to perpetuate itself, experiencing pleasure when things are in harmony with that striving and pain when they are not. He saw reason as the road to freedom, in which human nature finds its true purpose. An admirer of the French philosopher René Descartes and a correspondent of the German philosopher Gottfried Wilhelm von Leibniz, Spinoza contributed to the progress of rationalism over the forces of blind passion and to the rational ordering of human activity.

Nadler, Steven M. *Spinoza: A Life*. New York: Cambridge University Press, 1999.

Scruton, Roger. *Spinoza*. New York: Routledge, 1999.

Standard Minimum Rules for the Administration of Juvenile Justice (Beijing Rules)

Juveniles accused of crimes should be separated from adults in detention, the International Covenant on Civil and Political Rights (1966) recommends, adding that "their age and the desirability of promoting their rehabilitation" should be taken into consideration during any encounters with the justice system. Two decades later more detailed standards for national governments to follow in dealing with juvenile offenders were set out in the Standard Minimum Rules for the Administration of Juvenile Justice, drafted by a committee that met in Beijing in May 1984. The next summer the Seventh United Nations Congress on the Prevention of Crime and the Treatment of Offenders, meeting in Milan, recommended that the UN General Assembly adopt these so-called Beijing Rules, which it did on November 29, 1985.

Part One, General Principles, article 1, Fundamental Perspectives, declares in paragraphs 1.1 and 1.2: "Member States shall seek, in conformity with their respective general interests, to further the well-being of the juvenile and her or his family. Member States shall endeavor to develop conditions that will ensure for the juvenile a meaningful life in the community, which, during that period of life when she or he is most susceptible to deviant behavior, will foster a process of personal development and education that is as free from crime and delinquency as possible." "These Rules shall be implemented," states paragraph 1.5, "in the context of economic, social and cultural conditions prevailing in each Member State."

Adds paragraph 1.6: "Juvenile justice services shall be systematically developed and coordinated with a view to improving and sustaining the competence of personnel involved in the services, including their methods, approaches and attitudes." A commentary section provides, among other things, that "[t]hese broad fundamental perspectives refer to comprehensive social policy in general and aim at promoting juvenile welfare to the greatest possible extent, which will minimize the necessity of intervention by the juvenile justice system, and in turn, will reduce the harm that may be caused by any intervention. Such care measures for the young, before the onset of delinquency, are basic policy requisites designed to obviate the need for the application of the Rules."

According to article 2, Scope of the Rules and Definitions Used, paragraph 2.1, "The [rules] shall be applied to juvenile offenders impartially, without distinction of any kind, for example as to race, color, sex, language, religion, political or other opinions, national or social origin, property, birth or other status." Definitions under paragraph 2.2 include: "(a) A *juvenile* is a child or young person who, under the respective legal systems, may be dealt with for an offense in a manner which is different from an adult. . . . (c) A *juvenile offender* is a child or young person who is alleged to have committed or who has been found to have committed an offense." Adds paragraph 2.3: "Efforts shall be made to establish, in each national jurisdiction, a set of laws, rules and provisions specifically applicable to juvenile offenders and institutions and bodies entrusted with . . . the administration of juvenile justice. . . ."

Under article 3, Extension of the Rules, paragraphs 3.1 to 3.3 provide that the rules "shall be applied not only to juvenile offenders but also to juveniles who may be proceeded against for any specific behavior that would not be punishable if committed by an adult," as well as to those "dealt with in welfare and care proceedings" and "young adult offenders."

Article 4, Age of Criminal Responsibility, provides that "[i]n those legal systems recognizing the concept of the age of criminal responsibility for juveniles, the beginning of that age shall not be fixed at too low an age level, bearing in mind the facts of emotional, mental and intellectual maturity." Article 5, Aims of Juvenile Justice, directs that the juvenile justice system "shall emphasize the well-being of the juvenile and shall ensure that any reaction to juvenile offenders shall always be in proportion to the circumstances of both the offender and the offense."

Basic procedural safeguards are set out in article 7, Rights of Juveniles, which cites rights including the presumption of innocence, notification of the charges, the choice of silence, representation by counsel, the presence of a parent or a guardian, cross-examination of witnesses, and appeal to a higher authority. Article 8, Protection of Privacy, seeks to shield young offenders from "undue publicity" and "the process of labeling," as well as public identification.

Part Two, Investigation and Prosecution, sets forth guidelines for handling juvenile cases, such as requiring immediate notification of parents or guardians and judicial consideration of release. Article 11, Diversion, suggests, where appropriate, dealing with offenders "without resorting to formal trial" and other discretionary disposition of cases, including referral to community services, temporary supervision, restitution, and compensation of victims. Article 12, Specialization within the Police, calls for special training and units devoted to juveniles. In article 13, Detention Pending Trial, imprisonment is deemed "a measure of last resort," one that wherever possible should be replaced by alternative measures such as close supervision or placement with a family or in an educational setting. "Juveniles under detention pending trial," states paragraph 13.3, "shall be entitled to all rights and guarantees of the Standard Minimum Rules for the Treatment of Prisoners [1955] adopted by the United Nations." Paragraph 13.4 adds that they "shall be kept separate from adults and shall be detained in a separate institution or in a separate part of an institution also holding adults."

Part Three, Adjudication and Disposition, paragraph 14.2, requires that formal "proceedings shall be conducive to the best interests of the juvenile and shall be conducted in an atmosphere of understanding, which shall allow the juvenile to participate therein and to express herself or himself freely." Other paragraphs secure access to a legal adviser and the participation of parents and guardians as well as a "social inquiry report" into the juvenile's background. "Deprivation of personal liberty," notes paragraph 17.1(c), "shall not be imposed unless the juvenile is adjudicated of a serious act involving violence against another person or of persistence in committing other serious offenses and unless there is no other appropriate response." Adds paragraph 17.1(d): "The well-being of the juvenile shall be the guiding factor in the consideration of her or his case."

Article 18, Various Disposition Measures, lists alternatives to institutionalization, including guidance and supervision, probation, community service, financial penalties and restitution, foster care, and court orders "to participate in group counseling and similar activities." Placing a juvenile in an institution, states paragraph 19.1, "shall always be a disposition of last resort and for the minimum necessary period." Article 21, Records, mandates that juvenile records "be kept strictly confidential and closed to third parties" and that they "not be used in adult proceedings in subsequent cases involving the same offender."

Noninstitutional and institutional treatments are addressed in Parts Four and Five, including issues such as objectives of each and release of the juvenile. Research, planning, policy formulation, and evaluation are covered in Part Six, the last section of the rules.

In view of the special care and assistance young people

require to mature into responsible citizens without getting into trouble, the General Assembly on December 14, 1990, adopted two additional sets of guidelines for juveniles: Rules for the Protection of Juveniles Deprived of Their Liberty, which assist professionals who manage juvenile justice systems; and Guidelines for the Prevention of Juvenile Delinquency (Riyadh Guidelines), which encourage governments to steer young people away from criminal activities and toward "lawful, socially useful activities."

United Nations High Commissioner for Human Rights, 8–14 avenue de la Paix, 1211 Geneva 10, Switzerland. ☎ 41-22-917-9000. 🖷 41-22-917-9016. 🖳 webadmin.hchr@unog.ch. 🖳 www.unhchr.ch.

United Nations Youth Unit, One United Nations Plaza, Room DC 2-1318, New York, N.Y. 10017. ☎ 212-963-1380. 🖷 212-963-3062. 🖳 youth@un.org. 🖳 www.un.org/esa/socdev/unyin/yth-unit.

Accused; Detention; Guidelines for the Prevention of Juvenile Delinquency (Riyadh Guidelines); Rules for the Protection of Juveniles Deprived of Their Liberty; Prisoners; Standard Minimum Rules for the Treatment of Prisoners; Youth

Standard Minimum Rules for the Treatment of Prisoners

Punishment of offenders is the obligation of the state, but in civilized countries punishment must be humane and not "cruel and unusual," a term used in the U.S. Bill of Rights (1791). Although those convicted of crimes have forfeited many rights by breaking the law, they are still entitled to some basic human rights. To reflect generally accepted principles and practices for the treatment of prisoners and the management of penal institutions, the Standard Minimum Rules for the Treatment of Prisoners were adopted by the First United Nations Congress on the Prevention of Crime and the Treatment of Offenders in Geneva in 1955 and then approved by the Economic and Social Council (ECOSOC) on July 31, 1957. On May 13, 1977, ECOSOC added a new section on Persons Arrested or Detained without Charge.

Other related UN human rights documents on prisoners include the Declaration on the Protection of All Persons from Being Subjected to Torture and Other Cruel, Inhuman or Degrading Treatment or Punishment (1975), Convention against Torture and Other Cruel, Inhuman or Degrading Treatment or Punishment (1984), Body of Principles for the Protection of All Persons under Any Form of Detention or Imprisonment (1988), and Basic Principles for the Treatment of Prisoners (1990). In the latter document the UN General Assembly affirmed the right of all prisoners to "be treated with the respect due their inherent dignity and value as human beings."

The 1955 rules begin with Preliminary Observations, paragraph 1 of which notes: "The following rules are not intended to describe in detail a model system of penal institutions. They seek only . . . to set out what is generally accepted as being good principle and practice in the treatment of prisoners and the management of institutions." More observations follow in paragraphs 2 and 3: "In view of the great variety of legal, social, economic and geographical conditions of the world, it is evident that not all of the rules are capable of application in all places and at all times. . . . On the other hand, the rules cover a field in which thought is constantly developing. They are not intended to preclude experiment and practices, provided these are in harmony with the principles and seek to further the purposes which derive from the text of the rules as a whole." According to paragraph 5, "young persons should not be sentenced to imprisonment."

Part I, Rules of General Application, Basic Principle, paragraph 6, states that "[t]here shall be no discrimination on grounds of race, color, sex, language, religion, political or other opinion, national or social origin, property, birth or other status," but adds that "it is necessary to respect religious beliefs and moral precepts of the group to which a prisoner belongs." Register, paragraph 7, mandates that a register of vital information about each prisoner be maintained at every place of imprisonment.

Under Separation of Categories, paragraph 8, it is recommended that separate prisons or parts of institutions be created for men and women, untried detainees and convicted prisoners, civil and criminal offenders, and youths and adults. Living, working, and sleeping accommodations are addressed under Accommodation, paragraphs 9 through 14, as are sanitary conditions. One item calls for windows "large enough to enable the prisoners to read or work by natural light," together with fresh air. Additional sections, encompassing paragraphs 15 through 55, address issues of personal hygiene, including shaving and hair care; clothing and bedding, including clean beds; food, including wholesome food "well prepared and served"; exercise and sport, including at least one hour of open-air exercise daily; medical services, including prenatal and postnatal care for imprisoned mothers; discipline and punishment, including "no more restriction than is necessary"; prohibitions on instruments of restraint, including "handcuffs, chains, irons and strait-jackets"; information to and complaints by prisoners, including the right to complain to prison authorities; contact with the outside world, including communication with "family and reputable friends"; books, including recreational and instructional titles; religion, including the right to satisfy one's religious life; personal property, including return of all items held; notification of illness, death, and transfer, including notice to a spouse or the nearest relative; removal of prisoners, including protection from public "insult, curiosity and publicity";

institutional personnel, including reliable and competent employees; and inspection, including review of adherence to applicable laws.

Part II, Rules Applicable to Special Categories, A, Prisoners under Sentence, Guiding Principles, paragraph 57, provides that "[i]mprisonment and other measures which result in cutting off an offender from the outside world are afflictive by the very fact of taking from the person the right of self-determination by depriving him of his liberty. Therefore the prison system shall not, except as incidental to justifiable segregation or the maintenance of discipline, aggravate the suffering inherent in such a situation." Paragraphs 59 through 61 deal with, among other things, the goal of returning prisoners to society when their sentences have been served and safeguards "to the maximum extent compatible with the law and the sentence, the rights relating to civil interests, social security rights and other social benefits of prisoners." "The treatment [of prisoners]," states Treatment, paragraph 65, "shall be such as will encourage their self-respect and develop their sense of responsibility." Other items addressed regarding prisoners under sentence concern classification of prisoners, privileges, work, education and recreation, social relations, and aid after release from prison.

Part II concludes by setting out rules for insane and "mentally abnormal" prisoners, prisoners under arrest or awaiting trial, and civil prisoners—debtors, for example, who may be legally incarcerated in some countries.

The final item, section E, Persons Arrested or Detained without Charge, paragraph 95, was added by ECOSOC in 1977. Persons not charged, it states, are to be extended "the same protection as that accorded" under the document's rules for prisoners under arrest or awaiting trial and under sentence "where their application may be conducive to the benefit of this special group of persons in custody. . . ." However, the rules add, "no measure shall be taken implying that re-education or rehabilitation is in any way appropriate to persons not convicted of any criminal offense."

✉

United Nations High Commissioner for Human Rights, 8–14 avenue de la Paix, 1211 Geneva 10, Switzerland. ☎ 41-22-917-9000. 🖨 41-22-917-9016. 🖳 webadmin.hchr@unog.ch. 🖳 www.unhchr.ch.

Basic Principles for the Treatment of Prisoners; Beccaria, Cesare; Body of Principles for the Protection of All Persons under Any Form of Detention or Imprisonment; Convention against Torture and Other Cruel, Inhuman or Degrading Treatment or Punishment; Declaration on the Protection of All Persons from Being Subjected to Torture and Other Cruel, Inhuman or Degrading Treatment or Punishment; Prisoners; Punishment; Rules for the Protection of Juveniles Deprived of Their Liberty; Standard Minimum Rules for the Administration of Juvenile Justice; Torture

Standard of Living

The broad right to an adequate standard of living encompasses the more specific rights to sufficient food, shelter, health care, education, employment, and social security. This concept is implicit in the notions of economic and social rights embodied in the International Covenant on Economic, Social and Cultural Rights (1966). But even if a national government adopts a policy of guaranteeing all its citizens an adequate standard of living (a term used in English since the early eighteenth century to indicate a level of wealth or quality of life), the country's economic conditions will determine whether and how well such a policy can be implemented.

Recognition of an adequate standard of living as an international goal took a major step forward in 1919, with the International Labor Organization's adoption of its constitution. It declared that "all human beings, irrespective of race, creed, or sex, have the right to pursue both their material well-being and their spiritual development in conditions of freedom and dignity, of economic security and equal opportunity."

Although there is no general agreement among nations about how to implement the right to an adequate standard of living, President Franklin D. Roosevelt included "freedom from want" in his famous four freedoms in 1941. In the United States the debate often focuses on whether a government guarantee of economic freedom and opportunity is sufficient to promote an adequate standard of living for all citizens, allowing for a "safety net" of minimal government support for those who fail to attain such a standard, or whether the government should guarantee to all citizens a minimum standard of living above the poverty level.

Few national constitutions expressly guarantee an adequate standard of living, but a number of international human rights documents do, including the Universal Declaration of Human Rights (1948), International Covenant on Economic, Social and Cultural Rights (1966), and Convention on the Rights of the Child (1989). Other international human rights documents, such as the Declaration on the Right to Development (1986), promote the idea of raising the standard of living for all people.

Constitution of the Philippines (1987), article II, section 5: "The maintenance of peace and order, the protection of life, liberty, and property, and the promotion of the general welfare are essential for the enjoyment by all the people of the blessings of democracy."

International Covenant on Economic, Social, and Cultural Rights (1966), article 11, section 1: The states parties to the covenant "recognize the right of everyone to an adequate standard of living for himself and his family, including adequate food, clothing and housing, and to the continuous improvement of living conditions

... [and] will take appropriate steps to ensure the realization of this right, recognizing to this effect the essential importance of international co-operation based on free consent."

Supreme Court of Japan (1982): Although Japan's constitution (1947), article 25, states that people shall have "the right to maintain a minimum standard of wholesome and cultured living," section 1 does not make the government liable to citizens for fulfilling this requirement in specific terms. Such matters must be left to the wide discretion of the legislative branch of the government.

European Court of Human Rights (1993): Serious delay in a proceeding to determine payment of a disability allowance under a social security statute in Italy was a breach of the claimant's right under the European Convention for the Protection of Human Rights and Fundamental Freedoms (1950), article 6, which guarantees a fair hearing on the determination of a person's civil rights.

Khusro, Ali M. *The Poverty of Nations.* New York: St. Martin's, 1999.

Owens, Sarah, and Paris Yeros, eds. *Poverty in World Politics: Whose Global Era?* New York: St. Martin's, 1999.

Wealth, Work, Well-being: Cunningham Lecture and Annual Symposium, 1997. Canberra: Academy of Social Sciences in Australia, 1998.

Convention on the Rights of the Child; Declaration on the Right to Development; Economic Rights; Food; Housing; International Covenant on Economic, Social and Cultural Rights; Social Rights; Universal Declaration of Human Rights; Welfare

Stanton, Elizabeth Cady

Elizabeth Cady Stanton (1815–1902) spent her life opposing discrimination on many fronts. She fought for women's suffrage and in 1848 launched the first convention on women's rights in America, although she did not live to see American women win the right to vote in 1920. As an abolitionist she worked equally hard for the rights of blacks both before and after the Civil War.

Born on November 12, 1815, in Johnstown, New York, Stanton studied law with her father, a judge, even though only men were admitted into the profession at that time. After hearing her father advise married women abused by their husbands that they had no recourse, she embarked on a lifetime of activism.

In 1840 she married Henry Stanton, an abolitionist, with whom she had five children. She once traveled to London with her husband to attend an antislavery convention, only to learn that she and other women would not be permitted to participate. Even with her family responsibilities, Stanton found time to write and speak out for feminist causes. She wrote a declaration of principles for the 1848 Women's Rights Convention held in Seneca Falls, New York, where she lived, and pushed through a resolution at the convention demanding the vote for women.

During the Civil War, Stanton and Susan B. Anthony created the National Women's Loyal League to promote adoption of a constitutional amendment prohibiting slavery; the measure became the Thirteenth Amendment to the Constitution in 1865. The ensuing campaign to enfranchise black freedmen split the women's organization into two camps: one wanting to link suffrage for women and blacks and one wanting to work first for suffrage for black men. In 1890, however, the camps reunited to form the National American Woman Suffrage Association and elected Stanton as the first president.

In addition to contributing numerous articles to magazines, Stanton helped write the *History of Woman Suffrage* and edited *The Woman's Bible*, a feminist critique of the Bible. In the Seneca Falls Declaration of Sentiments and Resolutions, she proclaimed: "The history of mankind is a history of repeated injuries and usurpations on the part of man towards woman, having in direct object the establishment of an absolute tyranny over her. To prove this, let the facts be submitted to a candid world." She died on October 26, 1902.

Women's Rights National Historical Park, 136 Fall Street, Seneca Falls, N.Y. 13148. ℂ 315-568-2991. 🖨 315-568-2141. 🖳 www.nps.gov/wori.

Cullen-DuPont, Kathryn. *Elizabeth Cady Stanton and Women's Liberty.* New York: Facts on File, 1992.

Davis, Lucile. *Elizabeth Cady Stanton.* Mankato, Minn.: Bridgestone, 1998.

Stanton, Elizabeth Cady. *The Selected Papers of Elizabeth Cady Stanton and Susan B. Anthony.* New Brunswick, N.J.: Rutgers University Press, 1997.

Waggenspack, Beth Marie. *The Search for Self-Sovereignty.* New York: Greenwood, 1989.

Discrimination; Equality; Seneca Falls Declaration of Sentiments and Resolutions; Sex Discrimination; Slavery; Voting; Women

Statelessness

"In the case of statelessness, which is the opposite of dual nationality or multiple nationality, an unfortunate individual is placed in the unenviable position of being without any country at all," noted an English author of a 1930 work on nationality in the British Commonwealth. The number of stateless people today, while difficult to determine, is estimated by the Office of the United Nations High Commissioner for Refugees to be several million worldwide.

Statelessness can occur in various ways. A person of legal age may renounce citizenship of one country and yet not become a citizen of another. For a person born outside a country that bases citizenship on one's place of birth rather than on the nationality of one's parents, a positive act by the person seeking citizenship may be required under national law. Individuals and groups may become stateless if stripped of their citizenship by their own government, as Jews in Germany were "denationalized" in the 1930s under Nazi laws that stripped their rights to German citizenship. In an extreme case, if a country loses its sovereignty under international law as the result of a war or an international agreement, its whole population may become stateless. During World War II, when the United States acquired the Philippine Islands by conquest from the Japanese, the Filipinos lost their sovereignty and citizenship and became U.S. nationals, not U.S. citizens, a situation that obtained until July 4, 1946, when the United States relinquished its sovereignty over the islands.

The concept of nationality developed as an accepted part of international law in the late eighteenth century. The status of a citizen of a sovereign country is basically a matter of domestic law. The Hague Convention on Certain Questions Relating to the Conflict of Nationality Laws (1930) declares: "It is for each State to determine under its own law who are its nationals." However, the convention did not address the loss of nationality resulting from the transfer of territory, which was the major cause of statelessness at the time.

Even before the adoption of the Universal Declaration of Human Rights (1948), the Economic and Social Council (ECOSOC) requested the UN secretary-general to conduct a study on the problems of statelessness. Although drafts of conventions on the subject were submitted to the UN General Assembly in 1954, it was not until 1961 that action was taken by the United Nations Conference on the Elimination or Reduction of Future Statelessness, which met first in Geneva and later reconvened at the UN headquarters in New York City. The conference representatives adopted the Convention on the Reduction of Statelessness but not the draft Convention on the Elimination of Statelessness, although they did agree that every effort should be made to avoid the statelessness of children.

Similarly, Europe's emphasis has been on ensuring a basis of nationality for a child born to stateless parents. In 1977 and 1983 the Committee of Ministers of the Council of Europe adopted resolutions inviting member countries to facilitate nationality for foreign-born spouses and for children with one parent who was already a national and urging measures to reduce the stateless character of nomads.

In addition to the 1961 Convention on the Reduction of Statelessness, international human rights documents that address statelessness include the Convention Relating to the Status of Refugees (1951) and its Protocol Relating to the Status of Refugees (1967), Convention Relating to the Status of Stateless Persons (1954), Convention on the Nationality of Married Women (1957), Convention on the Elimination of All Forms of Racial Discrimination (1965), and Convention on the Elimination of All Forms of Discrimination against Women (1979).

Constitution of Germany (1949), I, Basic Rights, article 16: "(1) No one may be deprived of his German citizenship. Citizenship may be lost only pursuant to a statute, and it may be lost against the will of the person affected only where such person does not become stateless as a result thereof."

Universal Declaration of Human Rights (1948), article 15: "1. Everyone has the right to a nationality. 2. No one shall arbitrarily be deprived of his nationality nor denied the right to change his nationality."

Supreme Administrative Court of Finland (1995): The passport of a child of mixed Finnish-Russian parentage cannot be canceled simply on the basis of Russian legislation in 1992 automatically extending Russian citizenship to certain categories of persons and without sufficient evidence of the factual grounds for the purported loss of Finnish citizenship.

European Court of Human Rights (1985): Although the European Convention for the Protection of Human Rights and Fundamental Freedoms (1950) does not include the right to nationality, this omission does not preclude the possibility that deprivation of nationality might raise other issues under the convention.

United Nations High Commissioner for Refugees, C.P. 2500, 1211 Geneva 2, Switzerland. 41-22-739-8111. 41-22-739-7377. hqpioo@unhcr.ch. www.unhcr.ch.

Vertovec, Steven, and Robin Cohen, eds. *Migration, Diasporas, and Transnationalism.* Northampton, Mass.: Edward Elgar, 1999.

Weis, Paul. *Nationality and Statelessness in International Law.* Westport, Conn.: Hyperion, 1979.

Convention on the Elimination of All Forms of Discrimination against Women; Convention on the Elimination of All Forms of Racial Discrimination; Convention Relating to the Status of Refugees; European Convention for the Protection of Human Rights and Fundamental Freedoms; Nationality; Refugees; Universal Declaration of Human Rights

Statutory Rights

See Constitutional Rights

Students

Although the rights of students traditionally have not been separately recognized, their rights, especially beyond the elementary school level, are a microcosm of adult human rights. In addition to the right to education, these rights traverse such issues as freedom of speech and the press, privacy, religion, security, and punishment.

The primary right of students is the right to a free public education through secondary school without discrimination on account of race, color, sex, religion, national origin, disability, or learning ability. In addition, students have a basic right to be treated with dignity and respect. The Convention on the Rights of the Child (1989), article 28, sets forth, among other things, that states parties to the convention must "recognize the right of the child to education . . . on the basis of equal opportunity, . . . [m]ake primary education compulsory and available free to all; . . . [m]ake educational and vocational information and guidance available and accessible to all children; . . . [and] take all appropriate measures to ensure that school discipline is administered in a manner consistent with the child's human dignity. . . ." The child's education, according to article 29, "shall be directed to: (a) The development of the child's personality, talents and mental and physical abilities to their fullest potential; (b) the development of respect for human rights and fundamental freedoms, and for the principles enshrined in the Charter of the United Nations. . . ." Thus, teachers, administrators, other school staff, and school board members have a duty to respect student rights and foster in young people a similar respect for the human rights of others.

Other student rights involve freedom of speech, in the case of school publications; personal security, with respect to supervision and the right to a weapon-free environment; the right to healthful facilities free of drugs; and humane treatment with respect to disciplinary measures by school officials. One of the most contentious student issues occurs over religion: when students or faculty members of one faith want to use public school facilities or time for religious expression such as praying and displaying or using religious material, including wearing religious symbols. Privacy, regarding personal possessions, school lockers, and records, is another concern of students. Records, for example, often contain subjective determinations such as teachers' evaluations. The Family Educational Rights and Privacy Act (1974) grants students and parents access to some of these records at federally funded schools.

In the United States, student rights have been well litigated in the courts. In a case involving censorship of a high school newspaper containing interviews with students about divorce and teenage pregnancy, the U.S. Supreme Court found that school administrators had wide latitude to determine "whether to disseminate student speech on potentially sensitive topics." The Court has also held that students are not entitled to the same protections as adults with respect to searches. Students' right to privacy must be balanced against the "substantial interests of teachers and administrators in maintaining discipline in the classroom and on school grounds."

National constitutions generally do not address student rights in detail or at all except indirectly with respect to the right to an education. The constitution of Sweden (1975) authorizes financial support for students, while the constitution of Ecuador (1979) guarantees that education "will stimulate development of the critical capacity of the student to fully understand the Ecuadorian reality. . . ."

Many international human rights documents, in addition to the Convention on the Rights of the Child, touch on aspects of student rights, among them the African Charter on the Rights and Welfare of the Child (1990) and Convention against Discrimination in Education (1962), which provides that countries party to it must, among other things, "ensure, by legislation where necessary, that there is no discrimination in the admission of pupils to educational institutions. . . ." Student rights may also be supported by general human rights documents, such as the European Convention for the Protection of Human Rights and Fundamental Freedoms (1950).

Constitution of Italy (1948), part one, The Duties and Rights of the Citizen, title II, Ethical and Social Problems, article 33: "By laying down the rights and obligations of private schools which request equality, the law shall assure those schools have total freedom and their students enjoy a school treatment equal to that of the students of state schools."

Convention against Discrimination in Education (1960), article 1: "1. For the purposes of this Convention, the term 'discrimination' includes any distinction, exclusion, limitation or preference which, being based on race, color, sex, language, religion, political or other opinion, national or social origin, economic condition or birth, has the purpose or effect of nullifying or impairing equality of treatment in education and in particular . . . (d) Of inflicting on any person or group of persons conditions which are incompatible with the dignity of man."

U.S. Supreme Court (Opinion of Justice Abe Fortas) (1969): "In our system, state-operated schools may not be enclaves of totalitarianism. School officials do not possess absolute authority over students. Students in school as well as out of school are 'persons' under our Constitution."

European Court of Human Rights (1982): In the context of the European Convention for the Protection of Human Rights and Fundamental Freedoms (1950), the right not to be denied access to education is "the right of the child" and not the right of the parent.

American Civil Liberties Union (ACLU), 125 Broad Street, 18th Floor, New York, N.Y. 10004-2400. (212-549-2500. 📠 212-549-2646. 🖳 aclu@aclu.org. 🖳 www.aclu.org.

Student Rights Forum. 🖳 www.tentler.com/studentrightsforum.

Cate, Fred H. *The Internet and the First Amendment: Schools and Sexually Explicit Expression.* Bloomington, Ind.: Phi Delta Kappa Educational Foundation, 1998.

Lane, Robert Wheeler. *Beyond the Schoolhouse Gate: Free Speech and the Inculcation of Values.* Philadelphia: Temple University Press, 1995.

Weeks, J. Devereux. *Student Rights under the Constitution: Selected Federal Decisions Affecting the Public School Community.* Athens, Ga.: Carl Vinson Institute of Government, University of Georgia, 1992.

African Charter on the Rights and Welfare of the Child; Children; Convention against Discrimination in Education; Convention on the Rights of the Child; Discrimination; Education; The Press; Privacy; Religion; Teachers; Youth

Subcommission on the Promotion and Protection of Human Rights

Established in 1947 under the authorization of the Economic and Social Council (ECOSOC), the Subcommission on the Prevention of Discrimination and the Protection of Minorities was renamed in 1999 the Subcommission on the Promotion and Protection of Human Rights to reflect its broader current responsibilities. The subcom-

mission is the main subsidiary body of the Commission on Human Rights, which was created under the authority of the Charter of the United Nations (1945). Because its twenty-six members, each of whom is an expert on human rights issues, are elected in their personal capacities, the subcommission may be more effective in addressing human rights concerns than the commission itself, whose members officially represent their governments.

The activities of the subcommission, as initially set out by the commission, include studying provisions that "should be adopted in defining the principles to be applied in the field of prevention of discrimination on the grounds of race, sex, language, or religion, and in the field of the protection of minorities, and to make recommendations to the Commission on urgent problems in these fields." It also performs "any other functions which may be entrusted to it by the Economic and Social Council or the Commission on Human Rights." In 1949, following adoption of the Universal Declaration of Human Rights (1948), the subcommission's mission was strengthened to focus it on undertaking studies and making recommendations to the commission on ways to prevent discrimination and protect racial, national, religious, and linguistic minorities.

Reporting to the subcommission are working groups and special rapporteurs (experts), as well as UN study groups. Several working groups meet before each session. One, the Working Group on Communications, reviews complaints to determine if they reveal "a consistent pattern of gross and reliably attested violations of human rights" by governments and also reviews any replies by the countries involved. This work is authorized by ECOSOC Resolution 1503 (1970) and is referred to as the Resolution 1503 Procedure. Other working groups concentrate on the problems of contemporary forms of slavery, minorities, and indigenous populations.

Areas covered by special rapporteurs and studies include traditional practices affecting the health of women and children, race discrimination, cultural property of indigenous peoples, compensation for victims of gross violations of human rights, population transfers, the administration of justice, transnational corporations, and the environment. Advisory services, training, fellowships, and promotional activities of the subcommission cover support for national plans of action, constitutions, free and fair elections, the judiciary and legal professions, and conflict resolution.

The subcommission meets in Geneva once a year in August for four weeks. Twenty-six members are elected by the commission, and then lots are drawn to select thirteen members and thirteen alternates. They serve for two- to four-year terms based on an equitable geographical distribution. Most recently, seven members were from Africa, five from Asia, five from Latin America, three from Eastern Europe, and six from Western Europe and other nations. Observers from national governments, UN agencies, and nongovernmental organizations that maintain consultative status with the UN also attend.

Subcommission on the Promotion and Protection of Human Rights, 8–14 avenue de la Paix, 1211 Geneva 10, Switzerland. (41-22-917-9000. 📠 41-22-917-9011. ✉ webadmin.hchr@unog.ch. 💻 www.unhchr.ch.

Commission on Human Rights; Complaints; Economic and Social Council (ECOSOC); Remedies; Reporting Violations; Resolution 1503 Procedure; Violations; Working Groups

Suffrage

See Stanton, Elizabeth Cady; Voting; Women

Summary Executions

Executions carried out quickly, or summarily (from the Latin *summatim,* meaning briefly), have been an expedient way of dispatching people throughout history, particularly in time of war or emergency. There is little difference between summary execution and murder, except that technically a state cannot commit murder. Anyone acting on behalf of the state who convicts and executes a person without a fair trial is acting outside the scope of legitimate state authority in a civilized nation. Executions after communist show trials in the Soviet Union in the 1930s shocked the world, as did mass summary executions of minorities and citizens in territory occupied by German and Japanese military forces during World War II.

Summary executions are symptomatic of a lapse in the rule of law—in particular, the principle that a person must be tried and convicted by due process of law, including a fair trial by an impartial court, before any sentence or punishment may be meted out by the state. Arbitrary executions of individuals are acts of lawlessness that violate the fundamental human right: the right to life.

"No one shall be arbitrarily deprived of his life," states the International Covenant on Civil and Political Rights (1966). Other international human rights documents condemn the death penalty under any circumstance. Some national constitutions also ban the death penalty. Mozambique's constitution (1990), for example, states that "there shall be no death penalty." And the constitutions of countries that permit the death penalty generally prohibit summary executions. The language used may vary, but in essence the state may not take a person's life without due process of law or procedures established by law, including a fair and impartial trial with procedural safeguards for the accused, such as the rights to counsel and to appeal a guilty verdict. Japan's constitution (1947) provides: "No person shall be deprived of life

or liberty . . . except according to procedures established by law. . . . [I]n all criminal cases the accused shall enjoy the right to a speedy and public trial by an impartial tribunal."

After a number of political executions, especially in Argentina and Chile, were brought to the world's attention, the Sixth United Nations Congress on the Prevention of Crime and Treatment of Offenders, held in Caracas, Venezuela, in 1980, condemned "the practice of killing and executing political opponents or suspected offenders carried out by armed forces, law enforcement or other governmental agencies or by paramilitary or political groups," under the overt or tacit authority of government officials. A special rapporteur appointed by the Economic and Social Council (ECOSOC) in 1982 now submits an annual report to the Commission on Human Rights containing processed communications of summary or arbitrary executions to the governments concerned and their replies. On the recommendation of the Committee on Crime Prevention and Control, ECOSOC adopted the Principles on the Effective Prevention and Investigation of Extra-legal, Arbitrary and Summary Executions on May 24, 1989.

U.S. Constitution, Fifth Amendment (1791): "No person shall be held to answer for a capital, or otherwise infamous crime, unless on a presentment or indictment of a Grand Jury, except in cases arising in the land or naval forces, or in the Militia, when in actual service in time of War or public danger; nor shall any person . . . be deprived of life, liberty, or property, without due process of law. . . ."

Principles on the Effective Prevention and Investigation of Extra-Legal, Arbitrary and Summary Executions (1989), Prevention: "1. Governments shall prohibit by law all extra-legal, arbitrary and summary executions and shall ensure that any such executions are recognized as offenses under their criminal laws, and are punishable by appropriate penalties which take into account the seriousness of such offenses."

Federal Court of Argentina (1985): "Acts prohibited at all times [under international law] in respect of [persons protected by provisions of the Geneva Conventions (1949)] include: violence to life and persons, in particular murder of all kinds, mutilation, cruel treatment and torture; also passing sentences and the carrying out of executions without previous judgment pronounced by a regularly constituted court, affording all the judicial guarantees which are recognized by civilized people."

Nuremberg International Military Tribunal (1946): "The provisions [of the Charter of the International Military Tribunal (1945, article 8)] are in conformity with the law of all nations. That a soldier was ordered to kill or torture in violation of the international law of war has never been recognized as a defense to such acts of brutality, though, as the Charter here provides, the order may be urged in mitigation of the punishment."

Summary or Arbitrary Executions. Fact Sheet no. 11. Geneva: Center for Human Rights, 1990.

Capital Punishment; Commission on Human Rights; Due Process; Economic and Social Council (ECOSOC); Fair Trial; Geneva Conventions; International Covenant on Civil and Political Rights; International Covenant on Civil and Political Rights, Second Optional Protocol, Aiming at the Abolition of the Death Penalty; Principles on the Effective Prevention and Investigation of Extra-Legal, Arbitrary and Summary Executions; War Crimes

Suzman, Helen

The daughter of Lithuanian Jewish immigrants to South Africa, Helen Suzman (b. 1917) helped found the Progressive Party and shaped its political platform, which called for the elimination of apartheid and advocated universal political participation in South Africa's government. In addition to other awards, she received a United Nations human rights prize in 1978 for her efforts on behalf of racial equality and peace.

Suzman was born on November 7, 1917, in South Africa's Transvaal region. Educated at the Parktown Convent in Johannesburg, she later obtained a degree in commerce from the University of Witwatersrand. In 1937 she married Moses B. Suzman, a doctor from a prominent Johannesburg family.

After working as a statistician for the South African War Supplies Board, in 1945 Suzman was hired by her alma mater as a lecturer in economics. From her studies she became acutely aware of the economic plight of the nonwhite population of South Africa, especially in the country's urban areas, and this concern drew her into politics. She joined the political party opposing the pro-apartheid National Party and was elected to the South African parliament in 1953.

In 1959, together with eleven other liberal legislators, Suzman formed the aggressively anti-apartheid Progressive Party. She was the only member of her party to be reelected in 1961 and remained the only anti-apartheid member of parliament until 1974. Suzman was an articulate spokesperson for the cause, using her position as the lone voice for human rights to obtain national and international recognition. When South Africa's minister of justice proposed legislation allowing the government to arrest and detain people for up to ninety days without filing charges, she cast the only opposition vote in the parliament's lower house.

During the 1960s and early 1970s Suzman continued her strong dissent against harsh apartheid measures imposed by the government. Finally, in 1974 six more candidates from her Progressive Party were elected to parliament, and by 1985 party legislators totaled twenty-seven. As a member of parliament for more than three decades, Suzman always remained true to her political goals for the country: a multiracial society, equal opportunity for all citizens, and free and democratic elections in which all citizens, regardless of race, could participate equally.

Although Suzman chose not to run again for parliament in 1989, her vision was realized in 1991 with the signing of a national peace accord ending apartheid. The South African Parliament later honored her for her service to the nation. She also has received honorary degrees from Oxford, Harvard, and Columbia universities as well as the Moses Mendelssohn Prize in 1988 and the B'Nai B'Rith Dor L'Dor Award in 1992.

Lee, Robin, ed. *Values Alive: A Tribute to Helen Suzman.* Johannesburg: J. Ball, 1990.

Suzman, Helen. *In No Uncertain Terms: A South African Memoir.* New York: Knopf, 1993.

Apartheid; Mandela, Nelson; Race Discrimination; Tutu, Desmond

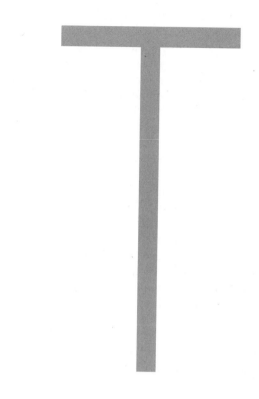

Tallinn Guidelines

See Guidelines for Action on Human Resources Development in the Field of Disability

Teachers

The instruction of young persons, which is a basic responsibility of parents, developed over time into a system of professional instruction for children who had reached a certain age. Regarded as *in locus parentis* (standing in the place of the parents), teachers have been held responsible for their acts while a student is in their care for instruction. They have also been entitled to certain special rights in view of their special duties, but these rights—including to convey a broad spectrum of ideas and to assert authority—have been eroded, particularly in many Western nations. In countries such as the United States, the recent emphasis on children's and parents' rights has greatly circumscribed the parental authority that a teacher may legally exercise.

Germany's constitution (1949) and a few other national constitutions expressly refer to teachers' rights. A number of others, in addition to addressing education, contain provisions related to teaching. Ireland's constitution (1937) provides that three members of the upper house of the Irish parliament are to be elected by the National University of Ireland and three by the University of Dublin. Sweden's constitution (1975) includes teacher training under the jurisdiction of the parliament's education committee.

One international human rights document that specifically addresses teachers is the Recommendation Concerning the Status of Teachers (1966), which was sponsored jointly by the International Labor Organization and the United Nations Educational, Scientific and Cultural Organization (UNESCO). The recommendation, recognizing "the essential role of teachers in educational advancement and the importance of their contribution to the development of man and modern society," defines *teachers* as "all those persons in schools who are responsible for the education of pupils" and t*eachers' status* as "both the standing or regard accorded them, as evidenced by the level of appreciation of the importance of their function and of their competence in performing it, and the working conditions, remuneration and other material benefits accorded them relative to other professional groups." The recommendation extends its scope to "all teachers in both public and private schools up to the completion of secondary stage of education." Why instructors at institutions of higher learning are not included is not clear, although it may be because they have more academic freedom and are not always or preponderantly government employees.

The recommendation's major divisions include Guiding Principles, Educational Objectives and Policies, Preparation for the Profession, Further Education for Teachers, Employment and Career, The Rights and Responsibilities of Teachers, Conditions for Effective Teaching and Learning, Teachers' Salaries, Social Security, and The Teacher Shortage.

Under The Rights and Responsibilities of Teachers, the recommendation addresses professional freedom, participation by teachers in course and textbook development, supervision directed at encouraging and assisting teachers, consideration of teachers' recommendations regarding students' abilities, and promotion of close cooperation between teachers and parents. Specific rights of teachers include participation in social and public life to further their personal development, the field of education, and society as a whole; the exercise of "all civic rights generally enjoyed by citizens," including job protection when elected to public office; participation in salary negotiations through teacher organizations; and machinery for settlement of disputes between teachers and their employers.

Besides the possibility of conflict between the rights of teachers and the rights of students, parents, and educational authorities, there is a long history of conflict between teachers and religious interests. The establishment of parochial (church) schools to incorporate the indoctrination of religion along with general education mitigates this problem, but where members of supervising bodies such as boards of education are intent on injecting religious beliefs into secular education, the rights of teachers may be compromised. In 1999, for example, members of the Kansas state school board acted to require that "creationism"—the belief that all species of life on Earth were created by God as described in the Bible—be taught alongside the scientifically accepted theory of the evolution of the species propounded by Charles Darwin in 1859.

Education International, formerly the World Confederation of Organizations of the Teaching Profession, is an international nongovernmental organization that works on behalf of the rights of teachers, equality of opportunity through education, and better education around the world.

Constitution of Germany (1949), I, Basic Rights, article 5, Freedom of Expression: "(3) Art and science, research and teaching shall be free. Freedom of teaching shall not release anybody from his allegiance to the constitution."

Convention against Discrimination in Education (1960), article 4: "The States Parties to this Convention undertake furthermore to formulate, develop and apply a national policy which, by methods appropriate to the circumstances and national usage, will tend to promote equality of opportunity and of treatment in the matter of education and in particular: . . . (d) To provide training for the teaching profession without discrimination."

Supreme Court of Nova Scotia, Canada (1953): A schoolteacher is entitled to "administer reasonable corporal punishment to a pupil to maintain discipline and order" and thus was not liable for the consequential accidental striking of the pupil's head against a desk or floor, especially when there were no serious results.

European Court of Human Rights (1982): The European Convention for the Protection of Human Rights and Fundamental Freedoms (1950), Protocol no. 1, Securing Certain Rights and Freedoms Other Than Those Already Included in the Convention (1952), distinguishes between *education* and *teaching*: "[E]ducation . . . is the whole process whereby, in any society, adults endeavor to transmit their beliefs, culture and other values to the young, whereas teaching or instruction refers in particular to the transmission of knowledge and to intellectual development."

Education International, 5 boulevard du Roi Albert II, Eighth Floor, 1210 Brussels, Belgium. (32-2-224-06-11. 🖳 32-2-224-06-06. 🖂 educint@ei-ie.org. 🖥 www.ei-ie.org.

Fischer, Louis, David Schimmel, and Cynthia Kelly. 5th ed. *Teachers and the Law.* New York: Longman, 1999.

Poch, Robert K. *Academic Freedom in American Higher Education: Rights, Responsibilities, and Limitations.* ERIC Clearinghouse on Higher Education, The George Washington University, in cooperation with the Association for the Study of Higher Education. Washington, D.C.: School of Education and Human Development, The George Washington University, 1993.

Education; International Labor Organization; Students; United Nations Educational, Scientific and Cultural Organization (UNESCO)

Teresa, Mother

Mother Teresa of Calcutta (1910–97), a Roman Catholic nun, won worldwide fame for her lifelong mission of ministering to the poorest of the poor, including the blind, aged, and dying, as well as lepers, disabled persons, and abandoned children. During her lifetime she received numerous awards for her selfless dedication to human rights, including the Nobel Peace Prize in 1979.

Agnes Gonxha Bojaxhiu was born on August 27, 1910, in Shkup, Albania (now Skopje, Yugoslavia). In 1928 she entered the Institute of the Blessed Virgin Mary in Ireland as a Catholic nun in the Sisters of Loretto, a missionary order. Six weeks later she sailed to India, where she began teaching. She requested the opportunity to work with Calcutta's poor, and, after receiving training as a nurse and being released from her vows by the Vatican, she moved to the slums of Calcutta.

In 1948 she became an Indian citizen and founded the Congregation of the Missionaries of Charity, dedicated to fulfilling the needs of the most destitute people. In addition to their normal vows, members of the order also pledge to give "whole-hearted free service to the poorest of the poor—to Christ in his distressing disguise." The congregation was sanctioned by the pope in 1950 and in 1965 came under his direct authority.

Mother Teresa's order opened many places of refuge, and in 1957 it focused on working with lepers as well. With her organization spreading to some fifty cities in India and more than twenty-five other countries, Mother Teresa became a world-renowned figure and symbol of selfless dedication to serving society's most unfortunate.

The Indian government recognized Mother Teresa in 1963 with the Padma Shri ("Lord of the Lotus") award for her service to its people. On a visit to India in 1964, Pope Paul VI gave her a ceremonial limousine, which she used to obtain funding for her Town of Peace leper colony. Other honors, in addition to India's Jawaharlal Nehru Award, include awards from the Philippines, the Good Samaritan Prize, the first Pope John XXIII Peace Prize, and the Albert Schweitzer Award for her service to humanity. Mother Teresa used the money and gifts she received to fund her missions. She died on September 5, 1997.

Spink, Kathryn. *Mother Teresa: A Complete Authorized Biography*. New York: HarperCollins, 1997.

Teresa, Mother. *Life in the Spirit: Reflections, Meditations, Prayers*. New York: Harper and Row, 1983.

———. *Mother Teresa: In My Own Words*. New York: Gramercy Books, Random House, 1997.

———. *No Greater Love*. Novato, Calif.: New World Library, 1997.

———. *A Simple Path*. Compiled by Lucinda Vardey. New York: Ballantine, 1995.

Territorial Jurisdiction

The territorial instinct is a primal one: a number of animals, including humans, will fight over a piece of land to defend or expand their domain. National and international political systems likewise are deeply rooted in the idea of territorial jurisdiction and the right to exclusive political dominion within well-defined borders. Two hundred separate territorial or political jurisdictions exist today, each with its own definition of what constitutes human rights and adequate enforcement of those rights. Territorial jurisdiction also raises its own human rights issues, such as war, peace, refugees, statelessness, freedom of movement, diplomatic and consular rights, indigenous peoples, natural resources, security, self-determination, sovereignty, nationality, and the environment.

The concept of territorial (from the Latin *terra*, meaning earth) jurisdiction is the foundation of international law. Sometimes called territorial sovereignty, it is the authority of a state or a nation that physically occupies a part of the surface of the Earth and has control over everything therein to the exclusion of other states, except as limited by custom or treaty. The concept is derived from the Roman law of property and the founding of nations on the theory of the absolute right of monarchs, who treated their territory and people as personal property.

Territorial jurisdiction establishes the exclusive right of national governments to extend, promote, and enforce human rights within their domains. By ratifying international agreements that include enforcement provisions, countries may voluntarily permit outside intervention in human rights matters. There are, however, a number of methods for protecting and enforcing human rights in national territories short of armed intervention, such as political, social, and economic sanctions enacted both internally and externally.

But territorial jurisdiction theoretically precludes any interference with the internal affairs of a nation for any reason except war, including enforcement of human rights norms and international agreements. International tribunals to prosecute war crimes in Rwanda and the former territory of Yugoslavia, however, have recently been given limited international jurisdiction to prosecute and punish gross violations of human rights. In 1998 representatives from many countries meeting in Rome went a step further and adopted a statute for an International Criminal Court, which will have permanent international jurisdiction for crimes involving the worst human rights abuses once a sufficient number of countries accept its jurisdiction.

Actions within a nation also have extraterritorial effects. Pollution of the environment, persecution resulting in mass expulsions of refugees, and support of external terrorism seriously affect other territories. A more benign example is the creation of policies by an importing state that alter the production of goods in an exporting state, such as a ban on imports of goods made by slave or child labor.

Countries whose territorial jurisdiction is disputed may set out their claims in their constitutions. Disregarding the existence of Northern Ireland and the fact that it was under British jurisdiction, Ireland's constitution (1937) proclaimed that "the national territory consists of the whole island of Ireland, its islands and its territorial seas." Germany's constitution (1949) declared in its preamble that it is "valid for the entire German People," despite the country's division at the time into West and East Germany.

Territorial jurisdiction remains a question of international law to be settled by countries themselves, although international courts—the Permanent Court of International Justice and its successor, the International Court of Justice (World Court)—have occasionally been called on to resolve territorial disputes. Conflicts may also be solved by negotiations among the countries involved, by war, or by international military intervention, as in the case of the

Persian Gulf War (1990–91), when Iraq's attempt to add new territory taken from its neighbors was prevented by an international military operation under UN auspices.

As operations such as the Gulf War indicate, external aggression for the purpose of taking territory from other nations may increasingly be dealt with by the international community acting in concert. But despite recent actions such as military intervention in Kosovo by the North Atlantic Treaty Organization (NATO) in 1999, it is difficult for the international community of nations—or one or several of them alone—to protect a country's citizens from internal human right abuses carried out by their own government within their own territorial jurisdiction.

Constitution of the Philippines (1987), article I, National Territory:
"The national territory comprises the Philippine archipelago, with all the islands and waters embraced therein, and all other territories over which the Philippines has sovereignty or jurisdiction, consisting of its terrestrial, fluvial, and aerial domains, including its territorial sea, the seabed, the subsoil, the insular shelves and other submarine areas."

International Covenant on Civil and Political Rights (1966), part II, article 2: "1. Each State Party to the present Covenant undertakes to respect and to ensure to all individuals within its territory and subject to its jurisdiction the rights recognized in the present Covenant. . . ."

High Court of Australia (1958): A law of the Australian parliament relating to the government of the territories may operate beyond the limits of the subject territory because the parliament has nation-wide jurisdiction.

Permanent Court of Arbitration (1928): "Territorial sovereignty . . . involves the exclusive right to display the activities of a state. This right has as a corollary a duty: the obligation to protect within the territory the rights of other states, in particular their right to integrity and inviolability in peace and in war, together with rights which each state may claim for its nationals in foreign territory."

Goertz, Gary. *Territorial Changes and International Conflict.* London: Routledge, 1992.

Meessen, Karl M., ed. *Extraterritorial Jurisdiction in Theory and Practice.* The Hague: Kluwer Law International, 1996.

Diplomats and Consuls; Enforcement; Expulsion; International Criminal Court; International Court of Justice (World Court); International Law; Nationality; North Atlantic Treaty Organization (NATO); Refugees; Sovereignty; Statelessness; War

Terrorism

As an instrument of both legitimate governments and insurrectionists, terrorism has probably been around as long as humans have fought one another. The ancient Greeks used terroristic acts to intimidate the Persians, and in medieval Italy the Guelphs terrorized the Ghibellines. The infamous Vlad the Impaler of Eastern Europe (possibly a model for Bram Stoker's Count Dracula) impaled his enemies on stakes outside his castle to warn away others who might try to attack him. The word *terrorism* (from the Latin *terror*, meaning dread) found its way into the English language by the end of the eighteenth century to describe France's Reign of Terror following the French Revolution of 1789.

Today's terrorists are more likely to plant bombs on airplanes, or hijack them, or place explosives in areas of civilian activity. Their goal is to strike fear in the minds of citizens, aiming at such basic human rights as peace, personal security, freedom of movement, and privacy. By threatening the rights to life, liberty, and property, terrorism represents an illegitimate attempt to bring about a change in policy through cowardice rather than by persuasion or political organization. In addition to revolutionaries and governments themselves, many groups may resort to terrorism: criminal organizations, racists, anti-abortionists, religious fanatics, individual malcontents, and civilian paramilitary groups.

The International Law Commission has described terrorist acts as "(i) Any act causing death or grievous bodily harm or loss of liberty [assassination or hostage taking] to a Head of State, persons exercising the prerogatives of the Head of State, their hereditary or designated successors, the spouse of such persons, or persons charged with public functions or holding public positions when the act is directed against them in their public capacity; (ii) Acts calculated to destroy or damage public property . . . ; (iii) Any act likely to imperil human lives through the creation of a public danger, in particular the seizure of aircraft, the taking of hostages and any form of violence directed against persons who enjoy international protection or diplomatic immunity; (iv) The manufacture, obtaining, possession or supplying of arms, ammunition, explosives or harmful substances with a view to the commission of a terrorist act."

A problem with defining terrorism is that it is sometimes used as a weapon to achieve human rights, such as in self-determination and resistance movements against totalitarian regimes. Although it is difficult to conclude that there is any "good" terrorism, as opposed to "bad" terrorism, the frustrations of oppressed peoples offer an explanation for the use of terrorism in some instances. Terrorism is generally a peacetime phenomenon.

Antiterrorism weapons available to national governments and the international community include the military and police as well as laws and legal systems. Most nations have laws dealing with terrorism, and a number of regional and international documents are directed at combating it. The European Union has adopted conventions on Extradition (1957), Judicial Cooperation (1969), and Suppression of Terrorism (1978). Broader international conventions address Offenses and Certain Other Acts Committed on Board Aircraft (1963), Suppression of Unlawful Acts against the Safety of Civil Aviation (1971), Suppression of Unlawful Seizure of Aircraft (1971), Terrorism Taking the Form of Crimes against Persons and Related Extortion that are of International Significance (1971), Prevention and Punishment of Crimes against Internationally Protected Persons including Diplomatic Agents (1974), and Taking of Hostages (1979).

U.S. Antiterrorism and Effective Death Penalty Act of 1996, title III, International Terrorism Prohibitions, subtitle A, Prohibition on International Terrorist Fundraising, section 302, Designation of Foreign Terrorist Organizations (amending the Immigration and Nationality Act [1952], chapter II, by adding section 219, Designation of Foreign Terrorist Organizations): "The Secretary [of State] is authorized to designate an organization as a foreign terrorist organization in accordance with this subsection if the Secretary finds that—(A) the organization is a foreign organization; (B) the organization engages in terrorist activity (as defined in section 212(a)(3)(B)); and (C) the terrorist activity of the organization threatens the security of United States nationals or the national security of the United States."

Geneva Convention Relative to the Protection of Civilian Persons in Time of War (1949), Additional Protocol no. 1 (1977), article 51, paragraph 2: "Acts or threats of violence the primary purpose of which is to spread terror among the civilian population are prohibited."

Recommendation Concerning International Cooperation in the Prosecution of Terrorism, Council of Europe (1982), part III, Prosecution and Trial of Offenses of an International Character, paragraph 7: "Where one or several acts of terrorism have been committed in the territory of two or several member States and there is a link between those acts or their authors, the member States concerned should examine the possibility of having the prosecution and the trial conducted in only one State."

U.S. District Court, District of Columbia (1998): The plaintiff, whose daughter was killed by a suicide bomber who attacked a public bus, was granted a default judgment against the Islamic Republic of Iran and others in the amount of $225 million as punitive damages based on recent amendments to the U.S. Foreign Sovereign Immunities Act (1976), "which grant jurisdiction over foreign states and their officials, agents and employees, and create federal causes of action related to personal injury or death resulting from state-sponsored terrorist attacks."

Combs, Cindy C. *Terrorism in the Twenty-First Century*. Upper Saddle River, N.J.: Prentice Hall, 1999.

Egendorf, Laura K., ed. *Terrorism: Opposing Viewpoints*. San Diego: Greenhaven, 2000.

Elagab, O. *International Law Documents Relating to Terrorism*. London: Cavendish, 1995.

Malik, S., and S. N. Gaur, eds. *Encyclopaedia of Terrorist Law*. Allahabad, India: Law Publishers, 1997.

Crimes against Humanity; Diplomats and Consuls; Geneva Conventions; Hostages; Movement; Security

Thomas Aquinas, St.

Influenced by the ancient Greek philosopher Aristotle, the medieval religious scholar Thomas Aquinas (ca. 1224–74) argued that human reason was capable of functioning within the concept of Christian faith, thus setting in motion the development of natural law as a derivative of natural reason. His writings provided a foundation for the human rights concepts later developed by natural rights and natural law scholars.

The son of an official of Frederick II, emperor of Germany and king of Naples, Thomas Aquinas was born in 1224 or 1225 at his family's castle near Aquino, in the kingdom of Sicily. After studying in Naples, he joined the Dominican religious order in 1244 against the wishes of his family, who abducted him and brought him home. He studied in Paris and Cologne from 1245 to 1255, quickly becoming a master of theology.

Aquinas taught in Paris until opposition by secular colleagues forced him to return to Italy, and between 1252 and 1273 he devoted himself to writing. His views on just governance are found in his greatest work, *Summa Theologica*, and the short fragment *On Kingship*. Unlike St. Augustine, who lived and worked eight hundred years earlier, Aquinas criticized Plato and instead built his philosophy on the works of Aristotle, in particular *The Politics* and *The Ethics*, even though Aristotle's ideas were often at odds with Church dogma.

Aquinas's conclusion about the necessity of secular government—that while dominion of one person over another is slavery and therefore wrong, dominion as a manner of governing free people is not—made a fundamental contribution to the later development of human rights. Following Aristotle, he further argued that secular government must be based on the superior morality and wisdom of the ruler for the benefit of the ruled. He also developed the concept of human justice derived from divine justice by human reason: the human mind, being God-given, is capable of discovering the principles of divine law and justice and applying them in the secular world.

Because the church's influence on secular government remained strong for many centuries after Aquinas's death in 1274, his development of the theory of natural law and natural rights was significant in the evolution of modern human rights concepts.

Kretzmann, Norman, and Eleanor Stump, eds. *The Cambridge Companion to Aquinas*. New York: Cambridge University Press, 1996.

Sigmund, Paul E., ed. and trans. *St. Thomas Aquinas on Politics and Ethics: A New Translation*. New York: Norton, 1988.

Aristotle; Augustine, St.; Justice; Natural Rights; Plato

Thought

"Everyone has the right to freedom of thought, conscience and religion," states the Universal Declaration of Human Rights (1948), a concept echoed in the International Covenant on Civil and Political Rights (1966). Both tie the right to maintain personal ideas predominantly to the right to hold—or not hold—religious beliefs.

In analyzing the 1966 covenant, the Human Rights Committee, which was established to implement its provisions, observed in 1993 that the right to one's thoughts is "far-reaching and profound; it encompasses freedom of thought on all matters, personal conviction and the commitment to religion or belief, whether manifested individually or in community with others." Noting that freedom of thought cannot be suspended, even in times of emergency, the committee stated that freedom of thought, conscience, and religion "protects theistic, non-theistic and atheistic beliefs, as well as the right not to profess any religion or belief." Freedom of thought is separate from "the freedom to manifest religion or belief," the committee added, and it may not be limited in any way.

Closely related to the freedoms of speech, expression, conscience, communication, the press, and religion, freedom of thought or its expression has often been circumscribed—monarchs, for example, did not want to hear their subjects expressing a desire to overthrow the throne and punished such thoughts as treason. Reactions from ostracism to corporal punishment might result for a yeoman who simply found fault with his social superiors. In the democracies of ancient Greece, the need to hear citizens' opinions on issues and candidates made some

freedom of thought not only acceptable but also necessary. These same Greeks, however, were equally quick to condemn certain types of thought, especially when they went against ingrained traditions.

The spread of democracies around the world and the influence of international human rights documents such as the Universal Declaration of Human Rights and the International Covenant on Civil and Political Rights have made freedom of thought an absolute and inalienable right in all freedom-loving societies. The benefits that accrue when everyone has the right to think and speak freely about his or her thoughts far outweigh any damage that may occasionally occur from the irresponsible exercise of freedom of thought.

Constitution of Portugal (1976), title II, Rights, Freedoms and Guarantees, chapter I, Personal Rights, Liberties and Guarantees, article 37, Freedom of Expression and Information: "1. All have the right to express and publicize their thoughts freely, by words, images or other means. . . ."

American Convention on Human Rights (1969), part I, State Obligations and Rights Protected, chapter II, Civil and Political Rights, article 12, Freedom of Thought and Expression: "Everyone has the right to freedom of thought and expression. This right includes freedom to seek, receive, and impart information and ideas of all kinds, regardless of frontiers, either orally, in writing, in print, in the form of art, or through any other medium of one's choice."

U.S. Supreme Court (1992): "The First Amendment [to the U.S. Constitution, added in 1791] generally prevents government from proscribing speech, or even expressive conduct, because of disapproval of the ideas expressed."

European Court of Human Rights (1993): Freedom of thought, conscience, and religion, as contained in the European Convention for the Protection of Human Rights and Fundamental Freedoms (1950), article 9, collectively form one of the foundations of a "democratic society" within the meaning of that document.

Symons, Ann K., and Sally Gardner Reed, eds. *Speaking Out! Voices in Celebration of Intellectual Freedom*. Chicago: American Library Association, 1999.

Communication; Conscience; European Convention for the Protection of Human Rights and Fundamental Freedoms; Expression; International Covenant on Civil and Political Rights; Opinion; The Press; Religion; Speech; Universal Declaration of Human Rights

Timerman, Jacobo

Jacobo Timerman (b. 1923) founded a newspaper in Argentina through which he denounced human rights abuses by left- and right-wing activists in the 1970s. His continuing criticism of the country's military rulers resulted in his arrest in 1977, followed by exile after two and a half years of torture and harassment.

Born in the town of Bar, Ukraine, on January 6, 1923, Jacobo Timerman immigrated to Argentina to escape anti-semitism when he was five years old. His family lived in the Jewish section of Buenos Aires with other Jews who had fled Eastern Europe. As in other parts of the world, the rise of Nazism in Germany encouraged right-wing elements in Argentina in the 1930s. Timerman sought refuge in Jewish history, culture, and youth activities, which led to his fervent support of Zionism and a Jewish homeland.

He began a career in journalism in the 1940s, when the fascist-style political leader Juan Perón was coming to power in Argentina. Timerman gained popularity for his reporting in the 1950s and became active in radio, television, and magazine publishing. In 1971 he founded the newspaper *La Opinión*, whose editorials condemned human rights violations in Argentina as well as in Chile, Cuba, Israel, and the Soviet Union. Soon he was publishing the names of those who were known as the *desaparecidos* (the disappeared)—missing persons who had been abducted, tortured, raped, or killed with government acquiescence. In 1976 the paper supported the military's overthrow of Isabel Perón, who had succeeded her late husband in 1974.

When Timerman was arrested (but never officially charged) in April 1977, tortured, placed under house arrest with his wife and sons, and then exiled forcibly, the matter was reported internationally. In his book *Prisoner without a Name, Cell without a Number* (1981), he described his ordeal. Even the intervention of the Vatican and President Jimmy Carter and three court decrees could not bring about the family's release. Finally Timerman's citizenship was cancelled, and he was expelled from Argentina in 1979.

After leaving Argentina Timerman appealed to the world through his book, which was translated into several languages. He and his family took up residence in Israel, where he continued his support of human rights and criticized the Israeli occupation of Lebanon in a 1982 book. When civilian government was restored in Argentina in 1984 and began prosecuting the former military rulers for gross human rights violations, he returned that year to testify against the people who tortured him and to reestablish his newspaper.

Jacobo Timerman has received several international awards for his support of human rights and his role in improving inter-American relations. His other books include *Chile: Death in the South* (1987), which strongly condemns the rule of the Chilean dictator General Augusto Pinochet, and *Cuba: A Journey* (1991).

Timerman, Jacobo. *Chile: Death in the South*. New York: Knopf, 1987.

————. *Prisoner without a Name, Cell without a Number*. 1981. Reprint, New York: Vintage Books, 1988.

Disappearance; The Press

Tolerance

Tolerance, like equality and respect for human dignity, is a keystone of all human rights. To accept diversity and treat fairly and equally people of different races, sexes, ethnic backgrounds, and opinions is a goal set for government officials in many human rights documents at the national and international levels. But it is one thing not to discriminate and another to tolerate those who break the law or abuse the human rights of others. Tolerance, therefore, often requires a logical balance between nondiscrimination and intolerance for illegal or immoral behavior.

Tolerance—the capacity to allow or respect the beliefs and behavior of others—and its opposite—intolerance—have been human attributes throughout history. One early effort toward religious tolerance was England's Toleration Act (1689), which repealed a number of statutory obstacles to freedom of religion. However, the English philosopher John Locke came under criticism for his *Letters on Tolerance*, published around the same time, in which he advocated tolerance of religious diversity.

Locke's ideas nonetheless had a positive effect on the framers of the U.S. Constitution (1789) and were expressed in the First Amendment (1791), which specified the separation of church and state and tolerance for all religions. Today most other national constitutions also guarantee religious freedom and prohibit discrimination on the basis of religion or belief, although even some democratic constitutions provide either directly or indirectly for a state-authorized religion.

The concept of tolerance holds that all individuals have a right to respect regardless of their beliefs or lack of beliefs and should be treated equally irrespective of race, sex, religion, or ethnic origin. Tolerance also comes into play regarding freedom of conscience, thought, and communication. In determining if certain types of communications or expressions of art violate the standards of public decency, a court may consider evidence of what the community involved has tolerated in the past regarding similar communications or expressions.

Most national constitutions contain language prohibiting discrimination specifically on the basis of race, religion, or national origin, for example. The framers of Bulgaria's constitution (1991), however, in the preamble to that document simply expressed their loyalty to "the universal human ideals of freedom, peace, humanism, equality, justice, and tolerance. . . ."

A number of international human rights documents mandate tolerance and prohibit discrimination on the basis of race, sex, religion, or ethnic or national origin. In 1981 the UN General Assembly adopted the Declaration on the Elimination of All Forms of Intolerance and of Discrimination Based on Religion or Belief, which notes that for many people a religion or belief "is one of the fundamental elements in [a person's] conception of life" and that "manifestations of intolerance and the existence of discrimination in matters of religion or belief [are] still in evidence in some areas of the world."

Constitution of Japan (1947), preamble: "We, the Japanese people . . . desire to occupy an honored place in an international society striving for the preservation of peace, and the banishment of tyranny and slavery, oppression and intolerance for all time from the earth."

African Charter on Human and Peoples' Rights (1981), part I, Rights and Duties, chapter II, Duties, article 29: "Every individual shall also have the duty: . . . 7. To preserve and strengthen positive African cultural values in his relations with other members of the society, in the spirit of tolerance, dialogue and consultation and, in general, to contribute to the promotion of the moral well-being of society. . . ."

Supreme Court of Tennessee (1979): "The noun 'tolerance' means '1. The capacity for or practice of allowing or respecting the nature, beliefs, or behavior of others. . . .'"

European Court of Human Rights (1981): "[P]luralism, tolerance and broadmindedness are the hallmarks of 'democratic society.'"

Cohen, Mark Nathan. *Culture of Intolerance: Chauvinism, Class, and Racism in the United States.* New Haven, Conn.: Yale University Press, 1998.

Walzer, Michael. *On Toleration.* Castle Lectures in Ethics, Politics, and Economics. New Haven, Conn.: Yale University Press, 1997.

Communication; Conscience; Declaration on the Elimination of All Forms of Intolerance and of Discrimination Based on Religion or Belief; Dignity; Discrimination; Equality; Expression; Locke, John; Pluralism; Race Discrimination; Religion; Separation of Church and State; Sex Discrimination; Thought

Torture

The prohibition against torture and other inhuman or degrading treatment by agents of the state is a basic human right derived from the inherent dignity of the person. The right to respect as a person and to security of the person, even if accused or convicted of heinous crimes, is an acknowledgment by a civilized society of the humane nature of the state that represents its citizens. Inhumane treatment or cruel or unusual punishment of fellow human beings is a hallmark of a society that lacks a basic sense of humanity and the worth of the individual.

Throughout history people have used torture (from the Latin *torqueo*, meaning to twist or torture) to accomplish some end—obtain information, punish, or intimidate—or for sadistic pleasure. In the Roman republic, torture could be used only on slaves; later, during the period of the empire, it was reserved for those suspected of treason. The definition of torture given by Azo, a thirteenth-century Roman lawyer—"the inquiry after truth by means of torment"—was adopted by the Roman Catholic Church, which incorporated torture into its canon law and used it extensively against suspected heretics during the infamous Spanish Inquisition, which began in 1480. William Blackstone, the eighteenth-century commentator on the laws of England, noted that although the English courts had disallowed the use of the rack to extract information, certain ministers of Henry VI had erected one derisively called "the Duke of Exeter's daughter" in the tower of London, "where it was occasionally used as an engine of state, not of law, more than once in the reign of Queen Elizabeth [I]."

When the former British colonists in America ratified the first ten amendments to the world's first written constitution in 1791, that Bill of Rights contained two prohibitions against torture and cruelty as instruments of the government. The Fifth Amendment mandates that no person "shall be compelled in any criminal case to be a witness against himself," while the Eighth Amendment states that no "cruel and unusual punishments [shall be] inflicted." These prohibitions have not meant the end of torture and brutality in the enforcement of law in the United States, but they do provide redress for violations of these rights.

Even in the modern age governments have practiced torture and cruelty. The record of officially sanctioned torture in Nazi Germany and throughout its jurisdiction during World War II; Stalin's massacre of U.S.S.R. citizens; military juntas in the "Southern Cone" of South America, including Argentina and Chile; Idi Amin's regime in Uganda and Pol Pot's in Cambodia; and the Serbian government's atrocities in the former territory of Yugoslavia are only a few recent examples of unbridled state brutality.

The use of torture by the government or its agents is considered a violation of an individual's right to be secure in his or her person. Cruelty, torture, or any type of degrading or dehumanizing treatment by a government agent is prohibited by most national constitutions as well as many international human rights documents. Of particular note are provisions in the Universal Declaration of Human Rights (1948) and the International Covenant on Civil and Political Rights (1966).

International human rights instruments dealing specifically with torture include the Convention on the Prevention and Punishment of the Crime of Genocide (1948), Declaration on the Protection of All Persons from Being Subjected to Torture and Other Cruel, Inhuman or Degrading Treatment or Punishment (1975), Principles of Medical Ethics Relevant to the Role of Health Personnel, Particularly Physicians, in the Protection of Prisoners and Detainees against Torture and Other Cruel, Inhuman or Degrading Treatment or Punishment (1982), and Convention against Torture and Other Cruel, Inhuman or Degrading Treatment or Punishment (1984). Regional human rights documents also address the subject of torture, among them the American Convention on Human Rights (1969), Inter-American Convention to Prevent and Punish Torture (1985), and European Convention for the Prevention of Torture and Inhuman or Degrading Treatment or Punishment (1987).

Constitution of Nicaragua (1987), title IV, Rights, Duties, and Guarantees of the Nicaraguan People, chapter I, article 39: "In Nicaragua the penitentiary system is humane, and it has as a fundamental objective the transformation of the interned in order to reintegrate him or her into society."

American Convention on Human Rights (1969), article 5, Right to Humane Treatment: "1. Every person has the right to have his physical, mental, and moral integrity respected. 2. No one shall be subjected to torture or to cruel, inhuman, or degrading punishment or treatment. All persons deprived of their liberty shall be treated with respect for the inherent dignity of the human person."

U.S. Court of Appeals, Ninth Circuit (1992): "[W]e conclude that the right to be free from official torture is fundamental and universal, a right deserving of the highest status under international law. . . . The crack of the whip, the clamp of the thumb screw, the crush of the iron maiden, and, in these more efficient modern times, the shock of the electric cattle prod are forms of torture that the international order will not tolerate."

Committee against Torture (1996): Switzerland's return to Turkey of a Turkish citizen of Kurdish background, in view of the past and current practices of torture in Turkey, would be a violation of the Convention against Torture and Other Cruel, Inhuman or Degrading Treatment or Punishment (1984), article 3, which prohibits "the return ('*refouler*') or [extradition of] a person to another State where there are substantial grounds for believing that he would be in danger of being subjected to torture."

Committee against Torture, 8–14 avenue de la Paix, 1211 Geneva 10, Switzerland. Telephone 41-22-917-3456. 41-22-917-0213. webadmin.hchr@unog.ch. www.unhchr.ch.

Survivors International, 447 Sutter Street, Suite 811, San Francisco, Calif. 94108. 415-765-6999. 415-765-6995. survivors intl@msn.com. www.survivorsintl.org.

Torture Survivors Network, 120 17th Avenue, S.W., Third Floor, Calgary, Alberta T2S 2T2, Canada. 403-262-2006. 403-262-2033. galbi@pacinfo.com. www.pacinfo.com/eugene/tsnet/dspcenterhla.

United Nations High Commissioner for Human Rights, 8–14 avenue de la Paix, 1211 Geneva 10, Switzerland. 41-22-917-9000. 41-22-917-9016. webadmin.hchr@unog.ch. www.unhchr.ch.

Boulesbaa, Ahcene. *The U.N. Convention on Torture and the Prospects for Enforcement.* The Hague: Martinus Nijhoff, Kluwer Law International, 1999.

Evans, Malcolm, and Rod Morgan. *Preventing Torture: A Study of the European Convention for the Prevention of Torture and Inhuman or Degrading Treatment or Punishment.* Oxford, England: Clarendon Press, Oxford University Press, 1998.

Innes, Brian. *The History of Torture.* New York: St. Martin's, 1998.

Beccaria, Cesare; Convention against Torture and Other Cruel, Inhuman or Degrading Treatment or Punishment; Declaration on the Protection of All Persons from Being Subjected to Torture and Other Cruel, Inhuman or Degrading Treatment or Punishment; European Convention for the Prevention of Torture and Inhuman or Degrading Treatment or Punishment; Geneva Conventions; Genocide; Inter-American Convention to Prevent and Punish Torture; Principles of Medical Ethics Relevant to the Role of Health Personnel, Particularly Physicians, in the Protection of Prisoners and Detainees against Torture and Other Cruel, Inhuman or Degrading Treatment or Punishment; Prisoners; Punishment; *Refoulement;* War Crimes

Transitional Justice

See Impunity; Justice

Travel

See Immigrants; Movement

Treaties

A treaty—an international agreement—may be viewed as a contract between or among countries. Under international law, a country's ratification of a treaty binds it to perform the document's obligations. International and regional human rights law has developed to a large extent as the result of human rights treaties such as the UN charter (1945), the paired International Covenant on Civil and Political Rights (1966) and International Covenant on Economic, Social and Cultural Rights (1966), and the American Convention on Human Rights (1969).

The ancient Greeks entered into bilateral treaties *(symbola)* with other states to ensure fair treatment in their dealings with one another, and such treaties became a part of the laws of each state. The Romans established the fundamental principle of international law—*pacta sunt servanda* (meaning treaties must be performed in good faith). By the fifteenth century, a treaty *(foedus* in Latin) and an agreement *(pacta* in Latin) referred to contracts between two or more states relating to a truce, an alliance, commerce, or other international relations. The English term *treaty* (from the Scandinavian *traitee* and the Old French *traite,* among other words) has been in use since at least the fifteenth century. "By advantageous treaties of commerce," wrote Adam Smith in *The Wealth of Nations* in 1776, "particular privileges were procured in some foreign state for the goods and merchants of the country." A contemporary definition of the term *treaty* appears in the Vienna Convention on the Law of Treaties (1969), which calls it "an international agreement concluded between States in written form and governed by international law, whether embodied in a single instrument or in two or more related instruments and whatever its particular designation. . . ."

Treaties, whether called conventions, covenants, instruments, or protocols, are one form of international human rights document. They differ from declarations, recommendations, rules, guidelines, and standards in that they invite countries to sign and ratify them, thereby binding signatory countries to implement the treaty provisions. Sometimes a human rights treaty will allow exceptions or ratification of less than all the provisions. Some human rights treaties—for example, the European Convention for the Protection of Human Rights and Fundamental Freedoms (1950) and the International Covenant on Civil and Political Rights—have several protocols. A protocol can be a preliminary draft of a treaty, but with respect to human rights treaties the term generally refers to additional provisions and obligations. Such protocols have to be ratified separately in order for a country to be bound by these additional provisions.

Certain UN agencies and bodies created by an international treaty are referred to as treaty organizations. These committees—such as the Human Rights Committee, called for in the covenant on civil and political rights—are established under the authority of specific international conventions, while charter operations—such as the Commission on Human Rights—are established by or carried out under the authority of the UN charter.

Unlike a country's domestic laws, which can be enforced using the government's police power, there are few ways to enforce treaty provisions beyond the sanctions available under international law for enforcement of any kind of treaty. Such sanctions include diplomatic pressure, moral and intellectual arguments, public opinion, and loss of reciprocal benefits for the nation that fails to abide by its agreements.

Constitution of the Netherlands (1814), chapter 5, Legislation and Administration, section 2, Miscellaneous Provisions, article 91: "1. The Kingdom shall not be bound by treaties, nor shall such treaties be denounced without prior approval of the States General [national legislature] . . . 3. Any provisions of a treaty that conflict with the Constitution or which lead to conflicts with it may be approved by the Chambers of the States General only if at least two-thirds of the votes cast are in favor."

European Convention for the Protection of Human Rights and Fundamental Freedoms (1950), section IV, article 65: "1. A High Contracting Party may denounce the present Convention only after the expiry of five years from the date on which it became a Party to it and after six months' notice contained in a notification addressed to the Secretary General of the Council of Europe, who shall inform the other High Contracting Parties."

Supreme Court of California (1952): "It is not disputed that the charter [of the United Nations (1945)] is a treaty, and our federal Constitution [1789] provides that treaties made under the authority of the United States are part of the supreme law of the land. . . . It is clear[, however,] that the provisions of the preamble and of Article 1 of the charter which are claimed to be in conflict with [a domestic law of the United States] are not self-executing, . . . and do not purport to impose legal obligations on the member nations or to create rights in private persons."

European Court of Justice (1974): Although the European Community is not itself a party to the European Convention for the Protection of Human Rights and Fundamental Freedoms (1950), "international treaties for the protection of human rights on which the Member States have collaborated or of which they are signatories, can supply guidelines which should be followed within the framework of Community law."

Leigh, Monroe, and Merritt R. Blakeslee, eds. *National Treaty Law and Practice: France, Germany, India, Switzerland, Thailand, United Kingdom.* Washington, D.C.: American Society of International Law, 1995.

Charter of the United Nations; Commission on Human Rights; Human Rights Committee; International Covenant on Civil and Political Rights; International Covenant on Economic, Social and Cultural Rights; International Human Rights Instruments; Enforcement; International Law; Ratification; Regional Human Rights Systems; Sovereignty; United Nations

Tubman, Harriet

A slave who escaped to Philadelphia in 1849, Harriet Tubman (ca. 1820–1913) helped run the Underground Railroad to aid other runaway slaves on their route to freedom. After the Civil War, she continued to work for the betterment of African Americans and was active in the temperance and women's rights movements.

Born the daughter of slaves on the Eastern Shore of Maryland, Harriet Ross defied custom by rejecting the name Araminta given to her by her master, taking her mother's name instead. In 1844 her mother forced her to marry John Tubman, a free man. When her master died in 1849, she fled to the North for fear of being sold in the Deep South, even though her husband threatened to expose her.

Unable to enjoy her new freedom while knowing that others were enslaved, Tubman became a conductor on the Underground Railroad, helping free some three hundred slaves over the next ten years. Although the penalties were harsh for aiding an escaped slave, and there was a $40,000 bounty on her head, she continued to help slaves move clandestinely from the South to Canada. After the 1859 capture of John Brown, whom she supported, Tubman undertook a speaking tour, calling not only for the abolition of slavery but also for expanded women's rights.

During the Civil War, Tubman was a nurse, spy, and scout for the Union army, but after the war she was denied a pension for her service. To help support her, a friend wrote her biography and contributed its sales proceeds to her. Tubman was later granted a small pension. Much of her time after the Civil War was spent setting up schools for freed slaves in the South. Toward the end of her life she made her home in Auburn, New York, in a home for the elderly and needy.

Bradford, Sarah H. *Harriet Tubman: The Moses of Her People.* 1869. Reprint, Bedford, Mass.: Applewood, 1993.

Janney, Rebecca Price. *Harriet Tubman.* Minneapolis: Bethany House, 1999.

Race Discrimination; Slavery; Stanton, Elizabeth Cady; Women

Tutu, Desmond

In 1978 the Anglican priest Desmond Tutu (b. 1931) became the first black secretary-general of the interfaith South African Council of Churches, a position he would use to combat the racial segregation policy known as apartheid. Along with other opponents of apartheid, including Steve Biko, who was beaten to death while in police custody in 1977, and Nelson Mandela, who would become the first black president of South Africa, Tutu worked to bring the promise of equal rights to all South Africans and was awarded the Nobel Peace Prize in 1984.

Born on October 7, 1931, in Klerksdorp, South Africa, Desmond Mpilo ("life") Tutu almost died as an infant. A good student, he planned a medical career, but visits from an Anglican priest during his recovery from a bout with tuberculosis at the age of fourteen and the high cost of medical school influenced his decision to become a priest. A teacher at first, he resigned when forced by the white government to teach only the tribal language to black children.

After two years of training at St. Peter's Theological College in Johannesburg, Tutu became an Anglican priest in 1961. He served as a teacher and pastor until 1975, when he was named bishop of Lesotho and dean of Johannesburg. Three years later he was elevated to secretary-general of the interdenominational South African Council of Churches. Because black political movements were generally banned in South Africa at this time, Tutu was able to use the council as a platform for opposition to apartheid.

Tutu's advocacy, which included withdrawal of foreign investment in South Africa as a nonviolent method of protesting the country's discriminatory policy, resulted in revocation of his passport on several occasions. After being awarded the Nobel Peace Prize in 1984, he redoubled his efforts to topple the "whites only" national government. In 1985 he was named bishop of Johannesburg, and the following year he became archbishop of Cape Town and head of the Anglican Church in South Africa.

Beginning in 1996 Archbishop Tutu led the country's emotional investigation into abuses under apartheid conducted by its Truth and Reconciliation Commission. "You cannot hold people down forever," he wrote in the book *The Rainbow People of God* (1994), "because people are made for something more glorious."

DuBoulay, Shirley. *Tutu: Voice of the Voiceless.* Grand Rapids, Mich.: Eerdmans, 1988.

Tutu, Desmond, and John Allen, ed. *The Rainbow People of God.* New York: Doubleday, 1994.

Apartheid; Mandela, Nelson; Race Discrimination

UNIVERSAL DECLARATION OF HUMAN RIGHTS

WHEREAS *recognition of the inherent dignity and of the equal and inalienable rights of all members of the human family is the foundation of freedom, justice and peace in the world,*

WHEREAS *disregard and contempt for human rights have resulted in barbarous acts which have outraged the conscience of mankind, and the advent of a world in which human beings shall enjoy freedom of speech and belief and freedom from fear and want has been proclaimed as the highest aspiration of the common people,*

WHEREAS *it is essential, if man is not to be compelled to have recourse, as a last resort, to rebellion against tyranny and oppression, that human rights should be protected by the rule of law,*

WHEREAS *it is essential to promote the development of friendly relations between nations,*

WHEREAS *the peoples of the United Nations have in the Charter reaffirmed their faith in fundamental human rights, in the dignity and worth of the human person and in the equal rights of men and women and have determined to promote social progress and better standards of life in larger freedom,*

WHEREAS *Member States have pledged themselves to achieve, in co-operation with the United Nations, the promotion of universal respect for and observance of human rights and fundamental freedoms,*

WHEREAS *a common understanding of these rights and freedoms is of the greatest importance for the full realization of this pledge,*

Now, Therefore,

THE GENERAL ASSEMBLY

PROCLAIMS

THIS UNIVERSAL DECLARATION OF HUMAN RIGHTS *as a common standard of achievement for all peoples and all nations, to the end that every individual and every organ of society, keeping this Declaration constantly in mind, shall strive by teaching and education to promote respect for these rights and freedoms and by progressive measures, national and international, to secure their universal and effective recognition and observance, both among the peoples of Member States themselves and among the peoples of territories under their jurisdiction.*

Article 1. All human beings are born free and equal in dignity and rights. They are endowed with reason and conscience and should act towards one another in a spirit of brotherhood.

Article 2. Everyone is entitled to all the rights and freedoms set forth in this Declaration, without distinction of any kind, such as race, colour, sex, language, religion, political or other opinion, national or social origin, property, birth or other status.

Furthermore, no distinction shall be made on the basis of the political, jurisdictional or international status of the country or territory to which a person belongs, whether it be independent, trust, non-self-governing or under any other limitation of sovereignty.

Article 3. Everyone has the right to life, liberty and security of person.

Article 4. No one shall be held in slavery or servitude; slavery and the slave trade shall be prohibited in all their forms.

Article 5. No one shall be subjected to torture or to cruel, inhuman or degrading treatment or punishment.

Article 6. Everyone has the right to recognition everywhere as a person before the law.

Article 7. All are equal before the law and are entitled without any discrimination to equal protection of the law. All are entitled to equal protection against any discrimination in violation of this Declaration and against any incitement to such discrimination.

Article 8. Everyone has the right to an effective remedy by the competent national tribunals for acts violating the fundamental rights granted him by the constitution or by law.

Article 9. No one shall be subjected to arbitrary arrest, detention or exile.

Article 10. Everyone is entitled in full equality to a fair and public hearing by an independent and impartial tribunal, in the determination of his rights and obligations and of any criminal charge against him.

Article 11. (1) Everyone charged with a penal offence has the right to be presumed innocent until proved guilty according to law in a public trial at which he has had all the guarantees necessary for his defence.

(2) No one shall be held guilty of any penal offence on account of any act or omission which did not constitute a penal offence, under national or international law, at the time when it was committed. Nor shall a heavier penalty be imposed than the one that was applicable at the time the penal offence was committed.

Article 12. No one shall be subjected to arbitrary interference with his privacy, family, home or correspondence, nor to attacks upon his honour and reputation. Everyone has the right to the protection of the law against such interference or attacks.

Article 13. (1) Everyone has the right to freedom of movement and residence within the borders of each state.

(2) Everyone has the right to leave any country, including his own, and to return to his country.

Article 14. (1) Everyone has the right to seek and to enjoy in other countries asylum from persecution.

(2) This right may not be invoked in the case of prosecutions genuinely arising from non-political crimes or from acts contrary to the purposes and principles of the United Nations.

Article 15. (1) Everyone has the right to a nationality.

(2) No one shall be arbitrarily deprived of his nationality nor denied the right to change his nationality.

Article 16. (1) Men and women of full age, without any limitation due to race, nationality or religion, have the right to marry and to found a family. They are entitled to equal rights as to marriage, during marriage and at its dissolution.

(2) Marriage shall be entered into only with the free and full consent of the intending spouses.

(3) The family is the natural and fundamental group unit of society and is entitled to protection by society and the State.

Article 17. (1) Everyone has the right to own property alone as well as in association with others.

(2) No one shall be arbitrarily deprived of his property.

Article 18. Everyone has the right to freedom of thought, conscience and religion; this right includes freedom to change his religion or belief, and freedom, either alone or in community with others and in public or private, to manifest his religion or belief in teaching, practice, worship and observance.

Article 19. Everyone has the right to freedom of opinion and expression; this right includes freedom to hold opinions without interference and to seek, receive and impart information and ideas through any media and regardless of frontiers.

Article 20. (1) Everyone has the right to freedom of peaceful assembly and association.

(2) No one may be compelled to belong to an association.

Article 21. (1) Everyone has the right to take part in the government of his country, directly or through freely chosen representatives.

(2) Everyone has the right of equal access to public service in his country.

(3) The will of the people shall be the basis of the authority of government; this will shall be expressed in periodic and genuine elections which shall be by universal and equal suffrage and shall be held by secret vote or by equivalent free voting procedures.

Article 22. Everyone, as a member of society, has the right to social security and is entitled to realization, through national effort and international co-operation and in accordance with the organization and resources of each State, of the economic, social and cultural rights indispensable for his dignity and the free development of his personality.

Article 23. (1) Everyone has the right to work, to free choice of employment, to just and favourable conditions of work and to protection against unemployment.

(2) Everyone, without any discrimination, has the right to equal pay for equal work.

(3) Everyone who works has the right to just and favourable remuneration ensuring for himself and his family an existence worthy of human dignity, and supplemented, if necessary, by other means of social protection.

(4) Everyone has the right to form and to join trade unions for the protection of his interests.

Article 24. Everyone has the right to rest and leisure, including reasonable limitation of working hours and periodic holidays with pay.

Article 25. (1) Everyone has the right to a standard of living adequate for the health and well-being of himself and of his family, including food, clothing, housing and medical care and necessary social services, and the right to security in the event of unemployment, sickness, disability, widowhood, old age or other lack of livelihood in circumstances beyond his control.

(2) Motherhood and childhood are entitled to special care and assistance. All children, whether born in or out of wedlock, shall enjoy the same social protection.

Article 26. (1) Everyone has the right to education. Education shall be free, at least in the elementary and fundamental stages. Elementary education shall be compulsory. Technical and professional education shall be made generally available and higher education shall be equally accessible to all on the basis of merit.

(2) Education shall be directed to the full development of the human personality and to the strengthening of respect for human rights and fundamental freedoms. It shall promote understanding, tolerance and friendship among all nations, racial or religious groups, and shall further the activities of the United Nations for the maintenance of peace.

(3) Parents have a prior right to choose the kind of education that shall be given to their children.

Article 27. (1) Everyone has the right freely to participate in the cultural life of the community, to enjoy the arts and to share in scientific advancement and its benefits.

(2) Everyone has the right to the protection of the moral and material interests resulting from any scientific, literary or artistic production of which he is the author.

Article 28. Everyone is entitled to a social and international order in which the rights and freedoms set forth in this Declaration can be fully realized.

Article 29. (1) Everyone has duties to the community in which alone the free and full development of his personality is possible.

(2) In the exercise of his rights and freedoms, everyone shall be subject only to such limitations as are determined by law solely for the purpose of securing due recognition and respect for the rights and freedoms of others and of meeting the just requirements of morality, public order and the general welfare in a democratic society.

(3) These rights and freedoms may in no case be exercised contrary to the purposes and principles of the United Nations.

Article 30. Nothing in this Declaration may be interpreted as implying for any State, group or person any right to engage in any activity or to perform any act aimed at the destruction of any of the rights and freedoms set forth herein.

Adopted by the General Assembly on 10 December 1948

UNITED NATIONS

The Universal Declaration of Human Rights, drafted by the Commission on Human Rights and adopted by the UN General Assembly in 1948, set the community of nations on the road to identifying, promoting, and protecting human rights. In the half century following the declaration's adoption, hundreds of other international instruments were drawn up to secure rights for all. [Library of Congress]

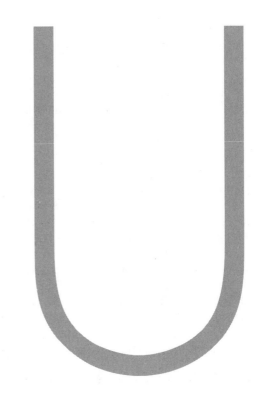

United Nations

The United Nations is an international organization established by treaty in 1945 to maintain peace among the nations of the world and to promote human rights for all people in all nations. Membership is open to all peace-loving countries willing and able to accept and carry out the obligations of the UN charter (1945). New members are admitted by a vote of the General Assembly on the recommendation of the Security Council. Today 189 countries, nearly all the world's sovereign nations, are members of the UN, which is headquartered in New York City.

The successor to the League of Nations, which was established in 1920 and dissolved in 1946, the UN grew out of World War II. The road to its formation began with a joint declaration by the president of the United States and the prime minister of Great Britain on August 14, 1941: the Atlantic Charter, which declares that the two nations "hope to see established a peace . . . which will afford assurance that all the men in all the lands may live out their lives in freedom from fear and want." President Franklin D. Roosevelt is credited with naming the organization. Other documents, including the Joint Declaration by United Nations (1942) and agreements creating the International Monetary Fund (1944), led to formation of the new international organization.

The Charter of the United Nations, ratified on October 24, 1945, by fifty-one nations, sets out the rights and obligations of the member states and establishes the UN

agencies and their procedures. This treaty also codifies major principles of international relations, recognizing the sovereign equality of nation-states and the basic human rights to which all people are entitled; it additionally prohibits the use of force in international relations. As set forth in the charter, the purposes of the UN include the maintenance of international peace and security; development of friendly relations among nations based on equal rights and self-determination of peoples; assistance with international economic, social, cultural, and humanitarian problems; promotion of respect for human rights and fundamental freedoms; and creation of a center for harmonizing national actions to attain these goals.

Beginning with the Universal Declaration of Human Rights (1948), a major contribution of the UN has been the preparation and adoption of numerous declarations and conventions on human rights. Some of the most important include the Convention on the Prevention and Punishment of the Crime of Genocide (1948), International Convention on the Elimination of All Forms of Racial Discrimination (1965), International Covenant on Civil and Political Rights (1966), International Covenant on Economic, Social and Cultural Rights (1966), Convention on the Elimination of All Forms of Discrimination against Women (1979), Convention against Torture and Other Cruel, Inhuman or Degrading Treatment or Punishment (1984), Convention on the Rights of the Child (1989), Vienna Declaration and Program of Action (1993), and Declaration on the Right and Responsibility of Individuals, Groups and Organs of Society to Promote and Protect Universally Recognized

Human Rights and Fundamental Freedoms (1998). The conventions and covenants bind signatory nations to enforce the declared principles in their own nations and in their relations with other countries of the world.

The major divisions of the UN include the General Assembly, Security Council, Economic and Social Council (ECOSOC), Trusteeship Council (now essentially redundant), International Court of Justice, and Secretariat, all located at UN headquarters except for the court, which is in The Hague.

The General Assembly is the UN's deliberative body, but unlike a national legislature it cannot enact laws. Each member country is entitled to one voting representative in the assembly. Important questions regarding peace and security, the admission of new members, and the budget require a two-thirds majority vote; other decisions need only a simple majority. The assembly also elects the non-permanent members of the Security Council, the members of ECOSOC, some members of the Trusteeship Council, and, jointly with the Security Council, the judges of the International Court of Justice. On the recommendation of the Security Council, the assembly appoints the UN secretary-general.

The Security Council has primary responsibility for maintaining international peace and security. It includes five permanent members: China, France, Russia, the United Kingdom, and the United States. Ten other members are elected by the General Assembly for two-year terms, each of whom has one vote. Nine of the fifteen votes are required on procedural matters; substantive matters also call for nine votes, including the concurring votes of all five permanent members. This requirement of "great Power unanimity" is a veto power for each of the permanent members. To implement its duty to maintain international peace, the council in the 1990s established two international criminal tribunals to prosecute war crimes in Rwanda and the former Yugoslavia.

The Secretariat is the UN's administrative arm. It consists of an international staff to carry out day-to-day operations. The head of the Secretariat is the secretary-general, who is appointed by the General Assembly on the recommendation of the Security Council for a renewable five-year term. The Secretariat's duties include overseeing peacekeeping operations, mediating disputes, analyzing economic and social forces, preparing reports on such topics as human rights and the environment, organizing international conferences, monitoring implementation of UN decisions, and providing public relations for UN activities. Article 100 of the UN charter requires that the member states respect the Secretariat's exclusively international character and responsibilities and refrain from unduly influencing them.

The mission of the UN includes promoting a number of human rights causes, including the prevention of extrajudicial execution, arbitrary detention, torture, racial discrimination, and disappearances; the promotion of the rights of women, children, disabled persons, and migrant workers; the successful struggle against apartheid in South Africa; and the provision of humanitarian assistance and assistance to refugees.

The Office of the High Commissioner for Human Rights, created in 1993 under the secretary-general, is now responsible for supporting most of the UN's human rights functions. These include the Commission on Human Rights and its Subcommission on the Promotion and Protection of Human Rights, which are under ECOSOC, and treaty-monitoring bodies such as the Human Rights Committee, established under the International Covenant on Civil and Political Rights (1966), as well as the Committee against Torture, Committee on the Elimination of Racial Discrimination, Committee on the Rights of the Child, and Committee on Economic, Social and Cultural Rights.

Commissions on the Status of Women, Sustainable Development, Human Settlements, and Crime Prevention and Criminal Justice report to ECOSOC, while a Special Committee to Investigate Israeli Practices Affecting Human Rights of the Palestinian People reports to the General Assembly. The UN also creates working groups to study specific problems and inform the parent commissions on their findings and recommendations. For example, the Subcommission on the Promotion and Protection of Human Rights of the Commission on Human Rights maintains a working group on Contemporary Forms of Slavery.

Some other specialized UN-related agencies and bodies devoted to human rights include the High Commissioner for Refugees, who aids people who have fled war or persecution; International Labor Organization (ILO), which addresses union rights, child labor, bonded labor, and worker rights in general; United Nations Educational, Scientific and Cultural Organization (UNESCO), which promotes education rights and human rights education; World Health Organization (WHO), which furthers health rights and HIV-AIDS efforts; UN Development Program, which pursues the right to development; Food and Agricultural Organization (FAO), which supports freedom from hunger and the right to food; United Nations Children's Fund (UNICEF), which promotes the rights of the child; and the so-called Bretton Woods institutions, such as the World Bank and the International Monetary Fund, which promote economic and development rights.

United Nations, One United Nations Plaza, New York, N.Y. 10017. (212-963-4475. 🖨 212-963-0071. 🖳 inquiries@un.org. 🖳 www. un.org.

Department of Public Information. *Basic Facts About the United Nations*. New York: United Nations, 1995.

O'Flaherty, Michael. *Human Rights and the UN: Practice before the Treaty Bodies*. London: Sweet and Maxwell, 1996.

☞

Charter of the United Nations; Commission on Human Rights; Economic and Social Council (ECOSOC); High Commissioner for Human Rights; High Commissioner for Refugees; Human Rights Committee; International Court of Justice; International Human Rights Instruments; International Labor Organization; United Nations Children's Fund (UNICEF); United Nations Educational, Scientific and Cultural Organization (UNESCO); Treaties; Working Groups; *and other specific UN agencies and instruments*

United Nations Children's Fund (UNICEF)

Created by the UN General Assembly in 1946, the United Nations Children's Fund (UNICEF) advocates children's rights by helping young people meet their basic needs and expand their opportunities. The only UN activity dedicated exclusively to children, UNICEF works within the UN system and with nongovernmental organizations to aid children in developing countries through community-based services in primary health care, basic education, and safe water and sanitation. It is committed to helping the most disadvantaged children—ensuring a "first call for children"—and responds in emergencies to protect children's rights and meet humanitarian needs.

UNICEF's first mission after World War II was to help children in war-torn Europe and China. Today it has an extensive network of field operations in developing countries around the world; thirty-seven national committees, most in industrialized nations, support advocacy and fundraising efforts. UNICEF carries out its work though eight regional offices and 125 country offices, including the Innocenti Research Center in Florence, Italy. Among its most well known fund-raising activities is publication of cards, calendars, and stationery.

The agency's international programs for children's rights include the ratification and implementation of the Convention on the Rights of the Child (1989) and the World Summit for Children in 1990. A 1996 mission statement noted that the agency "is guided by the Convention on the Rights of the Child and strives to establish children's rights as enduring ethical principles and international standards of behavior towards children." Through its country programs it asserts the equal rights of girls and women and supports their full participation in political, social, and economic development. It also encourages sustainable development and healthful motherhood and advocates against land mines, AIDS, and child labor.

Information currently available through UNICEF's Web site on the plight of children around the world includes items on the Convention on the Rights of the Child, *Cartoons for Children's Rights* (a broadcast initiative about children's rights), *NetAid* (a program to end extreme poverty),

The Progress of Nations (documenting development and human rights achievents), and *The State of the World's Children.*

UNICEF also provides an electronic discussion forum for children and youth about issues that affect them. Called Voices of Youth, it contains a "Meeting Place," where young people under twenty-one years of age can express their views, and a "Teacher's Place" for sharing thoughts about online learning. There is also a "Learning Place," which offers a series of interactive global projects in which young people can work together on common activities.

An executive board, following the overall policy guidance of the General Assembly and the Economic and Social Council (ECOSOC), is responsible for providing intergovernmental support to UNICEF and supervision of its activities. The board includes thirty-six members elected for three-year terms from five regions of the world and meets annually in New York City. Five officers—the president and four vice presidents, representing different regions—are called the bureau. Activities of the board and UNICEF staff are coordinated by an administrative office.

United Nations Children's Fund (UNICEF), Three United Nations Plaza, New York, N.Y. 10017. ✆ 212-326-7000. 🖨 212-887-7465. 🖥 netmaster@unicef.org. 🖥 www.unicef.org.

Voices of Youth (UNICEF): 🖥 www.unicef.org/voy.

Children; Convention on the Rights of the Child; Youth

United Nations Educational, Scientific and Cultural Organization (UNESCO)

A separate and autonomous body related to the United Nations by a special agreement, the United Nations Educational, Scientific and Cultural Organization (UNESCO) is devoted to promoting peace and security by encouraging cooperation among nations in the fields of education, science, culture, and communications. "[S]ince wars begin in the minds of men," states its 1946 constitution (as amended in 1976), "it is in the minds of men that the defenses of peace must be constructed." Ignorance of one another has led to suspicion, mistrust, and war, observes the document, which was adopted on November 16, 1945, in London by representatives of forty-four governments.

The organization was formally established on November 4, 1946, with the deposit of twenty instruments of acceptance. Before UNESCO's creation, a number of international organizations were dedicated to some of its goals: the International Committee of Intellectual Co-operation, founded in 1922; International Institute of Intellectual Co-operation, founded in 1925; and International Bureau of Education, also founded in 1925. The first two organizations were dissolved in 1946, and the latter became part of the UNESCO secretariat in 1969.

The main objective of UNESCO, according to its constitution, is to "contribute to peace and security by promoting collaboration among the nations through education, science and culture in order to further universal respect for justice, for the law and for the human rights and fundamental freedoms which are affirmed for the peoples of the world . . . by the Charter of the United Nations [1945]." Its principal functions include preparing prospective studies on the future of education, science, culture, and communications; training and teaching to promote the advancement, transfer, and sharing of knowledge; setting international standards; providing expertise to member nations; and facilitating information exchange in its areas of expertise.

UNESCO focuses on education so that countries can control their own development, on scientific and technological knowledge so that they can maximize their own resources, and on cultural identity and diversity to help them preserve their historical legacies. Other activities involve preventing discrimination and improving women's access to education; promoting freedom of the press and pluralistic media; emphasizing sustainable development; and encouraging research on conflicts, violence, obstacles to disarmament, and the role of international law and organizations in building peace.

In addition to its special agreement with the UN, UNESCO has entered into agreements with the International Labor Organization, Food and Agricultural Organization, World Health Organization, World Intellectual Property Organization, International Atomic Energy Agency, and UN Relief Agency for Palestine Refugees in the Near East. Membership in the UN automatically includes membership in UNESCO, but other countries may join with its approval. As of late 1999, the agency had 188 members (the United States having terminated its membership).

UNESCO's structure consists of a general conference comprising representatives of the member nations, who meet every two years. Intergovernmental conferences on education, the sciences, and the humanities may be convened by the general conference. An executive board and a secretariat administer the agency. A director-general is nominated by the board and appointed by the general conference for a renewable six-year term.

United Nations Educational, Scientific and Cultural Organization (UNESCO), 7 place de Fontenoy, 75352 Paris 07 SP, France. (33-1-45-68-10-00. 33-1-45-67-16-90. webmaster@unesco.org. www.unesco.org.

Symonides, Janusz, and Vladimir Volodin. *UNESCO and Human Rights: Standard-Setting Instruments.* Paris: UNESCO, 1996.

Convention Concerning the Protection of the World Cultural and Natural Heritage; Education

United Nations Program of Technical Cooperation in the Field of Human Rights

"[I]t is essential," observes the Universal Declaration of Human Rights (1948), "if man is not to be compelled to have recourse, as a last resort, to rebellion against tyranny and oppression, that human rights should be protected by the rule of law." To provide assistance to governments requesting help in promoting and protecting the rights of women and minorities, eliminating race discrimination, and facilitating freedom of information, the UN General Assembly authorized the secretary-general to create the Program of Advisory Services and Technical Cooperation in the Field of Human Rights in 1955. Commonly called the Program of Technical Cooperation in the Field of Human Rights, its mission is to assist countries in building and strengthening democratic national institutions that have a direct impact on the overall observance of human rights and the rule of law.

According to the Center for Human Rights, the basic elements for building human rights institutions in a country include "(a) a strong Constitution, which, as the highest law of the land, [among other things]: (i) incorporates internationally recognized human rights and fundamental freedoms, as enumerated in the International Bill of Human Rights; (ii) establishes effective and justiciable remedies at law for violations of those rights." Other building blocks include an independent judiciary, a strong electoral and legal system, and reliable human rights institutions, such as independent human rights commissions and an ombudsman.

The Program of Technical Cooperation operates in conjunction with the Office of the High Commissioner for Human Rights and is funded from the regular UN budget as well as the Voluntary Fund for Technical Cooperation in the Field of Human Rights, which became operational in 1988 and in little more than a decade received in excess of $19 million in contributions and pledges. The dramatic increase in this program's work is reflected in the fact that ten years ago it conducted an average of two projects per year but has since become involved in hundreds of activities in more than forty countries.

Major forms of assistance offered by the program consist of national plans of action; constitutional, electoral, and legislative reform assistance; help in establishing and strengthening national institutions; and training for judges, lawyers, prosecutors, police, prison officials, and armed forces. The program also provides support to parliaments, curriculum development and education for human rights, training for government officials in treaty reporting and international obligations, support for nongovernmental human rights organizations, and training for peacekeeping forces and international civil servants. The General Assembly's 1955 resolution creating the program also called for fellowships to be awarded to candidates nominated by their governments. Participants receive intensive training in a variety of human rights issues.

The technical cooperation program, says the Center for Human Rights, "is a vital element within the United Nations system of comprehensive assistance for the strengthening of the rule of law, on the basis of relevant United Nations standards embodied in half a century of human rights standard setting by the Organization."

United Nations Program of Advisory Services and Technical Cooperation in the Field of Human Rights, 8–14 avenue de la Paix, 1211 Geneva 10, Switzerland. ☎ 41-22-917-9000. 🖷 41-22-917-0213. ▣ www.unhchr.ch/html/menu2/techcoop.

Advisory Services and Technical Cooperation in the Field of Human Rights. Fact Sheet no. 3 (rev. 1). Geneva: Center for Human Rights, 1996.

Center for Human Rights; High Commissioner for Human Rights

Universal Copyright Convention

The world's first written national constitution, the U.S. Constitution (1789), authorized Congress to "promote the Progress of Science and useful Arts, by securing for limited Times to Authors and Inventors the exclusive Right to their respective Writings and Discoveries." Most nations now have some type of copyright law to protect creators' rights to the fruits of their labors for a specified time. Copyright protection furthers the rights of personality and property.

The Universal Copyright Convention, an international supplement to national copyright laws, was adopted in Geneva on September 6, 1952, and revised and adopted again in Paris on July 24, 1971, by a conference called by the United Nations Educational, Scientific and Cultural Organization (UNESCO). The revised convention, which entered into force on July 10, 1974, applies not only to authors but also to creators of works such as music, plays, films, paintings, engravings, sculpture, and designs. Two protocols added to the convention by the 1971 conference extend copyright protection to works by refugees and stateless persons as well as those of the United Nations, its agencies, and the Organization of American States.

The convention begins by noting the contracting nations' "desire to ensure in all countries copyright protection of literary, scientific and artistic works," adding that "a system of copyright protection appropriate to all nations of the world and expressed in a universal convention, additional to, and without impairing international systems already in force, will ensure respect for the rights of the individual and encourage the development of literature, the sciences and the arts."

"Each Contracting State," declares article 1, "undertakes to provide for the adequate and effective protection of the rights of authors and other copyright proprietors in literary, scientific and artistic works, including writings, musical, dramatic and cinematographic works, and paintings, engravings, and sculpture." According to article 2, "Published works of nationals of any Contracting State and works first published in that State shall enjoy in each other Contracting State the same protection as that other State accords to works of its nationals first published in its own territory, as well as the protection specially granted by this Convention." Similar protections are granted to unpublished works as well.

"Any Contracting State which, under its domestic law, requires as a condition of copyright, compliance with formalities such as deposit, registration, notice, notarial certificates, payment of fees or manufacture or publication in that Contracting State," provides article 3, "shall regard these requirements as satisfied with respect to all works protected in accordance with this Convention and first published outside its territory and the author of which is not one of its nationals, if from the time of the first publication all the copies of the work published with the authority of the author or other copyright proprietor bear the symbol © accompanied by the name of the copyright proprietor and the year of first publication placed in such manner and location as to give reasonable notice of claim of copyright." Four following paragraphs set forth limitations and mandate that in each participating nation "there shall be legal means of protecting without formalities the unpublished works of nationals of other Contracting States."

Article 4 specifies that "[t]he duration of protection of a work shall be governed, in accordance with the provisions of Article 2 and this Article, by the law of the Contracting State in which protection is claimed. The term of protection for works protected under this Convention shall not be less than the life of the author and twenty-five years after his death." A number of exceptions and limitations follow, together with a final section specifying that the "rights referred to in Article 1 shall include the basic rights ensuring the author's economic interests, including the "exclusive right to authorize reproduction by any means, public performance and broadcasting."

Article 5 provides for "the exclusive right of the author to make, publish and authorize the making and publication of translations of works protected under this Convention." It also allows developing countries to avail themselves of certain exceptions, for example, reducing the length of time in which literary works may be translated by someone other than the author.

Article 6 defines *publication* to mean "the reproduction in tangible form and the general distribution to the public of copies of a work from which it can be read or otherwise visually perceived." However, article 7 exempts "works or rights in works which, at the effective date of this Convention in a Contracting State where protection is claimed, are permanently in the public domain in the said Contracting State." Article 10 requires each nation to adopt its own measures necessary for application of the convention.

Article 11 creates an intergovernmental committee to, among other things, study problems concerning the convention's application and operation and to prepare for periodic revisions. The eighteen-member committee "shall be selected with due consideration to a fair balance of national interests on the basis of geographical location, population, languages and stage of development." A Resolution concerning Article 11 at the end of the convention specifies in part that the committee is to include representatives of the twelve state members of the committee established under the 1952 convention, plus representatives of Algeria, Australia, Japan, Mexico, Senegal, and Yugoslavia. Article 12 requires the committee to "convene a conference for revision whenever it deems necessary, or at the request of at least ten States party to this Convention."

An Appendix Declaration relating to Article 17 details provisions for the copyright convention's relationship to the Berne Convention for the Protection of Literary and Artistic Works and membership in the union it created.

✉

United Nations Educational, Scientific and Cultural Organization (UNESCO), 7 place de Fontenoy, 75352 Paris 07 SP, France. ☎ 33-1-45-68-10-00. 🖨 33-1-45-67-16-90. 📧 webmaster@unesco.org. 🖥 www.unesco.org.

U.S. Copyright Office, Library of Congress, 101 Independence Avenue, S.E., Washington, D.C. 20559-6000. ☎ 202-707-3000. 🖨 202-707-2600 (on demand). 📧 copyinfo@loc.gov. 🖥 www.loc.gov/copyright.

World Intellectual Property Organization, 34 chemin des Colombettes, 1211 Geneva 20, Switzerland. ☎ 41-22-730-9111. 🖨 41-22-733-5428. 📧 wipo@wipo.int. 🖥 www.wipo.int.

Artists; Economic Rights; Personality; Property

Universal Declaration of Human Rights

One of the most significant human rights documents, the Universal Declaration of Human Rights (1948) was drafted to carry out the mandate of the Charter of the United Nations (1945): "promoting and encouraging respect for human rights and fundamental freedoms." The first attempt to establish a universal standard of human and fundamental rights for every person, the declaration was adopted by the UN General Assembly on December 10, 1948, by a vote of forty-eight in favor, none opposed, with eight abstentions (December 10 is now observed internationally as Human Rights Day). The declaration became the first document of what is now referred to as the International Bill of Human Rights, which also includes the International Covenant on Civil and Political Rights (1966) and its two optional protocols as well as the International Covenant on Economic, Social and Cultural Rights (1966).

Under the chairmanship of Eleanor Roosevelt, the widow of President Franklin D. Roosevelt, the declaration was produced by the Commission on Human Rights, created in 1946. She believed that the world "could not have peace, or an atmosphere in which peace could grow, unless we [recognize] the rights of individual human beings . . . their importance, their . . . dignity. . . ." Others who made significant contributions to the document include Alexandre Bogomolov and Alexei Pavlov of the Soviet Union, René Cassin of France, Peng Chun Chang of China, Lord Dukeston and Geoffrey Wilson of the United Kingdom, William Hodgson of Australia, John Humphrey of Canada, Charles Malik of Lebanon, and Hernán Santa Cruz of Chile.

The declaration, as proclaimed by the General Assembly, is to serve "as a common standard of achievement for all peoples and all nations, to the end that every individual and every organ of society, keeping this Declaration constantly in mind, shall strive by teaching and education to promote respect for these rights and freedoms and by progressive measures, national and international, to secure their universal and effective recognition and observance, both among the peoples of Member States themselves and among the peoples of territories under their jurisdiction."

The declaration consists of a preamble and thirty articles. The preamble begins with a series of seven clauses providing justification for the document. According to the fifth clause, "the peoples of the United Nations have in the Charter reaffirmed their faith in fundamental human rights, in the dignity and worth of the human person and in the equal rights of men and women and have determined to promote social progress and better standards of life in larger freedom[.]"

Article 1 sets forth the declaration's basic philosophy: "All human beings are born free and equal in dignity and rights. They are endowed with reason and conscience and should act towards one another in a spirit of brotherhood."

Fundamental rights and remedies for violations of those rights are described in articles 2 through 8. Fundamental rights, the document states, may not be denied on the basis of "race, color, sex, language, religion, political or other opinion, national origin, property, birth or other status." Any distinction based on territorial jurisdiction is also prohibited. Each person has the rights to life, liberty, and personal security; torture and "cruel, inhuman or degrading treatment or punishment" are prohibited; each person must be recognized as a person before the law; all people are equal before the law; and "[e]veryone has the right to an effective remedy by the competent national tribunals for acts violating the fundamental rights granted him by the constitution or by law."

Articles 9, 10, and 11 address basic rights for persons accused of crimes. "No one shall be subjected to arbitrary interference with his privacy, family, home or correspondence, nor to attacks upon his honor and reputation," provides article 12 in part. Articles 13 through 20 enumerate additional rights, including freedom of movement and residence; the rights to asylum, nationality, marriage and family, and property ownership; freedom of thought, conscience, and religion; freedom of opinion and expression; and the right of peaceful assembly.

The right of each person to participate in the government and equal access to public services of his or her country is extended in article 21. Article 22 states that everyone has the right to social security, and article 23 endorses equal pay for equal work, a just and favorable rate of pay, and the right to form and join trade unions. Articles 24 through 27 provide for the right to rest and leisure; an adequate standard of living, clothing, housing, and medical care as well as "special assistance" for motherhood and childhood; education; and participation in the community's cultural life, the benefit of "scientific advancement and its benefits," and protection of interests of scientific and artistic creations.

According to article 28, "Everyone is entitled to a social and international order in which the rights and freedoms set forth in this Declaration can be fully realized." Article 29 notes that, as well as rights, everyone has "duties to the community" and that rights and freedoms have limitations. The final article, article 30, states: "Nothing in this Declaration may be interpreted as implying for any State, group or person any right to engage in any activity or to perform any act aimed at the destruction of any rights and freedoms set forth herein."

In an address at the University of Tehran, Iran, on December 10, 1997, UN Secretary-General Kofi Annan noted: "The growth in support for the Declaration of Human Rights over the past fifty years has given it new life and reaffirmed its universality. The basic principles of the Declaration have been incorporated into national laws of countries from all cultural traditions."

United Nations High Commissioner for Human Rights, 8–14 avenue de la Paix, 1211 Geneva 10, Switzerland. (41-22-917-9000. 📠 41-22-917-9016. 🖥 webadmin.hchr@unog.ch. 🖥 www.unhchr.ch.

Alfredsson, Gudmundur, and Asbjorn Eide, eds. *The Universal Declaration of Human Rights: A Common Standard of Achievement.* The Hague: Kluwer Law International, 1999.

Human Rights: The International Bill of Human Rights. UN Fact Sheet no. 2 (rev. 1). Geneva: Center for Human Rights, 1996.

Morsink, Johannes. *The Universal Declaration of Human Rights.* Philadelphia: University of Pennsylvania Press, 1999.

Bills of Rights; Charter of the United Nations; Commission on Human Rights; Fundamental Rights; High Commissioner for Human Rights; International Bill of Human Rights; International Covenant on Civil and Political Rights; International Covenant on Economic, Social and Cultural Rights; Roosevelt, Eleanor

Universal Declaration on the Eradication of Hunger and Malnutrition

"Every man, woman and child has the inalienable right to be free from hunger and malnutrition," declared the World Food Conference in 1974. Despite its apparent logic, this lofty ideal remains more a goal for all nations than a right that can be immediately enforced nationally or internationally. Along with the right to adequate health care, housing, and other social and economic needs, the human right to adequate food has nevertheless occasionally been reaffirmed by the United Nations and other human rights organizations. An adequate standard of living, for example, is guaranteed in the Universal Declaration of Human Rights (1948) and restated in the International Covenant on Economic, Social and Cultural Rights (1966), while the Declaration on Social Progress and Development (1969) includes the elimination of hunger and malnutrition as one of its objectives.

Meeting in Rome at the request of the UN General Assembly, the World Food Conference on November 16, 1974, adopted the Universal Declaration on the Eradication of Hunger and Malnutrition, which was endorsed by the General Assembly on December 17, 1974. The document's purpose was to develop methods by which the international community could attack the problem of world hunger. In 1988 the General Assembly reaffirmed the declaration, noting, however, that in the 1980s the number of people suffering from hunger and malnutrition had increased, making the efforts underscored by the declaration even more urgent.

The declaration begins by noting in paragraph (a) that the "grave food crisis that is afflicting the peoples of the developing countries where most of the world's hungry and ill-nourished live and where more than two thirds of the world's population produce about one third of the world's food ... actively jeopardizes the most fundamental principles and values associated with the right to life and human dignity as enshrined in the Universal Declaration of Human Rights." Paragraph (c) attributes hunger to "historical circumstances, especially social inequalities, including in many cases alien and colonial domination, foreign occupation, racial discrimination, *apartheid* and neo-colonialism in all its forms. ..." Aggravating these conditions, according to paragraph (d), are economic problems, inflation, high import costs, external debt, and "a rising food demand partly due to demographic pressure. ..."

A world food security system, according to paragraph (g), "would ensure adequate availability of, and reasonable prices for, food at all times. ..." Recognizing that "peace and justice" may help solve various economic problems, paragraph (h) states that "it is necessary to eliminate threats and resort to force and to promote peaceful co-operation. ..." Paragraph (i) calls for eliminating the "widening gaps" separating developed and developing countries; paragraph (j) asks developing countries to "reaffirm their belief that the primary responsibility for ensuring their own rapid development rests with themselves"; and paragraph (k) urges international action, "free of political pressures," to help developing countries meet their food needs when they cannot do so themselves.

The formal text of the declaration proclaims in paragraph 1: "Every man, woman and child has the inalienable right to be free from hunger and malnutrition in order to develop fully and maintain their physical and mental faculties. Society today already possesses sufficient resources, organizational ability and technology and hence the competence to achieve this objective. Accordingly, the eradication of hunger is a common objective of all countries of the international community, especially of the developed countries and others in a position to help." According to paragraph 2, governments have the "fundamental responsibility ... to work together for higher food production and a more equitable and efficient distribution of food between countries and within countries."

Paragraphs 3, 4, and 6, respectively, provide that each country should emphasize humanitarian issues such as food problems in national plans and programs; shoulder responsibility "to remove the obstacles to food production ... [and] recognize the key role of women in agricultural production and rural economy in many countries"; and "promote a rational exploitation" of marine and inland

water resources. The role of highly industrialized countries is discussed in paragraphs 7, 8, and 10. Paragraph 9 focuses on "the preservation of the environment" to aid in food production; and paragraph 11 urges countries to "readjust, where appropriate, their agricultural policies to give priority to food production."

Paragraph 12 outlines procedures for establishing "an effective system of world food security," including participating in the Global Information and Early Warning System on Food and Agriculture, earmarking food stocks for international emergencies, and cooperating in providing "food aid for meeting emergency and nutritional needs as well as for stimulating rural employment through development projects."

"Time is short," concludes the declaration. "Urgent and sustained action is vital. The Conference, therefore, calls upon all peoples expressing their will as individuals, and through their Governments, and non-governmental organizations, to work together to bring about the end of the age-old scourge of hunger."

Cooperative Assistance Relief Everywhere (CARE), 151 Ellis Street N.E., Atlanta, Ga. 30303-2439. (404-681-2552. 404-589-2657. info@care.org. www.care.org.

Food and Agriculture Organization of the United Nations, Viale delle Terme di Caracalla, 00100 Rome, Italy. (39-6-57051. 39-6-57053152. webmaster@fao.org. www.fao.org.

International Fund for Agricultural Development, 107 Via del Serafico, 00142 Rome, Italy. (39-6-54591. 39-6-5043463. ifad@ifad.org. www.ifad.org.

Oxfam International, 267 Banbury Road, Second Floor, Oxford OX2 7HT, England. (44-186-531-3939. 44-186-531-3935. administration@oxfaminternational.org. www.oxfaminternational.org.

United Nations High Commissioner for Human Rights, 8–14 avenue de la Paix, 1211 Geneva 10, Switzerland. (41-22-917-9000. 41-22-917-9016. webadmin.unhchr@unog.ch. www.unhchr.ch.

World Food Program, Via Cesare Giulio Viola, 68 Parco de Medici, Rome 00148, Italy. (39-6-65131. 39-6-6590632. webadministrator@wfp.org. www.wfp.org.

Barbour, Scott, and William Dudley, eds. *Hunger*. San Diego, Calif.: Greenhaven, 1995.

Declaration on Social Progress and Development; Food; Health; International Covenant on Economic, Social and Cultural Rights; Oxfam International; Social Rights; Standard of Living; Welfare

Universal Declaration on the Human Genome and Human Rights

Beginning with the Nuremberg Code (1947), which states that the "voluntary consent of the human subject is absolutely essential," the international scientific and medical communities have sought to set rules for research and experimentation on humans. The 1947 statement of principles, adopted after the international community reacted to the World War II experiments of Nazi Germany, also specified that medical research should be designed to produce "fruitful results for the good of society," avoid unnecessary physical and mental suffering and injury to subjects, and be conducted only by qualified persons.

In 1993 the United Nations Educational, Scientific and Cultural Organization (UNESCO) created the International Bioethics Committee (IBC) and charged it with drafting an international instrument to protect human rights during scientific research on the human genome. The human genome is a map of the complete set of chromosomes of a germ cell (a sperm or an egg cell), which contains the genetic code triggering human development from the embryo to adulthood.

The IBC's Universal Declaration on the Human Genome and Human Rights, unanimously adopted by UNESCO's General Conference on November 11, 1997, begins by recognizing that "research on the human genome and the resulting applications open up vast prospects for progress in improving the health of individuals and of mankind as a whole," but it emphasizes that "such research should fully respect human dignity, freedom and human rights, as well as the prohibition of all forms of discrimination based on genetic characteristics."

A, Human Dignity and the Human Genome, article 1, declares: "The human genome underlies the fundamental unity of all members of the human family, as well as the recognition of their inherent dignity and diversity. In a symbolic sense, it is the heritage of humanity." According to article 2: "a) Everyone has a right to respect for their dignity and for their rights regardless of their genetic characteristics. b) That dignity makes it imperative not to reduce individuals to their genetic characteristics and to respect their uniqueness and diversity." Article 3 notes that the human genome, "which by its nature evolves, is subject to mutations. It contains potentialities that are expressed differently according to each individual's natural and social environment including the individual's state of health, living conditions, nutrition and education." Adds article 4, "The human genome in its natural state shall not give rise to financial gains."

Pursuant to B, Rights of the Persons Concerned, article 5: "a) Research, treatment or diagnosis affecting an individual's genome shall be undertaken only after rigorous and prior assessment of the potential risks and benefits pertaining thereto and in accordance with any other requirement of national law. b) In all cases, the prior, free and informed consent of the person concerned shall be obtained. ... c) The right of each individual to decide whether or not to be informed of the results of genetic examination and the resulting consequences should be respected. d) In the case of research, protocols shall ... be submitted for prior review in accordance with relevant ... standards or guidelines." Articles 6 through 9, respectively, prohibit discrimination, require confidentiality, assert the right to reparation for damage, and specify that "limitations to the principles of consent and confidentiality may only be prescribed by law, for compelling reasons within the bounds of ... human rights."

Under C, Research on the Human Genome, article 10 provides that research or its applications may not "prevail over respect for the human rights, fundamental freedoms and human dignity" of individuals and groups. Article 11 mandates: "Practices that are contrary to human dignity, such as reproductive cloning of human beings, shall not be permitted." It invites nations and international organizations "to co-operate in identifying such practices" and taking measures that follow the declaration's principles. Under article 12, the benefits of human genome research "shall be made available to all, with due regard to the dignity and human rights of each individual." It adds that such research "shall seek to offer relief from suffering and improve the health of individuals and humankind as a whole."

Other recent international human rights documents addressing similar issues include the International Ethical Guidelines for Biomedical Research Involving Human Subjects (1993), Convention on Human Rights and Biomedicine (1996), and Cloning in Human Reproduction (1997), adopted by the World Health Organization.

American Association for the Advancement of Science (AAAS), 1200 New York Avenue, N.W., Washington, D.C. 20005. (202-326-6400. 🖷 202-789-0455. 🖳 webmaster@aaas.org. 🖳 www.aaas.org.

United Nations Educational, Scientific and Cultural Organization (UNESCO), 7 place de Fontenoy, 75352 Paris 07 SP, France. (33-1-45-68-10-00. 🖷 33-1-45-67-16-90. 🖳 webmaster@unesco.org. 🖳 www.unesco.org.

Marshall, Elizabeth L. *The Human Genome Project: Cracking the Code within Us.* New York: Watts, 1996.

Health; United Nations Educational, Scientific and Cultural Organization (UNESCO); World Health Organization

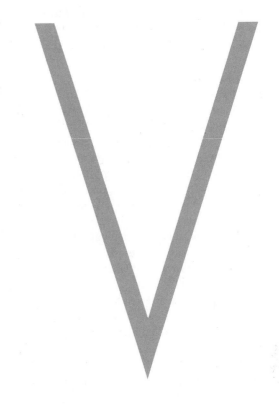

Although Iran is a theocracy, the Iranian constitution provides for regular parliamentary elections, at one of which women voted at a mosque in 2000. All citizens' participation in the governing of their country by voting in elections and holding public office regardless of sex, race, or minority status is a basic human right.

[Henghameh Fahimi, Agence France-Presse

Vancouver Declaration on Human Settlements

The right to decent housing, along with an adequate standard of living, universal health care, and other economic and social rights, is declared in the International Covenant on Economic, Social and Cultural Rights (1966). Other instruments such as the European Social Charter (1961, revised in 1996) also guarantee everyone the right to housing. To stimulate interest in making good on this guarantee by solving one of the greatest problems facing humankind—how to adequately house the world's growing population—conferees met at HABITAT in Vancouver, British Columbia, Canada, from May 31 to June 11, 1976. Formally known as the UN Conference on Human Settlements, the meeting was held at the recommendation of the UN Conference on the Human Environment and the UN General Assembly.

On the conference's final day, the Vancouver Declaration on Human Settlements, which calls adequate shelter "a basic human right," was adopted. It recognizes "that the establishment of a just and equitable world economic order through necessary changes in the areas of international trade, monetary systems, industrialization, transfer of resources, transfer of technology, and the consumption of world resources, is essential for socio-economic development and improvement of human settlement, particularly in developing countries." Taking note of the declaration,

the General Assembly that year urged nations to consider it when determining their own housing policies.

The declaration begins by noting that "the condition of human settlements largely determines the quality of life, the improvement of which is a prerequisite for the full satisfaction of basic needs, such as employment, housing, health services, education and recreation." It goes on to state that "the circumstances of life for vast numbers of people in human settlements are unacceptable, particularly in developing countries. . . ." World population growth was expected to double in the next twenty-five years, observed the declaration, "thereby more than doubling the need for food, shelter and all other requirements for life and human dignity which are at the present inadequately met." The document cites a number of related problems, among them uncontrolled urbanization, overcrowding, pollution, psychological tensions, "rural backwardness," and involuntary migrations and expulsions of people, admitting that "these problems pose a formidable challenge to human understanding, imagination, ingenuity and resolve. . . ."

"Mankind must not be daunted by the scale of the task ahead," declares part I, Opportunities and Solutions, paragraph 1. It urges governments and the international community to create "more livable, attractive and efficient settlements which recognize human scale, the heritage and culture of people and the special needs of disadvantaged groups," develop "effective participation by all people in the planning, building and management of their human settlements," and support "economic opportunities conducive to full employment where, under healthy, safe conditions, women and men will be fairly compensated for their labor. . . ." Paragraph 2 calls human settlements "an instrument and object of development," adding that the "goals of settlement policies are inseparable from the goals of every sector of social and economic life."

Part II, General Principles, sets forth principles and guidelines for housing policies. Paragraph 1 states that "improvement of the quality of life of human beings is the first and most important objective of every human settlement policy." In addition, "priority must be given to the needs of the most disadvantaged people," notes paragraph 2. According to paragraph 4, "Human dignity and the exercise of free choice consistent with over-all public welfare are basic rights which must be assured in every society." Other items refer to the illegality of settlements in occupied territories; freedom of movement; the desirability of preserving cultural heritage, historic settlements, monuments, and other parts of a nation's heritage; and international cooperation. The world's countries, notes paragraph 11, "must avoid the pollution of the biosphere and the oceans and should join in the effort to end irrational exploitation of all environmental resources. . . ."

Part III, Guidelines for Action, focuses on government responsibilities in setting human settlement policies. Among the policies recommended are reduction of disparities between rural and urban areas, more orderly and humane urbanization, protection of agricultural land, public control over land use and tenure, recapture of increased land values for society as a whole, better planning processes, improved design, greater personal and family privacy, and conservation and recycling strategies.

"Adequate shelter and services," states paragraph 8, "are a basic human right which places an obligation on Governments to ensure their attainment by all people, beginning with direct assistance to the least advantaged through guided programs of self-help and community action." The declaration urges increased technical and financial cooperation between the developed and developing countries, stating that because "resources of Governments are inadequate to meet all needs, the international community should provide the necessary financial and technical assistance, evolve appropriate institutional arrangements and seek new effective ways to promote them."

United Nations Center for Human Settlements (Habitat), P.O. Box 30030, Nairobi, Kenya. (254-2-621234. 🖨 254-2-624266. 🖥 habitat@unchs.org. 🖥 www.unchs.org.

United Nations Commission on Human Settlements, P.O. Box 30030, Nairobi, Kenya. (254-2-623149. 🖨 254-2-624040. 🖥 habitat@unchs.org. 🖥 www.unchs.org.

United Nations High Commissioner for Human Rights, 8–14 avenue de la Paix, 1211 Geneva 10, Switzerland. (41-22-917-9000. 🖨 41-22-917-9016. 🖥 webadmin.hchr@unog.ch. 🖥 www.unhchr.ch.

Development; Economic Rights; European Social Charter; Housing; International Covenant on Economic, Social and Cultural Rights; Standard of Living; Welfare

Victims

It is traditionally considered that crimes are committed against the state or the people of the state; the victims (from the Latin *victima,* meaning a person who is put to death or subjected to torture by another) is simply the object of the crime, although civil as well as criminal liability may result from the same act. But since World War II the notion that victims of crimes may have certain rights vis-à-vis their government in prosecuting the perpetrator has gained currency, and victims' rights are now firmly a part of the lexicon of human rights concepts.

The Holocaust carried out by the Nazi regime in Germany and Japanese oppression during World War II created victims whose particularly horrific plight raised the world's awareness of victims of human rights abuses, and these events continue to have repercussions—among them investigations into Swiss banks that in 1999 still held property taken by the Nazis from their victims and the German government's pledge in 2000 of $5 billion to compensate "elderly victims" of Nazi policies of slave and forced labor. In 1985 the UN General Assembly adopted the Declaration of Basic Principles of Justice for Victims of Crime and Abuses of Power, and the UN Model Treaty on the Transfer of Proceedings in Criminal Matters (1990) includes an article that addresses victims' rights, urging states to ensure that the transfer of criminal matters between them does not adversely affect a victim's "right to restitution or compensation."

Although the concept of victims' rights has not historically been recognized in Anglo-American law, a number of states of the United States have instituted victims' bills of rights—constitutional or statutory provisions extending certain guaranteed rights to the victims of crime—and have established funds to compensate victims. A typical victims' bill of rights provides that victims of crime be treated with fairness and dignity; be advised in a timely manner about the disposition of the case against the accused; be given the opportunity to attend court proceedings, confer with the prosecution, and make a statement to the court about the disposition of the case; be given reasonable protection from the accused; be provided information on the outcome of the case and the release of the accused; and be entitled to restitution and compensation. There has also been a movement in Congress to amend the U.S. Constitution (1789) to add a victims' bill of rights that would, in addition to the rights mentioned earlier, give victims the right to testify about parole, plea agreements, and sentencing and to be notified of any consideration of executive clemency; however, many believe that balancing victims' rights with rights of those accused of a crime is yet to be resolved satisfactorily. In some European civil law systems, such as France's, the victim or the victim's family has the right to separate representation at the trial of the defendant.

At the international level, victims' rights are at the heart of the remedy process for violations of human rights. The Universal Declaration of Human Rights (1948) provides in article 8: "Everyone has the right to an effective remedy by the competent national tribunals for acts violating fundamental rights granted him by the constitution or by law." The International Covenant on Civil and Political Rights (1966) refers to victims' rights to compensation, and the First Optional Protocol (1966) to that document expressly provides for communications from individuals claiming to be victims of human rights violations.

The Declaration of Basic Principles of Justice for Victims of Crime and Abuse of Power, adopted by the UN General Assembly in 1985, is a significant document because of its increased emphasis on victims' rights. The declaration, in addition to extending to victims certain considerations such as the right to be informed of their rights, also addresses restitution, compensation, and assistance for victims. Additional Protocols I and II (1977) to the Geneva Conventions (1949) address protection of victims of international and noninternational conflicts.

Various international and regional forums for handling human rights complaints, such as the Commission on Human Rights, have adopted procedures to assist and protect victims. The World Society of Victimology, a nongovernmental organization established in 1979, aids victims by promoting research and publishing research findings on victims of crime and human rights violations.

New Zealand Criminal Injuries Compensation Act of 1963 (1964): This act, based on the philosophy that the community has a "duty towards those who suffer misfortune," provides "for the compensation of persons injured by certain criminal acts, and of dependents of persons killed by such acts."

International Covenant on Civil and Political Rights (1966), part III, article 9: "5. Anyone who has been the victim of unlawful arrest or detention shall have an enforceable right to compensation."

U.S. Supreme Court (1991): New York's "Son of Sam" law, named for a serial killer who contracted to write a book about his crimes, required that persons accused or convicted of crimes who derived income from works describing their crimes may not profit from such works but must make such income available to the victims. Such a law is "presumptively inconsistent" with the U.S. Constitution's First Amendment (1791), guaranteeing freedom of speech. Whether the "speaker" is a person accused of or convicted of a crime or the pub-

lisher of such works, the "Son of Sam" law "singles out speech on [a] particular subject for [a] financial burden that it places on no other [type of] speech and no other income" and therefore is unconstitutional.

European Court of Human Rights (1986): The European Convention for the Protection of Human Rights and Fundamental Freedoms (1950), article 25, provides that anyone claiming to be the victim of a violation of the convention may file a complaint. "Article 25 . . . in its use of the word 'victim' denotes 'the person directly affected by the act or omission which is in issue.'"

National Center for Victims of Crime, 1211 Wilson Boulevard, Suite 300, Arlington, Va. 22201. (703-276-2880. 🖷 703-276-2889. 🖳 ncvc@ncvc.org. 🖳 www.ncvc.org.

World Society of Victimology, University of Applied Sciences, Department of Social Work, Rheydter Strasse 232, D-41065, Mönchengladbach, Germany. (49-2161-186-161. 🖷 49-2161-186-633. 🖳 kirchhoff@bigfoot.com. 🖳 wsv-international.com.

Bassiouni, M. Cherif, ed. *International Protection of Victims*. Toulouse, France: Erès, 1988.

Tobolowsky, Peggy M., ed. *Understanding Victimology: Selected Readings*. Cincinnati: Anderson, 1999.

Accused; Compensation; Complaints; Declaration of Basic Principles of Justice for Victims of Crime and Abuse of Power; Geneva Conventions; International Covenant on Civil and Political Rights; International Covenant on Civil and Political Rights, First Optional Protocol; Rehabilitation; Remedies; Reporting Violations; Universal Declaration of Human Rights; Violations

Vienna Declaration and Program of Action

Forty-five years after adoption of the Universal Declaration of Human Rights (1948) and twenty-five years after the first World Conference on Human Rights had met in Tehran in 1968, another World Conference on Human Rights convened in Vienna in 1993 to assess the progress made toward human rights. Plans for the conference began in 1989, shortly after the Berlin Wall had fallen, "carrying away with it a certain vision of the world," noted UN Secretary-General Boutros Boutros-Ghali in his opening remarks.

A year earlier, the UN General Assembly had set an extensive agenda for the conference, asking it to evaluate the effectiveness of UN actions, identify financial resources to promote human rights, and study the links among economic, social, cultural, and political rights. The conference, which was attended by seven thousand participants, including representatives from 171 national governments as well as from UN agencies and bodies, national institutions, and 841 nongovernmental organizations, produced the Vienna Declaration and Program of Action. Adopted on June 25 with the consent of the 171 nations represented and endorsed by the General Assembly in December 1993, the lengthy document contains ambitious proposals and goals for addressing human rights problems.

The declaration begins by noting that the conference "affords a unique opportunity to carry out a comprehensive analysis of the international human rights system and of the machinery for the protection of human rights, in order to enhance and thus promote a fuller observance of those rights, in a just and balanced manner." It goes on to note "the major changes taking place on the international scene and the aspirations of all peoples for an international order based on the principles enshrined in the Charter of the United Nations [1945], including promoting and encouraging respect for human rights and fundamental freedoms for all and respect for the principle of equal rights and self-determination of peoples, peace, democracy, justice, equality, rule of law, pluralism, development, better standards of living and solidarity." It adds its deep concern over "various forms of discrimination and violence, to which women continue to be exposed all over the world."

"The World Conference on Human Rights reaffirms the solemn commitment of all States to fulfill their obligations to promote universal respect for, and observance and protection of, all human rights and fundamental freedoms for all in accordance with the Charter of the United Nations, other instruments relating to human rights, and international law," declares part I, paragraph 1. "All peoples have the right of self-determination," adds paragraph 2. "By virtue of that right they freely determine their political status, and freely pursue their economic, social and cultural development."

According to paragraph 5, "All human rights are universal, indivisible and interdependent and interrelated." Paragraph 8 notes that "[d]emocracy, development and respect for human rights and fundamental freedoms are interdependent and mutually reinforcing." Part I, among other things, also calls on nations to take action on such matters as promoting development and protecting the environment, and it challenges the international community to deal with a number of human rights problems by "strengthening and promoting . . . democracy," encouraging "effective international cooperation for the realization of the right to development," and making "all efforts to help alleviate the external debt burden of developing countries," as well as taking steps to alleviate poverty and racial discrimination, "including xenophobia and related intolerance," and to combat terrorism, which is "aimed at the destruction of human rights, fundamental freedoms

and democracy, threatening territorial integrity, security of States and destabilizing legitimately constituted Governments."

Paragraph 18 highlights discrimination and violence against women and girls and calls on the international community to guarantee "full and equal participation of women in political, civil, economic, social and cultural life" and to eradicate "all forms of discrimination on grounds of sex." Other aspects addressed include gross violations of human rights such as "genocide, 'ethnic cleansing' and systematic rape of women in war situations," as well as the rights of minority and indigenous peoples, children, disabled persons, refugees, asylum seekers, migrant workers, and displaced persons. "[F]ood should not be used as a tool for political pressure," it adds, mentioning obstacles to trade among nations. Paragraph 27 urges every nation to "provide an effective framework of remedies to redress human rights grievances or violations," stressing the "administration of justice, including law enforcement and prosecutorial agencies and, especially, an independent judiciary and legal profession in full conformity with applicable standards contained in international human rights instruments. . . ."

Part II, section A, Increased Coordination on Human Rights within the United Nations System, discusses resources for human rights activities and information about the Center for Human Rights. Section B addresses in detail equality, dignity, and tolerance, targeting topics such as racial discrimination, minorities, indigenous peoples, migrant workers, women, children, and disabled persons, as well as torture and enforced disappearance. Section C focuses on international cooperation, development, and strengthening human rights; section D singles out human rights education; and sections E and F, respectively, address implementation and monitoring methods and ideas for following up on the activities of the conference.

The ambitious 1993 Vienna Declaration and Program of Action concludes by recommending to the UN, among other activities, that ways and means be considered "for the full implementation, without delay, of the recommendations" contained in the document and that the Commission on Human Rights "annually review the progress towards this end."

✉

United Nations High Commissioner for Human Rights, 8–14 avenue de la Paix, 1211 Geneva 10, Switzerland. ☎ 41-22-917-9000. 🖷 41-22-917-9016. 🖳 webmaster.hchr@unog.ch. 🖳 www.unhchr.ch.

☞

Center for Human Rights; Charter of the United Nations; Commission on Human Rights; Development; International Covenant on Civil and Political Rights; International Covenant on Economic, Social and Cultural Rights; Self-Determination; Universal Declaration of Human Rights

Violations

In a perfect world, all acts by government officials would strictly conform to the human rights guarantees contained in national laws and international human rights documents. But because people are imperfect, a government of laws becomes, in fact, a government of individuals who may unintentionally or willfully violate citizens' rights. Violation, abuse, denial, or infringement of human rights by agents of the state are crimes that should trigger enforcement procedures, punishment for violators, redress, and compensation for the victims.

Violations of human rights take many forms. In extreme cases, such as under dictatorships, abuses may include arbitrary imprisonment, torture, and even summary execution simply on the basis of one's religion, ethnic origin, or political beliefs. By denying equal rights, discrimination on the basis of race, sex, religion, national origin, social status, or birth—in economic opportunities, participation in a community's political life, or education or other benefits—is another form of abuse.

Some violations (from the Latin *violare*, meaning to treat with violence or dishonor) involve direct participation by government officials, such as the passage of discriminatory legislation or the uneven enforcement of laws. In other instances discrimination is more subtle, as in the government's failure to pass laws against discrimination or to take action in cases of private discrimination. One example is the failure by the United States to ensure the rights of former slaves and their descendants until after World War II, even though they had been granted freedom following the Civil War.

Preventing violations from occurring is, of course, preferable to having to stop violations, redress wrongs, and punish guilty parties. Humans may always harbor some individual prejudices, but increasingly the world community expects governments to take the necessary actions to limit and punish the effect of prejudicial behavior. If violations of human rights are to be minimized, if not eradicated, citizens and government officials alike—legislators, administrators, judges, and law enforcement officials—must be educated as to what constitutes human rights, who is entitled to which rights, and what remedies are available for violations. Public awareness, a professional and aggressive legal system, watchful activity by nongovernmental organizations, and community support for human rights efforts also help reduce the opportunity for violations of a variety of rights.

Most national constitutions spell out rights guaranteed to citizens and leave enforcement of violations to their legal system and such specialized institutions as ombudsmen or human rights commissions. Some international human rights documents, such as the European Convention for the Protection of Human Rights and Fundamental Freedoms (1950) and the International Covenant on Civil and Political Rights (1966), provide a mechanism for filing complaints and seeking remedies. Many others, such as the Universal Declaration of Human Rights (1948), Declaration on the Rights of Disabled Persons (1975), and Declaration on the Protection of All Persons from Enforced Disappearance (1992), simply rely on countries to adapt their laws to conform to the documents and provide remedies for violations of the rights specified.

A number of international institutions also address human rights violations. The United Nations and some of its subsidiary bodies, particularly the Office of the High Commissioner for Human Rights, assist with preventing, monitoring, reporting, and correcting government actions that violate international standards of human rights. The International Court of Justice (World Court) acts on cases involving human rights abuses, as do regional courts and commissions in Europe, Latin America, and Africa. Committees established under certain conventions, such as the International Convention on the Elimination of All Forms of Racial Discrimination (1966) and the Convention on the Elimination of All Forms of Discrimination against Women (1979), also play a role in preventing and redressing specific violations of human rights.

Constitution of India (1949), part III, Fundamental Rights, Right to Constitutional Remedies, notes to article 32: "The jurisdiction conferred on the Supreme Court by Article 32 is an important and integral part of the basic structure of the Constitution. The violation of a fundamental right is the sine qua non of the exercise of the right under Article 32 [to remedies for enforcement of constitutional rights]."

Procedure for Dealing with Communications Relating to Violations of Human Rights and Fundamental Freedoms (1970): "The Economic and Social Council [ECOSOC] . . . 5. Requests the [Subcommission on the Promotion and Protection of Human Rights] to consider . . . the communications brought before it . . . with a view to determining whether to refer to the Commission on Human Rights particular situations which appear to reveal a consistent pattern of gross and reliably attested violations of human rights requiring consideration by the Commission. . . ."

Supreme Court of Canada (1986): In holding unconstitutional a law requiring the defendant to prove that his or her possession of drugs was not for the purposes of trafficking in them, the court said that such a requirement would violate the guarantee of a presumption of innocence.

International Court of Justice (Advisory Opinion) (1971): "To establish . . . and to enforce distinctions, exclusions, restrictions and limitations exclusively based on grounds of race, color, descent, or national or ethnic origin which constitute a denial of fundamental human rights is a flagrant violation of the purposes and principles of the Charter [of the United Nations (1945)]."

Bröhmer, Jürgen. *State Immunity and the Violation of Human Rights.* International Studies in Human Rights, vol. 47. The Hague: Kluwer Law International, 1997.

Commission on Human Rights; Compensation; Complaints; Enforcement; High Commissioner for Human Rights; Human Rights Committee; International Court of Justice; International Covenant on Civil and Political Rights; International Criminal Court; Law Enforcement; Ombudsmen; Regional Human Rights Systems; Remedies; Reporting Violations; Resolution 1503 Procedure; Subcommission on the Promotion and Protection of Human Rights; Victims

Voting

The right to vote for public officials is a hallmark of democratic government. Regular elections in which all citizens have the right to participate both as voters and as candidates for office, conducted fairly and using the secret ballot, are the primary means of ensuring accountability of those who hold and wield political power on behalf of the citizens in any political jurisdiction. Because the right to vote is one way of protecting citizens from arbitrary and capricious acts by government officials, it is a key element in protecting human rights.

In a representative democracy, citizens have the right to cast a ballot in an election to select members of the executive, legislative, and judicial branches of government (although most judges at the national level are appointed and confirmed rather than elected). *Vote* derives from the Latin *votum*, meaning a promise or desire, although the Latin word meaning vote is *suffragim*, the precursor of the English word *suffrage.*

The practice of citizens voting for public officials and on public policy began in ancient Greece, although voting was then and for much of history has been a right reserved for free adult males. Women did not obtain the right to vote until 1893 (in New Zealand) and until 1920 in the United States, where blacks were discriminated against particularly in the southern states before passage of the 1964 Civil Rights Act. In 1994, after the collapse of the racist policies of apartheid, all the citizens of South Africa were finally eligible to vote in national elections. Even today in some countries, however, some citizens are still disenfranchised.

The right to vote is considered an attribute of national citizenship. The constitutional concept of popular sovereignty requires that all citizens have an equal right to vote in periodic elections for government leaders and representatives. Abridgment of the right to vote is a form of discrimination, although in some countries a person can lose the right to vote if convicted of a crime. The right to vote also generally involves a number of procedural require-

ments, including registering to vote, getting to the polls, and actually casting a ballot. Democratic principles require that voting must be free and open to all registered citizens and done by secret ballot (also called Australian ballot).

Most nations provide for elections and voting in their laws and often in their constitutions. At the international level, the right to vote is considered a universal civil and political human right. In 1989 the UN General Assembly adopted a resolution stressing its conviction that "periodic and genuine elections are a necessary and indispensable element of sustained efforts to protect the rights and interests of the governed and that . . . the right of everyone to take part in the government of his or her country is a crucial factor in the effective enjoyment by all of a wide range of other human rights and fundamental freedoms. . . ."

Constitution of Norway (1814), C, Rights of Citizens and Legislative Power, article 55: "The polls shall be conducted in the manner prescribed by law. Disputes regarding the right to vote shall be settled by the poll officials, whose decision may be appealed to the Storting [national legislature]."

International Covenant on Civil and Political Rights (1966), part III, article 25: "Every citizen shall have the right and the opportunity, without any . . . distinctions . . . and without unreasonable restrictions; . . . (b) To vote and to be elected at genuine periodic elections which shall be by universal and equal suffrage and shall be held by secret ballot, guaranteeing the free expression of the will of the electors. . . ."

Supreme Court of Japan (1976): Provisions of Japan's constitution "require that the content of the right to vote at the election of both houses of the Diet [national legislature], that is the value of votes of each and every electorate, must be equal."

Inter-American Commission on Human Rights (1993): Regarding a complaint of "numerous irregularities" in elections held in Mexico between March and November 1990, the commission expressed its hope that, "as it was told by the authorities of that country, these amendments [to Mexican law on political organizations and electoral processes] will effectively allow greater 'authenticity, equality, and transparency' in current and future electoral processes. . . ."

Human Rights and Elections: A Handbook on the Legal, Technical and Human Rights Aspects of Elections. Professional Training Series, no. 2. Geneva: Center for Human Rights, 1994.

Civil Rights; Seneca Falls Declaration of Sentiments and Resolutions; Stanton, Elizabeth Cady; Women

An all-male audience before World War I listens to a woman speaking on behalf of extending the vote to women. The women's rights movement has been closely linked with human rights causes. Many women who were active in the movement to abolish slavery in the United States before the Civil War, for example, went on to work actively for women's right to vote and hold office.
[Corbis-Bettmann]

Walesa, Lech

As the tenacious leader of the Polish workers' Solidarity movement, Lech Walesa (b. 1943) helped engineer the downfall of the communist regime in Poland in 1989, which led to the establishment of constitutional democracy and the restoration of human rights. For his efforts he was awarded the Nobel Peace Prize in 1984 and shared the European Human Rights Prize in 1989. The Nobel Prize Committee commended him for his "defense of human rights and his determination to solve his country's problems through negotiation and cooperation without resorting to violence."

Born on September 29, 1943, in Wroclaw, Poland, Walesa was trained as an automobile mechanic. After serving for two years in the army, he began working as an electrician at the shipyard in Gdansk. Walesa was fired in 1976 for criticizing the communist trade unions and with other workers began organizing an independent labor union.

His actions followed by a year the Polish communist government's agreement to abide by the Helsinki Final Act (1975), which recognized many basic human rights. To publicize violations of the Helsinki agreement, the Movement in Defense of Human Rights sprang up in 1976.

In 1980 the shipyard workers went on strike, with Walesa at the lead. Even after the strike was settled in Gdansk, it continued in other parts of Poland as a show of solidarity among the workers. When the newly legalized labor groups formed the National Committee on Solidarity in 1980,

Walesa was chosen as its chair. The committee, which became known in Polish simply as *Solidarnosc* (Solidarity), was the first trade union in Poland not controlled by the Soviet Union through the Communist Party.

"Without this basic freedom [of expression], human life becomes meaningless," Walesa later wrote, "and once the truth of it hit me, it became a part of my whole way of thinking. From that moment, I began to see myself as part of a vast pattern, woven from scraps of knowledge of our own history and tradition and from everyday experiences. . . ."

Even after Poland threw off the yoke of communism in 1989, Walesa continued to criticize the government. Still the head of Solidarity, he ran for president under Poland's newly revised constitution and on December 21, 1990, was elected with seventy-five percent of the vote. During his term, the constitution was further revised to incorporate the principles and procedures of a truly democratic government. After losing his bid for reelection in 1996, he returned to Gdansk to reapply for his old job as an electrician.

Walesa, Lech. *The Struggle and the Triumph: An Autobiography*. New York: Arcade, 1992.

————. *A Way of Hope*. New York: Henry Holt, 1987.

Helsinki Final Act; Workers

Wallenberg, Raoul

A Swedish businessman who posed as a diplomat in Hungary during World War II, Raoul Wallenberg (1912–47?), at great personal risk, assisted tens of thousands of Hungarian Jews in escaping death at the hands of the Nazis. Taken into custody by the Russians in 1945, he presumably died shortly afterward.

Wallenberg was born into one of Sweden's wealthiest families on August 4, 1912, three months after his father had died of cancer. A precocious child, he received an extensive education, learned a number of languages, and traveled and studied abroad, graduating with honors from the University of Michigan in 1935. During business trips to central Europe, Wallenberg became aware of the plight of the Jews under Hitler's government. He began working for a Jewish-owned export company in Stockholm in 1941, and on trips to Budapest, Hungary, he gained a familiarity with the city that later proved invaluable.

In 1944 the Nazis sent forces commanded by Adolf Eichmann to Hungary to round up Jews for deportation to death camps. In a desperate effort by the U.S. Refugee Board to save as many Hungarian Jews as possible, Wallenberg volunteered to pose as a Swedish diplomat (Sweden had declared its neutrality during the war). By opening numerous Swedish embassy annexes in Budapest that were in reality safe houses, forging passports, and bribing Hungarian government officials, he was able save more than twenty thousand Jews from the Holocaust.

When Russian troops entered Budapest early in 1945, Wallenberg reported to their commander. His whereabouts since then have been a mystery, although the Soviet Union reported at one time that he had died in prison in 1947. An investigation initiated by President Boris Yeltsin of Russia in 1991 turned up no new information.

Wallenberg's unselfish bravery in the face of genocide has earned him the status of an international hero. In 1981 he was made an honorary citizen of the United States, joining a select company consisting only of the marquis de Lafayette and Winston Churchill.

Established in the memory of this defender of human rights, the Raoul Wallenberg Institute of Human Rights and Humanitarian Law in Sweden offers a master's program in international law and human rights, humanitarian law, and refugee law, mainly for young lawyers and officials with governments and nongovernmental organizations. Associated closely with the University of Lund, the institute is a private foundation financed in part by the Swedish Ministry of Foreign Affairs and the Swedish International Development Corporation Agency.

Raoul Wallenberg Institute of Human Rights and Humanitarian Law, P.O. Box 1155, SE-221 05 Lund, Sweden. (46-46-222-12-00. 📠 46-46-222-12-22. 📧 secretariat@rwi.lu.se. 🖥 www.rwi.lu.se.

Rosenfeld, Harvey. *Raoul Wallenberg*. Rev. ed. New York: Holmes and Meier, 1995.

Skoglund, Elizabeth. *A Quiet Courage: Per Anger, Wallenberg's Co-Liberator of Hungarian Jews.* Grand Rapids, Mich.: Baker, 1997.

Crimes against Humanity; Defenders of Human Rights; Genocide

War

"For what can Warr, but endless warr still breed, Till Truth, and Right from Violence be freed," mourned the English poet John Milton in *Sonnets to Fairfax* (1648). It is estimated that 150 million persons have died in wars around the world since the first century, with some 111 million of those deaths occurring in the twentieth century alone. While the French Revolution and the Napoleonic wars claimed nearly five million victims at the turn of the nineteenth century, the tallies rose to twenty-six million in World War I and more than fifty-three million in World War II. In the 1990s six million persons died in more than a dozen wars worldwide, which were fought with the aid of more than 250,000 children under the age of eighteen years. Statisticians put the ratio of war deaths at 3.2 per 1,000 population in the sixteenth century but at 44.4 in the twentieth century.

Why men fight wars has been the subject of much study. War (from the Old High German *werra*, meaning discord or strife) is the continuation "of political intercourse with the intermixing of other means," suggested Carl von Clausewitz in his 1830s work *On War*. A more straightforward definition can be found in the U.S. General Order 100 (1863): "Public war is a state of armed hostility between sovereign nations or governments." Organized aggression seems to have been a part of human history even before written records were kept. The seminal literary works of Western culture, Homer's *Iliad* and *Odyssey*, vividly portray the Trojan War and its aftermath.

What is clear is that war denies a fundamental human right of all people: the right to peace. Some wars, however, are more just than most, such as wars of liberation and wars to defend against aggression and threats to human rights. The soldier and the pacifist have at least one thing in common in that both are willing to surrender their lives for authority, the former for the authority of the state and the latter for the moral authority of one's own principles. And even though the twentieth century witnessed the most devastating wars in human history, a few have resulted in unexpected benefits, including the formation of the United Nations in 1945, together with the promulgation of the Universal Declaration of Human Rights in 1948 and other international human rights documents in the wake of World War II.

Much progress in the humane conduct of wars has developed alongside the atrocities. The seventeenth-century Dutch jurist and politician Hugo Grotius wrote *On the Law of War and Peace* (1625), laying the foundation for modern international law. Later humanitarian rules of warfare such as the Hague Conventions (1907) and the Geneva Conventions (1864, 1929, 1949)—if their terms are honored by the combatants—create conditions for limiting war and its impact, addressing both the conduct of war and consequences such as wounded and sick soldiers, prisoners of war, and civilian casualties.

Most national constitutions authorize the government to declare war and specify the war powers of officials, including designation of a commander in chief of the armed forces. In addition to the Geneva Conventions, a number of multilateral humanitarian treaties and international human rights documents address war or aspects of war, among them the Declaration on the Prohibition of the Use of Nuclear and Thermo-Nuclear Weapons (1961), Convention on Prohibitions or Restrictions on the Use of Certain Conventional Weapons Which May Be Deemed to Be Excessively Injurious or to Have Indiscriminate Effects (1981), and Declaration on Fundamental Principles Concerning the Contribution of the Mass Media to Strengthening Peace and International Understanding, to the Promotion of Human Rights and to Countering Racialism, Apartheid and Incitement to War (1978).

Constitution of Japan (1947), chapter II, article 9: "Aspiring sincerely to an international peace based on justice and order, the Japanese people forever renounce war as a sovereign right of the nation and the threat or use of force as means of settling international disputes."

Charter of the United Nations (1945), preamble: "We the Peoples of the United Nations [are] determined to save succeeding generations from the scourge of war. . . ."

U.S. District Court, Southern District of New York (1970): A doctor in the U.S. Army could not avoid being assigned to duty in Vietnam on the grounds that the war was being waged in contravention of the U.S. Constitution (1789) or because it was possible that U.S. forces in Vietnam might be violating the laws of war.

International Court of Justice (1986): The Declaration on Principles of International Law Concerning Friendly Relations and Co-operation among States in Accordance with the Charter of the United Nations (1970) demonstrates that "the States represented in the [UN] General Assembly regard the exception to the prohibition of force constituted by the right of individual or collective self-defense as already a matter of customary law."

Art, Robert J., and Kenneth N. Waltz, eds. *The Use of Force: Military Power and International Politics*. Lanham, Md.: Rowman and Littlefield, 1999.

Keegan, John. *A History of Warfare*. New York: Knopf, 1993.

Welch, David A. *Justice and the Genesis of War*. New York: Cambridge University Press, 1993.

Conscience; Convention on Prohibitions or Restrictions on the Use of Certain Conventional Weapons Which May Be Deemed to Be Excessively Injurious or to Have Indiscriminate Effects; Crimes against Humanity; Declaration on Fundamental Principles Concerning the Contribution of the Mass Media to Strengthening Peace and International Understanding, to the Promotion of Human Rights and to Countering Racialism, Apartheid and Incitement to War; Declaration on the Prohibition of the Use of Nuclear and Thermo-Nuclear Weapons; Declaration on the Protection of Women and Children in Emergency and Armed Conflict; Geneva Conventions; Grotius, Hugo; Military Personnel; Peace; War Crimes; Weapons

War Crimes

War by its very nature violates the basic right to peace and opens the door to other human rights violations. Sun Tzu's *Art of War*, written in the sixth century B.C.E., contained rules for sparing the sick, wounded, and elderly during war (from the Old High German *werra*, meaning discord or strife). Some codes of military conduct dating to the Middle Ages in Europe have addressed the lawful use of force during armed conflict, and some violations of customary laws of war were punished during the nineteenth century. But with a few exceptions, such as centuries-old prohibitions against piracy, the international law of war crimes had its beginnings in the twentieth century.

Among the first attempts to define war crimes were the Geneva Convention (1906) and the Hague Convention no. X (1907)—both of which required states parties, among other things, to enact laws criminalizing the misuse of protective markings, such as the Red Cross symbol—and the Treaty of Washington (1922), which limited submarine warfare. According to the International Military Tribunal's London Charter (1945), article 6(b), war crimes are "violations of the laws and customs of war. Such violations shall include, but are not limited to, murder, ill-treatment or deportation to slave labor or for any other purpose of civilian population of or in occupied territory, murder or ill-treatment of prisoners of war or persons on the seas, killing of hostages, plunder of public or private property, wanton destruction of cities, towns or villages, or devastation not justified by military necessity." During the Nuremberg war crime trials of Nazis in Germany after World War II, the definition of war crimes was expanded to encompass such actions as medical experiments on unwilling patients, the taking of hostages, and economic exploitation of occupied territories.

An addendum to the Nuremberg trials is the case of Adolf Eichmann, a Nazi war criminal who was abducted from Argentina by Israeli forces in 1960 and taken to Israel, where he was tried for war crimes, including genocide, convicted, and executed in 1962. Israel had not been in existence at the time of Eichmann's crimes but claimed jurisdiction as an agent of enforcement of the Nuremberg Principles (1946) and the Convention on the Prevention and Punishment of the Crime of Genocide (1948). More recent tribunals have been established under the auspices of the UN Security Council to adjudicate war crimes in the former territory of Yugoslavia and in Rwanda.

In addition to gross violations of human rights occurring outside the rules of war—such as mistreatment of prisoners and genocide—war crimes now include all actions proscribed in treaties on the conduct of warfare. In 1968 the UN General Assembly adopted the Convention on the Non-Applicability of Statutory Limitations to War Crimes and Crimes against Humanity, which entered into force in 1970. A European convention with a similar title, adopted by the Council of Europe, was opened for signature in 1974.

A problem with making conduct during warfare between sovereign nations a crime is how to enforce violations. The victors may or may not punish violations by the vanquished, but who will punish violations by the victors? The International Criminal Court, a new institution for prosecuting, trying, and punishing war criminals, was created in 1998 under the provisions of the Rome Statute. As proposed, this court will have international jurisdiction to investigate and bring to justice individuals (not nations) who commit the most serious crimes, including war crimes.

U.S. Army Manual on the Law of Land Warfare (1956): "The term 'war crime' is the technical expression for a violation of the law of war by any person or persons, military or civilian. Every violation of the law of war is a war crime."

European Convention on the Non-Applicability of Statutory Limitations to Crimes against Humanity and War Crimes (1974): "[C]rimes against humanity and the most serious violations of the laws and customs of war constitute a serious infraction of human dignity."

U.S. Supreme Court (1981): A person who fails to reveal on his application for U.S. admission that he was a guard in a German concentration camp, where he committed crimes against the inmates, may be stripped of his citizenship obtained by naturalization.

Nuremberg Military Tribunals under Control Council Law no. 10 (1950): The claim that a defendant was "following superior orders" was not always automatically rejected during the Nuremberg trials. Therefore, "to find a field commander criminally responsible for the transmittal of such an order, he must have passed the order to the chain of command and the order must be one that is criminal upon its face, or one which he is shown to have known was criminal."

Coalition for International Justice, 740 15th Street, N.W., Eighth Floor, Washington, D.C. 20005-1009. (202-662-1595. 📠 202-662-1597. 📧 coalition@cij.org. 🌐 www.cij.org.

Coalition for International Justice, Javastraat 119, 2585 AH, The Hague, Netherlands. (31-70-363-9721. 📠 31-70-363-9721. 📧 coalition@cij.org. 🌐 www.cij.org.

International Criminal Court, 777 United Nations Plaza, 12th Floor, New York, N.Y. 10017. (212-599-1320. 📠 212-599-1332. 📧 wfm@igc.org. 🌐 www.igc.org/icc.

McCormack, Timothy L. H., and Gerry J. Simpson, eds. *The Law of War Crimes: National and International Approaches.* The Hague: Kluwer Law International, 1996.

Sunga, Lyal S. *Individual Responsibility in International Law for Serious Human Rights Violations.* The Hague: Martinus Nijhoff, Kluwer Law International, 1992.

Convention on the Prevention and Punishment of the Crime of Genocide; Crimes against Humanity; Declaration on the Protection of Women and Children in Emergency and Armed Conflict; Geneva Conventions; Genocide; International Criminal Court; Prisoners; Refugees; Rome Statute of the International Criminal Court; Torture; War

Weapons

For some people the perceived need for weapons to defend against lawlessness and aggression makes the right to bear arms a human right. Access to weapons, however, may help arm those intent on violating the rights of others. In the second half of the twentieth century, "ban the bomb" demonstrators attempted to equate the nuclear arms race between the West and the Soviet Union with violations of human rights such as the right to peace, security, and a safe environment. Despite some progress signaled by international agreements limiting nuclear weapons, the availability of weapons of mass destruction continues to threaten the peace and security of much of the world.

The human facility for making tools is the same as that for making weapons, which have been used ever since the first combatant picked up a rock or a fallen tree limb to protect himself or attack another. In *The Laws*, written in the fourth century B.C.E., the Greek philosopher Plato suggests replacing the *pankration,* a sport combining wrestling and kick-boxing, with "a general contest of light-infantry; the weapons of the competitors are to be bows, javelins, and stones cast by hand and sling."

The history of warfare includes the development of weapons (a word derived from Teutonic languages) as well as military strategies, and the introduction of new or improved weapons has played a key role in the outcome of many battles. Leonardo da Vinci, the Italian Renaissance painter, sculptor, architect, and engineer, also busied himself with designing weapons. More recently, the arms race between the former Soviet Union and the United States and its North Atlantic Treaty Organization (NATO) allies has had worldwide repercussions, even without the actual use of nuclear weapons by the adversaries.

Prohibitions against some kinds of weapons have been sought throughout the history of warfare. An ancient principle of the laws of war provides that the right of warring nations to adopt means of injuring the enemy is not unlimited. Another customary rule of warfare, which was codified by the Hague Land War Regulations (1907), article 23, provides that it is "especially forbidden to employ poison or poisoned weapons." Additional Protocol I (1977) to the Geneva Conventions (1949) provides in article 35(2): "It is prohibited to employ weapons, projectiles and materials and methods of warfare of a nature to cause superfluous injury or unnecessary suffering." During the darkest days of World War II for both the United Kingdom and Germany, neither resorted to the internationally prohibited practice of chemical warfare.

Although national constitutions often outline the government's military aspects, most do not directly address weapons. Some exceptions are the U.S. Constitution (1789) and Germany's constitution (1949), article 26(2) of which states: "Weapons designed for warfare may not be manufactured, transported or marketed except with the permission of the Federal Government."

At the international level, the overwhelming increase since the end of World War II in conventional weapons as well as nuclear and other weapons of mass destruction has brought about a number of human rights documents aimed at limiting, reducing, and ultimately abolishing if not all at least the most dangerous and devastating military weapons. The UN Convention on Certain Conventional Weapons (1981), Protocol no. 1, prohibits the use of any weapon "the primary effect of which is to injure by fragments which in the human body escape detection by X-rays" (and thus cannot be found or removed by a surgeon, dooming the injured person to live with the fragments and the resulting pain). The Convention on the Prohibition, Production, Stockpiling and Use of Chemical Weapons and on Their Destruction, drafted in 1993 by the UN Standing Conference on Disarmament, prohibits "not only the chemical agents as such, but also their means of delivery and any device designed for the use of chemical weapons."

Some international treaties have provisions banning or reducing weapons of mass destruction, among them the Nuclear Test Ban Treaty (1963), Convention on the Prohibition of the Development, Production and Stockpiling of Bacteriological (Biological) and Toxic Weapons and on their Destruction (1972), SALT (Strategic Arms Limitation Treaty) I and II agreements (1972 and 1979, respectively), and START (Strategic Arms Reduction Treaty) I and II agreements (1991 and 1993, respectively).

U.S. Constitution, Second Amendment (1791): "A well regulated Militia, being necessary to the security of a free State, the right of the people to keep and bear Arms, shall not be infringed."

Declaration on the Prevention of Nuclear Catastrophe (1981), preamble: "The General Assembly, . . . Recognizing that all the horrors of past wars and all other calamities that have befallen people would pale in comparison with what is inherent in the use of nuclear weapons capable of destroying civilization on earth, . . . Solemnly proclaims . . . 5. Nuclear energy should be used exclusively for peaceful purposes and only for the benefit of mankind."

Saskatchewan District Court, Canada (1977): The accused was acquitted on the charge of possessing an unregistered restricted weapon, a sten (rapid firing) gun, because the gun had been rendered permanently inoperable and thus did not meet the definition of a restricted weapon in the criminal code, which "implies that a restricted weapon is a firearm that *is* capable of firing bullets in rapid succession."

Human Rights Committee (1993): In a communication to the committee, 6,588 citizens of the Netherlands claimed that their rights under the International Covenant on Civil and Political Rights (1966), article 6, which concerns the right to life, had been violated by the Netherlands government, which had agreed to the deployment of cruise missiles fitted with nuclear warheads on Netherlands territory. The communication was held to be inadmissible, however, because none of the 6,588 citizens were, according to the committee's findings, "victims whose right to life was then violated [during the relevant period] or under imminent prospect of violation."

International Atomic Energy Agency, P.O. Box 100, Wagramer Strasse 5, A-1400 Vienna, Austria. (43-1-20600. 🖴 43-1-20607. 🖳 official.mail@iaea.org. 🖳 www.iaea.org.

UN Department for Disarmament Affairs, Room S-3170, United Nations, New York, N.Y. 10017. (212-963-5584. 🖴 212-963-1121. 🖳 rydell@un.org. 🖳 www.un.org/depts/dda.

Conference of Government Experts on the Use of Certain Conventional Weapons. Report of the Second Session, Lugano, January 28–February 26, 1976. Geneva: International Committee of the Red Cross, 1976.

Stockholm International Peace Research Institute. *The Law of War and Dubious Weapons.* Stockholm: Almqvist and Wiksell International, 1976.

Convention on Prohibitions or Restrictions on the Use of Certain Conventional Weapons Which May Be Deemed to Be Excessively Injurious or to Have Indiscriminate Effects; Declaration on the Prohibition of the Use of Nuclear and Thermo-Nuclear Weapons; Declaration on the Use of Scientific and Technological Progress in the Interests of Peace and for the Benefit of Mankind; Geneva Conventions; North Atlantic Treaty Organization (NATO); Peace; War

Wei Jingsheng

As an impassioned young communist, Wei Jingsheng (b. 1950) embraced the cultural revolution that began in China in 1966. But after a period of internal exile and a stint in the Chinese army, during which time he saw firsthand the country's poverty and the upheavals wrought by Mao Zedong's policies, he became an ardent supporter of democracy and human rights in his homeland. For this he was arrested and imprisoned for eighteen years. Wei has been nominated for the Nobel Peace Prize.

Born in Beijing to parents who were high-ranking officials in the communist regime, Wei was indoctrinated in communist philosophy and came to know Mao and his wife, Jiang Qing. As a young man and a member of the Red Guards, he zealously participated in the cultural revolution of the 1960s, later becoming a member of the elite United Action Committee. In 1969 he joined the Chinese army for four years.

While Wei was serving in the army, his parents were discredited within the Communist Party, his father was sent to a labor camp, and his family lost its high position. Wei was forced to question the values he had been taught since childhood. After Mao's death in 1976, Wei was working as an electrician at the Beijing Zoo, the only job he could get. Soon student unrest began to coalesce around Democracy Wall near Tiananmen Square in Beijing, where large opposition posters were plastered. To these posters, Wei added his own in which he called for a "fifth modernization"—democracy—in addition to the four modernizations touted by the authorities: in industry, science and technology, defense, and agriculture. He soon became a leader in the democracy movement and an advocate for human rights in his homeland.

Wei's activities resulted in his arrest and conviction, and in 1979 he was sentenced to fourteen years in prison. Although he was released in 1993, his continued promotion of democracy and human rights, as well as his criticism of China's leaders for their actions in Tibet, led to another trial and an additional fourteen-year sentence. In 1997 a friend and assistant, Tong Yi, wrote an article urging President Bill Clinton to call for Wei's release. Within a month and a half, Wei was released and permitted to travel to the United States, where he received medical treatment and accepted a position as a visiting scholar at Columbia University's Center for the Study of Human Rights.

For his efforts on behalf of democracy and human rights, Wei has received Sweden's Olof Palme Award, the European Parliament's Sakharov Award for Freedom of Thought, and the Robert F. Kennedy Human Rights Award. In a speech to Amnesty International, Wei recalled a discussion with a prison guard during his long imprisonment: "I suddenly realized that my determination to help others was the great cause which had been helping me to withstand physical and mental suffering and helped me maintain my optimism and strength. Once I realized this point, I became aware that I could not shake off my life-long responsibility to other people."

Wei Jingsheng. Translated and edited by Kristina M. Torgeson. *The Courage to Stand Alone: Letters from Prison and Other Writings.* New York: Viking Penguin, 1997.

Yang Jian-li, ed., with John Downer. *Wei Jingsheng: The Man and His Ideas.* Pleasant Hill, Calif.: Foundation for China in the 21st Century, 1995.

Defenders of Human Rights; Democracy; Sakharov, Andrei

Welfare

In its primary sense, welfare means the general well-being or prosperity, but in a second sense it has come to mean public assistance for needy persons and families. Welfare rights are part of the bundle of economic rights, which are considered second-generation human rights (following first-generation civil and political rights). Because they are positive rights—requiring governments to take steps to implement them—the welfare rights to which citizens are entitled vary from country to country.

A number of national constitutions, including those of the United States (1789), India (1950), and the Philippines (1987), refer to the general welfare in broad policy terms. The preamble to the U.S. Constitution speaks of establishing the constitution in order to, among other things, "promote the general Welfare," and article I directs Congress "to lay and collect Taxes" in order to "provide for the . . . general Welfare." Sweden's Instrument of Government (1974), part of its constitution, states in chapter 1, The Basic Principles of the Constitution, article 2: "The personal, economic and cultural welfare of the individual shall be fundamental aims of public activity."

The term *welfare state* is used to describe countries that implement socialist economic policies as opposed to strict capitalist policies. The basic difference between a welfare state, such as Sweden and Denmark, and a more traditional capitalist state, such as the United States, is the degree to which citizens receive services, benefits, and assistance—that is, welfare—from the government as a right or entitlement. An extreme form of the socialist or welfare state is seen in communist countries, in which the government controls and manages the state's economy with little or no private capitalistic incentives. Such systems have failed in most countries to foster sufficient economic growth to maintain the goals of the communist welfare state. The collapse of the communist regimes in the Soviet Union and other Eastern European states was due in part to their inability to develop and maintain the economic base necessary to provide the tremendous output of goods and services to which citizens were entitled. The level of welfare rights a country provides is also related to its current economic policies. The United Kingdom, for example, began deemphasizing its socialist welfare policies during Prime Minister Margaret Thatcher's tenure.

The International Covenant on Economic, Social and Cultural Rights (1966) is the premier global document in which welfare rights are enshrined. It advocates "the widest possible protection and assistance" for the family, special protection for mothers, and protection and assistance for all children and young persons. It also endorses each person's right to adequate food, clothing, and housing, to the continuous improvement of his or her living conditions, and to the enjoyment of the highest attainable standards of physical and mental health and to social security. One important element of social security is social insurance, which includes government assistance in the event of loss of work, disability, or illness and is often paid for through a special tax on employees and employers.

Regional human rights documents that contain provisions for welfare rights include the Inter-American Charter of Social Guarantees (1948), African Charter on the Rights and Welfare of the Child (1990), and European Social Charter (1961, revised in 1996). These documents all contain provisions for state assistance for people in need.

Constitution of India (1950), part IV, Directive Principles of State Policy, article 38(1): "The state shall strive to promote the welfare of the people by securing and protecting as it may a social order in which justice, social, economic, and political, shall inform all the institutions."

African Charter on the Rights and Welfare of the Child (1990), chapter one, Rights and Welfare of the Child, article 20, Parental Responsibilities: "2. States Parties to the present Charter shall in accordance with their means and national conditions take all appropriate measures: (a) to assist parents and other persons responsible for the child and in case of need provide material assistance and support programs particularly with regard to nutrition, health, education, clothing and housing. . . ."

Constitutional Court of Germany (1970): Welfare legislation that terminates state benefits to orphans when they marry conflicts with constitutional provisions that guarantee equality before the law, protect marriage and the family, and define the Federal Republic of Germany as "a democratic and social federal state." If the married orphan receives no support from his or her spouse, such legislation, therefore, is unconstitutional.

European Court of Human Rights (1993): In previous cases the court had determined that the procedural rights to a fair trial under the European Convention for the Protection of Human Rights and Fundamental Freedoms (1950), article 6(1), were applicable to disputes involving social insurance. While "there are differences between [social insurance and welfare benefits] . . . , they cannot be regarded as fundamental . . . [or] sufficient to establish that [article 6 (1)] is inapplicable [to disputes involving welfare benefits]."

Cavanna, Henry. *Challenges to the Welfare State: Internal and External Dynamics for Change.* Northampton, Mass.: Edward Elgar, 1998.

Dean, Hartley. *Welfare, Law, and Citizenship.* New York: Prentice Hall/Harvester Wheatsheaf, 1996.

African Charter on the Rights and Welfare of the Child; Declaration on Social Progress and Development; Economic Rights; European Social Charter; Inter-American Charter of Social Guarantees; International Covenant on Economic, Social and Cultural Rights; Social Rights

Wiesel, Elie

At the age of sixteen, Elie Wiesel (b. 1928), his family, and some fifteen thousand other Jews from his hometown in Romania were deported to Nazi concentration camps, where his mother, father, and younger sister died. Liberated in 1945, Wiesel has written many books and plays recounting the atrocities he suffered and witnessed during the Holocaust and pointing out revived antisemitism and similar abuses in South Africa, Vietnam, and Bangladesh.

Eliezer Wiesel was born on September 30, 1928, in Sighet, Romania, into a community of devout Jews. It remained untouched by World War II until 1944, when all of the inhabitants were taken by the Nazis to concentration camps. Wiesel was transported with his father from Auschwitz, where his mother and younger sister were killed, to Buchenwald, where they served as slave laborers and his father died.

After the war, Wiesel studied literature and philosophy at the Sorbonne in Paris and later became a journalist for a French newspaper. Immigrating to the United States in 1956, he worked on a Jewish newspaper in New York City and became a professor at City College of New York in 1972 and at Boston College in 1976. While in France, at the urging of the French novelist François Mauriac, Wiesel wrote a book in Yiddish, with the English title *And the World Has Remained Silent* (1956), about his experiences in the concentration camps. Thus began a series of some thirty works focusing on the plight of Jews during the Holocaust and other inhumanities around the world.

Wiesel's ability to translate his personal experiences and feelings into a body of works condemning all forms of violence, hatred, and prejudice have won him worldwide acclaim. In addition to other awards and honors, he received the Nobel Peace Prize in 1986. In his literature and his lectures, he has striven to ensure that the world will not soon forget just how inhuman people can be to others.

A Journey of Faith: A Dialogue between Elie Wiesel and John Cardinal O'Connor. WNBC-TV. New York: D. Fine, 1990.

Wiesel, Elie. *All Rivers Run to the Sea: Memoirs.* New York: Knopf, 1995.

Crimes against Humanity; Defenders of Human Rights; Genocide

Wiesenthal, Simon

A witness to atrocities carried out by the Soviet Union and Nazi Germany, Simon Wiesenthal (b. 1908) survived a number of work and concentration camps, but eighty-nine members of his and his wife's families were deported and murdered during World War II. Reunited with his wife after the war, he began a life-long campaign of gathering evidence against and apprehending Nazi war criminals so that they could be brought to justice for their crimes against humanity.

Born in what is now Buchach, Ukraine, on December 31, 1908, Simon Wiesenthal obtained a degree in architectural engineering from the Technical University of Prague in 1932. After his marriage to Cyla Muller, they settled in Lvov,

Poland (now Lviv, Ukraine). When the Soviet Union occupied the area in 1939, Wiesenthal escaped being sent to Siberia by bribing an official. Cyla was able to avoid harm by using "Aryan" identity papers, but when the Germans moved in in 1941, Simon was assigned to forced labor and concentration camps at Ostbahn, Janowska, and the infamous Mauthausen camp in Austria.

Liberated by the U.S. Army in May 1945, Wiesenthal began helping the army's war crimes operations gather evidence to prosecute Nazis. In 1947, together with thirty volunteers, he set up in Linz, Austria, the Documentation Center on the Fate of Jews and Their Persecutors, to assist Jewish refugees and provide evidence for the war crimes prosecutions. The most celebrated of the "Nazi hunters," Wiesenthal, with the cooperation of the governments of Israel, West Germany, and others, helped bring approximately 1,100 war criminals to justice.

The Linz office was closed in 1954, and the files were sent to Israel, but the whereabouts of the infamous architect of the Holocaust, Adolf Eichmann, still haunted Wiesenthal. With Eichmann's capture, trial in 1961, and subsequent execution, the documentation center reopened in Vienna. In 1966 Wiesenthal's efforts helped bring nine members of the dreaded Nazi SS to trial for the mass murder of Jews near Lvov. Other major war criminals were later apprehended as a result of his work.

Twice nominated for the Nobel Peace Prize, Wiesenthal has received honors and awards from Austria, France, and the United Nations as well as the Dutch and Luxembourg Medals of Freedom and the U.S. Congressional Medal of Honor. Wiesenthal's tireless pursuit of justice for the six million Jews who died in the Holocaust and the millions more who suffered from the Nazi atrocities is a monumental example of the sacrifice often required to ensure that violations of human rights do not go unpunished.

Simon Wiesenthal Center and Museum of Tolerance, 9760 West Pico Boulevard, Los Angeles, Calif. (800-900-9036. 📠 310-772-7655. 💻 webmaster@wiesenthal.com. 🖥 www.wiesenthal.com.

Jeffrey, Laura S. *Simon Wiesenthal: Tracking Down Nazi Criminals.* Springfield, N.J.: Enslow, 1997.

Pick, Hella. *Simon Wiesenthal: A Life in Search of Justice.* Boston: Northeastern University Press, 1996.

Wiesenthal, Simon. *Justice, Not Vengeance.* Translated by Ewald Osers. London: Weidenfeld and Nicolson, 1989.

Crimes against Humanity; Defenders of Human Rights; Genocide; Intolerance; War Crimes

Wollstonecraft, Mary

A British feminist, Mary Wollstonecraft (1759–97) wrote *A Vindication of the Rights of Woman* (1792), an influential book in the struggle for women's rights. In it, she argued that women's minds were capable of illumination and that females deserved equal educational opportunities as well as social equality. Wollstonecraft's life was both heroic and tragic. Married to William Godwin in 1797, the year she died, she was the mother of Mary Wollstonecraft Shelley, who married the English poet Percy Bysshe Shelley and wrote the classic horror story *Frankenstein*.

Born to the wife of a young silk weaver on April 27, 1759, Wollstonecraft had a relatively wealthy grandfather whose income provided economic stability for the family for more than sixty years. Her education included lessons from the father of a childhood friend, John Arden, a teacher and philosopher who influenced her early intellectual life.

In 1787 Wollstonecraft wrote *Thoughts on the Education of Daughters*, a collection of short essays on raising and educating children, especially girls. The ideas expressed in it would be more thoroughly developed in *A Vindication of the Rights of Woman*. After working for a publisher in London, she went to France in 1792 to observe the French Revolution. While there she had an affair with an American, giving birth to a daughter in 1794. Returning to London and the publishing business, she become part of an influential radical group that included Thomas Paine, William Wordsworth, William Blake, and William Godwin. After becoming pregnant by Godwin, she married him but died eleven days after giving birth to her daughter Mary.

"The power of generalizing ideas, of drawing comprehensive conclusions from individual observations," Wollstonecraft wrote in *A Vindication of the Rights of Woman*, "is the only acquirement for an immortal being, that really deserves the name knowledge. . . . This power has not only been denied to women; but writers have insisted that it is inconsistent, with a few exceptions, with their sexual character. Let men prove this, and I shall grant that woman only exists for man."

Lorch, Jennifer. *Mary Wollstonecraft: The Making of a Radical Feminist*. New York: St. Martin's, 1990.

Mazel, Ella. *Ahead of Her Time: A Sampler of the Life and Thought of Mary Wollstonecraft*. Larchmont, N.Y.: Bernel, 1995.

Sunstein, Mary. *A Different Face: The Life of Mary Wollstonecraft*. New York: Harper and Row, 1995.

Equality; Paine, Thomas; Seneca Falls Declaration of Sentiments and Resolutions; Sex Discrimination; Women

Women

Biological differences alone—women's reproductive responsibilities and men's greater physical strength—cannot explain the historical reluctance of men to acknowledge the right of women to participate in all aspects of society. Cultural and religious practices have also contributed significant obstacles to the struggle faced by women (from the Old English *wifmann*, a combination of *wife* and *man*) who simply seek to be treated equally in the political, economic, and social life of their families, communities, and countries. The phrase *women's rights* has been used in English since at least the seventeenth century to refer to the goal of attaining rights and opportunities equal with those of men. Women's rights today involve many areas of concern, among them equal rights before the law, freedom from discrimination, health care, education, economic opportunity and equal pay, reproductive freedom, marriage and divorce, domestic violence, sexual harassment, rape, commercial slavery and prostitution, protection during military occupation and as refugees, and the now widely denounced practice of genital mutilation.

The Enlightenment and the French Revolution in the eighteenth century introduced new philosophical reasoning that supported the women's rights movement. "Among the various sorts of mental progress most important for the general good," wrote the marquis de Condorcet, an aristocratic sympathizer of the French Revolution, in 1795, "we must count the total destruction of those prejudices which have established between the two sexes an inequality of rights. . . ." Some otherwise enlightened thinkers, however, including the French philosopher Jean-Jacques Rousseau, could justify limiting women to a subservient role on the grounds that their nature differed from that of men's.

Great Britain's industrial revolution, which occurred roughly between 1760 and 1840, changed the makeup of the workforce: by the 1830s more than half the adult labor force consisted of women. In 1792, anticipating a cultural revolution in women's social position, Mary Wollstonecraft wrote her seminal work, *A Vindication of the Rights of Woman*, and some eighteen years later the first women's reform societies were established in England. In *The Subjection of Women* (1869), the British philosopher John Stuart Mill, a proponent of women's rights, observed that women were protesting their condition of inequality not only in England but also in France, Italy, Switzerland, Russia, and the United States. The world was changing, he declared, and the presumption that women were born into a subservient station in life was wrong.

In the United States, women were becoming more active in political affairs, especially in the movement to abolish slavery. Along with this new activism came organizations dedicated to expanding women's rights, specifically the rights to vote and hold political office. The women's suffrage movement in the United States culminated in the ratification of the Nineteenth Amendment (1920) to the

U.S. Constitution, which granted women the right to vote. Eight years later British women gained universal suffrage. The first country to grant suffrage to women, however, was New Zealand in 1893, and the second was Finland in 1906.

The trade union and socialist movements also influenced the twentieth-century struggle to expand women's rights. After World War II the campaign for equal rights gained greater momentum, a result of the increased number of women in the workforce and gains such as improved and accepted means of contraception, which allowed women greater control over their reproductive functions. Although the proposed Equal Rights Amendment (1972) to the U.S. Constitution was not ratified by the required number of states by 1982, the period allotted by Congress, many countries passed laws guaranteeing women equal work, pay, and other opportunities during the second half of the twentieth century.

While equality between the sexes remains elusive, women have made great strides in the industrial and postindustrial nations. Unchanged, however, is the plight of women in the Third World and in countries dominated by religions that condone subjection of all but privileged females and selective abortion of female fetuses. According to a recent UN publication, women have not achieved equality with men in any country. Only twenty-four women were elected heads of state or government during the twentieth century, and women hold only about ten percent of the seats in the world's legislatures—yet they constitute more than half of the population. Women also account for a significantly higher percentage of the world's 1.3 billion poor persons and one billion illiterate adults. Women earn on average only three-fourths of the amount as men for the same work. Between twenty and fifty percent of them experience domestic violence during marriage, and together with children civilian women are the primary victims of armed conflict. Each year an estimated two million girls suffer genital mutilation.

A number of recent national constitutions specifically support women's rights and equality. Brazil's constitution (1988) expressly provides that "men and women have equal rights and duties under the terms of this Constitution," and several articles of Cambodia's constitution (1993) regarding rights and obligations begin: "Cambodian citizens of both sexes. . . ." Some international human rights documents expressly address women's rights, including several conventions adopted by the United Nations: the Convention on the Political Rights of Women (1952), Convention on the Nationality of Married Women (1957), and Convention on the Elimination of All Forms of Discrimination against Women (1979). The International Labor Organization adopted the Convention Concerning Equal Remuneration for Men and Women Workers for Work of Equal Value (1951). Other pertinent documents include the Declaration on the Elimination of Discrimination against Women (1967), Convention on the Elimination of All Forms of Discrimination against Women (1979); Declaration on the Participation of Women in Promoting International Peace

and Co-operation (1982), Declaration on the Elimination of Violence against Women (1993), and Vienna Declaration and Program of Action, adopted by the World Conference on Human Rights in Vienna in 1993.

Regional human rights conventions addressing women's rights include the Inter-American Convention on the Granting of Civil Rights to Women (1948), Inter-American Convention on the Granting of Political Rights to Women (1948), and Inter-American Convention on the Prevention, Punishment and Eradication of Violence against Women (Convention of Belém do Para) (1994).

Constitution of Russia (1993), part one, chapter 2, Human and Civil Rights and Freedoms, article 19: "3. Men and women shall have equal rights and freedoms and equal opportunities to exercise them."

Vienna Declaration and Program of Action (1993), part I: "The human rights of women and of the girl-child are an inalienable, integral and indivisible part of universal human rights. The full and equal participation of women in political, civil, economic, social and cultural life, at the national, regional and international levels, and the eradication of all forms of discrimination on the grounds of sex are priority objectives of the international community."

Supreme Court of Canada (1996): Denial of a woman's request for admission into a fraternal order on the grounds that she was a woman does not constitute a violation of her human rights under Canadian law, even though the order may publish historical information distorted in favor of men's role.

European Court of Human Rights (1991): The United Kingdom's denial of applications by women who had settled in the country to allow their husbands to join them, while allowing wives to join husbands, was a case of sexual discrimination and a violation of the European Convention for the Protection of Human Rights and Fundamental Freedoms (1950).

Commission on the Status of Women, United Nations, Two United Nations Plaza, DC2-12th Floor, New York, N.Y. 10017. (212-963-4248. 🖨 212-963-3463. 🖳 daw@un.org. 🖳 www.un.org/womenwatch/daw/csw.

Division for the Advancement of Women, United Nations, Two United Nations Plaza, DC2-12th Floor, New York, N.Y. 10017. (212-963-4248. 🖨 212-963-3463. 🖳 daw@un.org. 🖳 www.un.org/womenwatch/daw.

National Organization for Women (NOW) Legal Defense Fund, 395 Hudson Street, New York, N.Y. 10014. (212-925-6635. 🖨 212-226-1066. 🖳 lir@nowldef.org. 🖳 www.nowldef.org.

UN Development Fund for Women, 304 East 45th Street, 15th Floor, New York, N.Y. 10017. (212-906-6400. 📠 212-906-6705. 📖 unifem@undp.org. 📖 www.unifem.undp.org.

Bolt, Christine. *The Women's Movements in the United States and Britain from the 1790s to 1920s.* Amherst: University of Massachusetts Press, 1993.

Martin, J. Paul, and Mary Lesley Carson, eds. *Women and Human Rights: The Basic Documents.* New York: Center for the Study of Human Rights, Columbia University, 1996.

Abortion; Convention on the Elimination of All Forms of Discrimination against Women; Convention on the Political Rights of Women; Equality; Declaration on the Elimination of Discrimination against Women; Declaration on the Elimination of Violence against Women; Domestic Violence; Inter-American Commission of Women; Inter-American Convention on the Granting of Civil Rights to Women; Inter-American Convention on the Granting of Political Rights to Women; Inter-American Convention on the Prevention, Punishment and Eradication of Violence against Women; International Labor Organization; Marriage; Maternity; Mill, John Stuart; Rousseau, Jean-Jacques; Sex Discrimination; Slavery; Stanton, Elizabeth Cady; Vienna Declaration and Program of Action; Voting; Wollstonecraft, Mary

Workers

Since the establishment of large-scale human settlements, workers who produce goods or provide services have often been characterized as a distinct class, separate from and socially inferior to their employers. Although the struggle of working people to profit from their own labor is as old as human history, the issue of workers' rights has seriously engaged world attention for only the past two centuries.

In *The Laws*, written in the fourth century B.C.E., the Greek philosopher Plato lauds the "class of craftsmen who have enriched our lives by their arts and skills"; however, he suggested a harsh penalty should they fail to complete their work "within the stipulated time." In ancient Rome the two major classes consisted of patricians (aristocrats) and plebians (common working men). On occasion, to protest their ill treatment, the plebians would stage a strike and leave the city. After a series of such controntations the plebians were finally granted rights as Roman citizens to participate in the governing process on a relatively more equal footing with the patricians. Even today, political parties tend to represent either the business class or the working class; examples of such distinctions are the Republican and Democratic Parties in the United States and the Conservative and Labor Parties in the United Kingdom.

At the beginning of the industrial revolution in the mid-eighteenth century, an important change took place. Workers, especially those in factories, began to organize into labor unions to protect their rights, particularly to bargain equally with employers or factory owners for wages, benefits, and better working conditions. As espoused by Karl Marx, communism—predicated on the assumption of inevitable class conflict between the workers (the proletariat) and the owners of the means of production (the capitalists)—was intended to avoid such conflict by putting the means of production in the hands of the workers. The International Labor Organization (ILO), founded in 1919, however, has been more effective and had a more lasting worldwide impact on the advancement of the rights of workers.

The labor union movement of the twentieth century brought about many constructive changes in the conditions of workers and employees. As a result, many national constitutions and laws guarantee the rights of workers. Freedom of association generally includes the right of workers to form and join unions. Other issues relating to workers' rights include child labor, migrant labor, equality of treatment and pay for women workers, the right of workers to strike, the intellectual rights of professionals—authors, artists, and inventors, for example—and the rights of public employees. Recognized rights of workers include the right to earn a minimum wage that will provide an adequate standard of living, rest periods, and leave; the right to share in the profits of the company for which they work; safe and healthy working conditions; health and disability insurance; retirement benefits; and protection against unjust suspension and termination.

A number of international documents have been adopted in support of workers' rights, including many conventions sponsored by the ILO, including the Convention Concerning Freedom of Association and Protection of the Right to Organize (1948) and Convention Concerning the Application of Principles of the Right to Organize and to Bargain Collectively (1949), as well as others sponsored by the United Nations, including the Universal Declaration of Human Rights (1948). Subsequent ILO conventions have covered the protection and facilities afforded to workers' representatives (1971), the right to organize and procedures for determining conditions of employment in the public service (1978), promotion of collective bargaining (1981), and employment promotion and protection against unemployment (1988). Regional human rights documents that provide for workers' rights include the Inter-American Charter of Social Guarantees (1948) and the European Social Charter (1961, revised in 1996).

Constitution of South Africa (1997), chapter 2, Bill of Rights, article 23: "(2) Every worker has the right—(a) to form and join a trade union; (b) to participate in the activities and programs of a trade union; and (c) to strike."

International Covenant on Civil and Political Rights (1966), part II, article 22: "1. Everyone shall have the right to freedom of association with others, including the right to form and join trade unions for the protection of his interests. 2. No restrictions may be placed on the exercise of this right other than those which are prescribed by law and which are necessary in a democratic society in the interests of national security or public safety, public order . . . , the protection of pubic health or morals or the protection of the rights and freedoms of others. This article shall not prevent the imposition of lawful restrictions on members of the armed forces and of the police in their exercise of this right."

U.S. Supreme Court (1937): Congress has the power to regulate labor relations in the United States and the constitutional authority to safeguard the right of employees to self-organization and freedom of choice of representatives for the purposes of collective bargaining.

European Commission of Human Rights (1980): "The Commission has on various occasions recognized the character of a civil right in the case of certain rights whose common characteristic is that they are attached to the person. . . . For the same reason the right to work, which in all its forms is as closely attached to the person as is for example the right to found a family, must be recognized as a civil right. The right to choose and be admitted to practice a profession is an indispensable manner of exercising the right to the free development of the personality. . . ."

International Labor Organization, 4 route des Morillons, 1211 Geneva 22, Switzerland. (41-22-799-6111. 🖳 41-22-798-8685. 🖳 somavia@ilo.org. 🖳 www.ilo.org.

Cropanzano, Russell, ed. *Justice in the Workplace: From Theory to Practice.* 2d ed. Mahwah, N.J.: Lawrence Erlbaum, 2000.

Gregory, Robert J. *Your Workplace Rights and How to Make the Most of Them: An Employee's Guide.* New York: American Management Association, 1999.

Raynauld, Andre, and Jean-Pierre Vidal. *Labour Standards and International Competitiveness: A Comparative Analysis of Developing and Industrialized Countries.* Northampton, Mass.: Edward Elgar, 1998.

Association; Convention Concerning Freedom of Association and Protection of the Right to Organize; Economic Rights; Forced Labor; Inter-American Charter of Social Guarantees; International Labor Organization; International Covenant on Economic, Social and Cultural Rights; Standard of Living; Universal Declaration of Human Rights

Working Groups

The Commission on Human Rights and its Subcommission on the Promotion and Protection of Human Rights, like other permanent UN agencies, often use working groups to study specific human rights problems, investigate complaints lodged against a country, or draft international instruments. Members of these groups, created for a specific purpose, tend to be drawn from the parent body and are chosen for their individual expertise. Sometimes, rather than a group of experts, a single rapporteur (French for reporter) is appointed to study a problem and report his or her findings to the permanent human rights body. Although established as temporary, many working groups have become permanent.

One of the subcommission's most important working groups accepts communications (complaints) that "appear to reveal a consistent pattern of gross and reliably attested violations of human rights and fundamental freedoms," as provided in a 1970 resolution of the Economic and Social Council (ECOSOC). In carrying out what is known as the Resolution 1503 Procedure, the group's five members—representing Africa, Asia, Latin America, Eastern Europe, and Western Europe—meet two weeks before the subcommission's annual session in August. With each taking responsibility for different types of abuse, the group reviews thousands of communications and then votes on which complaints to forward to the subcommission. That body conducts a similar process, referring selected problems to the Commission on Human Rights, which maintains its own working group for complaints of abuse.

Other working groups under the Subcommission on the Promotion and Protection of Human Rights, called pre-sessional working groups because they meet before the subcommission's annual sessions, address contemporary forms of slavery, indigenous populations, and minorities. In addition, a working group on the administration of justice operates during subcommission sessions.

The Commission on Human Rights's own working groups address topics including arbitrary detention, enforced disappearance, migrants, a permanent UN forum for indigenous peoples, the right to development, and enhancing the effectiveness of the commission itself. Although considered temporary, many working groups have operated for several decades or more.

Working groups are sometimes created to draft human rights instruments. One established in 1984 produced a draft Declaration on the Right and Responsibility of Individuals, Groups and Organs of Society to Promote and Protect Universally Recognized Human Rights and Fundamental Freedoms, which was adopted by the UN General Assembly in 1998. Other draft documents have included the Declaration on the Rights of Persons Belonging to National, Ethnic, Religious and Linguistic Minorities, adopted in 1992, and the Declaration on the Right to Development, adopted in 1986. More recent groups have worked to draw up documents on torture, children in armed conflict, and child prostitution and pornography.

Eight working groups have addressed environmental concerns for the UN Environment Program. Established in 1994 as a response to the Rio Declaration on Environment and Development (1992), the Working Group on Sustainable Product Development has been supported by the Dutch government and the city and University of Amsterdam. A key activity has been the creation of an international network of experts from some seven hundred fifty organizations in fifty-five countries.

United Nations High Commissioner for Human Rights, 8–14 avenue de la Paix, 1211 Geneva 10, Switzerland. (41-22-917-9000. 🖥 41-22-917-9016. 🖳 webadmin.hchr@unog.ch. 🖳 www.unhchr.ch.

☞

Commission on Human Rights; Complaints; Declaration on the Right and Responsibility of Individuals, Groups and Organs of Society to Promote and Protect Universally Recognized Human Rights and Fundamental Freedoms; Declaration on the Right to Development; Economic and Social Council (ECOSOC); Environment; Remedies; Reporting Violations; Resolution 1503 Procedure; Rio Declaration on Environment and Development; Subcommission on the Promotion and Protection of Human Rights

World Council of Churches

In 1998 the World Council of Churches, an ecumenical organization that works for the unity and renewal of Christian denominations, celebrated its fiftieth anniversary in Amsterdam, the city of its founding. Begun as a mainly Protestant and European fellowship of 147 churches, it has become the world's largest ecumenical body, with 337 member churches in more than 120 countries, and has plans to include the Roman Catholic Church. Over the years the organization has assisted in human rights, peace, and humanitarian relief efforts throughout the world.

In 1920 a League of Churches similar to the League of Nations was proposed by a Christian church in Constantinople (now Istanbul). During that decade other churches and church leaders joined in seeking such a league. In 1937 representatives of two Christian church organizations, the Life and Work Movement and the Faith and Order Movement, met in London to establish a worldwide organization of Christian churches to be called the World Council of Churches, the first assembly of which convened in Amsterdam in 1948.

The council's work today focuses on "a renewed vision of ecumenism," church relations, and interchurch aid and assistance to refugees. Its current projects in Africa involve workshops for church refugee workers, refugee and emergency administration, advocacy, human resources development, and emergency response programs. Its Commission of the Churches on International Affairs includes a program for combating race discrimination worldwide, which since 1970 has distributed about $12 million in grants including grants for general work on racism, "women under racism," and indigenous peoples.

An assembly that meets roughly every six years at different locations around the world directs the organization. The assembly selects the 150 members of a central committee, which in turn chooses a twenty-six-member executive committee. Other organizational units include specialized committees and copresidents to act between assembly meetings. A general secretary is in charge of the staff at the organization's headquarters in Geneva.

World Council of Churches, Commission of the Churches on International Affairs, 150 route de Ferney, 1211 Geneva 20, Switzerland. (41-22-98-9400. 🖥 41-22-791-0361. 🖳 info@wcc-coe.org. 🖳 www.wcc-coe.org.

Race Discrimination; Refugees; Religion

World Court

See International Court of Justice

World Declaration on the Survival, Protection and Development of Children

"The children of the world are innocent, vulnerable, and dependent," states the World Declaration on the Survival, Protection and Development of Children, adopted on September 30, 1990. "They are also curious, active, and full of hope. Their time should be one of joy and peace, of playing, learning, and growing. Their future should be shaped in harmony and cooperation. Their lives should mature, as they broaden their perspectives and gain new experiences. But for many children," adds the document, "the reality of childhood is altogether different."

The declaration, which gained the approval of more than seventy heads of state and government and other high-level officials who met in New York City at the World Summit for Children, set out goals to be reached by 2000 in areas such as infant mortality, education, and protection of children in especially difficult circumstances, such as armed conflict. While some progress has undoubtedly been made toward these goals, the United Nations has reported that in the last decade two million children were killed in conflicts in fifty countries and many millions more were injured and displaced by war.

A year before the conferees met to approve the declaration and an accompanying plan of action, the UN General Assembly had adopted the Convention on the Rights of the Child (1989). On December 21, 1990, it endorsed the provisions of the World Declaration on the Survival, Protection and Development of Children and the Plan of Action. (The United Nations Children's Fund [UNICEF] suggested the use of the term *survival*, which is not often found in human rights materials.)

"Each day, countless children around the world are exposed to dangers that hamper their growth and development," notes the declaration's section entitled The Challenge, which describes the appalling conditions under which many children in the world live: neglect, cruelty, exploitation, hunger, malnutrition, homelessness, epidemics, AIDS, lack of clean water and adequate sanitation, war, race discrimination, environmental degradation, and exposure to drugs. It notes that forty thousand children die daily from malnutrition, disease, and unclean water.

Stating that the Convention on the Rights of the Child "provides a new opportunity to make respect for children's rights and welfare truly universal," The Opportunity section stresses "international cooperation and solidarity" to revitalize economic growth, protect the environment, prevent diseases, and achieve greater social and economic justice. "The current moves toward disarmament also mean that significant resources could be released for purposes other than military ones," it adds. "Improving the well-being of children must be a very high priority when these resources are reallocated."

According to The Task, "Enhancement of children's health and nutrition is a first duty and also a task for which solutions are now within reach." It also urges attention to disabled and other children in "very difficult circumstances." Improving women's status and responsible family planning will accrue to children's benefit as well, it notes. The Commitment section "requires political action at the highest level . . . to give high priority to the rights of children, to their survival, and to their protection and development." A number of specific areas are addressed, including health, hunger, family planning, education, and support for parents and other caregivers. The special problems of victims of apartheid and foreign occupation, orphans, street children, children of migrant workers, displaced children, disaster victims, the disabled, the abused, the socially disadvantaged, and the exploited, among others, are also enumerated.

The Next Steps directs attention to the role of regional and international organizations, including the United Nations and nongovernmental organizations, in achieving the declaration's goals; children are also urged to participate. "We do this not only for the present generation," it states, "but for all generations to come. There can be no task nobler than giving every child a better future."

The Plan of Action, described as "a framework for more specific national and international undertakings," called for achieving certain major goals by 2000, including reducing rates of child and maternal mortality as well as malnutrition among children under five years; facilitating universal access to safe drinking water and sanitation; providing primary education; reducing adult illiteracy; and protecting particularly endangered children. The plan also addresses children's health, calling for eradication of diseases including AIDS; food and nutrition, including promotion of breast feeding; and the role of women and the family, noting the importance of intact families. Detailed suggestions for education, illiteracy, poverty, and special problems such as child labor, drug abuse, and protection of children during armed conflict are also offered.

"The goals enunciated in the Declaration and this Plan of Action are ambitious," states the final section, "and the commitments required to implement them will demand consistent and extraordinary effort on the part of all concerned. . . . There is no cause that merits a higher priority than the protection and development of children, on whom the survival, stability, and advancement of all nations—and indeed, of human civilization—depends."

United Nations Children's Fund (UNICEF), Three United Nations Plaza, New York, N.Y. 10017. (212-326-7000. 📠 212-887-7465. 📧 netmaster@unicef.org. 🖥 www.unicef.org.

United Nations High Commissioner for Human Rights, 8–14 avenue de la Paix, 1211 Geneva 10, Switzerland. (41-22-917-9000. 📠 41-22-917-9016. 📧 webadmin.hchr@unog.ch. 🖥 www.unhchr.ch.

☞

Adoption; African Charter on the Rights and Welfare of the Child; Children; Convention on the Rights of the Child; Declaration of the Rights of the Child; Declaration on Social and Legal Principles Relating to the Protection and Welfare of Children, with Special Reference to Foster Placement and Adoption Nationally and Internationally; Declaration on the Protection of Women and Children in Emergency and Armed Conflict; Families; Maternity; United Nations Children's Fund (UNICEF); Youth

World Health Organization

"The enjoyment of the highest attainable standard of health is one of the fundamental rights of every human being without distinction of race, religion, political belief, economic and social conditions," asserted the World Health Organization (WHO) in its 1946 constitution. "Without health," adds this autonomous intergovernmental agency established in 1948, "other rights have little meaning. . . . WHO considers that the basic health services essential for the provision of adequate health protection to the community should cover: care of mothers and children including midwifery; nutrition; prevention and control of communicable diseases; sanitation and water supply; health education; occupational health."

In the wake of the 1830 cholera epidemic in Europe, a conference held in Paris in 1851 tried but failed to produce an international sanitary convention. Such a document, restricted to cholera, was adopted only in 1892. Early health organizations included the International Sanitary Bureau (the forerunner of the Pan American Health Organization), established in Washington, D.C., in 1902, and the International Office of Public Hygiene, set up in Paris in 1907. Beginning in 1921 the International Labor Organization (ILO) proposed and issued some international health agreements, and three years later the Pan American Union produced a sanitary code to help prevent the spread of communicable diseases.

Around this time the League of Nations created an international health organization to work with the International Office of Public Hygiene. After the League's demise in 1945, a UN conference in San Francisco decided to create the World Health Organization. The following year WHO's constitution was approved by an international health conference in New York City and entered into force in 1948 as soon as twenty-six UN members had ratified it.

WHO's mission is to help the peoples of the world achieve "a state of complete physical, mental and social well-being and not merely the absence of disease or infirmity." Its ongoing work includes directing and coordinating international health projects; assisting governments with health services on request, including in emergencies; developing international standards for health products and standardizing diagnostic procedures; and promoting technical cooperation on health as well as on related needs such as housing, working conditions, nutrition, sanitation, and recreation. WHO also coordinates biomedical and

health services research; fosters mental health activities; proposes international health conventions, agreements, and regulations; makes recommendations regarding foods, diseases, causes of death, and public health practices; and assists with teaching and training health care personnel. Among its important health initiatives have been a program begun in 1974 for immunizing children against poliomyelitis, measles, diphtheria, whooping cough, tetanus, and tuberculosis and a global AIDS program launched in 1987.

WHO's governing body is the World Health Assembly, which consists of representatives from 190 member states who meet annually. An executive board of thirty-two members from as many countries is responsible for executing the assembly's decisions. Some activities of WHO have been decentralized into regional organizations, each with its own office and committee composed of representatives from the countries of the region. A WHO policy information retrieval system has been established online to provide direct access to policy documents, information about regional activities, and selected booklets from WHO's Health for All series.

World Health Organization, 20 avenue Appia, 1211 Geneva 27, Switzerland. (41-22-791-2111. 🖨 41-22-791-3111. 🖳 info@who.int. 🖳 www.who.int.

AIDS; Health; International Labor Organization; Maternity

World Heritage Committee

See Convention Concerning the Protection of the World Cultural and Natural Heritage

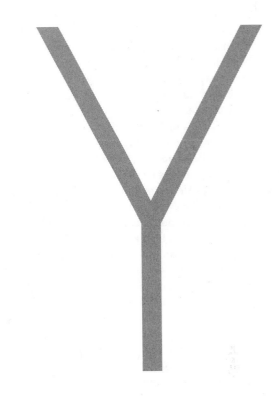

Youth hold the future of the world in their hands. Demonstrating that the denial of the human rights of some people is a threat to the human rights of others, Czech students held a solidarity march in December 1989 to show their support for the student democracy movement in China, which had been crushed by the Chinese communist government six months earlier. [Reuters/Corbis]

Youth

The rights of young people or juveniles—persons between childhood and adulthood—have only recently been identified as a distinct category of human rights. However, the field of youth or juvenile rights, like the field of children's rights, is evolving and expanding rapidly. The stake that young people have in the future of the world they will inhabit as adult citizens obligates them to take an active part in understanding and developing their rights, and governments have a special obligation to guarantee and protect those rights. "Governments are responsible for ensuring compliance with the Convention on the Rights of the Child [1989], which applies to children up to the age of 18," commented a youth delegate from the Netherlands to the UN General Assembly in 1992. "That is an arbitrary age limit. Young people aged between 15 and 25 have specific problems, a fact which has been recognized by the General Assembly. . . ." That same year Malta created a ministry for youth and a national youth council that has worked toward a universal definition of the term *youth* as well as national and international documents setting forth youth rights.

"Developments in the contemporary world convincingly demonstrate that young people have a more and more important role to play in attaining the objectives of progress and development set by all peoples," stated an update to a report entitled *Human Rights and Youth* issued by the UN secretary-general in 1989. "Their right to life, to education and to work and their freedoms are of particular impor-

tance and significance." The report recognizes, among other things, young people's "important role in the life of society for the achievement of social justice and the attainment of the objectives of economic and social progress and the maintenance of international peace and security" and "the need to ensure the full exercise of youth's fundamental rights to life, education, vocational training, work, social assistance, the elimination of all forms of social and racial discrimination, so that youth can participate actively in the decision-making process. . . ."

The human rights of youth overlap in some instances with the rights of children—for example, education, students' rights, an adequate standard of living, prohibitions against child labor and forced labor, and protection from sexual exploitation. Regarding the latter, the Recommendation Concerning Sexual Exploitation, Pornography, Prostitution of, and Trafficking in, Children and Young Adults, adopted by the Council of Europe's Committee of Ministers in 1991, states that "sexual exploitation of children and young adults for profit-making purposes in the form of pornography, prostitution and traffic of human beings has assumed new and alarming dimensions at [the] national and international level. . . ."

The rights of youth also overlap with many adult rights, a primary one being freedom from discrimination on the grounds of race, sex, religion, national or ethnic origin, social or other status, or political opinion. As the U.S. Supreme Court held in 1976, "Constitutional rights do not mature and come into being magically only when one attains the state-defined age of majority. Minors, as well as adults, are protected by the Constitution and possess constitutional rights."

The administration of juvenile justice is a special issue that has been the focus of increased attention. In 1985 the UN General Assembly adopted the Standard Minimum Rules for the Administration of Juvenile Justice (Beijng Rules). These supplement provisions of the International Covenant on Civil and Political Rights (1966) recommending that treatment for juveniles accused of crimes or under detention be separate from treatment for adults. The document encourages families, schools, and community groups to provide young people with "a meaningful life" and an alternative to "deviant behavior." The rules also require that in the administration of juvenile justice the age of the offenders be taken into account and that they be given access to an ombudsman. According to the document, the rights of young people accused of crimes include the right to privacy and "[b]asic procedural safeguards such as the presumption of innocence, the right to be notified of the charges, the right to remain silent, the right to counsel, the right to the presence of a parent or a guardian, the right to confront and cross-examine witnesses and the right to appeal. . . ."

Because many juveniles are in fact placed in detention for actions ranging from breaking curfew laws to street-gang killings, the General Assembly in 1990 adopted Rules for the Protection of Juveniles Deprived of Their Liberty. Underscoring that "[i]mprisonment should be used as a last resort," the document sets out detailed procedures for juveniles under arrest and awaiting trial as well as the management of juvenile facilities, including the physical conditions, education, recreation, religion, medical care, discipline, and return to the community.

Mindful of the need to keep juveniles out of detention in the first place, in 1990 the General Assembly also adopted the Guidelines for the Prevention of Juvenile Delinquency (Riyadh Guidelines). These are to "be interpreted and implemented within the broad framework of the Universal Declaration of Human Rights [1948] . . . as well as other instruments and norms relating to the rights, interests and well-being of children and young persons," the guidelines note.

Other international human rights documents directly related to youth include the Declaration on the Promotion among Youth of the Ideals of Peace, Mutual Respect and Understanding among Peoples (1965), which expresses the consensus of the General Assembly that the education of young people, including the interchange of ideas, is important for improving international relations and ensuring world peace and security.

Constitution of Italy (1948), part one, The Duties and Rights of the Citizens, title III, Economic Relations: "37. . . . The Republic protects the work of minors by means of special regulations and grants them equal pay for equal work."

Declaration on the Promotion among Youth of the Ideals of Peace, Mutual Respect and Understanding between Peoples (1965), principle 1: "Young people shall be brought up in the spirit of peace, justice, freedom, mutual respect and understanding in order to promote equal rights for all human beings and all nations, economic and social progress, disarmament and the maintenance of international peace and security."

Supreme Court of Estonia (1996): The constitutional right to form nonprofit associations is not dependent on an individual's legal capacity under civil law; therefore the constitutional freedom of association must also be guaranteed to minors.

Inter-American Commission on Human Rights (1987): The U.S. government violated the American Declaration of the Rights and Duties of Man (1948), articles I (right to life) and II (right to equality before the law), in executing a South Carolinian who was seventeen years old when he murdered a fourteen-year-old girl and her seventeen-year-old boyfriend.

Angel, William D., ed. *The International Law of Youth Rights: Source Documents and Commentary.* The Hague: Martinus Nijhoff, Kluwer Law International, 1995.

Nunez, Sandra Joseph, and Trish Marx. *And Justice for All: The Legal Rights of Young People.* Brookfield, Conn.: Millbrook, 1997.

Puritz, Patricia, et al. *A Call for Justice.* Chicago: ABA, 1995.

United Nations Association Youth (UNA Youth), Three Whitehall Court, London, SW1A 2EL England. (44-207-930-2932. info@unayouth.org.uk. www.unayouth.org.uk.

United Nations High Commissioner for Human Rights, 8–14 avenue de la Paix, 1211 Geneva 10, Switzerland. (41-22-917-9000. 41-22-917-9016. webadmin.hchr@unog.ch. www.unhchr.ch.

Voices of Youth (UNICEF): www.unicef.org/voy.

Youth Unit, United Nations, One United Nations Plaza, Room DC2-1318, New York, N.Y. 10017. (212-963-1380. 212-963-3062. youth@un.org. www.un.org/esa/socdev/unyin/yth-unit.

Children; Declaration on the Promotion among Youth of the Ideals of Peace, Mutual Respect and Understanding between Peoples; Education; Guidelines for the Prevention of Juvenile Delinquency (Riyadh Guidelines); Rules for the Protection of Juveniles Deprived of Their Liberty; Standard Minimum Rules for the Administration of Juvenile Justice (Beijing Rules); Students; Teachers

INDEX